JONSON

FOUR COMEDIES

LONGMAN ANNOTATED TEXTS

GENERAL EDITORS
Charlotte Brewer, *Hertford College, Oxford*
H. R. Woudhuysen, *University College London*
Daniel Karlin, *University College London*

PUBLISHED TITLES
Michael Mason, *Lyrical Ballads*
Alexandra Barratt, *Women's Writing in Middle English*
Tim Armstrong, *Thomas Hardy: Selected Poems*
René Weis, *King Lear: A Parallel Text Edition*
James Sambrook, *William Cowper: Selected Poems*
Douglas Brooks-Davies, *Edmund Spenser: Selected Shorter Poems*
J. P. Phelan, *Clough: Selected Poems*
Priscilla Bawcutt, *William Dunbar: Selected Poems*

JONSON
FOUR COMEDIES

Volpone, or The Fox
Epicoene, or The Silent Woman
The Alchemist
Bartholomew Fair

EDITED BY
HELEN OSTOVICH

LONGMAN

LONDON   NEW YORK

Wesley Longman
ıburgh Gate
CM20 2JE, England
panies throughout the world.

*Published in the United States of America
by Addison Wesley Longman Inc., New York.*

First published 1997

ISBN 0 582 07067 8   CSD
ISBN 0 582 07066 X   PPR

British Library Cataloguing-in-Publication Data

A catalogue record of this book is
available from the British Library

Library of Congress Cataloging-in-Publication Data

Jonson, Ben, 1573?–1637.
[Plays.   Selections]
Jonson, four comedies / edited by Helen Ostovich.
p.   cm. – (Longman annotated texts.)
Includes bibliographical references and index
ISBN 0–582–07066–X (pbk.). – ISBN 0–582–07067–8 (cased)
I. Ostovich, Helen.   II. Title.   III. Series.
PR2602.O86   1996
822'.3–dc20   96-2274

Set by 33 in Sabon 9½/12 pt
Produced by Longman Singapore Publishers (Pte) Ltd.
Printed in Singapore

CONTENTS

vi   Contents

ACKNOWLEDGEMENTS

Some of the material in the General Introduction is revised from '"Jeered by Confederacy": Group Aggression in Jonson's Comedies', *Medieval and Renaissance Drama in England* 3 (1986), pp. 115–28; and 'Ben Jonson and the Dynamics of Misogyny: A Cultural Collaboration', *Elizabethan Theatre* 15 (forthcoming). I am grateful to the publishers for permission to make use of this material. The latter paper was delivered at the 15th International Conference on Elizabethan Theatre, University of Waterloo, 26–29 July 1993; I am indebted to Lynne Magnusson and C. Edward McGee for their encouragement, and also to the listeners who, at the end of a very hot and intellectually gorged day, were able to rouse themselves to express some enthusiasm over my words, especially Guy Hamel, Irene Makaryk, Skip Shand, and Michael Shapiro. I am also indebted to the members of Barbara Traister's seminar 'The Stage and the Occult' at the Shakespeare Association of America Meeting, Kansas City, 16–18 April 1992, who commented usefully on 'Heywood's Wise-Woman, Jonson's Cunning-Man, and the Ideology of Witchcraft on the Early Jacobean Stage', especially John Mebane; and for discussion at the Center for Medieval and Early Renaissance Studies Conference at SUNY–Binghamton, 15–16 October 1993, where I first presented '"Besotted on Sleights and Forgeries": Widows and Witchcraft in *The Puritan* and *The Alchemist*'.

For their less formal but even more valuable assistance, I have relied on Karen Bamford, Mark Houlahan, Jean Nielsen, and Linda Phillips, who read drafts, offered suggestions, and (best of all) expressed support and praise for my efforts. My most confident backer was my husband, Rick, a Jonson-lover from his undergraduate days, who actually enjoyed helping me check my texts. He died of cancer before this book was completed, six weeks short of his fiftieth birthday.

ABBREVIATIONS

Alch	*The Alchemist*
BF	*Bartholomew Fair*
Cat	*Cataline*
CisA	*The Case is Altered*
Conv	*Conversations with Drummond*
CR	*Cynthia's Revels*
DisA	*The Devil is an Ass*
Disc	*Timber, or Discoveries*
EH!	*Eastward Ho!*
EMI	*Every Man In his Humour*
EMO	*Every Man Out of his Humour*
H&S	C. H. Herford and Percy and Evelyn Simpson (eds) (1925–52), *Ben Jonson*, 11 vols, Oxford
NI	*The New Inn*
OED	*Oxford English Dictionary*
Poet	*The Poetaster*
Sej	*Sejanus*
StN	*The Staple of News*
SW	*Epicoene, or The Silent Woman*
Volp	*Volpone, or The Fox*

Citations of Jonson's plays not in this volume are from H&S. Shakespeare is cited from the Arden Shakespeare series.

CHRONOLOGY

Note: Each play listing is followed parenthetically by the name of the company which performed it. Masques are followed by dates of performance.

1573   Ben Jonson born 11 June in London, posthumous son of a gentleman who lost his estate during Queen Mary's reign and became a minister. His mother remarried a bricklayer.

1589   Left Westminster School, where he had studied under William Camden. Apprenticed as a bricklayer.

1591–92   Served as a soldier in the Netherlands, where he killed an enemy in single combat.

1593   Returned briefly to bricklaying.

1594   Married Anne Lewis, whom he described later as 'a shrew yet honest'. Began to find work as an actor.

1596   Collaborated on plays for Henslowe.

1597   *The Case is Altered* (Children of the Chapel Royal).
    The Isle of Dogs (Pembroke's Men), a collaboration with Thomas Nashe, for which Jonson was imprisoned with two actors, Gabriel Spencer and Robert Shaw, for sedition.

1598   *Every Man In his Humour* (Lord Chamberlain's Men).
    Killed Gabriel Spencer in a duel, but was released on plea of benefit of clergy; converted to Roman Catholicism by priest (Father Thomas Wright) while awaiting trial in prison, and remained in that faith until 1610.

1599   Collaborated with Dekker on two tragedies, now lost, *Page of Plymouth* and *Robert II, King of Scots*.
    Every Man Out of his Humour (Lord Chamberlain's Men), one of the first plays performed at the new Globe theatre, began the trend for comical satire and city comedy, dominant modes on the stage for the next century.

1600   *Every Man Out of his Humour* became a best-seller, selling out three printings within about eight months.
    Cynthia's Revels (Children of the Chapel Royal).

1601   *The Poetaster* (Children of the Chapel Royal). The 'Dialogue' appended to this play, suppressed by the authorities, ended the so-called War of the Theatres (*poetomachia*), Jonson's satirical battles with Marston and Dekker.
    Daughter Mary dies.

1602   Paid by Henslowe for additions to Kyd's *The Spanish Tragedy*.

1603   *Sejanus* (King's Men) failed on stage. Jonson questioned by the Privy Council for popery and treason.

Son Ben died of plague; probably second son Joseph also.

The Entertainment at Althorpe (June) began long career at court writing entertainments and masques.

1604   *King's Coronation Entertainment* (15 March); *The Entertainment at Highgate* (1 May).

1605   *The Masque of Blackness* (6 January), commissioned by Queen Anne, began his long and later acrimonious association with Inigo Jones.

Eastward Ho! (Children of the Queen's Revels), a collaboration with Chapman and Marston. Chapman and Jonson imprisoned for anti-Scottish satire.

Jonson involved in spying related to the Gunpowder Plot.

1606   *Hymenaei* (5 January) and *Barriers* (6 January). *The Entertainment of the Two Kings at Theobalds* (24 July).

Volpone (King's Men) later performed at Oxford and Cambridge.

1607   *The Entertainment of King James and Queen Anne at Theobalds* (22 May).

1608   *The Masque of Beauty* (10 January); *The Haddington Masque* (*Hue and Cry After Cupid*) (9 February).

1609   *Epicoene* (Children of the Queen's Revels).

The Masque of Queens (2 February).

1610   *The Alchemist* (King's Men).

Prince Henry's Barriers (6 January).

Returned to the Anglican faith.

1611   *Oberon, the Fairy Prince* (1 January); *Love Freed from Ignorance and Folly* (3 February).

Cataline (King's Men) failed on stage, but the published text was praised for its literary and poetic merits.

1612   *Love Restored* (6 January).

Travelled in France as tutor to Sir Walter Ralegh's son.

1613–14 *A Challenge at Tilt* (December/January); *The Irish Masque* (29 December, 3 January).

Bartholomew Fair (Lady Elizabeth's Men).

1615   *Mercury Vindicated from the Alchemists at Court* (6 and 8 January).

1616   *The Golden Age Restored* (1 and 6 January).

The Devil is an Ass (King's Men).

Publication of *Works* in folio. Received royal pension.

Christmas his Masque (Christmas).

1617   *Lovers Made Men* (22 February); *The Vision of Delight* (Christmas).

1618   *Pleasure Reconciled to Virtue* (6 January); *For the Honour of Wales* (17 February).

Walking tour to Scotland, where he was given the freedom of the city of Edinburgh, and visited poet William Drummond of Hawthornden, who recorded their conversations.

1619   Formally inducted as Master of Arts at Oxford.
1620   *Pan's Anniversary* (?).
          The Entertainment at Blackfriars (20? May).
1620–23   Lecturer in rhetoric at Gresham College.
1621   *News from the New World* (6 January); *The Gypsies Metamorphosed* (3
          and 5 August, and early September).
1622   *The Masque of Augurs* (6 January, 6 May).
1623   *Time Vindicated* (6 January).
          Fire in Jonson's lodgings destroyed his library and current work.
1624   *Neptune's Triumph* (6 January); *The Masque of Owls* (19 August).
1625   *The Fortunate Isles* (9 January).
1626   *The Staple of News* (King's Men).
1629   Paralysed by stroke.
          The New Inn (King's Men).
1631   *Love's Triumph Through Callipolis* (9 January); *Chloridia* (22 Feb-
          ruary).
1632   *The Magnetic Lady* (King's Men).
1633   *The King's Entertainment at Welbeck* (May).
          A Tale of a Tub (Queen Henrietta's Men), containing satire on Inigo
          Jones.
1634   *Love's Welcome at Bolsover* (30 July).
          Died in Westminster, 6 August, and buried in Westminster Abbey.
          Incomplete works: *The Sad Shepherd* and *Mortimer his Fall*.
1640   *Works* published in two folio volumes by Sir Kenelm Digby.

To Rick
1942–1992

To have so soon 'scaped world's and flesh's rage
And, if no other misery, yet age!
Rest in soft peace.

GENERAL INTRODUCTION

JONSON'S CHOICES: A PLAYWRIGHT'S LIFE

Jonson entered the theatrical scene in London during an explosive period of urban growth. The city's population was teeming and sprawling outside the walls; commerce, tourism, and conspicuous consumption were expanding; and in the suburbs and liberties, theatres were springing up and competing for plays from a new breed of writers, professional playwrights. Many of them, like Marlowe, Greene, and Kyd, were Oxford and Cambridge graduates who turned to writing when the glut of educated men on the market closed doors on more conventional career opportunities. These 'university wits' and others, like Shakespeare, had been making names for themselves since about 1589, shaping public audiences eager for dramatic entertainment. That year, Ben Jonson, sixteen years old, left Westminster School, the elite academy which he had attended for nine years, supported by an anonymous patron. Denied the advantage of a university education, Jonson faced a problematic future. As the posthumous son of an impoverished gentleman, he may have hoped to regain his father's lost estate, but circumstances forced him into an apprenticeship in his stepfather's trade, bricklaying. The situation was not a happy one. In 1591, he quit his training to join the army in the Netherlands, and, after a brief return to bricks following his year abroad, he married Anne Lewis, thus rashly ending his apprenticeship before he qualified for any secure alternative employment. Like other over-educated, witty, and ambitious young gentlemen with no prospects, Jonson gravitated towards the theatre.

Although acting was not his forte, by 1597 Jonson began to enjoy success and even notoriety as a playwright. Thomas Nashe admired *The Case is Altered* (1597), Jonson's one surviving early comedy, and collaborated with him on *The Isle of Dogs* (1597), a satire so slanderous that Nashe fled to Yarmouth to avoid arrest, while Jonson and two of the actors, Gabriel Spencer and Robert Shaw, languished for eight weeks in Marshalsea prison. Satire nevertheless became Jonson's favourite theatrical mode, despite praise he received for his early tragedies (now lost), despite later incarceration for anti-Scottish satire in *Eastward Ho!* (1605), and despite suppression of or censure for material in *Every Man Out of his Humour* (1599), *Poetaster* (1601), *Sejanus* (1603), and *Epicoene* (1609). Why this preference for satire? The answer lies partly in Jonson's classical education and scholarly interests, partly in the intellectual vogue for corrosive verse satire during the 1590s, partly in the anti-authoritarian reaction to the book-burnings ordered by the Archbishop of Canterbury and the Bishop of London on 1 June 1599, as a way of containing satirical attacks on the establishment, and partly, too, in Jonson's aggressive temperament, which required an outlet other than physical violence. He had already escaped hanging by pleading benefit of clergy after killing Gabriel Spencer in a duel in 1598; the brand on his thumb reminded him that a second charge of manslaughter would not be treated so leniently.

No list of reasons can wholly explain Jonson's satisfaction in defining himself as the satiric commentator on social follies, a role he adopted in creating 'comical satire'. He devised this genre for *Every Man Out of his Humour* and continued to develop it with subtle variations throughout his career. Comical satire allowed him to show off his own learning, to tease his friends, and to chastise the ignorant. His originality appears in his distinctively contemporary and English redefinition of ancient forms. He deftly recycled Greek and Roman masterworks, notably Aristophanes' bawdy satirical fantasies, not for plot, but rather for techniques of lively social criticism. As the annotations in this volume indicate, Jonson borrowed extensively from ancient sources, such as Juvenal's vituperative harangues, Plautus's irreverent farces, and Horace's self-deprecating ironies, to support the tangle of actions through which his egocentric characters expose their limitations. But, although other classical influences modify the rowdy tone of old comedy, the shape of Jonson's plays remains unrepentantly Aristophanic.

In Aristophanes' comedies, a malcontent/outsider generally turns his back on the 'reality' of a world that either excludes or repels him, amd looks for ways to displace it. In a supreme effort of will, he imposes his own private fantasy of uncurbable power, sometimes triumphantly, as in *The Birds*, where the hero makes himself king of the universe, sometimes ambivalently, as in *The Clouds* or *The Wasps*, where the hero registers his defiance and incorrigibility by raging out of control. While reconstructing the world to fit his fantasy, the hero engages his antagonists in battles of witty exploitation, and then celebrates his victory by parodying the power he has just defeated. That is, he punishes impostors who try to capitalise upon his success, and rewards himself with community approbation, usually in the form of willing sexual partners and lavish feasts.

In englishing Aristophanes for the seventeenth-century audience, Jonson demonstrates his view of the creative artist as an intelligent innovator who digests his predecessors' methods but revises their material to fit his own times. From Aristophanes he borrows the flexible shape of the contest for personal power, with satirical butts illustrating the range of follies in society, and an elastic sense of the ridiculous that incorporates jesting and jeering, absurdity and abuse, reductive clowning and flights of literary wit. He also borrows the unruly egotism of Aristophanes' eccentric protagonists in order to revise the Renaissance notion of 'humours' dominating his own obsessive-compulsive characters. Like Aristophanes, Jonson writes comedy that is urban, scoffing, earthy, and technically original. Jonson's comedy, like old comedy, relies on farce to express serious social and political concerns, with frequent metatheatrical shifts of perspective to force his audience into observing and judging the performance from different points of view. He transforms Aristophanes' chorus into his own characteristically crowded scene, busily exposing itself as corrupt and complacent. Community 'morality' becomes just another mask in the social performance of injustice and greed. As one contemporary remarked in 1602, Jonson 'has become nowadays something humorous and too-too satirical up and down, like his great grandfather Aristophanes' (Bradley and Adams 1922: p. 33).

But by 1602 Jonson had halted his experiments with comical satire. Possibly his popularity with young intellectuals prompted him to go too far: John Marston, then an Inns of Court student-satirist, wrote an admiring portrait of Jonson as a social critic into his revision of *Histriomastix* (1599), and the Cambridge playwrights' *II Return from Parnassus* (1601/2) imitated Jonson's theatrical mode, thus suggesting his status as a cult figure. But Aristophanes had licence for personal abuse; Jonson did not. Jonson had been adjusting Aristophanic comedy to suit modern taste in part by imitating the complex theatricality of the Inns of Court revels, where in-jokes, insulting banter with the audience, and aggressive mockery of current fads and questionable legal practices vied with rhetorical games and political commentary in what was essentially a burlesque rehearsal for future careers in government. But the revels too had special licence to criticise the powerful within a closed community. When Jonson took a similar liberty in *The Poetaster*, he was threatened with a lawsuit. Luckily, his friendships among the lawyers at the Inns of Court provided more than intellectual and artistic rapport. Richard Martin, a former 'Prince' in the Middle Temple revels (to whom Jonson later dedicated the play), vouched for him, and the suit was dismissed.

The following year, his tragedy *Sejanus* failed at the Globe, and its political content prompted the Privy Council to question him for Roman Catholic sympathies and treason. (Jonson had converted to Roman Catholicism while awaiting trial for murder in 1598, and remained in that faith until 1610.) He suffered more personal anguish over the deaths of his two sons in the plague of 1603 (his daughter had died in 1601), and sometime during that period, Jonson and his wife separated, living apart until at least the spring of 1605, perhaps until 1607. The accession of James I, however, brought Jonson new professional opportunity. Beginning with the success of *The Masque of Blackness*, written for Queen Anne in 1604, he found favour creating entertainments for the court, a favour apparently not seriously jeopardised either by his imprisonment in September 1605 with Chapman for anti-Scots jokes in *Eastward Ho!*, or by his failure to provide any real assistance as a spy in the Gunpowder Plot of 5 November. In fact, his involvement in prison and spying seems to have done him more good than harm: he used the experience to work out the plot of *Volpone*, which, according to the Prologue, he then wrote in only five weeks.

Jonson's career after *Volpone* confirmed his status as a major writer. The chief disappointment was that his second tragedy, *Cataline* (1611), met with literary but not popular praise, and worse, like his first tragedy, coincided with personal loss, the death of his son Ben, the last of his legitimate children. His marriage apparently crumbled again, and for about five years, up to 1618, Jonson lived with Lord Aubigny. On the other hand, the combined success of the court masques and the city comedies – *Epicoene* (1609), *The Alchemist* (1610), *Bartholomew Fair* (1614), and *The Devil is an Ass* (1616) – culminated in the publication of Jonson's *Works* in 1616, a folio volume that set a precedent for considering other playwrights as writers of literature instead of producers of ephemera, and the granting of a royal pension of 100 marks, effectively making him Britain's poet laureate. The fact that Jonson stopped writing for the public theatre until 1626 suggests that his celebrity committed him, or allowed him to commit himself, to other projects. During his summer walking tour from London to Scotland in 1618, he was honoured by the city of Edinburgh, and spent three weeks at Hawthornden visiting the Scottish poet William Drummond, who recorded their conversations. The following summer of 1619, he was formally inducted as Master of Arts at Oxford; apparently Oxford and Cambridge had already honoured him *in absentia*, perhaps as early as 1607, as the dedication of the *Volpone* quarto implies. He certainly claimed honorary degrees from both universities, according to Drummond. In 1620, he took up residence at Gresham College, which had since 1575 offered free instruction to all who attended the lectures; Jonson was apparently the professor of rhetoric, a position he held for about three years. To judge from his list of losses in 'An Execration upon Vulcan' (Parfitt 1975: pp. 181–7) after his library burned in 1623, aside from 'parcels of a play', he had been working on translations of Horace and Aristotle, a grammar text, an epic about his journey to Scotland, a history of Henry V, and 'humble gleanings in divinity'. In 1621, he was granted the reversion of the office of Master of the Revels, although he did not live long enough to claim it.

With the death of James in 1625, however, the honours ceased, and Jonson suffered financial difficulties, multiplied by illness, possibly minor strokes during 1626–28, until a final paralytic stroke confined him permanently to bed in January 1629. During this period, his former court collaborator Inigo Jones, after an acrimonious struggle, took over as Charles I's masque-maker, and Jonson's plays – *The Staple of News* (1626), *The New Inn* (1629), *The Magnetic Lady* (1632), and *The Tale of a Tub* (1633) – had little success. Although the king made him London's city chronologer in 1629, and in 1630 raised his annual pension to £100, actual payment was either erratic or withheld. Jonson nevertheless continued to support himself by writing epigrams and occasional poetry, and ninety of the poems were eventually published posthumously as *The Underwood* in 1640, both as a separate volume and as part of the two-volume 1640 folio of Jonson's *Works*. In 1631, Jonson himself arranged for the publication in folio of three plays not in the 1616 folio – *Bartholomew Fair*, *The Devil is an Ass*, and *The Staple of News* – but they were never issued.

If Jonson lacked financial support in his final years, his friends and admirers were lavish in emotional and intellectual support. His room was filled with visitors and books, and he was working on a pastoral romance, *The Sad Shepherd*, possibly even considering further work on an early tragedy, *Mortimer his Fall*, when he died on 6 August 1637. He left less than £9 in goods. Although he was buried in Westminster Abbey, there were insufficient funds for a monument. The spot is marked by a blue marble square, briefly engraved (thanks to an obscure gentleman's gift of 18 pence) O RARE BEN JONSON. The inscription happily puns on the Latin *orare* ('pray for') and simple English praise that would have gratified Jonson, the master of the plain style.

Further reading

David Riggs's biography (1989) uses a psychoanalytical approach to the material, finally failing to give a very vivid impression of Jonson's charismatic and volatile personality. Rosalind Miles (1986) manages, especially in her final chapter, to communicate Jonson's sensitivities, passions, and contradictions as a man and an artist, although she glosses over the political and cultural tensions in his experience. The best evaluation of Jonson's life is W. David Kay's succinct and learnedly balanced volume (1995). For an unusual appraisal of Jonson's final years as poet after his early success up to 1616, see Jennifer Brady (1991). Bradley and Adams (1922) and Herford and Simpson (1925–52: vol. II, pp. 305–494) are both good sources for contemporary comments on Jonson. To hear his own teasing (and probably tipsy) voice, read *Conversations with Drummond* (Parfitt 1975: pp. 459–80), and for demonstrations of his plain prose style and gift for idiomatic translation of classical ideas, see Jonson's commonplace book, *Timber; or Discoveries* (Parfitt 1975: pp. 373–458).

VOLPONE, OR THE FOX

A potent blend of Aristophanic and revels comedy, *Volpone* tells the story of a middle-aged recluse who, despite being a *magnifico*, has not played a powerful role at court since his magnetic performance of 'graceful gesture, note, and footing' as Antinous, twenty-one years earlier in the Doge's entertainment for the new king of France (see 3.7.155ff.). In the Jacobean court as well, literally dancing attendance upon a ruler was a formidable method of gaining influence, to judge from the career of James I's current favourite, Robert Carr, later Earl of Somerset. But instead of continuing to dance for favour in Venetian politics and commerce, Volpone rejects the competition. He prefers to dominate his own golden sphere at home, mocking and defeating challengers who try to share it, glorying in his absolute authority. His treasure-hoard, his freaks, his parasite, his pretence of dying, and his sick-bed visitors, all express Volpone's contempt for a world he sees as diseased and twisted, a 'wrong' reality which he miniaturises and torments, thus freeing himself from an otherwise intransigently oppressive system.

Jonson treats Volpone's household as a context for darkly witty perceptions of the contemporary scene, rather than a 'plot' in the usual dramatic sense. The play does not 'develop' as a unified plot, although it burgeons with delusion and conspiracy in every scene. Volpone's secret and profitable victory in games-playing provides the large controlling concept; specific situations laterally augment and reinforce that concept by showing variations on the theme, dazzling the audience with rapid comic pacing, balances, contrasts, and incongruities. The structuring of this comedy depends on hostile wit, which, as Freud defines it, requires at least three persons: the perpetrator of the witticism, the dupe victimised by the hostile aggression, and the audience who enjoys the result (Freud n.d.: p. 144). Jonson illustrates the elasticity of this comedy throughout the play as Volpone and Mosca juggle all three roles implicit in hostile wit, ridiculing conventional goals and behaviour, setting up even themselves as straw men to be knocked down, and appreciating each other's performances. Volpone preens himself as the profane miser gloating over his hoard (1.1) and the prodigal sensualist wooing his mistress with jewels (3.7), the ingenious entrepreneur accumulating wealth without the stain of trade (1.3–5), and the vulgar mountebank working the crowd with drastic price-cutting (2.2). He plays each role with conviction. He coughs on cue, feigns deafness when Mosca and Corvino bawl insults into his ears, and holds his pose as the 'impotent' exhibit in court, even when Lady Would-be embraces him (4.6). As the supporting actor, Mosca sticks wittily to one role: the transparently oily factotum who begs the question with tongue in cheek and hand out for a tip, a role he overplays broadly for Volpone's amusement, but tones down (with caustic asides) for the three legacy-hunters, and even reduces to weepy sincerity for Bonario (3.2). The almost incestuous intensity with which Volpone and Mosca match irreverent wits and puncture their own nimble role-playing sustains even the table-turning of the finale.

Models for satire: Sutton, Aristophanes, and *commedia dell'arte*

Jonson's seventeenth-century audience consistently recognised in Volpone a broad representation of Thomas Sutton, the founder of the London Charterhouse. Samuel Herne, the Restoration historian of Charterhouse, assumed, as John Aubrey did in *Brief Lives*, that Sutton was the original of Volpone (Hotine 1991: p. 79; Evans 1989: pp. 303–5). Herne recognised the spirit behind the satire when he compared Jonson's sketch of Sutton to Aristophanes' spoof of Socrates in *The Clouds* (Shipley 1992: p. 368). Sutton accumulated vast wealth by moneylending, but not at extortionate rates; Volpone too denies 'usure private', which Mosca defines as exploitative practices (1.1.40–51). Like Volpone, Sutton was reclusive, and kept his money in chests in his lodgings, but spent lavishly on personal luxuries. He surrounded himself with hangers-on who believed they were his heirs, but from 1604 he drafted a new will every six months, and public opinion sided with Sutton in his games of using and outwitting these legacy-hunters. He relied heavily on his agent, John Lawe, a garrulous 'Mosca' who managed much of Sutton's business. Sutton first considered a plan to endow a charitable hospital in 1595, but did not begin conveying properties to finance the foundation until 1606. At about the same time, Sir John Harington, another would-be plotter whom Jonson held in contempt, tried to interest him in a less philanthropic political scheme that would net Sutton an earldom and Harington appropriate rake-offs from Sutton and the government. Sutton ended up rejecting both plans, and did not reconsider the hospital project until 1611, when he finalised all the arrangements between 9 May and 28 November, just before his death on 12 December. The confiscation of Volpone's estate to fund the hospital for the *Incurabili* indicates Jonson's view of the proper disposition of Sutton's wealth.

These correlations between Sutton and Volpone are too extensive to be accidental, and too topical to be ignored. The fact that Sutton later gave Jonson a £40 pension may be evidence that Sutton took the satirical advice seriously. At any rate, he did not consider it libellous. Indeed, why should he? Volpone, if anything, glamorises Sutton into an intellectually adventurous and charismatic hero. Only the barest outline of the circumstances provides 'a key for the deciphering of everything' (Epistle). The rest of the play satirises social venality generally, rather than Sutton particularly. Jonson's dedicatory epistle goes to great lengths to justify the play's intention, and to deny particular satire in 'uncharitable thought' or 'malicious slander', asserting instead the poet's duty to 'inflame grown men to all great virtues, keep old men in their best and supreme state'. In other words, instead of refuting all 'application', he merely denies his creation of anything 'obnoxious to construction', except against 'creatures for their insolencies worthy to be taxed'. This is a significant proviso, one that undercuts his vigorous protests at personal satire, whether of Sutton or any other plotter.

Jonson enjoyed great latitude in treating satiric targets as figures of farce. Despite the current modern critical acceptance of his bluffs at face value, Jonson, like Aristophanes, did use obscenity and crude physical comedy to dilute his satire and make it acceptable: 'not too refined and dainty for *you*, of course, but rather more intelligent than smutty farce', as Aristophanes says to the audience in *The Wasps* (D. Parker 1961: p. 26). Jonson protests that his purpose differs substantially from that of his contemporaries, whose only aim is to provoke laughter at any cost. He claims to loathe 'the use of such foul and unwashed bawdry as is now made the food of the scene' – 'nothing but ribaldry, profanation, blasphemy, all licence of offence to God and man, is practised' (Epistle 39, 31–2). 'If you find their plays funny,' remarks Aristophanes of his rivals in *The Clouds*, 'then don't laugh at mine' (McLeish 1979: pp. 13–14). Both playwrights dare the audience, at peril of appearing stupid, to recognise the satire and not to complain about it.

Perhaps Jonson's cleverest method of imbedding particular satire in *Volpone* is to represent it in *commedia dell'arte* skits which disguise the English plot within an Italian mode. *Commedia* actors each play a caricature dominated by one obsession, not unlike a Jonsonian humour, performed in characteristic verbal or physical routines, like Corbaccio's hobble and deafness, or Corvino's jealous rages. The actors wear grotesque masks, which have an effect similar to that suggested by the beast-fable names of *Volpone*, and follow scenarios full of intrigues and unsolvable situations with ludicrous pay-backs. The usual butt is the *pantalone*, sometimes a weak old curmudgeon, as Volpone pretends to be; sometimes a despotic father, like Corbaccio, whose child, like Bonario, eventually escapes his control; sometimes an ageing husband whose young wife cuckolds him, as Corvino believes when he calls himself '*Pantalone di Besogniosi*' and Celia '*Francescina*', a saucy wench (2.3.8, 4). The alternate butt is the *dottore*, a pedantic lawyer or doctor, pompously grandiloquent like Voltore in court (4.4.22–92), or deliberately abstruse like Volpone in his mountebank performance. Usually a thrashing is the only way to make him stop talking about his professional reputation; hence the appropriateness of Corvino's stage direction, '*He beats away the mountebank*' (2.3.2), and Voltore's self-inflicted fit (5.12.20–40). The chief comic trickster is *Arlecchino* (Harlequin), the pantaloon's outrageously ribald rival, who woos and sometimes wins the serious *inamorata*, the love-interest. The Harlequin's traditional costume of mask and fox-tail and his chameleon-like nature suggest the similarity between the *commedia* trickster, originally a demon-figure, and Volpone, himself a role-player *par excellence*. The Harlequin may be followed by a zany, or comic servant, whose competitive imitations of his master, like Mosca's in Act 5, escalate into a grotesque race for victory. The stock villain, *il capitano*, is as crude as Volpone's *commendatore*. These traditions of Italian comedy temporise the Volpone-as-Sutton satire by separating the relatively naive English from the Italians on stage, and by making the Italians appear even more greedy, even more conniving, even more jealous, and finally even more *foreign* to English eyes than they could possibly appear without the *commedia* perspective.

Three questions of interpretation

The differentiation between the English and the Italian modes of intrigue accounts for some, but not all, of the play's digressions and inconsequence. Interpretations of *Volpone* cluster around three vexing questions aroused by the play's fluid plot and tone. Why allow Sir Politic Would-be so much stage room when he has no direct connection with Volpone at all? Why clutter up the middle acts of the play with elaborate side-issues (the mountebank performance, the attempted seduction of Celia, and the gulling of Lady Would-be) that have only a tenuous bearing on the main fable of the wily old fox and his attendant fly luring the three birds of prey? Why end the play with harsh decisions in a courtroom where characters who have not been tried for a crime are found guilty and sentenced by judges who have no idea of what the case is about until Volpone confesses in the last few minutes of the final scene? All three of these questions arise because critics tend to see Jonson as a dogmatic moralist instead of a playful iconoclast whose models in ancient Athens and contemporary practice rely on physical reductivity, rhetorical variety, and inspired lunacy.

Sir Politic Would-be and plots

How does Sir Politic Would-be fit into *Volpone*'s slippery structure? His first appearance in the opening scenes of Act 2 provides the paradigm. Although Sir Pol and Volpone are on stage together in the mountebank scenes, neither knows the other: while Volpone, the virtuoso performer, commands attention, Sir Pol stays on the margins, commenting inaccurately. This is his role for the entire play. After the exotic atmosphere of Act 1 – with its echoes of Turkish extravagance in the heat, the indolent lounging in bed, the fabulous wealth, freakish retainers, sycophantic guests – the English audience can immediately recognise one of their own, as if Sir Pol had just wandered off the street and on to the stage by mistake. In Sir Pol, Jonson reconstructs the quintessential English booby as the self-important cosmopolitan, busybody, and know-it-all whose trendy ambitions and asinine pronouncements on state affairs make him a byword of sophisticated fatuity. His propensity for needless complication appears most graphically in his design for a plague-detecting machine (4.1.100–125) – and that same delight in intricacy for its own sake dominates his view of international intrigue. In the relation between subplot and main plot in *Volpone*, what we are seeing, by way of Sir Pol, is not simply an Italianate gentleman, a conspiracy-ridden variation on the modish Frenchified courtiers satirised later in *Epicoene*. Rather, following his habit of englishing Aristophanic plots for early modern tastes, Jonson uses Sir Pol to italianise, not quite unrecognisably, English plots which he himself had, like Sir Pol, observed from the margins. Sir Pol is a double agent theatrically, if not politically. On one hand, the audience feels comfortably superior to him as an absurd English eccentric abroad, fervently playing the Machiavel masterminding plots everywhere. On the other hand, they share his alarmist belief in plots within plots and his conviction that secret agents are undermining the governments of Europe. Indeed, current events in England seemed to prove this state of affairs beyond doubt.

From his first speech, Sir Pol identifies himself peripherally with several figures and incidents in the news, beginning with references to 'shifting a religion' and 'disaffection to the state' that apply to Jonson's own circumstances. As a convert to Roman Catholicism and as a satirical playwright periodically accused of sedition, Jonson had brushes with government agents reporting on recusants and other subversives. As early as 1599, he may himself have become an agent for Sir Robert Cecil, Elizabeth's investigator into conspiracy. Although Jonson had contacts with people on the fringes of the Essex rebellion, he was more likely asked to watch certain prominent Catholics. After Cecil used his influence to release Jonson from prison following the *Eastward Ho!* incident (9 October 1605), Jonson celebrated at a supper given by Robert Catesby and other conspirators implicated in the Gunpowder Plot. Of the people at Catesby's party, only Jonson and his friend Sir John Roe, also assumed to be a government agent, escaped later interrogation and trial. The plot was exposed on 4 November, one day before Guy Fawkes was to explode thirty-six barrels of gunpowder in the cellar of the Parliament building as James opened a joint session of the Lords and the Commons. Cecil asked Jonson on 7 November to locate a certain priest to help with further inquiries; in his report of 8 November, Jonson protested his own loyalty, but could not produce the priest. Subsequently Jonson and his wife were harassed by repeated charges of recusancy, and the association with Cecil cooled. Jonson may have perceived himself during this period as an unwitting victim of circumstance, enmeshed in state stratagems beyond his control in a world where even accident could not be dismissed as accidental. He parodies this bewildering and blackly comic experience in Sir Pol's neurotic belief that conspiratorial menace underlies all apparently innocent activities. Even his solemn notes on shopping and urinating have the authority of evidence: 'Sir, I do slip / No action of my life, thus, but I quote it' (4.1.145–6). Sir Pol's entrapment in the tortoise shell is the perfect physical correlative: an escape device in his secret-agent fantasy becomes the proof of his guilt and the instrument of his shame at the hands of masquerading 'agents' in a counterplot engineered by Peregrine, who mistakenly sees himself as a victim of Sir Pol's 'plot' to pander to Lady Would-be's sexual appetites!

Jonson did not have to look far to find other models for Sir Pol. Sir Henry Wotton, an eccentric friend of John Donne's and Jonson's at the Inns of Court, was named ambassador to Venice in 1604. Like Wotton, Sir Politic is a credulous gossip and an earnest student of foreign customs and language; the diminutive 'Pol' suggests his willingness to parrot whatever he hears. In 'To Sir Henry Wotton', Donne suggests Wotton's interest in 'news' or rumour of any kind and his alertness to suspicious 'ears' and 'tongues' plotting at court as if in a play. In 'To Sir H. W., at his going Ambassador to Venice', Donne mentions Wotton's habit of keeping notes and papers, a constant concern of Sir Pol's. In yet another poem to Wotton, Donne advises him, if 'continuance maketh hell', to imitate the prudent snail which, 'Carrying his own house still, still is at home' wherever it travels. Sir Pol finally admits that his notes were largely 'Drawn out of play-books' (5.4.42), before he seeks refuge in the tortoise shell, the 'house' Jonson prefers as a more workable stage emblem of prudence. Wotton's political career actually began with his discovery of a Catholic plot to poison James in 1601; he visited Scotland to bring the king an antidote allegedly recommended by the Duke of Tuscany. Volpone's *oglio del Scoto* may pun on this oil for the Scot. Like Wotton, Sir Pol had been in Venice for about fourteen months and had also furnished his household on credit from Jewish merchants. According to his letters, Wotton saw the Gunpowder Plot of November 1605 as part of an international Catholic conspiracy originated by Spain and the Pope; Sir Pol too fears secret attacks by Spain, or the Archdukes in the Spanish Netherlands, and secret weapons invented by their general, Spinola (2.1.50–51). Sir Pol fears specifically that enemy agents might explode the ships and weapons kept in the Arsenale (4.1.85–99), and has figured out their plans 'to sell this state now to the Turk' (130). Similar fears prompted Wotton to attempt to form a league of Protestant nations to oppose Catholic power; he believed that Venice, then resisting papal domination, would assist, and even convert to Protestantism. Sir Pol's description of spy networks led by Stone the English fool, a certain cheesemonger in Rotterdam, and a common sergeant in Venice suggests the same concern with international alliance, although Jonson reduces its object to literal red herrings. This satirical stage portrait is not necessarily malicious, although, in Peregrine's words, 'he that should write / But such a fellow should be thought to feign / Extremely' (2.1.58–60). Its apparent pillorying of Wotton merely reflects the jeering tradition of an Inns of Court roasting. In fact, Jonson admired Wotton's wit; he told Drummond that he had memorised Wotton's poem 'Character of a Happy Life', and could still recite it nearly twenty years later.

Jonson may have found another model for Sir Pol in Sir Anthony Sherley, the adventurer who captured the English imagination in 1595–98 as a buccaneer and world traveller, but finally overreached himself when his plots to become ambassador to Persia offended the English government. Sherley's political and financial deals are even more complicated than Sir Pol's imaginings. By 1600, Sherley successfully negotiated a trade agreement with Persia by figuring out a trade route to Germany, the Low Countries, and England by way of Moscow, thus avoiding the Mediterranean sea-lanes controlled by Turkey, Venice, and Spain. He was at that time acting as a double agent, spying for Cecil (but often acting separately for his kinsman Essex), and for James in Scotland as well. England, an ally of Turkey, exiled him for plotting against national interests and interfering in Levantine trade. Sir Pol's plot to shift the red-herring trade to Venice suggests similar interference in English commerce. Between 1600 and 1603, Sherley complicated matters further by attempting to forge a Persian–Christian alliance against Turkey, a goal antithetical to Venice's interests as well as England's. He lived in Venice without licence, trying to curry favour with the English by reporting Jesuit plots, spied upon by various agents, Venetian, Spanish, and English, and yet still working to corner the Persian silk market. Sir Pol's worry about licences (2.1.14–15) hinges on claims that he, like Sherley, has been under surveillance and 'all my advices, all my letters, / They have been intercepted' (2.3.13–14). After a silk merchant complained of intimidation by Sherley's gang of hired thugs, the Doge and Council had him arrested and his papers confiscated. Peregrine's avenging *mercatori* may comment on Sherley's terrorist tactics. James, upon his accession, reinstated Sherley's licence, and negotiated for his release. By the spring of 1604, however, Sherley was up to his old tricks, intercepting reports from the English ambassador at Constantinople and selling the information to Emperor Rudolf II. He was abruptly banished from Venice, but his quest for political power continued in Morocco as the joint representative of James, Philip III of Spain, and the Emperor, on yet another anti-Turkish mission. Sir Pol is expelled less formally from Venice, and unlike Sherley he promises to 'shrink' quietly into his 'politic shell' (5.4.89).

The important thing about Sir Pol is that he trails clouds of paranoia with him wherever he goes. The fact that he is wrong about specific plots emphasises the political anxieties of the age, and the fact that multiple nefarious plots tangle the action of the play demonstrates that his anxieties are not unfounded, even if they are wrongly identified. Sir Pol sniffs out the doubleness of Volpone's performance as the mountebank, although he attributes it to 'Some trick of state' (2.3.10) instead of a private conspiracy to view Celia. Actual tricks of state did justify his anxiety over omens in London's birds, lions, and fish. Anxiety over a world gone wrong because of ceaseless plotting for money and personal power – an anxiety endemic in Jonson's London – underpins the Would-be world-view, and corresponds to the darker disaffections of Volpone's Venice. Sir Pol's comic misapprehension alerts the audience to the difficulty of recognising and the need for exposing plots in public and private performances.

Celia, Lady Would-be, and domestic disorder

Domesticity in Jonson's plays tends to be inverted or perverse. Private life mirrors the claustrophobia, paranoia, and aggressive greed in public life among groups of men. Corvino has Celia watched by 'a guard of ten spies thick' (1.5.123); Peregrine mistakes the women who run the Would-be household for whores (5.4.14), based on his conjecture that Sir Politic is a bawd (4.3.20); Volpone allows no women in his literally freakish ménage. Assumptions about female promiscuity and duplicity, especially in a city famous for its courtesans, add to the play's atmosphere of conspiracy. Lady Would-be and Celia sexualise plots already concerned with the prostitution of values, which they equivocally embody, putatively as cures. Instead of restoring value, however, they simply confirm its loss. Although Celia approximates the ideal wife as chaste, silent, and obedient, Jonson is no supporter of the Griselda model of wifehood. A woman married to an unworthy husband ought not to consent to his follies or to abase herself, but Celia only draws the line at agreeing to be raped. Neither Celia nor Lady Would-be is the conventionally good wife – companionable, efficient, and fecund – and neither has married the conventionally good husband, an affliction common to all Jonsonian wives (Ezell 1987: ch. 1). Both owe their characterisations to Jonson's reinvention of two Aristophanic types of womanhood: the Amazon and the silent bride.

Lady Would-be embraces an Amazonian style akin to Aristophanes' female intruders on masculine territory. The women in *Lysistrata*, *Thesmophoriazusae*, and *Ecclesiazusae* reject submissive domesticity, and debate social and literary issues. By refusing obedience to the prevailing cultural construction of the wife, Lady Would-be joins the ranks of what Knox called 'monstrous women', women whose humanist education paradoxically helps to denigrate their sex (King 1991: pp. 189–90). Eloquent women cannot be chaste: freedom of speech and thought suggests other, more libertine freedoms. Volpone reads Lady Would-be's sexual openness in the freedom of movement allowed by English husbands, who 'dare let loose / Their wives, to all encounters!' (1.5.101–2). Celia, by contrast, is 'kept as warily as is your gold' (118), never allowed out except to church. Sir Politic admits that the trip to Venice was 'a peculiar humour of my wife's / ... to observe, / To quote, to learn the language, and so forth –' (2.1.11–13), and agrees with Peregrine's interpretation of Lady Would-be's studies as a female version of espionage: 'intelligence / Of tires, and fashions, and behaviour / Among the courtesans' (27–9). This ambivalent link between female education and whoredom is particularly pungent in Lady Would-be's parody of elegant Venetian courtesans, many of whom were poets, painters, and musicians, sought out for their discourse as well as their sexual arts. But Lady Would-be's artistic skill, vulgarised in lavish dress, coarse makeup, and a *Book of Lists* approach to conversation, reveals in her verbal and social aggressiveness a travesty of cultivated womanhood. Her ludicrous herbal and philosophical prescriptions at Volpone's bedside (3.4.51ff.) precede an offer to revitalise him with ambiguously platonic 'time and loves together' such as she had apparently enjoyed during a six-year affair with another man (115–24). Lady Would-be's obsession with her Venetian masquerade even makes her believe that Peregrine is a fashionable transvestite courtesan out to seduce Sir Politic – an assumption she transfers to evidence against Celia during the trial (4.6.1–5) – and she begs Peregrine, as an act of solidarity between 'one fair gentlewoman' (4.2.39) and another, to desist. Convinced that both the Would-bes have been trying to seduce him, he rejects her later apologies. The final occasion of Lady Would-be's identification with courtesans comes from Mosca's threat to reveal 'what you said e'en your best madams did / For maintenance, and why not you?' (5.3.42–3). The only way to restore the distinction between wife and whore is to leave town; Lady Would-be 'will straight to sea for physic' (5.4.86).

Celia is a variant of the silent bride, an eroticised abstraction of peace and plenty who appears in most Aristophanic comedies to reward the wily hero with her wanton compliance. Despite the heavenly promise of her name, Celia resembles her Aristophanic forebears in body only. She looks like a 'wonder' of soft lips and melting flesh (1.5.107–13). After one glimpse Volpone burns to possess her. Corvino accuses her of flaunting her body like a *commedia* actress or a common 'whore' (2.6.69). Both men interpret the tossing of her handkerchief from her window to the mountebank as a sexual provocation rather than an offer to purchase a love-potion, presumably to cure her jealous husband. Clearly there is a considerable discrepancy between the desiring male reading of Celia's voluptuous appearance and her chaste state of mind. This disjunction sets up the comedy of cross-purposes in the seduction scene, a bizarre reversal of Lady Would-be's earlier offer of medicinal intercourse. What Lady Would-be seems hideously eager to give,

Celia piously withholds. Ironically, Celia's disquisition against 'sensual baits' and her naming of 'breasts', 'face', 'ears', 'eyes', 'heart', 'Or any part' draw Volpone's attention to those very sites from which she wants to deflect him. Her dilemma, distended by farce, is the alienated, even schizophrenic, experience of a woman whose unruly body issues invitations that her staid mind rejects. Despite her chastity, men see only her sex appeal: she is accused of hustling, prostituted by her husband, propositioned by Volpone, and convicted of adultery and fraud. Even though Celia is eventually freed from both imprisonment and marriage, the judge's final warning to her – 'You hurt your innocence, suing for the guilty' (5.12.106) – smears her good name.

As with Lady Would-be, the truth of the charges is not what matters. Jonson finally makes no distinction between the offensive self-assertion of the one woman and the pathetic self-effacement of the other – literalised when Celia pleads with Volpone to flay her face or make her sprout leprous sores as punishment for arousing him (3.7.249–57). Both women are silenced and eliminated. Lady Would-be, however, has the satisfaction of a husband willing not only to apologise (5.4.30), but also to accompany her on her sea-quest for 'physic'. Celia is simply a cancelled debt, returned to her father with triple the money back. Lady Would-be's brush with adultery and jealousy counterpoints Celia's, and both convey, by means of sexual shock, the depravity inherent in social codes that entrench quantitative values. For those who judge by such codes, like the *avocatori*, the sheer volume of calumny heaped on Celia is enough to reverse the opinion initially held of her innocence. They find Volpone not guilty of attempted rape, partly because he demonstrates that disease incapacitates him as the 'rider on men's wives' (4.6.24), but mostly because the accrued testimonies induce the judges to blame the victim. Although the *avocatori* recognise Celia as being 'Of unreproved name' (4.5.4) and pity her for fainting (132), they respond to the cumulative attacks on her virtue by registering suspicion: 'This woman has too many moods' (142). Once Lady Would-be identifies her as a harlot, they accept all the other lies and condemn Celia for colluding with Bonario to murder Corbaccio and defame Volpone, regardless of the lack of corroborating evidence. Lady Would-be's error in bearing false witness – whether she recognises it as a convenient lie, or whether she has been misled by Mosca – illustrates how the wrongness of public life among men and whores seeps into and contaminates private life, disabling it as the restorative or refuge from the effects of the outside world.

The final judgments

Although the middle acts of the play show Volpone and Mosca toying heartlessly with the legacy-hunters – disinheriting Bonario, seducing Celia, and spurning Lady Would-be – none of these entanglements leads directly to defeat. The Act 4 trial ends in Volpone's favour. Despite his anxiety, expressed in nervous drinking (5.1.11–12) and the 'sweat' Mosca keeps twitting him about (5.2.37, 98), he feels the urge, perhaps aggravated by Mosca's conviction that 'This is our masterpiece' (13), to outdo the experience. The result is the 'jig' in which Mosca plays the new heir whose inventory-taking galls the dupes, an entertainment which Volpone first watches from behind a curtain, and then extends, in his *commendatore* disguise, by jeering the disappointed men through the streets. Volpone's pleasure in harassing his victims in public, taunting them into squirms and denials, is what really causes his downfall. The game implodes on itself in the final trial scenes. Voltore and Corvino bicker over changing their testimony (how much Corbaccio hears is comically uncertain), Mosca tries to squeeze Volpone out of his wealth and position, and Volpone decides to 'uncase' rather than let Mosca have such an impertinent victory.

The sentencing is what exercises audiences and critics alike. The verdict seems wrongheaded in the arbitrary branding of Mosca as 'chiefest minister' of the 'lewd impostures' and anticlimactic in the gradual emptying of the stage before all the judgments are heard. It also seems unduly punitive to give Mosca a life sentence on the galleys and Volpone a slow death 'cramped with irons'. But Jonson claims in the dedicatory epistle that he chose deliberately 'to put the snaffle in their mouths that cry out, we never punish vice in our interludes', following 'some lines of example' in the ancients, whose comedies do not always end joyfully. Although Plautus and Terence offer no models of unhappy comedy, one workable precedent is Aristophanes' *Ecclesiazusae*, a play in which everyone is satirically 'mulcted'. Annoyed by the waste and inequity of patriarchal democracy, Athenian women take over the legislative assembly, and impose a form of communism which inverts traditional concepts of property, family, and sex. The city becomes a great mother, clothing and feeding its people at public expense, thus eliminating capitalist consumerism; children greet all men as fathers, thus abolishing the stigma of bastardy; and men simply become sexual objects regulated by women according to age and need, with the old women satisfied before the young, ironically reversing the female experience of prostitution. The play ends with these concepts firmly entrenched: the brothels are closed, the bumboys are reassigned to pleasure bickering old hags, with the oldest and ugliest rival winning the handsomest youth, young lovers are separated, and masters return home as the pampered playthings of their households.

Through black comedy, Aristophanes mocks the oppressive Athenian patriarchy by grotesquely duplicating its errors under a matriarchal rule. He fulfils his duty as a poet by exposing the city's flaws to theatrical derision. So does Jonson when he argues that 'the office of a comic-poet' is 'to imitate justice and instruct to life', even if the justice is biased and the instruction cynical. The judges in Act 5 of *Volpone* are confused by the contradictory evidence of Voltore's notes and equally contradictory reports of Volpone's death. Although Mosca's attractiveness as the 'heir' sways them – one wants him for a son-in-law – all the judges hide behind pompous self-righteousness when Volpone contemptuously reveals the truth. Their venality, denied other outlets, asserts itself in their severity. Jonson's own experience with justice in the courts may have some bearing here, particularly his recent incarceration for *Eastward Ho!* His collaborator and cellmate, George Chapman, seems to share Jonson's view in the final scene of *The Widow's Tears* (written in 1605), which represents a governor discharging 'justice': he ignores the evidence, bullies officers who try to correct him, decides upon execution because of his prejudice in the case, boasts of his impartiality (which turns out to mean he will take bribes from anyone), and shrugs off his own ineptness with inappropriate diatribes against lechery, envy, and pride. So too Jonson's first *avocatore* lectures the audience about studying the rewards of vice. Chapman, however, prevents the enforcement of any verdicts. Jonson appears to insist on it.

But the satiric corollary of *Volpone* is the epilogue, arguably a loophole through which Volpone slips. Volpone's scorn for Venice's ingrained corruption – its commercial ethic of greed, sycophancy, and exploitation – seems justified by his adroit escape out of the plots of the play and into the theatre, where the audience's applause acquits him. The play's many theatrical contrivances support this artistic displacement of crude realism, as do the bizarre preferences of all of the characters for fantasy lives: even Bonario wants to believe that his father's perjury is the result of coercion (4.5.110). Like the fox-tailed Harlequin-actor, Volpone survives his role in the play, following the tradition of the fox. In the medieval Reynard the Fox beast-epic, the fox appears in many guises (false doctor, serenading seducer, insolent trickster) and, though he is tried for his crimes, including rape and feigning death, he always escapes the court's final sentence (see R. B. Parker 1976a). The general feeling in the epic as in the play is that fox, victims, and court are all corrupt and therefore, as King Lear says, 'None does offend'; retribution is pointless. Even faced with punishment, Reynard or Harlequin, like Volpone, shrugs it off, a physically and spiritually resilient figure with a life beyond the context of the particular tales in which other characters are imbedded. Liberated from the roles his ingenuity has constructed, distilling them into the vitality that formerly infused them, Volpone rises to myth, heroically transcending the substance that chains others:

> What should I do
> But cocker up my *genius* and live free
> To all delights my fortune calls me to?
> (1.1.70–72)

EPICOENE, OR THE SILENT WOMAN

The world of *The Silent Woman* is, as the subtitle suggests, a paradoxical place; it posits, like Joseph Hall's *Mundus Alter et Idem* (see the Introduction to *Epicoene*, 'Sources'), an alternative satirical world that is also identical with the real world of Jacobean London. The inhabitants are cliques of fools, rogues, consumers, and status-seekers who mark off their territories with aggressive displays of food, drink, dress, and noise. At the centre of this social map-making is the enigmatic Epicoene. Swirling around her, busy crowds of dilettantes and toadies violate boundaries of taste, common sense, personal privacy, discretion, and gender. They offend, attract, disorient, titillate, and frighten others, but, more to the point, their fascinating bustle almost eliminates our awareness of Dauphine's plot against his uncle. Instead we are caught up in the confusion of unstable social changes, fluid sexual identities, and the hostility such fluctuations usually arouse.

The volatile world of the play depends on its unnerving liminality. Jonson's London is on the threshold of major social upheaval as a town elite thrusts its way between court and country life. The old standards are vanishing, and distortion, ambiguity, randomness, and risk are taking their place. The characters try to compensate for their feelings of insecurity by closing their eyes to contradictions and seeking approval in conformity. They race, hunt, gamble, and gossip; as Truewit shrugs, 'These be the things wherein your fashionable men exercise themselves, and I for company' (1.1.34–5). To reduce the pressures of uncertainty, the characters seek out talismanic alliances with privileged groups who proclaim themselves powerful wits, braveries, ladies collegiate, or knights. At best, such 'clubs' give their members psychic support by seeming to share certain codes of behaviour and, as among Morose's guests, by encouraging the solidarity of noise in the carnival revelry of 'The spitting, the coughing, the laughter, the neezing, the farting, dancing, noise of the music, and [Epicoene's] masculine and loud commanding and urging the whole family' (4.1.6–8). This new society is both monstrous and charismatic, and despite the barricades Morose throws up, he is helpless to impede its growth. In fact, in desiring Epicoene and in attempting to thwart Dauphine's status-seeking, he unwittingly lets it 'mushroom' (2.4.131) into his house. Dauphine, on the other hand, works within the new social dynamic to achieve more power for himself: he begins with a purchased knighthood and friends at court, and he ends with the income he needs to support the idle life he covets. This world has no heroes, only winners, desperate hangers-on, and losers.

Why Dauphine wins

Whereas his friends and the other social butterflies vie for the intangibles conferred by social power, sexual reputation, and admiration, or at least attention, Dauphine competes primarily for money, although he achieves the other ends as well. The final victory of Dauphine is to flaunt Epicoene's peruke in one hand and the signed contract in the other, demonstrating his superiority by disgracing his uncle and profiting himself. The mere public humiliation of Morose, as demonstrated by the peruke, would not have won him any profit. Morose already believed that Dauphine's crowd had maligned his reputation by circulating 'ridiculous' stories about him (1.2.8–10); hence, the plan to disinherit his nephew. But the contract giving Dauphine control of Morose's estate routs the uncle definitively.

The strength of Dauphine's plot lies in its single-minded objective: to train, set up, and introduce to Morose a silent bride who will turn into a shrew after the wedding, and disappear once Morose signs over his estate to Dauphine. Dauphine is fearful of the involvement of others. He lies to Truewit about 'some business now' (1.2.40) to avoid introducing him to Epicoene and her agent, Cutbeard. Later he cautions Epicoene against going to La Foole's party (2.3.9–11), apparently out of the same fear of shrewd eyes piercing the masquerade. His secretiveness asserts itself as a protective cover even when he thinks all is lost after Truewit's stunt with the post-horn. Dauphine claims Truewit has 'undone' him: 'That which I have plotted for and been maturing now these four months, you have blasted in a minute'; yet he goes on to misrepresent his plot as depending on a 'gentlewoman' – his 'entire friend' – who after marrying Morose would have made Dauphine 'ample conditions' (2.4.33–40). This version is not quite the same story that he tells Morose at the end of the play, when he reveals the 'gentleman's son that I have brought up this half year at my great charges, and for this composition which I have now made with you' (5.4.176–9). But prevarication is a habit with Dauphine. Just as he misrepresents himself to his friends as victimised, he also misrepresents himself to his uncle as sympathetic at the end of 4.2, and as worthy of trust at the beginning of 4.4. The truth seems to be that he himself is incapable of trusting anyone fully, especially anyone who needs to boast of superior power or knowledge, like his friends Clerimont and Truewit. He reproaches Clerimont for gossiping about Morose (1.3), and jeers at Truewit's promises – 'Ay, you have many plots! So you had one to make all the wenches in love with me' (4.5.17–18) – and at Truewit's 'vanity' for needing his 'every jest ... published'. Dauphine's longest speech in the play suppresses the true source of his joy at his uncle's marriage paradoxically with a gush of words, an elaborate lie uttered in Truewit's giddy style, conning La Foole into dressing as a sewer and delivering a feast to Morose's house (3.3.54–65). Dauphine needs few words to amplify the indisputable evidence of his victory in the final scene: the contract signed before witnesses is firmly in his grasp, as is Epicoene's peruke, and both are tangible proofs that the groom, now his nephew's ward, is 'no man' and the bride, Dauphine's ward all along, is no woman.

Dauphine's plot illustrates the dystopian idea – developed in all the other characters – of a society in the process of emerging into new and possibly monstrous shapes by way of dubious androgyny, gender transgressions and inversions which the play sets out but makes no attempt to resolve. Clerimont's first appearance, for example, '*making himself ready*' in fashionable dress, suggests an artful trans-formation to which the audience is privy, and provides a contradictory context for Clerimont's song praising 'sweet neglect' and 'simplicity' over 'th'adulteries of art', the formal attire, cosmetics, and perfume which may hide impairment. The singer of the song is also paradoxical: he is 'the welcom'st thing under a man' – 'and above a man too', kept as Clerimont's 'ingle' but, as the boy himself confesses, the plaything of ladies who kiss him and dress him up in a peruke and gown. Since the song addresses a lady and assumes that the art of dressing is feminine, what are we to make of the poet who exposes to the audience his own art in dressing throughout this act? Clerimont seems to be trapped in an inconsistent pattern of aggression and retreat. He sends his ingle to woo his lady – a medium in conflict with the message? or is the medium the message? – and resents her acceptance of the boy in his place. He denies knowledge of the Ladies Collegiate, but Lady Haughty, their leader, is the subject of his song. After seeing her again, he finds himself still drawn to her despite his 'dispraise of her i' the morning' (4.1.27), and yet he says nothing to her, nor does she recognise him as a prospective suitor, or speak to him even after he leads the ladies in to watch the humiliation of Daw and La Foole (4.5). Should we interpret Clerimont's silence as extreme diffidence, tact, or counter-rejection? How similar is he to Daw, another poet who, rejected by his lady, retaliates with silent melancholy (2.4.118–28)?

Truewit's antagonistic chatter is as peculiar as Clerimont's relative silence. In his rebuttal of Clerimont's song, Truewit supports women's use of cosmetics, but then defies his own argument with an anecdote of how he and another 'rude fellow' intruded for an hour upon the privacy of a woman who, startled, put her wig on backwards. The incident suggests that he finds something both erotic and laughable in the woman's vulnerability to male intrusion and in her need for the protection that he withholds. But this anecdote, like his diatribe against wives (2.2) and his boasts of sexual expertise (4.1), seems to have nothing to do with his actual behaviour with women. He visits at the college, but none of the Ladies Collegiate greets him as a particular 'friend' or lover. He is as polite to Mistress Otter, even in 4.3 when he refuses to kiss her, as he is to Epicoene, and is more interested in pulling off his grand theatrics – the bullying of Morose in 2.2, the heralding of the Ladies Collegiate in 3.5 and 3.6, the kicking and tweaking of the fools in 4.5, and the annulment debate in 5.3 – than he is in either shaming or winning a mistress. Even in his final speech to the assembled gulls, he lashes Daw and La Foole, but spares the ladies with ingratiating promises of secrecy. The degree of sarcasm or spite is open to question. Perhaps, as in the anecdote about the woman and the wig, Truewit disguises his passive aggression with hypocritical denial.

Dauphine also likes to pose as an 'innocent' bystander because the ruse distracts everyone from the real plot that he has constructed. As he tells Clerimont, 'with the fewer a business is carried, it is ever the safer' (1.3.6–7). Dauphine owes his victory to his secretiveness, shutting out even his closest friends so that he can spring the final surprise on them too. The in-group dynamic among the three friends operates on distrust, competition, and gibes, each man trying to impress and outdo the others. Clerimont even feels a testy rivalry with his boy, who has proved a more acceptable visitor at the college than himself. Truewit needles Clerimont about his indolent way of life, with his 'ingle at home' and 'mistress abroad', picks up on Clerimont's annoyance at Lady Haughty's declining his visits to her bedroom, and pointedly tells his own tale of the woman with the reversed wig – that is, the story of a woman incapable of resisting Truewit's entrance. Conceivably, Clerimont tells Truewit details of Morose's quest for a silent bride as a tit-for-tat, implying a confidential alliance with Dauphine that excludes Truewit. Clerimont may also enjoy needling Dauphine, who irritably refuses to give Truewit any information whatsoever. During forty lines of 1.2, Dauphine speaks only twice to Truewit, both negative replies. Neither Truewit nor Clerimont is allowed full knowledge of the plot, perhaps because Dauphine blames them for his 'predicament' with his uncle and prefers to be seen as refusing to oppose Morose's 'least fancy': 'Let it lie upon my stars to be guilty, I'll be innocent' (47–8). Because he mouths all the correctly deferential attitudes towards his uncle, he deludes his friends with views of himself as a victim. As a result, they support Dauphine's real 'business' at Morose's house by plotting absurd distractions as camouflage: moving La Foole's feast and detouring the Ladies Collegiate to celebrate the bridal; fomenting quarrels between the Otters and between Daw and La Foole; and spinning out legal debate over the prospective annulment. These diversions, like relations generally among the three friends, have a double dynamic: the escalating practical jokes spur them on in their in-group competition for dominance, but also unite them in a common goal to vex Morose into relenting so that Dauphine will not 'be poor, and beg' (49) – exactly the fate that Morose wants for him at the end of 2.5. But, because Morose is so vindictive in his fantasy of his nephew's defeat, we, the audience, tend to discount the accuracy of his view of Dauphine as a one-upping plotmeister. For all these reasons, Dauphine's final success jolts us.

Despite his apparently decisive control of the plot, Dauphine is still part of the liminality and confusion that rule the rest of the play, feelings that Jonson relates specifically to sexual identity. Although Dauphine creates a perfect parody of the feminine in Epicoene, he is frightened of women, and, like his uncle, reclusive generally. According to Truewit, Dauphine spends far too much time reading romances in his room alone, when he should 'come abroad where the matter is frequent' to meet women at court, tiltings, public shows and feasts, plays and church, and by experience learn 'whom to love, whom to play with, whom to touch once, whom to hold ever' (4.1.47–53). But although Dauphine, like Clerimont, desires older married women, he is happier with his boy, the 'entire friend' who wins him Morose's estate. Like the other characters in *Epicoene*, Dauphine is on the threshold of change, but change into what? Equal pulls of attraction and repulsion, transmutation and deviation, magnify his choices and yet promise only unstable metamorphosis. Even his name, 'Sir Dauphine', combines the masculinity of his purchased knighthood with the femininity of the given name, 'Princess', or more accurately 'Heiress Apparent'. 'Epicoene', 'Otter', 'Centaur', 'La Foole', 'Ladies

Collegiate', all have similarly hermaphroditic implications that suggest the forma-
tion of a third sex (see notes on The Persons of the Play). The contradictions
between speech and behaviour in Clerimont and Truewit hint at a similar
indeterminacy.

Although Dauphine, Clerimont, and Truewit may display individual weaknesses, as a group united against an outside target they are cohesive and supportive,
even without being fully informed of one another's activities. Projecting power as
a group is the key to their success, not honesty within the group. They all lie to one
another. Honesty, even to oneself, is not a prized value. Image is what counts. A
group's vitality in Jonson's plays usually expresses itself by jeering, and the
strongest group co-ordinates its attacks and crushes its targets through its verbal
alacrity and poise. The jeering may range from light teasing to sneers, malicious
gossip, mimicry and parody, name-calling, exclusion, and outright denunciation. At
any point, the verbal hostility may erupt into physical threat or assault. The verbal
sparring with Morose in 3.5 and 3.6, for example, ends in Truewit's unspecified
physical threat to 'begin' to Morose 'in a very sad cup' (3.6.98), followed by
Clerimont's onslaught of noise in *'Music of all sorts'* (3.7). Mistress Otter responds
to Otter's drunken slurs by beating him (4.2.84ff.). Jeering is a manipulative sport.
In the drinking competition, for example, a combination of jeering and praise
compels Daw and La Foole to participate, although neither can hold his liquor, and
La Foole especially fears that his cousin Mistress Otter will blame him for
encouraging Otter's cups. Skill in jeering also separates the weak from the strong.
While the inept group of Otter, Daw, and La Foole drink, the proficient trio –
Dauphine, Clerimont, and Truewit – celebrate their secret confederacy by inciting
Otter's mockery of his wife and the subsequent beating. Otter utters his jeers
because he believes mistakenly that he has the unified support of all the other men.
Instead, he has been their scapegoat.

Both kinds of jeering – castigating a group member for failing to conform to
group standards, and scapegoating a target outside the group – alternate when
Truewit seems at first to have disrupted Morose's plans to marry and then to have
precipitated them (2.4). Clerimont jeers Truewit with sarcasm and name-calling,
and Dauphine denounces both men, but when the reversal is announced, Truewit
retaliates with mimicry: 'No, I was "ignorantly officious", "impertinent". This was
the "absurd weak part"' (2.4.62). Finally, Dauphine reunifies the group by
placating the other two with 'Nay, gentlemen, 'tis well now' and eventually
promising to conspire with them 'for any device of vexation' (2.6.19–20), a scheme
that scapegoats virtually everyone else in the play. A group legitimates its jeering
tactics by imposing order on its members' frustrations; it lets them assert their
masculinity by symbolically killing their enemies with verbal barbs, or at least by
intimidating them with threatening postures. The severest risk in this game is that
a counter-attack will destroy the group utterly, scattering and isolating its members.
Being alone, as Morose's experience attests, is a kind of death.

Male bonding actually stimulates the testing and violating of group boundaries,
as groups root out the unmanly or the cowardly, whether by temporary exclusion
or complete ostracism. When Dauphine learns (inaccurately) that Daw and La

Foole called him 'a pitiful poor fellow' who had 'nothing but three suits of apparel and some few benevolences that lords ga' [him] to fool to 'em and swagger', he asserts his maleness by threatening to 'beat 'em . . . bind 'em . . . and have 'em baited' (4.5.8–13). The degradation of Daw and La Foole involves locking them into separate closets and jeering them into abject displays of submission, witnessed by the Ladies Collegiate. Co-ordinated jointly by Truewit and Clerimont, the inspired stage management presents Dauphine as manly and witty, and induces all the Ladies to fall in love with him. This group-sponsored power takes direct aim at Morose in Act 5, and achieves what Dauphine could not have done on his own: the utterly humiliating defeat of Morose before jeering witnesses. This punishment reconfirms the unity and power of the successful group, even though Dauphine's degradation of Morose began as a private war whose secret weapon Clerimont and Truewit knew nothing about.

Why Morose loses

The humiliation planned for Morose is far more elaborate than that of the other gulls, in proportion to his outrageous crime against Dauphine: Morose attempts to destroy Dauphine's masculinity by cutting off his finances. Truewit's foray with the post-horn into Morose's house is merely the first sally in the larger encounters that escalate after the wedding. In subsequent retaliations, Morose, most vulnerable because he is the only non-group-member in the play, is systematically invaded, forced to confess to sexual and social incompetence – 'I am no man, ladies' (5.4.38); 'I will become thy ward' (149) – and finally ostracised: '[B]e as private as you will, sir. I'll not trouble you till you trouble me with your funeral, which I care not how soon it come' (185–7).

The mock-divorce and mock-death that end *Epicoene* hardly seem the stuff of comedy. Nevertheless, the play has most of the elements of Aristophanic comedy – bizarrely skewed. If Aristophanes had been the playwright, Morose would have been the comic hero, rather than the Jonsonian butt. As a grouchy patriarch, he pursues the Aristophanic quest for peace – reduced by Jonson to a desire for silence – on private terms that exclude the rest of society as barbaric and unworthy impostors: this is the scenario of *Acharnians*, *Peace*, and *The Birds*. Morose imposes his fantasy of self-centred power upon his household, in which his is the only voice, interminably talking, while his dependants communicate in dumb show. He needs the final fillip of a mute bride as testimonial and guarantee of his continuing power, like Peisthetairos in *The Birds*, or Trygaeus in *Peace*. But instead of repelling the belligerent intruders from his version of cloud-cuckoo-land, Morose helplessly allows his house to become a clamorous thoroughfare: the intruders take over, the bride metamorphoses into a monster, and the scoffing antagonist wins the struggle by means of a mock-trial, the usual Aristophanic battleground. Although Morose begins with his private paradise in place, he cannot prevent its destruction when exposed to public infiltration and ridicule.

The attack on Morose is successful largely because of his isolation. He has no chorus of supporters. As the head of the household, he is so repressive that he has fired servants for wearing squeaky shoes – not a condition that inspires loyalty in the staff. And he persists in shutting out and condemning change in society without instituting a counteractive model of behaviour, as Aristophanic heroes do. Instead he proposes only negative and rigid silence. His objections to the new society are clear in his contempt for Dauphine, whom he describes as 'insolent' and manipulative (2.5.86–112): he sees Dauphine's knighthood as an attempt to obtain precedence over his uncle and win favour among the titled at court. Without the income appropriate for the high life, however, Dauphine cannot gamble, squander, and fornicate as other modern gentlemen do, and the only use for his knighthood in the end will be to impress a whore ('Dol Tearsheet or Kate Common') into marrying and supporting him, a fit conclusion to his dissolute life. Although Morose's resentment biases his view of Dauphine's career, the play's other descriptions of fashionable life bear out some of his charges. Clerimont 'can melt away his time ... between his mistress abroad and his ingle at home, high fare, soft lodging, fine clothes' (1.1.21–3), gambling with lords at horse-races, and gossiping with ladies in the evenings, because he apparently has the money to live well. Truewit 'for company' does the same. Dauphine emulates the life without the advantage of the income: he too desires mistresses abroad, and, it turns out, has an ingle at home who plays out Dauphine's scripts (instead of singing his songs, like Clerimont's boy), cross-dresses in a gown and peruke, and chats intimately with the Ladies Collegiate. Daw and La Foole lead similar lives, complete with 'boys' (5.1.3) and mistresses, including Epicoene, they say.

Morose has no social set with whom he shares values. The court life he recalls from his youth is ludicrously outdated (2.5.28). He is fooled by his apparently impregnable house, the apparently loyal Cutbeard, and the apparently innocent Epicoene into thinking that he can form his own team to defeat Dauphine's. What he does not know is that his team is only a mock-team whose real loyalty is to Dauphine. The verbal abuse he endures from Truewit (2.2) angers Morose, but does not entirely incapacitate him; rather, it makes him act precipitately. But the post-marital abuse eventually breaks him. Epicoene refuses to countenance silence: 'I'll have none of this coacted unnatural dumbness in my house, in a family where I govern' (3.4.46–7). The Ladies Collegiate bait Morose with recipes to cure his madness, allowing him to 'breathe' between attacks 'a quarter of an hour or so' (4.4.131). By Act 5, the Ladies have, through direct and indirect abuse, so thoroughly stigmatised and demoralised Morose that he feels merely to be among them exposes him to intolerable invasions of privacy. In fact, the Ladies even threaten to strip him and check out his claim to be a 'bridegroom uncarnate' (5.4.43). He attempts to deflect their attacks with hostile bravado, but achieves only temporary success in the sword-brandishing of 4.2 and 4.6. His house, once his fortress, becomes his prison. Having lost credibility by spurning his 'wife', he also loses freedom of movement and of speech: he is physically constrained to greet his guests in 3.5–7, interrupted when he speaks, and forced to hear the Ladies' diagnosis of his insanity in 4.4. Otherwise his choices are either to hide in the attic 'sitting over a cross-beam o' the roof' where he is 'peeped' at by the sniggering Dauphine (4.1.17–21), or to run out of the house 'in's night-caps' to find a divorce lawyer (4.5.3–4). He has no privacy. The environment that before nurtured his eccentric fantasies now becomes the site of nightmares robbing him of self-respect, dignity, and other personal defences. With no hope of an annulment, Morose's final tactic, defensive covering by claiming impotence, fails because it evokes even more jeering once the jeerers know he is helpless with dread. Shocked by his noisy wife and bullying guests, forced into passivity at his loss of authority in his household, and afflicted by bouts of hysteria, Morose finds himself lulled into dependency on Dauphine, who sympathetically offers aid and then humiliates him in the presence of hostile spectators. The accumulated power of their derision strips him of his self-respect and the respect of his peers. All that remains is abandonment and death by emotional starvation.

The new women and the boy-players

In *Conversations with William Drummond*, Jonson recollects *Epicoene*'s unfavourable reception: 'When his play of a *Silent Woman* was first acted, there was found verses after on the stage against him, concluding that that play was well named *The Silent Woman*, there was never one man to say "plaudite" to it' (Parfitt 1975: p.480). The anonymous critic suggests that neither men nor women in the audience appreciated the play, and the deliberate reference to gender implies that Jonson's depiction of the sexes may have caused this adverse reaction. The Ladies Collegiate and their admirers, as exemplars of social change, represent human nature as evolving into sexual dead ends. Barren creatures who batten on noise, material consumption, and social status, they displace or deflect heterosexual desire. Truewit, like Daw and La Foole, talks sex instead of doing it. Dauphine pursues money and independence by means of a liaison with a boy. Clerimont lives with a boy, and Morose marries one. The Ladies Collegiate transform themselves into mock-men who debunk patriarchal authority by burlesquing male behaviour. But the salient fact of the play is that men and women alike are drawn to the powers of the 'autumnal' Lady Haughty and her set, and strive for their favour. No matter how destructive their social excesses, the middle-aged women exert such a seductive magnetic pull that no one can resist.

The mock-masculinity of the Ladies Collegiate gets a thorough examination in the many inversions of gender-role-playing that dominate the text. As members of a rapidly expanding group, these women live apart from their husbands and 'cry down, or up, what they like or dislike in a brain or a fashion with most masculine or rather *hermaphroditical* authority' (1.1.67–9). In an amusing inversion of the sexual double standard, they make passes at pages, lure lovers with gifts of jewels, and kiss other women's husbands with their wives' 'leave ... to use a becoming familiarity' (3.6.20). Their jeering epitomises and exploits the cruelty of a society so competitive that the only concept of honour comes from successful one-upmanship. Although the Ladies do not appear on stage until the end of Act 3, references to their collegiate activities and related discussions of women and marriage dominate virtually every scene in the play. Clerimont evokes Lady Haughty's influence in song; Truewit describes the college's membership; and La

Foole, in his invitation (1.4), makes clear the social cachet of attending the same parties as the Ladies. For that reason, Truewit decides to redirect 'the college-honours' (2.6.36) to Morose's house to add to the feast. The Ladies arrive in a stultifying explosion of noise (3.6–7), criticising Morose and testing Epicoene. Although the Collegiates initially enter Morose's house to laugh at his silent wife, they stay 'Withdrawn with the bride in private ... instructing her i' the college-grammar' (4.1.23–4). Most of this anti-marital instruction involves the management of her husband, the taking of lovers, and the secret of effective prophylaxis. During the humiliation of Daw and La Foole, their physical presence 'above' dominates the stage itself. The staging particularly suggests that the gratification of matriarchs is the high point, if not the only point, of male pleasure.

The fact that Jonson wrote *Epicoene* for a boys' company increases possibilities for satiric inversion. While it is quite likely that in *Volpone* an adult clown played Lady Would-be as a 'dame' role, leaving Celia for a conventionally androgynous boy-actor, we cannot be so sure about how Jonson loaded the dice in *Epicoene*. Did larger, older boys play the Ladies Collegiate as grotesques? Or was Mistress Otter the only grotesque 'dame'? Who played Epicoene? How unsettling was the play's metatheatrical focus on boys trained to sing and act, dress as women, wear cosmetics, act as ingles, prattle, and pull youthful pranks? How might large boys as women and smaller boys as men affect an audience's perception of the play's ideas about sexuality, marriage, motherhood, and the inheritance of property? Such casting might readjust the audience's view of male power-games as childish fancies, particularly Dauphine's insidious and successful inversion of the natural order of things: he eliminates the wife as the producer of the legitimate heir, not only creating himself heir to his uncle's wealth, but also inheriting it before his uncle's death.

Fear of adult women with equal rights in the domestic and public spheres activates all the conflicts in *Epicoene*. Jonson reinvented this plot based on Aristophanes' female-intruder plays, in which the women trespass on the public male world, and take charge, usually because men abuse their social responsibilities (Zeitlin 1980–82: p. 135). In *Ecclesiazusae*, for example, women disguised in their husbands' garments pack the legislature to vote themselves into power because the men have been lining their own pockets instead of serving public interests. As part of the new social milieu set up by the comedy, the role reversal allows women to compete openly with men and to assume rights usually allocated only to men. At the same time, the men of *Ecclesiazusae* experience womanhood, first by wearing women's clothes, then by being confined to the domestic sphere where they drink and behave irrationally, and finally, if they are attractive enough, by becoming sex objects to gratify ugly old crones. In *Epicoene*, a similar satirically reductive pattern emerges. The Ladies Collegiate adopt male manners and doublets as signs of their successful intervention in the male world. Leaving their husbands to drudge at home, the wives assemble in a college/bordello where they invite suitably effeminate lovers, and broadcast opinions on trends and people with 'hermaphroditical authority'. Their education and their aggressiveness upset social place, and their status as heads of household, presumably secured through a marriage contract such as Mistress Otter describes, means that they cannot be ignored. In the Otters' agreement, a parodic reversal of the usual family hierarchy, the wife is the 'princess' and reigns in the house, where the husband is the obedient 'subject', dependent on her for food, clothing, spending-money, and social standing, and liable to her 'correction' if he speaks out of turn (3.1.9, 23ff.).

At their most terrifying, the Ladies Collegiate imitate male privilege by wielding the power of sexual choice, a choice that includes neither monogamy nor procreation on demand. They refuse to admit Clerimont as a lover (remember the sour-grapes song he has written for Lady Haughty), they tolerate Daw and La Foole as useful hangers-on, and they gossip with Truewit, but they actively court Dauphine, who, infatuated with all the Collegiates, is too diffident to pursue them. The Ladies seem to be living refutations of Truewit's argument that 'A man should not doubt to overcome any woman', and that rape is 'an acceptable violence, and has oft-times the place of the greatest courtesy' (4.1.61, 72–3). The threatening presence of strong females on stage exposes Truewit's remarks as empty blather. The Ladies' 'autumnal' age and perhaps their size, if large actors did play the roles, make them impervious to attackers, like mothers dealing with naughty boys. Such matriarchal figures are more likely to resist physical intimidation or psychological domination by infantilising their seducers. The doubleness of the play's ending explores this notion. In the final proposition, intended to dispel doubts cast on their sexual adequacy, the men promise not to tell the women's secrets, if the women let the men visit at the college. The Ladies' silence seems to give consent to sexual blackmail that will preserve their public reputations. But are they cowed by the men's knowledge, or aroused by Epicoene's bold invasion of their ranks? Are they cannily sizing up, in terms of advantages to themselves, the cockiness of the men's little rebellion? Perhaps by letting the men think themselves victors, the women will find other methods of asserting female domination. A flicker of shared glances and smirks is all the women need to arm themselves for the contest to come. By thus reversing and challenging the spatial, economic, and sexual boundaries that should have kept the women enclosed and dominated within their households (Foley 1982: p. 6), the Ladies Collegiate assert matriarchal composure, and puncture the bravado of their puny men.

The attraction and the fear aroused by such controlling women suggest the public discomfort with the feminised social scene and the erosion of masculine authority in a play that represents men as barely pubescent, still under their mothers' thumbs. It asks, or perhaps begs, the question, 'What is the difference between a cultivated lady of opinion and a shrew?' In Aristophanes, as in Jonson, feminisation is a double-edged concept on stage: how should an audience react to the male actor who successfully creates a positive female role such as Lysistrata (Zeitlin 1980–82: p. 140), or, more complicatedly, Epicoene? Aristophanes regards temporary feminisation as a positive cure for male depravity: when the Magistrate orders the women to stop their anti-war sex-strike, Lysistrata and her companions force him to understand the female position by decking him with a veil and the accessories of women's work. In figures like Lysistrata, or Praxagora in *Ecclesiazusae*, the male actor playing a heroic female character creates a superwoman who fuses a woman's concern for the household with a man's concern for the public weal. The misogyny that normally diminishes female behaviour on stage is temporarily abrogated to allow her to undermine or denounce abusive male authority. So too with Epicoene. Although we know Dauphine has coached her and continues to cue her during the play, we also respect her independent improvisational ability in creating a strong sympathetic female response to an intolerable marital situation. Instantly following the Morose wedding, Epicoene drops the pretence of silence and launches into just criticisms of oppressive male attitudes towards wives: 'Why, did you think you had married a statue? or a motion only? one of the French puppets with the eyes turned with a wire? or some innocent out of the hospital, that would stand with her hands thus, and a plaice-mouth, and look upon you?' (3.4.33–6). Epicoene intends to behave in the manner 'competent to the estate and dignity of [a] wife' (40–41), and reasonable conduct requires open channels of communication, 'none of this coacted, unnatural dumbness', whether among members of the household, or between the household and the community. Morose's hysterical denunciations of his wife as 'a Penthesilia, a Semiramis' (48–9) undermine his authority and support Epicoene's by associating her with classical heroines of androgynous strength. As Truewit remarks, 'she speaks but reason, and methinks is more continent than you' (3.5.35–6). Morose's argument that he has been tricked into marrying a whore wins no credibility in view of Epicoene's calm civilised demeanour. Fraudulent though she is, Epicoene complicates the view of sexual relations by representing a wife with sensible and recognisably female feelings, trapped in a marriage that refuses to acknowledge her virtues. With the sole exception of her husband, Epicoene is the focus of universal admiration from the other characters and from the audience as well. When she cries, 'I am undone, I am undone!' (5.4.101), we all feel horrified disbelief.

But Epicoene's unmasking puts a different spin on the whole question of contradictory gender roles, dramatically and metatheatrically. The idea of Epicoene as a boy-actor playing the part of a boy who plays the silent bride reverses the usual direction of cross-dressing in drama, and inverts the idea of the female intruder into legitimate male space. Like the transgressive male characters who cross-dress to penetrate the secret but legitimate world of women in *Thesmophoriazusae*, Epicoene trespasses on the Ladies Collegiate's social and sexual domain (legitimate within the satirical construct of the play) to spy upon them and disclose their secrets. In the course of committing this transgression, Epicoene also exposes multiple male intrigues: the minor anti-feminist plot, urged by Dauphine's gang and perpetrated by Jack Daw and La Foole, to ruin a woman's reputation by baselessly accusing her of whoredom (5.4.95–9), and the larger plot, suggested by the mock-divorce and the boy-bride, to eliminate wives altogether, thus leaving women to the college/brothel of their choice – and leaving men to invent a witty substitute for patrilineal succession. In the illogical world of *Epicoene*, most men refuse to be husbands, and most women marry for the privilege of living as widows. But are they women? Once Epicoene's peruke is off, do we not look askance at the perukes and gowns of the Ladies Collegiate? Metatheatrically, the boy-actors posit a world which excludes heterosexuality except in terms of coy role-playing and games-playing, a never-never land which assumes that adults have trivial intellects and contract barren or broken marriages, and that life among boys is more fun, so long as no one grows up.

THE ALCHEMIST

The Alchemist is ostensibly about magic, though its magic does not seriously undertake to harness the occult power of the natural world, except in a satirical sense. Jonson represents the magic as a con-game which profits from the hidden desires and fantasies of natural fools. As for alchemy itself, he is sceptical of its claims as a scientific or pseudo-scientific study. Unlike the verifiable and repeatable experimentation that Bacon defines as the scientific method, the alchemical process promises to unlock the mystery of creation through ritualised experiments that depend on the practitioner's subjective quirks, rather than on objective criteria. In theory, if the alchemist can release the naturally occurring spirit or soul in matter, he can intensify its power through distillation and crystallisation until it achieves quintessence, a purer component of matter impervious to corruption and time. This potent powder is the philosopher's stone. With its immediate perfectibility of matter, the alchemist in his laboratory can imitate God, and re-create the prelapsarian universe, but without the allowance for free will, and hence without prospective flaw. All base metals 'would be gold, if they had time' (2.3.136); all life would be free of disease, struggle, and famine, all people would be good, and their dreams would come true, if only they had time to achieve perfection. With a grain of the philosopher's stone, the transformation is instant.

The goal of alchemy – understanding the secrets of matter in order to improve it – is not that far from the ideals of modern science generally. But Jonson's point of view is socially and rationally pragmatic, geared to observable reality, and he jeers satirically, not so much at the scientific assumptions (with which he is learnedly familiar), but at fraudulent practitioners and their credulous and self-serving clientele. Esoteric knowledge, by stimulating unprincipled minds, opens the door to abuse. The popular prejudice against science, whether mathematics, navigation, astronomy, or natural philosophy, crops up in the uncertain division between legitimate study and unlawful dabbling in magic, a dilemma that coloured attitudes towards Paracelsus, for example: was he the first modern physician, or was he a fiendish magician? In *The Alchemist*, Jonson suggests a similar confusion. Subtle's expertise in natural science and mathematics has equal weight with his experience as an alchemist, conjurer, thief, and jack-of-all-trades – none of them successful. Face reminds Subtle of his ragged and hunger-pinched destitution before the set-up in Lovewit's house,

> When all your alchemy, and your algebra,
> Your minerals, vegetals, and animals,
> Your conjuring, cozening, and your dozen of trades,

Could not relieve your corps, with so much linen
Would make you tinder but to see a fire.

(1.1.38–42)

The association of Subtle with mathematics and later with medicine places him beside John Dee, Della Porta, and Cornelius Agrippa, who actively investigated the occult alongside more conventional study. Scholars not actively interested in alchemy or conjuring, like Kepler or Cornelius Drebbel, conducted experiments in natural science that at least seemed magical, or, like Walter Ralegh, accepted astrology as legitimate. According to Drummond, Jonson himself 'can set horoscopes, but trusts not in them' (Parfitt 1975: p. 469). Even Francis Bacon's empiricism relied on hermetic and neoplatonic concepts of cosmic analogies, the hidden sympathies and antipathies by which the universe was thought to operate.

The alchemy of Jonson's play shows how magic intersects fact and fantasy, process and product, experiment and experience. It may represent itself teasingly as piety, wealth, wit, luck, love, or empire, but its real power is the illusion of absolute, even permanent, self-fulfilment. It celebrates male and female, survives life and death, punishes, transforms, and perfects. At the literal level, the alchemical fraud holds the plot together. Satirically, it turns the base metal of the dupes into gold to line the rogues' pockets. Metaphorically, it supplies the language of transformation upward into a higher state of being. During the argument in the opening scene, Subtle claims in alchemical terms to have 'Sublimed', 'exalted', and 'fixed' Face from a household drudge into a fashionable military gentleman, and then 'Wrought [him] to spirit, to quintessence', making him the perfect shill or lure for enticing customers; now Face threatens to 'fly out i' the projection' – rebel, thus exploding the experiment, rather than work the final change that will bring them all wealth (1.1.67–70, 79). The rogues' characters also conform to the alchemical process, which requires mercury and sulphur to engender changes in the metal. Dol's mercurial temper and sexual association with heat and volatility – 'She'll mount you up like quicksilver / Over the helm' (2.3.254–5) – are paired with Subtle's stench, blackened face, and vitriolic properties of flask and tongue. Face, whether as the inflammatory huckster who brings in the raw material (the customers) or the 'Lungs' who blows the fire, steadily increases the temperature of the dupes' desires. According to Subtle, the process begins with slow dry heat and gradually switches to more intense steaming, cooling, and steaming again: 'For look, how oft I iterate the work, / So many times I add unto his virtue' (2.3.106–7). The combination of heat, suspenseful delay, and the closed environment of a chemical bath keeps the dupes paying until their money is spent and their dreams turn to ashes.

Alchemy assumes the existence of natural affinities that bind the microcosm and the macrocosm, both of which aspire to a perfect spiritual and physical state. Essentially, Jonson inverts this assumption by using alchemy as a compendiously cynical test-tube in which parasitic elements mix and match, reveal their venal natures, and through corrupt aspirations prove themselves unworthy of the prosperity they desire. Jonson demonstrates his theory of inverse alchemy by linking puritanism with business enterprise, altruism with narcissism, and theatre with witchcraft.

Puritanism and business enterprise

Puritan tradesmen were transforming London commerce with their work ethic and amassing wealth at rates and in commodities (like feathers, tobacco, or other imported luxuries) that seemed at odds with their ascetic preaching. In the literal correspondences that puritans understood linked this life with the life to come, prosperity was a sign of the elect. The successful merchant worked long hours improving his shop, took no holidays except for prayer, and with his coffers full could expect his spiritual reward in heaven to equal his financial worth on earth. Although many condemned this mercenary scheme as hypocritical, puritans justified it as a direct revelation of God's judgment, setting them above the moral and legal codes of the national church and state.

Extremist sects like the Anabaptists countered public criticism by pointing out the state of sinfulness in which most people lived, particularly reading civil unrest, debauchery, famine, and plague as signs of the approaching apocalypse, during which the wicked would perish and the elect would enter bliss. Out of millenarianist zeal (see the note on 4.5 for Broughton's version of how history prophesies the end of the world), the Anabaptists advocated sweeping reforms to the social, religious, and political order, so that the faithful who survived the four kingdoms of corruption (Babylonian, Assyrian, Greek, and Roman, including the realm of the Holy Roman Empire – not necessarily millennia, though they do have a time frame) would be ready to enter the fifth, the kingdom of God. This final kingdom is the millennium, the thousand years of Christ's reign before the last judgment (see Revelation 20). Radical activists like John of Leyden and Bernt Knipperdollinck, to whom Tribulation and Ananias are linked, led a violent revolution in Münster, where they founded their republic on communal ownership of goods and equal rights, thus inspiring a series of minor but unsuccessful uprisings elsewhere in Europe, and ended with the tyrant-'king' John ordering bloodbaths and keeping a harem (see notes to 2.5). This union of reformist enthusiasm, mystical revelation, and reductive thinking suggests certain broad affinities between puritanism and alchemy. Both follow a tradition of purification through persecution: Subtle is a 'smoky persecutor of nature' (1.3.100), and the Anabaptists suffer 'chastisements' and 'rebukes' (3.1.1–2). Both dedicate themselves to a pattern of separation, death, and resurrection which can be interpreted allegorically or symbolically, but which they choose to understand literally. Both dream of reformed social and spiritual life based on the miraculous transformation of corrupt matter into an idealised state. Both play similar number games in which four corruptible elements/millennia ultimately produce a perfect fifth. Both comprehend gold as a sign of God's approval. Both arouse suspicion because of their anarchic tendency, stated or implied, to undermine or dissolve established authority with secret powers of their own.

Jonson confirms these parallels by balancing the alchemical fanatics against the

Anabaptist zealots. After Subtle and Face out-babble Ananias with sectarian cant
in 2.5, Tribulation repeats the silencing of his co-enthusiast with hair-splitting
debate in 3.1, and then joins Subtle in squelching Ananias's scruples over popish
bells and traditions in 3.2. All three agree on the lawfulness of casting over coining,
an indication of their shared cupidity. The Anabaptists in *The Alchemist* bear out
the worst censure of puritans as hypocritical, mercenary, even innately criminal,
and thus due for come-uppance. Tribulation and Ananias drive hard bargains in
deals for widows' and orphans' goods, exact forfeits on barely overdue bonds, pile
up material wealth, and finally plan an international takeover with counterfeit
Dutch dollars, all the while claiming the benefits of the austere spiritual life (3.2 and
4.7). Despite recognising that Subtle is a heathen, they are more than willing to use
him for their own profit. With Subtle's metallurgical skills, they can bribe English
magistrates into restoring the silenced ministers, eventually pay 'an army in the
field' to topple opposing governments in the name of their 'glorious cause', and
become 'temporal lords' themselves, like the leaders of the Münster Uprising
(3.2.45, 99, 52).

The English puritans of *The Alchemist* are represented as a much tamer lot
than the Amsterdam or Münster variety. They seem to be mild dissenters rather than
fervent sectarians. Lovewit's neighbours are law-abiding and harmless, if rather
suggestible; when Face denies their reports of coaches and guests at the house, the
neighbours change their stories, because 'Jeremy / Is a very honest fellow'
(5.2.25–38). Puritans were considered particularly credulous where magic was
concerned. Drugger, for example, visits Subtle for his skill as a cunningman or
neighbourhood witch, not as an alchemist. (Though Drugger is not an Anabaptist
– he denies being a 'Brother', belongs to the Grocers' guild, and frequents the
theatre, where the players lend him a Spanish costume – he looks enough like a
puritan in dress that Lovewit '*beats him away*' from the house after Tribulation
and Ananias.) When Drugger asks for a necromantic interior design to enhance
trade in his new shop, Subtle proves to him by metaposcopy and chiromancy
instead that his business success is guaranteed. All he need do is:

> Beneath your threshold, bury me a lodestone
> To draw in gallants that wear spurs; the rest,
> They'll seem to follow.

(1.3.69–71)

Such sympathetic magic, like writing names of protective spirits on the east
and north walls (64–8), or calculating 'ill-days' for business from an almanac
(94–6), are staples of divination. The same magic works in the naming of
John Dee in Drugger's new logo. The appearance of Dee as a capital letter on
Drugger's sign confers the power of the celebrated magus on the tradesman and
his shop:

> He shall have *a bell*, that's *Abel*;
> And by it standing one whose name is *Dee*,
> In a *rug* gown, there's *D*, and *Rug*, that's *drug*;

And right anenst him a dog snarling *Er*;
There's *Drugger*, Abel Drugger. That's his sign.
(2.6.19–24)

Like the Anabaptists who dream of temporal lordship through crafty business dealings with the philosopher's stone, Abel dreams on a smaller scale of becoming a powerful merchant and marrying the rich widow. Both of these 'alchemical' projections upward in class take root in the indentured commercial contract signed by Subtle, Dol, and Face, the 'venture tripartite' in which the three have equal shares, and which relies, like legally constituted firms, on reputation, judgment, credit, and the steady accumulation of carefully counted cash. Just as the puritan dupes try to use magic to increase their commercial and spiritual worth, so the three frauds use puritan reformist analogues to aggrandise their worth as rogues exploding established religious and social institutions. Their magic factory is their '*republic*' in which Subtle is 'Sovereign', Face is 'General', and Dol is 'Queen'. But the titles do not indicate 'priority'; they hold 'All things in common', even sexual favours. Jonson's representation of the con-game as a legitimate business venture of unimpeached integrity proclaims his satirical equating of criminal activity with capitalist expansion and religio-social innovation.

Altruism and narcissism

Where Jonson commercialises desire in Drugger and the Anabaptists, he sensualises it in Dapper and Mammon. Dapper's dream of leaving the law for an exciting life of indulgence pampered by his 'aunt of Fairy' (1.2.149) is a small-scale version of Mammon's anarchic fantasy in which he is the only potent male in a realm of willing women, the prodigal philosopher-king who opts out of the United Kingdom to set up his own 'free state' of sexual bliss (4.1.120–69). Both men long to kick free of the randomness of fortune and the uncertainties of competition, to spring into social dominance and 'Give lords th' affront' (2.2.8). One sees himself as the foster-child of benevolent fairies, receiving life-enhancing gifts, the other as the 'lord of the philosopher's stone', dispensing them. For each, Dol Common epitomises the perpetually golden future.

But Dol as the queen of their dreams is really Dol the *quean*, part of Jonson's bawdy reduction of the alchemy of human relations. Before metals can be 'married' in a flask (2.4.72), they must first undergo cleansing and softening preliminaries – ablution, maceration, and malleation – in the laboratory. Likewise, a bath and massage are preludes to coition in a hot-house. Preparations for the Spanish Don include 'perfumes, delicate linen, / The bath in chief, a banquet, and [Dol's] wit, / For she must milk his *epididymis*' (3.3.20–22). Surly, however, immediately recognises the rogues' masquerade as a bawdy-house subversion (2.3.226ff.) and means to expose it when he returns in Spanish disguise. More naive, Dapper comes to visit the 'cunning-man' (1.2.8) and learns of the 'Queen' only subsequently. Thus he is subject to different purification ceremonies, reminiscent of ritual healing, to ensure his credulous obedience: the fasting, the barely disguised crossing ('take /

Three drops of vinegar in at your nose, / Two at your mouth, and one at either ear'),
and the hint of holy water ('bathe your fingers' ends') are all papist practices
associated with witchcraft, only slightly redeemed by the aping of puritan prayer
in the *hum* and *buz* that finish the initial purging process (1.2.165–70). The next
stage of Dapper's ordeal is a crudely explicit brothel tease combining bondage and
masochism with regressive fetishism. During about eighty lines of scatological
humiliations, he is dressed in a petticoat (worn by young children, particularly
before toilet-training); made '*blind*' with a 'smock' (that is, aroused by a whore,
whose undergarment he wears over his face); searched, pinched, and tickled by
'elves' who strip him of his valuables; then, in a bizarre approximation of a return
to the womb, gagged and locked into 'Fortune's privy lodgings' where 'the
fumigation's somewhat strong' (3.5.10–15, 31, 79–81). To help him endure this
discomfort, Subtle stuffs this favoured nephew with the traditional treat of
cunningwomen, who sweetened their cures of children by giving them cake. In the
last stage of his erotic infantilisation, Dapper is forced to 'wriggle' at the Queen of
Fairy's feet and 'kiss her departing part' (5.4.21, 57). This sequence illustrates the
ludicrous bawdry of the alchemy game. It kindles vile desires while inducing
regression to childhood, and leaves the customer grateful for the experience, willing
to pay for more. No audience could leave the theatre untouched by this vivid lesson
in narcissistic folly.

Like Dapper, Mammon wants to have his cake and eat it too, though on a less
literal and more deliberate level. Just as irresponsible and childish, he is more
culpable than Dapper, partly because he is older and, according to Surly, should
have been prudent:

> Heart! Can it be
> That a grave sir, a rich, that has no need,
> A wise sir, too, at other times, should thus
> With his own oaths and arguments make hard means
> To gull himself?
>
>   (2.3.278–82)

Where Dapper is not much more than a posturing boy anxious to be a fashionable
gentleman of leisure, not unlike Kastril in his desire for aggressive social eminence,
Mammon aspires to complete dominance that far exceeds the select circle that the
younger men aim at impressing.

Mammon lives up to his name by assuming that riches can buy anything,
including piety and the fruit of piety, the philosopher's stone. He pays lip-service
to philanthropy, because he likes the idea of himself as an imitation *homo frugi*,
piously curing the world's ills – pox, plague, leprosy, old age, poverty:

> He will make
> Nature ashamed of her long sleep when art,
> Who's but a step-dame, shall do more than she,
> In her best love to mankind, ever could.
>
>   (1.5.25–8)

What he hopes to gain in return for his altruism, aside from fabulous wealth, is nothing less than undisputed supremacy as a public benefactor, controlling all social relationships: 'confer honour, love, respect, long life, / Give safety, valour, yea, and victory / To whom he will' (2.1.50–52). He sees no contradiction in his right to the philosopher's stone as a business investment, or in his plans to combine its employment for 'public good', 'pious uses, and dear charity' with satisfaction of his 'own particular lusts', despite Subtle's warnings (2.3.16–20). Nor can he pierce Subtle's charade as 'A notable, superstitious, good soul' who 'Has worn his knees bare and his slippers bald / With prayer' (2.2.102–4). A true alchemist lives a secluded life, avoids necromancy and astrology, and keeps his mind and his laboratory in accord with the rigorous patience required by his work. According to Thomas Norton of Bristol, a fifteenth-century alchemist, he must work without disturbances or any hint of lechery, and must delegate menial work, like the collecting of raw materials, to his servant, while he performs the subtle science in strict secrecy (Kieckhefer 1989: pp. 135–8). Mammon's knowledge of the process is based entirely on quantity, not quality. He retails scholarship indiscriminately, merely listing syncretistic rereadings of alchemical lore (2.1.80–104). His altruistic urge is simply a cover for megalomaniacal narcissism, a refined egotism that expresses itself in exhibitionistic display.

Mammon's obsessive desire is to restore his sexual potency, and then augment it with aphrodisiacs and other epicurean aids. The emphasis is always on the quantity of sexual acts, partners, beds, pictures, mirrors, perfumes, baths. Everything is plural. His desire for social dominance declares itself as the desire for sexual dominance that includes alchemical refinements in class and practice. He plans to purify and exalt all who tend his ego: 'Lungs' will be gelded before becoming master of his harem; his toadies will be clergymen, and his fools, members of Parliament; and 'no bawds, / But fathers and mothers' will provide the '*succubae*' that service his desires (2.2.57–8, 48). Even his tableware, food, and clothing will be unique or extraordinary commodities.

Mammon recognises Dol too as falling under this category of the phenomenal or wondrous. She is a 'Claridiana' (1.1.175), a heroine of romance, and 'a most rare scholar', whose learned discourse in religion, politics, and mathematics drives men mad. Because Mammon sees himself now as exceptional, he perceives no bar against paying Lungs to procure the favours of a lord's mad sister: 'Is she no way accessible? no means, / No trick to give a man a taste of her – wit – / Or so?' (2.3.258–60). Like Mammon himself, Dol represents hedonism masquerading as humanitarian reform; with her, Mammon can remake the world in his own lustful image (Mebane 1989: p. 152). In fact, once he meets Dol, his utopian urge evaporates. She distils for him what he really wants: absolute dictatorship in his own empire, out-Neroing Nero in 'a perpetuity / Of life and lust' (4.1.165–6). He no longer wants to transform the world into a place of moral and religious purpose, or physical health, but rather into a platform for his own self-display and self-celebration. This little 'chrysosperm' of truth is all that remains when, just at the moment of projection, the whole alchemical apparatus explodes, and 'All the works / Are flown *in fumo*. Every glass is burst' (4.5.57–8). Mammon acknowledges his 'voluptuous mind' and 'base affections' (74, 76) as the cause, and, since his own future has vanished, it is not surprising that he should choose finally to 'mount a turnip cart, and preach / The end of the world within these two months' (5.5.81–2). This last pose at least gives him a way of asserting a benevolent intent, thereby recovering some of his badly damaged ego, without any public admission of fault. He still insists, when Lovewit remarks, 'What a great loss in hope have you sustained!': 'Not I. The commonwealth has' (5.5.75–6).

Theatre and witchcraft: performative magic

Performative magic works when the audience desiring the entertainment believes, supports, participates in, and applauds the illusion. In *The Alchemist*, witchcraft and delusion succeed when the actors convince their spectators that they are hearing and seeing magic, that the performers have power over nature. Evidence from court records and pamphlets indicates that practitioners of witchcraft abounded in early modern England, and that their clientele was loyal, numerous, and class-mingled. William Perkins (1602), in *A Discourse from the Damned Art of Witchcraft*, may be expressing a clergyman's professional jealousy when he complains that people regard the neighbourhood cunningman as a blessing from God (Haining 1974: p. 126). Alexander Roberts (1616), in *A Treatise of Witchcraft*, grumbles that credulous lawyers purchase cauls from cunningwomen/ midwives as guarantees of eloquence and persuasive speech (Green 1971: p. 66). 'There be thousands in the land deceived', George Gifford writes in 1593, in *A Dialogue concerning Witches and Witchcraft* (H1 r–v), indicating how hard it is to counter popular beliefs when supported by the kindness and efficacy of 'these cunning men and women, unto whom so many run for help, which are thought to do very much good, and no hurt at all'. Hence the ease with which the charlatans in Jonson's play acquire their customers.

Although Subtle's main fraud is obviously the alchemy game, he is in other respects the conventional 'cunning-man' (1.2.8). During their quarrel, Face calls him 'Conjurer!' and 'Witch!' (1.1.107), and lists some of his 'tricks' as 'Searching for things lost, with a sieve and shears, / Erecting figures in your rows of houses, / And taking in of shadows with a glass' (95–7): all typical witchcraft activities of foretelling, making horoscopes, and crystal-gazing. Drugger comes to Subtle for charms to increase trade, Dapper comes for a gambling fly to help him win at dice, and Dame Pliant comes to have her fortune told and to see her future husband in a glass. These exercises invest Subtle's practice with the authority traditionally wielded by wisemen and honoured by their customers. The house is clogged with clients clamouring to get in. The puritan neighbours tell Lovewit later that they have seen visitors of all classes: 'some as brave as lords', 'Ladies and gentlewomen', 'Citizens' wives', 'knights', 'oyster-women', 'Sailors' wives', and 'Tobacco men', a good cross-section of the Blackfriars community. The only absentees are actors, but they are already inside the house, putting on the show.

Jonson virtually forces the off-stage audience to connect theatricality with witchcraft. The rogues argue over top billing, make illusion-puncturing asides, and shift their role-playing for each of the clients, who are themselves co-opted to perform. True to theatrical tradition, a costume change is an impenetrable disguise. Surly recognises Face's name as that of a famous pimp, 'The superintendent / To all the quainter traffickers in town' (2.3.302–3), but does not recognise Face as Lungs, or later as Jeremy, though he exclaims, 'This's a new Face?' (5.3.21). The rogues change costume frequently, notably Face's on-stage quick-change into 'Lungs' during the last twenty-five lines of 3.5. Mammon imagines himself parading naked before mirrors and Dol as his empress constantly dressing up; Surly changes costume and language as the Spanish Don; and the second Spanish costume passes from hand to hand in the last act, from Drugger, to Face, to Lovewit. Even the alchemical fluids change colour. Some scenes are products of careful rehearsal – the apparently accidental appearance of Dol in 2.3 as Bathsheba to Mammon's Solomon; Face's alchemical catechism in 2.5; and the explosion of 4.5 – and some require dextrous improvisation, like cajoling Dame Pliant to stand in for Dol, forcing Surly's exit at the end of Act 4, or cutting roles after Lovewit arrives in Act 5. These last two alterations to the rogues' script are good illustrations of Face's expertise in performative magic. He prompts, reblocks movement, invents a chorus in Drugger to echo Kastril's 'angry tongue', inspires Subtle to mention 'Zeal' and 'Spanish slops' (4.7.47–8) as a way of inciting Ananias's puritanical abuse, and directs the now elated hurlers of invective ('Did I not quarrel bravely?' asks Kastril) to follow Surly off stage with more jeering. Face's ability to control the scene and force his partner to follow his cues – 'Bear up, Subtle' (18) – predicts his later proficiency in evicting Subtle and Dol, and satisfying Lovewit.

The most impressive theatrical illusions are the alchemical laboratory tricks, which have powerful effects that derive from but go well beyond the physical. Even though the off-stage lab is merely a source of props, the audience hears more than anyone ever wanted to know about the base ingredients (merds, piss, women's terms, man's blood, powdered bones, and phlegm), fuel (*equi clibanum, fimus equinus*), solvents and residues (*menstrue, faeces*) used in the experiments. Face is associated with dung (Face's name even puns on 'faeces'), and Subtle's weapon of choice is the fart. Dol calls them both 'stinkards' (1.1.115). All this animal waste suggests that the whole alchemical obsession with gold is foul and debasing. Jonson uses the juxtaposition of gold and manure more graphically in his earliest extant play, *The Case is Altered*: Jaques de Prie, a miser who buries his gold in a dung-heap, digs it up periodically with his bare hands to check its safety and enjoy 'oh, how sweet it smells' (4.8.65).

In his conception of alchemy, Jonson echoes Reginald Scot, who declared in *The Discoverie of Witchcraft* that alchemy's three general principles were flattery, subtle speech, and the extortion of money (1584; rpt 1964: p. 299). The explosion of the alchemical apparatus is a particularly cunning illusion, like the trick Scot explains of Brandon's pigeon, an instance of natural magic based on ethology. When a juggler, pointing out pigeons on a roof, stabs a picture of a pigeon, a real pigeon drops down dead. Actually, the pigeon, poisoned and released before the perform-ance, naturally flies up to rejoin the other birds, while the trickster times his act to coincide with the anticipated death (Scot, pp. 245, 258–9). In Subtle's version of this trick, he may even resurrect the pigeon (that is, the elixir) with Mammon's conscience money: 'For some good penance you may have it yet; / A hundred pound to the box at Bedlam –' (4.6.85–6).

The play's final trick of legerdemain is the transmutation of the original 'indenture tripartite' into a legitimate social contract: the marriage of Lovewit and Dame Pliant displaces the unsavoury coupling of the witch and the whore, Subtle and Dol, while Jeremy the butler supplants Face the pimp. Aside from metaphorical connections between alchemy and sexuality, the deceptively simple question of why Jonson set his role-players in a bawdy-house opens up a complex of assumptions about witchcraft rooted in the denigration of women. According to *Malleus Maleficarum*, the *locus classicus* of witchcraft beliefs, all witchcraft comes from carnal lust, insatiable in women; the argument rests on Eve, blamed for original sin. Later commentators insist likewise on the moral incapacity of women, associating female sexual behaviour with irrationality, malice, intemperance, credulity, and pride, evident in women's scolding and cursing tongues. The association of ungoverned female sexuality with witchcraft was a habit of thought, and any unruly behaviour in women – adultery, vengeful cursing, or other laxness – tended to be understood as a demonic threat to the social order. Persistent linking of witchcraft with aberrant or criminal sexual behaviour suggests the importance to the community of raising the level of social control over women and of attacking nonconformity by extinguishing the voices of independent women.

Ironically, the only women with the power to be independent were whores and widows. The prejudice against such independence encouraged the denigration of widows as whores who must be either criminalised or re-absorbed by the patriarchy. Jonson's wry pairing of Dame Pliant and Dol Common illustrates the widow–whore dichotomy as a shape-shifting and reversible accommodation of two contradictory roles that reflect ironically upon each other and upon the men who try to appropriate them. In making an initial distinction between the whore and the widow, Jonson relies on the contrast between the Amazon and the silent bride. Dol dominates the opening scene as the roaring-girl, physically able to punish men and impudently refusing subjection to male partners (Shepherd 1981: pp. 69–71). When Subtle and Face quarrel, ignoring her feminine pleas for peace, sanity, and civil behaviour, she wrenches the sword out of Face's hand, smashes the vial of acid which Subtle has been threatening to throw at Face, and swears that she will cut both their throats unless they co-operate. She ends the argument by throttling Subtle into submission. Her concern is the principle of 'equality' within the partnership. Yet the men celebrate this equality by drawing straws to see who will sleep with Dol that night (176–9); Dol herself has no straw and no veto. The meaning of equality with men – the state Dol desires – shrinks into free sexual access for men – the state she achieves.

Although Dol dismisses marriage as a goal, Dame Pliant has come to town with her brother expressly to find a husband. She is suitably obedient and silent – she has only nine and a half lines – but her status as a widow assumes that she cannot be chaste. When Drugger first mentions 'A rich young widow –', Face interjects to complete the poetic line with 'Good! A *bona roba*' (2.6.30); that is, a good-looking whore. Despite all their other differences in station, personality, and education, this reductive sexual assumption is the chief factor that makes Dol and Dame Pliant interchangeable in the plot. Dame Pliant's sole advantage over Dol is her widow's portion, ultimately a decisive magic more beguiling than Subtle's wizardry or Dol's bawdry. But the money does not protect her from abuse. In terms of sexual attractiveness, Dol and Dame Pliant are opposite types. Dol is a Bradamante (2.3.225), a dominatrix who inspires both fear and lust. Subtle and Face dread Dol's anger; when they bicker over who will marry Dame Pliant, each threatens to tell Dol that the other is breaking their partnership agreement, and the terror of that prospect keeps the rivals in line. Dame Pliant, on the other hand, projects a simpler view of receptive nature satisfying appetite: a 'soft and buxom widow' who 'melts' like ripe fruit at a kiss, 'a delicate dab-chick' (4.2.37, 41, 60). Dame Pliant is artless, guileless, and stupid. She agrees with any man whether he threatens like her brother, reasons like Surly, or rushes her off her feet like Lovewit. Dol is argumentative, resentful of interference, and clever enough to recycle her knowledge of puritan millenarianist tracts into a convincing portrayal of a lady-scholar driven mad by abstruse learning, a fate that parodies male prejudice against female intellectuals (McLuskie 1989: p. 176). But no matter how acute the one and how foolish the other, a woman's 'wit' is punningly reduced to her 'whit', or genitalia, when Mammon asks for what he bawdily calls 'a taste of her – wit' (2.3.259). Similarly, Subtle and Face promise each other, in competing for Dame Pliant's hand: 'We'll e'en draw lots, and he that fails shall have / The more in goods, the other has in tail' (2.6.86–7). Later deciding to use Dame Pliant to 'work' the Spanish Count while Dol entertains Mammon, Face argues, 'It is but one man more', since 'There is no maidenhead to be feared or lost' (4.3.66, 68). But Subtle is not so philosophical. Because he will not 'marry a whore' (90), he loses his interest in Dame Pliant, except for the crude jokes about Kastril's becoming 'brother / To a great Count' (4.4.86–7) and Dame Pliant being made 'a Countess' – the words 'count' and 'cunt' being aurally indistinguishable. When money hangs in the balance, however, chastity has no value. Surly's sexual restraint costs him the fortune which Lovewit's priapic ardour wins. Kastril completes Dame Pliant's transition from widow to whore when he stands outside Lovewit's door in Act 5, bellowing for 'Punk, cockatrice, my suster' (5.3.34).

When Jonson expels the whore and the witch, powerless and unheard, in the penultimate scene of *The Alchemist*, he replaces them with the bird-brained Dame Pliant as the legitimate (though hardly dominant) female power. She is the new elixir whose nubile form and widow's portion will rejuvenate her husband Lovewit, making him 'seven years younger, and a rich one' (5.3.86), a magic more potent than Subtle's 'black arts', his cover for 'the more thriving skill / Of bawdry' (1.1.48–9). While Face ejects Dol from the house with the offer of a reference to another brothel, Dame Pliant consummates her marriage with Lovewit, who manages to 'prime his powder, and give fire, and hit, / All in a twinkling' (5.5.57–8). Lovewit shows the same efficiency in ridding his house of Anabaptists and other erstwhile clients of the alchemist. His role in the last act of the play – laying down the law and winning the prize bride – seems justified as an integral part of life in Blackfriars, where gentlemen can profit from the same immunity as outlaws and dissenters. Although the sexual morality may seem conventional here, with the whore expelled and the respectable widow remarried, the parallels drawn by placing the two women in the same house and engaging them in the same activity confirm smugly hostile classifications of female roles – and simultaneously expose them as absurd.

Jonson's brothel- and magic-shop overflows with impostors, apparently ordinary citizens, who harbour extraordinary, egotistical visions of rising above and victimising their community. Subtle fills his cunningman role by facilitating his clients' paranoid delusions, which are, despite their comic presentation, as dark as those in Genet's *The Balcony*. The innocent, the immature, and the frustrated come to be transformed into the worldly successes that they cannot become on their own. Even Lovewit, seduced by what is left of the cunningman game, abdicates responsibility while regressing into angry-boy jollity with his new brother-in-law Kastril: 'I will be ruled by thee in anything, Jeremy' (5.5.143), he tells the erstwhile 'Face'. And Jeremy too, in his self-conscious epilogue, defends his 'part' by citing the audience's desire to be charmed by the performers' magic. The larceny is forgiven and forgotten.

BARTHOLOMEW FAIR

The carnival atmosphere of *Bartholomew Fair* and its heroless structure help to contrive an almost cinematic flow to its place-related plots. If Jonson had written the play 360 years later, it might have become a shooting script for Fellini, whose *Amarcord* (1974) relies on a similarly panoramic pastiche of intertwining lives, young and old, in a circumscribed place, overflowing with hilarious, warmhearted, bawdy anecdotes of love, sex, family, neighbours, and politics, all of which conclude in a wonderfully heightened marriage feast, as a classic comedy should. Jonson's fairground has the same evanescently quirky glow of a temporary space that must be enjoyed at the moment or lost – at least for a year, if not forever. His festive crowd, like Fellini's, indulges voraciously in physical and verbal excess: food, drink, abuse, obscenity, and raucous laughter. No authority escapes attack, no hypocrisy eludes hissing, no pretentiousness evades come-uppance. Through reversals and inversions, magnifications and trivialisations, the issues of class, gender, and age blur, and the common denominator, lusty humanity, takes the foreground.

In its treatment of place as magic space, Jonson's play also resembles Victor Fleming's film *The Wizard of Oz* (1939). The grey realism of the first act at the Littlewit house gives way in the subsequent acts to the wild, surreal colour of the fairground with its odd denizens, noise, and constant movement. Although the fair has no trees that throw apples or horses that change colour, no cowardly lion, weeping tin man, or dancing scarecrow, it does boast a fat lady with a skinny tapster, stocks with disappearing prisoners, and puppets with voices to rival any Munchkin's. The search in Oz, like the fairground paper-chase after licences and warrants, is for bureaucratic sanction of desire in the form of some tangible confirmation. To have social recognition of the value of heart, brain, or courage, the tin man needs (or feels he does) the ticking clockwork, the scarecrow needs the diploma, and the lion needs the medal. And Dorothy needs official permission to return home, even though the power of returning was hers all along. But she takes a while to open her eyes to the truth, even when her dreams turn into nightmares. Jonson's characters variously experience the same phenomenon: Overdo is beaten, Busy is out-sermonised by a puppet, and Grace escapes one wardship only to fall prey to another. In what is perhaps the most graphic representation, Cokes loses purses, clothes, sister, tutor, purchases, and bride, and by 4.2 fears that he can never find his way back to his brother-in-law's house. In Oz, Dorothy only understands her responsibility to herself after she exposes, however accidentally and ironically, the humbug of authority. Essentially, this recognition also effects the homeward journey that ends *Bartholomew Fair*. When Overdo sees the humbug in himself, he decides to celebrate, not revile, his flesh-and-blood bond with the other chastened citizens: suspending all notion of rank or legitimacy, he invites everyone home to supper.

This levelling finale comes about because of the collision between the hucksters' world and the middle-class world of landowners and urbanites who go as tourists to the fair. Smithfield supplies the scene, but the Londoners and their guests have the dramatic experience. Although the play ends in the promise of a feast and the toasting of two brides, the upside-down world of the fair makes no sweeping claims about happy endings. Its genial cynicism shrugs at what it knows will be buried again in the grey world outside Smithfield.

The anarchy of the fair

The cony-catchers of the fair regulate themselves within a criminal anti-order whose crafty dealers and guileless customers crudely parody legitimate city trade. This anti-order is densely, palpably physical, dependent upon exciting acquisitive appetites and blotting out restraint and rationality. Everywhere are booths, stands, and baskets crammed with food or toys; passers-by and itinerant sellers jostle and gawk in perpetual chaotic waves; seductive scents and sounds – tobacco, ginger-bread, roasting pork, street cries, ballads – congest the air. People breathe in the infection of desire. Busy surrenders to gluttony, Dame Purecraft pursues madness, and Grace tosses herself into a marriage lottery. This anti-order, ritualised in the game of vapours, relies on '*nonsense*' – deranged logic and the befuddlement of the senses, whether through drink or some other euphoric stimulant – both to incite and exploit the hedonism temporarily reigning in Smithfield.

Within the fairground, all standards invert. Commercial infractions abound: Joan Trash hawks stale cake; Ursula sells more froth than ale; and both Trash and Leatherhead abscond without delivering goods Cokes has paid for. Civic, domestic, and spiritual ideals turn inside out to expose injustice in a justice of the peace, incompetence in a governor, and bigotry in a spiritual leader. Youth wrests control of family, property, and marriage from oppressive elders. But the most festive and exhilarating reversal, dominating and containing all the others, directs lower bodily urges to supplant rule by heart and brain. Reflexes oust reflection. The sheer expansiveness of this misrule expresses itself in the fertile figure of Ursula, whose huge body preserves the first rib, Eve, and waters the earth with her sweat 'like a great garden-pot' (2.2.48–9): she is the grotesque 'mother o' the pigs', 'juicy and wholesome' (2.5.66, 74; for her mythic dimension, see the note on 2.5). Her amazing booth, 'the very womb and bed of enormity' (2.2.96), houses, besides the 'bower' in front, a 'backside' that seems infinitely elastic with its restaurant, kitchen, warehouse for stolen goods, wardrobe of whores' gowns, privy, and brothel. Like Ursula's chair, which needs to be 'let out o' the sides' so that her 'hips might play' (2.2.58–9), the booth enlarges to accommodate any increase or longing.

The fellowship of the fair people mirrors this same swelling flexibility. Unlike traditional guilds or societies, they avoid organising themselves by rank or privilege, preferring the frank free-flow of camaraderie (Ostovich 1986: p. 122), a kind of golden rule that expects mutual consideration without territorial infringements. Ramping Alice attacks Mistress Overdo because Alice perceives her as non-union labour treading on harlots' rights. When Leatherhead warns Joan Trash not to 'hinder the prospect of my shop', she retorts, 'I pay for my ground as well as thou dost' (2.2.4, 14–15); their bickering results from a fear that this year's fair, apparently 'pestilence dead' early in the day, will remain unprofitable. Later in 3.4, as Cokes runs to Trash's wares before settling his purchases with Leatherhead, another quarrel erupts, only settled when Cokes agrees to buy up both shops. At that point, Trash and Leatherhead join forces to prevent Wasp from stopping the sale. This same give-and-take operates when Nightingale distracts the crowd with a song while Edgworth picks Cokes's pocket, or when the costermonger helps set up another robbery of Cokes by spilling a basket of pears. Ironically, these characters of the petty-criminal underworld survive as a group with more integrity than the respectable middle-class fair-goers, who disperse and deteriorate.

The camaraderie of the fair people nurtures itself on superficially antagonistic raillery: sarcasm, threats, complaints, name-calling, and slurs. This in-group ridicule is a social game that emerges in situations in which everyone knows everyone else, and each participant expects the others to know what the rules are, so that no one takes offence at the tone or content of the language. Their invective conceals mutual affection. Ursula may call Mooncalf 'false faucet', 'rascal', 'changeling', 'stote', 'vermin', and 'errant incubee', but she has an almost motherly concern to teach him to 'discharge his place of trust' as 'tapster, a man of reckoning' (2.2 *passim*). Mooncalf has an almost filial admiration for Ursula's proficiency in execration. He boasts to Overdo: 'She'll do forty such things in an hour, an you listen to her, for her recreation, if the toy take her i'the greasy kerchief: it makes her fat, you see. She battens with it' (2.3.30–32). Despite the abuse that flies back and forth between Knockem and Ursula, Knockem asserts: 'Come, there's no malice in these fat folks' (17–18), and Ursula placates his belligerence by feeding him: 'You angry? You are hungry. Come, a pig's head will stop your mouth and stay your stomach at all times' (42–3). As Freud, among others, has pointed out, sharing laughter at the same jokes demonstrates positive psychological accord within a group (Freud n.d.: p.233). The hostile wit of the fair people is as much an attribute of their solidarity as is their use of Ursula's premises for the distribution of stolen goods and wenches, or their ready sharing of funds and information.

When the ridicule is aimed at outsiders, however, its effect is intended to be crude and degrading, and the laughter that it evokes, derisive. Konrad Lorenz (1967: p. 253) speculates that laughter probably evolved from the ritualisation of a redirected threat. By producing fellow-feeling among the in-group and joint aggressiveness against an enemy, it draws a line between insider and outsider. Jonson literalises this process in the game of vapours when Val Cutting draws a circle on the ground and jeers Quarlous into entering it to fight. Laughter directed at someone outside the laugher's group conveys the scorn associated with aggression and triumph. Quarlous's scalding mockery of Ursula's appearance and his laughter in face of her profanities end in her physical scalding with a pan of hot pork-drippings: the word is literalised on the flesh. Here, the in-group loyalty of the fair people asserts itself, as the rogues of the fair co-operate to help Ursula. Mooncalf watches Joan Trash's basket while she fetches cream for the burns. Leatherhead, Nightingale, Edgworth, and Knockem settle Ursula in her chair, tend her wounds, and salve her self-esteem.

The distinction between in-group and out-group laughter in the game of vapours marks off the levels of play. For Wasp, the game is a formalised contest in reviling, a festive occasion on which he can, for a change, get as good as he gives. The roarers play a double game. They play the same game that Wasp plays, defined by Jonson's stage direction as '*nonsense: every man to oppose the last man that spoke, whether it concerned him or no*' (4.4.24.1–2). But they also use it as a trick to divert Wasp while the pickpocket steals the marriage licence and later to divert the outsiders while Whit steals their cloaks. Knockem is the moderator for both levels of game, scoring vapours by rating them 'sweet', 'sufficient', 'gross', or 'noisome', and at the same time giving Whit signals to brawl ('Strike, Whit!') or steal ('Gather up, Whit!'). He ends both games with a compliment: 'Good vapours!' The second level of game is as saturnalian for the roarers as the first level of game is for Wasp. The roarers have found the perfectly patterned release for their aggressive and anti-social impulses (and the perfect cover for crime) by the deviousness of staging a violent quarrel with friends in front of the real target. They assail their friends with ridicule really meant for the target, who willingly participates in the abuse because he does not feel personally attacked. At the same time, the friends profit, and everyone feels better for having reviled someone (Elliott 1960: p. 81). Although the roarers cheat, they sustain the game's magic while manipulating it, and the dupes feel no let-down. The roarers do not spoil the game, as some of the tourists try to do, by carping at pleasures they are actually enjoying.

Just as the in-group camaraderie of the fairgrounders is condensed in the game of vapours, with its roarer-loyalty and double-play aggressiveness against outsiders, so the game of vapours is itself parodied on an even smaller scale in the puppet-play of Act 5. To capitalise on the effects of automatic mindless aggression carried to absurd extremes, Jonson accelerates the bickering by presenting it as a series of redirected activities. Damon and Pythias vilify each other until Leatherhead insults them both, whereupon the friends join forces to revile and beat him. An example of 'friendship's true trial', they quarrel with each other only until 'friendly together, / at the next man they meet, / They let fly their anger, as here you might see't' (5.4.230–31). Later, responding to Leatherhead's taunts, Damon and Pythias slander and kick Hero. Further insults from Leatherhead and Jonas galvanise Leander into joining the brawl and abuse. The *pièce de résistance* is the impudence of the dispute between the puppet Dionysius and Zeal-of-the-land Busy, whose puritanical argument is confounded by a physical, not logical, exposure – just as Overdo's oratorical attempt to mete out justice is silenced by his wife's vomiting. In an inversion of earlier scuffles, here the frailty of the flesh defeats the word. The appeal to the senses overwhelms the appeal to the inadequate intellect. Through the conditions established by the fairground characters, Jonson seems to be directing us towards a recognition of our world's failure to find a moral centre. All we have is a games centre where the player with the best trick wins. If we deny the flesh that plays the game, we lose.

Authority, licence, and warrant

What are the rules of the game? The induction initiates the question of who has the right to do what in the course of play. The stage-keeper complains that the performance misrepresents the Smithfield milieu, and feels offended at Jonson's unjust reception of his opinions: the playwright has kicked him 'three or four times about the tiring-house . . . for but offering' the benefit of his experience, and called him 'an ass'. The book-holder disdains both the stage-keeper's judgment and the play itself, forestalling further criticism from the pit by imposing a contract 'drawn out in haste' which the spectators must approve before the author will let his play go on. The contract itself is comically insolent. A kind of blackmail, it forces the audience punningly to give their hands to the document before they watch the play they have already paid to see. Furthermore, the articles demand that the audience sit patiently for two to three hours, and afterwards criticise only in proportion to the exact amount they have paid. This specious condition, intended to silence the audience entirely, smacks of the legalistic word-play by which, in *The Merchant of Venice*, Portia entraps Shylock, who may take his pound of flesh only if he spills no blood and takes not a hair more or less than a pound. How will a judge measure the exactness of a six penn'orth opinion compared to twelve or eighteen penn'orth? How will a court penalise a spectator who changes his opinion after he leaves the theatre? Or one who laughs at implications the author did not intend?

Authority of this kind amounts to no authority at all. At best, it rules by whim; at worst, by intolerance and extortion. No character or document in the play has genuine authority. The marriage licence, a document purchased, stolen, and altered by the play's end, is issued for one bride and groom and forged for use by another. Overdo signs a blank warrant, the object of Troubleall's quest, in order to supply a madman with food and shelter; Quarlous, formerly a student at the Inns of Court, uses it feloniously to transfer to himself the wardship of Grace, thus gaining superfluous funds. The Court of Wards itself, from which Overdo purchased his interest in Grace's estate, was generally considered a legalised abuse of wealthy orphaned minors (see the note on 3.5). Dame Purecraft confesses that she has used her office as deaconess to steal alms, and to extort money from women whose marriages she has arranged, upon the threat of 'reprobation and damnation' (5.2.57–8). As a baker in Banbury, Busy had cheated a grocer over a sale of currants; now, as a preacher, he cheats heirs out of their inheritance by claiming to act as trustee for deceased brethren who granted him absolute gifts of their estates. Even Littlewit, an ecclesiastical lawyer, pays a shilling bribe to have officers arrest Busy. Such authority, based upon questionable civil and religious practices, transgresses the spirit of the law; as Wasp puts it, 'There's nothing in't but hard words' (1.5.30).

This shrivelling of authoritative models of behaviour into trivial lip-service or petty display accounts for the breakdown in the conduct of the visitors to the fair.

Unlike the fairground hucksters, whose relatively egalitarian community depends upon the free association of self-actuated tricksters sharing scams, money, and pleasure together in an openly predatory counter-system, the visitors operate within institutionalised ideals which, like Wasp's black box, turn out to be empty. In Act 1, two parallel groups of citizens meet: Littlewit and Cokes, as the names indicate, are foolish heads of household (see notes on The Persons of the Play); Win Littlewit, the young wife, corresponds to Grace Welborn, soon to be married to Cokes; Dame Purecraft and Mistress Overdo equate as older married women, the former now a widow; and Busy and Wasp act as imposing shepherds to their respective flocks. The only connection between the two family groups initially is the marriage licence which Littlewit has drawn up for Cokes and Grace. When Cokes leads his group to visit the fair, however, the puritan family soon follows. One other group visits the fair, Winwife and Quarlous, at first scornfully. They claim to find only Cokes entertaining, but really intend to trail after Grace. Both are attracted by her manner, and appalled at the prospect of her marrying Cokes. The fact that Winwife willingly gives up his widow-hunt, 'for today' at least, suggests that he may already be hoping to win Grace for himself. His excuse that the fair will provide amusing 'sport' does not seem to fool Quarlous, whose response, 'A man that has but a spoonful of brain would think so', seems to acknowledge their shared motive and competition.

Once the visitors arrive at the fair, the alliances based on kinship, friendship, business, religion, and marriage dissolve, and other surprising or absurd associations take their places, linking members of opposite groups together in contradictory ways, like little echoes of the game of vapours. Sometimes the pairings have an absurd logic in the closed cycle of consumption and elimination among the fairground clientele. Win and Mistress Overdo both seek a jordan in Ursula's booth, and both end up together as whores in Jordan Knockem's stable. Grace and Dame Purecraft share the same suitors, each picking up the other's rejected lover, each as a result of seeing and speaking to Troubleall. Busy and Wasp sit in the same stocks, a spoof of the sacred and the profane. Cokes and Littlewit, together at the puppet theatre, are victims of loss: just as Cokes has lost his toys and his bride, so Littlewit, in trying to find his wife, misses the performance of his puppet-play. Some of the displacements and realignments beg the question. Winwife displaces Cokes as Grace's husband, but the differences between the two men may not be as significant as the similarities. Cokes's obsession with purchasing pleasure at the fair resembles Winwife's obsession with marrying money. Perhaps Winwife is simply a more presentable and conversational Cokes.

Similarly, Quarlous displaces Busy as Dame Purecraft's husband: like Busy, Quarlous is hypocritical and larcenous in his determination to manipulate events for his own profit. He even preaches a sermon against widow-hunting (1.3), though he himself ends up marrying 'an old reverend smock' for her money. Neither Winwife nor Quarlous can be regarded as trustworthy choric figures; although they set themselves up as supercilious observers of the fairground scenes, that role slips away as they become participants in the action. The opportunist Quarlous is especially identified with fairground characters. As quarrelsome as Knockem, Quarlous is also not averse to buying and selling women. Like Edgworth, he looks and talks almost like a gentleman, but in The Persons of the Play, Jonson calls him a 'gamester', a designation that implies a player at any game, an actor, a gambler, a merry trickster, and a lewd trifler with women. Ironically, Quarlous spurns any notion of equality with Edgworth and his 'companions in beastliness' (4.6.19). Winwife, his Nightingale, sings a good song, but is not in on the game as the ballad-singer is with Edgworth; Quarlous outwits Winwife without a qualm. And like Troubleall, Quarlous fixates on the warrant for action, but instead of asking others 'Have you a warrant?', he grasps at unfair advantages, asking himself instead 'Why should I not?' Quarlous's and Winwife's value as triumphant bridegrooms at the end of the play is dubious. Quarlous's possession of both the licence and the warrant (like Dauphine's clutching the contract and the wig at the end of *Epicoene*) may win him the money, but acquisitiveness has not been hailed as a virtue in the play. He has committed himself to sterility and pretended madness in his marriage to Dame Purecraft, and has broken his gentleman's agreement with Winwife and Grace, who may end up with even less money than they originally bargained for.

The critical touchstone for folly at the fair is Adam Overdo, whose disguises, transgressions, and moralistic commentary connect him to visitors and hucksters alike. Like Wasp, he fails as a guardian; neither is able to control his ward, but at least Wasp has some genuine concern for Cokes's well-being. Like Busy, Overdo fails at preaching and abuses his parochial power. His oration on 'the fruits of bottle-ale and tobacco' (2.6.1) does not convert the wicked, any more than Busy's diatribe against the World, the Flesh, and the Devil convinces those who have just seen him devour two and a half suckling pigs and a pailful of ale in Ursula's booth. By drawing a crowd to hear his oration, Overdo unwittingly gives Edgworth the opportunity of robbing Cokes, and himself a beating for being 'the patriarch of the cutpurses'. And by neglecting his duties in the Pie-Powders court, he obstructs justice, just as Busy does by meddling in the estates of deceased puritans. Like Littlewit, Overdo fails in his duty as a husband, abandoning his wife to her own devices and thus to the devices of pimps. Whereas Overdo ignores his wife in order to play a devious double role at the fair, Whit lavishes attention on her to persuade her to do likewise. Like Quarlous, Overdo tries to give a choric commentary on the fair, and assumes the disguise of a madman. But where Quarlous at least recognises the pimps and thieves for what they are, Overdo focuses on minor infractions, and completely misses the real crimes. He even thinks Edgworth is a 'civil young gentleman' who needs to be rescued from 'debauched company'. In their inter-actions with the real madman, Troubleall, it is difficult to tell whose behaviour, Overdo's or Quarlous's, is more reprehensible. Other officers of the court describe Overdo as an 'upright' judge, but also 'parantory', one who will 'swell like a boil, God bless us, an he be angry' (4.1.65–6). Perhaps he thinks that his wrath makes his judgment more thunderingly righteous, but in fact his decisions are both irrational and binding: 'when he is angry, be it right or wrong, he has the law on's side ever'. Overdo's unpredictable cantankerousness is responsible for Troubleall's insanity, a direct result of his being dismissed from his job as an officer in the Pie-Powders court. Overdo at least tries to make amends by giving him (as he thinks) a blank warrant as a cure. Troubleall is so deranged that his wife 'cannot get him make his water or shift his shirt without his warrant' (4.1.52–3). Quarlous, however, exploits and worsens Troubleall's condition by taking over the madman's personality, clothing, and blank warrant, thereby increasing his own healthy financial advantage.

As the tracing of these displacements and rearrangements suggests, the visitors at the fair undergo a shrinking of their spiritual, intellectual, or moral pretensions into crude physical fact. The history of the game of vapours offers the clearest paradigm for this regression, and incidentally reveals why the game takes place in a pig-booth. John Stow explains (1908; rpt 1971: vol. 1, pp. 74–5) that formerly, on the Eve of St Bartholomew, scholars of various grammar schools met in the churchyard of the Smithfield priory for a public-speaking contest: each student in turn mounted a platform erected under a tree (like Ursula's bower roofed with leafy branches) to oppose and answer arguments from his peers until he was overcome by some better scholar who then took his place on the platform. In those days, the best scholars were from St Anthony's Hospital and St Paul's. The latter called their rivals 'Anthony pigs', based on the emblem of St Anthony figured with a pig following him; in retaliation, the St Anthony boys called them 'pigeons of Paul's', for the many birds nesting in the cathedral. (Ursula's tent is famous for pigs and 'birds o' the game'.) After the disputations themselves were discontinued, the sole vestige of the contest was puerile disorder, as schoolboys provoked one another to fisticuffs with the old invitation to debate: *'Placet tibi mecum disputare?'* – *'Placet'* ['Will it please you to argue with me?' – 'It will']. Thus, Stow reports, 'they usually fall from words to blows with their satchels full of books, many times in great heaps that they troubled the streets and passengers'. The reduction of scholarly argument in the game of vapours to the mere noise of contradiction, jeering, and blows is part and parcel of all the fair's trivialisations of former authority. Busy, full of pig, battles the gingerbread saints and other relics of idolatry: hobby-horses, drums, fiddles, pipes, rattles, and bells (3.6). The schoolmaster Wasp uses a schoolboy trick to escape his detention: *'As they open the stocks, Wasp puts his shoe on his hand, and slips it in for his leg'* (4.6). Bristle and Haggis bicker with Troubleall, and the watchmen's threats turn to jabs: *'The madman fights with 'em, and they leave open the stocks'*. As an emblem of civic childishness, the figures illustrate senselessness battling apes of judgment, just as later Cokes is pestered by the mocking *'boys o'the fair'* (5.3), Busy is defeated by a puppet, and Overdo is silenced by his wife.

Overdo, reduced to 'Adam flesh and blood' in the final scene, discovers his true kinship with the fair's Eve, Ursula: she is the fleshly mother of excess, as he is the father of philosophical and administrative enormity. His own dereliction is plain in Mistress Overdo's upheaval. In her, Overdo sees what comes of dissociating himself from the appetites aroused by the fair, and discounting the physical instincts that share the body with the soul. Overdo has been stoically trying to preserve the soul by ignoring the humiliations and urges of the body, but he discovers that he denies them at his peril. They will not be regimented, reprimanded, and infinitely repressed. At the puppet show he tries to segregate the physically sinful from the spiritually good, and finds himself at a loss to place people accurately. His rigid and narrow interpretations of behaviour cannot accommodate the humanity that confronts him. Though Quarlous smugly warns him to remember his own 'frailty' before judging others, the sentiment is self-serving, considering his own abuse of weaknesses at the fair. The range of 'enormities' represented on the crowded stage of the finale certainly points to a need for some compromise that rejects zealous or mean-spirited condemnation in favour of toleration and acceptance of difference. Through the play's Adam and Eve, Jonson suggests that the compromise include both the expansive embrace of Ursula's fertile realm and the public-spiritedness of Overdo's good intentions, without the vaporous excesses.

The daughters of Eve: wives and whores

When Win Littlewit asks, in Act 4 of *Bartholomew Fair*, 'Is an honest woman's life a scurvy life?' (4.5.27), she is weighing her marriage to John Littlewit against the prospect of independence as 'a free-woman and a lady'. By conventional standards, her marriage to a lawyer in the Court of Arches is a good one. Why then should she feel that offers made her by two fairground pimps promise a less scurvy life? Perhaps Win's experience tells her that a husband who, after 'a hot night' (1.3.13) of drinking and bragging about his wife's attractions, invites his companion home to fondle and kiss her, is not a husband who cares much about her sense of propriety. When Win objects to the sexual harassment, he rebukes her for unfeminine behaviour: 'Be womanly, Win', he orders. Her response, 'I'faith, you are a fool, John', sums up his complacency, and so does her attacker's emendation, 'apple-John', or pimp. Winwife stops Quarlous's assault, but his reason for doing so is obscure: he may be responding sensitively to Win's discomfort, or fastidiously to his own. He certainly enjoys her 'strawberry-breath, cherry lips, apricot-cheeks, and a soft velvet head like a melicotton' when he kisses her, but he at least recognises the difference between a respectable wife and a whore. Win has been made to feel that there *is* no difference, and that her protests at this lack of difference have somehow placed *her* in the wrong. So later, when the fairground pimps assure Win that the new fashion in honesty is for wives 'to cuckold' husbands resolved 'not to suspect' (4.5.43–4), the scales fall from her eyes. If there is to be no difference between a wife and a whore, at least the lack of difference will be of her own choosing.

Win Littlewit's situation illustrates the confusion that results when women discover they are to play two contradictory roles at once. The ideological shift, instigated by puritan theology, towards more liberal partnership in marriage confused categories of female sexuality, mingling wife and whore in ways contrary to the binary oppositions of pre-Reformation thinking (Kahn 1991: 249–51). A wife who seeks pleasure in marital sex legitimises whoredom, and reconfirms the ancient suspicion that all women are sexually voracious – the subject of jokes since Aristophanes. Even their fertility seems to brand women as unstable and shape-shifting; Win's pregnancy, like the play of Ursula's hips, testifies to her sexual appetite. Once men perceive women as blurring distinctions between roles that should allow reliable classification and control, then patriarchal authority totters (Leinwand 1986: p. 140). Yet John Littlewit stimulates Win's shape-shifting by dressing her fashionably: he selects the velvet cap, the high-heeled shoes, and the lace-trimmed habit to arouse his own desire and to flatter himself by arousing the lust of other men, despite his wife's distaste for both the clothing and the men. The marital situation reflects the problems of larger social change in the emergence of affluent middle-class women with the leisure and freedom to develop a social life but, unlike noblewomen, without a tradition of acceptable social behaviour to guide them (Maclean 1980: p. 88). The resulting conflicts place the sexes in the liminal realm of what Judith Butler calls 'gender trouble', where female identities coalesce and dissolve according to time and circumstance, often simultaneously consenting to and disrupting inventions of gender that support masculine ascendancy (J. Butler 1990: pp. 16, 34). Women like Win become both victims and agents of the new social constructions of woman.

Bartholomew Fair represents this contradictory cultural collaboration against women in the predicament of Grace Wellborn. Grace may seem an ironic comment on God's grace, as she is bought and sold rather than freely bestowed. Nevertheless, she fits the ideology that woman, made from Adam's rib in man's image, has her intelligence by God's grace (Maclean 1980: p. 13). Her name recollects Castiglione's *grazia*, the nonchalance of the diplomatic, the charming art of weighing words and deeds in shifting contexts in order to gain the good will of a worthy audience. Her graceful qualities obscure her Amazonian insistence on having her own choice, even if her choice is limited to the decision not to marry Cokes, and to gamble on marrying one of two rational gentlemen she happens to fall in with at the fair. Her wit grants her the licence of the 'woman on top' as social critic (Davis 1978: pp. 162–3), first tacitly by being 'melancholy' in the company of fools (3.4), then explicitly by commenting, albeit with restraint, on the folly of Cokes, the whole Overdo household (3.5), and particularly the wardship system. Through what Grace calls 'a common calamity', she has been sold as an orphaned heiress to Justice Overdo in the Court of Wards, and must marry Cokes according to her guardian's wishes, or 'pay value' of her land (3.6). She escapes the trap of Overdo's wardship only to fall into Quarlous's. Despite her confidence in her own propriety, her independent action cannot disconnect her from the appearance of whoredom: she knows her lot is a gamble between two fortune-hunters, and to that extent she is still for sale. She does not deceive herself with superficial partiality or allow her suitors to deceive her with promises of love or aggressive display. Having found two 'equal and alike' suitors who are 'reasonable creatures' with 'understanding and discourse', however, she is convinced that her 'own manners' will make either man a good husband (4.3). She therefore accepts the suitor that mad destiny selects. Her accomplishment lies in preferring an equal match of intelligence to an unequal union which would demean her wit by forcing her to coddle a fool.

Her ideal of marriage based on mutual respect separates Grace from the other women, whose notions of marriage throughout the play are chipping, if not shattering. Dame Purecraft, the play's other bride, also has the opportunity to choose between Winwife and Quarlous, and makes a choice just as precipitate, but she chooses emotionally, not rationally. Where wit and reticent gentility govern Grace, superstition and hypocrisy govern Dame Purecraft, despite her guile. Even though the widow has run her own business for seven years successfully enough to keep her family 'like gentlefolks' (1.5.143), when fortune-tellers warn her to marry a madman within the week – a plot device typical of the prejudice against independent women – she obeys. Quarlous's diatribe against marrying widows (1.3.48–86) makes the usual claims that widows are sexually insatiable and physically repellent, but Jonson offers no evidence that Dame Purecraft is either. Instead, he stresses her sharp practices in commerce and religion: 'she is not a wise wilful widow for nothing, nor a sanctified sister for a song' (1.5.144–5). When she proposes to her madman – Quarlous in disguise – she confesses to profiting from suitors' gifts and from alms stolen under cover of her church office, but her major source of revenue is matchmaking, for which service she virtually blackmails new wives in the church's name. In thus gaining from the couplings of others, her livelihood most resembles Ursula's. Both rule and cheat others by exploiting appetites. Ursula literalises the male prejudice that independent women are monsters: while feeding others with a sharp eye on the profits, she has obviously given rein to her own gargantuan sensuality in eating, drinking, smoking, quarrelling, and obscene joking. But her agenda is transparent. Dame Purecraft's pious shape-shifting makes her a far more insidious and inscrutable figure. Under the patriarchally approved covers of indulgent mother and obedient churchwoman, she secretly manipulates men and male institutions for her own advantage.

Ursula's shape cannot shift; stable and accommodating at once, she massively incorporates the needs and greeds of her male customers. The women who pass through her bower, however, do shift their shapes when touched by fervent male appetite. They give in to the anarchy of the place, betraying themselves into their opposites, either suddenly blurting out the truth, like Dame Purecraft, or losing all claim to judgment, like Mistress Overdo. Their instability emerges especially when they are cast adrift on their own, freely walking in public areas and freely speaking to strangers. Grace wanders through the fair unsullied by shape-shifting, though accompanied by strangers, perhaps because, like Persephone in the underworld, she has no appetite. But Dame Purecraft falls in love with the madman as a result of losing her companions after a pig-feast. Mistress Overdo eats, drinks, and speaks out of turn as she tries to regulate the game of vapours; once Wasp is arrested, she is abandoned to the care of bawds and pimps. Misogynistic views of the fluidity of women's nature as 'leaky vessels' equate incontinence in controlling their urine with sexual promiscuity (Paster 1987: pp. 48–9). Both Mistress Overdo and Win Littlewit disappear into Ursula's booth to use a makeshift privy, and end up transformed into whores. The 'punk of Turnbull, Ramping Alice' resents the competition when she beats Mistress Overdo, crying: 'The poor common whores can ha' no traffic for the privy rich ones. Your caps and hoods of velvet call away our customers, and lick the fat from us' (4.5.61–3). The fact that Mistress Overdo's first name is also Alice makes the equation between wife and whore plainer. In another reductive equation, tiny Win Littlewit and the puppet Hero both play parts as punks created by John Littlewit. Once the women put on their green gowns and crimson petticoats, the wives and the whores are virtually indistinguishable: 'How should my husband know me, then?' asks Win (5.4.42).

When her husband does finally recognise her, he does not explain or moralise his shock – he simply expresses it, faced with the contradictory roles he has culpably elicited from his wife. So too Justice Overdo, faced with the raw come-uppance to his sense of superiority: the stage direction simply indicates, '*Mistress Overdo is sick, and her husband is silenced*'. When Quarlous, stripped of his mad disguise, crows over his bride, Dame Purecraft sees in her new spouse what the other couples have been forced to see in each other: a failure of reciprocity, a violation of trust, a drying up of expectation, that places the integrity of each, as an individual and as a collaborating partner, in jeopardy. This recognition is essentially the recognition lurking in all the social contracts in all the plays in this volume. Volpone sees it in Mosca; Bonario sees it in his father Corbaccio. Subtle recognises it in Face, and everyone, from close relatives to mere acquaintances, feels it in *Epicoene*. The betrayals cross gender lines and to some extent render those lines irrelevant. No one emerges morally superior, or wins an unambiguous reward. Even Grace has to pay unfairly for her witty improvement of her fate.

The circularity of the play's logic mimics the debating tactics of the puppet Dionysius, who argues that an idol is a lawful calling because Busy called him idol, and Busy's calling is lawful. The antonymical switch neutralises both arguments. Why, Dionysius asks, are puppets considered profane, if puritan feather-makers, tirewomen, and other fashioners of trifles are not equally labelled '*pages of Pride and waiters upon Vanity*'? Let him who is without sin cast the first stone. Dionysius's very genderlessness refutes Busy's charges of sexual abomination: '*The puppet takes up his garment*' to show there is nothing sexual underneath. Where Busy's zealous imagination sees 'all licence, even licentiousness itself', Lantern Leatherhead sees only the Master of the Revels's signature licensing the show. This logical confusion as words slip from their meanings corresponds to all the documents which start out authorising one purpose and end up with another, and to the women who follow the same paradigm, rotating between wifedom and whoredom. It asks the question, when is a dripping-pan a dripping-pan, and when is it a makeshift chamberpot, or an outsized codpiece to preserve male modesty? The answer seems to be, whenever time and circumstance require it – whenever the failure of one meaning or function demands the construction of another. In *Bartholomew Fair*, the constructions are finally open-ended: no doors are closed, no spouses rejected, no classes excluded, no law laid down. If Jonson promises no authoritatively happy future, at least he gives a moderately festive one where the feasting, the coupling, and the playing will go on.

NOTE ON THE TEXTS

Volpone appeared originally in quarto, published by Thomas Thorpe in 1607, and probably printed by George Eld, who had already printed *Sejanus* and *Eastward Ho!* in 1605, and later printed *The Masques of Blackness and of Beauty* in 1608. The folio text appeared in Jonson's *Works*, printed by William Stansby in 1616, and, despite evidence of revision, by and large reproduces the quarto text, even its errors in speech-headings. For specifics, see the Textual Notes.

The sole authoritative text for *Epicoene* is the 1616 folio. Although the Stationers' Register indicates that Walter Burre acquired the publishing rights of *Epicoene* on 28 September 1612, he apparently did not bring out a quarto when he printed *The Alchemist*, possibly for political reasons associated with the Arabella Stuart case (see the note on 5.1). Part of the folio text of *Epicoene*, from the prologues to 2.2.64, exists in two states. Apparently the compositors had made too many errors, and had also created confusion between the speech-prefix for Dauphine (DAV) and the one for Daw (DAW). DAV was changed to DAVP, and Jonson made various other changes that may be scanned in the Textual Notes.

The Alchemist was printed first in quarto in 1612, and then in the folio of 1616. The revisions seem to arise from fear of prosecution for blasphemy; many oaths are modified to secular equivalents. These may be tracked in the textual notes.

Bartholomew Fair was first prepared in folio in 1631, either for a volume with *The Devil is an Ass* and *The Staple of News*, or for a second companion folio of Jonson's works since 1614. However, the volume was neither released nor completed (if the intention was to print all of Jonson's later works), and the 1631 folios were incorporated into the second folio of 1640. There are, therefore, no textual notes for this play, since changes in the 1640 folio have no authority.

In modernising the texts, where there has been a choice, I have followed the folio, largely because the stage directions seem to reflect general stage practice, although their inexactness suggests they were not culled from prompt-books. Even though various editors have criticised these directions as unnecessary guides to actions already clear from the dialogue, the likelihood is that Jonson inserted them recognising that many readers have difficulty visualising actions that actors or frequent theatre-goers might think too obvious to mention. In fact, Jonson's failure to insert directions that might strike the novice play-reader as vital (such as the precise moment when Lady Would-be embraces Volpone during 4.6.20–57, or the exact point at which Celia appears in the window during 2.2) actually reveals, not how limiting, but how liberating familiarity with theatrical practice can be. A good playwright builds flexibility into the text, so that many production choices are possible. I have attempted, nevertheless, to control the flexibility by expanding or adding stage directions in square brackets to give support to the dialogue and to make further annotation irrelevant. But readers should remember that my stage directions are not the only acting choices validated by the text.

Jonson's idiosyncratic spellings (*windore* for window, *venter* for venture, *moyle* for mule, *porcpisces* for porpoises, etc.) have all been modernised along with the then-current failure to distinguish clearly between *ingenious* and *ingenuous*, *then* and *than*, *off* and *of*. In two instances, there seems to be confusion between *affect* and *effect* in *Volpone*: in the last lines of the Epistle, Jonson refers to those 'who never affected an act worthy of celebration'; and at 3.7.124, Corvino declares that Celia wishes 'spitefully to affect my utter ruin'. In both lines, either *effect*, meaning 'bring about' or 'achieve', or *affect*, in the sense of 'inspire', may be appropriate, and consequently I have kept the original spelling. Also in *Volpone* I have attempted to support Jonson's Italianate spelling of *cecchines* by preferring *zecchins* to alternatives in the *OED* ('chequeens', 'chequins', or even 'sequins'), all of which reflect French renderings of the Italian.

I have also modernised Jonson's contractions, since his system is puzzling to modern readers: Jonson indicated *I'm* by writing *I' am*, for example, and *they're* appeared as *they' are*. Unusual contractions, made to regularise the poetic metre, are annotated.

THE PLAYS

—

VOLPONE, OR THE FOX

INTRODUCTION

The setting: Venice

Venice, the crossing-point between east and west, was the most cosmopolitan city in the Renaissance world, with a large population of foreigners temporarily or permanently enjoying the climate, the culture, and the opportunities for international trade. As a world power, Venice by 1605 was on the decline, but it still dominated the realms of commerce and high finance. Venice monopolised the European market in such luxuries as silk and spices from the near and far east, brought by merchant-ships from the Levant, whose ruler, the Grand Turk, amazed and terrified the rest of the world. The decadent splendour of the Ottoman Empire seemed to spill over into Venice, with its wealth, its political intrigues, its reputation for sophisticated sexual practices, and its architectural beauty. The English fascination with the degeneracy and perversion they assumed dominated Venetian life animates the whole play, particularly in the figures of the English tourists and their references to the famous courtesans. The casting of the plots and characters into the general shape of a scenario from the *commedia dell'arte*, Venice's indigenous dramatic tradition, also injects a strong foreign flavour (see General Introduction, p. 10).

Although Venice was a popular destination for merchants and travellers, it was not often selected as a background for English plays, perhaps because playwrights feared seeming to support its republican values. Shakespeare used it twice, in *The Merchant of Venice* (1596/7?) and in *Othello* (1603/4), but relied on Venice's exotic reputation to create the setting, rather than the many concrete allusions Jonson makes to Italian literature, coins, topography, language, fashion, and entertainment. Shakespeare's references to the Rialto, the Jewish merchants, the courtesans, the navy, and the justice system represent only the most general and largely inaccurate knowledge of Venice circulating among the untravelled in the rest of Europe. Middleton's Venetian setting in *Blurt, Master Constable* (1602) relies solely on the licentious reputation of the courtesans; it has otherwise no local colour at all. Nevertheless, Jonson was impressed enough with Middleton's introduction to Imperia and her women (2.2.1–50) to draw on it for Lady Would-be's grumbles at 3.4.1–37 and 4.2.3–6: both women complain about the effects of hot weather on their makeup and about the fit of their gowns; Lady Would-be grouses at length about her coiffure. Jonson expands the comic vanity by moving the scene from Middleton's setting in the courtesan's private chamber, where such conversation seems appropriate, to a reception room in Volpone's house (3.4) and then to a public street (4.2). Marston probably set *What You Will* (1606) in Venice following the success of *Volpone*. He names his play's loyal wife Celia, and the first reference to her involves a suitor who serenades her under a window, like Volpone in the mountebank scene. Some local allusions to Venice, mostly occurring in Act 1, are sprinkled through the dialogue (the Rialto, the importance of merchants in the Republic, the black clothing of high-ranking gentlemen, and the oaths swearing by St Mark), but otherwise the Venetian setting has nothing like the impact of place in *Volpone*. In fact, *Volpone*'s pervasive attention to setting, fixed in the local area near the Piazza di San Marco, is unique among Jacobean plays.

Sources

Since Jonson had never visited Italy, *Volpone*'s local allusions to the Arsenale, the Procuratia, the Piazza di San Marco, the Rialto, the shipping, the markets, mountebanks, and courtesans are all borrowed from secondary sources. Jonson's Italian friends Antonio Ferrobosco, the musician who set the songs for the play, and John Florio, the author of the English–Italian dictionary *The World of Words*, supplied local expressions and customs. Although his acquaintance Thomas Coryat had not yet written his travelogue of Europe, *The Crudities* (1611), many of Coryat's observations of Venice attest to the accuracy of details in Jonson's play. The overview of the Venetian government and legal system came from Gasparino Contarini's *De Magistratibus et Republica Venetorum* (1589), translated by Samuel Lewkenor (1599) with an appendix of other related historical information.

Jonson's vast reading in classical literature pointed him towards the legacy-hunting device central to his play: Horace's *Satires*, 2.5, Petronius's *Satyricon*, and Lucian's *Dialogues of the Dead*, 5–9, all tell stories of vicious flattering heirs outwitted by their wealthy victim. Experimenting with sources he was to use more extravagantly later in *Epicoene*, Jonson invented Lady Would-be out of misogynist sketches in Libanius of Antioch's declamation 26, *The Loquacious Woman*, and Juvenal's offensively learned lady in *Satire vi*. Volpone's opening prayer to gold parodies Ovid's description of the golden age in *Metamorphoses* I, his mockery of decrepit old age (1.4.144ff.) derives from Juvenal's *Satire x*, and his song to Celia (3.7) magically translates Catullus's fifth ode to Lesbia. Lucian's *The Dream, or The Cock* is the main source for the freak-show of 1.2, with some extra details from Diogenes Laertius's *De Philosophorum Vitis*. The annotations point out other fainter echoes from Jonson's classical library.

The strongest medieval and Renaissance influence on the play also comes from a classical source, Aesop's *Fables* (the fox-and-the-grapes story appears at 1.1.121, and the fox-and-the-cheese at 5.3.13), but the beast-fable and the bestiary abounded as moral conventions and analogues not only in emblem books, but also in church decorations, manuscript iconography, and domestic embroidery. This moral tradition has a complex history. Its effects on Jonson are perhaps best seen in his use of the beast-epic of Reynard the Fox, translated by William Caxton (1481) as *The History of Reynard the Fox*; it also tells the story of a crafty fox who pretends to be dying in order to entrap predatory birds and to rape the crow's wife (see General Introduction, p. 18, and R. B. Parker 1976a). The lesson of Sir Pol in the tortoise shell echoes emblem book cautions recommending prudence and the wisdom of staying at home (Creaser 1976: p. 511).

Other more or less contemporary influences include Erasmus's *The Praise of Folly* (1511), especially for the fool's song in 1.2, and Cornelius Agrippa's *The Vanity and Uncertainty of Arts and Sciences* (trans. 1575), chapters 83 and 93 on doctors and lawyers.

Stage history

The King's Majesty's Servants, also known as the King's Men (Shakespeare's company), first performed *Volpone* at the Globe, in 1605 by the old calendar, which would make it February or March 1606 by the modern calendar, assuming the play was written in December–January, following the Gunpowder Plot. It played subsequently at Oxford and Cambridge in 1606 or 1607, with several revivals up to 1638. The six 'principal comedians' or actors in the original production were listed at the end of the printed play, but how the roles were assigned can only be guessed at.

After the Restoration, *Volpone* was frequently performed at the Theatre Royal and the Dorset Garden, and in the eighteenth century at Drury Lane and Covent Garden. The play was dropped from the Covent Garden repertory in 1753 and not revived until 1771; it then survived in cut form (omitting coarseness and indecencies) until 1785. There were no further performances until 1921. Since then it has become the most frequently revived non-Shakespearean play of the Renaissance period (see R. B. Parker 1978). The most famous Volpone, Donald Wolfit, reduced Mosca's part and often cut out Sir Politic entirely (see R. B. Parker 1976b). Other famous Volpones include Ralph Richardson in 1952 (Royal Shakespeare Company) with Anthony Quayle as Mosca, Eric Porter in 1955 (Bristol Old Vic), Colin Blakeley in 1968 (National Theatre) and Paul Scofield in 1977 (National Theatre) with Ben Kingsley as Mosca and Sir John Gielgud in the restored part of Sir Pol. Most modern productions since 1955 have tended to stress the beast-fable in costume and characterisation; the National Theatre production of 1968 (dir. Tyrone Guthrie) first represented the Would-bes as parrots.

As testament to the play's enduring popularity, *Volpone* has also been adapted for radio, television, and even opera and musical comedy (*Foxy*), and modernised in several versions and languages (Stefan Zweig's play was translated from German into French by Jules Romains for a cinematic treatment), for Broadway stage (Larry Gelbart's *Sly Fox*, 1976), and film (Joseph Mankiewicz's *The Honeypot*, 1966).

Further reading

John Creaser (1975) and Ian Donaldson (1971) offer impressive interpretations of the play's ending with a close study of Volpone's character. For two views of the Would-be subplot, John Creaser (1976) analyses its implications thoroughly, and

David M. Bergeron (1986) adds a delightful whimsicality by reading Sir Pol as a romantic. John D. Rea's introduction to his edition (1919) defends Sir Pol as a parody of Sir Henry Wotton. William W. E. Slights (1985) and John Sweeney (1982) relate themes of conspiracy and theatricality. Robert C. Evans (1989) analyses the personal satire of Thomas Sutton, and B. N. De Luna (1967) gives background on the 'popish plot' in chapters 4 and 5. R. B. Parker (1976a) explores the beast-fable motif, and in two other articles (1976b, 1978) addresses practical theatre performance.

VOLPONE,

OR

THE FOX

A Comedy

Acted in the year 1605, by
the King's Majesty's
Servants

The Author, Ben Jonson

HORACE:

Simul et iucunda et idonea dicere vitae.

LONDON,
Printed by WILLIAM STANSBY

1616

[DEDICATION]

To the most noble and most equal sisters,
the two famous universities,
for their love and acceptance
shown to his poem in the presentation,
Ben Jonson,   5
the grateful acknowledger,
dedicates both it and himself.

1. *equal*] Identical in excellence; balanced in judgment.
2. Cambridge and Oxford. The Inns of Court in London were known as the 'Third University'.
4 *poem*] Play. Jonson used the original Greek term, meaning any created work. *presentation*] Performance. The play was performed at both universities some time during 1606/7.
7. *and himself*] Jonson received honorary MA degrees from both Oxford and Cambridge, probably as a result of *Volp*'s academic success.
After 7] Q adds: 'There follows an epistle, if you dare venture on the length.' Like the dedication, the epistle is addressed to the two universities.

[EPISTLE]*

Never, most equal sisters, had any man a wit so presently excellent as that
it could raise itself, but there must come both matter, occasion, commenders, and favourers to it. If this be true, and that the fortune of all
writers doth daily prove it, it behoves the careful to provide well toward
these accidents and, having acquired them, to preserve that part of   5
reputation most tenderly wherein the benefit of a friend is also defended.
Hence is it that I now render myself grateful, and am studious to justify the
bounty of your act, to which, though your mere authority were satisfying,
yet, it being an age wherein poetry and the professors of it hear so ill on all
sides, there will a reason be looked for in the subject.   10
  It is certain, nor can it with any forehead be opposed, that the too much
licence of poetasters in this time hath much deformed their mistress, that
every day their manifold and manifest ignorance doth stick unnatural
reproaches upon her. But for their petulancy, it were an act of the greatest
injustice either to let the learned suffer, or so divine a skill (which indeed   15

---

*   In this open letter Jonson attempts to justify both his reputation as a writer and the
     universities' discrimination as his patrons. He argues that poetry at this time has a bad
     name simply because too many undisciplined and tasteless minds are aspiring to an art
     beyond their capacity, but urges that the mere existence of 'poetasters', or trashy verse-
     writers, cannot corrupt a true talent who inspires all that is best in those who read or
     hear him. He finally defends *Volp* as a comedy adhering to classical form and moral law
     even in the seriousness of its ending. But tongue-in-cheek self-justification is a hallmark
     of Aristophanic comedy, and Jonson's hyperbolic defensiveness should not be construed
     too literally as high-minded knight-errantry rescuing Poetry in distress.
1.   *wit*] Imagination, intellectual power. *presently*] Directly.
2.   *raise*] Create, develop. *matter*] Subject matter.
5.   *accidents*] Concomitants of success; cf. 'matter, occasion, commenders, and favourers'.
6.   *benefit*] Beneficence.
8.   *bounty of your act*] Generosity of your patronage.
9.   *professors of it*] Those who claim to be writers. The wording suggests both the well-
     qualified or scholarly professional, and the hack or amateur who merely pretends to
     have talent. *hear so ill*] Have such a bad reputation.
11. *forehead*] Impudence, confidence.
12. *poetasters*] Writers of shoddy verse; paltry rimesters. Jonson's play on this topic, *Poet*,
     was printed in 1602. *mistress*] Poetry. *that*] So that, in that.
14. *But*] Except. *petulancy*] Insolence.

should not be attempted with unclean hands) to fall under the least
contempt. For if men will impartially and not asquint look toward the
offices and function of a poet, they will easily conclude to themselves the
impossibility of any man's being the good poet without first being a good
man. He that is said to be able to inform young men to all good disciplines,   20
inflame grown men to all great virtues, keep old men in their best and
supreme state or, as they decline to childhood, recover them to their first
strength; that comes forth the interpreter and arbiter of nature, a teacher of
things divine no less than human, a master in manners; and can alone, or
with a few, effect the business of mankind: this, I take him, is no subject for   25
pride and ignorance to exercise their railing rhetoric upon.

But it will here be hastily answered that the writers of these days are other
things; that not only their manners but their natures are inverted, and
nothing remaining with them of the dignity of poet but the abused name,
which every scribe usurps; that now, especially in dramatic or (as they term   30
it) stage poetry, nothing but ribaldry, profanation, blasphemy, all licence of
offence to God and man is practised. I dare not deny a great part of this, and
am sorry I dare not, because in some men's abortive features (and would
they had never boasted the light) it is over-true. But that all are embarked
in this bold adventure for hell is a most uncharitable thought and, uttered,   35
a more malicious slander.

For my particular, I can, and from a most clear conscience, affirm that
I have ever trembled to think toward the least profaneness, have loathed the
use of such foul and unwashed bawdry as is now made the food of the scene.
And, howsoever I cannot escape from some the imputation of sharpness but   40
that they will say I have taken a pride or lust to be bitter, and not my

16. *unclean*] Impure, or unsanctified. The ancients believed that true poets were inspired
directly by the gods.
19–20. *impossibility ... good man*] Conventional belief that moral superiority led to
worldly superiority; Shakespeare's Duke (*Measure for Measure* 1.1.30–41) makes a
similar claim for the good ruler.
20. *inform*] Shape.
22. *decline to childhood*] Slip into senility.
25. *effect the business of*] Demonstrate solicitude for.   *subject*] Subordinate person.
30. *scribe*] Writer, but generally a copyist, not a creative or intellectual talent.
31. *all licence*] Complete disregard for propriety.
33. *abortive features*] Undeveloped and unsuccessful plays.
37–9. *For my particular ... of the scene*] Aristophanes also inserted such wry disclaimers,
insisting that his comedies could escape charges of profanity because his plays had
higher intellectual and moral purposes than those of his contemporaries.
37. *For my particular*] As for me.
40. *sharpness*] Severity.
41. *lust*] Vicious pleasure.

youngest infant but hath come into the world with all his teeth, I would ask
of these supercilious politics: what nation, society, or general order, or state
I have provoked? what public person? whether I have not in all these
preserved their dignity, as mine own person, safe? My works are read, 45
allowed (I speak of those that are entirely mine): look into them. What
broad reproofs have I used? Where have I been particular? Where personal,
except to a mimic, cheater, bawd, or buffoon, creatures for their insolencies
worthy to be taxed? Yet to which of these so pointingly as he might not
either ingenuously have confessed or wisely dissembled his disease? 50

But it is not rumour can make men guilty, much less entitle me to other
men's crimes. I know that nothing can be so innocently writ or carried but
may be made obnoxious to construction; marry, whilst I bear mine
innocence about me, I fear it not. Application is now grown a trade with
many; and there are that profess to have a key for the deciphering of 55
everything. But let wise and noble persons take heed how they be too
credulous or give leave to these invading interpreters to be over-familiar
with their fames, who cunningly and often utter their own virulent malice
under other men's simplest meanings.

As for those that will, by faults which charity hath raked up or common 60
honesty concealed, make themselves a name with the multitude or, to draw
their rude and beastly claps, care not whose living faces they entrench with

42. *youngest infant*] Most recent play; probably a reference to *Eastward Ho!*, for which
    the collaborators Marston, Jonson, and Chapman were charged, and the latter two
    imprisoned, for satirising James I's practice of selling knighthoods for ready cash.
    with all his teeth] Bitingly satirical.
43. *politics*] Cynical contrivers.
46. *allowed*] Passed uncensored by the Master of Revels and licensed for the stage.
    entirely mine] Not a collaboration like *The Isle of Dogs* (1597), *Sej* (1603), or *EH!*
    (1605), for which he had been imprisoned and questioned by the Privy Council.
47. *broad*] Explicit, outspoken. *reproofs*] Insulting language. *particular*] Critical of
    specific persons.
48. *mimic*] Burlesque actor. *buffoon*] Clown.
49. *taxed*] Censured.
51. *entitle me*] Ascribe or impute to me.
53. *obnoxious to construction*] Liable to harmful interpretation. *marry*] Common
    expletive, originally alluding to the Virgin Mary.
54. *Application*] Twisting or 'deciphering' a writer's language to reveal libel.
55. *there are that*] There are those that.
58. *fames*] Reputations *utter*] Circulate counterfeit money (here, information) as though
    it were legitimate.
60. *raked up*] Buried.
61. *honesty*] Decency.
62. *rude and beastly claps*] Applause of the ignorant and crude.
62–3. *entrench … styles*] Disfigure with their pens (Latin, *stilus*, pen, writing style).

their petulant styles – may they do it without a rival for me. I choose rather
to live graved in obscurity than share with them in so preposterous a fame.
Nor can I blame the wishes of those severe and wiser patriots who,   65
providing the hurts these licentious spirits may do in a state, desire rather
to see fools and devils and those antique relics of barbarism retrieved, with
all other ridiculous and exploded follies, than behold the wounds of private
men, of princes, and nations. For, as Horace makes Trebatius speak, among
these   70

> – *Sibi quisque timet, quanquam est intactus, et odit.*

And men may justly impute such rages, if continued, to the writer as his
sports. The increase of which lust in liberty, together with the present trade
of the stage, in all their miscellane interludes, what learned or liberal soul
doth not already abhor? where nothing but the filth of the time is uttered,   75
and that with such impropriety of phrase, such plenty of solecisms, such
dearth of sense, so bold prolepses, so racked metaphors, with brothelry able
to violate the ear of a pagan and blasphemy to turn the blood of a Christian
to water. I cannot but be serious in a cause of this nature, wherein my fame
and the reputations of divers honest and learned are the question, when   80
a name so full of authority, antiquity, and all great mark is through their
insolence become the lowest scorn of the age, and those men subject to the
petulancy of every vernaculous orator that were wont to be the care of kings
and happiest monarchs.

64. *graved*] Buried.   *preposterous*] Monstrous, unnatural.
65. *patriots*] Fellow countrymen.
66. *providing*] Foreseeing.
67–8. *fools … follies*] Revival of clownish figures from medieval mystery and morality
    drama, and other old-fashioned nonsense worthy only of being jeered and hooted off
    the stage.
71. *– Sibi … odit*] From Horace, *Satires* II.i.23. Jonson had already translated this passage
    in *Poet* 3.5.41–2: 'In satyres, each man (though untoucht) complaines / As he were hurt;
    and hates such biting straines' (H&S).
72–3. *men … sports*] People may rightly assume that, satirically attacking others, the
    writer is simply playing his own eccentric game.
73. *lust*] Vicious pleasure.
74. *miscellane interludes*] *Ludi miscelli*, Roman variety shows, similar to music-hall
    entertainments.
76. *solecisms*] Irregularities in diction, or faulty agreements in grammar; generally, incor-
    rect use of language.
77. *prolepses*] Misattributions of time, such as anachronisms.   *racked*] Twisted,
    stretched.
81. *a name*] That is, poet.
82. *those men*] Poets; also the antecedent of the 'that'-clause ending the sentence.
83. *vernaculous*] Low-bred, scurrilous.

This it is that hath not only rapt me to present indignation, but made me   85
studious heretofore and by all my actions to stand off from them; which
may most appear in this my latest work – which you, most learned
arbitresses, have seen, judged, and to my crown approved – wherein I have
laboured, for their instruction and amendment, to reduce not only the
ancient forms but manners of the scene: the easiness, the propriety, the   90
innocence, and, last, the doctrine which is the principal end of poesy, to
inform men in the best reason of living. And though my catastrophe may,
in the strict rigour of comic law, meet with censure, as turning back to my
promise, I desire the learned and charitable critic to have so much faith in
me to think it was done of industry; for with what ease I could have varied   95
it nearer his scale, but that I fear to boast my own faculty, I could here insert.
But my special aim being to put the snaffle in their mouths that cry out we
never punish vice in our interludes, etc., I took the more liberty, though not
without some lines of example drawn even in the ancients themselves, the
goings out of whose comedies are not always joyful, but oft-times the   100
bawds, the servants, the rivals, yea and the masters are mulcted; and fitly,
it being the office of a comic poet to imitate justice and instruct to life, as
well as purity of language, or stir up gentle affections. To which I shall take
the occasion elsewhere to speak.

For the present, most reverenced sisters, as I have cared to be thankful for   105
your affections past, and here made the understanding acquainted with
some ground of your favours, let me not despair their continuance to the
maturing of some worthier fruits, wherein, if my muses be true to me, I shall
raise the despised head of poetry again and, stripping her out of those rotten
and base rags wherewith the times have adulterated her form, restore her to   110

---

85. *rapt me*] Carried me away.

88. *to my crown*] As my crowning honour.

89. *reduce*] Bring back.

90. *ancient forms*] Classical dramatic structures for comedy, including the unities of time
and place (see Prologue 31n.). *manners of the scene*] Dramatic conventions, listed in
the rest of the sentence; i.e., informal and uncontrived style, action suitable for comedy,
entertainment both artistically sound and morally instructive.

92. *catastrophe*] Final scene.

95. *of industry*] On purpose.

100. *goings out*] Conclusions.

101. *mulcted*] Punished.

103. *affections*] Emotional influences on the mind.

104. *elsewhere to speak*] Jonson intended to publish a commentary on Horace's *Ars
Poetica*, as he had announced in *Sej*, but he kept working on it until the fire in his study
finally destroyed it, along with other works and most of his library, in 1623. See
Jonson's poem 'An Execration upon Vulcan' (Parfitt 1975: p. 181) for details of the
loss.

106. *understanding*] Those who understand.

her primitive habit, feature, and majesty, and render her worthy to be
embraced and kissed of all the great and master spirits of our world. As for
the vile and slothful who never affected an act worthy of celebration, or are
so inward with their own vicious natures as they worthily fear her, and
think it a high point of policy to keep her in contempt with their   115
declamatory and windy invectives: she shall out of just rage incite her
servants (who are *genus irritabile*) to spout ink in their faces that shall eat,
farther than their marrow, into their fames; and not Cinnamus the barber
with his art shall be able to take out the brands, but they shall live and be
read till the wretches die, as things worst deserving of themselves in chief
and then of all mankind.   120

111. *primitive habit*] Original clothing.

117. *genus irritabile*] Class of people easily aroused (Horace).

117–18. *spout ink ... fames*] Satire was commonly described as corrosive, capable of
maiming and even killing its victims.

118. *Cinnamus the barber*] In Martial, *Epigram* VI, 24–6; barbers and surgeons belonged
to the same guild, and had the same training. According to another of Martial's poems,
Cinnamus had to close his shop apparently because of investigations into his
qualifications.

119. *brands*] Burns, caused by the corrosive satire. Criminals who escaped hanging were
branded with a hot iron; Jonson himself was branded on the thumb in 1599 for the
murder of a fellow-actor.

After last line] Q adds: 'From my house in the Blackfriars, this 11 of February, 1607.'

THE PERSONS OF THE PLAY*

[Major roles]	[Supporting roles]
VOLPONE, *a Magnifico*	POLITIC WOULD-BE, *a Knight*
MOSCA, *his Parasite*	PEREGRINE, *a Gentleman-Traveller*
VOLTORE, *an Advocate*	BONARIO, *a young Gentleman*
CORBACCIO, *an old*	FINE MADAM WOULD-BE, *the*
Gentleman	Knight's Wife

*   This edition's list of the characters imitates the two-column format printed in the folio, but adds labels to explain the structural significance of the arrangement. The main roles, characters introduced in Act 1, are listed in order of their appearance in the play. The secondary roles, introduced in Acts 2 and 3 as complications, are also listed in order of appearance, not in the order of their family or business relationships to the major characters with whom they share lines. Bonario has no connection with Voltore, any more than Lady Would-be has with Corbaccio, although the latter pairing is convenient for the compositor. The fact that Celia appears on the same line as Corvino, her husband, is fortuitous. The minor roles appear in Acts 4 and 5 as testing figures who provoke the final catastrophes in the main plot and the subplot. The fourth group of characters require either doubling (using the actors playing the minor roles), super-numerary, or specialised performers. The three freaks in particular seem to demand entertainers who combine the skills of musicians, clowns, acrobats, jugglers, and mimes.

    The names suggest Jonson's debt to his friend John Florio, author of *A World of Words* (1598), an Italian–English dictionary. Jonson inscribed a presentation copy of *Volp*, 1607, to Florio, gratefully calling him the 'aid of his muses' and his 'father', indications that Florio assisted Jonson on things Italian.

1. *VOLPONE*] '[A]n old fox ... an old crafty sly subtle companion, sneaking lurking wily deceiver' (Florio). He has the characteristic red hair of the fox (cf. 2.4.30), and Jonson reminds us of two of Aesop's fables: The Fox and the Grapes (1.1.121) and The Fox, the Raven, and the Cheese (5.3.13). *Magnifico*] Honorary title for wealthy noblemen in Venice. *POLITIC WOULD-BE*] Would-be crafty schemer, thus an aspiring Venetian. His nickname, Sir Pol, identifies him as a poll-parrot, symbolising a thoughtless mimic.

2. *MOSCA*] '[A]ny kind of fly' (Florio), including parasites. *Parasite*] A toady or obsequi-ous hanger-on who flatters the wealthy in exchange for hospitality or patronage. *PEREGRINE*] Pilgrim-hawk, apt name for a traveller. In Greek myth, hawks, sacred to Apollo, the god of enlightenment, attacked ignorant fools.

3. *VOLTORE*] '[A] ravenous bird called a vulture ... a greedy cormorant' (Florio). Legacy-hunters were commonly called vultures, because they lived off the dead. *Advocate*] Barrister acting as defence counsel. *BONARIO*] '[H]onest, good, uncorrupt' (Florio); suggests a good-natured naivety.

4. *CORBACCIO*] '[A] filthy great raven' (Florio). A raven's croaking presaged death. Its keen sight and hearing are burlesqued in Corbaccio's myopia and deafness. The Elizabethan notion of the raven as a negligent parent has since been disproved by ethologists like Konrad Lorenz.

[Major roles]	[Supporting roles]	
CORVINO, *a Merchant*	CELIA, *the Merchant's Wife*	5

[Minor roles]
AVOCATORI, *four Magistrates*   COMMANDATORI, *Officers*
NOTARIO, *the Register*   MERCATORI, *three Merchants*

[Servants/Extras]
NANO, *a Dwarf*   ANDROGYNO, *a Hermaphrodite*
CASTRONE, *an Eunuch*   SERVITORE, *a Servant [in Corvino's house]*
GREGE, *[a crowd]*   [TWO] WOMEN, *[in the Would-be   10 household]*

[PORTERS, *for Corbaccio's chair*]

The scene: Venice

5. *CORVINO*] A gorcrow, or carrion crow. The crow, which mates for life, is an ironic symbol of Corvino's marital fidelity. *CELIA*] Heavenly woman (Latin).
6. *AVOCATORI*] Public prosecutors for crimes against citizens. They conducted hearings and recommended punishments to the court, but were not responsible for final judgments as Jonson mistakenly indicates in Act 5. See 5.12.145–6n. *COMMANDATORI*] Acted as process-servers or bailiffs, summoning witnesses to court and issuing proclamations.
7. *Register*] Court clerk.
8. *NANO*] Dwarf (Latin, *nanus*). Dwarf entertainers were fashionable at court. *ANDROGYNO*] '[H]e that is both male and female' (Florio). Hermaphrodites were thought to be the monstrous result of their parents' sexual excesses.
9. *CASTRONE*] '[A] gelded man ... a ninny' (Florio).
10. *GREGE*] '[A] troop or multitude of men or women' (Florio).
12. *Venice*] Elizabethans regarded this city-state as the European hub of political intrigue and sophistication. See the Introduction to *Volp.*

THE ARGUMENT*

V olpone, childless, rich, feigns sick, despairs,
O ffers his state to hopes of several heirs,
L ies languishing; his parasite receives
P resents of all, assures, deludes; then weaves
O ther cross-plots, which ope themselves, are told.   5
N ew tricks for safety are sought; they thrive: when, bold,
E ach tempts th'other again, and all are sold.

---

* Jonson uses the acrostic here and in *Alch* to prefix a summary of the plot, self-consciously echoing classical comedy by following Plautus's usual practice.
1. *despairs*] Gives up hope of life.
2. *state*] Estate.
5. *told*] Exposed.
7. *sold*] Cheated; made to pay for their crimes.

PROLOGUE*

Now luck yet send us, and a little wit
    Will serve, to make our play hit,
According to the palates of the season.
    Here is rhyme not empty of reason.
This we were bid to credit from our poet,   5
    Whose true scope, if you would know it,
In all his poems still hath been this measure:
    To mix profit with your pleasure;
And not as some, whose throats their envy failing,
    Cry hoarsely, 'All he writes is railing',   10
And, when his plays come forth, think they can flout them
    With saying, 'He was a year about them'.
To these there needs no lie but this his creature,
    Which was, two months since, no feature;
And, though he dares give them five lives to mend it,   15
    'Tis known, five weeks fully penned it
From his own hand, without a coadjutor,
    Novice, journeyman, or tutor.
Yet thus much I can give you as a token

---

*   The rough metre of the verse may mean that Nano, with or without Androgyno and Castrone, played the prologue.

1–4. This cocky assertion is in the style of Aristophanes: A play needs only luck, and relatively little talent, to please public taste. But *this* play is different: it has something to say.

1. *yet*] Replaces 'God' in Q, probably to avoid charges of blasphemy.

5. *credit*] Believe. *our poet*] Jonson.

7. *measure*] Both 'proposition' and 'poetic metre'.

8. The idea is from Horace (*Ars Poetica* 343), and appears frequently in Jonson and other writers of the period.

9. *as some*] Both Dekker (*Satiromastix*, 1601) and Marston (*The Dutch Courtesan*, 1605) had accused Jonson of being overly didactic.

12. *a year*] Jonson answered gibes at slowness in composition in the 'Apologetical Dialogue' appended to *Poet*. He always affirmed the value of careful revision: even Shakespeare, whom he admired 'this side idolatry', could have improved by rewriting.

13. *needs no lie*] Requires no rebuttal. *creature*] That is, his play, *Volp*.

14. Which did not exist two months ago.

17. *coadjutor*] Collaborator.

18. *novice*] An assistant or apprentice learning the business. *journeyman*] A writer hired to compose only certain scenes. *tutor*] One who superintends or corrects another's work.

Of his play's worth: no eggs are broken,   20
Nor quaking custards with fierce teeth affrighted,
   Wherewith your rout are so delighted;
Nor hales he in a gull, old ends reciting,
   To stop gaps in his loose writing,
With such a deal of monstrous and forced action   25
   As might make Bedlam a faction;
Nor made he his play fro' jests stol'n from each table,
   But makes jests to fit his fable –
And so presents quick comedy refined
   As best critics have designed: 30
The laws of time, place, persons he observeth.
   From no needful rule he swerveth.
All gall and copperas from his ink he draineth;
   Only a little salt remaineth
Wherewith he'll rub your cheeks till, red with laughter,   35
   They shall look fresh a week after.

20–28. Jonson lists various tricks of cheap farce, contrasting his own 'quick comedy refined'.

21. *quaking custards*] At city feasts, a fool jumped into a huge custard set on the Lord Mayor's table. The phrase also parodies John Marston's 'cowardy custards' bitten by the 'sharp-fanged satirist' (*Satires* ii).

22. *rout*] Rabble.

23. *gull, old ends reciting*] A fool repeating hackneyed proverbs and jokes.

25. *monstrous and forced action*] Distorted and artificial acting.

26. A performance that might do well at Bedlam, the London lunatic asylum of St Mary of Bethlehem. Tourists visited the madhouse for entertainment.

27–8. He does not piece a play together out of scavenged jokes, but invents jokes that rise naturally out of the plot.

29. *quick*] Lively.

30. *critics*] Classical authorities like Aristotle and Horace.

31. The 'Unities' recommended by Aristotle and codified by Renaissance Italian critics: stage time should not exceed twenty-four hours; stage locations should conform to expectations of real travel; and characters should consistently reflect the genre and milieu of the play.

33. *gall and copperas*] Oak-gall and sulphuric acid, used in making ink; figuratively, bitterness and virulence.

34. *salt*] Sediment; also, satiric wit. The use of salt in preserving flesh (pork, beef, or fish) sets up 'fresh' (36).

ACT 1

Act 1 scene 1*

[Enter] Mosca [and draws the bed-curtains, revealing] Volpone

VOLPONE   Good morning to the day – and, next, my gold!
    Open the shrine, that I may see my saint.

[Mosca opens the treasure chest]

    Hail, the world's soul, and mine! More glad than is
    The teeming earth to see the longed-for sun
    Peep through the horns of the celestial ram   5
    Am I to view thy splendour darkening his;
    That, lying here amongst my other hoards,
    Show'st like a flame by night, or like the day
    Struck out of chaos, when all darkness fled

*   All the scenes of this act take place in Volpone's bedroom, in which the chief prop is Volpone's curtained bed; the cupboard housing his gold may merely have been suggested at the Globe by one of the stage doors or the discovery-space. The scene begins with a blasphemous prayer to the supreme power of money which overrules moral and social codes, thanks to the greed in men's hearts. The prayer parodies Ovid's account of the Golden Age in *Metamorphoses*, Book 1, and inverts Seneca's argument that gold is a superficial distraction from the pursuit of wisdom (*Epistles* CXV). Volpone's house, to judge from the reference at 5.7.7–15, is located on the south side of the Piazza di San Marco near the *Piscaria*, the wharf for the fish-market. All the action of the play takes place in or near the Piazza.

2. *shrine ... saint*] A profane celebration of gold in the form of a mock-*matins*, in which Volpone, with deliberate irony, abuses conventional Christian terms of prayer (especially 12–14); the sun substitutes for God, and gold for the son of God.

3. *world's soul*] Refers ambiguously to the sun (*sol* is Latin for sun and sun-god) as the source of life, but also facetiously to the Platonic deity, and cynically to gold. *mine!*] My soul; the sun is to the world what gold is to Volpone. He continues to gloat punningly on soul/sol, as at 10.

5. *horns of the celestial ram*] An image from the zodiac. The sun is in Aries, the Ram, at the vernal equinox, beginning the spring season.

7. *lying here*] Suggests that Volpone is still abed, luxuriating in self-display among his 'hoards' of treasure. At this point he wants only to 'view' his gold; he does not fondle it until 11.

8. *flame by night*] Combines a classical image of gold (as in Pindar, or Lucian) with a biblical image of God appearing as a pillar of fire to guide the Israelites to the Promised Land (Exodus 13:21).

9. *struck out of chaos*] Another combination of the classical and the biblical, based on the creation myth (Genesis 1:2–4).

Unto the centre. [*Rises*] O thou son of Sol,   10
But brighter than thy father, let me kiss,
With adoration, thee and every relic
Of sacred treasure in this blessèd room!
Well did wise poets by thy glorious name
Title that age which they would have the best,   15
Thou being the best of things, and far transcending
All style of joy in children, parents, friends,
Or any other waking dream on earth.
Thy looks when they to Venus did ascribe,
They should have giv'n her twenty thousand Cupids: 20
Such are thy beauties and our loves! Dear saint!
Riches, the dumb god that giv'st all men tongues –
That canst do nought and yet mak'st men do all things!
The price of souls! Even hell, with thee to boot,
Is made worth heaven! Thou art virtue, fame,   25
Honour, and all things else! Who can get thee,
He shall be noble, valiant, honest, wise –
MOSCA   And what he will, sir. Riches are in fortune
A greater good than wisdom is in nature.
VOLPONE   True, my beloved Mosca. Yet I glory   30
More in the cunning purchase of my wealth
Than in the glad possession, since I gain

10. *son of Sol*] Punning on son/sun, Sol/soul. Sol is the alchemical symbol for gold.

14. *poets*] Such as Ovid in *Metamorphoses* 1.89–112 and 15.96ff.

15. *Title that age*] The Golden Age, a mythical time when life was perfect, and men needed no laws or labour to regulate their days.

16–18. An ironic foreshadowing of the selfish pursuit of gold that destroys all the characters' happiness by the play's end.

17. *style*] Legal, official, or honorific title or entitlement; method or custom of performing actions or functions, especially one sanctioned by usage or law.

20. *twenty thousand Cupids*] Gold's beauty generates more potent and acquisitive pleasures than mere sexual or procreative bliss (Venus). This 'cupidity' is inordinate lust for wealth.

22. *dumb god*] Proverbially, silence is golden.

24. *price of souls*] Pure gold represents Christ's sacrifice (see 1 Corinthians 6:20). *to boot*] As prize (or booty).

28. *fortune*] Luck; also position or prosperity in life. Mosca is philosophically a gambler.

31. *cunning*] Clever, skilled; perhaps suggesting the conjuring power of a *cunningman*, or wizard. *purchase*] Acquisition.

No common way. I use no trade, no venture.
I wound no earth with ploughshares; fat no beasts
To feed the shambles; have no mills for iron,   35
Oil, corn, or men, to grind 'em into powder.
I blow no subtle glass; expose no ships
To threat'nings of the furrow-facèd sea.
I turn no moneys in the public bank;
Nor usure private –
MOSCA   No, sir, nor devour   40
Soft prodigals. You shall ha' some will swallow
A melting heir as glibly as your Dutch
Will pills of butter, and ne'er purge for't;
Tear forth the fathers of poor families
Out of their beds and coffin them alive   45
In some kind clasping prison, where their bones
May be forthcoming when the flesh is rotten.
But your sweet nature doth abhor these courses.
You loathe the widow's or the orphan's tears
Should wash your pavements, or their pitious cries   50
Ring in your roofs and beat the air for vengeance –
VOLPONE   Right, Mosca, I do loathe it.
MOSCA   And besides, sir,
You are not like the thresher that doth stand
With a huge flail watching a heap of corn,

33–40. Volpone, as mock social critic, deliberately misrepresents Golden Age values (a time
when there was no commerce or finance, no mining or industry, no shipbuilding or
exploration, no agriculture), thus exculpating his own practice of generating wealth and
condemning modern money-making endeavours as decadent.
33. *venture*] Speculation.
35. *shambles*] Meat-market or slaughterhouse.
36. *Oil*] Olive oil.
37. *subtle glass*] Fine glassware, for which Venice is famed. Glass was made on the island
of Murano, where the craftsmen could be kept isolated from commercial spies.
39. *turn*] Speculate with. *public bank*] The first public bank, Banco della Piazza di
Rialto, founded in 1587, allowed depositors to make payments by transfer (*per scritta*),
thus facilitating speculative ventures.
40. *usure*] Moneylending.
41. *soft*] Gullible. The Renaissance was an era of conspicuous consumption, during which
young men of fashion frequently lost their estates in unscrupulous deals for ready cash.
42. *melting*] Squandering.
42–3. *Dutch ... butter*] The Dutch were ridiculed for eating too much butter. *pills*]
Mouthfuls. *purge*] Take a laxative.
46. *clasping*] Holding in chains or manacles.

And, hungry, dares not taste the smallest grain,   55
But feeds on mallows and such bitter herbs;
Nor like the merchant who hath filled his vaults
With Romagnia and rich Candian wines,
Yet drinks the lees of Lombard's vinegar.
You will not lie in straw whilst moths and worms   60
Feed on your sumptuous hangings and soft beds.
You know the use of riches and dare give, now,
From that bright heap to me, your poor observer,
Or to your dwarf, or your hermaphrodite,
Your eunuch, or what other household-trifle   65
Your pleasure allows maintenance –

VOLPONE   Hold thee, Mosca,
Take of my hand. [*Gives money*] Thou strik'st on truth in all,
And they are envious, term thee parasite.
Call forth my dwarf, my eunuch, and my fool,
And let 'em make me sport.

[*Exit Mosca*]
                            What should I do   70
But cocker up my genius and live free
To all delights my fortune calls me to?
I have no wife, no parent, child, ally,
To give my substance to, but whom I make
Must be my heir, and this makes men observe me.   75
This draws new clients daily to my house:
Women and men, of every sex and age,
That bring me presents, send me plate, coin, jewels,
With hope that when I die (which they expect

---

55. *mallows*] Common wild plants having a gummy texture when cooked.
58. *Romagnia*] Rumney wine, a sweet Greek import.   *Candian*] Malmsey, a wine from Candia, Crete.
59. *Lombard's vinegar*] A barely potable wine from Lombardy, northern Italy, a Venetian mainland possession.
63. *poor observer*] Humble attendant.
65. *household-trifle*] Menial servant.
66. *Hold thee*] Stop.
69. Noblemen frequently kept freaks or grotesques as household pets and companions, sometimes for pious or charitable reasons, sometimes as scapegoats to deflect the evil eye. See the note on 1.2.
71. *cocker up my genius*] Indulge my appetites or whims; pamper my ego.
74. *make*] Designate.
75. *observe*] Venerate, pay flattering attentions to.
76. *clients*] Followers relying on his patronage.

Each greedy minute) it shall then return   80
Tenfold upon them; whilst some, covetous
Above the rest, seek to engross me whole
And counter-work the one unto the other,
Contend in gifts, as they would seem in love –
All which I suffer, playing with their hopes,   85
And am content to coin 'em into profit,
And look upon their kindness, and take more,
And look on that, still bearing them in hand,
Letting the cherry knock against their lips,
And draw it by their mouths, and back again. – How now!   90

Act 1 scene 2*

[*Enter*] Mosca, [*presenting*] Nano, [*holding a manuscript*], Androgyno,
    [*and*] Castrone, [*performing*]
NANO   *Now, room for fresh gamesters, who do will you to know*

83. *counter-work*] Undermine.
88. *bearing them in hand*] Leading them on.
89. *the cherry*] Alluding to the game of chop-cherry or bob-cherry, in which the player tries
     to bite a suspended cherry.
90. *How now!*] An extra-metrical exclamation, breaking off the soliloquy and introducing
     the freak-show of the next scene.
*   Freaks were not uncommon in noble Mediterranean households. A dwarf was most
     commonly retained as a child-minder or as a jester, the latter particularly if hunch-
     backed or mentally deficient. Nano seems to be relatively alert. The other two freaks
     associate Volpone with the exotic extravagances of the Turkish court. Castrone may be
     a mute eunuch, performing only as a musician. The hermaphrodite Androgyno may
     have been the result of recent interest in such cases as Marin/Marie le Marcis, the
     Hermaphrodite of Rouen, tried in 1601 and convicted of perversion for cohabiting with
     and wishing to marry a young widow. Of Volpone's three freaks, only Androgyno
     classifies himself as 'fool', though he may not mean a natural fool or imbecile; certainly,
     all are treated like children (i.e., as if lacking adult competence; see 5.11.8–11), with
     Nano their spokesman and manager. Possibly Volpone's 'natural' children (1.5.46–7,
     but see his denial at 1.1.73), they symbolise his folly and corruption despite the
     advantages of wealth, learning, and respectability.
         The freaks' interlude, like the freaks themselves, is emblematic of the degenerate
     tastes of their audience. Their emphasis on greed and amorality reflects Volpone's
     jeering contempt for society. A similarly deflating satiric principle operates in the
     puppet-show of *BF* 5.4 and 5.5.
1.   *room*] The traditional performers' cry to the audience for access to the playing space,
     particularly where there was no clearly defined performance area or stage entrance.
     gamesters] Players.

They do bring you neither play nor university show,
And therefore do entreat you that whatsoever they rehearse
May not fare a whit the worse for the false pace of the
    verse.
If you wonder at this, you will wonder more ere we pass,   5
    For know, here *[Indicates Androgyno]* is enclosed
    the soul of Pythagoras,
That juggler divine, as hereafter shall follow;
    Which soul, fast and loose, sir, came first from Apollo,
And was breathed into Aethalides, Mercurius his son,
    Where it had the gift to remember all that ever was done.   10
From thence it fled forth and made quick transmigration
    To goldilocked Euphorbus, who was killed in good
    fashion
At the siege of old Troy by the Cuckold of Sparta.
    Hermotimus was next (I find it in my charta)
To whom it did pass, where no sooner it was missing,   15

2. *play nor university show*] Neither a public theatre play nor a learned entertainment. But this interlude does contain obscure classical references of the kind found in Oxbridge parodies.

3. *rehearse*] Recite.

4. *false pace of the verse*] Clumsy four-stressed 'galloping' metre of early English drama, intended to complement these amateur theatricals.

6–62. A burlesque of Pythagoras's doctrine of the transmigration of souls, based on Lucian's satirical dialogue *The Dream, or The Cock*, an attack on the worship of wealth. In the interlude, transmigration is progressively debasing as the soul moves from the philosopher to the freak.

6. *Pythagoras*] Greek philosopher of the sixth century BC who believed in metempsychosis. The fallen soul, divine in itself, was trapped in a cycle of reincarnation from which it could free itself by cultivating Apollonian purity through the study of nature, music, and especially mathematics, the basis of the cosmic order. Pythagoreans accepted both sexes as equal (hence the hermaphrodite) and followed strict rules of silence, vegetarian diet, and self-examination according to severe ethical precepts.

7. *juggler*] Trickster; conjuror, because of the magical transformations of identity.

8. *fast and loose*] Impossible to guess accurately. The expression is based on a gambling game in which the gambler thrusts a skewer into an intricately folded belt and bets that the belt is either fixed 'fast' to the table, or 'loose'.

9. *Aethalides*] The herald of the Argonauts, gifted with omniscient memory.

12. *goldilocked Euphorbus*] The Trojan who wounded Patroclus and was killed by Menelaus. Euphorbus tied back his hair in a gold net before battle (*Iliad* 17). The name means 'Well-fed', an ironic attribute for an abstemious Pythagorean.

13. *Cuckold of Sparta*] Menelaus, Helen's husband.

14. *Hermotimus*] Greek philosopher of about 500 BC. *charta*] A manuscript, perhaps the script for the interlude, or perhaps a 'map' of Pythagoras's transmigrations.

> But with one Pyrrhus of Delos it learned to go a-fishing,
> And thence did it enter the Sophist of Greece.
>   From Pythagore she went into a beautiful piece
> Hight Aspasia, the meretrix; and the next toss of her
>   Was again of a whore she became a philosopher,   20
> Crates the cynic (as itself doth relate it).
>   Since, kings, knights and beggars, knaves, lords and
>   fools gat it,
>   Besides ox, and ass, camel, mule, goat, and brock,
>   In all which it hath spoke as in the cobbler's cock.
> But I come not here to discourse of that matter,   25
>   Or his one, two, or three, or his great oath, by quater,
> His musics, his trigon, his golden thigh,
>   Or his telling how elements shift. But I
> Would ask how of late thou hast suffered translation,
>   And shifted thy coat in these days of reformation?   30

ANDROGYNO *Like one of the reformed, a fool, as you see,*
          Counting all old doctrine heresy.

16. *Pyrrhus of Delos*] Greek philosopher, formerly a fisherman.
17. *Sophist of Greece*] Pythagoras.
18. *piece*] Contemptuous term for a woman.
19. *Aspasia*] Mistress of Pericles, fifth century BC. *meretrix*] prostitute. *the next toss of her*] The next trick she turned; punning on sexual bout and reincarnation.
20. *again*] logically, the word belongs after 'philosopher'. *of*] From.
21. *Crates the cynic*] Greek philosopher, 364–285 BC, a student of Diogenes; he became a wanderer who advocated voluntary poverty, independence, and equanimity.
23. *brock*] Badger.
24. *cobbler's cock*] Lucian's *Dream* is a dialogue between a cobbler and a cock who recounts the transformations.
26–7. *one, two, or three ... quater ... trigon*] In the Pythagorean system, the principles of astronomical and ethical harmony were based on the 'quaternion', or first four whole numbers (1, 2, 3, 4) which add up to 10, demonstrated in the equilateral triangle of four units per side, called the 'trigon'.
27. *musics*] Numerical ratios which determine the principal intervals of the musical scale, discovered by Pythagoras and then related to the spacing of the cosmic spheres in the harmony of the universe. *golden thigh*] Traditional proof that Pythagoras was a god.
28. *how elements shift*] Pythagoras taught that the four elements were constantly changing into one another.
29. *translation*] Transformation.
30. *shifted thy coat*] Changed your religion. *reformation*] The then-current Puritan reforms, not the earlier Protestant Reformation.
32. *old doctrine*] Both high Anglican and Roman Catholic teachings, condemned by Puritans as vanity. In 1606, Jonson, a converted Catholic, was questioned by the authorities for refusing to take Church of England communion.

NANO	*But not on thine own forbid meats hast thou ventured?*	
ANDROGYNO	*On fish, when first a Carthusian I entered.*	
NANO	*Why, then thy dogmatical silence hath left thee?*	35
ANDROGYNO	*Of that, an obstreperous lawyer bereft me.*	
NANO	*O wonderful change! When sir lawyer forsook thee,*	
	For Pythagore's sake, what body then took thee?	
ANDROGYNO	*A good dull mule.*	
NANO	*And how! By that means,*	
	Thou wert brought to allow of the eating of beans?	40
ANDROGYNO	*Yes.*	
NANO	*But from the mule into whom didst thou pass?*	
ANDROGYNO	*Into a very strange beast, by some writers called*	
	an ass;	
	By others a precise, pure, illuminate brother	
	Of those devour flesh and sometimes one another;	
	And will drop you forth a libel or a sanctified lie	45
	Betwixt every spoonful of a nativity-pie.	
NANO	*Now quit thee, for heaven, of that profane nation,*	
	And gently report thy next transmigration.	
ANDROGYNO	*To the same that I am.*	
NANO	*A creature of delight,*	
	And – what is more than a fool – an hermaphrodite?	50
	Now pray thee, sweet soul, in all thy variation,	
	Which body wouldst thou choose to take up thy station?	
ANDROGYNO	*Troth, this I am in, even here would I tarry.*	
NANO	*'Cause here the delight of each sex thou canst vary?*	
ANDROGYNO	*Alas, those pleasures be stale and forsaken.*	55

33. *forbid meats*] Pythagoreans were vegetarian, with an arbitrary additional ban on beans.
34. *Carthusian*] Monk of an austere Benedictine order that ate fish but not meat.
35. *dogmatical silence*] Both Pythagoreans and Carthusians took a vow of silence, the former for only two to five years.
36. *obstreperous*] Clamorous.
39. *mule*] Ridden by dignified benchers to the law courts.
40. *beans*] Used mainly for fodder.
43. *precise, pure, illuminate brother*] A puritan; *precise* because strict, and *illuminate* because he has seen the light.
44. *devour ... one another*] Metaphorical cannibalism, descriptive of puritan business tactics.
45. *libel*] Puritan tracts attacked opponents by name-calling.
46. *nativity-pie*] Christmas pie. Puritans avoided the 'papist' syllable *-mas*, referring instead to Christ-tide or Nativity.
47–81. The details in the song derive from Erasmus's *The Praise of Folly.*
47. *nation*] Sect.
54. Can enjoy the sexual pleasures of both male and female.

>   No, 'tis your fool wherewith I am so taken,
>   The only one creature that I can call blessed,
>   For all other forms I have proved most distressed.

NANO   Spoke true, as thou wert in Pythagoras still.
                 [*To Castrone*] This learnèd opinion we celebrate will,   60
              Fellow eunuch, as behoves us, with all our wit and art,
                 To dignify that whereof ourselves are so great and
                    special a part.

VOLPONE   Now very, very pretty! Mosca, this
     Was thy invention?

MOSCA   If it please my patron,
     Not else.   65

VOLPONE   It doth, good Mosca.

MOSCA   Then it was, sir.

[*Nano and Castrone sing*]

> **song**
> Fools, they are the only nation
> Worth men's envy or admiration;
> Free from care or sorrow-taking,
> Selves and others merry making:
> All they speak or do is sterling.   70
> Your fool, he is your great man's dearling,
> And your lady's sport and pleasure;
> Tongue and bauble are his treasure.
> E'en his face begetteth laughter,
> And he speaks truth, free from slaughter;   75
> He's the grace of every feast
> And, sometimes, the chiefest guest;
> Hath his trencher and his stool
> When wit waits upon the fool.
>   O, who would not be   80
>   He, he, he?

71. *dearling*] Darling.
72–3. Equivocal references to sexual games. *Tongue* suggests both witticism and cunni-
     lingus; *bauble*, punning on 'babble', is both the court jester's baton, usually surmounted
     by a grotesque head with ass's ears, and a symbol of the phallus.
75. *free from slaughter*] With impunity. Licensed fools had permission to joke about any
     subject. But see note on Stone, 2.1.53.
77. *chiefest guest*] Fools often headed the table at feasts.
78. *trencher*] Plate.
79. The witty have to wait for the fool to finish eating before they have 'food' for their jests.
81. *He, he, he*] Complement of the sentence and sniggering laughter, perhaps pointing at
     Androgyno the fool.

One knocks without

VOLPONE   Who's that? Away!

[*Exeunt Nano and Castrone*]

Look, Mosca

MOSCA   Fool, begone!

[*Exit Androgyno*]

'Tis Signior Voltore, the advocate.
I know him by his knock.

VOLPONE   Fetch me my gown,
My furs, and night-caps. Say my couch is changing,   85
And let him entertain himself awhile
Without i' th' gallery.

[*Exit Mosca*]

Now, now, my clients

Begin their visitation! Vulture, kite,
Raven, and gorcrow, all my birds of prey
That think me turning carcass, now they come.   90
I am not for 'em yet.

[*Re-enter Mosca with costume and make-up, and dresses Volpone
during the following dialogue*]

How now? The news?

---

84. *I know ... knock*] Voltore's characteristic comic knock, distinct from others' knocking, is a bit of stage business probably derived from *commedia dell'arte* buffoonery.

85. *furs*] Worn by the sick for warmth, but appropriate for the 'fox'. *couch is
changing*] Bed is being changed.

87. *gallery*] In Venice, 'a pretty walk ... betwixt the wall of the house and the brink of the
river's bank ... for men to stand in without their houses, and behold things'; 'somewhat
above the middle of the front of the building ... they have right opposite unto their
windows, a very pleasant little terrace, that jutteth or butteth out from the main
building' (Coryat, 1611; rpt 1905: p. 307). The reference is also a self conscious
theatre-joke. The gallery, sometimes called the upper stage, offered playing spaces in the
window-like openings of the tiring house facade at the level of the first gallery. Celia
appears at a window in 2.2, and Bonario may wait in one during 3.7, as may Voltore
at 90–125.

88. *kite*] A kind of falcon formerly common in England; used of a rapacious person, here
probably Lady Would-be.

89. *gorcrow*] Carrion crow, or corbie.

91. *for 'em*] Ready for their visit; or prepared to die to further their purposes.

MOSCA   A piece of plate, sir.

VOLPONE   Of what bigness?

MOSCA   Huge,
    Massy, and antique, with your name inscribed
    And arms engraven.

VOLPONE   Good! And not a fox
    Stretched on the earth with fine delusive sleights,   95
    Mocking a gaping crow? Ha, Mosca?

MOSCA   [*Laughing*]   Sharp, sir!

VOLPONE   Give me my furs. Why dost thou laugh so, man?

MOSCA   I cannot choose, sir, when I apprehend
    What thoughts he has without now, as he walks:
    That this might be the last gift he should give;   100
    That this would fetch you; if you died today
    And gave him all, what he should be tomorrow;
    What large return would come of all his ventures;
    How he should worshipped be and reverenced;
    Ride with his furs and foot-cloths; waited on   105
    By herds of fools and clients; have clear way
    Made for his mule, as lettered as himself;
    Be called the great and learnèd advocate;
    And then concludes there's nought impossible.

VOLPONE   Yes: to be learnèd, Mosca.

MOSCA   O, no: rich   110
    Implies it. Hood an ass with reverend purple,

92. *plate*] Silver- or gold-plated tableware.

94–6. *fox . . . crow*] Aesop's fable of the fox who tricks a crow into singing, thus dropping the cheese in its beak; may also refer to the fox's habit of 'playing dead' in order to catch scavengers.

98. *apprehend*] Imagine.

99. *without*] Outside, referring to Voltore who is pacing in the gallery while he waits to visit Volpone.

101. *fetch you*] Win you over.

102. *be*] Be worth.

103. *ventures*] Investments, perhaps referring to the money he has invested in wooing Volpone.

105. *foot-cloths*] Ornamental drapery for a horse or mule, a mark of the rider's status.

111–13. *Hood . . . doctor*] Recurrent joke in Erasmus, *The Praise of Folly*, and a common observation in Shakespeare; e.g., Lear's rant on injustice in *King Lear* (1605) 4.6, 'Robes and furr'd gowns hide all'. Ambition was generally stigmatised as asinine; see note at 112 below.

111. *reverend purple*] Robes of a Doctor of Divinity.

So you can hide his two ambitious ears,
And he shall pass for a cathedral doctor.
VOLPONE My caps, my caps, good Mosca. Fetch him in.
MOSCA Stay, sir, your ointment for your eyes.   115
VOLPONE   That's true.
Dispatch, dispatch! I long to have possession
Of my new present.
MOSCA [*Applying cosmetics*] That and thousands more
I hope to see you lord of.
VOLPONE   Thanks, kind Mosca.
MOSCA And that, when I am lost in blended dust,
And hundred such as I am in succession –   120
VOLPONE Nay, that were too much, Mosca.
MOSCA   – you shall live
Still to delude these harpies.
VOLPONE   Loving Mosca!

[*Checks his appearance and returns to bed*]

'Tis well. My pillow now, and let him enter.

[*Exit Mosca*]

Now, my feigned cough, my phthisic, and my gout,
My apoplexy, palsy, and catarrhs,   125

---

112. *ambitious*] Latinate pun, denoting a person striving after excessively high honours, or ears towering ostentatiously.
113. *cathedral doctor*] Doctor of Divinity.
114. *caps*] Possibly ear-caps rather than night caps. Volpone's request adds mute point to Mosca's contention that any ass can pass for what he is not, with the right costume.
115. *ointment . . . eyes*] To make them look gummy with mucus, a sign of disease.
116. *Dispatch*] Hurry.
120. Mosca flatters Volpone by projecting for him an incredibly long life, outliving Mosca and a hundred similar attendants.
122. *harpies*] The hideously rapacious and filthy birds of Greek myth, sent to exact divine vengeance. The term has ironic pertinence for the outcome of the play.
124. *phthisic*] Tuberculosis, as a possible source of the 'feigned cough' at 128 and elsewhere. The 'fox's cough', so named for its hoarse barking, is the chronic cough of the old and dying. *gout*] Painful inflammation of the joints.
125. *apoplexy*] Stroke destroying part of the brain, usually accompanied by paralysis and coma. *palsy*] Chronic disorder of the nervous system afflicting the elderly with symptoms of slow movement, weakness, muscular rigidity, and tremors. *catarrhs*] Profuse discharge from the nose and eyes, caused by inflammation of the mucous membranes.

Help with your forcèd functions this my posture,
Wherein this three year I have milked their hopes.
He comes; I hear him. [*Coughs*] Uh! Uh! Uh! Uh! [*Groans*] 0 –

Act 1 scene 3*

[*Enter*] *Mosca* [*with*] *Voltore*, [*holding a piece of plate*]

MOSCA   [*To Voltore*] You still are what you were, sir. Only you,
        Of all the rest, are he commands his love;
        And you do wisely to preserve it thus
        With early visitation and kind notes
        Of your good meaning to him, which, I know,   5
        Cannot but come most grateful [*Loudly, to Volpone*] Patron, sir!
        Here's Signor Voltore is come –
VOLPONE   [*Weakly*]   What say you?
MOSCA   [*Louder*]   Sir, Signor Voltore is come this morning
        To visit you.
VOLPONE   I thank him.
MOSCA   And hath brought
        A piece of antique plate, bought of St Mark,   10
        With which he here presents you.
VOLPONE   He is welcome.
        Pray him to come more often.
MOSCA   Yes.
VOLTORE   [*Straining to hear*]   What says he?
MOSCA   He thanks you and desires you see him often.
VOLPONE   Mosca.
MOSCA   My patron?
VOLPONE   Bring him near. Where is he?
        I long to feel his hand.   15
MOSCA   The plate is here, sir.
VOLTORE   How fare you, sir?
VOLPONE   I thank you, Signor Voltore.
        Where is the plate? Mine eyes are bad.
VOLTORE   I'm sorry

---

126. *forced*] Artificially induced.   *posture*] Imposture.
*   The basis of this and the following two scenes is the Roman *salutio*, or morning visit
     of clients to a patron, frequently the subject of satirists. In Lucian's *Dialogues of the
     Dead*, 19, an old man describes how he deluded his morning visitors by promising to
     make each the sole heir.
 4. *notes*] Tokens; i.e., gifts.
 5. *meaning to*] Wishes for.
10. *of St Mark*] From a goldsmith's shop in the Piazza di San Marco.

To see you still thus weak.

MOSCA   [*Aside*]   That he is not weaker.

VOLPONE   You are too munificent.

VOLTORE   No, sir, would to heaven
    I could as well give health to you as that plate.   20

VOLPONE   You give, sir, what you can. I thank you. Your love
    Hath taste in this, and shall not be unanswered.
    I pray you, see me often.

VOLTORE   Yes, I shall, sir.

VOLPONE   Be not far from me.

MOSCA   [*To Voltore*]   Do you observe that, sir?

VOLPONE   Harken unto me still. It will concern you.   25

MOSCA   You are a happy man, sir. Know your good.

VOLPONE   I cannot now last long –

MOSCA   [*Aside to Voltore*]   You are his heir, sir.

VOLTORE   Am I?

VOLPONE   I feel me going – uh! uh! uh! uh! –
    I am sailing to my port – uh! uh! uh! uh! –
    And I am glad I am so near my haven.   30

MOSCA   Alas, kind gentleman! Well, we must all go –

VOLTORE   But Mosca –

MOSCA   Age will conquer.

VOLTORE   Pray thee, hear me.
    Am I inscribed his heir for certain?

MOSCA   Are you?
    I do beseech you, sir, you will vouchsafe
    To write me i' your family. All my hopes   35
    Depend upon your worship. I am lost,
    Except the rising sun do shine on me.

VOLTORE   It shall both shine and warm thee, Mosca.

MOSCA   Sir,
    I am a man that have not done your love
    All the worst offices. Here I wear your keys,   40
    See all your coffers and your caskets locked,
    Keep the poor inventory of your jewels,
    Your plate, and moneys: am your steward, sir,

22. *Hath taste*] Shows judgment.   *unanswered*] Unrewarded.
30. *haven*] Punning on 'heaven'.
33. *inscribed*] Officially entered in the document.
35. *write … family*] Enter my name in your household book. Mosca returns the same
    legalistic point, wanting to confirm his place in Voltore's household register of servants
    and dependants.
40. *your keys*] Implying that Mosca, officially Volpone's agent, is really serving the heir,
    Voltore. But Mosca does not have possession of all the keys until 5.4.

Husband your goods here.

VOLTORE   But am I sole heir?

MOSCA   Without a partner, sir, confirmed this morning.   45
　　The wax is warm yet, and the ink scarce dry
　　Upon the parchment.

VOLTORE   Happy, happy me!
　　By what good chance, sweet Mosca?

MOSCA   Your desert, sir.
　　I know no second cause.

VOLTORE   Thy modesty
　　Is loath to know it. Well, we shall requite it.   50

MOSCA   He ever liked your course, sir; that first took him.
　　I oft have heard him say how he admired
　　Men of your large profession that could speak
　　To every cause, and things mere contraries,
　　Till they were hoarse again, yet all be law;   55
　　That with most quick agility could turn
　　And re-turn, make knots and undo them,
　　Give forkèd counsel, take provoking gold
　　On either hand and put it up: these men,
　　He knew, would thrive with their humility.   60
　　And for his part, he thought he should be blessed
　　To have his heir of such a suffering spirit,
　　So wise, so grave, of so perplexed a tongue,
　　And loud withal, that would not wag nor scarce
　　Lie still without a fee; when every word   65

46. *wax*] Of the official seal.

51. *course*] Skill at manipulating the law.

53. *large profession*] Impressive vocation, or extensive practice; in religion, a sweeping declaration of faith; in general, high-sounding but empty claims.

54. `*cause*] Legal case or action.   *mere contraries*] Completely contradictory suits.

58. *forked*] Capable of two or more interpretations.

58–9. *provoking ... hand*] bribes to influence the judge or court for either side of the lawsuit.

59. *put it up*] Pocket it.

60. *humility*] A puritan virtue; also, ironically commenting on lowliness and perhaps obsequiousness of lawyers who accept fees from any source.

62. *suffering*] In puritan usage, referring to hardships endured for the sake of one's religion; here, to Voltore's dedication to making money by his *profession* (see 53), another equivocation mixing law with divinity.

63. *perplexed*] Full of complicated argument or involved language.

Your worship but lets fall is a *zecchin*!

Another knocks

Who's that? One knocks. I would not have you seen, sir.
And yet – pretend you came and went in haste.
I'll fashion an excuse. And, gentle sir,
When you do come to swim in golden lard,   70
Up to the arms in honey, that your chin
Is borne up stiff with fatness of the flood,
Think on your vassal. But remember me.
I ha' not been your worst of clients.
VOLTORE   Mosca –
MOSCA   When will you have your inventory brought, sir?   75
Or see a copy of the will?

[*Knocks again*]

                          – Anon!
[*To Voltore*] I'll bring 'em to you, sir. Away, begone,
Put business i' your face.

[*Exit Voltore*]

VOLPONE   Excellent, Mosca!
Come hither. Let me kiss thee!
MOSCA   Keep you still, sir.
Here is Corbaccio.   80
VOLPONE   Set the plate away.
The vulture's gone, and the old raven's come.

---

66. *zecchin*] Gold coin from Venice's mint, the *Zecca*. Coryat's 'chiquin' gives the
    Englishman's attempt at pronunciation. Jonson approximated an Italian spelling in *F*
    and *Q*, *cecchine*, which may have had dialectal authority; he may also have wanted to
    add to the bird-allusions with a coin that sounds like 'chicken' to the English ear.
70–72. Ambivalent images of sensual bliss, projecting the erotic pleasure Voltore finds in
    money. To *swim* meant to float or swoon orgasmically; *lard*, like *honey*, meant sexual
    vigour or supply of semen (see *Alch* 3.3.47–9); *arms* equivocated between the military
    and sexual 'weapon'; *chin* was a euphemism for penis; *stiff*, erect; *fatness* referred to
    sexual rankness (like Ursula, the fat bawd in *BF*); *flood* suggested ejaculation.
73. *But*] Only.
76. *Anon!*] Coming!
78. *Put . . . face*] Look business-like.

Act 1 scene 4*

MOSCA   Betake you to your silence and your sleep.
  [*Adds the plate to the treasure chest*] Stand there and multiply.
    – Now shall we see
  A wretch who is indeed more impotent
  Than this can feign to be, yet hopes to hop
  Over his grave.   5

  [*Enter Corbaccio*]

                          Signior Corbaccio!
    You're very welcome, sir.
CORBACCIO   How does your patron?
MOSCA   Troth, as he did, sir: no amends.
CORBACCIO   [*Mishearing*]   What? Mends he?
MOSCA   No, sir. He is rather worse.
CORBACCIO   That's well. Where is he?
MOSCA   Upon his couch, sir, newly fallen asleep.
CORBACCIO   Does he sleep well?   10
MOSCA   No wink, sir, all this night,
    Nor yesterday, but slumbers.
CORBACCIO   Good! He should take
    Some counsel of physicians. I have brought him
    An opiate here, from mine own doctor –
MOSCA   He will not hear of drugs.
CORBACCIO   Why? I myself
    Stood by while 'twas made; saw all th' ingredients;   15
    And know it cannot but most gently work.
    My life for his, 'tis but to make him sleep.
VOLPONE   [*Aside*] Aye, his last sleep, if he would take it.
MOSCA   Sir,

---

*   Volpone portrays a dying man by adding new postures of decrepitude for each
    successive visitor. For Voltore, he was blind and weakly coughing. For Corbaccio, he is
    drowsy and incapable of speech. For Corvino, in the next scene, he adds deafness. Part
    of the comedy depends (a) on the tension between the two scheming actors as Mosca
    gives cues for Volpone's performance, and (b) on the contrast between Volpone's
    apparent illness and his hearty mirth at his successful acting, exploding with laughter
    after each visitor exits.
  2. *Stand ... multiply*] Profane restatement of the biblical injunction 'Be fruitful and
    multiply'. *Stand* meant 'have an erection'.
  4. *this*] Contemptuous reference to Volpone, a clue to Mosca's later behaviour.
  10. *wink*] Deep sleep.
  11. *slumbers*] Dozes.
  18. *last sleep*] That is, death.

He has no faith in physic.
CORBACCIO   Say you? Say you?
MOSCA   He has no faith in physic. He does think   20
    Most of your doctors are the greater danger
    And worse disease t'escape. I often have
    Heard him protest that your physician
    Should never be his heir.
CORBACCIO   Not I his heir?
MOSCA   Not your physician, sir.   25
CORBACCIO   O, no, no, no,
    I do not mean it. [*Puts the medicine away*]
MOSCA   No, sir. Nor their fees
    He cannot brook. He says they flay a man
    Before they kill him.
CORBACCIO   Right, I do conceive you.
MOSCA   And then they do it by experiment,
    For which the law not only doth absolve 'em,   30
    But gives them great reward, and he is loath
    To hire his death so.
CORBACCIO   It is true they kill
    With as much licence as a judge.
MOSCA   .   Nay, more;
    For he but kills, sir, where the law condemns,
    And these can kill him too.   35
CORBACCIO   Aye, or me,
    Or any man. How does his apoplex?
    Is that strong on him still?
MOSCA   Most violent.
    His speech is broken, and his eyes are set,
    His face drawn longer than 'twas wont –
CORBACCIO   How? How?
    Stronger than he was wont?   40

---

21. *your doctors*] Doctors generally. *Your* is indefinite, not possessive. So too at 23, 25.
27. *flay*] Skin; metaphorically, strip of money.
28. *conceive*] Understand.
29. *by experiment*] By guessing at cures.
34. *he*] The judge.
35. *these*] Doctors.
36–54. As Mosca comments on each symptom, Volpone embodies it.
36. *apoplex*] Stroke, suffering recurrent loss of consciousness and paralysis.
38–44. Speech disturbances, vacant staring, blank face, gaping mouth, rigid muscles, greasy pale skin: all are symptoms of advanced palsy. Leaden pallor also indicates anaemia, which may accompany phthisis (tuberculosis).

MOSCA   No, sir: his face
    Drawn longer than 'twas wont.
CORBACCIO   O, good!
MOSCA   His mouth
    Is ever gaping, and his eyelids hang.
CORBACCIO   Good.
MOSCA   A freezing numbness stiffens all his joints
    And makes the colour of his flesh like lead.
CORBACCIO   'Tis good.
MOSCA   His pulse beats slow and dull.   45
CORBACCIO   Good symptoms still.
MOSCA   And from his brain –
CORBACCIO   Ha? How? Not from his brain?
MOSCA   Yes, sir, and from his brain –
CORBACCIO   I conceive you. Good.
MOSCA   – Flows a cold sweat, with a continual rheum
    Forth the resolvèd corners of his eyes.
CORBACCIO. Is't possible? Yet I am better, ha!   50
    How does he with the swimming of his head?
MOSCA   O, sir, 'tis past the scotomy. He now
    Hath lost his feeling and hath left to snort.
    You hardly can perceive him that he breathes.
CORBACCIO   Excellent, excellent! Sure I shall outlast him!   55
    This makes me young again a score of years.
MOSCA   I was a-coming for you, sir.
CORBACCIO   Has he made his will?
    What has he given me?
MOSCA   No, sir.
CORBACCIO   Nothing? Ha?
MOSCA   He has not made his will, sir.
CORBACCIO   O, O, O.
    What then did Voltore, the lawyer, here?   60
MOSCA   He smelled a carcass, sir, when he but heard
    My master was about his testament –
    As I did urge him to it, for your good –
CORBACCIO   He came unto him, did he? I thought so.

46. Drainage of brain fluid, eagerly anticipated by Corbaccio, was thought to signal death
    from apoplexy.
48. *rheum*] Mucus discharge (cf. *catarrhs*, 1.2.125), associated with phthisis.
49. *resolved*] Soft, spongy.
52–3. Symptoms of apoplexy. *scotomy*] Dizziness and dimness of vision. *lost … feel-
    ing*] Become numb. *left to snort*] Stopped snoring. Stertorous respiration is common
    in comatose patients.
54. In advanced phthisis, breath sounds may become diminished.

MOSCA   Yes, and presented him this piece of plate.   65
CORBACCIO   To be his heir?
MOSCA   I do not know, sir.
CORBACCIO   True,
    I know it too.
MOSCA   [*Aside*]   By your own scale, sir.
CORBACCIO   Well,
    I shall prevent him yet. See, Mosca, look,
    Here I have brought a bag of bright *zecchins*
    Will quite weigh down his plate.   70
MOSCA   [*Taking the bag*]   Yea, marry, sir!
    This is true physic, this your sacred medicine:
    No talk of opiates to this great elixir.
CORBACCIO   'Tis *aurum palpabile*, if not *potabile*.
MOSCA   It shall be ministered to him in his bowl?
CORBACCIO   Aye, do, do, do!   75
MOSCA   Most blessèd cordial!
    This will recover him.
CORBACCIO   Yes, do, do, do!
MOSCA   I think it were not best, sir.
CORBACCIO   What?
MOSCA   To recover him.
CORBACCIO   O, no, no, no, by no means!
MOSCA   Why, sir, this
    Will work some strange effect, if he but feel it.
CORBACCIO   'Tis true; therefore, forbear. I'll take my venture.   80
    Give me 't again. [*Reaches for the bag*]
MOSCA   At no hand, pardon me.
    You shall not do yourself that wrong, sir. I
    Will so advise you, you shall have it all.
CORBACCIO   How?
MOSCA   All, sir, 'tis your right, your own. No man
    Can claim a part. 'Tis yours, without a rival,   85
    Decreed by destiny.
CORBACCIO   How? How, good Mosca?
MOSCA   I'll tell you, sir. This fit he shall recover –

---

67. *By ... scale*]   Measuring him by your own behaviour.
68. *prevent*]   Outstrip.
72. *great elixir*]   The final alchemical essence, supposed to guarantee eternal life and wealth.
73. *Aurum potabile*, a drinkable as opposed to a merely touchable (*palpabile*) form of gold, was considered a potent medicine.

CORBACCIO   I do conceive you.
MOSCA   – and, on first advantage
    Of his gained sense, will I re-importune him
    Unto the making of his testament,   90
    And show him this. [*Indicates the bag of money*]
CORBACCIO   Good, good!
MOSCA   'Tis better yet,
    If you will hear, sir.
CORBACCIO   Yes, with all my heart.
MOSCA   Now, would I counsel you, make home with speed.
    There, frame a will, whereto you shall inscribe
    My master your sole heir.   95
CORBACCIO   And disinherit
    My son?
MOSCA   O, sir, the better, for that colour
    Shall make it much more taking.
CORBACCIO   O, but colour?
MOSCA   This will, sir, you shall send it unto me.
    Now, when I come to enforce (as I will do)
    Your cares, your watchings, and your many prayers,   100
    Your more than many gifts, your this day's present,
    And last produce your will, where – without thought,
    Or least regard unto your proper issue,
    A son so brave and highly meriting –
    The stream of your diverted love hath thrown you   105
    Upon my master and made him your heir,
    He cannot be so stupid or stone dead,
    But out of conscience and mere gratitude –
CORBACCIO   He must pronounce me his?
MOSCA   'Tis true.
CORBACCIO   This plot
    Did I think on before.   110
MOSCA   I do believe it.
CORBACCIO   Do you not believe it?
MOSCA   Yes, sir.
CORBACCIO   Mine own project.
MOSCA   Which, when he hath done, sir –

88. *advantage*] Opportunity.
94. *frame*] Compose.
96. *colour*] Outward appearance concealing the truth.
97. *taking*] Acceptable.
99. *enforce*] Emphasise.
103. *proper issue*] Legitimate offspring.
104. *brave*] Fine.

CORBACCIO	Published me his heir?
MOSCA And you so certain to survive him –	
CORBACCIO	Aye.
MOSCA Being so lusty a man –	
CORBACCIO	'Tis true.
MOSCA	Yes, sir –

CORBACCIO I thought on that too. See how he should be   115
    The very organ to express my thoughts!

MOSCA You have not only done yourself a good –

CORBACCIO But multiplied it on my son?

MOSCA   'Tis right, sir.

CORBACCIO Still my invention.

MOSCA   'Las, sir, heaven knows
    It hath been all my study, all my care   120
    (I e'en grow grey withal) how to work things –

CORBACCIO I do conceive, sweet Mosca.

MOSCA   You are he
    For whom I labour here.

CORBACCIO   Ay, do, do, do.
    I'll straight about it. [*Leaving*]

MOSCA [*Aside*]   Rook go with you, raven!

CORBACCIO I know thee honest.   125

MOSCA [*Aside*]   You do lie, sir –

CORBACCIO   And –

MOSCA [*Aside*] Your knowledge is no better than your ears, sir.

CORBACCIO I do not doubt to be a father to thee.

MOSCA [*Aside*] Nor I, to gull my brother of his blessing.

CORBACCIO I may ha' my youth restored to me. Why not?

MOSCA [*Aside*] Your worship is a precious ass –   130

CORBACCIO   What sayest thou?

MOSCA I do desire your worship to make haste, sir.

CORBACCIO 'Tis done, 'tis done. I go. [*Exit*]

VOLPONE [*Writhing in laughter*]   O, I shall burst!
    Let out my sides, let out my sides –

MOSCA   Contain
    Your flux of laughter, sir. You know, this hope
    Is such a bait, it covers any hook.   135

---

114. *lusty*] Vigorous, ironically contradicting Corbaccio's doddering state.

116. *organ*] Mouthpiece.

119. *invention*] Plan. Corbaccio takes credit for Mosca's scheme, as at 111.

124. *Rook ... raven*] You thieving fraud! *Rook*] A common crow, related to the raven
    (= Corbaccio), but also punning on the verbs *rook*, 'cheat', and *raven*, 'plunder'.

128. *my brother*] Bonario, if Corbaccio acts as Mosca's father; possibly alluding to Jacob's
    theft of Esau's birthright (Genesis 27).

VOLPONE   O, but thy working and thy placing it!
          I cannot hold! Good rascal, let me kiss thee.
          I never knew thee in so rare a humour.
MOSCA   Alas, sir, I but do as I am taught;
          Follow your grave instructions; give 'em words;   140
          Pour oil into their ears, and send them hence.
VOLPONE   'Tis true, 'tis true. What a rare punishment
          Is avarice to itself!
MOSCA   Aye, with our help, sir.
VOLPONE   So many cares, so many maladies,
          So many fears attending on old age,   145
          Yea, death so often called on, as no wish
          Can be more frequent with 'em, their limbs faint,
          Their senses dull, their seeing, hearing, going,
          All dead before them; yea, their very teeth,
          Their instruments of eating, failing them: 150
          Yet this is reckoned life! Nay, here was one
          Is now gone home that wishes to live longer!
          Feels not his gout nor palsy, feigns himself
          Younger by scores of years, flatters his age
          With confident belying it, hopes he may   155
          With charms, like Aeson, have his youth restored;
          And with these thoughts so battens, as if fate
          Would be as easily cheated on as he,
          And all turns air!

          Another knocks
                        Who's that there now? A third?

MOSCA   Close, to your couch again. I hear his voice.   160
          It is Corvino, our spruce merchant.
VOLPONE   [*In bed, as before*]   Dead.
MOSCA.   Another bout, sir, with your eyes. [*Applies more make-up*]
          – Who's there?

138. *rare a humour*] Outrageous a mood.
140. *give 'em words*] Deceive them.
141. *Pour . . . ears*] Trick them with flattery.
148. *going*] Movement.
154–5. *flatters . . . belying it*] Lies unabashedly about his age.
156. *Aeson*] Jason's father, restored to youth by Medea's magic.
157. *battens*] Gloats; grows fat.
159. *all turns air*] Everything becomes a delusion.
160. *Close*] Quiet.
161. *spruce*] Dapper, fashionably dressed.   *Dead*] Playing dead; cf. 1.2.94–6.

Act 1 scene 5*

   [Enter] Corvino

MOSCA Signor Corvino! come most wished for! O,
    How happy were you, if you knew it, now!
CORVINO Why? What? Wherein?
MOSCA   The tardy hour is come, sir.
CORVINO He is not dead?
MOSCA   Not dead, sir, but as good:
    He knows no man.   5
CORVINO   How shall I do then?
MOSCA   Why, sir?
CORVINO I have brought him here a pearl.
MOSCA   Perhaps he has
    So much remembrance left as to know you, sir.
    He still calls on you; nothing but your name
    Is in his mouth. Is your pearl orient, sir?
CORVINO Venice was never owner of the like.   10
VOLPONE *[Weakly]* Signor Corvino.
MOSCA   Hark.
VOLPONE   Signor Corvino.
MOSCA He calls you. Step and give it him. *[To Volpone]* He's here, sir,
    And he has brought you a rich pearl.
CORVINO   How do you, sir?
    [To Mosca] Tell him it doubles the twelfth carat.
MOSCA *[To Corvino]*   Sir,
    He cannot understand, his hearing's gone,   15
    And yet it comforts him to see you –
CORVINO   Say
    I have a diamond for him too.
MOSCA   Best show 't, sir.
    Put it into his hand. 'Tis only there
    He apprehends: he has his feeling yet.

---

*   This scene sums up the dupes' gullibility and their viciousness. Whereas Mosca only
    suspects that Corbaccio in the previous scene has arrived with poison disguised as
    medicine (but see 3.9.14, where murderous intent is clear), Corvino is eager to have
    Volpone murdered – he is 'scrupulous' (73) only about witnessing the crime, not about
    having it performed. The second half of the scene introduces the names of the two
    women who manage to unnerve Volpone: Celia appears in Act 2, and Lady Would-be,
    denied a visit now, returns to pay her call in 3.4.
  8. *still*] Always.
  9. *orient*] Eastern pearls had superior lustre and value.
14. *doubles . . . carat*] 24 carats, a weight suggesting a considerable size.

See how he grasps it!   20
CORVINO   'Las, good gentleman!
    How pitiful the sight is!
MOSCA   Tut, forget, sir.
    The weeping of an heir should still be laughter
    Under a visor.
CORVINO   Why? Am I his heir?
MOSCA   Sir, I am sworn. I may not show the will
    Till he be dead. But here has been Corbaccio,   25
    Here has been Voltore, here were others too –
    I cannot number 'em, they were so many –
    All gaping here for legacies; but I,
    Taking the vantage of his naming you,
    'Signor Corvino, Signor Corvino', took   30
    Paper and pen and ink, and there I asked him
    Whom he would have his heir? 'Corvino.' Who
    Should be executor? 'Corvino.' And,
    To any question he was silent to,
    I still interpreted the nods he made   35
    Through weakness for consent, and sent home th'others,
    Nothing bequeathed them but to cry and curse.
CORVINO   O my dear Mosca!

    They embrace

                        Does he not perceive us?
MOSCA   No more than a blind harper. He knows no man,
    No face of friend, nor name of any servant,   40
    Who 'twas that fed him last, or gave him drink;
    Not those he hath begotten or brought up
    Can he remember.
CORVINO   Has he children?
MOSCA   Bastards,
    Some dozen or more that he begot on beggars,
    Gypsies, and Jews, and black-moors, when he was drunk. 45
    Knew you not that, sir? 'Tis the common fable.

23. *visor*] Mask.
28. *gaping*] Suggests the open beaks of nestlings waiting to be crammed with food. Forms
     of 'gape' appear frequently in the play.
30, 32, 33. *'Signor . . . Corvino'*] Mosca mimics Volpone's feeble cry from 11.
35–6. *nods . . . weakness*] The tremors caused by palsy. Volpone illustrates the symptom, as
     in the previous scene.
39. *blind harper*] Proverbial, explained by the subsequent lines; Volpone sees them only as
     anonymous shapes.
46. *common fable*] Subject of common talk.

The dwarf, the fool, the eunuch are all his.
He's the true father of his family
In all, save me, but he has given 'em nothing.
CORVINO That's well, that's well. Art sure he does not hear us?   50
MOSCA Sure, sir? Why, look you, credit your own sense.
[*Shouts in Volpone's ear*] The pox approach and add to your diseases,
If it would send you hence the sooner, sir.
For your incontinence, it hath deserved it
Throughly and throughly, and the plague to boot!   55
[*To Corvino*] You may come near, sir. [*To Volpone*] Would you
    would once close
Those filthy eyes of yours, that flow with slime
Like two frog-pits, and those same hanging cheeks,
Covered with hide instead of skin – [*To Corvino*] Nay, help, sir. –
That look like frozen dish-clouts set on end.   60
CORVINO Or like an old smoked wall, on which the rain
Ran down in streaks.
MOSCA   Excellent, sir! Speak out.
You may be louder yet. A culverin
Dischargèd in his ear would hardly bore it.
CORVINO His nose is like a common sewer, still running.   65
MOSCA 'Tis good! And what his mouth?
CORVINO   A very draught.
MOSCA [*Offering a pillow*] O, stop it up –
CORVINO   By no means.
MOSCA   Pray you, let me.
Faith, I could stifle him rarely with a pillow
As well as any woman that should keep him.

48. *father ... family*] *paterfamilias*, head of the household.
49. *save*] Except for.
52. *pox*] Syphilis.
54. *incontinence*] Lack of sexual restraint or discretion. *it ... it*] Your debauchery
    deserves the punishment of syphilis.
55. *Throughly and throughly*] Through and through, thoroughly.
58. *frog-pits*] Scummy puddles or ponds. Possibly a printer's error for 'frog-bits', small
    white water lilies with yellow centres found floating in ditches, ponds, or standing
    water in marshy areas; mentioned in contemporary herbals as a cure for diarrhoea and
    gonorrhoea, and, applied externally, a preventative for 'venerous nightmares'.
60. *dish-clouts*] Dish-cloths.
63. *culverin*] Hand-gun.
64. *bore*] Penetrate; i.e., make itself heard.
66. *draught*] Privy, cesspool.
68–9. Suggests that smothering a sleeping victim is a woman's crime; that Mosca will do it
    as tenderly as any female nurse; and that such smothering punningly resembles a

CORVINO   Do as you will, but I'll be gone.   70
MOSCA   Be so.
    It is your presence makes him last so long.
CORVINO   I pray you, use no violence.
MOSCA   No, sir? Why?
    Why should you be thus scrupulous, pray you, sir?
CORVINO   Nay, at your discretion.
MOSCA   Well, good sir, be gone.
CORVINO   I will not trouble him now to take my pearl?   75
MOSCA   Pooh! Nor your diamond. What a needless care
    Is this afflicts you? Is not all here yours?
    Am not I here? Whom you have made? Your creature?
    That owe my being to you?
CORVINO   Grateful Mosca!
    Thou art my friend, my fellow, my companion,   80
    My partner, and shalt share in all my fortunes.
MOSCA   Excepting one.
CORVINO   What's that?
MOSCA   Your gallant wife, sir.

    [*Exit Corvino*]

    Now is he gone. We had no other means
    To shoot him hence but this.
VOLPONE   My divine Mosca!
    Thou hast today outgone thyself.   85

    Another knocks

                Who's there?
    I will be troubled with no more. Prepare
    Me music, dances, banquets, all delights.
    The Turk is not more sensual in his pleasures
    Than will Volpone.

    [*Exit Mosca*]

           Let me see: a pearl?

    woman's smothering her lover with her body when she receives (*keeps*) him sexually,
    letting him 'die' in orgasm.
75, 76. *pearl ... diamond*] Volpone is still clutching both.
78. *made*] Caused to devote himself to you.
82. *gallant*] Good-looking.
88. *The Turk*] Mahomet III, the Ottoman Sultan, known as the Grand Turk, famous for his
    extravagant tastes and sexual prowess.

A diamond? plate? *zecchins*? – good morning's purchase.   90
Why, this is better than rob churches, yet,
Or fat by eating, once a month, a man.

[*Enter Mosca*]

Who is't?
MOSCA   The beauteous Lady Would-be, sir,
Wife to the English knight, Sir Politic Would-be
(This is the style, sir, is directed me),   95
Hath sent to know how you have slept tonight,
And if you would be visited.
VOLPONE   Not now.
Some three hours hence –
MOSCA   I told the squire so much.
VOLPONE   When I am high with mirth and wine, then, then.
'Fore heaven, I wonder at the desperate valour   100
Of the bold English, that they dare let loose
Their wives to all encounters!
MOSCA   Sir, this knight
Had not his name for nothing. He is politic,
And knows, howe'er his wife affect strange airs,
She hath not yet the face to be dishonest.   105
But had she Signor Corvino's wife's face –
VOLPONE   Has she so rare a face?
MOSCA   O, sir, the wonder,
The blazing star of Italy! A wench
O'the first year! A beauty, ripe as harvest!
Whose skin is whiter than a swan, all over,   110
Than silver, snow, or lilies! A soft lip,
Would tempt you to eternity of kissing!
And flesh that melteth in the touch to blood!
Bright as your gold! And lovely as your gold!
VOLPONE   Why had not I known this before?   115

90.   *purchase*] Haul, booty.
92.   Refers to monthly interest charged by usurers.
95.   *style*] Mode of address.
100. *desperate*] Reckless.
101–2. *let ... encounters*] Suggesting that English husbands ignored their wives' sexual
      adventures. Englishwomen, unlike Mediterranean women, were not heavily chaper-
      oned or restricted.
105. *face ... dishonest*] Physical beauty to attract lovers; the impudence or shamelessness
      to take a lover.
109. *O' ... year*] In the first season of her womanhood.
113. *blood*] Passionate sexual response.

MOSCA   Alas, sir,
    Myself but yesterday discovered it.
VOLPONE   How might I see her?
MOSCA   O, not possible.
    She's kept as warily as is your gold:
    Never does come abroad, never takes air,
    But at a window. All her looks are sweet   120
    As the first grapes or cherries, and are watched
    As near as they are.
VOLPONE   I must see her –
MOSCA   Sir,
    There is a guard of ten spies thick upon her:
    All his whole household, each of which is set
    Upon his fellow, and have all their charge,   125
    When he goes out, when he comes in, examined.
VOLPONE   I will go see her, though but at her window.
MOSCA   In some disguise, then.
VOLPONE   That is true. I must
    Maintain mine own shape still the same. We'll think.

    [*Exeunt*]

ACT 2

Act 2 scene 1*

[*Enter Sir*] *Politic Would-be* [*and*] *Peregrine*

119. *abroad*] Out of the house.
122. *near*] Closely, carefully.
125–6. *charge ... examined*] The servants have to report on their assigned spying duties whenever Corvino enters or leaves his house.
129. *Maintain ... same*] Continue my pose as a dying man.
*   By 1600, travel had become an important feature of humanist education. The English government had, since the days of Henry VIII, supported scholars in Italy with the object of promoting greater diplomatic skills, both in the use of language and in state practices. Travellers went to France for fashion and gallantry, to Germany and Holland for first-hand contact with the ideas of the Reformation, and to Italy, especially Venice, for political intrigue, Near Eastern trade, and licentious living. The intrepidly adventurous journeyed as far as Constantinople and Jerusalem. Accounts of English travellers abroad, such as Robert Dallington, Fynes Moryson, Thomas Dallam, and Thomas Coryat, were popular reading both for tourists and for armchair travellers. Stage-plays like Heywood's *The Four Prentices of London* or his later *The English Traveller*, Day's *The Travels of Three English Brothers*, and Beaumont's *The Knight of the Burning*

SIR POLITIC   Sir, to a wise man, all the world's his soil.
    It is not Italy, nor France, nor Europe
    That must bound me, if my fates call me forth.
    Yet I protest it is no salt desire
    Of seeing countries, shifting a religion,   5
    Nor any disaffection to the state
    Where I was bred (and unto which I owe
    My dearest plots) hath brought me out; much less
    That idle, antique, stale, grey-headed project
    Of knowing men's minds and manners, with Ulysses;   10
    But a peculiar humour of my wife's,
    Laid for this height of Venice, to observe,
    To quote, to learn the language, and so forth –
    I hope you travel, sir, with licence?
PEREGRINE   Yes.
SIR POLITIC   I dare the safelier converse. How long, sir,   15
    Since you left England?
PEREGRINE   Seven weeks.
SIR POLITIC   So lately!
    You ha' not been with my lord ambassador?
PEREGRINE   Not yet, sir.
SIR POLITIC   Pray you, what news, sir, vents our climate?
    I heard last night a most strange thing reported
    By some of my lord's followers, and I long   20
    To hear how 'twill be seconded!

Pestle capitalised on the English fascination with foreign travel.
    The first four scenes of this act take place near Corvino's house in a corner of the
Piazza, presumably illustrating in the crowd the variety of visitors to St Mark's Square.
  1. Proverbial: A wise man may live everywhere.   *soil*] Country.
  4. *salt*] Wanton, inordinate.
  5. *shifting*] Converting to.
  8. *plots*] Projects.   *out*] Abroad, out of England.
11. *peculiar humour*] Particular whim.
12. *height*] Latitude.
13. *quote*] Make note of in his diary; see 1.1.133ff.
14. *licence*] Travel permit, obtained from the Privy Council; the traveller had to present his
     licence to the English ambassador in the country visited.
15. *I dare ... converse*] I may talk to you with greater security. A licensed traveller was
     prohibited from communicating with unlicensed travellers.
17. *my lord ambassador*] Sir Henry Wotton, at Venice from 1604 to 1612, a poet and
     friend of Jonson's, caricatured in some of Sir Pol's mannerisms.
18. *what news*] This question frequently began farce routines in satiric jigs, which
     combined nonsense with mockery of the popular passion for gossip and sensationalism.
     vents] Publishes.

PEREGRINE   What was't, sir?
SIR POLITIC   Marry, sir, of a raven that should build
     In a ship royal of the king's.
PEREGRINE   [*Aside*]   This fellow,
     Does he gull me, trow? Or is gulled? [*To Sir Politic*]   – Your name, sir?
SIR POLITIC   My name is Politic Would-be.   25
PEREGRINE   [*Aside*]   O, that speaks him.
     – A knight, sir?
SIR POLITIC   A poor knight, sir.
PEREGRINE   Your lady
     Lies here in Venice for intelligence
     Of tires and fashions, and behaviour
     Among the courtesans? The fine Lady Would-be?
SIR POLITIC   Yes, sir, the spider and the bee oft-times   30
     Suck from one flower.
PEREGRINE   Good Sir Politic!
     I cry you mercy. I have heard much of you.
     'Tis true, sir, of your raven.
SIR POLITIC   On your knowledge?
PEREGRINE   Yes, and your lion's whelping in the Tower.
SIR POLITIC   Another whelp!   35
PEREGRINE   Another, sir.
SIR POLITIC   Now, heaven!
     What prodigies be these? The fires at Berwick!
     And the new star! These things concurring, strange!

22. *raven*] Portends disaster.   *should build*] Is said to have built.
24. *gull*] Fool.   *trow?*] Do you think?
26. *poor*] Insignificant, a self-deprecating comment; but both Wotton and Sherley complained of indigence while in Venice.
27. *intelligence*] Information.
28. *tires*] Attires, head-dresses.
29. *courtesans*] Venetian courtesans were famed for their stylish dress, cosmetics, and coiffures, as well as their skill in music and elegant conversation.
30–31. *spider ... flower*] Proverbially, 'Where the bee sucks honey, the spider sucks poison', suggesting that Lady Would-be (the bee) will not be sullied by being in the same city as courtesans (spiders).
32. *I cry you mercy*] I beg your pardon.
35. *Another whelp!*] Stow, *Annals* (1615), reports that on 5 Aug. 1604, a lioness in the Tower of London bore a whelp that lived barely a day; on 26 Feb. 1605, when her second whelp was born, James ordered it raised by hand, but it died 16 days later.
36. *fires at Berwick*] Alluding to reports of ghostly warfare near Halidon Hill on 7 Dec. 1604, alarming both sides of the border; probably *aurora borealis*.
37. *new star*] A supernova explosion in the constellation Serpens, first appearing 30 Sept. 1604, and remaining visible for 17 months. Kepler described it as brighter than Jupiter.

And full of omen! Saw you those meteors?
PEREGRINE   I did, sir.
SIR POLITIC   Fearful! Pray you, sir, confirm me:
  Were there three porpoises seen above the Bridge,   40
  As they give out?
PEREGRINE   Six, and a sturgeon, sir.
SIR POLITIC   I am astonished!
PEREGRINE   Nay, sir, be not so.
  I'll tell you a greater prodigy than these –
SIR POLITIC   What should these things portend!
PEREGRINE   The very day
  (Let me be sure) that I put forth from London,   45
  There was a whale discovered in the river
  As high as Woolwich, that had waited there
  – Few know how many months – for the subversion
  Of the Stode fleet.
SIR POLITIC   Is't possible? Believe it,
  'Twas either sent from Spain or the Archdukes!   50
  Spinola's whale, upon my life, my credit!
  Will they not leave these projects? Worthy sir,
  Some other news.
PEREGRINE   Faith, Stone the fool is dead,
  And they do lack a tavern-fool extremely.

38. *meteors*] Considered ill omens because they suggest disruption in the cosmic order.

40, 46. *three porpoises ... a whale*] Stow reported that on 19 Jan. 1606, a porpoise was captured alive at West Ham in a small creek over a mile inland; days later, a whale came up the Thames to Woolwich, 8 miles east of London. *above the Bridge*] An exaggeration. Both sightings occurred below London Bridge.

41. *sturgeon*] Common in the Thames then, though perhaps not commonly seen, since sturgeons are bottom-feeders; deemed by Edward II and still remaining a royal fish.

49. *Stode fleet*] The English Merchant Adventurers, without a continental harbour since being expelled in 1597 from Stade on the Elbe estuary, 22 miles NW of Hamburg; the merchant ships of the Hanseatic League now controlled the port although some independent English traders continued to deal there.

50. *Archdukes*] The Infanta Isabella and her husband Albert, joint rulers of the Spanish Netherlands under Philip II. The peace signed in 1604 by James I, Philip III, and the Archdukes was an unpopular treaty in some parts of England.

51. *Spinola's whale*] Ambrosio Spinola (1569–1630), general of the Spanish army in the Netherlands from 1604, was thought to have developed bizarre secret weapons, such as a whale trained to inundate London by spewing Thames water on to it.

53. *Stone the fool*] James's outspoken court jester, whipped in Bridewell in the spring of 1605 after criticising the Lord Admiral and his two sons for their negotiations with Spain.

SIR POLITIC   Is Mas' Stone dead?   55
PEREGRINE   He's dead, sir. Why, I hope
   You thought him not immortal? [*Aside*] O, this knight
   (Were he well known) would be a precious thing
   To fit our English stage. He that should write
   But such a fellow should be thought to feign
   Extremely, if not maliciously.   60
SIR POLITIC   Stone dead!
PEREGRINE   Dead. Lord, how deeply, sir, you apprehend it!
   He was no kinsman to you?
SIR POLITIC   That I know of.
   Well, that same fellow was an unknown fool.
PEREGRINE   And yet you knew him, it seems?
SIR POLITIC   I did so. Sir,
   I knew him one of the most dangerous heads   65
   Living within the state, and so I held him.
PEREGRINE   Indeed, sir?
SIR POLITIC   While he lived, in action.
   He has received weekly intelligence,
   Upon my knowledge, out of the Low Countries,
   For all parts of the world, in cabbages;   70
   And those dispensed again t'ambassadors
   In oranges, musk-melons, apricots,
   Lemons, pome-citrons, and such like; sometimes
   In Colchester oysters and your Selsea cockles.
PEREGRINE   You make me wonder!   75
SIR POLITIC   Sir, upon my knowledge.
   Nay, I have observed him at your public ordinary
   Take his advertisement from a traveller
   (A concealed statesman) in a trencher of meat,

---

55. *Mas'*] Abbreviation of Master.
60. *Stone dead!*] Ridiculous play on words. The expression is used idiomatically at
     1.4.107.
61. *apprehend*] Feel.
63. *unknown*] Unrecognised for his true work (as a spy).
67. *in action*] Engaged in subversive activities.
70. *in cabbages*] A major Dutch export at the time.
73. *pome-citrons*] Like lemons, but less acidic and more thick-skinned.
74. *Colchester oysters*] Oysters from Colchester, Essex, famous since Roman days. *Selsea*
     cockles] Selsea, a Sussex village, provided shellfish delicacies to the court.
76. *public ordinary*] Tavern or restaurant.
77. *advertisement*] Information or instructions.
78. *concealed statesman*] Secret agent. *trencher*] Dinner-plate.

And instantly, before the meal was done,
Convey an answer in a toothpick.   80
PEREGRINE   Strange!
How could this be, sir?
SIR POLITIC   Why, the meat was cut
So like his character, and so laid, as he
Must easily read the cipher.
PEREGRINE   I have heard
He could not read, sir.
SIR POLITIC   So 'twas given out
In polity by those that did employ him,   85
But he could read, and had your languages,
And to't as sound a noddle –
PEREGRINE   I have heard, sir,
That your baboons were spies, and that they were
A kind of subtle nation near to China.
SIR POLITIC   Ay, ay, your *Mamaluchi*. Faith, they had   90
Their hand in a French plot or two, but they
Were so extremely given to women as
They made discovery of all; yet I
Had my advices here on Wednesday last
From one of their own coat, they were returned,   95
Made their relations (as the fashion is),

80. *toothpick*] Fashionable accessory, often elaborately carved of ebony or ivory, and kept in fanciful cases such as little *memento mori* coffins that could accommodate a spy's message.
81–2. *meat ... character*] Serving meat cut into fantastic shapes was a fashionable amusement. *character*] Code.
85. *(In polity)*] As a cover.
87. *noddle*] Brain.
88. *baboons*] Records in Southwark, Leicester, and Norwich indicate that baboons were shown as curiosities either in permanent displays or on tour.
89. *subtle*] Cunning.
90. *Mamaluchi*] Mamelukes, formerly Circassian slaves, who seized power in Egypt in 1254 and maintained control even after the Turkish takeover in 1517, when 24 Mameluke beys ruled under a nominal Ottoman viceroy. Sir Pol describes the Mamelukes as womanisers, but in fact the most powerful among them were eunuchs; baboons, however, were reputedly lascivious. The name was also applied figuratively to the fighting slaves of the Pope, but they had no connection with baboons or China.
93. *made discovery*] Revealed.
94. *advices*] Dispatches, news.
95. *one ... coat*] One of their own kind.
96. *relations*] Reports.

And now stand fair for fresh employment.
PEREGRINE [*Aside*]   'Heart!
    This Sir Pol will be ignorant of nothing.
    – It seems, sir, you know all.
SIR POLITIC   Not all, sir. But
    I have some general notions; I do love   100
    To note and to observe. Though I live out,
    Free from the active torrent, yet I'd mark
    The currents and the passages of things
    For mine own private use, and know the ebbs
    And flows of state.   105
PEREGRINE   Believe it, sir, I hold
    Myself in no small tie unto my fortunes
    For casting me thus luckily upon you,
    Whose knowledge (if your bounty equal it)
    May do me great assistance in instruction
    For my behaviour and my bearing, which   110
    Is yet so rude and raw –
SIR POLITIC   Why, came you forth
    Empty of rules for travel?
PEREGRINE   Faith, I had
    Some common ones from out that vulgar grammar
    Which he that cried Italian to me taught me.
SIR POLITIC Why, this it is that spoils all our brave bloods, 115
    Trusting our hopeful gentry unto pedants:
    Fellows of outside and mere bark. You seem
    To be a gentleman of ingenuous race –
    I not profess it, but my fate hath been

97. *'Heart!*] By God's heart!
102. *Free ... torrent*] Not in the political swim; not actively plunging into political intrigue. Sir Pol's metaphor is mannered and 'precious'.
106. *tie*] Obligation.
113–14. *vulgar ... me*] Foreign languages are still taught by means of published dialogues set in the foreign country and illustrating customs as well as use of the vernacular (*vulgar*) idiom. The sixth dialogue of John Florio's *Second Frutes* (1591) is a satirical rule-book for travellers. But *grammar* here may simply mean 'guide to acceptable conduct' (see 'college-grammar', *SW* 4.1.24), and no text may be implied.
114. *cried Italian*] Gave lessons in Italian, putting the tutor in the same category as street-vendors 'crying' their wares.
115. *brave bloods*] Splendid young gentlemen.
117. *outside ... bark*] Mere externals; concern for the letter, not the spirit, of what they teach.
118. *ingenuous*] Noble.
119. *profess it*] Teach professionally.

To be where I have been consulted with   120
In this high kind, touching some great men's sons,
Persons of blood and honour –
PEREGRINE   Who be these, sir?

Act 2 scene 2*

[*Enter*] *Mosca* [*and*] *Nano* [*disguised as zanies, followed by*] *Grege*

MOSCA   Under that window, there't must be. The same.

[*Mosca and Nano erect a platform*]

SIR POLITIC   Fellows to mount a bank! Did your instructor

121. *In . . . kind*] In this important capacity.
*   St Mark's Square, Stephanus Pighius remarked in 1587, was the forum not of the city
        but of the world. Visitors thronged Venice, the 'Queen of the Sea', particularly the
        Piazza di San Marco and the Piazzetta, where politicians from the Procuratia, members
        of the Doge's retinue at the Palace, and religious officials from the Cathedral mingled
        with retailers and consumers of every nation and degree. The Carnival of Venice,
        loosely evoked by the fun-seeking crowd in this scene, featured masquerading and
        commedia dell'arte performances, where the principal figures were the magnifico, or
        pantaloon as he later became (Volpone's fluctuations between powerful grandee and
        impotent old man reflect this duality), the doctor, the role Volpone adopts in his
        medicine show, and the zany, or clown. According to Sansovino, ladies like Celia placed
        themselves at upper windows to watch the festivities below. The *commedia* drew on
        that custom in one of its most common scenes: the serenade by a suitor, assisted by
        zanies, at the window of a beautiful woman, whose husband/master/guardian subse-
        quently chases him away.
            Explanations of herbs and medications given below and in 3.4 come largely from
        two herbals, one used in Jonson's day, John Gerard's *The Herball* (1587), and a
        standard later seventeenth-century reference, Robert Lovell's *A Compleat Herball*
        (1665).
0.1. *zanies*] Clowns, mountebank's assistants, who provoked laughter by awkwardly
        imitating their master.
1.   *that window*] The opening in the tiring-house facade at the gallery level. See 1.2.87n.
2.   *mount a bank*] In Italian, *monta in banco*, climb up on a bench. Mountebanks, or
        itinerant quacks, performed on a stage formerly made of benches pushed together, as
        opposed to charlatans who performed on the ground (see 47). Venetian mountebanks
        performed regularly, morning and afternoon, in St Mark's Square between the churches
        of St Mark and St Geminian. The show began with clowns and musicians, both vocal
        and instrumental, until the mountebank began his eloquent and witty sales pitch, up to
        an hour in length, including impromptu joking with purchasers in the audience. The
        entertainment often incorporated comic dialogues with actresses; hence Corvino's
        reactions at 2.3.1–9 and 2.5.1–10.

In the dear tongues never discourse to you
  Of the Italian mountebanks?
PEREGRINE   Yes, sir.
SIR POLITIC   Why,
  Here shall you see one.   5
PEREGRINE   They are quacksalvers,
  Fellows that live by venting oils and drugs?
SIR POLITIC Was that the character he gave you of them?
PEREGRINE As I remember.
SIR POLITIC   Pity his ignorance.
  They are the only knowing men of Europe!
  Great general scholars, excellent physicians,   10
  Most admired statesmen, professed favourites
  And cabinet counsellors to the greatest princes!
  The only languaged men of all the world!
PEREGRINE And, I have heard, they are most lewd impostors,
  Made all of terms and shreds; no less beliers   15
  Of great men's favours than their own vile med'cines,
  Which they will utter upon monstrous oaths,
  Selling that drug for twopence ere they part,
  Which they have valued at twelve crowns before.
SIR POLITIC Sir, calumnies are answered best with silence.   20
  Yourself shall judge. [*To Mosca and Nano*] Who is it mounts,
     my friends?
MOSCA Scoto of Mantua, sir.
SIR POLITIC   Is't he? Nay, then
  I'll proudly promise, sir, you shall behold
  Another man than has been fancied to you.
  I wonder yet that he should mount his bank   25

---

3. *dear*] Esteemed, worthy.
5. *quacksalvers*] Now simply 'quacks', from a Dutch word meaning 'impostors who boast about their knowledge of medical remedies'; 'snake-oil salesmen' in the USA.
6. *venting*] Vending.
9. *knowing*] Knowledgeable.
12. *cabinet counsellors*] Private advisers.
13. *languaged men*] Skilled or educated speakers.
14. *lewd*] Ignorant.
15. *terms and shreds*] Jargon and scraps of quotations.   *beliers*] Misrepresenters.
17. *utter*] Sell fraudulently. See Epistle 58.
22. *Scoto of Mantua*] Professional actor who toured England between 1576 and 1583, impressing audiences with his juggling and sleight-of-hand. The name gives some indication of the style of Volpone's performance, especially in stage-business with the vial, the bill, and Celia's handkerchief.
24. *fancied*] Imagined, visualised.

Here, in this nook, that has been wont t'appear
In face of the Piazza! Here he comes.

[*Enter Volpone, disguised as a mountebank*]

VOLPONE   *[To Nano] Mount, zany.*
GREGE   [*Gathering excitedly*]   Follow, follow, follow, follow, follow.
SIR POLITIC   See how the people follow him! He's a man
May write ten thousand crowns in bank here. Note: 30

[*Volpone mounts the platform*]

Mark but his gesture. I do use to observe
The state he keeps in getting up!
PEREGRINE   'Tis worth it, sir.
VOLPONE   *Most noble gentlemen and my worthy patrons: it may
seem strange that I, your Scoto Mantuano, who was ever wont to fix
my bank in face of the public Piazza, near the shelter of the portico*   35
*to the Procuratia, should now, after eight months' absence from this
illustrious city of Venice, humbly retire myself into an obscure nook
of the Piazza.*
SIR POLITIC   Did not I now object the same?
PEREGRINE   Peace, sir.
VOLPONE   *Let me tell you: I am not (as your Lombard proverb saith)*   40
*cold on my feet, or content to part with my commodities at a cheaper
rate than I accustomed. Look not for it. Nor that the calumnious
reports of that impudent detractor and shame to our profession
(Alessandro Buttone, I mean) who gave out in public I was condemned* a 'sforzato *to the galleys for poisoning the Cardinal Bembo's*   45

26. *nook*]   Retired corner of the Square.
29. *Follow ... follow*]   Indicates confused crowd-noises, or 'rhubarb'.
32. *state*]   Dignified bearing, stateliness.
35–6. *portico ... Procuratia*]   The arcade running along the north side of St Mark's Square, fronting the residence for the procurators, or senior members of government.
41. *cold ... feet*]   The proverb is explained by the rest of the sentence; i.e., his poverty forcing him to sell his wares for little or no profit.
44. *Alessandro Buttone*]   An imaginary rival whose last name merely sounds Italian. The translation, Alexander the Button or the Insignificant, suggests a mock-heroic Alexander the Great. The name is synonymous with cowardice and the spreading of filth: Florio records *Il culo gli fa lappe*, 'His tail makes buttons', describing faecal droppings in a state of terror.
45. *a 'sforzato*]   A forced labourer as a prisoner or galley-slave.
45–6. *Cardinal Bembo's – cook*]   Pietro Bembo (1470–1547), the humanist; he appeared in Castiglione's *The Courtier* defending the spiritual value of kissing. The dash suggests a coy substitution for 'mistress'.

– cook, hath at all attached, much less dejected me. No, no, worthy
gentlemen, to tell you true, I cannot endure to see the rabble of these
ground ciarlitani *that spread their cloaks on the pavement as if they
meant to do feats of activity, and then come in lamely with their
mouldy tales out of Boccaccio, like stale Tabarin the fabulist, some of*   50
them discoursing their travels and of their tedious captivity in the
Turks' galleys, when indeed (were the truth known) they were the
Christians' galleys, where very temperately they ate bread and drunk
water as a wholesome penance (enjoined them by their confessors) for
base pilferies.*   55

SIR POLITIC   Note but his bearing and contempt of these.

VOLPONE   *These turdy-facy-nasty-paty-lousy-fartical rogues, with one
poor groatsworth of unprepared antimony, finely wrapped up in
several* scartoccios, *are able very well to kill their twenty a week, and
play; yet these meagre starved spirits, who have half stopped the*   60
organs of their minds with earthy oppilations, want not their
favourers among your shrivelled salad-eating artisans, who are
overjoyed that they may have their ha'p'orth of physic, though it
purge 'em into another world, 't makes no matter.*

SIR POLITIC   Excellent! Ha' you heard better language, sir?   65

VOLPONE   *Well, let 'em go. And, gentlemen, honourable gentlemen,
know that for this time our bank, being thus removed from the*

46. *attached*] Drawn the attention of the authorities.

48. *ciarlitani*] Charlatans.

49. *feats of activity*] Acrobatics.

50. *Boccaccio*] Giovanni Boccaccio (1313–75), author of the *Decameron*, salacious tales
frequently used by later writers as a source for plots. Along with Petrarch, he is
considered the founder of Renaissance humanism, and promoter of vernacular
literature, but virtually his only other vernacular work was a satire called *Il Corbaccio*.
Tabarin] A zany in a troupe of Italian comedians who visited France in 1572; he later
moved to Paris, where he was a favourite of Charles IX, who became godfather to
Tabarin's son.   *fabulist*] Story-teller, one of a zany's roles in attracting and warming
up a crowd before the main performance.

57. *turdy- . . . fartical*] An Aristophanic compound.

58. *groatsworth*] Fourpence worth.   *unprepared antimony*] A native trisulphide (*stibium*) used in alchemical experiments, medicines, and cosmetics.

59. *several*] Separate.   *scartoccios*] Paper containers for spice or medication, used by
apothecaries.

61. *earthy oppilations*] Gross obstructions; suggesting mental constipation. In humours
theory, the *earthy* element produced a phlegmatic or sluggish temperament.

62. *salad-eating*] Then an Italian dining custom; the English ate bread and meat. Lettuce
was prescribed as a laxative to relieve heartburn and biliousness; see 63–4 and 5.3.104.

63. *ha'p'orth*] halfpennyworth.

67. *bank*] Platform.

clamours of the canaglia, *shall be the scene of pleasure and delight, for
I have nothing to sell, little or nothing to sell.*

SIR POLITIC   I told you, sir, his end.   70
PEREGRINE   You did so, sir.
VOLPONE   *I protest, I and my six servants are not able to make of
this precious liquor* [Holds up a glass vial] *so fast as it is fetched
away from my lodging by gentlemen of your city, strangers of the* terra
firma, *worshipful merchants, ay, and senators too, who ever since my
arrival have detained me to their uses by their splendidous liberalities.*   75
*And worthily! For what avails your rich man to have his magazines
stuffed with* moscadelli *or of the purest grape when his physicians
prescribe him on pain of death to drink nothing but water cocted with
aniseeds? O, health, health! The blessing of the rich! The riches of the
poor! Who can buy thee at too dear a rate, since there is no enjoying*   80
*this world without thee? Be not then so sparing of your purses,
honourable gentlemen, as to abridge the natural course of life –*

PEREGRINE   You see his end?
SIR POLITIC   Aye, is't not good?
VOLPONE   *For when a humid flux or catarrh, by the mutability of
air, falls from your head into an arm or shoulder or any other part,*   85
*take you a ducat or your zecchin of gold, and apply to the place
affected. See what good effect it can work. No, no, 'tis this blessed
unguento, this rare extraction, that hath only power to disperse all
malignant humours that proceed either of hot, cold, moist, or windy
causes –*   90
PEREGRINE   I would he had put in dry too.
SIR POLITIC   Pray you, observe.
VOLPONE   *– to fortify the most indigest and crude stomach, ay, were
it of one that (through extreme weakness) vomited blood, applying*

68. *canaglia*] Rabble, riff-raff.
73–4. *strangers ... terra firma*] Foreigners from the mainland communities controlled by
    Venice.
75. *splendidous*] Inflated form of 'splendid'.
76. *magazines*] Storehouses.
77. *moscadelli*] Muscatel wine.
78. *cocted*] Boiled.
84–90. *when a humid ... windy causes*] Again relying on the medical theory of the four
    humours and their pathological relationship with the four elements, Scoto argues that
    a change in the weather (air) causes a corresponding physiological change, creating an
    overflow of the watery humour (*humid flux*) into various parts of the body, thus
    causing physical imbalance and discomfort; here, rheumatism.
88. *unguento*] Ointment.
92. *crude*] Undigested.

only a warm napkin to the place, after the unction and fricace; for the
vertigine *in the head, putting but a drop into your nostrils, likewise*   95
behind the ears: a most sovereign and approved remedy; the mal-
caduco, *cramps, convulsions, paralyses, epilepsies,* tremor-cordia,
retired nerves, ill vapours of the spleen, stoppings of the liver, the
stone, the strangury, hernia ventosa, iliaca passio; *stops a* dysenteria
immediately; easeth the torsion of the small guts; and cures melancho-   100
lia hypocondriaca, *being taken and applied according to my printed*
receipt.

> Pointing to his bill and his glass

For this is the physician, this the medicine; this counsels, this cures;
this gives the direction, this works the effect; and (in sum) both
together may be termed an abstract of the theoric and practic in the   105
Aesculapian art. 'Twill cost you eight crowns. [To Nano] *And, Zan*
Fritada, pray thee sing a verse extempore *in honour of it.*

SIR POLITIC   How do you like him, sir?
PEREGRINE   Most strangely, I!
SIR POLITIC   Is not his language rare?
PEREGRINE   But alchemy,
I never heard the like, or Broughton's books.   110

94. *unction*] Application of ointment.   *fricace*] Massage.
95. *vertigine*] Dizziness.
96–7. *mal-caduco*] Falling sickness, epilepsy.
97. *tremor-cordia*] Palpitation of the heart.
98. *retired nerves*] Shrunken sinews.   *ill ... spleen*] Hysteria or depression; the spleen
    was thought to be the seat of melancholy, the earthy humour.   *stoppings*] Obstruc-
    tions, probably gallstones.
99. *stone*] Kidney stone.   *strangury*] Impeded urination.   *hernia ventosa*] Swollen
    scrotum caused by a rupture?   *iliaca passio*] Painful obstruction of the small intestine,
    frequently fatal.   *dysenteria*] Severe diarrhoea, with passage of blood and mucus.
100. *torsion. . . guts*] Spasmodic pain in the bowels; colic.
100–1. *melancholia hypochondriaca*] Depression. The *hypochrondria* refers to parts of the
    abdomen immediately under the ribs and on each side of the stomach. See *spleen*, 98n.
    above.
102. *receipt*] Recipe.
106. *Aesculapian*] Medical, after Aesculapius, god of medicine.
106–7. *Zan Fritada*] Literally 'Jack Pancake', a zany in Venice famous for his stories, songs,
    and improvisations.
109. *But*] Except for.
110. *Broughton's books*] Hugh Broughton (1549–1612), puritan minister and scholar
    whose many monographs and pamphlets explaining obscure biblical points are also
    satirised in *Alch* 2.3.237–8 and 4.5.1–32.

[*Nano sings*]

song

Had old Hippocrates or Galen
(That to their books put med'cines all in)
But known this secret, they had never
(Of which they will be guilty ever)
Been murderers of so much paper,   115
Or wasted many a hurtless taper.
No Indian drug had ere been famed,
Tobacco, sassafras not named;
Ne yet of guacum one small stick, sir,
Nor Raymond Lully's great elixir.   120
Ne had been known the Danish Gonswart,
Or Paracelsus with his long sword.

PEREGRINE   All this yet will not do. Eight crowns is high.
VOLPONE   [*To Nano*] No more.   Gentlemen, if I had but time to
discourse to you the miraculous effects of this my oil, surnamed *oglio*   125
del Scoto, *with the countless catalogue of those I have cured of*
th'aforesaid and many more diseases; the patents and privileges of
all the princes and commonwealths of Christendom; or but the

111. *Hippocrates or Galen*] Medical authorities up to the sixteenth century; Hippocrates
    (460–350 BC) originated the humours theory and Galen (AD 130–200) expounded it in
    almost five hundred treatises.
116. *hurtless*] Harmless.
118. *Tobacco, sassafras*] Both recent American imports used medicinally, especially as mild
    sedatives and cures for syphilis.
119. *guacum*] Guaiacum tree, native to the West Indies; the wood, bark, and resin were
    used medicinally as diuretics, purges for syphilis and digestive disturbances, and
    stimulants of the menstrual flow (Gerard).
120. *Raymond Lully*] Spanish scholar, missionary, and astrologer (1235–1315), wrongly
    believed to have been an alchemist who discovered the elixir of eternal life.
121. *Danish Gonswart*] Not identified, probably a printer's error, but apparently not a
    person. *Worts*, however, are herbs used to prepare medicine. The likeliest of these is
    Danewort, or Dwarf Elder, used like guaiacum in curing disorders of the digestive tract
    and stimulating menstrual flow, and most frequently prescribed for gout and syphilis,
    two diseases often confused because of similar symptoms of 'bone-ache'. Another herb,
    Goutwort, was thought to be a variety of Danewort, and to have the same property of
    healing gout (Lovell). Conceivably, Jonson is referring here to 'Danish Goutwort'.
122. *Paracelsus*] The pioneer of chemical medicine (1493–1541), supposed to have hidden
    a familiar spirit, or secret cures, or the philosopher's stone itself, in the pommel of his
    sword.

depositions of those that appeared on my part before the Signiory
of the Sanitá and the most learned College of Physicians, where   130
I was authorised upon notice taken of the admirable virtues of my
medicaments and mine own excellency in matter of rare and unknown
secrets, not only to disperse them publicly in this famous city, but in
all the territories that happily joy under the government of the most
pious and magnificent states of Italy. But may some other   135
gallant fellow say, 'O, there be divers that make profession to have as
good and as experimented receipts as yours.' Indeed, very many have
assayed, like apes, in imitation of that which is really and essentially
in me, to make of this oil; bestowed great cost in furnaces, stills,
alembics, continual fires, and preparation of the ingredients (as   140
indeed there goes to it six hundred several simples, besides some
quantity of human fat for the conglutination, which we buy of the
anatomists); but, when these practitioners come to the last decoction,
blow, blow, puff, puff, and all flies in fumo. Ha, ha, ha! Poor
wretches! I rather pity their folly and indiscretion than their loss of   145
time and money, for those may be recovered by industry, but to be a
fool born is a disease incurable. For myself, I always from my youth
have endeavoured to get the rarest secrets and book them, either in
exchange or for money. I spared nor cost nor labour where anything
was worthy to be learned. And, gentlemen, honourable gentlemen, I   150
will undertake, by virtue of chemical art, out of the honourable hat
that covers your head to extract the four elements; that is to say, the
fire, air, water, and earth, and return you your felt without burn or
stain. For, whilst others have been at the balloo, I have been at my
book, and am now past the craggy paths of study, and come to the   155
flowery plains of honour and reputation.

SIR POLITIC   I do assure you, sir, that is his aim.
VOLPONE   *But to our price.*
PEREGRINE   And that withal, Sir Pol
VOLPONE   *You all know, honourable gentlemen, I never valued this*

129–30. *Signiory of the Sanitá*] Ministry of health, organised 1485, which licensed
   physicians, mountebanks, and charlatans.
140. *alembics*] Distilling apparatus.
141. *several simples*] Separate herbs.
142. *conglutination*] Gluing together.
143. *decoction*] Boiling down.
144. *in fumo*] Up in smoke. See *Alch* 4.5.58.
148. *book*] Record.
153. *felt*] Hat made of felt.
154. *balloo*] Or balloon, a game played by six or seven young men equipped with a
   wooden brace on one arm, with which they strike a large inflated ball of double
   leather, tossing it considerable distances upwards and across to one another.

ampulla *or vial at less than eight crowns, but for this time I am con-* 160
tent to be deprived of it for six; six crowns is the price, and less, in
courtesy, I know you cannot offer me. Take it or leave it howsoever,
both it and I am at your service. I ask you not as the value of the thing,
for then I should demand of you a thousand crowns, so the Cardinals
Montalto, Fernese, the great Duke of Tuscany, my gossip, with divers 165
other princes, have given me, but I despise money. Only to show my
affection to you, honourable gentlemen, and your illustrious state
here, I have neglected the messages of these princes, mine own offices,
framed my journey hither, only to present you with the fruits of my
travels. [To Nano and Mosca] Tune your voices once more to the 170
touch of your instruments, and give the honourable assembly some
delightful recreation.

PEREGRINE   What monstrous and most painful circumstance
    Is here, to get some three or four *gazets*!
    Some threepence, i'th' whole, for that 'twill come to! 175

[*Enter Celia at the window above while Nano sings, Mosca*
  accompanying him]

    song
    You that would last long, list to my song:
    Make no more coil, but buy of this oil.
    Would you be ever fair? and young?
    Stout of teeth? and strong of tongue?
    Tart of palate? quick of ear? 180
    Sharp of sight? of nostril clear?
    Moist of hand? and light of foot?
    (Or I will come nearer to't)
    Would you live free from all diseases?

160. ampulla] Vial of thin glass.
164–5. *Cardinals ... Tuscany*] Felice Peretti became Cardinal of Montalto in 1570, and
    Pope Sixtus V in 1585. Alessandro Ferneze (1520–89) was a cardinal at about the same
    time. Cosimo de Medici became the first Archduke of Tuscany in 1569.
165. *gossip*] Godfather of one's child; hence, close friend. Princes often sponsored the
    children of favoured actors; see *Tabarin*, 50n. above. Tristano Marinelli, the famous
    Harlequin who achieved phenomenal success between 1596 and 1626, corresponded
    with several French and Italian princes who competed for the honour of being
    godparents to his children.
168. *offices*] Duties.
174. *gazets*] Coined at Venice for circulation in the Levant, and worth less than a penny.
177. *coil*] Fuss, argument.
182. *Moist of hand*] Sign of libidinousness.

> Do the act your mistress pleases,   185
> Yet fright all aches from your bones?
> Here's a med'cine for the nones.

VOLPONE   Well, I am in a humour, at this time, to make a present
of the small quantity my coffer contains: to the rich, in courtesy, and
to the poor, for God's sake. Wherefore, now mark. I asked you six   190
crowns, and six crowns at other times you have paid me; you shall not
give me six crowns, nor five, nor four, nor three, nor two, nor one; nor
half a ducat; no, nor a muccenigo. Six – pence it will cost you, or six
hundred pound – expect no lower price, for by the banner of my front,
I will not bate a bagatine, that I will have only a pledge of your loves, 195
to carry something from amongst you to show I am not contemned by
you. Therefore, now, toss your handkerchiefs cheerfully, cheerfully,
and be advertised that the first heroic spirit that deigns to grace me
with a handkerchief I will give it a little remembrance of something
beside, shall please it better than if I had presented it with a double   200
pistolet.

PEREGRINE   Will you be that heroic spark, Sir Pol?

Celia at the window throws down her handkerchief

O, see! The window has prevented you.

VOLPONE   *[Retrieving and kissing the handkerchief]* Lady, I kiss your
bounty, and for this timely grace you have done your poor Scoto   205
of Mantua, I will return you, over and above my oil, a secret of that
high and inestimable nature shall make you forever enamoured on
that minute wherein your eye first descended on so mean – yet not
altogether to be despised – an object. Here is a powder concealed in
this paper of which, if I should speak to the worth, nine thousand   210
volumes were but as one page, that page as a line, that line as a word:
so short is this pilgrimage of man (which some call life) to the

---

185. *Do the act*] Make love.
186. *aches ... bones*] Venereal disease, called the 'bone-ache'. See note on *Danish
    Gonswart*, 121n. above.
187. *nones*] Nonce, occasion.
193. *muccenigo*] Coin worth about 9 old pence.
194. *banner ... front*] The banner hanging before the platform, advertising his wares.
195. *bagatine*] Small coin worth about one-twelfth of a penny.
197. *toss your handkerchiefs*] Mountebanks customarily asked for money tied into the
    corner of the customer's ornamental handkerchief, which might be decorated at the
    corners with strings or tassels for that purpose; the purchase was returned in the same
    way. Celia's act is not flirtatious.
200–1. *double pistolet*] Spanish gold coin worth about 18 shillings.
203. *prevented*] Thwarted; reached a goal ahead of another.

expressing of it. Would I reflect on the price, why, the whole world were but
as an empire, that empire as a province, that province as a bank, that bank
as a private purse, to the purchase of it. I will only tell you it is   215
the powder that made Venus a goddess (given her by Apollo), that kept her
perpetually young, cleared her wrinkles, firmed her gums, filled her
skin, coloured her hair; from her derived to Helen, and at the sack of
Troy (unfortunately) lost – till now, in this our age, it was as happily
recovered by a studious antiquary out of some ruins of Asia, who   220
sent a moiety of it to the court of France (but much sophisticated) wherewith
the ladies there now colour their hair. The rest, at this present, remains with
me, extracted to a quintessence, so that wherever it but touches, in youth
it perpetually preserves, in age restores, the complexion; seats your
teeth, did they dance like virginal jacks, firm as a wall; makes them   225
white as ivory, that were black as –

Act 2 scene 3 *

[*Enter*] *Corvino*, [*enraged by the performers*]

CORVINO   Spite o' the devil, and my shame! [*To Volpone*]
            Come down here!
        Come down! No house but mine to make your scene?
        Signor Flaminio, will you down, sir? Down?

216–22. *powder … colour their hair*] The powder declines from a god-given gift of eternal
    youth to a hair-dye, a cheapening process similar to the corruption of Pythagoras's soul
    in 1.2, or of Volpone's career in the course of the play.
221. *moiety*] Part. *sophisticated*] Adulterated.
223. *quintessence*] The fifth essence of life that remains after earth, air, fire, and water have
    been reduced in the alchemical process, thus releasing the quintessential ingredient of
    the elixir, or philosopher's stone.
224. *seats*] Fixes firmly.
225. *virginal jacks*] Keys of a small spinet; or the pegs attached to the quills which pluck the
    strings when the keys are depressed.
*   The point of view in this scene shifts comically in a very short space of time: Volpone's
    masterly display turns to ignominious flight when threatened by Corvino's hysterical
    rage. The Englishmen puzzle over Italian excess.
 2. *scene*] Set. In Roman comedy, as in later Italian comedy, the scene was a public street
    overlooked by private houses. Window scenes were common in the *commedia dell'arte*,
    improvised farce based on certain stock characters and situations.
 3. *Flaminio*] One of the young lovers in some versions of the *commedia dell'arte*, or
    perhaps one of two famous *commedia* actors: Flaminio Scala, also a playwright and
    director in the Gelosi company; or Flaminio Curtezze, who performed with his troupe
    before Queen Elizabeth in August 1602.

What, is my wife your Franciscina, sir?
No windows on the whole Piazza here   5
To make your properties but mine? But mine?

He beats away the mountebank, etc. [*Volpone, Mosca, and Nano*
hide while the Grege disperses; exit Celia from her window]

Heart! Ere tomorrow I shall be new christened,
And called the Pantalone di Besogniosi
About the town. [*Exit*]
PEREGRINE   What should this mean, Sir Pol?
SIR POLITIC   Some trick of state, believe it. I will home.   10
PEREGRINE   It may be some design on you.
SIR POLITIC   I know not.
I'll stand upon my guard.
PEREGRINE   It is your best, sir.
SIR POLITIC   This three weeks, all my advices, all my letters,
They have been intercepted.
PEREGRINE   Indeed, sir?
Best have a care.   15
SIR POLITIC   Nay, so I will. [*Exit*]
PEREGRINE   This knight,
I may not lose him for my mirth till night. [*Exit*]

Act 2 scene 4[*]

Mosca [*tends to*] *Volpone* [*while Nano dismantles the platform*]

VOLPONE   O, I am wounded!
MOSCA   Where, sir?
VOLPONE   Not without;
Those blows were nothing. I could bear them ever.
But angry Cupid, bolting from her eyes,
Hath shot himself into me like a flame,
Where now he flings about his burning heat   5

---

4. *Franciscina*] The saucy maidservant of the *commedia dell'arte*. Marston used the name
   for the eponymous whore in *The Dutch Courtesan* (1605).
6. *properties*] Stage sets.
8. *Pantalone di Besogniosi*] A stock Venetian character in the *commedia*, a lean old miser
   commonly depicted as a jealous dotard or as a cuckold.
*   During this scene, while Volpone and Mosca hide from Corvino, presumably Nano and
     other helpers are dismantling the mountebank's platform.
1. *without*] Externally.
3. *bolting*] Shooting arrows (bolts).

As in a furnace an ambitious fire
Whose vent is stopped. The fight is all within me.
I cannot live except thou help me, Mosca.
My liver melts and I, without the hope
Of some soft air from her refreshing breath,   10
Am but a heap of cinders.

MOSCA   'Las, good sir!
Would you had never seen her.

VOLPONE   Nay, would thou
Hadst never told me of her.

MOSCA   Sir, 'tis true.
I do confess I was unfortunate
And you unhappy, but I'm bound in conscience,   15
No less than duty, to effect my best
To your release of torment, and I will, sir.

VOLPONE   Dear Mosca, shall I hope?

MOSCA   Sir, more than dear,
I will not bid you to despair of aught
Within a human compass.   20

VOLPONE   O, there spoke
My better angel. Mosca, take my keys.
Gold, plate, and jewels: all's at thy devotion.
Employ them how thou wilt. Nay, coin me too,
So thou in this but crown my longings. Mosca?

MOSCA   Use but your patience.   25

VOLPONE   So I have.

MOSCA   I doubt not
To bring success to your desires.

VOLPONE   Nay, then,
I not repent me of my late disguise.

MOSCA   If you can horn him, sir, you need not.

VOLPONE   True.
Besides, I never meant him for my heir.
Is not the colour o' my beard and eye-brows   30

---

6. *ambitious*] Rising, swelling.
7. *stopped*] Blocked.
9. *liver*] Believed the seat of love and violent passion.
22. *devotion*] Disposal, punning on the religious 'charitable offering' or 'dedication to sacred use', and the mundane 'loyalty'.
24. *crown*] Consummate or fulfil, punning on 'coin', 23.
28. *horn*] Cuckold.
30. *colour*] Red, the fox's colour.

To make me known?

MOSCA   No jot.

VOLPONE   I did it well.

MOSCA   So well, would I could follow you in mine
        With half the happiness; and yet I would
        Escape your epilogue.

VOLPONE   But were they gulled
        With a belief that I was Scoto?   35

MOSCA   Sir,
        Scoto himself could hardly have distinguished!
        I have not time to flatter you now. We'll part,
        And as I prosper, so applaud my art.

[*Exeunt*]

Act 2 scene 5 *

[*Enter*] *Corvino* [*and*] *Celia*

CORVINO   Death of mine honour, with the city's fool?
        A juggling, tooth-drawing, prating mountebank?
        And at a public window? Where, whilst he
        With his strained action and his dole of faces
        To his drug-lecture draws your itching ears,   5
        A crew of old, unmarried, noted lechers
        Stood leering up like satyrs? And you smile
        Most graciously! And fan your favours forth
        To give your hot spectators satisfaction!
        What, was your mountebank their call? Their whistle? 10

---

33. *happiness*] Success in performance.
34. *epilogue*] The beating from Corvino.
*   The remaining scenes in this act take place at Corvino's house. Possibly these scenes were played on the upper stage at Celia's window overlooking the Piazza. Certainly Corvino could display his hatred of crowds in this scene to advantage if he could look down at spectators who illustrate some of his remarks. The upper stage, however, was a small playing space; perhaps scene 6 was performed on the main stage, with only scenes 5 and 7 played above.
2.   *tooth-drawing*] A service performed by barbers and mountebanks.
4.   *strained action*] Overacting. *dole of faces*] Quick-changes of facial expression, mugging. The wording suggests the broad acting style Volpone used for Scoto.
8.   *fan your favours*] Flirt, perhaps referring to a literal fan.
9.   *hot*] Aroused; see 6, 'lechers', 7, 'satyrs', and 18–20.
10. *call ... whistle*] Bird lures.

Or were y'enamoured on his copper rings?
His saffron jewel, with the toad-stone in't?
Or his embroidered suit with the cope-stitch,
Made of a hearse cloth? Or his old tilt-feather?
Or his starched beard? Well! You shall have him, yes!   15
He shall come home, and minister unto you
The fricace for the mother. Or, let me see,
I think you'd rather mount? Would you not mount?
Why, if you'll mount, you may. Yes, truly, you may.
And so you may be seen, down t' th' foot.   20
Get you a cittern, Lady Vanity,
And be a dealer with the virtuous man.
Make one. I'll but protest myself a cuckold,
And save your dowry. I am a Dutchman, I!
For if you thought me an Italian,   25
You would be damned ere you did this, you whore!
Thou'dst tremble to imagine that the murder

11–15. Satiric catalogue of the gaudy mountebank costume.
11. *copper rings*] Cheap substitutes for gold.
12. *saffron*] Yellow-stained, to imitate gold. *toad-stone*] Toad-coloured stone supposed to be found in a toad's head and believed to have therapeutic and magical properties; hence its popularity in rings and amulets.
13. *cope-stitch*] Embroidery stitch to decorate edges.
14. *hearse cloth*] Drape for a coffin. *tilt-feather*] Large plume, usually ostrich, worn at an angle either backwards to trail over the broad brim of a cocked hat, or upwards drooping over the crown of a narrow-brimmed hat. The fashion derives from plumes worn on jousting helmets in the Tilt-yard.
15. *starched*] Stiffened with gum or egg-white to hold a fashionable shape.
17. *fricace for the mother*] Massage for hysteria, believed to originate in the womb; also suggesting the sexual act.
18. *you'd*] You had.
18–20. *mount … foot*] Climb upon the mountebank's platform where spectators can look up her skirts; or perform sexually upon the mountebank himself, exposing herself from the waist down.
21. *cittern*] A wire-stringed guitar, commonly played by *commedia* and mountebank actresses, and by prostitutes. *Lady Vanity*] A character in several morality plays; see the interlude in *Sir Thomas More* (159-?) 4.1, or *The Contention between Liberality and Prodigality* (1602).
22. *be a dealer*] Solicit sexual acts, prostitute yourself. *virtuous*] Manly, implying 'sexually vigorous or active'.
23. *Make one*] Copulate.
24. *save your dowry*] An adulterous wife forfeited her financial security. *Dutchman*] Considered temperamentally phlegmatic, because of his cold and watery clime, as opposed to the hot-tempered and vengeful Italian.

Of father, mother, brother, all thy race,
Should follow as the subject of my justice!

CELIA   Good sir, have patience!   30

CORVINO   [*Drawing his dagger*] What couldst thou propose
Less to thyself than, in this heat of wrath
And stung with my dishonour, I should strike
This steel unto thee with as many stabs
As thou wert gazed upon with goatish eyes?

CELIA   Alas, sir, be appeased! I could not think   35
My being at the window should more now
Move your impatience than at other times.

CORVINO   No? Not to seek and entertain a parley
With a known knave? Before a multitude?
You were an actor with your handkerchief!   40
Which he, most sweetly, kissed in the receipt,
And might (no doubt) return it with a letter,
And point the place where you might meet: your sister's,
Your mother's, or your aunt's might serve the turn.

CELIA   Why, dear sir, when do I make these excuses?   45
Or ever stir abroad, but to the church?
And that so seldom –

CORVINO   Well, it shall be less;
And thy restraint before was liberty
To what I now decree, and therefore mark me.
First, I will have this bawdy light dammed up;   50
And, till't be done, some two or three yards off
I'll chalk a line, o'er which, if thou but chance
To set thy desp'rate foot, more hell, more horror,
More wild remorseless rage shall seize on thee
Than on a conjurer that had heedless left   55
His circle's safety ere his devil was laid.

---

28. *race*] Kin.
34. *goatish*] Lecherous.
43. *point*] Appoint.
44. *aunt*] Slang for bawd or madam. *serve the turn*] Serve the purpose, punning lewdly
    on 'provide the sexual service'.
50. *light*] Window.
53. *desp'rate*] Irreclaimable.
56. *circle's safety*] Conjurors could raise spirits with impunity so long as they remained
    within the magic circle (pentagram) until the spirit was 'laid' or returned to hell.
    Corvino also crudely puns on 'conjuring in a circle' meaning sexual intercourse; see
    2.6.65–6.

Then, [*Showing a chastity belt*] here's a lock which I will hang
    upon thee –
And, now I think on't, I will keep thee backwards:
Thy lodging shall be backwards; thy walks backwards;
Thy prospect – all be backwards; and no pleasure   60
That thou shalt know but backwards. Nay, since you force
My honest nature, know: it is your own
Being too open makes me use you thus.
Since you will not contain your subtle nostrils
In a sweet room, but they must snuff the air   65
Of rank and sweaty passengers –

Knock within
                                 One knocks.

Away, and be not seen, pain of thy life;
Not look toward the window. If thou dost –

[*Celia begins to leave*]

Nay, stay, hear this – let me not prosper, whore,
But I will make thee an anatomy,   70
Dissect thee mine own self, and read a lecture
Upon thee to the city, and in public.
Away!

[*Exit Celia and enter Servitore*]

         Who's there?
SERVITORE   'Tis Signior Mosca, sir.

Act 2 scene 6

CORVINO   Let him come in.

[*Exit Servitore*]

                 His master's dead! There's yet
Some good to help the bad.

[*Enter*] *Mosca*

                 My Mosca, welcome!

57. *lock*] Chastity belt.
58. *backwards*] At the rear of the house; but suggesting the anal-erotic, especially 60–61,
    and 'open' and 'use', 63. Sodomy was considered an Italian vice, particularly associated
    with Venice because of its large population of homosexual-transvestite prostitutes.
67. *pain of*] On pain of.
70. *anatomy*] Both a corpse for dissection, and a moral analysis.

I guess your news.

MOSCA   I fear you cannot, sir.

CORVINO   Is't not his death?

MOSCA   Rather the contrary.

CORVINO   Not his recovery?   5

MOSCA   Yes, sir.

CORVINO   I am cursed!
I am bewitched! My crosses meet to vex me!
How? How? How? How?

MOSCA   Why, sir, with Scoto's oil!
Corbaccio and Voltore brought of it
Whilst I was busy in an inner room –

CORVINO   Death! That damned mountebank! But for the law,   10
Now I could kill the rascal. 'T cannot be
His oil should have that virtue. Ha' not I
Known him a common rogue, come sidling in
To th'*osteria* with a tumbling whore,
And, when he has done all his forced tricks, been glad   15
Of a poor spoonful of dead wine, with flies in't?
It cannot be. All his ingredients
Are a sheep's gall, a roasted bitch's marrow,
Some few sod earwigs, pounded caterpillars,
A little capon's grease, and fasting spittle.   20
I know 'em to a dram.

MOSCA   I know not, sir,
But some on't there they poured into his ears,
Some in his nostrils, and recovered him,
Applying but the fricace.

CORVINO   Pox o' that fricace!

MOSCA   And since, to seem the more officious   25
And flatt'ring of his health, there they have had
(At extreme fees) the college of physicians
Consulting on him how they might restore him:
Where one would have a cataplasm of spices,
Another a flayed ape clapped to his breast,   30

6. *crosses*] Afflictions.

14. *osteria*] Inn. *tumbling whore*] Either an acrobat serving as Scoto's assistant, or a prostitute; 'tumbling-trick' was a cant-word for sexual intercourse.

16. *dead*] Stale.

19. *sod*] Boiled, sodden.

20. *fasting spittle*] Saliva of a starving man (Scoto's own?).

25. *officious*] Zealous.

27. *extreme fees*] Great cost.

29. *cataplasm*] Poultice.

A third would ha'it a dog, a fourth an oil
With wild cats' skins. At last, they all resolved
That to preserve him was no other means
But some young woman must be straight sought out,
Lusty and full of juice, to sleep by him;   35
And to this service (most unhappily
And most unwillingly) am I now employed,
Which here I thought to pre-acquaint you with,
For your advice, since it concerns you most,
Because I would not do that thing might cross   40
Your ends, on whom I have my whole dependence, sir.
Yet, if I do it not, they may delate
My slackness to my patron, work me out
Of his opinion, and there all your hopes,
Ventures, or whatsoever, are all frustrate.   45
I do but tell you, sir. Besides, they are all
Now striving who shall first present him. Therefore –
I could entreat you, briefly, conclude somewhat.
Prevent 'em if you can.
CORVINO   Death to my hopes!
This is my villainous fortune! Best to hire   50
Some common courtesan?
MOSCA   Ay, I thought on that, sir.
But they are all so subtle, full of art,
And age again doting and flexible,
So as – I cannot tell – we may perchance
Light on a quean may cheat us all.   55
CORVINO   'Tis true.
MOSCA No, no. It must be one that has no tricks, sir:
Some simple thing, a creature made unto it,
Some wench you may command. Ha' you no kinswoman?
God's so– Think, think, think, think, think, think, think, sir.
One o' the doctors offered there his daughter.   60
CORVINO How!

34–5. In I Kings 1, Abishag attempted this cure for King David.
35. *lusty*] Healthy and energetic. *juice*] Lubricity; eagerness to make love.
40–41. *cross … ends*] Thwart your plans.
42. *delate*] Report, denounce; the original Latin meant 'bring charges before a judge'.
47. *present him*] That is, with a young woman.
48. *conclude somewhat*] Decide on something.
49. *Prevent 'em*] Act first, forestall them.
55. *quean*] Harlot, whore.
57. *made unto it*] Biddable, fit for the task.
59. *God's so–*] Corruption of 'by God's soul'; sounds like *cazzo*, Italian for 'penis'.

MOSCA   Yes, Signor Lupo, the physician.
CORVINO   His daughter?
MOSCA   And a virgin, sir. Why? Alas,
   He knows the state of's body, what it is;
   That nought can warm his blood, sir, but a fever,
   Nor any incantation raise his spirit: 65
   A long forgetfulness hath seized that part.
   Besides, sir, who shall know it? Some one or two –
CORVINO   I pray thee give me leave. [*Walks aside, brooding*]
    If any man
   But I had had this luck – The thing in'tself,
   I know, is nothing – Wherefore should not I   70
   As well command my blood and my affections
   As this dull doctor? In the point of honour,
   The cases are all one, of wife and daughter.
MOSCA   [*Aside*] I hear him coming.
CORVINO   [*Aside*]   She shall do't. 'Tis done.
   'Slight, if this doctor, who is not engaged   75
   Unless 't be for his counsel (which is nothing),
   Offer his daughter, what should I that am
   So deeply in? I will prevent him. Wretch!
   Covetous wretch! [*Aloud*] Mosca, I have determined.
MOSCA   How, sir?   80
CORVINO   We'll make all sure. The party you wot of
   Shall be mine own wife, Mosca.
MOSCA   Sir! The thing –
   But that I would not seem to counsel you –
   I should have motioned to you at the first!
   And, make your count, you have cut all their throats.
   Why, 'tis directly taking a possession!   85

61. *Lupo*] 'Wolf' in Italian; applied to a rapacious person, or in medicine (*lupus*) to a variety of malignant skin diseases with symptomatic ulceration.

65. Suggests the failure both of magic and of sexual potency, the latter directly commented on in the next line. 'Conjuring in a circle' was a common metaphor for sexual intercourse; see 2.5.55–6, or Shakespeare's *Henry V* 5.2.306–12.

69. *in'tself*] In itself.

74. *coming*] Yielding to persuasion.

75. *'Slight*] Corruption of 'by God's light'.   *not engaged*] Not deeply involved; i.e., not ingratiating himself in hopes of becoming an heir.

80. *wot*] Know.

83. *motioned*] Proposed.

84. *make your count*] Count on it.

85. *taking a possession*] Legally, the enjoyment of a thing either by the owner himself or by his proxy.

And in his next fit we may let him go.
'Tis but to pull the pillow from his head,
And he is throttled. 'T had been done before,
But for your scrupulous doubts.

CORVINO   Ay, a plague on't,
My conscience fools my wit. Well, I'll be brief,   90
And so be thou, lest they should be before us.
Go home, prepare him, tell him with what zeal
And willingness I do it. Swear it was
On the first hearing (as thou mayst do truly)
Mine own free motion.   95

MOSCA   Sir, I warrant you,
I'll so possess him with it that the rest
Of his starved clients shall be banished all,
And only you received. But come not, sir,
Until I send, for I have something else
To ripen for your good. – You must not know't.   100

CORVINO   But do not you forget to send now.

MOSCA   Fear not. [*Exit*]

Act 2 scene 7*

CORVINO   Where are you, wife? My Celia? Wife?

[*Enter Celia, crying*]
                                    What, blubbering?
Come, dry those tears. I think thou thought'st me in earnest?
Ha? By this light, I talked so but to try thee.
Methinks the lightness of the occasion
Should ha' confirmed thee. Come, I am not jealous.   5

CELIA   No?

CORVINO   Faith, I am not, I, nor never was.
It is a poor, unprofitable humour.
Do not I know, if women have a will,

90. *fools my wit*] Makes a fool of my common sense.
95. *Mine ... motion*] My voluntary proposition.
96. *possess*] Impress, influence convincingly.
* Given the bargain Corvino has just made with Mosca to prostitute his own wife, the dialogue with Celia here has an unnerving quality, particularly as Corvino denies and defends his jealousy simultaneously, while inviting his wife to display herself attractively.
3. *try*] Test.
5. *confirmed*] Assured.
8. *will*] Sexual appetite.

They'll do 'gainst all the watches o' the world?
And that the fiercest spies are tamed with gold?   10
Tut, I am confident in thee, thou shalt see't.
And see, I'll give thee cause too, to believe it.
Come, kiss me. – Go and make thee ready straight
In all thy best attire, thy choicest jewels,
Put 'em all on, and with 'em thy best looks.   15
We are invited to a solemn feast
At old Volpone's, where it shall appear
How far I am free from jealousy or fear.

[*Exeunt*]

ACT 3

Act 3 scene 1*

[*Enter*] *Mosca*

MOSCA   I fear I shall begin to grow in love
With my dear self and my most prosp'rous parts,
They do so spring and burgeon. I can feel
A whimsy i' my blood. I know not how –
Success hath made me wanton. I could skip   5
Out of my skin now like a subtle snake,
I am so limber. O, your parasite
Is a most precious thing, dropped from above,

9.   They'll take a lover despite all the watchfulness in the world.
16. *solemn feast*] Formal banquet.
*   In *Disc* (Parfitt 1975: pp. 406–7), Jonson comments, 'Though a man be hungry, he
     should not play the parasite': the parasite's effect is like 'honey distilling from a whorish
     voice; which is not praise, but poison'. Those who listen to parasites and believe them
     expect praise even for their vices, and eventually become incapable of distinguishing
     between friend and foe, truth and lies: 'Nay, they will hire fellows to flatter them, with
     suits, and suppers, and to prostitute their judgements'. Similar views appear in Plutarch,
     Moralia I.273–91, and Lucian, *The Parasite*.
          The first two scenes of this act take place in the Piazza; the rest are set in Volpone's
     house.
1–7. Mosca's secret glorying in his own power is sexually equivocal.
2.   *parts*] Talents.
3.   *burgeon*] Thrive; swell or grow larger.
4.   *whimsy*] Capricious humour; giddiness, a sign of lechery.
5.   *wanton*] Reckless, unrestrained by law or ethics.
6.   *subtle*] Physically agile, instinctively cunning; elusive.
8.   *dropped from above*] God-given.

Not bred 'mongst clods and clotpolls here on earth!
I muse the mystery was not made a science,   10
It is so liberally professed! Almost
All the wise world is little else in nature
But parasites or sub-parasites. And yet
I mean not those that have your bare town-art
To know who's fit to feed 'em; have no house,   15
No family, no care, and therefore mould
Tales for men's ears, to bait that sense; or get
Kitchen-invention and some stale receipts
To please the belly and the groin; nor those,
With their court-dog-tricks that can fawn and fleer,   20
Make their revenue out of legs and faces,
Echo my lord, and lick away a moth;
But your fine, elegant rascal that can rise
And stoop, almost together, like an arrow;
Shoot through the air as nimbly as a star;   25
Turn short as doth a swallow; and be here,
And there, and here, and yonder, all at once;
Present to any humour all occasion;

9. *clotpolls*] Blockheads.
10. *mystery*] Skill or craft, taught by apprenticeship rather than formal study. *science*] A branch of knowledge required for a degree in 'liberal arts' (= knowledge worthy of a free man).
11. *liberally*] Freely, but also referring to the well-educated. *professed*] Practised professionally; also, taught.
14. *bare town-art*] The minimal skills of a crude urban flatterer, described at 15–22.
16–17. *mould Tales*] Devise scandal.
17. *bait*] Entice, indulge.
18. *kitchen-invention ... stale receipts*] Common recipes; whore's tricks. A *stale* is a whore; kitchens and kitchen-stuff (grease rendered during cooking, often sold on the side as the cook's perquisite) were associated with pudenda and prostitution; see Ursula, the greasy cook/bawd in *BF*, or the fat kitchen-maid married to Dromio of Ephesus in *Comedy of Errors*.
19. *To ... groin*] as aphrodisiacs.
20. *court-dog-tricks*] Sycophancy of the courtier, as opposed to the cruder 'town-art'. *fleer*] Sneer, or smirk ingratiatingly.
21. *legs and faces*] Bowing and simpering.
22. *lick away a moth*] Behave sycophantically, as in brushing a speck off a patron's coat. A *moth* may be a mote of dust, or any insect-parasite; 'licking' at either suggests repellent physical vulgarity.
25. *star*] A falling star, or meteor.
28. Seem to offer gratification to any temperament or whim.

And change a visor swifter than a thought!
This is the creature had the art born with him;   30
Toils not to learn it, but doth practise it
Out of most excellent nature. And such sparks
Are the true parasites, others but their zanies.

Act 3 scene 2*

[*Enter*] *Bonario*

MOSCA   [*Aside*] Who's this? Bonario? Old Corbaccio's son?
    The person I was bound to seek. [*To him*] Fair sir,
    You are happ'ly met.
BONARIO   That cannot be, by thee.
MOSCA   Why, sir?
BONARIO   Nay, pray thee know thy way and leave me.
    I would be loath to interchange discourse   5
    With such a mate as thou art.
MOSCA   Courteous sir,
    Scorn not my poverty.
BONARIO   Not I, by heaven,
    But thou shalt give me leave to hate thy baseness.
MOSCA   Baseness?
BONARIO   Ay. Answer me, is not thy sloth
    Sufficient argument? Thy flattery?   10
    Thy means of feeding?
MOSCA   Heaven, be good to me.
    These imputations are too common, sir,
    And easily stuck on virtue when she's poor.
    You are unequal to me, and howe'er
    Your sentence may be righteous, yet you are not   15
    That, ere you know me, thus proceed in censure. [*Weeps*]
    St Mark bear witness 'gainst you, 'tis inhuman.
BONARIO   [*Aside*] What? Does he weep? The sign is soft and good!
    I do repent me that I was so harsh.

29. *visor*] Mask; hence, facial expression, or role.
33. *zanies*] Clownish imitators.
*   In a demonstration of his truth as an actor, Mosca weeps, thereby convincing the
    naively idealistic and conventional Bonario of the parasite's integrity.
2. *bound*] On the way.
3. *happ'ly*] By good chance.
6. *mate*] Fellow (term of contempt).
14. *unequal*] Unjust; also, of a higher social standing.
15. *sentence*] Opinion.

MOSCA   'Tis true that, swayed by strong necessity,   20
    I am enforced to eat my careful bread
    With too much obsequy; 'tis true, beside,
    That I am fain to spin mine own poor raiment
    Out of my mere observance, being not born
    To a free fortune. But that I have done   25
    Base offices in rending friends asunder,
    Dividing families, betraying counsels,
    Whispering false lies, or mining men with praises,
    Trained their credulity with perjuries,
    Corrupted chastity, or am in love   30
    With mine own tender ease, but would not rather
    Prove the most rugged and laborious course
    That might redeem my present estimation,
    Let me here perish in all hope of goodness.

BONARIO   [*Aside*] This cannot be a personated passion!   35
    [*To him*] I was to blame so to mistake thy nature.
    Pray thee forgive me, and speak out thy business.

MOSCA   Sir, it concerns you; and though I may seem
    At first to make a main offence in manners
    And in my gratitude unto my master,   40
    Yet for the pure love which I bear all right
    And hatred of the wrong, I must reveal it.
    This very hour, your father is in purpose
    To disinherit you –

BONARIO   How!

MOSCA   – and thrust you forth
    As a mere stranger to his blood. 'Tis true, sir.   45
    The work no way engageth me, but as
    I claim an interest in the general state
    Of goodness and true virtue, which I hear
    T'abound in you and for which mere respect,
    Without a second aim, sir, I have done it.   50

---

21. *careful*] Hard-earned.
22. *obsequy*] Submissiveness.
23–4. *spin ... observance*] Work for my living (literally, clothe myself) as a lowly servant.
28. *mining*] Undermining.
29. *Trained*] Lured, enticed.
32. *Prove*] Undergo as a test.
35. *personated passion*] Impersonated or false emotion.
39. *main*] Very great.
46. *engageth*] Concerns.
49. *for ... respect*] Only for this reason.
50. *Without ... aim*] Without ulterior motive.

BONARIO   This tale hath lost thee much of the late trust
    Thou hadst with me. It is impossible.
    I know not how to lend it any thought,
    My father should be so unnatural.
MOSCA   It is a confidence that well becomes   55
    Your piety, and formed (no doubt) it is
    From your own simple innocence, which makes
    Your wrong more monstrous and abhorred. But, sir,
    I now will tell you more. This very minute,
    It is, or will be, doing. And, if you   60
    Shall be but pleased to go with me, I'll bring you –
    I dare not say where you shall see, but – where
    Your ear shall be a witness of the deed:
    Hear yourself written bastard and professed
    The common issue of the earth.   65
BONARIO   I'm mazed!
MOSCA   Sir, if I do it not, draw your just sword
    And score your vengeance on my front and face.
    Mark me your villain. You have too much wrong,
    And I do suffer for you, sir. My heart
    Weeps blood in anguish –   70
BONARIO   Lead. I follow thee.

    [*Exeunt*]

Act 3 scene 3*

[*Enter*] Volpone [*with*] Nano, Androgyno [*and*] Castrone

VOLPONE   Mosca stays long, methinks. Bring forth your sports
    And help to make the wretched time more sweet.
NANO   *Dwarf, fool, and eunuch, well met here we be.*

---

56.   *piety*] Filial love (Latin, *pietas*).
65.   *common ... earth*] Of obscure or unknown parentage (Latin, *terrae filius*). *mazed*]
    Bewildered, confused.
67.   *score*] Mark, incise. *front*] Forehead. Bonario does inflict such a wound later; see
    3.8.
*   In the second freak-show, the competition among the three freaks farcically parallels the
    rivalry among the three legacy-hunters. Costume might enhance the correspondence
    between the two groups: Nano, for example, might wear a lawyer's 'biggin', or cap,
    Castrone might carry an ear-horn, a cane, and a large handkerchief to mimic
    Corbaccio's many infirmities, and Androgyno might carry a little effigy of Celia instead
    of a fool's bauble.

> A question it were now whether of us three,
>> Being all the known delicates of a rich man, 5
>> In pleasing him claim the precedency can?

CASTRONE   *I claim for myself.*

ANDROGYNO   *And so doth the fool.*

NANO   'Tis foolish indeed. Let me set you both to school.
> First, for your dwarf, he's little and witty,
>> And everything, as it is little, is pretty; 10
> Else why do men say to a creature of my shape,
>> So soon as they see him, 'It's a pretty little ape'?
> And why a pretty ape? But for pleasing imitation
>> Of greater men's action in a ridiculous fashion.
> Beside, this feat body of mine doth not crave 15
>> Half the meat, drink, and cloth one of your bulks will have.
> Admit your fool's face be the mother of laughter,
>> Yet, for his brain, it must always come after;
> And though that do feed him, it's a pitiful case
>> His body is beholding to such a bad face. 20

One knocks

VOLPONE   Who's there? My couch – Away! Look, Nano, see!
> Give me my caps first – Go, enquire.

[Exeunt Nano, Androgyno, and Castrone]

[Volpone gets into bed]

                                        Now Cupid
Send it be Mosca, and with fair return.

[Enter Nano]

NANO   It is the beauteous madam –

VOLPONE   Would-be – is it?

4. *whether*] Which.

5. *known delicates*] Acknowledged darlings or pets.

15. *Beside*] Besides. *[feat*] Dainty.

18. *come after*] Be less important or useful.

19. *that*] Laughter (see 17). *feed him*] Earn his keep.

20. *beholding*] Indebted.

22. *caps*] Unfashionable relics of the sixteenth century, usually worn indoors by old men. One style covered hair and ears, buttoning under the chin; another was a skull-cap with ear-flaps.

23. *return*] Reply; in law, the sheriff's report on how far he has been able to carry out the court's instructions.

NANO   The same.   25
VOLPONE   Now torment on me! Squire her in,
    For she will enter or dwell here forever.
    Nay, quickly, that my fit were past!

    [*Exit Nano*]

                                                I fear
    A second hell too, that my loathing this
    Will quite expel my appetite to the other.
    Would she were taking now her tedious leave.   30
    Lord, how it threats me, what I am to suffer!

    Act 3 scene 4*

    [*Enter*] Nano [*with*] Lady Would-be

LADY WOULD-BE   I thank you, good sir. Pray you signify
    Unto your patron I am here. – This band
    Shows not my neck enough. [*To Nano*] I trouble you, sir;
    Let me request you bid one of my women
    Come hither to me. [*Exit Nano*] In good faith, I am dressed   5
    Most favourably today. [*Adjusts curls*] It is no matter.

25. *Squire*] Escort. Presumably three hours have passed since Lady Would-be's last attempt
    to visit (see 1.5.98).
28. *hell*] Pudenda.
29. *appetite*] Sexual desire. *the other*] Celia.
*   Lady Would-be lives up to the earlier description of her as a lady visiting Venice to
    acquire the latest 'intelligence / Of tires, and fashions, and behaviour / Among the
    courtesans' (2.1.26–9). Like the courtesans, she wears a low-cut gown that reveals her
    breasts, thickly covered in make-up, as is her face, with her hair bleached and tightly
    curled. Venetian courtesans were famed not only for their beauty, but also for their
    sophisticated and learned 'discourse'; Lady Would-be attempts to emulate them with
    her inane chatter about the arts and medicine. Most significantly, she imitates their
    practice of offering sex in return for money, as her vamping in this scene suggests. See
    also her attempts on Mosca (4.6.69–101, 5.3.40–43) and Peregrine (4.3.16).
2. *band*] Neckband or collar, made of fine linen. The fashionable lady's band was large,
    open in the front, and held erect by a wired or starched support called a *rebato*.
3. *neck*] Referred to throat and breasts. Italian gentlewomen wore a low décolletage
    below an open collar. *sir*] Lady Would-be seems taken with Nano, addressing him
    more politely than the 'sirrah' (= fellow) commonly used for underlings, and wording
    her request as to an equal. See also 3.5.29.
6. *favourably*] Attractively (spoken sarcastically, given the complaints that follow).
    It is no matter] Lady Would-be's tag-expression, indicating her annoyance. See 37.

'Tis well enough.

[*Enter Woman 1 with Nano*]

                    Look, see – these petulant things,
How they have done this!
VOLPONE [*Aside*]   I do feel the fever
Ent'ring in at mine ears. O, for a charm
To fright it hence.   10
LADY WOULD-BE [*To Woman 1*] Come nearer. Is this curl
In his right place? Or this? Why is this higher
Than all the rest? You ha' not washed your eyes yet?
Or do they not stand even i'your head?
Where's your fellow? Call her.

[*Exit Woman 1*]

NANO [*Aside*]   Now, St Mark
Deliver us! Anon she'll beat her women   15
Because her nose is red.

[*Re-enter Woman 1 with Woman 2*]

LADY WOULD-BE   I pray you, view
This tire, forsooth. Are all things apt, or no?
WOMAN 2 One hair a little, here, sticks out, forsooth.
LADY WOULD-BE Does't so, forsooth? [*To Woman 1*] And where
    was your dear sight
When it did so, forsooth? What now? Bird-eyed?   20
[*To Woman 2*] And you too? Pray you both approach and mend it.

[*They fuss over her*]

Now, by that light, I muse you're not ashamed!

---

7. *petulant things*] Referring either to her women as insolent or saucy, or to her curls as
irritatingly unflattering.

10–12. *Is ... rest?*] The latest Venetian hair-style called for the hair to be dyed pale blonde,
the front and sides cut and curled with a curling iron into 'two frisled peaks standing
up like pretty pyramids' above the forehead (Coryat 1611; rpt 1905: p. 404), sometimes
held in place and framed by a wired head-dress shaped like a ram's horns. The back hair
was twisted up and pinned into a net or caul.

13. *even*] Balanced, in focus.

17. *tire*] Head-dress.

19, 20. *forsooth*] Sarcastic repetitions of Woman 2's insipid oath.

20. *Bird-eyed*] Beady with fear, like the eyes of a bird under attack.

I, that have preached these things so oft unto you,
Read you the principles, argued all the grounds,
Disputed every fitness, every grace,   25
Called you to counsel of so frequent dressings –
NANO   [*Aside*] More carefully than of your fame or honour.
LADY WOULD-BE   – Made you acquainted what an ample dowry
The knowledge of these things would be unto you,
Able alone to get you noble husbands   30
At your return; and you thus to neglect it?
Besides, you seeing what a curious nation
Th'Italians are, what will they say of me?
'The English lady cannot dress herself.'
Here's a fine imputation to our country!   35
Well, go your ways, and stay i'the next room.
This fucus was too coarse too. It's no matter.
[*To Nano*] Good sir, you'll give 'em entertainment?

[*Exit Nano with Women*]

VOLPONE   [*Aside*] The storm comes toward me.
LADY WOULD-BE   How does my Volp?
VOLPONE   Troubled with noise, I cannot sleep. I dreamt   40
That a strange fury entered now my house,
And with the dreadful tempest of her breath
Did cleave my roof asunder.
LADY WOULD-BE   Believe me, and I
Had the most fearful dream, could I remember 't –
VOLPONE   [*Aside*] Out on my fate! I ha' giv'n her the occasion   45
How to torment me: she will tell me hers.
LADY WOULD-BE   Methought the golden mediocrity,
Polite and delicate –
VOLPONE   O, if you do love me,
No more. I sweat and suffer at the mention

23–6. Lady Would-be scolds her women with formal rhetoric, more like a tutor than a
mistress.
27. *fame*] Reputation.
31. *return*] To England.
32. *curious*] Fastidious, carefully observant.
37. *fucus*] Make-up; the fashion was for pale skin, achieved with *cerussa* or white lead
skin-tint, *purpurissum*, a dark rouge, and *stibium*, or black antimony, to outline lids
and brows.
39. *Volp*] The cosy diminutive suggests an intimacy that Volpone's asides deny, but is
typical of Lady Would-be's brazen familiarity of manner.
41. *fury*] A dreadful hag from hell, sent to avenge and punish.
47. *golden mediocrity*] Travesty of Horace's 'golden mean'.

Of any dream. Feel how I tremble yet.   50
LADY WOULD-BE   [*Stroking him*] Alas, good soul! The passion
    of the heart.
    Seed-pearl were good now, boiled with syrup of apples,
    Tincture of gold, and coral, citron-pills,
    Your elecampane root, myrobalans –
VOLPONE   [*Aside*] Ay me, I have ta'en a grasshopper by the wing.   55
LADY WOULD-BE   – Burnt silk, and amber. You have muscadel
    Good i' the house –
VOLPONE   You will not drink and part?
LADY WOULD-BE   No, fear not that. I doubt we shall not get
    Some English saffron (half a dram would serve),
    Your sixteen cloves, a little musk, dried mints,   60
    Bugloss, and barley-meal –

51. *passion of the heart*] Heartburn (cardiac passion), or possibly palpitations. Lady Would-be's prescription (52–65) is an absurd compound of knowledge and ignorance.

52. *Seed-pearl*] Prepared in a cordial to stimulate the heart. *syrup of apples*] For heart and stomach ailments, especially palpitations; mixed in wine, it tempered melancholy (Lovell).

53. *tincture of gold*] Aurum potabile; see 1.4.73n. *coral*] Coralline, a moss used in pharmacoepia: 'the Arabian physicians use *moss* in their cardiac medicines' (Gerard). *citron-pills*] Made from the pome-citron, and considered 'good for vitality' in comforting and strengthening the heart; more frequently an ingredient in ointments to reduce facial blemishes (Lovell).

54. *elecampane*] Horse-heal, a plant with bitter aromatic leaves and root used as a tonic and stimulant. *myrobalans*] Astringent plum-like fruit whose distilled juices were thought to cure syphilitic and haemorrhoidal swellings (Lovell), but also were used in tonics to strengthen the heart (Gerard).

55. In mentioning his symptoms, he has inadvertently prompted Lady Would-be to do something she is quite eager to do without prompting – that is, prescribe medications. The grasshopper needs no assistance in high jumping.

56. *Burnt silk*] Dissolved in water as a cure for smallpox. *amber*] Perhaps ambergris, used to disguise the scent of medications. Oil of amber mixed in muscadel was thought to alleviate symptoms of gonorrhoea, known as Gomory or Gonor passion, which Lady Would-be perhaps confuses with cardiac passion. *muscadel*] A strong sweet wine.

59. *English saffron*] Grown at Saffron Walden, Essex, for use in medicine and cooking. Saffron was thought to strengthen the heart and chest, especially in poultices for palpitations (Lovell).

60. *cloves*] From the clove-gillyflower, used in cordials for the heart (Gerard). *musk*] A reddish-brown substance secreted by musk deer and used as a stimulant and anti-spasmodic. Gerard claims it 'comforts the heart, exhilarateth, helpeth the passions of the heart ... and causeth venery' (see 115 below and note). *mint*] A general strengthener, relieving 'choleric passion' or biliousness.

61. *bugloss*] A species of borage, used as a heart stimulant. Its syrup was considered

VOLPONE   [*Aside*]   She's in again.
    Before I feigned diseases; now I have one.
LADY WOULD-BE   – And these applied with a right scarlet cloth –
VOLPONE   [*Aside*] Another flood of words! A very torrent!
LADY WOULD-BE   Shall I, sir, make you a poultice?   65
VOLPONE   No, no, no!
    I'm very well. You need prescribe no more.
LADY WOULD-BE   I have a little studied physic, but now
    I'm all for music, save i' the fore-noons
    An hour or two for painting. I would have
    A lady indeed t'have all letters and arts,   70
    Be able to discourse, to write, to paint,
    But principal, as Plato holds, your music
    (And so does wise Pythagoras, I take it)
    Is your true rapture, when there is concent
    In face, in voice, and clothes, and is indeed ·   75
    Our sex's chiefest ornament.
VOLPONE   The poet
    As old in time as Plato and as knowing
    Says that your highest female grace is silence.
LADY WOULD-BE   Which o' your poets? Petrarch? Or Tasso?
    Or Dante?

effective for cardiac passion (Lovell). *barley-meal*] To thicken the preparation into a salve for spreading on a bandage; used generally for pains and swellings.

63. *scarlet cloth*] Bandages of red cloth were used for applying poultices to cure heartburn and smallpox pustules.

67–112. Lady Would-be emulates the broadly cultured gentlewomen of Castiglione's *The Courtier*. See 4.2.35 and note.

69. *painting*] Venice in 1605 was no longer the centre of the art world. Titian, Veronese, and Tintoretto were dead, and no masters replaced them until the late eighteenth century. In painting, as in everything else, Lady Would-be cannot distinguish between a cheap imitation and the real thing.

72–6. *Plato ... ornament*] Plato, in *The Republic*, argued that music shapes the soul, just as gymnastics shapes the body, but for him music included rhetoric and poetry. Harmony, or *concent*, far from the superficial feminine virtues Lady Would-be praises, was the complementary balance between a man's physical energy and his educated soul, moderating his brute strength through ideals of courage and non-violent persuasiveness. For Pythagoras's views on music, see notes at 1.2.6 and 27.

76. *The poet*] Sophocles, Euripides, and Homer have all had the remark attributed to them.

79. *Petrarch*] Francisco Petrarca, 1304–74, scholar, poet, and humanist, whose sonnet sequence to Laura began the Renaissance flowering of lyric poetry. *Tasso*] Torquato Tasso, 1544–95, whose epic poem *Gerusalemme Liberata* (1581) is based on the First Crusade. *Dante*] The greatest poet of the Renaissance, Dante Alighieri, 1265–1321,

Guarini? Ariosto? Aretine?   80
    Cieco di Hadria? I have read them all.
VOLPONE   [*Aside*] Is everything a cause to my destruction?
LADY WOULD-BE   [*Searching*] I think I ha' two or three of 'em
    about me.
VOLPONE   [*Aside*] The sun, the sea will sooner both stand still
    Than her eternal tongue! Nothing can scape it.   85
LADY WOULD-BE   [*Finding a book*] Here's *Pastor Fido* –
VOLPONE   [*Aside*]   Profess obstinate silence,
    That's now my safest.
LADY WOULD-BE   All our English writers,
    I mean such as are happy in th'Italian,
    Will deign to steal out of this author mainly,
    Almost as much as from Montaigne.   90
    He has so modern and facile a vein,
    Fitting the time and catching the court-ear.
    Your Petrarch is more passionate; yet he,
    In days of sonneting, trusted 'em with much.
    Dante is hard, and few can understand him.   95
    But for a desperate wit there's Aretine!
    Only his pictures are a little obscene –
    You mark me not?
VOLPONE   Alas, my mind's perturbed.

whose *Divine Comedy* is a landmark in world literature and the first major work
written in the vernacular.
80. *Guarini*] Giovanni Battista Guarini, 1537–1612, author of the widely influential
    pastoral, *Il Pastor Fido* (1590). *Ariosto*] Ludovico Ariosto, 1474–1533, author of
    the epic *Orlando Furioso*, considered the perfect expression of the art and spirit of the
    Italian Renaissance. *Aretine*] Pietro Aretino, 1492–1556, satirist, notorious for his
    pornographic sonnet sequence *Sonnetti Lussuriosi* (1523), which provided commentary
    on sixteen obscene drawings by Giulio Romano; see 96–7 below.
81. *Cieco di Hadria*] 'The blind man of Adria', Luigi Groto, 1541–85; a translator,
    playwright, and actor, but an obscure figure compared to the other poets in this list.
88. *happy ... Italian*] Lucky enough to speak Italian.
90. *Montaigne*] Michel Eyquem de Montaigne, 1533–92, the sceptical humanist whose
    Essais were translated by Florio in 1603. *Q*'s spelling, *Montagniè*, suggests a four-
    syllable pronunciation; *F*'s MONTAGNIE suggests only three, but printers usually
    omitted accents over capital letters.
91. *facile*] Fluent.
94. *trusted*] Entrusted; i.e., left them a considerable literary inheritance.
95. A variation on Florio's remark in the dedication to *A World of Words* (1598): '*Boccace*
    is pretty hard, yet understood: *Petrarch* harder, but explained: *Dante* hardest, but
    commented.'
96. *desperate*] Outrageous.

LADY WOULD-BE   Why, in such cases we must cure ourselves,
   Make use of our philosophy –   100
VOLPONE   *Ohimè*.
LADY WOULD-BE   – And, as we find our passions do rebel,
   Encounter 'em with reason, or divert 'em
   By giving scope unto some other humour
   Of lesser danger, as in politic bodies
   There's nothing more doth overwhelm the judgment   105
   And clouds the understanding than too much
   Settling, and fixing, and (as't were) subsiding
   Upon one object. For the incorporating
   Of these same outward things into that part
   Which we call mental leaves some certain faeces   110
   That stop the organs and, as Plato says,
   Assassinates our knowledge.
VOLPONE   Now the spirit
   Of patience help me!
LADY WOULD-BE   Come, in faith, I must
   Visit you more a-days, and make you well.
   Laugh and be lusty.   115
VOLPONE   My good angel save me!
LADY WOULD-BE   There was but one sole man in all the world
   With whom I ere could sympathise; and he
   Would lie you often three, four hours together
   To hear me speak; and be, sometime, so rapt
   As he would answer me quite from the purpose,   120
   Like you, and you are like him, just. I'll discourse
   (And 't be but only, sir, to bring you asleep)
   How we did spend our time and loves together
   For some six years.
VOLPONE   [*Groaning*] O, O, O, O, O, O!
LADY WOULD-BE   For we were *coaetanei*, and brought up –   125
VOLPONE   Some power, some fate, some fortune rescue me!

100. *Ohimè*] Italian for 'Alas'.
101. *passions*] Strong feelings aroused by fluctuating humours.
107. *Settling … fixing … subsiding*] Alchemical terms, referring to the separation (settling, subsiding) of sediment from the liquid, which then congeals (fixes).
110. *faeces*] Dregs.
111. *Plato*] Mere name-dropping.
115. *lusty*] Vigorously healthy; also, lustful, an innuendo that explains Volpone's fearful response.
118. *you*] Ethical dative, used for emphasis.
119. *rapt*] Entranced; emotionally carried away.
125. *coaetanei*] Of the same age (Latin).

Act 3 scene 5

[*Enter*] *Mosca*

MOSCA   God save you, madam.
LADY WOULD-BE   Good sir.
VOLPONE   Mosca? Welcome!
   Welcome to my redemption.
MOSCA   Why, sir?
VOLPONE   [*Aside to Mosca*]   O,
   Rid me of this my torture quickly: there,
   My madam with the everlasting voice.
   The bells in time of pestilence ne'er made   5
   Like noise, or were in that perpetual motion.
   The cock-pit comes not near it. All my house
   But now steamed like a bath with her thick breath.
   A lawyer could not have been heard, nor scarce
   Another woman, such a hail of words   10
   She has let fall. For hell's sake, rid her hence.
MOSCA   Has she presented?
VOLPONE   O, I do not care.
   I'll take her absence upon any price,
   With any loss.
MOSCA   [*To Lady Would-be*] Madam –
LADY WOULD-BE   I ha' brought your patron
   A toy, a cap here, of mine own work –   15
MOSCA   'Tis well.
   I had forgot to tell you, I saw your knight
   Where you'd little think it –
LADY WOULD-BE   Where?
MOSCA   Marry,
   Where yet, if you make haste, you may apprehend him,
   Rowing upon the water in a gondole
   With the most cunning courtesan of Venice.   20
LADY WOULD-BE   Is't true?

5–6. Church bells tolled for the dead almost continuously during periods of plague, as in
   1603.
7. *cock-pit*] Noise of cock-fights, a fashionable sport in London.
10. *woman*] Volubility was considered a woman's vice, just as silence was considered a
   woman's chief virtue (see 3.4.78).
12. *presented*] Given a gift.
14. *toy*] Trifle. *cap*] An outmoded gift. See 3.3.22n. *work*] Embroidery.
20. *gondole*] Common form during the seventeenth century (and here required by the
   scansion), when about 10,000 gondolas were in use, 4,000 as water-taxis. The chief

MOSCA   Pursue 'em, and believe your eyes.
    Leave me to make your gift.

    [*Exit Lady Would-be*]

                                    I knew 't would take.
    For lightly they that use themselves most licence
    Are still most jealous.
VOLPONE   Mosca, hearty thanks
    For thy quick fiction and delivery of me.   25
    Now, to my hopes, what sayst thou?

    [*Re-enter Lady Would-be*]

LADY WOULD-BE   But do you hear, sir? –
VOLPONE [*Aside*] Again! I fear a paroxysm.
LADY WOULD-BE   – Which way
    Rowed they together?
MOSCA   Toward the Rialto.
LADY WOULD-BE   I pray you, lend me your dwarf.
MOSCA   I pray you, take him.

    [*Exit Lady Would-be*]

    Your hopes, sir, are like happy blossoms, fair,   30
    And promise timely fruit, if you will stay
    But the maturing. Keep you at your couch.
    Corbaccio will arrive straight with the will.
    When he is gone, I'll tell you more. [*Exit*]
VOLPONE [*Bouncing up in the bed*] My blood,
    My spirits are returned. I am alive,   35
    And, like your wanton gamester at primero

transport of Venice since at least 697, it had been standardised in design, dimension, and colour (black) since 1562.
23. *lightly*] Often, commonly. *licence*] Personal freedom, here implying lack of sexual restraint.
24. *still*] Always.
26. *hopes*] Of an affair with Celia.
28. *Rialto*] Commercial centre of Venice; more specifically here, the Rialto Bridge, the only bridge across the Grand Canal, rebuilt of stone in 1588 after the wooden one collapsed in 1444. It was lined with rows of little shops, and several staircases led to two terraces at its top central point commanding impressive views.
34–5. *blood...spirits*] Equivocal references to sexual vigour.
36. *wanton gamester*] Equivocal, suggesting both 'reckless gambler' and 'incontinent lecher'. *primero*] Card-game similar to poker.

Whose thought had whispered to him, 'Not go less',
Methinks I lie and draw – for an encounter.

[*Volpone lies down and draws the bed-curtains*]

Act 3 scene 6

[*Enter*] *Mosca* [*with*] *Bonario* [*and shows him a hiding place*]

MOSCA   Sir, here concealed, you may hear all. But pray you
Have patience, sir.
   One knocks
                The same's your father knocks.
   I am compelled to leave you.
BONARIO   Do so.

   [*Exit Mosca*]
                          Yet

Cannot my thought imagine this a truth.   [*He hides*]

Act 3 scene 7*

[*Enter*] *Mosca* [*with*] *Corvino, Celia* [*trailing behind them*]

MOSCA   Death on me! You are come too soon. What meant you?
   Did not I say I would send?
CORVINO   Yes, but I feared
   You might forget it, and then they prevent us.
MOSCA   [*Aside*] Prevent? Did ere man haste so for his horns?
   A courtier would not ply it so for a place.   5
   [*To Corvino*] Well, now there's no helping it, stay here.
   I'll presently return. [*Goes to Bonario, still hidden*]
CORVINO   [*Looking back*] Where are you, Celia?

37. '*Not go less*'] In primero, match or top the highest wager.
38. *lie ... draw ... encounter*] Sexually allusive primero terms. 'Lie' means to place the bet;
    'draw', to take a card from the pack after bets are laid; and 'encounter', to match cards
    for a winning suit. Volpone may also use 'draw' as a cue to close the bed-curtains.
*   The black comedy of this 'seduction' scene relies on farcical contrasts: Volpone as the
    pathetically weak old man transformed into a robust lover ready to re-enact the virility
    of his youth, only to be deflated by the backfiring of his own ludicrous desires; the
    physically luscious Celia repelled by sexual advances and pornographically willing to
    destroy her own beauty; and Bonario, the dashing rescuer, revealed as melodramatically
    priggish.
3. *prevent*] Thwart, by arriving first.
4. *horns*] Sign of the cuckold.
5. *place*] Official position at court.

You know not wherefore I have brought you hither?
CELIA   Not well, except you told me.
CORVINO   Now I will.
    Hark hither. [*They talk privately*]   10
MOSCA   *To Bonario* Sir, your father hath sent word
    It will be half an hour ere he come,
    And therefore, if you please to walk the while
    Into that gallery – at the upper end
    There are some books to entertain the time;
    And I'll take care no man shall come unto you, sir.   15
BONARIO   Yes, I will stay there. [*Aside*] I do doubt this fellow. [*Exit*]
MOSCA   There, he is far enough. He can hear nothing.
    And for his father, I can keep him off.

[*Mosca opens the bed-curtains and confers with Volpone, while
Celia rejects Corvino's urgings*]

CORVINO   Nay, now, there is no starting back, and therefore
    Resolve upon it: I have so decreed.   20
    It must be done. Nor would I move't afore,
    Because I would avoid all shifts and tricks
    That might deny me.
CELIA   Sir, let me beseech you,
    Affect not these strange trials. If you doubt
    My chastity, why, lock me up forever.   25
    Make me the heir of darkness. Let me live
    Where I may please your fears, if not your trust.
CORVINO   Believe it, I have no such humour, I.
    All that I speak, I mean; yet I am not mad,
    Not horn-mad, see you? Go to, show yourself   30
    Obedient and a wife.
CELIA   O heaven!
CORVINO   I say it,

9. *except*] Except what.
13–14. Suggests that Bonario moves from his hiding-place on the main stage (behind the
    traverse curtain used later by Volpone in 5.3?) to the upper stage, and occupies himself
    with books as stage-business, waiting for his cue to re-enter at 265.1. See 1.2.87n.
21. *move*] Propose.
24. *Affect not*] Do not insist on or seek to obtain; perhaps, do not contrive (suggested by
    2.7.3). *strange trials*] Extraordinary tests (of her chastity).
30. *horn-mad*] Enraged at being cuckolded, either in fact or in anticipation.

Do so.

CELIA   Was this the train?

CORVINO   I've told you reasons:
What the physicians have set down; how much
It may concern me; what my engagements are;
My means; and the necessity of those means   35
For my recovery. Wherefore, if you be
Loyal and mine, be won, respect my venture.

CELIA   Before your honour?

CORVINO   Honour? Tut, a breath.
There's no such thing in nature: a mere term
Invented to awe fools. What, is my gold   40
The worse for touching? Clothes, for being looked on?
Why, this's no more. An old decrepit wretch
That has no sense, no sinew; takes his meat
With others' fingers; only knows to gape
When you do scald his gums; a voice; a shadow;   45
And what can this man hurt you?

CELIA   Lord! What spirit
Is this hath entered him?

CORVINO   And for your fame,
That's such a jig! As if I would go tell it,
Cry it on the Piazza! Who shall know it?
But he that cannot speak it, and this fellow   50
Whose lips are i' my pocket, save yourself.
If you'll proclaim 't, you may. I know no other
Should come to know it.

CELIA   Are heaven and saints then nothing?
Will they be blind or stupid?

CORVINO   How?

CELIA   Good sir,

---

32. *train*] Trick, trap.
34. *engagements*] Commitments, meaning either gifts Corvino has given to Volpone or more general financial obligations in Venice.
35. *means*] Steps taken in pursuing a course of action.
36. *recovery*] In law, the procedure of gaining possession of some property through a court judgment, here presumably probate.
38–40. A sentiment made famous by Falstaff, *1 Henry IV* 5.1.129–40, and frequently expressed by Iago in *Othello*, as at 1.3.319ff., 2.3.260ff., and 3.3.159ff.
43. *sense*] Sensory capability.
48. *jig*] Farce, laughable excuse.
49. *Cry*] Advertise, like a street-hawker.
50. That is, Volpone and Mosca.
51. *Whose lips ... pocket*] Whose silence I have bought. *save*] Except.

Be jealous still, emulate them, and think   55
What hate they burn with toward every sin.
CORVINO   I grant you, if I thought it were a sin,
I would not urge you. Should I offer this
To some young Frenchman or hot Tuscan blood
That had read Aretine, conned all his prints,   60
Knew every quirk within lust's labyrinth,
And were professed critic in lechery,
And I would look upon him and applaud him,
This were a sin. But here 'tis contrary:
A pious work, mere charity for physic,   65
And honest polity to assure mine own.
CELIA   O heaven! Canst thou suffer such a change?
VOLPONE   [*Aside to Mosca*] Thou art mine honour, Mosca, and
    my pride,
My joy, my tickling, my delight! Go, bring 'em!
MOSCA   [*Conducting Corvino*] Please you draw near, sir.   70
CORVINO   [*To Celia, who resists*]   Come on, what –
You will not be rebellious? By that light –

[*Corvino forces her to the bedside*]

MOSCA   [*To Volpone*] Sir, Signor Corvino here is come to see you –
VOLPONE   [*Moaning*] O!
MOSCA   – and, hearing of the consultation had
So lately for your health, is come to offer,
Or rather, sir, to prostitute –   75
CORVINO   Thanks, sweet Mosca.
MOSCA   – Freely, unasked, or unentreated –
CORVINO   Well.
MOSCA   – As the true, fervent instance of his love,
His own most fair and proper wife, the beauty
Only of price in Venice –
CORVINO   'Tis well urged.
MOSCA   – To be your comfortress and to preserve you.   80

60. *prints*] Obscene drawings. See 3.4.80n.
62. *critic*] Connoisseur; skilled judge of the merits of an art.
65–6. *charity ... polity*] Charitable cure, and honourable conduct.
75. *prostitute*] Offer selflessly, as an act of devotion; but with an ironic play on the cruder
    meaning.
78. *proper*] Beautiful, respectable, but also punning ironically on the legal sense of
    'belonging exclusively to him'.
79. *Only of price*] Of unsurpassed merit, unique.

VOLPONE   Alas, I am past already! Pray you, thank him
  For his good care and promptness, but, for that,
  'Tis a vain labour, e'en to fight 'gainst heaven,
  Applying fire to a stone – [*Coughs*] Uh! uh! uh! uh!
  Making a dead leaf grow again. I take   85
  His wishes gently, though, and you may tell him
  What I've done for him. Marry, my state is hopeless!
  Will him to pray for me, and t'use his fortune
  With reverence when he comes to't.
MOSCA   [*To Corvino*]   Do you hear, sir?
  Go to him with your wife.   90
CORVINO   Heart of my father!
  Wilt thou persist thus? Come, I pray thee, come.
  Thou seest 'tis nothing. Celia! By this hand,
  I shall grow violent. Come, do't, I say!
CELIA   Sir, kill me, rather. I will take down poison,
  Eat burning coals, do anything –   95
CORVINO   Be damned.
  Heart! I will drag thee hence home by the hair,
  Cry thee a strumpet through the streets; rip up
  Thy mouth unto thine ears; and slit thy nose
  Like a raw rotchet – Do not tempt me! Come,   100
  Yield! I am loath – Death! I will buy some slave
  Whom I will kill, and bind thee to him alive,
  And at my window hang you forth, devising
  Some monstrous crime which I, in capital letters,
  Will eat into thy flesh with aquafortis   105
  And burning cor'sives on this stubborn breast.
  Now, by the blood thou hast incensed, I'll do't!
CELIA   Sir, what you please, you may. I am your martyr.
CORVINO   Be not thus obstinate. I ha' not deserved it.
  Think who it is entreats you. Pray thee, sweet!
  Good faith, thou shalt have jewels, gowns, attires, 110
  What thou wilt think and ask. Do but go kiss him.
  Or touch him, but. For my sake. At my suit.
  This once. No? Not? I shall remember this.

81. *past*] Past curing.
95. *eat burning coals*] Like Brutus's wife, Portia.
99. *rotchet*] Rochet, from the French 'rouget', a local name for a fish now called red gurnard, for its colour.
101. *some slave*] Tarquin's threat to Lucrece in Shakespeare's *The Rape of Lucrece*, 515 and 671.
105. *aquafortis*] Nitric acid, used for etching.
106. *cor'sives*] Corrosives.

Will you disgrace me thus? D'you thirst my undoing?

MOSCA　Nay, gentle lady, be advised.　　　　　　　　　　　　　115

CORVINO　　　　　　　　　　　　No, no!
She has watched her time. God's precious, this is scurvy!
'Tis very scurvy! And you are –

MOSCA　　　　　　　　　　Nay, good sir.

CORVINO　　– An errant locust, by heaven, a locust! Whore!
Crocodile, that hast thy tears prepared,
Expecting how thou'lt bid 'em flow!　　　　　　　　　　　120

MOSCA　　　　　　　　　　　　Nay, pray you, sir,
She will consider.

CELIA　　　　　　　　Would my life would serve
To satisfy.

CORVINO　　　'Sdeath! If she would but speak to him
And save my reputation, 'twere somewhat –
But spitefully to affect my utter ruin!

MOSCA　Ay, now you've put your fortune in her hands.　　　125
Why, i'faith, it is her modesty: I must quit her.
If you were absent, she would be more coming.
I know it, and dare undertake for her.
What woman can, before her husband? Pray you,
Let us depart and leave her here.　　　　　　　　　　　130

CORVINO　　　　　　　　　　Sweet Celia,
Thou mayst redeem all yet. I'll say no more.
If not, esteem yourself as lost. – Nay, stay there.

[*Exeunt Corvino and Mosca*]

CELIA　O God and his good angels! Whither, whither
Is shame fled human breasts, that with such ease
Men dare put off your honours and their own?　　　　　135
Is that which ever was a cause of life
Now placed beneath the basest circumstance,
And modesty an exile made, for money?

116. *watched her time*] Waited for the opportunity to ruin me.　*God's precious*] 'Blood' is
　　understood.　*scurvy*] Shabby or contemptible.
118. *errant*] Straying, erring; punning on 'arrant', flagrant.　*locust*] Corvino sees Celia as
　　a wanton destroyer of his estate, like the biblical plague of locusts.
120. *Expecting*] Waiting to see.
126. *quit*] Acquit.
127. *coming*] Forthcoming.
136. *that . . . life*] That is, the sexual act.

[Volpone] leaps off from his couch

VOLPONE   Ay, in Corvino and such earth-fed minds
   That never tasted the true heav'n of love.   140
   Assure thee, Celia, he that would sell thee
   Only for hope of gain, and that uncertain,
   He would have sold his part of paradise
   For ready money, had he met a copeman.
   Why, art thou mazed to see me thus revived?   145
   Rather applaud thy beauty's miracle.
   'Tis thy great work that hath, not now alone,
   But sundry times raised me in several shapes,
   And but this morning like a mountebank
   To see thee at thy window. Ay, before   150
   I would have left my practice for thy love,
   In varying figures I would have contended
   With the blue Proteus or the hornèd flood.
   Now art thou welcome. *[Tries to embrace her]*
CELIA   Sir!
VOLPONE   Nay, fly me not.
   Nor let thy false imagination   155
   That I was bed-rid make thee think I am so.
   Thou shalt not find it. I am now as fresh,
   As hot, as high, and in as jovial plight
   As when – in that so celebrated scene
   At recitation of our comedy   160
   For entertainment of the great Valois –
   I acted young Antinous, and attracted

144. *copeman*] Dealer, tradesman.
147–8. Volpone's statement is a lie punning on a truth. He claims to have disguised himself on several occasions merely to view her beauty, but in fact saw her first only that morning. The innuendo is that the thought of her beauty has often aroused him sexually ('raised . . . shapes'), as at 1.5.106ff., 2.4.1–28, 3.3.29 and 3.5.26, 30–38.
151. *practice*] Struggling, with the suggestion of 'scheming'.
152. *figures*] Disguises.
153. *Proteus*] The sea-god who could change into any shape. *hornèd flood*] Achelous, the river-god, transformed himself into a bull, a serpent, and an ox-headed man when he fought Hercules for the hand of Deianeira. River-gods were depicted as vigorous men with horns, symbols of their strength.
158. *jovial*] Like Jove (Jupiter) in being a prodigious lover.
161. *Valois*] In 1574, the Doge and senators of Venice entertained Henry of Valois, Duke of Anjou and King of Poland, who was returning to France to be crowned Henry III.
162. *Antinous*] Possibly the beautiful boy who was Emperor Hadrian's catamite, but this figure does not seem likely to attract women; more likely the handsome Antinous who

The eyes and ears of all the ladies present
T'admire each graceful gesture, note, and footing.

[*He sings*]

song

> Come, my Celia, let us prove,   165
> While we can, the sports of love.
> Time will not be ours forever;
> He at length our good will sever.
> Spend not then his gifts in vain.
> Suns that set may rise again,   170
> But, if once we lose this light,
> 'Tis with us perpetual night.
> Why should we defer our joys?
> Fame and rumour are but toys.
> Cannot we delude the eyes   175
> Of a few poor household spies?
> Or his easier ears beguile,
> Thus removèd by our wile?
> 'Tis no sin love's fruits to steal,
> But the sweet thefts to reveal: 180
> To be taken, to be seen,
> These have crimes accounted been.

CELIA   Some serene blast me, or dire lightning strike
　　This my offending face!
VOLPONE　　　　　　　Why droops my Celia?
　　Thou hast in place of a base husband found   185
　　A worthy lover. Use thy fortune well,
　　With secrecy and pleasure. See, behold
　　What thou art queen of: not in expectation,
　　As I feed others, but possessed and crowned.

wooed Penelope in the *Odyssey*, and who appeared as an ideal courtly lover in Sir John
Davies' *Orchestra* (1596). If the latter, then the young Volpone's 'comedy' would have
enacted the heroic return of Ulysses as a loose parallel to Henry's return to France.
164. *footing*] Dance step.
165–82. Jonson's Italian friend Antonio Ferrabosco set this song to music for the theatrical
　　production, and later published it in his *Book of Ayres* (1609). The lyrics are loosely
　　based on Catullus, *Ode 5*.
168. *good*] Well-being.
174. *toys*] Trifles.
181. *taken*] Caught in the act.
183. *serene*] In hot countries, an evening mist or fine rain, once regarded as noxious.

[He shows her the treasure chest]

See here a rope of pearl, and each more orient	190
Than that the brave Egyptian queen caroused.	
Dissolve and drink 'em. See, a carbuncle	
May put out both the eyes of our St Mark;	
A diamond would have bought Lollia Paulina	
When she came in like starlight, hid with jewels	195
That were the spoils of provinces. Take these,	
And wear, and lose 'em; yet remains an earring	
To purchase them again, and this whole state.	
A gem but worth a private patrimony	
Is nothing. We will eat such at a meal.	200
The heads of parrots, tongues of nightingales,	
The brains of peacocks and of ostriches	
Shall be our food; and, could we get the phoenix,	
Though nature lost her kind, she were our dish.	

CELIA   Good sir, these things might move a mind affected   205
With such delights, but I, whose innocence
Is all I can think wealthy, or worth th'enjoying,
And which, once lost, I have nought to lose beyond it,
Cannot be taken with these sensual baits.
If you have conscience –   210
VOLPONE   'Tis the beggar's virtue.
If thou hast wisdom, hear me, Celia.
Thy baths shall be the juice of gillyflowers,

190. *orient*] Exquisite; see 1.5.9n.

191. According to Pliny (ix.120), Cleopatra defeated Antony in a wager to see who could spend more on one dinner; she dissolved one of her pearl earrings in vinegar and drank it.

192. *carbuncle*] Ruby.

193. *eyes ... Mark*] Possibly the nickname for Venice's two fine rubies, one kept in the Treasury, the other in the Doge's crown.

194. *Lollia Paulina*] Another classical extravagance. Caligula's bride, whose father had attained great wealth by looting the provinces, appeared at her betrothal party covered from head to foot with precious gems (Pliny, ix.117).

201–4. Details from feasts of the decadent Emperor Heliogabalus, who was destroyed eventually for his extravagances.

203. *phoenix*] Unique mythical bird that was supposed to regenerate itself every 500 years from its own funeral ashes.

204. *nature ... kind*] It became extinct.

212. *gillyflowers*] Clove-scented pinks, also called 'Venus looking-glass', a favourite Elizabethan flower. Its juice, reduced to an oil, was used as a soothing body-rub. The modern spelling indicates the pronunciation for Jonson's Q and F 'July-flowers'.

Spirit of roses and of violets,
The milk of unicorns, and panther's breath
Gathered in bags and mixed with Cretan wines.   215
Our drink shall be preparèd gold and amber,
Which we will take until my roof whirl round
With the vertigo; and my dwarf shall dance,
My eunuch sing, my fool make up the antic,
Whilst we, in changèd shapes, act Ovid's tales,   220
Thou like Europa now and I like Jove,
Then I like Mars and thou like Erycine;
So of the rest, till we have quite run through
And wearied all the fables of the gods.
Then will I have thee in more modern forms,   225
Attired like some spritely dame of France,
Brave Tuscan lady, or proud Spanish beauty;
Sometimes unto the Persian Sophy's wife,
Or the Grand Signor's mistress; and, for change,
To one of our most artful courtesans,   230
Or some quick Negro, or cold Russian.
And I will meet thee in as many shapes,
Where we may so transfuse our wand'ring souls
Out at our lips and score up sums of pleasures,

[*He sings*]

213. Distilled waters or perfumes.
214. *milk of unicorns*] Unusual reference, because unicorns were sexless and thus could not breed. Unicorn's horn (made of rhinoceros horn) was used as an antidote against poison. *panther's breath*] According to early naturalists, although the sight of a panther is terrifying, its seductive scent, when the animal is hidden, successfully lures prey to destruction.
215. *Cretan wines*] Malmsey.
216. That is, aurum potabile perfumed with ambergris, taken as a stimulant. See 1.4.73n. and 3.4.56n.
218–19. *dwarf ... eunuch ... fool*] May actually be on stage as voyeurs; in some modern productions, they block the exits preventing Celia's escape.
219. *antic*] Grotesque dance.
220. *changed shapes*] Fancy dress. *Ovid's tales*] *Metamorphoses*.
221. Jove transformed himself into a bull to abduct Europa.
222. *Erycine*] Venus, the Lady of Eryx in Sicily.
228. *Sophy*] Shah, or ruler.
229. *Grand Signor*] Sultan of Turkey, Mahomet III, famous for his harem.
231. *quick*] Lively, stimulating.
233. *transfuse*] Cause to flow from one to the other.

> That the curious shall not know   *235*
> How to tell them as they flow;
> And the envious, when they find
> What their number is, be pined

CELIA   If you have ears that will be pierced, or eyes
    That can be opened, a heart may be touched,   *240*
    Or any part that yet sounds man about you,
    If you have touch of holy saints, or heaven,
    Do me the grace to let me scape! If not,
    Be bountiful and kill me! You do know
    I am a creature hither ill betrayed   *245*
    By one whose shame I would forget it were.
    If you will deign me neither of these graces,
    Yet feed your wrath, sir, rather than your lust
    (It is a vice comes nearer manliness)
    And punish that unhappy crime of nature   *250*
    Which you miscall my beauty! Flay my face
    Or poison it with ointments for seducing
    Your blood to this rebellion! Rub these hands
    With what may cause an eating leprosy
    E'en to my bones and marrow! Anything   *255*
    That may disfavour me, save in my honour!
    And I will kneel to you, pray for you, pay down
    A thousand hourly vows, sir, for your health,
    Report and think you virtuous –
VOLPONE   Think me cold,
    Frozen, and impotent, and so report me?   *260*
    That I had Nestor's hernia, thou wouldst think.
    I do degenerate and abuse my nation
    To play with opportunity thus long

235–8. Like the earlier song, also from Catullus, *Ode 5*.

236. *tell*] Count.

238. *pined*] Tormented.

239–59. In Q, Celia's speech is heavily punctuated with dashes, indicating her near-hysterical terror.

241. Involuntary quibble. For Celia, true manliness demands a spiritual, not sexual, strength. *sounds man*] Proclaims manhood.

256. *disfavour*] Disfigure.

259–65. Volpone's view of what is 'virtuous' is diametrically opposed to Celia's; he is insulted by her promise to think him chaste.

261. *Nestor's hernia*] An old man's impotence. The aged Nestor was one of the Greek commanders in the *Iliad*.

262. *my nation*] The Italian standard for virility (see Corvino's comments, 2.5.24–9).

I should have done the act and then have parleyed.
Yield, or I'll force thee!   265
CELIA   O, just God!
VOLPONE   In vain –

[*Bonario*] *leaps out from where Mosca had placed him*

BONARIO   Forbear, foul ravisher! Libidinous swine!
Free the forced lady or thou diest, impostor.
But that I am loath to snatch thy punishment
Out of the hand of justice, thou shouldst yet
Be made the timely sacrifice of vengeance   270
Before this altar and this dross, thy idol!

[*He indicates the treasure chest*]

Lady, let's quit the place. It is the den
Of villainy. Fear nought: you have a guard,
And he ere long shall meet his just reward.

[*Exeunt Bonario and Celia*]

VOLPONE   Fall on me, roof, and bury me in ruin!   275
Become my grave, that wert my shelter! O!
I am unmasked, unspirited, undone,
Betrayed to beggary, to infamy –

Act 3 scene 8*

[*Enter*] *Mosca* [*wounded*]

MOSCA   Where shall I run, most wretched shame of men,
To beat out my unlucky brains?
VOLPONE   Here, here.
What! Dost thou bleed?
MOSCA   O, that his well-driv'n sword
Had been so courteous to have cleft me down
Unto the navel, ere I lived to see   5
My life, my hopes, my spirits, my patron, all

266. *swine*] Sensually degraded libertine, a condemnation of more force than the modern
   term of abuse.
277. *unspirited*] Deflated, drooping, with a sexual quibble on loss of potency.
*   Mosca's cries of humiliation interrupt Volpone's horrified grief at the disaster just
   befallen him. The overlap of scenes creates a comic echoing effect as each attempts to
   console the other.
2. *Here, here*] An unintentionally ironic reply.
3–5. Presumably Bonario has struck Mosca in the face, fulfilling 3.2.66–8.

　　　Thus desperately engagèd by my error!
VOLPONE　Woe on thy fortune!
MOSCA　　　　　　　　　　And my follies, sir.
VOLPONE　Th'hast made me miserable.
MOSCA　　　　　　　　　　And myself, sir.
　　　Who would have thought he would have hearkened so?　　　　　10
VOLPONE　What shall we do?
MOSCA　　　　　　　　　　I know not. If my heart
　　　Could expiate the mischance, I'd pluck it out.
　　　Will you be pleased to hang me? Or cut my throat?
　　　And I'll requite you, sir. Let's die like Romans,
　　　Since we have lived like Grecians.　　　　　　　　　　　　15

　　They knock without

VOLPONE　　　　　　　　　　Hark, who's there?
　　　I hear some footing: officers, the *Saffi*,
　　　Come to apprehend us! I do feel the brand
　　　Hissing already at my forehead. Now
　　　Mine ears are boring.
MOSCA　　　　　　　　　To your couch, sir; you
　　　Make that place good, however.　　　　　　　　　　　　　20

　　[*Volpone lies down*]

　　　　　　　　　　　　Guilty men
　　　Suspect what they deserve still.

　　[*Opens the door*]
　　　　　　　　　　　Signor Corbaccio!

7.　*engaged*] Entangled.
10.　*he*] Bonario. *hearkened*] eavesdropped
14.　*requite*] 'Return the favour', a ludicrous impossibility once Mosca is already dead;
　　　perhaps an indication of how much Bonario's surprise attack has rattled Mosca.
　　　like Romans] By stoically falling on their swords.
15.　*like Grecians*] In degenerate and reckless revelry. This view of the Greeks came to
　　　Renaissance Europe by way of the Romans, especially Plautus, who invented a verb for
　　　'going Greek'.
16.　*footing*] Footsteps. *Saffi*] Bailiffs or sergeants, subordinate to the commandatori.
17–19.　*brand ... boring*] Branding and ear-cropping, not piercing, were common punish-
　　　ments. Although Exodus 21:6 refers to ear-boring as a sign of perpetual slavery, for
　　　Volpone it symbolises fear of exposure as a criminal. Jonson himself was branded on the
　　　thumb for killing the actor Gabriel Spencer, and was threatened with ear-cropping and
　　　nose-slitting for his share in *Eastward Ho!*, just before writing *Volp*.
20.　*Make ... however*] Must keep up your role as invalid, no matter what.
21.　*Suspect*] Anticipate with dread.

Act 3 scene 9*

[*Enter*] *Corbaccio*

CORBACCIO Why, how now? Mosca!
MOSCA   O, undone, amazed, sir!

[*Enter Voltore, unseen*]

Your son, I know not by what accident,
Acquainted with your purpose to my patron
Touching your will and making him your heir,
Entered our house with violence, his sword drawn,   5
Sought for you, called you wretch, unnatural,
Vowed he would kill you.
CORBACCIO   Me?
MOSCA   Yes, and my patron.
CORBACCIO This act shall disinherit him indeed.
Here is the will.
MOSCA   'Tis well, sir.
CORBACCIO   Right and well.
Be you as careful now for me.   10
MOSCA   My life, sir,
Is not more tendered. I am only yours.
CORBACCIO How does he? Will he die shortly, thinkst thou?
MOSCA   I fear
He'll outlast May.
CORBACCIO [*Mishearing*] Today?
MOSCA   No, last out May, sir.
CORBACCIO Couldst thou not gi' him a dram?
MOSCA   O, by no means, sir.
CORBACCIO Nay, I'll not bid you.   15
VOLTORE   This is a knave, I see.
MOSCA [*Aside*] How! Signor Voltore! Did he hear me?
VOLTORE   Parasite!

---

*   Mosca shows expert management skills in turning both Corbaccio and Voltore against
     Bonario, now accused not only of the attempted murder of both Volpone and his father,
     but also of abducting Celia.
  1. *amazed*] Confused.
  8. That is, permanently. Originally the new will was an expedient to guarantee Volpone's
     favour, and ultimately Bonario would have inherited both Volpone's and Corbaccio's
     estates.
  9. *well*] In proper legal form.
 11. *more tendered*] Treated with more solicitous concern.
 14. *dram*] Dose of poison.

MOSCA   Who's that? [*To Voltore*] O, sir, most timely welcome –
VOLTORE   Scarce
    To the discovery of your tricks, I fear.
    You are his only? And mine also? Are you not?
MOSCA   Who? I, sir!   20
VOLTORE   You, sir. What device is this
    About a will?
MOSCA   A plot for you, sir.
VOLTORE   Come,
    Put not your foists upon me. I shall scent 'em.
MOSCA   Did you not hear it?
VOLTORE   Yes, I hear Corbaccio
    Hath made your patron there his heir .
MOSCA   'Tis true,
    By my device, drawn to it by my plot,   25
    With hope –
VOLTORE   Your patron should reciprocate?
    And you have promised?
MOSCA   For your good I did, sir.
    Nay, more, I told his son, brought, hid him here
    Where he might hear his father pass the deed,
    Being persuaded to it by this thought, sir,   30
    That the unnaturalness, first, of the act
    And, then, his father's oft disclaiming in him
    (Which I did mean to help on) would sure enrage him
    To do some violence upon his parent.
    On which the law should take sufficient hold,   35
    And you be stated in a double hope.
    Truth be my comfort and my conscience,
    My only aim was to dig you a fortune
    Out of these two old rotten sepulchres –
VOLTORE   I cry thee mercy, Mosca.   40
MOSCA   – worth your patience
    And your great merit, sir. And see the change!
VOLTORE   Why? What success?
MOSCA   Most hapless! You must help, sir.

20. *device*] Ruse.
22. *foists . . . scent*] Punning on 'foists', meaning 'cheating tricks' and 'silent farts'.
32. *disclaiming in*] Disinheriting or disowning.
36. *stated*] Established. *double hope*] Of two inheritances, but only if Corbaccio dies (murdered by Bonario?) before Volpone. Mosca's scheme has the spurious busy-ness of the newly invented.
42. *success*] Sequel. *hapless*] Unfortunate.

Whilst we expected the old raven, in comes
Corvino's wife, sent hither by her husband –
VOLTORE   What, with a present?   45
MOSCA   No, sir, on visitation –
I'll tell you how anon – and, staying long,
The youth, he grows impatient, rushes forth,
Seizeth the lady, wounds me, makes her swear –
Or he would murder her, that was his vow –   50
T'affirm my patron to have done her rape,
Which how unlike it is, you see! And hence
With that pretext he's gone t'accuse his father,
Defame my patron, defeat you –
VOLTORE   Where's her husband?
Let him be sent for straight.
MOSCA   Sir, I'll go fetch him.
VOLTORE   Bring him to the Scrutineo.   55
MOSCA   Sir, I will.
VOLTORE   This must be stopped.
MOSCA   O, you do nobly, sir.
Alas, 'twas laboured all, sir, for your good,
Nor was there want of counsel in the plot.
But fortune can at any time o'erthrow
The projects of a hundred learnèd clerks, sir.   60
CORBACCIO   What's that?
VOLTORE   [*To Corbaccio*] Will't please you, sir, to go along?

[*Exeunt Voltore and Corbaccio*]

MOSCA   [*To Volpone*] Patron, go in and pray for our success.
VOLPONE   [*Rising from his bed*] Need makes devotion. Heaven
        your labour bless.

[*Exeunt*]

55. *Scrutineo*] Law court of the senate-house, located in the Doge's Palace on the Piazzetta
    adjacent to St Mark's Square.
58. *counsel*] Prudence, sagacity.
60. *clerks*] Scholars.
62. *Will't*] Will it.

ACT 4

Act 4 scene 1*

[Enter] Sir Politic [and] Peregrine

SIR POLITIC   I told you, sir, it was a plot. You see
    What observation is! You mentioned me
    For some instructions. I will tell you, sir,
    Since we are met here in this height of Venice,
    Some few particulars I have set down   5
    Only for this meridian, fit to be known
    Of your crude traveller, and they are these.
    I will not touch, sir, at your phrase, or clothes,
    For they are old.

*   Ever since Erasmus exposed pilgimages as dissipations rather than exercises in piety (*Colloquies*), travel books attempted to promote high goals among travellers. Sir John Stradling's *A Direction for Travellers* (1592), a translation of Lipsius, contained practical hints for tourists and advice on correct behaviour abroad. *Profitable Instructions* (1595), possibly by Bacon, argued that experience and learning made the perfect man. Other guides, like Sir Robert Dallington's *Method for Travel* (1598), warned of the perils of conversion for Protestants visiting Roman Catholic countries, although the greater hazard of atheism lurked in Italy, especially in Venice, the city famous for its religious toleration. Still others warned indiscriminately of the dangers of adopting foreign affectations and of attack by Turks and pirates during voyages. The *bravi*, a particularly Venetian menace, were expatriate-gentlemen-adventurers-spies, whose unprincipled behaviour Sir Politic tries to imitate – thus bearing out the worst English fears of the corrupting effects of travel.

    Aside from satirising advice to travellers in this scene, Jonson mocks commercial and technological speculations, lumped under the label of 'projects' (see 46 below). Jonson similarly derides 'projectors' with improbable schemes in *DisA* and *NI*, as did later satirists such as Shadwell in *The Virtuoso* and Swift in Book 3 of *Gulliver's Travels*.

    The first three scenes of this act take place in the Piazza, and emphasise the continuous timing: while Celia has been refusing extramarital sex, thus causing Volpone's scheme to collapse, Lady Would-be has been out, squired by the dwarf, looking for evidence of her husband's sexual infidelity.

1.   *it was a plot*] Still convinced the mountebank incident was 'some trick of state' (2.3.10).
2.   *observation*] Scientific examination of any event, as advocated by Bacon.
2–3. *mentioned ... instructions*] Hinted that I might give you some travel tips. See 2.1.105–11, and Sir Pol's boast, 119–22.
4.   *this ... Venice*] A favourite phrase; see 2.1.12.
6.   *meridian*] Southern clime; figuratively, the tastes and habits of this part of the world.
7.   *crude*] Raw, inexperienced.
8.   *your*] Impersonal usage. Peregrine takes it as a personal criticism.   *phrase*] Language.

PEREGRINE   Sir, I have better.
SIR POLITIC   Pardon,
    I meant as they are themes.   10
PEREGRINE   O, sir, proceed.
    I'll slander you no more of wit, good sir.
SIR POLITIC   First, for your garb, it must be grave and serious;
    Very reserved and locked; not tell a secret
    On any terms, not to your father; scarce
    A fable but with caution. Make sure choice   15
    Both of your company and discourse. Beware
    You never spake a truth –
PEREGRINE   How!
SIR POLITIC   Not to strangers,
    For those be they you must converse with most;
    Others I would not know, sir, but at distance,
    So as I still might be a saver in 'em.   20
    You shall have tricks, else, passed upon you hourly.
    And then, for your religion, profess none,
    But wonder at the diversity of all,
    And, for your part, protest, were there no other
    But simply the laws o'th'land, you could content you.   25
    Nick Machiavel and Monsieur Bodin both
    Were of this mind. Then must you learn the use

10. *themes*] Topics.
11. I won't accuse you again of talking foolishly; I won't insult your intelligence again.
12. *garb*] Demeanour.
13. *locked*] Reticent, close-mouthed.
15. *fable*] Moral tale.
19. *Others*] Non-strangers, fellow countrymen. Englishmen were warned against consort-
    ing with unlicensed travellers. Sir Anthony Sherley, for example, was deprived of licence
    between 1599 and 1603 for visiting Persia and attempting to make an unsanctioned
    treaty with the Shah; Englishmen abroad were ordered to repudiate him.
20–21. The reference is to card-games: a *saver* is a player who escapes loss, though without
    gain; *tricks* are the cards won from (*passed upon*) one round of play. Sir Pol puns on
    deceits being imposed upon the unwary.
24–5. *no other ... land*] Only a single state-religion.
26. *Machiavel ... Bodin*] False attributions. Niccolò Machiavelli (1469–1527) subordi-
    nated all values to political expedience in *The Prince*, but made no claim for enforcing
    a single state religion. In *La République*, Jean Bodin (1530–96) advocated toleration
    solely on the rational grounds that a government should not destroy the state in an
    effort to obtain or maintain an impossibility like complete religious unity.

And handling of your silver fork at meals,
The metal of your glass – these are main matters
With your Italian – and to know the hour   30
When you must eat your melons and your figs.
PEREGRINE   Is that a point of state too?
SIR POLITIC   Here it is.
For your Venetian, if he see a man
Preposterous in the least, he has him straight,
He has. He strips him. I'll acquaint you, sir.   35
I now have lived here, 'tis some fourteen months.
Within the first week of my landing here,
All took me for a citizen of Venice.
I knew the forms so well –
PEREGRINE   [*Aside*]   And nothing else.
SIR POLITIC   I had read Contarine, took me a house,   40
Dealt with my Jews to furnish it with moveables –
Well, if I could but find one man, one man,
To mine own heart, whom I durst trust, I would –
PEREGRINE   What, what, sir?
SIR POLITIC   Make him rich, make him a fortune.

28. *fork*] Usual in Italy, but not in England, where full place-settings only gradually
     replaced fingers; knives and napkins were common after 1563, forks only relatively
     common after 1611.
29. *metal ... glass*] Quality of the molten material used to make glassware. *main
     matters*] Prime considerations.
31. *eat ... figs*] Coryat rhapsodises over the variety of fruit, especially the 'most tooth-
     some' melons, available in Venetian markets (1611· p. 395); also, a lewd quibble. 'Eat'
     meant satisfy the sexual appetite or 'stomach'; several fruits were euphemisms for the
     pudendum. 'Fig' or the Italian 'fico' was spoken as a sexually allusive expletive; to 'give
     the fico' usually meant an obscene gesture, but in a political context might mean a
     poisoned fig sent to destroy an adversary. Melons were aphrodisiacs, according to
     Lovell's *Herbal*: 'The Spaniards and Italians eat them to refresh the rage of lust.'
34. *Preposterous*] Behaving unnaturally or unconventionally, doing anything out of order
     or disorderly; also, sexual quibble on a preference for sodomy, suggesting 'posteriors
     first'. *has him straight*] Sees through him instantly; also quibbling on sodomy.
35. *strips*] Derides, taunts.
40. *Contarine*] Cardinal Gasparo Contarini, author of *De Magistratibus et Republica
     Venetorum* (1589), translated by Lewis Lewkenor (1599) as *The Commonwealth and
     Government of Venice*.
41. *Jews*] Moneylenders. Venice's large Jewish population, welcomed as intermediaries in
     Near-Eastern trade, lived in the Ghetto across the Grand Canal from the business centre
     in the Rialto. *moveables*] Furniture and other portable (as opposed to 'real' or 'fixed')
     possessions.

He should not think again. I would command it.   45
PEREGRINE   As how?
SIR POLITIC   With certain projects that I have,
    Which I may not discover.
PEREGRINE   [*Aside*]   If I had
    But one to wager with, I would lay odds now
    He tells me instantly.
SIR POLITIC   One is (and that
    I care not greatly who knows) to serve the state   50
    Of Venice with red herrings for three years,
    And at a certain rate, from Rotterdam,
    Where I have correspondence. [*Showing a letter*] There's a letter
    Sent me from one o'th'States and to that purpose.
    He cannot write his name, but that's his mark.   55
PEREGRINE   He is a chandler?
SIR POLITIC   No, a cheesemonger.
    There are some other too with whom I treat
    About the same negotiation,
    And I will undertake it. For 'tis thus
    I'll do't with ease; I've cast it all. Your hoy   60
    Carries but three men in her and a boy,
    And she shall make me three returns a year.
    So, if there come but one of three, I save;
    If two, I can defalk. But this is now
    If my main project fail.   65
PEREGRINE   Then you have others?
SIR POLITIC   I should be loath to draw the subtle air
    Of such a place without my thousand aims.

45. *think*] Consider the matter. *command*] Arrange.
46. *projects*] Speculations, quasi-scientific experiments.
51. *red herrings*] Smoked herrings, considered delicacies in Italy, though cheap and
plentiful in England and Holland. The political sense of 'laying a false trail' may not
have been current, although literal 'red herrings' were used in the hunt.
53. *correspondence*] Hinting at illicit communications.
54. *States*] Member of the States-General, the Dutch assembly.
56. *chandler*] A retail grocer or ship's provisioner, originally a dealer in candles; also used
as a term of contempt. Peregrine may be guessing by the greasiness of the letter, or by
the size of its wax seal. *cheesemonger*] Unlikely collaborator in a 'fishy' scheme, but
fits the stock image of the cheese-eating Dutch.
60. *cast*] Reckoned, worked out. *hoy*] Small Dutch sloop, used for short hauls along the
sea-coast.
63. *save*] Break even (see *saver*, 20n. above).
64. *defalk*] Pay off some debts or outstanding accounts.
66. *draw . . . air*] Inhale the atmosphere of intrigue.

I'll not dissemble, sir: where'er I come,
I love to be considerative, and 'tis true
I have at my free hours thought upon   70
Some certain goods unto the state of Venice,
Which I do call my cautions, and, sir, which
I mean (in hope of pension) to propound
To the Great Council, then unto the Forty,
So to the Ten. My means are made already –   75
PEREGRINE   By whom?
SIR POLITIC   Sir, one that, though his place b'obscure,
Yet he can sway and they will hear him. He's
A *commandatore*.
PEREGRINE   What, a common sergeant?
SIR POLITIC   Sir, such as they are put it in their mouths
What they should say sometimes, as well as greater.   80
I think I have my notes to show you – [*Searching*]
PEREGRINE   Good, sir.
SIR POLITIC   But you shall swear unto me, on your gentry,
Not to anticipate –
PEREGRINE   I, sir?
SIR POLITIC   Nor reveal
A circumstance – My paper is not with me.
PEREGRINE   O, but you can remember, sir.   85
SIR POLITIC   My first is
Concerning tinder-boxes. You must know
No family is here without its box.
Now, sir, it being so portable a thing,
Put case that you or I were ill affected

69. *considerative*] Hatching schemes, analysing theories.
71. *goods*] Benefits.
72. *cautions*] Precautionary measures, insurance.
74. *Great Council*] The supreme legislative body, composed of the 1200 nobles inscribed
     in the Book of Gold, the Venetian version of Debrett's Peerage, supposedly a closed
     book since 1297. From their ranks were elected the Doge, the Small Council (Senate),
     and the Collegio (Doge's Cabinet). *the Forty*] Court of appeal, drawn from the
     Senate.
75. *the Ten*] The Council of Ten, guardians of state security, who could interrogate, judge,
     and execute even the Doge. *means*] Contacts, approaches to the Council, Forty, and
     Ten. See 3.7.35n.
78. *commandatore . . . sergeant*] Officer charged with the arrest or summoning of offenders.
79–80. Common men, as well as important ones, may sometimes tell the government what
     to do.
86. *tinder-boxes*] Boxes to store tinder along with the flint and steel for striking sparks.
89. *Put case*] Say, for example.

Unto the state. Sir, with it in our pockets,   90
Might not I go into the Arsenale?
Or you? Come out again? And none the wiser?
PEREGRINE   Except yourself, sir.
SIR POLITIC   Go to, then. I therefore
Advertise to the state how fit it were
That none but such as were known patriots,   95
Sound lovers of their country, should be suffered
T'enjoy them in their houses, and even those
Sealed at some office and at such a bigness
As might not lurk in pockets.
PEREGRINE   Admirable!
SIR POLITIC   My next is how t'inquire and be resolved   100
By present demonstration whether a ship,
Newly arrivèd from Syria, or from
Any suspected part of all the Levant,
Be guilty of the plague; and, where they use
To lie out forty, fifty days sometimes   105
About the Lazaretto for their trial,
I'll save that charge and loss unto the merchant
And in an hour clear the doubt.
PEREGRINE   Indeed, sir?
SIR POLITIC   Or – I will lose my labour.
PEREGRINE   My faith, that's much.
SIR POLITIC   Nay, sir, conceive me. 'Twill cost me in onions   110
Some thirty *livres* –
PEREGRINE   Which is one pound sterling.

91. *Arsenale*] The shipyard, a prohibited military area at the east end of the city, accessible only by one land and one sea approach, where ships and ordnance were made and stored. Coryat (1611; rpt 1905) describes it as the most powerful munitions-store in Italy.

94. *Advertise to*] Warn, advise.

98. *Sealed*] Licensed.

100–125. Quarantine regulations were in effect since 1374; the first maritime quarantine station was established in 1402.

103. *Levant*] The Near-Eastern states.

106. *Lazaretto*] A pest-house, one of two built on islands in the Gulf of Venice after devastating plagues in 1423 and 1576.

110–25. Peeled onions, if left on the ground for ten days, were popularly thought to absorb plague infections. Herbalists recommended onion juice to cure plague and to expel wind. Incorporating both possibilities, Sir Pol's description is suggestive of male sexual organs ('onions ... Beside my waterworks') and bizarre acts of flatulence ('my bellows').

111. *livres*] French pounds.

SIR POLITIC   – Beside my waterworks. For this I do, sir.
    First, I bring in your ship 'twixt two brick walls
    (But those the state shall venture); on the one
    I strain me a fair tarpaulin, and in that   115
    I stick my onions, cut in halves; the other
    Is full of loopholes, out at which I thrust
    The noses of my bellows; and those bellows
    I keep with waterworks in perpetual motion
    (Which is the easiest matter of a hundred).   120
    Now, sir, your onion, which doth naturally
    Attract th'infection, and your bellows, blowing
    The air upon him, will show – instantly –
    By his changed colour if there be contagion,
    Or else remain as fair as at the first.   125
    Now 'tis known, 'tis nothing.
PEREGRINE   You are right, sir.
SIR POLITIC   I would I had my note.
PEREGRINE   Faith, so would I.
    But you ha' done well for once, sir.
SIR POLITIC   [*Searching again*]   Were I false,
    Or would be made so, I could show you reasons
    How I could sell this state now to the Turk,   130
    Spite of their galleys or their –
PEREGRINE   Pray you, Sir Pol.
SIR POLITIC   I have 'em not about me.
PEREGRINE   That I feared.
    They're there, sir? [*Sir Pol finds a book*]
SIR POLITIC   No, this is my diary,
    Wherein I note my actions of the day.
PEREGRINE   Pray you, let's see, sir. What is here? '*Notandum*   135
    A rat had gnawn my spur-leathers; notwithstanding,

114. *venture*] Invest in.

115. *strain*] Stretch.

126. *'tis nothing*] It's obvious. Peregrine ironically interprets the phrase as 'it means nothing'.

130. *the Turk*] The Ottoman Empire, Venice's chief rival in trade with the Levant and chief enemy: the Turks had captured key Venetian possessions, including Cyprus, by 1570. Venice regained Cyprus at the Battle of Lepanto, 7 Oct. 1571, but relinquished it to the Turks by a treaty in 1573.

135. *Notandum*] Something worthy of note, or worth investigating.

136–8. *A rat ... threshold*] Indicating that Sir Pol is superstitious.

136. *spur-leathers*] Laces for attaching spurs to boots. Spurs were worn for fashion, certainly not for riding in Venice. Sir Pol may insist on wearing them as a badge of his recently acquired knighthood; see 4.2.22n. and 29.

I put on new and did go forth. But first
I threw three beans over the threshold. *Item*,
I went and bought two toothpicks, whereof one
I burst immediately in a discourse   140
With a Dutch merchant 'bout *ragion' del stato*.
From him I went and paid a *moccenigo*
For piecing my silk stockings. By the way,
I cheapened sprats, and at St Mark's I urined.'
Faith, these are politic notes!   145

SIR POLITIC   Sir, I do slip
No action of my life thus but I quote it.
PEREGRINE   Believe me, it is wise!
SIR POLITIC   Nay, sir, read forth.

Act 4 scene 2*

[*Enter*] *Lady* [*Would-be*], *Nano*, [*and the two*] *Women*

LADY WOULD-BE   Where should this loose knight be, trow? Sure
          he's housed.
NANO   Why, then he's fast.
LADY WOULD-BE   Ay, he plays both with me. –
I pray you, stay. This heat will do more harm
To my complexion than his heart is worth. –
I do not care to hinder, but to take him –   5

139. *toothpicks*] Fashionable accoutrements. See 2.1.80n.
141. *ragion' del stato*] 'Reasons of state'; political matters.
142. *moccenigo*] Small coin.
143. *piecing*] Mending.
144. *cheapened*] Haggled for. Venetian gentlemen did the household shopping themselves.
145. *slip*] Let pass.
146. *quote*] Make a note of.
*   The comedy of this scene depends on Venice's reputation for homosexual-transvestite
     prostitutes who had infiltrated the city's profitable commerce in sex. The courtesans,
     resentful of the competition, had been unable to persuade the government to control
     the influx of male transvestites from the mainland; in retaliation, presumably to corner
     the sodomy market, the women began cross-dressing despite decrees against this
     practice in 1480 and 1578.
  1. *loose*] Wanton, unchaste; usually said of women.   *housed*] Accommodated in a
     brothel; sexually conjoined.
  2. *fast*] Quick-moving; closely connected, tightly gripping.   *plays both*] That is, fast and
     loose; see 1.2.8n.
  4. *complexion*] Applied cosmetics.
  5. I do not want to stop him, but to catch him in the act.

[*Checks her make-up*] How it comes off!
WOMAN 1   My master's yonder.
LADY WOULD-BE   Where?
WOMAN 1   With a young gentleman.
LADY WOULD-BE   That same's the party!
   In man's apparel. [*To Nano*] Pray you, sir, jog my knight.
   I will be tender to his reputation,
   However he demerit.   10
SIR POLITIC   [*Alerted by Nano*] My lady!
PEREGRINE   Where?
SIR POLITIC   'Tis she indeed. [*Walking towards her with Peregrine*]
     Sir, you shall know her. She is,
   Were she not mine, a lady of that merit
   For fashion and behaviour, and for beauty
   I durst compare –
PEREGRINE   It seems you are not jealous
   That dare commend her.   15
SIR POLITIC   Nay, and for discourse –
PEREGRINE   Being your wife, she cannot miss that.
SIR POLITIC   [*Introducing Peregrine*]   Madam,
   Here is a gentleman: pray you, use him fairly.
   He seems a youth, but he is –
LADY WOULD-BE   None?
SIR POLITIC   Yes, one
   Has put his face as soon into the world –
LADY WOULD-BE   You mean, as early? But today?   20
SIR POLITIC   How's this!
LADY WOULD-BE   Why, in this habit, sir. You apprehend me.
   Well, Master Would-be, this doth not become you.
   I had thought the odour, sir, of your good name
   Had been more precious to you, that you would not   25
   Have done this dire massacre on your honour.
   One of your gravity and rank, besides!
   But knights, I see, care little for the oath

6. *it*] The *fucus* complained of at 3.4.37.
8. *In man's apparel*] As a transvestite.
10. *demerit*] Deserve blame.
16. As your wife, she must have acquired the knack of talking.
19. *as soon*] At so early an age. Lady Would-be interprets this to mean that the 'youth' only
    recently put on the current disguise.
21. *habit*] Suit of clothes.
22. *Master*] This mode of address (also 38, 52) suggests that Sir Pol has not long been a
    knight, but rather that he was perhaps a well-to-do merchant who purchased his
    knighthood to satisfy social ambitions.

They make to ladies, chiefly their own ladies.
SIR POLITIC   Now, by my spurs – the symbol of my knighthood –
PEREGRINE   [*Aside*] Lord! How his brain is humbled for an oath.   30
SIR POLITIC   – I reach you not.
LADY WOULD-BE   Right, sir, your polity
  May bear it through thus. [*To Peregrine*] Sir, a word with you.
  I would be loath to contest publicly
  With any gentlewoman, or to seem
  Froward or violent, as *The Courtier* says;   35
  It comes too near rusticity in a lady,
  Which I would shun by all means. And, however
  I may deserve from Master Would-be, yet
  T'have one fair gentlewoman thus be made
  Th'unkind instrument to wrong another,   40
  And one she knows not, ay, and to persevere,
  In my poor judgment is not warranted
  From being a solecism in our sex,
  If not in manners.
PEREGRINE   How is this!
SIR POLITIC   Sweet madam,
  Come nearer to your aim.   45
LADY WOULD-BE   Marry, and will, sir.
  Since you provoke me with your impudence
  And laughter of your light land-siren here,
  Your Sporus, your hermaphrodite –
PEREGRINE   What's here?
  Poetic fury and historic storms!
SIR POLITIC   The gentleman, believe it, is of worth   50

30. *humbled*] Brought low – down to his spurs; a sneer at James's indiscriminate creation
    of new knights for a set fee.
31. *reach*] Understand. *polity*] Sly bluff.
32. *bear it through*] Carry it off.
35. *froward*] Refractory, perverse. *The Courtier says*] In Book 3 of Baldessare Casti-
    glione's definitive courtesy book, *The Courtier* (1528), translated by Thomas Hoby
    (1561).
40. *unkind*] Unnatural.
43. *solecism*] Strictly, a grammatical impropriety.
47. *light*] Immoral. *land-siren*] The mythical sirens were mermaids who lured men to
    destruction; Lady Would-be also sees Peregrine's transvestite status as half-woman,
    half-fish, playing on *fish*, a slang term for 'whore'.
48. *Sporus*] The favourite catamite of Nero, who had the youth castrated, dressed him as
    a woman, and married him in AD 67.
49. *Poetic fury*] Sarcastic reference to Plato's belief that poets were divinely inspired with
    a fine madness that allowed them to see truth; here applied to Lady Would-be's angrily

And of our nation.
LADY WOULD-BE   Ay, your Whitefriars nation?
Come, I blush for you, Master Would-be, I;
And am ashamed you should ha' no more forehead
Than thus to be the patron or St George
To a lewd harlot, a base fricatrice,   55
A female devil in a male outside.
SIR POLITIC   [*To Peregrine*]   Nay,
And you be such a one, I must bid adieu
To your delights! The case appears too liquid. [*Exit*]
LADY WOULD-BE   Ay, you may carry't clear with your state-face!
But for your carnival concupiscence,   60
Who here is fled for liberty of conscience
From furious persecution of the marshal,
Her will I disc'ple. [*Striking Peregrine*]
PEREGRINE   This is fine, i'faith!
And do you use this often? Is this part
Of your wit's exercise, 'gainst you have occasion?   65

creative use of 'siren'. *historic*] Referring to the Sporus analogy; perhaps playing on 'hysteric' or 'histrionic'.
51. *Whitefriars*] Located south of Fleet St and east of the Temple, an autonomous 'liberty' or free zone inhabited by debtors, criminals, and prostitutes; eventually abolished by Queen Anne.
53. *forehead*] Modesty.
54. *St George*] Protector of pure maidens.
55. *fricatrice*] Whore.
57. *And*] If.
58. *liquid*] Evidently proven; perhaps 'filled with tears', if Lady Would-be is weeping.
59. *state-face*] Hypocritical demeanour.
60. *carnival concupiscence*] Lechery appropriate to carnival festivities; or perhaps a malapropism for 'carnal'.
61. *liberty of conscience*] Usually 'freedom from religious persecution', but here implying amoral licence.
62. *marshal*] Either the prison warden, or more specifically the court of the Knight-Marshal of the royal household, with jurisdiction over crimes, including prostitution, committed in London and Westminster, the convicted offenders being sent to Marshalsea prison in Southwark. Jonson was imprisoned there in 1597 for his share in the slanderous satire *The Isle of Dogs*.
63. *disc'ple*] Discipline or chastise, especially as a religious practice.
64. *use this*] Behave like this.
65. *'gainst . . . occasion*] Whenever you have the opportunity.

Madam –
LADY WOULD-BE   Go to, sir.
PEREGRINE   – Do you hear me, lady?
      Why, if your knight have set you to beg shirts,
      Or to invite me home, you might have done it
      A nearer way by far.
LADY WOULD-BE   This cannot work you
      Out of my snare.   70
PEREGRINE   Why? Am I in it then?
      Indeed, your husband told me you were fair,
      And so you are, only your nose inclines –
      That side that's next the sun – to the queen-apple.
LADY WOULD-BE   This cannot be endured by any patience!   75

Act 4 scene 3

[Enter] Mosca

MOSCA   What's the matter, madam?
LADY WOULD-BE   If the Senate
      Right not my quest in this, I will protest 'em
      To all the world no aristocracy.
MOSCA   What is the injury, lady?
LADY WOULD-BE   Why, the callet
      You told me of, here, I have ta'en disguised.   5
MOSCA   Who? This? What means your ladyship? The creature
      I mentioned to you is apprehended now
      Before the Senate. You shall see her –
LADY WOULD-BE   Where?
MOSCA   I'll bring you to her. This young gentleman,
      I saw him land this morning at the port.   10
LADY WOULD-BE   Is't possible! How has my judgment wandered!

66. *sir*] Probably sarcastic, judging from Peregrine's reply, balancing her 'sir' against his
    'lady'. She still does not believe he is a man, and he implies that she does not behave like
    a lady. Possibly her line is a parting shot at Sir Pol, who may make a gradual exit during
    the quarrel.
67. *beg shirts*] Suggests Lady Would-be is grasping Peregrine's shirt to prevent his slipping
    away as Sir Pol has done.
69. *nearer*] More direct.
70. *snare*] Her grip on his shirt; Peregrine pretends to take it as a sexual advance.
74. *queen-apple*] A large red apple. See 3.4.16.
 2. *quest*] Petition.   *protest*] Proclaim publicly.
 3. *aristocracy*] Political system.
 4. *callet*] Whore.

– Sir, I must, blushing, say to you I have erred
And plead your pardon.
PEREGRINE   What! More changes yet?
LADY WOULD-BE I hope yo'ha' not the malice to remember
A gentlewoman's passion. If you stay   15
In Venice here, please you to use me, sir –
MOSCA Will you go, madam?
LADY WOULD-BE   Pray you, sir, use me. In faith,
The more you see me, the more I shall conceive
You have forgot our quarrel.

[*Exeunt Lady Would-be, Mosca, Nano, and Women*]

PEREGRINE   This is rare!
Sir Politic Would-be? No, Sir Politic Bawd!   20
To bring me thus acquainted with his wife!
Well, wise Sir Pol, since you have practised thus
Upon my freshmanship, I'll try your salt-head,
What proof it is against a counter-plot. [*Exit*]

Act 4 scene 4*

[*Enter*] *Voltore, Corbaccio, Corvino, Mosca*

VOLTORE Well, now you know the carriage of the business,
Your constancy is all that is required
Unto the safety of it.
MOSCA   Is the lie
Safely conveyed amongst us? Is that sure?

16. *use me*] Lady Would-be may mean only 'allow me to sponsor you socially', but
Peregrine understands her to mean that she is sexually available.
18. *see me*] Q repeats 'use me', but the extra repetition may have been a printer's
error. *conceive*] Understand; become pregnant.
20. *Bawd*] Pimp.
22. *practised*] Plotted.
23. *freshmanship*] Inexperience. *salt-head*] Seasoned experience (playing on salt used for
preserving or pickling fresh food); lewd frame of mind.
*   The remaining scenes of this act take place in the Scrutineo, located in the Doge's Palace
in the Piazzetta. The whispered conspiracies among the witnesses here act as a prelude
to the crowded courtroom scenes to follow. Extras as spectators may be filling up the
stage to prepare for the entry of the judges, clerks, guards, and prisoners.
1. *carriage*] Management, conduct.
3–4. *Is ... us?*] Are we all sure of our part in passing off this lie?

Knows every man his burden?   5
CORVINO   Yes.
MOSCA   Then shrink not.
CORVINO   [*Aside to Mosca*] But knows the advocate the truth?
MOSCA   O, sir,
  By no means. I devised a formal tale
  That salved your reputation. But be valiant, sir.
CORVINO   I fear no one but him, that this his pleading
  Should make him stand for a co-heir –   10
MOSCA   Co-halter,
  Hang him! We will but use his tongue, his noise,
  As we do Croaker's here. [*Indicates Corbaccio*]
CORVINO   Ay, what shall he do?
MOSCA   When we ha' done, you mean?
CORVINO   Yes.
MOSCA   Why, we'll think:
  Sell him for mummia – he's half dust already.
  [*Aside*] *to Voltore,* [*indicating Corvino*] Do not you smile to see
      this buffalo,   15
  How he doth sport it with his head? – I should,
  If all were well and past. – [*A loud aside*] *to Corbaccio* Sir, only you
  Are he that shall enjoy the crop of all,
  And these not know for whom they toil.
CORBACCIO   Ay, peace.
MOSCA   [*Aside*] *to Corvino* But you shall eat it. – Much! *and then*
      to Voltore again – Worshipful sir,   20

5. *burden*] Refrain or supporting line of harmony in a melody.
7. *formal*] Elaborately constructed, circumstantial.
8. *salved*] Preserved.
10. *Co-halter*] Playing on 'halter', a hangman's rope.
12. *Croaker's*] Suggests the tone of voice the actor should use for Corbaccio. See 5.3.76.
14. *mummia*] Powdered mummy, used in medical preparations. The substance was counterfeited by drying corpses in ovens, though Mosca suggests that Corbaccio will not need extensive preparation.
15. *buffalo*] Alluding to the size of the cuckold's horns put there by the lies they are all prepared to tell about Celia. Or perhaps he has told Voltore the truth about Corvino, despite his earlier disclaimer (6–8). A *buff* or *buffle* is also a term of contempt for a fool.
16–17. *I ... past*] May still be an aside to Voltore, or Mosca may be commenting to himself as he moves on to the next dupe.
20. *Much!*] Ironic. Corvino, presumably having overheard the loud aside to Corbaccio, needs reassuring that he shall 'eat' whatever 'crop' is gathered. Mosca's interjection, meaning 'So you'd like to think!', may be an aside to himself, or a conspiratorial aside to Voltore.

Mercury sit upon your thund'ring tongue,
Or the French Hercules, and make your language
As conquering as his club, to beat along,
As with a tempest, flat, our adversaries.
– But much more yours, sir.   25
VOLTORE   Here they come. Ha' done.
MOSCA   I have another witness, if you need, sir,
I can produce.
VOLTORE   Who is it?
MOSCA   Sir, I have her.   30

Act 4 scene 5*

[*Enter*] *four Avocatori, Bonario, Celia, Notario,* [*and*] *Commandatori*

AVOCATORE 1   The like of this the Senate never heard of.
AVOCATORE 2   'Twill come most strange to them when we report it.
AVOCATORE 4   The gentlewoman has been ever held
Of unreprovèd name.
AVOCATORE 3   So the young man.
AVOCATORE 4   The more unnatural part that of his father.   5
AVOCATORE 2   More of the husband.
AVOCATORE 1   I not know to give
His act a name, it is so monstrous!
AVOCATORE 4   But the impostor, he is a thing created
T'exceed example!
AVOCATORE [1]   And all after-times!
AVOCATORE 2   I never heard a true voluptuary   10
Described, but him.
AVOCATORE 3   Appear yet those were cited?
NOTARIO   All but the old magnifico, Volpone.

21. *Mercury*] God of eloquence and of theft.
22. *French Hercules*] Hercules fathered the Celts in Gaul (France) while returning from his
    tenth labour. Lucian depicted the Celtic Hercules as weakened by age, but powerfully
    eloquent.
23. *along*] At full length.
25. *But … yours*] That is, the other co-heirs will become Voltore's enemies, once they
    discover he means to be sole heir.
*   Like the mountebank scene in 2.2, the courtroom scenes in Acts 4 and 5 rely on a
    crowded stage for their effect. In addition to the thirteen speaking parts, most
    productions show officers, minor court officials, and spectators filling out the scene
    with noisy reactions to the evidence, even drowning out Bonario's protests, thus
    emphasising the perpetration of injustice.
9. *example*] Precedent. *after-times*] Future possibilities.

AVOCATORE 1   Why is not he here?
MOSCA   Please your fatherhoods,
    Here is his advocate. Himself's so weak,
    So feeble –   15
AVOCATORE 4 What are you?
BONARIO   His parasite,
    His knave, his pander! I beseech the court
    He may be forced to come, that your grave eyes
    May bear strong witness of his strange impostures.
VOLTORE   Upon my faith and credit with your virtues,
    He is not able to endure the air.   20
AVOCATORE 2   Bring him, however.
AVOCATORE 3   We will see him.
AVOCATORE 4   Fetch him.

    [*Exeunt Commandatori*]

VOLTORE   Your fatherhoods' fit pleasures be obeyed,
    But sure the sight will rather move your pities
    Than indignation. May it please the court
    In the meantime, he may be heard in me.   25
    I know this place most void of prejudice,
    And therefore crave it, since we have no reason
    To fear our truth should hurt our cause.
AVOCATORE 3   Speak free.
VOLTORE   Then know, most honoured fathers, I must now
    Discover to your strangely abusèd ears   30
    The most prodigious and most frontless piece
    Of solid impudence and treachery
    That ever vicious nature yet brought forth
    To shame the state of Venice. This lewd woman [*Indicating Celia*],
    That wants no artificial looks or tears   35
    To help the visor she has now put on,
    Hath long been known a close adulteress
    To that lascivious youth there [*Indicating Bonario*]; not suspected,
    I say, but known, and taken, in the act,

13. *fatherhoods*] Correct form of address, although Volpone later mimics Voltore's
    obsequious repetition of the title (5.2.33–7).
27. *it*] That is, being heard.
30. *abusèd*] Imposed upon.
31. *frontless*] Shameless.
35. *wants*] Lacks.
36. *visor*] Mask; the shocked and tearful innocence Voltore accuses her of hypocritically
    assuming.
37. *close*] Secret.

With him; and by this man [*Indicating Corvino*], the easy husband,   40
Pardoned; whose timeless bounty makes him now
Stand here, the most unhappy, innocent person
That ever man's own goodness made accused.
For these, not knowing how to owe a gift
Of that dear grace but with their shame, being placed   45
So above all powers of their gratitude,
Began to hate the benefit, and in place
Of thanks, devise t'extirp the memory
Of such an act. Wherein I pray your fatherhoods
To observe the malice, yea, the rage of creatures   50
Discovered in their evils, and what heart
Such take even from their crimes. But that anon
Will more appear. This gentleman, [*Indicating Corbaccio*] the father,
Hearing of this foul fact, with many others
Which daily struck at his too-tender ears,   55
And grieved in nothing more than that he could not
Preserve himself a parent (his son's ills
Growing to that strange flood), at last decreed
To disinherit him.
AVOCATORE 1   These be strange turns!
AVOCATORE 2   The young man's fame was ever fair and honest.   60
VOLTORE   So much more full of danger is his vice,
That can beguile so under shade of virtue.
But, as I said, my honoured sires, his father
Having this settled purpose (by what means
To him betrayed, we know not), and this day   65
Appointed for the deed, that parricide
(I cannot style him better), by confederacy
Preparing this his paramour to be there,
Entered Volpone's house (who was the man,
Your fatherhoods must understand, designed   70
For the inheritance), there sought his father.

40. *easy*] Good-natured; credulous.
41. *timeless*] Limitless.
44. *owe*] Own, acknowledge.
45. *dear grace*] Heartfelt kindness, generous pardon; the wording allies Corvino with God's grace or mercy.
48. *extirp*] Root out.
51. *heart*] Boldness, brazen insolence.
54. *fact*] Crime.
55. *too-tender*] Overly solicitous and sensitive, ironic considering Corbaccio's deafness.
57. *ills*] Evils.
67. *style him better*] Address or refer to him (Bonario) with a better title.

But with what purpose sought he him, my lords? –
I tremble to pronounce it, that a son
Unto a father, and to such a father,
Should have so foul, felonious intent! –   75
It was to murder him. When, being prevented
By his more happy absence, what then did he?
Not check his wicked thoughts. No, now new deeds:
(Mischief doth ever end where it begins)
An act of horror, fathers! He dragged forth   80
The agèd gentleman that had there lain bed-rid
Three years and more, out off his innocent couch,
Naked, upon the floor, there left him; wounded
His servant in the face; and, with this strumpet
The stale to his forged practice, who was glad   85
To be so active (I shall here desire
Your fatherhoods to note but my collections
As most remarkable), thought at once to stop
His father's ends, discredit his free choice
In the old gentleman, redeem themselves   90
By laying infamy upon this man
To whom, with blushing, they should owe their lives.
AVOCATORE 1   What proofs have you of this?
BONARIO   Most honoured fathers,
I humbly crave there be no credit given
To this man's mercenary tongue.   95
AVOCATORE 2   Forbear.
BONARIO   His soul moves in his fee.
AVOCATORE 3   O, sir!
BONARIO   This fellow,
For six *sols* more, would plead against his Maker.
AVOCATORE 1   You do forget yourself.

79. Misdeeds, once begun, persist in their harmful course.

82. *off*] Jonson's spelling in Q and F, meaning either 'off' or 'of'; altered to 'of' in
Restoration and later editions. Because 'off' wrenches the idiom, it makes the context
seem more violent.

85. *stale*] Prostitute used by thieves as a decoy. *forged practice*] Invented or fraudulent
plot.

86. *active*] As a participant in the plot, but also in sexual activity.

87. *collections*] Inferences, deductions.

88–9. *stop ... ends*] Put a stop to his father's intended plan of action; frustrate his father's
intentions.

90. *old gentleman*] Volpone.

91. *this man*] Corvino.

97. *sols*] Punning on 'soul', 96; a *sol* was a French coin worth about a halfpenny.

VOLTORE   Nay, nay, grave fathers,
    Let him have scope. Can any man imagine
    That he will spare's accuser, that would not   100
    Have spared his parent?
AVOCATORE 1   Well, produce your proofs.
CELIA   I would I could forget I were a creature!
VOLTORE   Signor Corbaccio.
AVOCATORE 4   What is he?
VOLTORE   The father.
AVOCATORE 2   Has he had an oath?
NOTARIO   Yes.
CORBACCIO   What must I do now?
NOTARIO   Your testimony's craved.   105
CORBACCIO   [*Mishearing*]   Speak to the knave?
    I'll ha' my mouth first stopped with earth! My heart
    Abhors his knowledge. I disclaim in him.
AVOCATORE 1   But for what cause?
CORBACCIO   The mere portent of nature.
    He is an utter stranger to my loins.
BONARIO   Have they made you to this?   110
CORBACCIO   I will not hear thee,
    Monster of men, swine, goat, wolf, parricide!
    Speak not, thou viper!
BONARIO   Sir, I will sit down
    And rather wish my innocence should suffer,
    Than I resist the authority of a father.
VOLTORE   Signor Corvino.   115
AVOCATORE 2   This is strange!
AVOCATORE 1   Who's this?
NOTARIO   The husband.
AVOCATORE 4   Is he sworn?
NOTARIO   He is.
AVOCATORE 3   Speak then.
CORVINO   This woman, please your fatherhoods, is a whore

---

100. *spare's*] Spare his.
102. *creature*] One of God's creatures (see 3.7.245); the context expresses Celia's humilia-
    tion, her longing not so much for death as for some undefined insensate state, like
    Marlowe's Faustus in his final trial, wanting to turn himself into thin air to escape
    torment by devils.
107. *his knowledge*] Acknowledging him. *disclaim in*] Disinherit, deny kinship to.
108. *portent*] Freak. Corbaccio equates his son with one of Volpone's freaks, who,
    reputedly his bastards, are also not named in their 'father's' will.

     Of most hot exercise, more than a partridge,
     Upon record –
AVOCATORE 1   No more.
CORVINO   – Neighs like a jennet.
NOTARIO   Preserve the honour of the court.   120
CORVINO   I shall,
     And modesty of your most reverend ears.
     And yet I hope that I may say these eyes
     Have seen her glued unto that piece of cedar,
     That fine well-timbered gallant [*Pointing to Bonario*]; and
        that here [*Gesturing at his own forehead*]
     The letters may be read thorough the horn   125
     That make the story perfect.
MOSCA   [*Aside to Corvino*]   Excellent, sir!
CORVINO   [*Aside to Mosca*] There is no shame in this now, is there?
MOSCA   None.
CORVINO   [*To the court*] Or if I said I hoped that she were onward
     To her damnation, if there be a hell
     Greater than whore and woman – a good catholic   130
     May make the doubt!
AVOCATORE 3   His grief hath made him frantic.
AVOCATORE 1   Remove him hence.

   [*Celia*] *swoons*

AVOCATORE 2   Look to the woman.
CORVINO   [*Taunting her*]   Rare!
     Prettily feigned! Again!
AVOCATORE 4   Stand from about her.

118. *hot exercise*] Ardent or eager sexual activity. *partridge*] Described as the most lecherous of creatures (Pliny, x.102).
119. *Neighs . . . jennet*] Whinnies like a mare in heat. A jennet is a small Spanish horse.
123. *cedar*] Referring to Bonario's height.
124. *well-timbered*] Well-built; crudely, well-equipped sexually.
125. *letters . . . horn*] Corvino makes forked signs with his fingers at his temples, indicating the cuckold's horns, but puns on the 'hornbooks' from which children learned the alphabet. These were boards mounted with a lesson-sheet under a thin layer of horn, like a protective plastic coating.
126. *perfect*] Complete, fully known.
130. *catholic*] Originally 'Christian' in Q, perhaps altered in F to refer more specifically to Venetians.
131. *frantic*] Hysterical.

AVOCATORE 1   Give her the air.
AVOCATORE 3   [*To Mosca*]   What can you say?
MOSCA   My wound,
  May't please your wisdoms, speaks for me, received   135
  In aid of my good patron when he missed
  His sought-for father, when that well-taught dame
  Had her cue given her to cry out a rape.
BONARIO   O, most laid impudence! Fathers –
AVOCATORE 3   Sir, be silent.
  You had your hearing free; so must they theirs.   140
AVOCATORE 2   I do begin to doubt th'imposture here.
AVOCATORE 4   This woman has too many moods.
VOLTORE   Grave fathers,
  She is a creature of a most professed
  And prostituted lewdness.
CORVINO   Most impetuous!
  Unsatisfied, grave fathers!   145
VOLTORE   May her feignings
  Not take your wisdoms. But this day, she baited
  A stranger, a grave knight, with her loose eyes
  And more lascivious kisses. This man [*Indicating Mosca*] saw 'em
  Together on the water in a gondola.
MOSCA   Here is the lady herself that saw 'em too,   150
  Without, who then had in the open streets
  Pursued them, but for saving her knight's honour.
AVOCATORE 1   Produce that lady.
AVOCATORE 2   Let her come.

  [*Exit Mosca*]

AVOCATORE 4   These things,
  They strike with wonder!
AVOCATORE 3   I am turned a stone!

---

136. *he*] Bonario.
139. *most laid*] Carefully planned or contrived.
140. *free*] Without interruption.
145. *Unsatisfied*] Insatiable.
146. *But this day*] Only today. *baited*] Enticed.
151. *Without*] That is, just outside the courtroom.

Act 4 scene 6*

[Enter] Mosca [with] Lady Would-be

MOSCA   Be resolute, madam.
LADY WOULD-BE   *[Identifying Celia]*   Ay, this same is she.
    Out, thou chameleon harlot! Now thine eyes
    Vie tears with the hyena. Durst thou look
    Upon my wronged face? *[To Avocatori]* I cry your pardons.
    I fear I have, forgettingly, transgressed   5
    Against the dignity of the court –
AVOCATORE 2   No, madam.
LADY WOULD-BE   – And been exorbitant –
AVOCATORE [1]   You have not, lady.
AVOCATORE 4   These proofs are strong.
LADY WOULD-BE   Surely I had no purpose
    To scandalise your honours or my sex's.
AVOCATORE 3   We do believe it.   10
LADY WOULD-BE   Surely you may believe it.
AVOCATORE 2   Madam, we do.
LADY WOULD-BE   Indeed you may. My breeding
    Is not so coarse –
AVOCATORE 4   We know it.
LADY WOULD-BE   – to offend
    With pertinacy –
AVOCATORE 3   Lady –
LADY WOULD-BE   – such a presence.
    No, surely.
AVOCATORE 1   We well think it.
LADY WOULD-BE   You may think it.
AVOCATORE 1   Let her o'ercome. *[To Bonario]* What witnesses have you   15
    To make good your report?
BONARIO   Our consciences.

---

*   This scene showcases the evidence against Celia: Lady Would-be's testimony, and the damning exhibit of the incapacitated Volpone, carried in on a litter.
3.   *chameleon*] Changing her clothes to suit the circumstance, as the chameleon changes its colour; Lady Would-be believes Celia is the transvestite courtesan whom she was seeking earlier (4.2, 3).
4.   *tears ... hyena*] A confused (and unscientific) reference to the luring of victims. Lady Would-be muddles the crocodile's artful tears and the hyena's human-like voice.
7.   *exorbitant*] Immoderate in her speech.
13.   *pertinacy*] A common seventeenth-century form of pertinacity, meaning perverse obstinacy in asserting an opinion. *presence*] Presence-chamber, or courtroom.
15.   *o'ercome*] Win, have the last word.

CELIA   And heaven, that never fails the innocent.
AVOCATORE 4   These are no testimonies.
BONARIO   Not in your courts,
    Where multitude and clamour overcomes.
AVOCATORE 1   Nay, then, you do wax insolent.   20

   Volpone is brought in as impotent
   [*Lady Would-be embraces him*]

VOLTORE   Here, here,
    The testimony comes that will convince
    And put to utter dumbness their bold tongues.
    See here, grave fathers: here's the ravisher,
    The rider on men's wives, the great impostor,
    The grand voluptuary! Do you not think   25
    These limbs should affect venery? Or these eyes
    Covet a concubine? Pray you, mark these hands.
    Are they not fit to stroke a lady's breasts?
    Perhaps he doth dissemble?
BONARIO   So he does.
VOLTORE   Would you ha' him tortured?   30
BONARIO   I would have him proved.
VOLTORE   Best try him, then, with goads or burning irons.
    Put him to the strappado. I have heard
    The rack hath cured the gout. Faith, give it him,
    And help him of a malady. Be courteous.
    I'll undertake, before these honoured fathers,   35
    He shall have yet as many left diseases
    As she has known adulterers, or thou strumpets.
    O, my most equal hearers, if these deeds,

19. *multitude*] That is, number of witnesses.
20.1. *impotent*] Completely disabled. Lady Would-be may embrace him here, or at his exit; or possibly as a show of sympathy or support after 30, or even during Voltore's speeches.
24. *rider ... wives*] Adulterer.
26. *affect venery*] Practise sexual indulgences.
30. *proved*] Tested.
32. *strappado*] A torture in which the victim, his wrists tied behind his back and attached to a pulley, is hoisted upwards and then let down half-way with a jerk that usually breaks the arms and pulls the bones out of joint.
33. *rack*] Instrument of torture, consisting of a frame with rollers at either end; the victim's wrists and ankles were attached to stretch the limbs out of joint, or break them.
34. *help*] Cure, relieve.
37. *known*] That is, known carnally.
38. *equal*] Just.

Acts of this bold and most exorbitant strain,
May pass with sufferance, what one citizen   40
But owes the forfeit of his life, yea, fame,
To him that dares traduce him? Which of you
Are safe, my honoured fathers? I would ask,
With leave of your grave fatherhoods, if their plot
Have any face or colour like to truth?   45
Or if, unto the dullest nostril here,
It smell not rank and most abhorrèd slander?
I crave your care of this good gentleman,
Whose life is much endangered by their fable;
And as for them I will conclude with this,   50
That vicious persons when they are hot and fleshed
In impious acts, their constancy abounds:
Damned deeds are done with greatest confidence.

AVOCATORE 1   Take 'em to custody and sever them.

[*Officers remove Bonario and Celia separately*]

AVOCATORE 2   'Tis pity two such prodigies should live.   55
AVOCATORE 1   Let the old gentleman be returned with care.
    I'm sorry our credulity wronged him.

[*Officers carry out Volpone*]

AVOCATORE 4   These are two creatures!
AVOCATORE 3   I have an earthquake in me!
AVOCATORE 2   Their shame, even in their cradles, fled their faces.
AVOCATORE 4   [*To Voltore*] You've done a worthy service to the   60
    state, sir,
    In their discovery.
AVOCATORE 1   You shall hear ere night
    What punishment the court decrees upon 'em.
VOLTORE   We thank your fatherhoods.

[*Exeunt Avocatori, Notario, Commandatori*]

                                   How like you it?
MOSCA
                                        Rare!

---

39. *exorbitant strain*] Outrageous kind.
40. *with sufferance*] With official toleration or impunity.
45. *face or colour*] Appearance or pretext.
51. *fleshed*] Inflamed and eager for more, said of initiating soldiers to bloodshed, hawks
    and hounds to the hunt, and virgins to sexual pleasures.
54. *sever*] Separate.
55. *prodigies*] Freaks, monsters.
58. *creatures*] Brutes; unlike Celia's use of the term, 4.5.102.

I'd ha' your tongue, sir, tipped with gold for this.
I'd ha' you be the heir to the whole city.   65
The earth I'd have want men, ere you want living.
They're bound to erect your statue in St Mark's.
Signor Corvino [*Taking him aside*], I would have you go
And show yourself, that you have conquered.

CORVINO   Yes.

MOSCA   It was much better that you should profess   70
Yourself a cuckold thus, than that the other
Should have been proved.

CORVINO   Nay, I considered that.
Now it is her fault.

MOSCA   Then it had been yours.

CORVINO   True. I do doubt this advocate still.

MOSCA   I'faith,
You need not. I dare ease you of that care.   75

CORVINO   I trust thee, Mosca.

MOSCA   As your own soul, sir.

[*Exit Corvino*]

CORBACCIO   Mosca!

MOSCA   Now for your business, sir.

CORBACCIO   How? Ha' you business?

MOSCA   Yes, yours, sir.

CORBACCIO   O, none else?

MOSCA   None else, not I.

CORBACCIO   Be careful then.

MOSCA   Rest you with both your eyes, sir.

CORBACCIO   Dispatch it.   80

MOSCA   Instantly.

CORBACCIO   And look that all,
Whatever, be put in: jewels, plate, moneys,
Household stuff, bedding, curtains.

MOSCA   Curtain-rings, sir.
Only the advocate's fee must be deducted.

CORBACCIO   I'll pay him now. You'll be too prodigal.

MOSCA   Sir, I must tender it.   85

CORBACCIO   Two *zecchins* is well?

66. *want living*] Lack a livelihood.
71. *the other*] That is, that he tried to prostitute his wife.
74. *do doubt*] Mistrust.
79. *Rest . . . eyes*] Sleep easy, relax without fear.
81. *put in*] Included in the inventory.

MOSCA No. Six, sir.
CORBACCIO   'Tis too much.
MOSCA   He talked a great while;
   You must consider that, sir.
CORBACCIO [*Giving money*] Well, there's three –
MOSCA I'll give it him.
CORBACCIO   Do so, and there's for thee.

  [*Corbaccio gives a coin, and exit*]

MOSCA [*Aside*] Bountiful bones! What horrid strange offence
   Did he commit 'gainst nature in his youth,   90
   Worthy this age? [*To Voltore*] You see, sir, how I work
   Unto your ends. Take you no notice.
VOLTORE   No,
   I'll leave you.
MOSCA   All is yours,

  [*Exit Voltore*]

            [*Aside*] the devil and all,
   Good advocate! [*To Lady Would-be*] Madam, I'll bring you home.
LADY WOULD-BE No, I'll go see your patron.   95
MOSCA   That you shall not.
   I'll tell you why. My purpose is to urge
   My patron to reform his will, and for
   The zeal you've shown today, whereas before
   You were but third or fourth, you shall be now   100
   Put in the first, which would appear as begged
   If you were present. Therefore –
LADY WOULD-BE   You shall sway me.

  [*Exeunt*]

89. *Bountiful bones!*] Comment on Corbaccio's stinginess, and aptly transferring it to his emaciated physique.
89–91. *What ... age*] Referring to the adage, 'Only the good die young'.
92. *Take ... notice*] If referring to Corbaccio or Lady Would-be, 'Don't pay attention to what I say to others'; if referring to the fee and tip he has just pocketed, 'Ignore this petty insult to your professional expertise, beneath your dignity to acknowledge'.
96–101. Mosca's speech may be construed as an oblique invitation to Lady Would-be, his promoting her as heir in return for her sexual favours. Her reply seems to agree to the proposition.
97. *reform*] Revise.
101. *sway*] Persuade.

ACT 5

Act 5 scene 1*

[Enter] Volpone

VOLPONE   Well, I am here, and all this brunt is passed.
　　　I ne'er was in dislike with my disguise
　　　Till this fled moment. Here, 'twas good, in private,
　　　But in your public – *cavè* whilst I breathe.
　　　'Fore God, my left leg 'gan to have the cramp,　　　　5
　　　And I apprehended straight some power had struck me
　　　With a dead palsy. Well, I must be merry
　　　And shake it off. A many of these fears
　　　Would put me into some villainous disease,
　　　Should they come thick upon me. I'll prevent 'em.　　10
　　　Give me a bowl of lusty wine, to fright
　　　This humour from my heart.

He drinks　　　　　　　　　Hum, hum, Hum!

　　　'Tis almost gone already. I shall conquer.
　　　Any device now of rare ingenious knavery,
　　　That would possess me with a violent laughter,　　　15

---

*　The first three scenes take place at Volpone's house, and scene 4 at the Would-bes'
　house. Scenes 5–9 and 11 are essentially street scenes; scene 5 is at the door of Volpone's
　house, and scene 11 suggests the same location (but see the note on scene 11 for further
　explanation). The rest are courtroom scenes.
　　This scene makes clear the effect of the tensions Volpone has been exposed to.
　Ironically, in drinking to calm his nerves, he impairs his judgment, and becomes
　entangled in a further scheme, with disastrous results.
1. *brunt*] Stress, strain of a sudden pressure.
3. *fled*] Past.
4. *cavè*] Beware (Latin). Volpone may be cautioning himself to calm down, or he may be
　addressing the audience directly to be on guard for him while he catches his breath.
6. *apprehended*] Felt; should be pronounced *apprênded*, as spelled in Q, to preserve the
　metre.　*straight*] Straight away.
7. *dead palsy*] Stroke causing complete paralysis.
10. *prevent 'em*] Cut them off.
13. *conquer*] That is, his fear.
14. *humour*] In the sense of 'disease', 9.

Would make me up again!

Drinks again   So, so, so, so!

This heat is life. 'Tis blood by this time. Mosca!

Act 5 scene 2

[*Enter*] *Mosca*

MOSCA   How now, sir? Does the day look clear again?
Are we recovered? And wrought out of error
Into our way? To see our path before us?
Is our trade free once more?
VOLPONE   Exquisite Mosca!
MOSCA   Was it not carried learnedly?   5
VOLPONE   And stoutly.
Good wits are greatest in extremities.
MOSCA   It were a folly beyond thought to trust
Any grand act unto a cowardly spirit.
You are not taken with it enough, methinks?
VOLPONE   O, more than if I had enjoyed the wench!   10
The pleasure of all womankind's not like it.
MOSCA   Why, now you speak, sir. We must here be fixed.
Here we must rest. This is our masterpiece:
We cannot think to go beyond this.
VOLPONE   True.
Thou'st played thy prize, my precious Mosca.   15
MOSCA   Nay, sir,
To gull the court –
VOLPONE   And quite divert the torrent
Upon the innocent.
MOSCA   Yes, and to make

16. *make . . . up*] Pull me together, restore me.
17. *heat*] Flushed euphoria caused by intoxication (or being 'foxed'), giving Volpone the
illusion of new energy or courage.   *'Tis blood*] That is, the wine transformed by the
humours and generating 'vital heat' or energy in his system.
2–3. *wrought . . . us*] Mocking puritan piety, as at 1.3.52–66.
  4. *Exquisite*] Consummately ingenious.
  6. *extremities*] Crises.
  9. *taken*] Satisfied, delighted.
10–11. Volpone is at least as drunk on successful trickstering as he is on wine, preferring
heady one-upmanship even to unrestricted sexual conquests.
12. *be fixed*] That is, stop playing games.
16. *gull*] Dupe.

So rare a music out of discords –
VOLPONE   Right.
That, yet, to me's the strangest! How th'hast borne it!
That these, being so divided 'mongst themselves,   20
Should not scent somewhat, or in me, or thee,
Or doubt their own side.
MOSCA   True, they will not see't.
Too much light blinds 'em, I think. Each of 'em
Is so possessed and stuffed with his own hopes
That anything unto the contrary,   25
Never so true, or never so apparent,
Never so palpable, they will resist it –
VOLPONE   Like a temptation of the devil.
MOSCA   Right, sir.
Merchants may talk of trade, and your great signors
Of land that yields well, but if Italy   30
Have any glebe more fruitful than these fellows,
I am deceived. Did not your advocate rare?
VOLPONE   O – 'My most honoured fathers, my grave fathers,
Under correction of your fatherhoods,
What face of truth is here? If these strange deeds   35
May pass, most honoured fathers' – I had much ado
To forbear laughing.
MOSCA   'T seemed to me you sweat, sir.
VOLPONE   In troth, I did a little.
MOSCA   But confess, sir,
Were you not daunted?
VOLPONE   In good faith, I was
A little in a mist, but not dejected: 40
Never but still myself.
MOSCA   I think it, sir.
Now, so truth help me, I must needs say this, sir,

18. See 4.4.5 for another version of the music analogy; here, the rival heirs are the 'discords' made to sing in harmony.
19. *strangest*] Most to be wondered at; a key word in Act 5. *borne it*] Carried it off.
21. *or ... or*] Either ... or.
24. *possessed*] Taken over by demonic possession; another key word.
31. *glebe*] Clod of earth; plot of land, usually used of a clergyman's benefice.
32. *rare*] Rarely, splendidly.
37. *you sweat*] That is, with fear. Mosca's accusation punctures Volpone's presentation of himself as confident enough to laugh.
39. *daunted*] See 40 for Volpone's qualification of the possible meanings of the term as stupefied or dazed ('A little in a mist'), but not overcome with fear, or downcast ('dejected').

And out of conscience, for your advocate:
He's taken pains, in faith, sir, and deserved
(In my poor judgment, I speak it, under favour,   45
Not to contrary you, sir) very richly –
Well – to be cozened.

MOSCA   Troth, and I think so too,
By that I heard him in the latter end.

MOSCA   O, but before, sir! Had you heard him, first,
Draw it to certain heads, then aggravate,   50
Then use his vehement figures — I looked still
When he would shift a shirt; and doing this
Out of pure love, no hope of gain –

VOLPONE   'Tis right.
I cannot answer him, Mosca, as I would,
Not yet. But for thy sake, at thy entreaty,   55
I will begin ev'n now to vex 'em all,
This very instant.

MOSCA   Good, sir.

VOLPONE   Call the dwarf
And eunuch forth.

MOSCA   Castrone! Nano!

  [*Enter Nano and Castrone*]

NANO   Here.

VOLPONE   Shall we have a jig now –

MOSCA   What you please, sir.

VOLPONE   Go,
Straight give out about the streets, you two,   60
That I am dead. Do it with constancy,
Sadly, do you hear? Impute it to the grief

44. *He's*] He has.
45. *under favour*] With your permission.
46. *contrary*] Contradict.
47. *cozened*] Cheated.
48. By what I heard of the end of his courtroom defence.
50. *heads*] Chief points of a discourse. *aggravate*] Intensify; exaggerate.
51. *vehement figures*] Either forceful gestures, or impassioned speech.
52. *shift a shirt*] Change his shirt (because of his sweaty vehemence).
54. *answer*] Repay.
59. *jig*] A burlesque song-and-dance skit that often followed Elizabethan stage perfor-
     mances; in later periods called an 'afterpiece'.
61. *with constancy*] With fidelity to the roles being played (i.e., mournful servants);
     perhaps, with straight faces.
62. *Sadly*] Seriously, gravely.

Of this late slander.

MOSCA   What do you mean, sir?

VOLPONE   O,
I shall have instantly my vulture, crow,
Raven, come flying hither, on the news,   65
To peck for carrion, my she-wolf and all,
Greedy and full of expectation –

MOSCA   And then to have it ravished from their mouths?

VOLPONE   'Tis true. I will ha' thee put on a gown
And take upon thee as thou wert mine heir.   70
Show 'em a will. Open that chest and reach
Forth one of those that has the blanks. I'll straight
Put in thy name.

MOSCA   It will be rare, sir.

VOLPONE   Ay,
When they e'en gape and find themselves deluded –

MOSCA   Yes.   75

VOLPONE   – and thou use them scurvily. Dispatch,
Get on thy gown.

MOSCA   [*Dressing*]   But what, sir, if they ask
After the body?

VOLPONE   Say it was corrupted.

MOSCA   I'll say it stunk, sir, and was fain t'have it
Coffined up instantly and sent away.

VOLPONE   Anything, what thou wilt. Hold, here's my will.   80
Get thee a cap, a count-book, pen and ink,
Papers afore thee. Sit as thou wert taking
An inventory of parcels. I'll get up
Behind the curtain on a stool and hearken;
Sometime peep over, see how they do look,   85
With what degrees their blood doth leave their faces.
O 'twill afford me a rare meal of laughter!

63. *mean*] Intend.
70. *take ... as*] Act as though.
72. *blanks*] Spaces for filling in a legatee's name.
78. *was fain*] I was obliged.
81. *cap*] As worn by clerks. *count-book*] Account book.
83. *parcels*] Lots, items.
84. *curtain*] The 'traverse', mentioned at 5.3.8.1, unlikely to be the bed-curtains if a stool
    is required; perhaps a curtain across an entrance-doorway, or a tapestry hung between
    the stage-doors under the gallery, to hide the recess used for eavesdropping and
    'discovery' scenes; or possibly a free-standing screen.

MOSCA   Your advocate will turn stark dull upon it.

VOLPONE   It will take off his oratory's edge.

MOSCA   But your *clarissimo*, old round-back, he   90
    Will crump you like a hog-louse with the touch.

VOLPONE   And what Corvino?

MOSCA   O, sir, look for him
    Tomorrow morning with a rope and a dagger
    To visit all the streets. He must run mad.
    My lady too that came into the court   95
    To bear false witness for your worship –

VOLPONE   Yes,
    And kissed me 'fore the fathers when my face
    Flowed all with oils.

MOSCA   And sweat, sir. Why, your gold
    Is such another med'cine, it dries up
    All those offensive savours! It transforms   100
    The most deformed and restores 'em lovely,
    As 'twere the strange poetical girdle. Jove
    Could not invent t'himself a shroud more subtle
    To pass Acrisius' guards. It is the thing
    Makes all the world her grace, her youth, her beauty.   105

VOLPONE   I think she loves me.

MOSCA   Who? The lady, sir?
    She's jealous of you.

VOLPONE   Dost thou say so?

[*Knocking at the door*]

MOSCA   Hark,

---

88. *dull*] Insensible; also, making 'blunt' the sharp edge of Voltore's elaborate legal oratory.

90. *clarissimo*] A Venetian grandee. *round-back*] Corbaccio, hunched with age.

91. *crump ... touch*] Curl up for you like a woodlouse at a touch; *you* is the ethical dative, used impersonally for vividness.

93. *rope ... dagger*] Stock emblems of suicidal despair.

102. *poetical girdle*] F adds *Cestus* in the right margin as a gloss for Venus's girdle, interwoven with all the transforming powers of love and gentle persuasion (*Iliad* 14.214–17).

104. *Acrisius' guards*] In the myth, Acrisius locked his daughter Danaë into a tower to prevent her conceiving a son that would kill him, but Zeus appeared to her in a shower of gold, thus fathering the hero Perseus. In Lucian's version, the cock claims the golden shower was a bribe for the guards.

106. *The lady*] Volpone may be thinking of Celia, but Mosca seems to refer to Lady Would-be.

107. *jealous of*] Devoted to your care; amorously lusting for your attentions; apprehensive of rivals for your favour.

There's some already.
VOLPONE   Look.
MOSCA   [*Looking out*]   It is the vulture.
   He has the quickest scent.
VOLPONE   [*Concealing himself*] I'll to my place.
   Thou to thy posture.   110
MOSCA   I am set.
VOLPONE   [*From behind the curtain*] But, Mosca,
   Play the artificer now. Torture 'em rarely!

Act 5 scene 3*

[*Enter*] Voltore

VOLTORE   How now, my Mosca?
MOSCA   [*Writing*]   Turkey carpets, nine –
VOLTORE   Taking an inventory? That is well.
MOSCA   Two suits of bedding, tissue –
VOLTORE   Where's the will?
   Let me read that the while.

[*Enter Servants carrying Corbaccio in a chair*]

CORBACCIO   So, set me down,
   And get you home.   5

[*Exeunt Servants*]

VOLTORE   [*Aside*]   Is he come now to trouble us?
MOSCA   Of cloth of gold, two more –
CORBACCIO   Is it done, Mosca?
MOSCA   Of several velvets, eight –
VOLTORE   [*Aside*]   I like his care.

---

109. *quickest scent*] The vulture's exceptional ability to sniff out a corpse from a distance.
110. *posture*] Imposture.
111. *artificer*] Craftsman (i.e., skilled torturer); trickster.
*   The inventory of goods at the beginning of this scene accurately reflects contemporary accounts of wealth, which frequently did not mean ready money. Turkish carpets, tapestries, brocades, velvets, gold-embroidered linens, and elaborately carved furniture, as well as jewellery and plate, figured largely in household account-books and were mentioned prominently in wills distributing estates among the heirs. Shakespeare, for example, left his second-best bed (including bedding and bed-curtains) to his wife.
1. *Turkey carpets*] Then used as table and wall coverings.
3. *suits of bedding*] Bed-covers and -curtains, probably of velvet or heavy silk. *tissue*] Cloth woven with gold or silver thread (see 6 for the completed phrase).
7. *several velvets*] Separate velvet hangings.

CORBACCIO   Dost thou not hear?

[Enter Corvino]

CORVINO   Ha? Is the hour come, Mosca?

Volpone peeps from behind a traverse

VOLPONE   [*Aside*]   Ay, now they muster!
CORVINO   What does the advocate here?
    Or this Corbaccio?   10
CORBACCIO   What do these here?

[Enter Lady Would-be]

LADY WOULD-BE   Mosca?
    Is his thread spun?
MOSCA   Eight chests of linen –
VOLPONE   [*Aside*]   O,
    My fine dame Would-be too!
CORVINO   Mosca, the will,
    That I may show it these, and rid 'em hence.
MOSCA   Six chests of diaper, four of damask – There.

[He tosses Corvino the will]

CORBACCIO   Is that the will?   15
MOSCA   [*Still writing*]   Down-beds and bolsters –
VOLPONE   [*Aside*]   Rare!
    Be busy still. Now they begin to flutter.
    They never think of me. Look, see, see, see!
    How their swift eyes run over the long deed
    Unto the name and to the legacies,
    What is bequeathed them there –   20
MOSCA   Ten suits of hangings –
VOLPONE   [*Aside*] Ay, i' their garters, Mosca. Now their hopes
    Are at the gasp.
VOLTORE   Mosca the heir!
CORBACCIO   [*Straining to hear*]   What's that?

8.1.   *traverse*] Possibly a screen that would allow the audience a better view of Volpone's
    reactions, rather than a conventional curtain; see 5.2.84n.
11.   *thread spun*] Pretentiously alluding to the Three Fates, who spin, measure, and then cut
    the thread of man's life.
14.   *diaper*] Linen with a diamond-patterned weave. *damask*] Used for tablecloths, twilled
    linen woven with elaborate designs that show up in opposite reflections of light at the
    surface.
20.   *suits of hangings*] Sets of tapestries.
21.   *i' their garters*] Punning on the common jibe, 'Hang yourself in your own garters'.
22.   *gasp*] Last gasp.

VOLPONE   [*Aside*] My advocate is dumb. Look to my merchant:
He has heard of some strange storm, a ship is lost,
He faints. My lady will swoon. Old glazen-eyes,   25
He hath not reached his despair yet.
CORBACCIO   [*Examining the will*]   All these
Are out of hope. I'm sure the man.
CORVINO   But, Mosca –
MOSCA   Two cabinets –
CORVINO   Is this in earnest?
MOSCA   One
Of ebony –
CORVINO   Or do you but delude me?
MOSCA   The other, mother of pearl – I am very busy.   30
Good faith, it is a fortune thrown upon me –
Item, one salt of agate – not my seeking.
LADY WOULD-BE   Do you hear, sir?
MOSCA   A perfumed box – pray you, forbear.
You see I am troubled – made of an onyx –
LADY WOULD-BE   How!
MOSCA   Tomorrow or next day I shall be at leisure   35
To talk with you all.
CORVINO   Is this my large hope's issue?
LADY WOULD-BE   Sir, I must have a fairer answer.
MOSCA   Madam!
Marry, and shall: pray you, fairly quit my house.
Nay, raise no tempest with your looks, but hark you:
Remember what your ladyship offered me   40
To put you in an heir. Go to, think on't.
And what you said e'en your best madams did
For maintenance, and why not you? Enough.
Go home and use the poor Sir Pol, your knight, well,
For fear I tell some riddles. Go, be melancholic.   45

[*Exit Lady Would-be*]

25. *glazen-eyes*] Corbaccio wears glasses (see 63).
31. *thrown*] Thrust. Mosca gives an impression of reluctance.
32. *salt*] Salt-cellar.
33. *perfumed box*] Vessel for perfume, made of onyx (34).
34. *troubled*] Busy; perhaps, vexed.
38. *fairly*] Completely, or courteously, playing on Lady Would-be's *fairer*, meaning more
    equitable.
40–43. An implication of sexual misconduct that may be deduced from intonation and
    gesture at 4.6.96–101.
45. *riddles*] Secrets.

VOLPONE   [*Aside*] O, my fine devil!
CORVINO   Mosca, pray you a word.
MOSCA   Lord! Will not you take your dispatch hence yet?
    Methinks, of all, you should have been th'example.
    Why should you stay here? With what thought? What promise?
    Hear you, do not you know I know you an ass?   50
    And that you would most fain have been a wittol,
    If fortune would have let you? That you are
    A declared cuckold on good terms? This pearl,
    You'll say, was yours? Right. This diamond?
    I'll not deny't, but thank you. Much here else?   55
    It may be so. Why, think that these good works
    May help to hide your bad. I'll not betray you.
    Although you be but extraordinary
    And have it only in title, it sufficeth.
    Go home – be melancholic too, or mad.   60

    [*Exit Corvino*]

VOLPONE   [*Aside*] Rare, Mosca! How his villainy becomes him!
VOLTORE   [*Aside*] Certain he doth delude all these for me.
CORBACCIO   [*Still reading the will*] Mosca the heir?
VOLPONE   [*Aside*]   O, his four eyes have found it!
CORBACCIO   I'm cozened, cheated, by a parasite-slave!
    Harlot, th'ast gulled me!   65
MOSCA   Yes, sir. Stop your mouth,
    Or I shall draw the only tooth is left.
    Are not you he, that filthy covetous wretch
    With the three legs, that here in hope of prey
    Have, any time this three year, snuffed about   70

49. Corvino should have set an example to the others by leaving first.
51. *wittol*] A complaisant cuckold.
53. *on good terms*] Fair and square.
58. *extraordinary*] In title only; used of an official with no defined function, attached as an extra to a place of employment.
61. *becomes*] Suits, shows to advantage.
63. *four eyes*] Slur on Corbaccio's glasses; see 25n.
65. *Harlot*] Rascally knave, without sexual connotation when used of men.
68. *three legs*] The third being Corbaccio's cane.
69–70. *snuffed ... nose*] Suggests that Corbaccio should be played with a sniffing or dripping nose, to accompany his hunched posture, lameness, weak eyesight, and deafness. 'Snuffed' implies nasal speech, associated then with the hypocritical canting of puritans. As an insult, it also implies dog-like activity equated with low breeding or menial status.

With your most grov'ling nose, and would have hired
Me to the pois'ning of my patron? Sir?
Are not you he that have today in court
Professed the disinheriting of your son?
Perjured yourself? Go home, and die, and stink.   75
If you but croak a syllable, all comes out.
Away, and call your porters. Go, go! Stink!

VOLPONE   [*Aside*] Excellent varlet!

VOLTORE   Now, my faithful Mosca,
   I find thy constancy.

MOSCA   Sir?

VOLTORE   Sincere.

MOSCA   [*Resumes writing*]   A table
   Of porphyry – I mar'l you'll be thus troublesome.   80

VOLTORE   Nay, leave off now. They are gone.

MOSCA   Why? Who are you?
   What? Who did send for you? O, cry you mercy,
   Reverend sir! Good faith, I am grieved for you
   That any chance of mine should thus defeat
   Your (I must needs say) most deserving travails.   85
   But I protest, sir, it was cast upon me,
   And I could almost wish to be without it,
   But that the will o' the dead must be observed.
   Marry, my joy is that you need it not.
   You have a gift, sir (thank your education)   90
   Will never let you want while there are men
   And malice to breed causes. Would I had
   But half the like, for all my fortune, sir.
   If I have any suits (as I do hope,
   Things being so easy and direct, I shall not)   95
   I will make bold with your obstreperous aid –
   Conceive me, for your fee, sir. In meantime,
   You that have so much law I know ha' the conscience
   Not to be covetous of what is mine.
   Good sir, I thank you for my plate. 'Twill help   100
   To set up a young man. Good faith, you look
   As you were costive. Best go home and purge, sir.

80. *porphyry*] A marble-like purple- or red-grained stone. *mar'l*] Marvel.
83. *chance*] Luck, good fortune.
92. *causes*] Lawsuits.
96. *obstreperous*] Noisy.
97. *Conceive ... fee*] You know I'll pay your regular fee.
100. *plate*] Voltore's gift to Volpone in 1.3.
102. *costive*] Constipated; figuratively, grasping, or stingy.

[Exit Voltore]

VOLPONE   [*Coming forward*] Bid him eat lettuce well. My witty
　　　mischief,
　　　Let me embrace thee! O, that I could now
　　　Transform thee to a Venus – Mosca, go   105
　　　Straight, take my habit of *clarissimo*,
　　　And walk the streets. Be seen, torment 'em more.
　　　We must pursue as well as plot. Who would
　　　Have lost this feast?
MOSCA   I doubt it will lose them.
VOLPONE   O, my recovery shall recover all.   110
　　　That I could now but think on some disguise
　　　To meet 'em in, and ask 'em questions.
　　　How I would vex 'em still at every turn!
MOSCA   Sir, I can fit you.
VOLPONE   Canst thou?
MOSCA   Yes. I know
　　　One o' the Commandatori, sir, so like you,   115
　　　Him will I straight make drunk and bring you his habit.
VOLPONE   A rare disguise, and answering thy brain!
　　　O, I will be a sharp disease unto 'em!
MOSCA   Sir, you must look for curses –
VOLPONE   Till they burst.
　　　The fox fares ever best when he is cursed.   120

　　　[Exeunt]

103. *lettuce*] Prescribed as a laxative.
106. *habit of clarissimo*] The clothing worn by a Venetian gentleman; usually a black
　　　gown with a flap on the left shoulder edged in black taffeta, and a flat black felt cap.
　　　Those with specific government appointments might wear signifying colours, but black
　　　was generally thought appropriate, because grave and decent (Coryat 1611:
　　　pp. 397–8).
109. *I doubt ... them*] I fear it [the *feast* of pleasure in gulling the victims] will eliminate
　　　them as future dupes.
115. *Commandatori*] Officers of the lawcourt.
115–16. *so ... habit*] Volpone, himself still drunk and eager to change clothes, misses the
　　　irony of this description.
120. A proverb; the hunter curses the fox for escaping.

Act 5 scene 4*

[*Enter*] *Peregrine* [*disguised, and*] *three Mercatori*

PEREGRINE   Am I enough diguised?
MERCHANT 1   I warrant you.
PEREGRINE   All my ambition is to fright him only.
MERCHANT 2   If you could ship him away, 'twere excellent.
MERCHANT 3   To Zant or to Aleppo?
PEREGRINE   Yes, and ha' his
   Adventures put i' th' *Book of Voyages*,   5
   And his gulled story registered for truth?
   Well, gentlemen, when I am in a while,
   And that you think us warm in our discourse,
   Know your approaches.
MERCHANT 1   Trust it to our care.

   [*Exeunt Merchants*]
   [*Enter Woman*]

PEREGRINE   Save you, fair lady. Is Sir Pol within?   10
WOMAN   I do not know, sir.
PEREGRINE   Pray you, say unto him,
   Here is a merchant upon earnest business
   Desires to speak with him.
WOMAN   I will see, sir.
PEREGRINE   Pray you.

---

*   Sir Pol's predicament, to be trapped by his own device, is also Volpone's by the end of
   the act: both must 'uncase' (5.12.85) to survive. The tortoise shell extends the bestiary
   motif by representing circumspect self-reliance and political safety; as a lesson to the
   foolish Would-bes, it also symbolises silence, and may recall the fable of the tortoise and
   the hare, where slow but steadfast behaviour wins the race.
1. *warrant*] Assure.
4. *Zant*] One of the Ionian islands owned by Venice, important in the currant trade.
   Aleppo] Syrian city described in Hakluyt (see next note) as the greatest inland trading
   mart of the eastern Mediterranean.
5. *Book of Voyages*] Probably Hakluyt's *Principal Navigations, Voyages and Discoveries
   of the English Nation* (1589, rev. 1598–1600), one of the many travel books popular
   at the time; possibly a pamphlet about Sir Anthony Sherley, an adventurer whose
   exploits in the Levant fascinated the Elizabethan public.
6. *his gulled story*] The story of his gulling.   *registered*] Formally recorded or entered in
   a register.
9. *Know your approaches*] Pick the moment for your entrances; *approaches* in a military
   sense meant hostile or offensive advances.
12. *earnest*] Serious, weighty.

[*Exit Woman*]

I see the family is all female here.

[*Re-enter Woman*]

WOMAN   He says, sir, he has weighty affairs of state   15
          That now require him whole. Some other time
          You may possess him.
PEREGRINE   Pray you, say again,
          If those require him whole, these will exact him
          Whereof I bring him tidings.

[*Exit Woman*]

                              What might be
          His grave affair of state now? How to make   20
          Bolognian sausages here in Venice, sparing
          One o' th' ingredients.

[*Re-enter Woman*]

WOMAN   Sir, he says he knows
          By your word 'tidings' that you are no statesman,
          And therefore wills you stay.
PEREGRINE   Sweet, pray you return him:
          I have not read so many proclamations   25
          And studied them for words as he has done,
          But –

[*Enter Sir Politic*]

          Here he deigns to come.

14. Peregrine may think he has come to a brothel, but other English travellers, like Fynes Moryson (*Itinerary*, 1616), observed that Italian households were composed entirely of women-servants.
16. *require him whole*] Occupy all his attention.
17. *possess him*] Pass on your information; perhaps, enjoy his company. If the latter, the words minimise whatever 'earnest business' Peregrine may wish to discuss.
18. *exact*] Compel unavoidably, or forcibly wrest away.
21. *Bolognian sausages*] Mortadella, imported to England via Rotterdam.   *sparing*] Omitting.
23. *tidings*] Sir Pol refers to 'intelligence' (2.1.68), 'advertisement' (77), 'advices' (94), and 'relations' (96). *statesman*] Government agent.
24. *return*] Reply to.
25–6. Sarcasm: I do not understand fine distinctions in political terminology as well as Sir Politic does.

[*Exit Woman*]

SIR POLITIC	Sir, I must crave

Your courteous pardon. There hath chanced, today,
Unkind disaster 'twixt my lady and me,
And I was penning my apology   30
To give her satisfaction, as you came now.

PEREGRINE   Sir, I am grieved I bring you worse disaster.
The gentleman you met at th' port today,
That told you he was newly arrived –

SIR POLITIC   Ay, was
A fugitive punk?   35

PEREGRINE   No, sir, a spy set on you.
And he has made relation to the Senate
That you professed to him to have a plot
To sell the state of Venice to the Turk.

SIR POLITIC   O me!

PEREGRINE   For which, warrants are signed by this time
To apprehend you and to search your study   40
For papers –

SIR POLITIC   Alas, sir! I have none but notes
Drawn out of play-books –

PEREGRINE   All the better, sir.

SIR POLITIC   And some essays. What shall I do?

PEREGRINE   Sir, best
Convey yourself into a sugar-chest,
Or, if you could lie round, a frail were rare;   45
And I could send you aboard.

SIR POLITIC   Sir, I but talked so
For discourse sake merely.

   They knock without

PEREGRINE   Hark, they are there.

SIR POLITIC   I am a wretch, a wretch!

PEREGRINE   What will you do, sir?

29. *Unkind*] Unaccustomed, untoward; unnaturally hostile or harsh.

35. *fugitive punk*] Slippery whore.

37–8. See 4.1.130.

42. *play-books*] Printed plays.

43. *essays*] Probably Montaigne's *Essais*; see 3.4.90n. Although Jonson's peers, among
   them Shakespeare and Bacon (who published his *Essays* in 1597), admired Montaigne,
   Jonson claimed to think him superficial and inconsistent (*Disc*, Parfitt 1975: p. 396).

45. *lie round*] Curl up. *frail*] Rush basket for shipping figs and raisins (see 3–4).

47. *for discourse sake*] In the name of small-talk.

Have you ne'er a currant-butt to leap into?
They'll put you to the rack. You must be sudden.   50
SIR POLITIC   Sir, I have an engine –
MERCHANT 3   [*Off-stage*]   Sir Politic Would-be?
MERCHANT 2   [*Off-stage*] Where is he?
SIR POLITIC   – that I have thought upon beforetime.
PEREGRINE   What is it?
SIR POLITIC   – I shall ne'er endure the torture! –
Marry, it is, sir, of a tortoise shell
Fitted for these extremities.   55

[*He shows the shell and begins to climb inside it*]

                              Pray you sir, help me.
Here I've a place, sir, to put back my legs:
Please you to lay it on, sir. With this cap
And my black gloves, I'll lie, sir, like a tortoise
Till they are gone.
PEREGRINE   And call you this an engine?
SIR POLITIC   Mine own device – Good sir, bid my wife's women   60
To burn my papers.

[*The three Merchants*] *rush in* [*followed by Woman;*
Peregrine speaks to her aside]

MERCHANT 1   Where's he hid?
MERCHANT 3   We must,

49. *currant-butt*] A cask or barrel of an agreed standard of measurement; see *frail*, 45.
50. *sudden*] Quick.
51. *engine*] Invention.
54. *tortoise shell*] Coryat (1611) reports that tortoises, rare in England, were commonly sold in the Venetian markets. As an emblem the tortoise represented both prudent self-containment and silence.
55. *Fitted*] Altered. *these extremities*] Such emergencies; not referring to arms and legs, although he goes on to describe their accommodation.
60. *device*] Something devised; also used of an emblem or crest.
61.1–2, 62.1. The burning of Sir Pol's papers might be arranged in other ways. Peregrine might exit with the papers during the Merchants' rough-and-tumble search, a comic routine of indeterminate length, and return at 62 to answer Merchant 1's question. If so, the Woman would not return after her exit at 27. The fire itself might be seen above in the gallery, or the smoke, the cue for 'funeral', might be wafted on stage by 76. For absurdly broad comedy, Peregrine and the Woman might burn the papers one by one between 62 and 76, within the tortoise's view, while the Merchants seem not to recognise their activities.

And will, sure find him.
MERCHANT 2   Which is his study?

[*Exit Woman with papers*]

MERCHANT 1   What
    Are you, sir?
PEREGRINE   I'm a merchant that came here
    To look upon this tortoise.
MERCHANT 3   How?
MERCHANT 1   St Mark!
    What beast is this?   65
PEREGRINE   It is a fish.
MERCHANT 2   [*Striking the shell*] Come out here!
PEREGRINE   Nay, you may strike him, sir, and tread upon him.
    He'll bear a cart.
MERCHANT 1   What, to run over him?
PEREGRINE   Yes.
MERCHANT 3   Let's jump upon him.
MERCHANT 2   Can he not go?
PEREGRINE   He creeps, sir.
MERCHANT 1   [*Poking with his foot*] Let's see him creep.
PEREGRINE   No, good sir, you will hurt him.
MERCHANT 2   [*Drawing his weapon*] Heart! I'll see him creep, or prick   70
    his guts!
MERCHANT 3   Come out here!
PEREGRINE   [*Restraining Merchant 2*] Pray you, sir – [*Aside to
    Sir Politic*] Creep a little.
MERCHANT 1   Forth!

[*Sir Politic creeps a few paces*]

MERCHANT 2   Yet further!
PEREGRINE   [*Restraining him*] Good sir! [*Aside to Sir Politic*] Creep!

[*Sir Politic creeps a few paces more*]

MERCHANT 2   We'll see his legs.

They pull off the shell and discover him

MERCHANT 3   God's so', he has garters!

---

67. According to Thomas Wilson's *Three Lords and Three Ladies of London* (1590), the
    shell is 'so hard that a loaden cart may go over and not break it'.
68. *go*] Move.
73. *God's so'*] By God's soul. *garters*] Ribbons tied and secured with intricate knots
    below the knee, with the loops and ends dangling by the calves.

MERCHANT 1   Ay, and gloves!
MERCHANT 2   Is this
    Your fearful tortoise?

[*They laugh, as Peregrine removes his own disguise*]

PEREGRINE   Now, Sir Pol, we are even.
    For your next project, I shall be prepared.   75
    I am sorry for the funeral of your notes, sir.
MERCHANT 1   'Twere a rare motion to be seen in Fleet Street.
MERCHANT 2   Ay, i' the term.
MERCHANT 1   Or Smithfield, in the fair.
MERCHANT 3   Methinks 'tis but a melancholic sight!
PEREGRINE   Farewell, most politic tortoise.   80

[*Exeunt Peregrine and Merchants*]
[*Enter Woman*]

SIR POLITIC   Where's my lady?
    Knows she of this?
WOMAN   I know not, sir.
SIR POLITIC   Inquire.

[*Exit Woman*]

    O, I shall be the fable of all feasts,
    The freight of the *gazetti*, ship-boy's tale,
    And, which is worst, even talk for ordinaries.

[*Re-enter Woman*]

WOMAN   My lady's come most melancholic home,   85
    And says, sir, she will straight to sea for physic.
SIR POLITIC   And I, to shun this place and clime forever,
    Creeping with house on back, and think it well
    To shrink my poor head in my politic shell.

[*Exeunt*]

74. *fearful*] Both 'frightening' and 'frightened'. *even*] Quits with each other, each having humiliated the other.
77. *motion*] Puppet-show.
78. *term*] One of the four annual law-terms when clients came to town to hear lawyers argue their cases in court; equivalent to a modern tourist season. *Smithfield*] Site of Bartholomew Fair, held in August.
82. *fable ... feasts*] Talk of the town, food for gossip.
83. *freight ... gazetti*] Topic of the newspapers.
84. *ordinaries*] Taverns; see 2.1.76n.
86. *for physic*] As a rest-cure.

Act 5 scene 5*

> [*Enter*] *Volpone* [*and*] *Mosca: the first in the habit of a commandatore;*
> *the other, of a clarissimo*

VOLPONE   Am I then like him?
MOSCA   O, sir, you are he!
   No man can sever you.
VOLPONE   Good.
MOSCA   But what am I?
VOLPONE   'Fore heaven, a brave *clarissimo*; thou becom'st it!
   Pity thou wert not born one.
MOSCA   If I hold
   My made one, 'twill be well.   5
VOLPONE   I'll go and see
   What news first at the court.
MOSCA   Do so.

> [*Exit Volpone*]

                         My fox
Is out on his hole and, ere he shall re-enter,
I'll make him languish in his borrowed case,
Except he come to composition with me.
Androgyno, Castrone, Nano!   10

> [*Enter Androgyno, Castrone, and Nano*]

ALL   Here.
MOSCA   Go recreate yourselves abroad. Go sport.

> [*Exeunt Androgyno, Castrone, and Nano*]

---

*   The disguises adopted in this scene focus the eye on the reversal in positions between
   servant and master, and the advantage Mosca intends to take of it with his 'fox-trap',
   locking Volpone and his freaks out of the house.
0.1–2. *habit ... commandatore*] A black gown and a red cap with two gold medallions of
   St Mark on either side.
  2. *sever*] Distinguish between.
  3. *brave*] Elegantly dressed.
  4. *hold*] Maintain.
  5. *made one*] Assumed status.
6–7. *fox ... hole*] Alludes to the boys' game in which players hop on one foot while striking
   at opponents with gloves tied to the end of leather thongs.
  8. *case*] Disguise.
  9. *composition*] Terms, agreement.
11. *recreate*] Amuse. *abroad*] Outside.

So, now I have the keys and am possessed.
Since he will needs be dead afore his time,
I'll bury him or gain by him. I'm his heir,
And so will keep me till he share at least.   15
To cozen him of all were but a cheat
Well placed. No man would construe it a sin.
Let his sport pay for't: this is called the fox-trap.

   [*Exit*]

Act 5 scene 6

   [*Enter*] Corbaccio [*and*] Corvino

CORBACCIO   They say the court is set.
CORVINO   We must maintain
   Our first tale good, for both our reputations.
CORBACCIO   Why? Mine's no tale. My son would there have killed me.
CORVINO   That's true, I had forgot. Mine is, I am sure.
   But for your will, sir.   5
CORBACCIO   Ay, I'll come upon him
   For that hereafter, now his patron's dead.

   [*Enter Volpone, disguised*]

VOLPONE   Signor Corvino! and Corbaccio! [*To Corvino*] Sir,
   Much joy unto you.
CORVINO   Of what?
VOLPONE   The sudden good
   Dropped down upon you –
CORBACCIO   Where?
VOLPONE   – And none knows how.
   [*To Corbaccio*] From old Volpone, sir.   10
CORBACCIO   Out, arrant knave!
VOLPONE   Let not your too much wealth, sir, make you furious.

12. *possessed*] In possession of the house; the audience may interpret this word as
   'possessed by demons', or 'mad'.
15. *keep me*] Remain.
18. Let him pay for his amusements.
 1. *set*] For the evening session; see 4.6.61.
 4. *Mine is*] That is, 'My tale is good too'.
 5. *come upon*] Make a claim or demand upon. *him*] Mosca.
11. *furious*] Mad.

CORBACCIO   Away, thou varlet!
VOLPONE   Why, sir?
CORBACCIO   Dost thou mock me?
VOLPONE   You mock the world, sir. Did you not change wills?
CORBACCIO   Out, harlot!
VOLPONE   [*Turns to Corvino*] O! Belike you are the man,
    Signor Corvino? Faith, you carry it well.   15
    You grow not mad withal. I love your spirit.
    You are not over-leavened with your fortune.
    You should ha' some would swell now like a wine-vat
    With such an autumn – Did he gi' you all, sir?
CORVINO   Avoid, you rascal!   20
VOLPONE   Troth, your wife has shown
    Herself a very woman! But you are well,
    You need not care. You have a good estate
    To bear it out, sir, better by this chance.
    Except Corbaccio have a share?
CORBACCIO   Hence, varlet!
VOLPONE   You will not be a'known, sir. Why, 'tis wise.   25
    Thus do all gamesters at all games dissemble.
    No man will seem to win.

   [*Exeunt Corbaccio and Corvino*]

                      Here comes my vulture,
    Heaving his beak up i'the air and snuffing.

Act 5 scene 7

[*Enter*] *Voltore*

VOLTORE   Outstripped thus by a parasite? A slave?
    Would run on errands? And make legs for crumbs?
    Well, what I'll do –

12. *varlet*] Sergeant; an abusive term for a knave or rascal (policing jobs were usually filled by menials).
13. *mock the world*] Can laugh at everyone.
17. *over leavened*] Puffed up, like bread with too much yeast.
19. *autumn*] Harvest.
20. *Avoid*] Go away.
21. *a very woman*] A typical female.
23. *bear it out*] Carry it off, have the upper hand.
25. *a'known*] Acknowledged as heir.
28. See 5.2.108–9n.
 2. *make legs*] Bow and scrape.

VOLPONE   The court stays for your worship.
    I e'en rejoice, sir, at your worship's happiness,
    And that it fell into so learnèd hands   5
    That understand the fingering –
VOLTORE   What do you mean?
VOLPONE   I mean to be a suitor to your worship
    For the small tenement out of reparations,
    That at the end of your long row of houses
    By the Piscaria. It was in Volpone's time,   10
    Your predecessor, ere he grew diseased,
    A handsome, pretty, customed bawdy-house
    As any was in Venice – none dispraised –
    But fell with him. His body and that house
    Decayed together.   15
VOLTORE   Come, sir, leave your prating.
VOLPONE   Why, if your worship give me but your hand
    That I may ha' the refusal, I have done.
    'Tis a mere toy to you, sir, candle-rents.
    As your learned worship knows –
VOLTORE   What do I know?
VOLPONE   Marry, no end of your wealth, sir, God decrease it.   20
VOLTORE   Mistaking knave! What, mock'st thou my misfortune?
VOLPONE   His blessing on your heart, sir. Would 'twere more!

    [*Exit Voltore*]

    Now to my first again, at the next corner.

5–6. *hands ... fingering*] Suggests both skilfully produced handiwork, and clever cheating, like the palming of coins.

  8. *tenement out of reparations*] House in need of repairs; perhaps Volpone's residence.

10. *Piscaria*] The fish-market on a wharf on the Grand Canal, south of St Mark's Square.

12. *customed*] Well-patronised.

13. *none dispraised*] No criticism intended of other houses.

17. *refusal*] That is, first refusal.

18. *candle-rents*] Rent from a deteriorating property (like a candle producing light [= rents] while depleting itself).

20. *decrease*] Calculated malapropism for 'increase', following Shakespeare's Dogberry in *Much Ado About Nothing*. Volpone apparently derives his impersonation of a policeman from the theatre, not from life.

22. *Would ... more*] Deliberately ambiguous; more wealth, or a greater decrease?

Act 5 scene 8

[*Enter*] *Corbaccio* [*and*] *Corvino* [*who watch*] *Mosca passing* [*over the stage*]

CORBACCIO   See, in our habit! See the impudent varlet!
CORVINO   That I could shoot mine eyes at him like gunstones!
VOLPONE   But is this true, sir, of the parasite?
CORBACCIO   Again t'afflict us? Monster!
VOLPONE   [*To Corbaccio*]   In good faith, sir,
   I'm heartily grieved a beard of your grave length   5
   Should be so overreached. I never brooked
   That parasite's hair. Methought his nose should cozen.
   There still was somewhat in his look did promise
   The bane of a *clarissimo*.
CORBACCIO   Knave –
VOLPONE   [*To Corvino*]   Methinks
   Yet you, that are so traded i' the world,   10
   A witty merchant, the fine bird Corvino,
   That have such moral emblems on your name,
   Should not have sung your shame and dropped your cheese,
   To let the fox laugh at your emptiness.
CORVINO   Sirrah, you think the privilege of the place   15
   And your red saucy cap, that seems to me
   Nailed to your jolt-head with those two *zecchins*,
   Can warrant your abuses. Come you hither.
   You shall perceive, sir, I dare beat you. Approach!
VOLPONE   No haste, sir. I do know your valour well,   20
   Since you durst publish what you are, sir.

1. *in our habit*] Dressed as a *clarissimo*.
2. *gunstones*] Cannonballs.
5. *beard ... length*] 'One so old and wise as you'; but also a literal description.
6. *never brooked*] Could never tolerate.
8. *still*] Always.
9. *bane*] Ruin.
10. *traded*] Experienced, but playing on Corvino's merchant status.
12–14. Referring to Aesop's fable of the fox who flatters the crow into singing, thus dropping the piece of cheese in its beak; see 1.2.94–6.
12. *moral emblems*] Drawings symbolising aspects of moral behaviour, accompanied by explanatory verses. Emblem books, common in well-to-do households, were considered suitable reading for women and children.
15. *privilege ... place*] Prerogative as an officer of the court; security within the precincts of the Scrutineo, located in the Doge's palace.
17. *jolt-head*] Blockhead. *zecchins*] The gold medallions of St Mark on either side of the commandatore's cap; see 5.5.0.1–2n.
18. *warrant*] Officially sanction.

CORVINO   Tarry!
    I'd speak with you.
VOLPONE   Sir, sir, another time –
CORVINO   Nay, now!
VOLPONE   O God, sir! I were a wise man
    Would stand the fury of a distracted cuckold.

    [*Enter*] *Mosca* [*and*] *walks by 'em*

CORBACCIO   What! Come again?   25
VOLPONE   [*Aside*]   Upon 'em, Mosca. Save me.
CORBACCIO   The air's infected where he breathes.
CORVINO   Let's fly him.

    [*Exeunt Corbaccio and Corvino*]

VOLPONE   Excellent basilisk! Turn upon the vulture.

Act 5 scene 9

    [*Enter*] *Voltore*

VOLTORE   Well, flesh-fly, it is summer with you now;
    Your winter will come on.
MOSCA   Good advocate,
    Pray thee, not rail, nor threaten out of place thus.
    Thou'lt make a solecism, as Madam says.
    Get you a biggin more. Your brain breaks loose.   5
VOLTORE   Well, sir.
VOLPONE   Would you ha' me beat the insolent slave?
    Throw dirt upon his first good clothes?
VOLTORE   This same
    Is doubtless some familiar!
VOLPONE   Sir, the court

23–4.   *I . . . stand*] Ironic; 'What a wise fellow I would be to withstand'.
27.   *basilisk*] Or cockatrice, a mythical reptile hatched by a serpent from a cock's egg, and
    capable of killing with its glance.
 1.   *flesh-fly*] Blow-fly, translating 'Mosca'; a fly which deposits its eggs in dead flesh.
    summer] Period when the flesh-fly flourishes.
 2.   The flesh-fly is dormant or dies in winter. Voltore's threat foreshadows his attempt to
    avenge himself on Mosca in 5.10.
 4.   See 4.2.43 and note. Presumably this is a favourite word of Lady Would-be's, since
    Mosca was not then present to hear it.
 5.   *a biggin more*] Another lawyer's cap.
 8.   *familiar*] Hanger-on, dependent on Mosca's household or 'family' (see 1.3.35 and
    note); also used of evil spirits attending on witches or inhabiting the possessed.

In troth stays for you. I am mad a mule,
That never read Justinian, should get up   10
And ride an advocate. Had you no quirk
To avoid gullage, sir, by such a creature?
I hope you do but jest; he has not done't.
This's but confederacy to blind the rest.
You are the heir?   15
VOLTORE   A strange, officious,
Troublesome knave! Thou dost torment me.
VOLPONE   I know –
It cannot be, sir, that you should be cozened.
'Tis not within the wit of man to do it.
You are so wise, so prudent, and 'tis fit
That wealth and wisdom still should go together.   20

[*Exit Voltore with Volpone heckling in pursuit*]

Act 5 scene 10*

[*Enter*] *four Avocatori, Notario, Commadatori, Bonario, Celia,
Corbaccio, Corvino*

AVOCATORE 1   Are all the parties here?
NOTARIO   All but the advocate.
AVOCATORE 2   And here he comes.

[*Enter Voltore holding papers, Volpone following*]

AVOCATORE 1   Then bring 'em forth to sentence.
VOLTORE   O, my most honoured fathers, let your mercy
Once win upon your justice to forgive –
I am distracted –   5
VOLPONE   [*Aside*]   What will he do now?
VOLTORE   O,

9–11. *mule . . . advocate*] Inverting the official mode of transport for benchers on their way
    to the lawcourts.
10. *Justinian*] *Corpus Juris Civilis*, the Roman code of law compiled by order of the
    Emperor Justinian, and required reading for seventeenth-century law students at the
    Inns of Court.
11. *quirk*] Law trick.
12. *gullage*] Being duped.
14. *confederacy*] That is, between Mosca and Voltore.
*   Voltore's bid to take control of the plot from Mosca by confessing and throwing himself
    upon the mercy of the court is accompanied by Corvino's insistence that the lawyer is
    mad, an accusation that sets up 5.12.22ff.
 4. *win upon*] Have the advantage of, override.

I know not which t'address myself to first,
    Whether your fatherhoods, or these innocents –
CORVINO   [*Aside*] Will he betray himself?
VOLTORE   – Whom equally
    I have abused, out of most covetous ends –
CORVINO   [*Aside*] The man is mad!   10
CORBACCIO   What's that?
CORVINO   He is possessed.
VOLTORE   – For which, now struck in conscience, here I prostrate
    Myself at your offended feet for pardon. [*He kneels*]
AVOCATORI 1, 2   Arise.
CELIA   O heaven, how just thou art!
VOLPONE   [*Aside*]   I'm caught
    I' mine own noose –
CORVINO   [*Aside to Corbaccio*] Be constant, sir! Nought now
    Can help but impudence.   15
AVOCATORE 1   [*To Voltore*] Speak forward.
COMMANDATORE   [*To courtroom*]   Silence!
VOLTORE   It is not passion in me, reverend fathers,
    But only conscience, conscience, my good sires,
    That makes me now tell truth. That parasite,
    That knave hath been the instrument of all.
AVOCATORE 1   Where is that knave? Fetch him.   20
VOLPONE   I go. [*Exit*]
CORVINO   Grave fathers,
    This man's distracted. He confessed it now;
    For, hoping to be old Volpone's heir,
    Who now is dead –
AVOCATORE 3   How?
AVOCATORE 2   Is Volpone dead?
CORVINO   Dead since, grave fathers –
BONARIO   O, sure vengeance!
AVOCATORE 1   Stay,
    Then he was no deceiver?   25
VOLTORE   O no, none.
    The parasite, grave fathers.
CORVINO   He does speak
    Out of mere envy, 'cause the servant's made

---

7. *innocents*] That is, Celia and Bonario.
10. *possessed*] By a devil; foreshadowing Voltore's trick at 5.12.
15. *Speak forward*] Continue.
16. *passion*] Madness.
24. *since*] That is, since his earlier court appearance.
27. *Out . . . envy*] Entirely out of envy. *made*] Grabbed.

The thing he gaped for. Please your fatherhoods,
This is the truth, though I'll not justify
The other, but he may be some-deal faulty.   30
VOLTORE   Ay, to your hopes as well as mine, Corvino.
But I'll use modesty. Pleaseth your wisdoms
To view these certain notes [*Hands them papers*] and but
confer them.
As I hope favour, they shall speak clear truth.
CORVINO   The devil has entered him!   35
BONARIO   Or bides in you.
AVOCATORE 4   We have done ill by a public officer
To send for him, if he be heir.
AVOCATORE 2   For whom?
AVOCATORE 4   Him that they call the parasite.
AVOCATORE 3   'Tis true.
He is a man of great estate now left.
AVOCATORE 4   Go you, and learn his name, and say the court   40
Entreats his presence here but to the clearing
Of some few doubts.
AVOCATORE 2   This same's a labyrinth!
AVOCATORE 1   Stand you unto your first report?
CORVINO   My state,
My life, my fame –
BONARIO   Where is't?
CORVINO   – are at the stake.
AVOCATORE 1   [*To Corbaccio*] Is yours so too?   45
CORBACCIO   The advocate's a knave,
And has a forkèd tongue –
AVOCATORE 2   Speak to the point.
CORBACCIO   So is the parasite too.
AVOCATORE 1   This is confusion.
VOLTORE   I do beseech your fatherhoods, read but those.

[*Indicating his papers*]

CORVINO   And credit nothing the false spirit hath writ.

28. *gaped for*] Hungered after.
30. *other*] Mosca. *some-deal*] Somewhat.
33. *confer them*] Make sense of them; discuss them together.
36. *public officer*] Volpone, as the commandatore.
40. *learn his name*] So far, Mosca has been introduced only as Volpone's 'parasite, knave, and pander' (4.5.15–16).
43. *state*] Status, or estate.
44. *Are . . . stake*] Are at stake; are guaranteeing the truth of Corvino's 'first report'.
49. *false spirit*] The demon possessing Voltore.

It cannot be but he is possessed, grave fathers.   50

[*The Avocatori examine the papers*]

Act 5 scene 11*

[*Enter*] *Volpone* [*on another part of the stage*]

VOLPONE To make a snare for mine own neck! And run
    My head into it wilfully! With laughter!
    When I had newly 'scaped, was free and clear!
    Out of mere wantonness! O, the dull devil
    Was in this brain of mine when I devised it,   5
    And Mosca gave it second. He must now
    Help to sear up this vein, or we bleed dead.

[*Enter Nano, Androgyno, and Castrone*]

    How now! Who let you loose? Whither go you now?
    What? To buy gingerbread? Or to drown kitlings?
NANO   Sir, Master Mosca called us out of doors,   10
    And bid us all go play, and took the keys.
ANDROGYNO   Yes.
VOLPONE   Did Master Mosca take the keys? Why, so!
I am farther in. These are my fine conceits!
I must be merry, with a mischief to me!
What a vile wretch was I that could not bear   15
My fortune soberly? I must ha' my crotchets!

---

*   In Q, scene xii is labelled as scene x, suggesting that this scene interrupts what was
originally the final court scene. The interpolation may be an afterthought, preparing the
audience for Volpone's decisions in the catastrophe (scene 12). Although the freaks may
perform some juggling and tumbling to imply childish jubilation at unexpected freedom
(see 8–11), the scene itself emphasises Volpone's self-entrapment. Its brevity suggests
that the courtroom activities still occupy centre-stage, perhaps frozen in posture, or
muted, while Volpone and the freaks perform at the edge of the apron stage (either at
the front, or to one side), or possibly above in the gallery.
4.   *wantonness*] Arrogance or self-satisfaction; frivolity.   *dull devil*] Perhaps the wine
which rendered Volpone stupid enough to conceive and act on his plan to twit the
ex-heirs.
6.   *gave it second*] Seconded it.
7.   *sear up*] Cauterise.   *bleed dead*] Will bleed to death; will be slaughtered. Opening a
vein is a technique for killing domestic animals for meat.
9.   *buy . . . kitlings*] Childish diversions.   *kitlings*] kittens.
13.   *farther in*] In deeper trouble, because he is locked out of his own house, and has
nowhere to make a safe retreat.   *conceits*] Ingenious schemes or practical jokes.
16.   *crotchets*] Whimsical fancies, perverse trickery.

And my conundrums! Well, go you and seek him.
His meaning may be truer than my fear.
Bid him, he straight come to me, to the court.
Thither will I and, if't be possible,   20
Unscrew my advocate upon new hopes.
When I provoked him, then I lost myself.

[*Exeunt*]

Act 5 scene 12*

AVOCATORE 1   [*With Voltore's notes*] These things can ne'er
    be reconciled. He here
Professeth that the gentleman was wronged,
And that the gentlewoman was brought thither,
Forced by her husband, and there left.
VOLTORE   Most true.
CELIA   How ready is heaven to those that pray!   5
AVOCATORE 1   But that
    Volpone would have ravished her, he holds
Utterly false, knowing his impotence.
CORVINO   Grave fathers, he is possessed – again I say,
    Possessed! Nay, if there be possession
And obsession, he has both.   10
AVOCATORE 3   Here comes our officer

[*Enter Volpone, still disguised*]

VOLPONE   The parasite will straight be here, grave fathers.
AVOCATORE 4   You might invent some other name, sir varlet.
AVOCATORE 3   Did not the notary meet him?

17. *conundrums*] Whims, crotchets, conceits.
18. *than my fear*] Than I fear it is.
21. *Unscrew*] Disengage, dissuade; shift or alter the behaviour of. *upon*] By means of.
*   The scene begins with the truth revealed in Voltore's notes, and devolves into lies and
    manipulations as Voltore fakes demonic possession, Mosca woos the judges while
    trying to whisper Volpone into submission, and Volpone retaliates by uncasing. The
    final judgments have been censured as anti-climactic in order, and too harsh for a
    comedy. See the General Introduction, pp. 16–18.
  5. *ready*] Responsive.
9–10. *possession ... obsession*] Opposite demonic activity; possession indicates entry of a
    demon into the body; obsession is demonic coercion from without. Ironically, Volpone
    acts as the obsessing demon in renewing his temptation of Voltore, who then undergoes
    an 'exorcism' of the possessing demon.
12. *invent*] Find. *varlet*] Sergeant, implying 'rascal'; see 5.6.12n.

VOLPONE	Not that I know.
AVOCATORE 4 His coming will clear all.	
AVOCATORE 2	Yet it is misty.
VOLTORE May't please your fatherhoods –	15

Volpone whispers [to] the advocate [Voltore]

VOLPONE   Sir, the parasite
    Willed me to tell you that his master lives,
    That you are still the man, your hopes the same,
    And this was only a jest –
VOLTORE   How?
VOLPONE   – sir, to try
    If you were firm and how you stood affected.
VOLTORE   Art sure he lives?   20
VOLPONE   Do I live, sir?
VOLTORE   O me!
    I was too violent.
VOLPONE   Sir, you may redeem it.
    They said you were possessed. Fall down and seem so.
    I'll help to make it good.

Voltore falls

        [*Aloud*] God bless the man!
  [*Aside to Voltore*] Stop your wind hard, and swell. [*Aloud*]
    See, see, see, see!
  He vomits crooked pins! His eyes are set   25
  Like a dead hare's hung in a poulter's shop!

19. *how ... affected*] How loyal you were to Volpone's interests.
20. *Do I live?*] Ironically suggesting that Volpone is as alive as anyone else; not a revelation of Volpone's true identity under the disguise. Voltore must continue to believe that Volpone is a sick old man from whom he might well inherit all.
21. *violent*] Aggressive, bold.
23–4. The course of the exorcism described here would be familiar to the reading public from similarly elaborate symptoms of possession detailed in pamphlets written between 1597 and 1605 on witch-trials (a particular interest of King James). See, for example, Samuel Harsnet, *A Discovery of the Fraudulent Practices of John Darrell* (1599) and *A Declaration of Egregious Popish Impostures* (1603).
24. *stop ... swell*] Hold your breath and puff up. These symptoms are recorded in Harsnet.
25. *vomits ... pins*] Ann Gunter of Windsor, in whose case James took particular interest, reputedly discharged pins from her nose and mouth. *set*] Staring.

His mouth's running away! [*To Corvino*] Do you see, signor?
Now 'tis in his belly –
CORVINO   Ay, the devil!
VOLPONE   – Now in his throat –
CORVINO   Ay, I perceive it plain.
VOLPONE   'Twill out, 'twill out! Stand clear. See where it flies!   30
In shape of a blue toad with a bat's wings!
[*To Corbaccio*] Do not you see it, sir?
CORBACCIO   What? I think I do.
CORVINO   'Tis too manifest.
VOLPONE   Look! He comes t'himself!
VOLTORE   Where am I?
VOLPONE   Take good heart, the worst is past, sir.
You are dispossessed.   35
AVOCATORE 1   What accident is this?
AVOCATORE [2]   Sudden and full of wonder!
AVOCATORE 3   [*Indicating Voltore's papers*] If he were
Possessed, as it appears, all this is nothing.
CORVINO   He has been often subject to these fits.
AVOCATORE 1   Show him that writing. [*To Voltore*] Do you
know it, sir?
VOLPONE   [*Aside to Voltore*] Deny it, sir, forswear it, know it not.   40
VOLTORE   Yes, I do know it well: it is my hand.
But all that it contains is false.
BONARIO   O practice!
AVOCATORE 2   What maze is this!
AVOCATORE 1   Is he not guilty then,
Whom you there name the parasite?
VOLTORE   Grave fathers,
No more than his good patron, old Volpone.   45
AVOCATORE 4   Why, he is dead!
VOLTORE   O no, my honoured fathers.

---

27. *mouth's ... away*] A common phenomenon in fraudulent possession cases. The jaws
move to distort the face, puffing out one side, then the other, before spreading such
twitches to the rest of the body; see next note.
28-9. *belly ... throat*] The rapidity of movements makes it appear as though a demon were
running about inside the body, seeking a hiding-place.
31. Toads and bats were associated with witchcraft and demons.
35. *accident*] Unexpected occurrence.
41. *hand*] Handwriting.
42. *practice*] Deceit.

                    He lives –
AVOCATORE 1 How! Lives?
VOLTORE   Lives.
AVOCATORE 2   This is subtler yet!
AVOCATORE 3 You said he was dead?
VOLTORE   Never.
AVOCATORE 3 [*To Corvino*]   You said so?
CORVINO   I heard so.
AVOCATORE 4 Here comes the gentleman. Make him way.

    [*Enter Mosca*]

AVOCATORE 3 [*To a commandatore*]   A stool.
AVOCATORE 4 [*Aside*] A proper man! And, were Volpone dead,   50
    A fit match for my daughter.
AVOCATORE 3   Give him way.
VOLPONE   [*Aside to Mosca*] Mosca, I was a'most lost. The advocate
    Had betrayed all, but now it is recovered.
    All's o' the hinge again – Say I am living.
MOSCA   [*Aloud*] What busy knave is this? Most reverend fathers,   55
    I sooner had attended your grave pleasures,
    But that my order for the funeral
    Of my dear patron did require me –
VOLPONE   [*Aside*]   Mosca!
MOSCA   – Whom I intend to bury like a gentleman.
VOLPONE   [*Aside*] Ay, quick, and cozen me of all.   60
AVOCATORE 2   Still stranger!
    More intricate!
AVOCATORE 1   And come about again!
AVOCATORE 4 [*Aside*] It is a match. My daughter is bestowed.
MOSCA   [*Aside to Volpone*] Will you gi'me half?
VOLPONE   [*Too loud*]   First I'll be hanged!
MOSCA   [*Quietly*]   I know
    Your voice is good. Cry not so loud.
AVOCATORE 1   Demand
    The advocate. Sir, did not you affirm   65

47. *subtler*] More intricate or complicated.
50. *proper*] Handsome.
54. *o' the hinge*] Running smoothly, in order again.
55. *busy*] Interfering.
60. *quick*] Alive; also, hastily.
61. *come about*] Reversed.
64. *Demand*] Let us question.
65. *Sir*] Addressing Voltore, although Volpone answers for him. The question is redirected
    to Voltore at 70.

Volpone was alive?

VOLPONE   Yes, and he is.

This gent'man [*Indicating Mosca*] told me so. [*Aside to Mosca*]
    Thou shalt have half.

MOSCA   Whose drunkard is this same? Speak some that know him.
    I never saw his face. [*Aside to Volpone*] I cannot now
    Afford it you so cheap.   70

VOLPONE   [*Aside*]   No?

AVOCATORE 1   [*To Voltore*]   What say you?

VOLTORE   The officer told me.

VOLPONE   I did, grave fathers,
    And will maintain he lives with mine own life.
    And that this creature [*Indicating Mosca*] told me. [*Aside*] I was born
    With all good stars my enemies!

MOSCA   Most grave fathers,
    If such an insolence as this must pass   75
    Upon me, I am silent. 'Twas not this
    For which you sent, I hope.

AVOCATORE 2   [*Pointing to Volpone*] Take him away.

VOLPONE   [*Aside to Mosca*] Mosca!

AVOCATORE 3   Let him be whipped –

VOLPONE   [*Aside to Mosca*]   Wilt thou betray me?
    Cozen me?

AVOCATORE 3   – And taught to bear himself
    Toward a person of his rank.   80

AVOCATORE 4   Away!

[*Officers seize Volpone*]

MOSCA   I humbly thank your fatherhoods.

VOLPONE   [*Aside*]   Soft, soft. Whipped?
    And lose all that I have? If I confess,
    It cannot be much more.

AVOCATORE 4   [*To Mosca*]   Sir, are you married?

VOLPONE   [*Aside*] They'll be allied anon. I must be resolute.
    The fox shall here uncase.   85

---

75. *pass*] Be allowed.
79. *bear himself*] Behave courteously.
80. *his*] That is, Mosca's.
81. *Soft, soft*] Hold on, stop.
84. *allied*] Related by marriage, and hence united by common financial interests against
     Volpone.
85. *uncase*] Remove the disguise.

He puts off his disguise

MOSCA   Patron!
VOLPONE   Nay, now
    My ruins shall not come alone. Your match
    I'll hinder sure. My substance shall not glue you
    Nor screw you into a family.
MOSCA   Why, patron!
VOLPONE   I am Volpone, and this [*Indicates Mosca*] is my knave;
    This [*Indicates Voltore*], his own knave; this [*Indicates*   90
        Corbaccio], avarice's fool;
    This [*Indicates Corvino*], a chimera of wittol, fool, and knave;
    And, reverend fathers, since we all can hope
    Nought but a sentence, let's not now despair it.
    You hear me brief.
CORVINO   May it please your fatherhoods –
COMMANDATORE   Silence!
AVOCATORE 1   The knot is now undone by miracle!   95
AVOCATORE 2   Nothing can be more clear.
AVOCATORE 3   Or can more prove
    These innocent. [*Indicates Celia and Bonario*]
AVOCATORE 1   Give 'em their liberty.

    [*Officers release Celia and Bonario*]

BONARIO   Heaven could not long let such gross crimes be hid.
AVOCATORE 2   If this be held the highway to get riches,
    May I be poor.   100
AVOCATORE 3   This's not the gain, but torment.
AVOCATORE 1   These possess wealth as sick men possess fevers,
    Which trulier may be said to possess them.
AVOCATORE 2   Disrobe that parasite.
CORVINO, MOSCA   Most honoured fathers –
AVOCATORE 1   Can you plead aught to stay the course of justice?
    If you can, speak.   105
CORVINO, VOLTORE   We beg favour.
CELIA   And mercy.

87–8. *My ... family*] My wealth will not be used to fix you firmly, through affection or
    extortion, in another household.
  91. *chimera*] A monster of Greek myth, part lion, part goat, and part serpent. *wit-
    tol*] Complaisant cuckold.
  93. *let's ... it*] Let's hear it; don't keep us waiting in suspense any longer.
  94. *You ... brief*] That's my story in a nut-shell.
106. This rejection of mercy is consistent with the office of the Avocatori: they were
    expected to enjoin severer penalties than would be sanctioned by an appeal held before
    the Council of Forty, who were more likely to issue lighter penalties.

AVOCATORE 1   [*To Celia*] You hurt your innocence, suing for the guilty.
    – [*To the others*]
    Stand forth, and first the parasite. You appear
    T'have been the chiefest minister, if not plotter,
    In all these lewd impostures, and now lastly
    Have with your impudence abused the court   110
    And habit of a gentleman of Venice,
    Being a fellow of no birth or blood,
    For which our sentence is first thou be whipped,
    Then live perpetual prisoner in our galleys.
VOLTORE   I thank you for him.   115
MOSCA   Bane to thy wolvish nature!
AVOCATORE 1   Deliver him to the Saffi.

   [*Exit Mosca with some Officers*]

                              Thou, Volpone,
    By blood and rank a gentleman, canst not fall
    Under like censure, but our judgment on thee
    Is that thy substance all be straight confiscate
    To the hospital of the Incurabili;   120
    And since the most was gotten by imposture,
    By feigning lame, gout, palsy, and such diseases,
    Thou art to lie in prison, cramped with irons,
    Till thou be'st sick and lame indeed. Remove him.
VOLPONE   This is called mortifying of a fox.   125

   [*Exit Volpone with some Officers*]

AVOCATORE 1   Thou, Voltore, to take away the scandal
    Thou hast giv'n all worthy men of thy profession,
    Art banished from their fellowship and our state.
    Corbaccio   bring him near. We here possess
    Thy son of all thy state, and confine thee   130
    To the monastery of San' Spirito,

108. *minister*] Agent.
109. *lewd*] Wicked.
115. *bane*] Poison. Wolf's-bane is a poisonous plant in the aconite family.
116. *Saffi*] Bailiffs, subordinate to the commandatori.
120. *Incurabili*] Incurables.
125. *mortifying*] Multiple pun: (1) neutralising or destroying power; (2) subjugating through bodily discipline; (3) humiliating; (4) disposing of property for charitable or public purposes (in Scottish law); (5) hanging game to make it tender for cooking.
130. *state*] Estate.
131. *San' Spirito*] Monastery of the Holy Spirit, located on a small island between the Giudeca and the mainland.

Where, since thou knew'st not how to live well here,
Thou shalt be learned to die well.

CORBACCIO   [*Straining to hear*]   Ha! What said he?

COMMANDATORE   You shall know anon, sir.

AVOCATORE 1   Thou, Corvino, shalt
Be straight embarked from thine own house and rowed   135
Round about Venice, through the Grand Canalé,
Wearing a cap with fair long ass's ears
Instead of horns, and so to mount, a paper
Pinned on thy breast, to the Berlino –

CORVINO   Yes,
And have mine eyes beat out with stinking fish,   140
Bruised fruit, and rotten eggs – 'Tis well. I'm glad
I shall not see my shame yet.

AVOCATORE 1   – And to expiate
Thy wrongs done to thy wife, thou art to send her
Home to her father with her dowry trebled.

[*To all three*]

And these are all your judgments –   145

ALL   Honoured fathers!

AVOCATORE 1   – Which may not be revoked. Now you begin,
When crimes are done and past and to be punished,
To think what your crimes are. Away with them!

[*Exeunt Voltore, Corbaccio, and Corvino with Officers*]

[*To audience*] Let all that see these vices thus rewarded
Take heart, and love to study 'em. Mischiefs feed   150
Like beasts till they be fat, and then they bleed.

[*Exeunt*]

136. *Grand Canale*] The S-shaped main canal of Venice, two miles long.

139. *Berlino*] Pillory.

143. This judgment is merely an official separation of husband and wife, not an annulment or a divorce, dispensations that only the Pope could grant.

145–6. *judgments ... revoked*] Not strictly accurate. The Council of Ten could supersede the Avocatori's judgments. In practice, the Avocatori only judged 'small causes'; in 'great causes', especially involving a clarissimo, the Avocatori could merely censure criminals without having the power to sentence them. Once a charge was brought and argued to a decision, then the final judgment for imprisonment, torture, or permission to appeal rested with the Council of Forty. In an appeal, the Avocatori acted as prosecutors, and the prisoners responded through lawyers for the defence. See Lewkenor's translation of Contarini (1599), p. 91.

150–51. *Mischiefs ... bleed*] Evil-doers are fattened like beasts on the success of their crimes, and then slaughtered.

[*Re-enter*] *Volpone* [*for the epilogue*]*

VOLPONE   The seasoning of a play is the applause.
    Now, though the fox be punished by the laws,
    He yet doth hope there is no suff'ring due
    For any fact which he hath done 'gainst you.
    If there be, censure him: here he doubtful stands.   5
    If not, fare jovially, and clap your hands.

THE END

[THE ACTORS]**

This comedy was first

acted in the year

1605.

By the King's Majesty's

Servants.   5

---

*   Volpone survives his role in the play, following the tradition of the fox and the Harlequin actor. For the parallels to Reynard the Fox, see Introduction, pp. 60–61. The Harlequin's traditional costume of mask and fox-tail and his chameleon-like nature also suggest the similarity between the *Commedia* trickster, originally a demon-figure, and Volpone, himself an actor in court revels (see 3.7.160–64) as well as in private life. Note the particular pleasure Volpone derives from playing the actor Scoto of Mantua (2.2).

4. *fact*] Crime.

**3. *1605*] Old calendar; probably February or March 1606.

4–5. *King's Majesty's Servants*] The King's Men, formerly the Lord Chamberlain's Men, the company at the Globe Theatre in which Shakespeare was a principal shareholder.

The principal comedians were:

Richard Burbage	John Hemminges
Henry Condel	John Lowin
William Sly	Alexander Cooke

With the allowance of the Master of Revels.   10

6. *comedians*] Actors.
7. *Richard Burbage*] 1567–1619. Son of James Burbage, manager of The Theatre, Shoreditch, where Richard was probably an apprentice; timbers from this play-house were used to build the first Globe in 1599. A principal shareholder of the Globe, he also owned the Blackfriars theatre, which became the winter house of the King's Men in 1609. Burbage was the most popular actor in London, particularly praised for his tragic parts; in *BF*, Jonson called him the 'best actor'. He probably played Volpone. *John Hemminges*] 1556–1630. A principal shareholder of the Globe, he apparently served as business manager; the Revels Accounts indicate that he received payments for court performances, and Jonson's *Christmas* portrays Hemminges and Burbage hiring a boy-actor for the company. With Henry Condel, he arranged for the publication of the first folio of Shakespeare's works in 1623. He may have played Sir Pol.
8. *Henry Condel*] d. 1627. Another major shareholder in the King's Men and by 1620 the company's leading figure. He, Hemminges, and Burbage were the only actors mentioned by name in Shakespeare's will and given money for memorial rings. He helped Hemminges edit the Shakespeare folio in 1623. He probably played Mosca. *John Lowin*] 1576–1659. A latecomer to the King's Men in 1603, later, after Burbage's death, taking over many leading roles, and becoming manager after Hemminges and Condel retired in 1623. He may have been the original Peregrine.
9. *William Sly*] d. 1608. Joined the company in 1594 and left in 1605. He is featured in Webster's Induction to Marston's *The Malcontent*, along with Burbage, Lowin, and Condel, playing themselves. He may have played Voltore. *Alexander Cooke*] d. 1614. Another latecomer, like Lowin, and may have played Bonario.
10. *Master of Revels*] Licensed all public and court performances; after 1607, he licensed plays for printing.

TEXTUAL NOTES

Selected Variants between the 1616 Folio and the 1607 Quarto Texts of *Volpone*

This list gives word-changes, additions, and omissions where Q differs from the F text. Since Q has no marginal stage directions, those omissions are not indicated here. The line-references and words in the lemmas are from the modernised text based on the folio. The variants are given in old spelling, but in standardised type. Because the punctuation in Q's 3.7 gives a vivid impression of the emotional state of the speaker, I have included it here. Obvious misprints are not listed.

Dedication

After 7, Q adds: There followes an Epistle, if you dare venture on the length.

Epistle

0.   *Q adds title:* The Epistle.
49.   *Yet*] F; or Q.
50.   *ingenuously*] F; ingeniously Q.
65.   *severe*] F; graue Q.
69.   *among*] F; in Q.
75.   *filth*] F; garbage Q.
103–4. *I shall ... speak*] F; Vpon my next opportunity toward the examining and digesting of my notes, I shall speake more wealthily, and pay the World a debt. Q.
105. *For the present*] F; In the meane time Q, *beginning a new paragraph.*
After 121, Q adds: From my house in the Black-Friars this 11. of February. 1607. Q *follows with several commendatory verses by Jonson's friends, including John Donne, Francis Beaumont, George Chapman, John Fletcher, and Nathan Field*

The Persons of the Play

PLAY] F; COMOEDYE Q.
10.   *Women*] F; Women 2 Q.
12.   *The scene: Venice*] F; *not in* Q.

Prologue

1.   *yet*] F; God Q.
27.   *fro'*] *this edition*; for Q, F.

Act 1

1.1.53.   *the*] F; a Q.
1.2.69.   *Selves*] F; Themselues Q.
1.2.74.   *E'en his*] F; His very Q.
1.2.79.   *waits*] F; shall waite Q.

1.2.87.	*Without*] F; Within Q.
1.2.99.	*without*] F; within Q.
1.2.125.	*catarrhs*] F; Catarrhe Q.
1.4.28.	*do*] F; *not in* Q.
1.4.40.	*MOSCA*] F; CORB. Q.
1.4.60.	*What then*] F; But what Q.

Act 2

2.1.50.	*Archdukes!*] F; Arch-duke, Q.
2.1.64.	*knew*] F; know Q.
2.2.64.	*'t makes*] F; makes Q.
2.2.77.	*of*] F; *not in* Q.
2.2.141.	*besides*] F; beside Q.
2.3.1.	*Spite o'*] F; Bloud of Q.
2.3.12.	*It is*] F; 'Tis Q.
2.4.6.	*an*] F; some Q.
2.4.37.	*now*] F; *not in* Q.
2.6.75.	*who*] F; that Q.

Act 3

3.4.90.	*Montaigne*] MONTAGNIE F; *Montagniè* Q. *See annotation.*
3.7.111.	*ask.*] F; aske – Q.
3.7.116.	*precious,*] F; precious – Q.
3.7.122.	*satisfy.*] F; satisfie – Q.
3.7.132.	*lost.*] F; lost, – Q.
3.7.239.	*pierced,*] pierc'd; F; pierc'd – Q.
3.7.240.	*opened,*] open'd; F; open'd – Q. *touched,*] touch'd; F; touch'd – Q.
3.7.241.	*you,*] you: F; you, – Q.
3.7.242.	*saints,*] F; Saints – Q. *heaven,*] F; Heauen – Q.
3.7.243.	*scape!*] scape. F; scape – Q.
3.7.244.	*me!*] me. F; me – Q.
3.7.246.	*were.*] were, F; were – Q.
3.7.248.	*lust*] lust; F; lust – Q.
3.7.251.	*beauty!*] beauty: F; beauty – Q.
3.7.253.	*rebellion!*] rebellion. F; rebellion – Q.
3.7.255.	*marrow!*] marrow: F; marrow – Q.
3.7.256.	*honour!*] honour. F; honour – Q.
3.7.258.	*health,*] F; health – Q.
3.8.9.	*Th'hast*] F; Thou hast Q.

Act 4

4.1.57.	*too*] F; two Q.
4.1.93.	*PEREGRINE*] F; POL. Q.
4.3.18.	*see*] F; use Q.
4.4.16.	*doth*] F; do's Q.
4.5.4.	*So the young man*] F; So has the youth Q.
4.5.43.	*goodness*] F; vertue Q.
4.5.55.	*Which*] F; That Q.
4.5.72.	*lords*] F; Sires Q.

4.5.127.   shame] F; harme Q.
4.5.130.   catholic] F; Christian Q.

Act 5

5.2.33–6.   'My ... fathers'] F prints this mimicry in roman type within parentheses; Q
            prints it in italics without parentheses.
5.2.102.   F adds in margin: Cestus.; not in Q.
5.3.1–78.   F gives the inventory in roman type; Q italicises it.
5.3.8.   the hour] F; th'houre Q.
5.4.55.   Fitted] F; Apted Q.
5.7.3.   your] Q; you F.
5.8.13.   your shame] Q; you shame F.
5.10.30.   some-deal] F; somewhere Q.
5.10.50.   but he is possessed, grave fathers] F; (my Sires) but he is possest Q.
5.12.54.   o' the hinge] F; on the henge Q.
5.12.130.   thy state] F; thy'estate Q.

EPICOENE, OR THE SILENT WOMAN

INTRODUCTION

The setting: London

Epicoene is the first Jonson play to make no bones about its London setting. *Every Man Out of his Humour* had fudged the location as 'The Fortunate Isle', although its streets and buildings were all in the London area. *Every Man In his Humour* was revised as a London play some time between 1606 and 1612, perhaps as a result of the success of *Eastward Ho!*, Jonson's city-comedy collaboration with Chapman and Marston. Even *Volpone* alludes to several London locales. Despite its expansive references to London, Southwark, and Westminster, however, the setting of *Epicoene* is actually confined to a small network of backstreets in the emerging West End just north of the Strand between St Martin's Lane and Drury Lane, where many new houses for the gentry were being erected. Quite aside from the artistic need for unity of place, Jonson selected this location for satiric and thematic reasons.

The Strand area was fast becoming the most fashionable address in London. It was also convenient for the socially ambitious and the politically powerful – the only thoroughfare for pedestrians or coaches going from the City or the Inns of Court to Westminster and Whitehall. Sir Amorous La Foole has prestigious lodgings directly on the Strand near the New Exchange and the china-houses, where the urban elite purchased luxuries. Truewit describes at length the quest for rich gowns and rejuvenating cosmetics, as well as the shop-at-home services supplied by 'embroiderers, jewellers, tirewomen, sempsters, feathermen, perfumers' (2.2.91–2). Morose woos Epicoene with talk of lineners, lace-women, wires, knots, ruffs, roses, girdles, fans, scarves, and gloves (2.5.62–9), and Mrs Otter, herself a seller of 'China stuffs' and a purchaser of damask, satin, and velvet (3.2.53–66), berates her husband for ingratitude, though she maintains him in silk stockings and fine linen (3.1.35–6). Quantity has supplanted quality. To borrow Otter's pun at the end of 3.3, '*decora*' – beautiful things – have replaced 'decorum', fitting behaviour.

Jonson set the play in this neighbourhood not only to take advantage of its reputation for conspicuous consumption, but also for its noise. If not for snobbery, why would Morose choose to live here, even with double walls, treble ceilings, caulked windows, and padded doors? Aside from the rattle of carts, coaches-and-four, and social chitchat, the streets echoed with the cries of fishwives, orange-women, chimney-sweeps, costermongers, broom-sellers, and smiths –

brass-workers, pewterers, and other hammermen. Itinerant musicians looking for dinner-parties to entertain, messengers with trumpets, and drummers advertising displays of bearbaiting, fencing, or tightrope-walking competed with the almost constant bellringing that tolled the parish deaths; 1609 had been a bad year for plague, keeping theatres closed until 9 December. Satirically, the Strand was the perfect setting for self-displaying Wits, Braveries, and Collegiates in their effusive social whirl, affirming Jonson's condemnations in *Discoveries* of affectation, imposture, and all the distempers of learning: 'wheresoever manners, and fashions are corrupted, language is. It imitates the public riot. The excess of feasts, and apparel, are the notes of a sick state; and the wantonness of language, of a sick mind' (Parfitt 1975: p. 403).

The concrete setting also enriches and familiarises the play for the London audience. Many of the play's first spectators were fashionable Inns of Court gentlemen and other near neighbours of the Whitefriars, the theatre closest to the Strand, just east of the Inner Temple. Intimate with city life and literature, such an audience would recognise how particular place names evoke the satirical types associated with them. Mistress Otter threatens to send the Captain back to Bankside and the Bear Garden to punish him for his vulgarity, ironically assuming her commercial breeding provides a superior standard of gentility. Otter dis-assembles his wife as a puppet of fashion whose teeth come from Blackfriars, eyebrows from the Strand, and hair from Silver Street. When Morose projects Dauphine's impoverished future, he imagines him in the seediest haunts of London, languishing in Coleharbour, drunk at the Three Cranes, and finally forced to flee England altogether, like other wastrels and criminals. To get rid of his wife, Morose volunteers to suffer the worst noises of Westminster Hall, Tower Wharf, London Bridge, Paris Garden, or Billingsgate. Truewit terrifies Daw with descriptions of a murderous La Foole, armed like a villain from St Sepulchre's parish. These city sites clarify social conditions generally by distinguishing class, gender, and type as features of place, uniting the audience through the common territorial bonds of tolerated discomfort, arbitrary loyalty, and shared urbanity.

Sources

Epicoene is more frequently seen as the source of the Restoration comedy of manners, rather than as having sources itself. The most commonly cited ancient sources are two declamations by Libanius of Antioch; the speaker of each is named Dyskalos, or Morosus in the Latin translation. In declamation 26, *The Loquacious Woman*, a noise-hating man marries an apparently quiet woman who then horrifies him with her loquacity and rowdy friends at the wedding feast; he begs the court to let him kill himself. Jonson borrowed many details from this source, even Morose's complaints of floods of noise, Mute's signs, and the parson's coughing. In declamation 27, *The Peevish Father*, a father disinherits his son for laughing at him. Jonson had to replace the son with a nephew to accommodate the marriage plot: Morose wants to disinherit Dauphine by producing a closer heir of his own.

Many of the anti-marriage sentiments derive from Juvenal's sixth satire on the miseries of marriage, compounded by Ovid's justification of cosmetics, promiscuity, and the irresponsible seduction of women in *The Art of Love*. The plot of the boy-bride resembles Aretino's *Il Marescalco* (1533), a comedy about a homosexual mysogynist victimised by a nasty practical joke: he is simultaneously forced into marriage and taunted with disgusting forecasts of life with a woman. When he tries to escape by pleading impotence, the instigator of the joke reveals that the bride is a boy, much to the groom's delight. Machiavelli's *Clizia* and Plautus's *Casina* also feature a boy-bride foisted on an old man, and if those plays have little bearing on Jonson's plot, they do echo, by way of the eroticism of boys, the suggestive sexual atmosphere of *Epicoene* and its boy-actors.

So too does the name 'Epicoene', a close approximation of 'Epicenes', the boy-lover of men and women in Aristophanes' *Ecclesiazusae*. The Ladies Collegiate themselves resemble Aristophanes' female legislators in their inversion of gender roles. They also resemble the women in Joseph Hall's *Mundus Alter et Idem* [*Another World and Yet the Same*] (1605), translated by John Healey in a crudely entertaining style, redolent of Thomas Nashe, as *The Discovery of a New World* (1609). In Book 2 of this work, Hall describes 'Viraginia' or 'Shee-landt' as a noisy 'Paradice for women' in which men do all the housework, and women rule by democratically raising their voices in a constant public squawking of opinion. Although all the women are equal, some are elevated in status as 'Gravesses', elected by elders. Jonson was clearly thinking of Healey's translation when he called Lady Haughty, the leader of the Ladies Collegiate, a 'grave and youthful matron' (1.1.71). Shee-landt is a land of parrots, full of fine feathers and empty heads mindlessly repeating what they hear, and bordered by blocs of lechers, hermaphrodites, fools, and rogues – not unlike Jonson's picture of the West End. Like Jonson's women, the Shee-landresses do not reproduce, but the population swells continually with women flocking from other countries where females are less privileged. They delight in cosmetics and perfumes, and are never at home except to dress. Otherwise, they spend their time at theatres or taverns dancing, singing, and seducing men with standard courtship practices: flirtation, pleading, bribes, or force. As Dauphine remarks of the Ladies' wooing: 'I was never so assaulted' (5.2.45). Shee-landt's military garrison is at 'Amazonia', or 'Shrewes-bourg', where the men are so subject to their wives that they seek permission to 'goe pisse' or 'passe a word with their best friend' (ch. 7). An uprising of husbands miscarried there, just as Otter's solitary rebellion fails. All men in Shee-landt have to swear to conditions of obedience to women: never to plot against a woman, or interrupt her; to cede authority to women; to avoid lechery and bad company; to be monogamous; never to betray the wife's secrets, or deny her ornaments; and always to praise women for beauty, wit, and eloquence, and defend them from detractors. The Otters' marriage 'instrument', and presumably the contracts signed by other Collegiate husbands, make similar promises. The premise of Hall's book on Shee-landt is that the narrator is true to his oath; the information given is not intended to discount women's power, he claims, but the failure of gender-role-switching speaks for itself in the slovenly men, ill-kept public buildings, and barren fields.

Stage history

Epicoene was first performed by the Children of her Majesty's Revels at Whitefriars either in December 1609 or January 1610, and was banned by early February after Lady Arabella Stuart complained of an allusion to herself and the Prince of Moldavia (see the note on 5.1). Jonson protested his innocence in another prologue, and no action was taken to prevent the play's publication intact in the 1616 folio. By 1619, the King's Men owned the play, and performed it twice at court in 1636.

After the Restoration in 1660, it was the first play to be performed when the theatres reopened. In 1663, Mrs Knepp played Epicoene, and subsequent performances through the first half of the eighteenth century – at least forty-two were recorded between 1711 and 1748 – continued to use a female in the role. When Garrick's revival failed in 1752, the play was assumed to have lost its popularity. In 1776, Garrick remounted a bowdlerised adaptation by George Colman, and for later performances, between 1777 and 1784, restored a boy-actor to play the silent woman. Those were the last performances until the twentieth century, except for the 1895 Harvard production using Colman's adaptation.

In 1909, the Marlowe Society at Cambridge returned to Jonson's 1616 folio script with an all-male cast, and Oxford followed suit in 1938. Despite many student productions after 1945, the records show few professional stagings in this century. After the Mermaid Repertory Company's performance in 1905 with a male Epicoene, the Phoenix Company, also with a male Epicoene, mounted a brief and modestly successful run in 1924, but the Birmingham Repertory staging in 1947 received bad reviews as a dirty play. The Bristol Old Vic production of 1959 staged it as a simple farce with the emphasis on physical gags. In Oxford 1964, the Margate Stage Company modernised the play apparently to emphasise its sexual relevance, but unaccountably cast a female Epicoene, thus short-circuiting its contemporary concept of juke-boxes and leather-jacketed gangs playing sexual games. The 1968 Oxford Playhouse production sensibly reverted to period. Most recently, the Manchester Umbrella Theatre mounted a production in 1980, as did the York Festival in 1984, and the Royal Shakespeare Company at the Swan in 1989. Like the 1980 production, the RSC emphasised the nastiness of the gallants, but did not make their hilariously nightcapped Morose unduly sympathetic. In these productions, a male actor performed Epicoene with satisfyingly androgynous charm.

Further reading

Steve Brown (1990) has written the indispensable text for understanding the effect of boy-actors on audiences. Huston D. Hallahan (1977) uses emblems to illustrate different concepts of gender behaviour. Barbara C. Millard (1984) discusses androgyny and the gap between cultural and actual representations of the masculine and the feminine. Karen Newman (1991) has very useful chapters on body politics, marriage, sartorial extravagance, femininity, and commodification in early modern London; Leo Salingar (1986: pp. 175–88) discusses fashion in the context of farce. For another view of fashionable life and Jonson's influence on Restoration comedy, see Emrys Jones (1982). Ian Donaldson focuses on Morose in '"A Martyr's Resolution": *Epicoene*', (1970: pp. 24–45), and John Gordon Sweeney examines Truewit in '*Epicene*: "I'le Doe Good To No Man Against His Will"' (1985: pp. 105–24). Finally, Helene Foley (1982) and Froma Zeitlin (1980–82), in their discussions of Aristophanes, elucidate by implication the classical models on which Jonson based his battle of the sexes.

EPICOENE

OR

THE SILENT WOMAN

A Comedy

Acted in the year 1609 by
the Children of her Majesty's
Revels

The Author B[en] J[onson]

HORAT[IO]

Ut sis tu similis Caeli, Byrrhique latronum,
Non ego sim Capri, neque Sulci. Cur metuas me?

LONDON
Printed by WILLIAM STANSBY

M DC XVI

Children of her Majesty's Revels] Formerly called the Children of the Chapel Royal, a company of boy-actors who acted at Blackfriars from 1597 to 1603; in 1600, they performed CR, and in 1601, *Poet*. Although the company was probably known by its new name earlier, it was offically changed by patent on 4 January 1610. The actors were authorised to use the Whitefriars Theatre, formerly the refectory hall of the monastery, renovated in 1606 on the model of the second Blackfriars playhouse. When they first

[DEDICATION]

TO THE TRULY
NOBLE, BY ALL
TITLES,
Sir Francis Stuart

Sir,   5
  My hope is not so nourished by example as it will conclude this dumb
piece should please you by cause it hath pleased others before, but by trust
that, when you have read it, you will find it worthy to have displeased none.
This makes that I now number you not only in the names of favour but the
names of justice to what I write, and do presently call you to the exercise   10
of that noblest and manliest virtue as coveting rather to be freed in my fame
by the authority of a judge than the credit of an undertaker. Read, therefore,
I pray you, and censure. There is not a line or syllable in it changed from
the simplicity of the first copy. And when you shall consider, through the

performed *SW* in December 1609 or January 1610, the manager was Nathan Field,
  formerly a chorister and boy-actor in the company.
  [*Ut sis . . . metuas me?*] From Horace, *Satires* 1.4.69–70: 'Though you may be like the
  robbers, Coelus and Byrrhus, I am not like Caprius and Sulcius [loud-mouthed
  professional informers]. Why are you afraid of me?'
  4. *Sir Francis Stuart*] By profession a naval officer; according to Aubrey (*Brief Lives*), 'He
      was a learned gentleman and one of the club at the Mermaid in Friday Street with Sir
      Walter Ralegh, etc.'
  6. *dumb*] Silent, because printed, not performed. The performance had been suppressed
      in 1610 (see 18 below; and the Introduction to *SW*, p. 233).
  7. *by cause*] Because.
  9. *makes that I*] Makes me.
  10. *presently*] Now, at this time.
  11. *be freed . . . fame*] Have my name cleared.
  12. *authority . . . judge*] Impartial decision of an expert.   *undertaker*] Financial sponsor
      or political backer, frequently in the pejorative sense of a partisan manipulator of
      opinion.
  13. *censure*] Judge, assess the evidence.
  14. *simplicity*] Honesty, candour (Latin, *simplicitas*), with an implication of artlessness.
      See the second stanza of Clerimont's song in 1.1.

certain hatred of some, how much a man's innocency may be endangered   15
by an uncertain accusation, you will, I doubt not, so begin to hate the
iniquity of such natures as I shall love the contumely done me, whose end
was so honourable as to be wiped off by your sentence.

Your unprofitable but true lover,

Ben Jonson   20

16. *uncertain accusation*] Jonson was accused of satirising Lady Arabella Stuart in La
    Foole's comments on the Prince of Moldavia and 'his mistress, Mistress Epicoene',
    5.1.20–21. See note, p. 344.
17. *contumely*] Defamation of character.
19. *unprofitable*] Modestly suggesting one whose friendship brings no advantages.

THE PERSONS OF THE PLAY

MOROSE, *a gentleman that loves no noise*
DAUPHINE EUGENIE, *a knight, his nephew*
CLERIMONT, *a gentleman, his friend*
TRUEWIT, *another friend*
EPICOENE, *a young gentleman supposed the silent woman*   5
JOHN DAW, *a knight, her servant*
AMOROUS LA FOOLE, *a knight also*
THOMAS OTTER, *a land and sea captain*
CUTBEARD, *a barber*
MUTE, *one of Morose his servants*   10

1. *MOROSE*] Derived from Latin for peevish, wayward, and unsocial. In casuistry, as defined by Aquinas and St Augustine, 'morose thoughts' are evil or unclean fantasies contemplated habitually and pleasurably.
2. *DAUPHINE EUGENIE*] A contradictory name for a man; in French, Princess Eugenia. The name associates him with effeminate mimics of French modishness and with the sexual ambivalence described variously in the play. The *dauphin* is the heir apparent to the King of France; Eugenie literally means fine offspring, although it may include a pun on fine wit (*génie*, wit).
3. *CLERIMONT*] A French-sounding name, possibly derived from a French romance by Des Escuteaux, *Les Chastes et Heureuses Amours de Clarimond et Antonide* (Paris, 1601); perhaps a variation on *clairement*, suggesting plain speaking or dealing. In either case, the meaning is ironically at odds with the character's behaviour.
4. *TRUEWIT*] 'Wit' means ingenuity, rather than the more modern sense of clever repartee. The addition of 'true' suggests a loyalty or legitimacy that his behaviour really lacks.
5. *EPICOENE*] One having the characteristics of both genders; a contradictory combination of sexual features. The term was used of masculine women and effeminate men. *silent woman*] Considered a paradox, or impossibility, like Middleton's *A Chaste Maid in Cheapside* or Dekker's *An Honest Whore*.
6. *JOHN DAW*] Thus permitting the nickname Jack Daw. A jackdaw, a small crow adapted to urban life, is easily tamed and taught to imitate the sounds of words; it is known for its loquacity and thefts. *servant*] Lover.
7. *AMOROUS LA FOOLE*] Another French-sounding feminine combination reflecting Jonson's contempt for 'Frenchified' English sophisticates. The name suggests the foolish would-be lover.
8. *OTTER*] A playful and agile animal with characteristics of both land and sea creatures, thus considered unclassifiable biologically and hence sexually; another paradoxical character. The Otter marriage further demonstrates the inversion of sexual roles in the dominant woman and the submissive male.
10. *MUTE*] The traditional term for an actor who has stage business but no lines; this mute paradoxically speaks at the end of 2.1.

MADAM HAUGHTY
MADAM CENTAUR   } *Ladies Collegiates*
MISTRESS MAVIS

MISTRESS TRUSTY, *the Lady Haughty's woman* }
 Pretenders   15
MISTRESS OTTER, *the captain's wife*

PARSON
PAGES
SERVANTS

The scene: London

11. *HAUGHTY*] High-ranking, as well as arrogant.

12. *CENTAUR*] In Greek mythology, a beast half-man, half-horse, representing wild life, animal desires, and barbarism. Typically centaurs hunted in packs, and were lustful and violent, especially when drunk. In the most notorious of their misdeeds, intoxicated centaurs attempted to rape the bride at the wedding feast of Pirithous and Hippodamia, the result was a battle between the centaurs and the groom's family. Applied to a female, the name suggests sexual paradox, since the centaurs were a race of males. *Ladies Collegiates*] Another contradiction. Women could not be members of traditional colleges or fraternities, whether religious or secular. The title suggests that the women have formed their own independent guild or self-governing association, with similarly exclusive rights and privileges.

13. *MAVIS*] A song-thrush, a bird known for its sweet song but associated contemptuously with other birds that seem to be types of human vanity like the popinjay or the peacock. The name may also be a variant on the Latin name Mavors, from Mars, the god of war; or, based on 5.2.30–1, may refer to the definition in Florio (1598): *maviso*, or *malviso*, an ill face. For Florio's influence on Jonson, see the Introduction to *Volp*, 'Sources', and the notes to The Persons of the Play.

15. *Pretenders*] Aspirants to College membership.

20. **London**] The first time Jonson openly set a play in London; subsequent plays followed suit.

PROLOGUE*

Truth says, of old, the art of making plays
    Was to content the people, and their praise
    Was to the poet money, wine, and bays.
But in this age a sect of writers are
    That only for particular likings care,   5
    And will taste nothing that is popular.
With such we mingle neither brains nor breasts;
    Our wishes, like to those make public feasts,
    Are not to please the cooks' tastes, but the guests'.
Yet, if those cunning palates hither come,   10
    They shall find guests' entreaty and good room;
    And though all relish not, sure there will be some
That, when they leave their seats, shall make 'em say,
    Who wrote that piece could so have wrote a play,
    But that he knew this was the better way.   15
For to present all custard, or all tart,
    And have no other meats to bear a part,
    Or to want bread and salt, were but coarse art.

---

*   Jonson claims a disingenuous intention to please his audience with this play. Despite the fact that he wrote it for the boy-actors to perform in a private theatre, its aim, he argues, is not elitist or satirically 'particular': he separates himself from writers who eschew the 'popular' and play up to the snobbery of private theatre patrons. The invitation to enjoy this play is inclusive: he has something for everyone, of whatever class or trade, and like the 'salt' that preserves the cheeks, 'red with laughter', of the *Volp* spectators, so too the leftovers from this feast of comedy will nourish the audience with entertainment for a week afterwards.

2. *content the people*] Elsewhere Jonson insists that the goal of playwrights is 'to profit and delight' the audience: see the next prologue ('Another'), l. 2, or *Volp* Prologue, 8.

3. *bays*] Acclaim; laurel leaves crowning a poet laureate.

5. *particular*] Narrowed to the interests of one group.

7. *mingle ... breasts*] Dissociate ourselves intellectually and emotionally.

9. *cooks'*] Referring to the writers' tastes (cf. lines 4–5), as opposed to the *guests'*, or audience's, tastes.

10. *cunning*] Refined, artistically knowledgeable.

11. *entreaty*] Entertainment.

14. *piece*] One part or scene of the play.

16. *custard*] From 'crustade', an open pie containing meat or fruit, thickened with broth, or milk, and egg.

17. *meats*] Dishes, not necessarily fowl or joints.

18. *bread and salt*] Basic staples at the table. *coarse*] Punning on 'course', or service of food.

The poet prays you, then, with better thought
   To sit; and when his cates are all in brought,   20
   Though there be none far-fet, there will dear-bought
Be fit for ladies, some for lords, knights, squires,
   Some for your waiting-wench and city-wires,
   Some for your men and daughters of Whitefriars.
Nor is it only while you keep your seat   25
   Here that his feast will last; but you shall eat
   A week at ord'naries on his broken meat,
         If his muse be true,
         Who commends her to you.

ANOTHER

Occasioned by some persons' impertinent exception

The ends of all who for the scene do write
   Are, or should be, to profit and delight.
And still 't hath been the praise of all best times,
   So persons were not touched, to tax the crimes.
Then in this play which we present tonight   5
   And make the object of your ear and sight,
On forfeit of yourselves, think nothing true,

20. *cates*] Provisions, delicacies.
21. *far-fet, dear-bought*] Imported, expensive. Proverbially, 'Far-fet and dear-bought is good for ladies'.
23. *city-wires*] Fashionable city women. Wires supported stiff collars, ruffs, and head-dresses.
24. *daughters of Whitefriars*] According to Lady Would-be (*Volp* 4.2.51), transvestite women who dressed in men's clothes in order to commit crimes. Whitefriars, a liberty in the city of London, was a sanctuary for thieves like the cross-dresser Mary Frith, known as Moll Cutpurse the Roaring Girl, as well as for more conventional lawbreakers. Whitefriars was also the indoor theatre in the disestablished Carmelite priory of Whitefriars where *SW* was performed; its 'daughters' were punningly the boys who played women's parts.
27. *ord'naries*] Taverns that served fixed-price meals; also a place to hear the latest gossip or jokes. *broken meat*] Leftovers.
 0. *persons'*] This prologue seems to address a complaint made by several people (see last line), but F reads '*Occasion'd by some persons impertinent exception*', not indicating singular or plural. *impertinent exception*] Irrelevant or silly objection.
 1. *scene*] Stage (Latin, *scena*).
 3. *still*] Always. *praise*] Worthwhile activity.

Lest so you make the maker to judge you,
For he knows poet never credit gained
   By writing truths, but things like truths well feigned.   10
If any yet will with particular sleight
   Of application wrest what he doth write,
And that he meant or him, or her, will say:
   They make a libel which he made a play.

---

8. *maker*] Poet.

11–14. Jonson frequently had to defend himself against charges of writing satires of particular persons, usually by claiming that his words were twisted by malicious spectators. See also the *Volp* Epistle or the induction to *BF*.

11. *sleight*] Trick, juggling.

13. *And ... will say*] Inverted syntax: 'And will say that he meant or him or her'; that is, will claim that Jonson intended to satirise either one or another particular man or woman.

ACT 1

Act 1 scene 1*

[*Enter*] *Clerimont. He comes out making himself ready,* [*attended by*]
    Boy

CLERIMONT   Ha' you got the song yet perfect I ga' you, boy?
BOY   Yes, sir.
CLERIMONT   Let me hear it.
BOY   You shall, sir, but i'faith let nobody else.
CLERIMONT   Why, I pray?   5
BOY   It will get you the dangerous name of a poet in town, sir,
    besides me a perfect deal of ill will at the mansion you wot of, whose
    lady is the argument of it, where now I am the welcom'st thing under
    a man that comes there.

---

*   This dressing scene became justly famous for wittily establishing the private London
    setting and manners among people of leisure. In his lodgings near the Strand, Clerimont
    idles his way through Act 1 drifting from music and gossip to ablutions and fashion,
    accepting social calls and dinner invitations. Much of the chatter is about other
    morning visits: Clerimont's boy describes how the Ladies Collegiate kiss, garb, and
    fondle him during their levee; Clerimont's song is about the art of dressing, and he
    prefers talk of 'pins and feathers and ladies' to morality; Truewit tells a story of a
    woman who put her wig on backwards when surprised at her morning toilet, and
    Dauphine's uncle always wears 'a huge turban of nightcaps on his head, buckled over
    his ears' to keep out the town's noises. Despite the casually inconsequential flow, all the
    information given here is vital to the development of the plot. Etherege borrowed this
    concept for Act 1 of *The Man of Mode*, and variations on the theme followed in the
    opening scenes of Wycherley's *The Country Wife* and *The Plain Dealer*, Congreve's
    Love for Love, and Sheridan's *School for Scandal*, to name only a few later playwrights
    influenced by Jonson.
1.1.0.1.   *making himself ready*] Dressing, stage business that may occupy all of this act.
  1.   *perfect*] Memorised; at 1.7, only emphasising a large amount.
  6.   *dangerous ... poet*] Refers both to the low social status of poets, and to the statutes
    against writing personal satire (labelled sedition, libel, or slander), for which Jonson
    had been imprisoned more than once. The second prologue specifically denies any such
    satire in this play.
7–8.   *mansion ... lady*] Quarters of the Ladies Collegiate, headed by Lady Haughty,
    described more fully later in this scene.
  7.   *wot*] know.
  8.   *argument*] Subject.   *under*] Sexual quibble, continued by *above*, 10.

CLERIMONT   I think, and above a man too, if the truth were racked   10
     out of you.

BOY   No, faith, I'll confess before, sir. The gentlewomen play with
     me, and throw me o' the bed, and carry me in to my lady, and she
     kisses me with her oiled face, and puts a peruke o' my head, and asks
     me an' I will wear her gown, and I say no, and then she hits me a blow   15
     o' the ear, and calls me innocent, and lets me go.

CLERIMONT   No marvel if the door be kept shut against your master
     when the entrance is so easy to you – Well, sir, you shall go there no
     more, lest I be fain to seek your voice in my lady's rushes a fortnight
     hence. Sing, sir.   20

     Boy sings
     [*Enter Truewit*]

TRUEWIT   Why, here's the man that can melt away his time, and
     never feels it! What between his mistress abroad and his ingle at home,
     high fare, soft lodging, fine clothes, and his fiddle, he thinks the hours
     ha' no wings, or the day no post-horse. Well, sir gallant, were you
     struck with the plague this minute, or condemned to any capital pun-   25
     ishment tomorrow, you would begin then to think and value every

10. *above*] Better than; taller than, joking on the small stature of the boy, and his stretched
     size if he were pulled on the rack.   *racked*] Tortured.
14. *oiled*] Greasy with cosmetic preparations.   *peruke*] Wig.
15. *an'*] If.
16. *innocent*] Idiot.
17–18. *door ... entrance*] Sexual quibble. Clerimont has been trying in vain to attract
     Haughty's attention as a lover.
19. *fain*] Forced.   *rushes*] Green rushes were strewn on bare floors to act as carpets and
     primitive air-fresheners. The allusion is to the whispering rushes that told of King
     Midas's ass's ears; the implication is that the boy will make a fool of his master by
     succeeding sexually where Clerimont has failed. Since boy sopranos lose their voices as
     they develop sexually, possibly Clerimont fears that precocious experience may cause
     his singing page's voice to break prematurely (Adams 1979).
20.1. *Boy sings*] Presumably he begins the song that he sings in its entirety later in this
     scene.
22. *ingle*] Catamite; boy kept for homosexual use.
23. *high fare*] Sumptuous meals.   *fiddle*] Clerimont may be accompanying the boy on a
     stringed instrument. The viola da gamba was in fashion especially for love-songs and
     often appeared metaphorically as the beloved in poems and paintings.
24. *post-horse*] Ridden by an express messenger. Suggests that for Clerimont, time has no
     meaning.

article o' your time, esteem it at the true rate, and give all for't.

CLERIMONT   Why, what should a man do?

TRUEWIT   Why, nothing, or that which, when 'tis done, is as idle. Harken after the next horse-race or hunting-match. Lay wagers. Praise Puppy or Peppercorn, Whitefoot, Franklin. Swear upon White-mane's party. Spend aloud, that my lords may hear you. Visit my ladies at night and be able to give 'em the character of every bowler or better o' the green. These be the things wherein your fashionable men exercise themselves, and I for company.   30   35

CLERIMONT   Nay, if I have thy authority, I'll not leave yet. Come, the other are considerations when we come to have grey heads and weak hams, moist eyes and shrunk members. We'll think on 'em then; then we'll pray and fast.

TRUEWIT   Ay, and destine only that time of age to goodness which our want of ability will not let us employ in evil?   40

CLERIMONT   Why, then 'tis time enough.

TRUEWIT   Yes, as if a man should sleep all the term, and think to effect his business the last day. O Clerimont, this time, because it is an incorporeal thing and not subject to sense, we mock ourselves the fineliest out of it with vanity and misery indeed, not seeking an end of wretchedness, but only changing the matter still.   45

CLERIMONT   [*Prompting him*]   Nay, thou'lt not leave now –

TRUEWIT   See but our common disease! With what justice can we complain that great men will not look upon us nor be at leisure to give our affairs such dispatch as we expect, when we will never do it to ourselves: nor hear nor regard ourselves.   50

CLERIMONT   Foh, thou hast read Plutarch's *Morals* now, or some such tedious fellow, and it shows so vilely with thee, 'fore God, 'twill spoil thy wit utterly. Talk me of pins and feathers and ladies and rushes and such things, and leave this *stoicity* alone, till thou mak'st sermons.   55

TRUEWIT   Well, sir! If it will not take, I have learned to lose as little

27. *article o' your time*] Moment.
30. *Harken after*] Seek out.
31–2. *Puppy … Whitemane*] 'Horses o' the time', a marginal note in *F1*.
32. *party*] Side in a contest.   *Spend aloud*] Make noise, used of hounds baying at game.
33. *give … the character of*] Gossip.
34. *green*] Bowling green. The popularity of lawn-bowling at court, instead of manly sports like archery, was seen as decadent.
36. *leave*] Leave off.
38. *hams*] Back of the knees, or hind-quarters in general.
43. *term*] One of the periods for trying cases in the law courts.
49. *common disease*] Commonly found shortcoming.
56. *stoicity*] Loosely meaning puritanical severity.

of my kindness as I can. I'll do good to no man against his will,
certainly. When were you at the college?

CLERIMONT   [*Feigning ignorance*] What college?   60

TRUEWIT   As if you knew not!

CLERIMONT   No, faith, I came but from court yesterday.

TRUEWIT   Why, is it not arrived there yet, the news? A new foundation, sir, here i' the town, of ladies that call themselves the Collegiates,
an order between courtiers and country-madams that live from their   65
husbands and give entertainment to all the wits and braveries o' the
time, as they call 'em, cry down or up what they like or dislike in a
brain or a fashion with most masculine, or rather, *hermaphroditical*
authority, and every day gain to their college some new probationer.

CLERIMONT   Who is the president?   70

TRUEWIT   The grave and youthful matron, the Lady Haughty.

CLERIMONT   A pox of her autumnal face, her pieced beauty! There's
no man can be admitted till she be ready nowadays, till she has
painted and perfumed and washed and scoured, but the boy here, and
him she wipes her oiled lips upon like a sponge. I have made a song,   75
I pray thee hear it, o' the subject.

[*Boy sings again*]

> song
> *Still to be neat, still to be dressed,*
> *As you were going to a feast;*

66. *wits and braveries*] Fashionable cliques of clever talkers and trendy dressers.

67. *cry down or up*] Decry or praise. Such public verbal freedoms suggest sexual freedoms
as well. Silence would show virtue.

68. *hermaphroditical*] Mannishly feminine, as opposed to genuinely masculine. Truewit
echoes Stubbes's criticism in *The Anatomy of Abuses* (Furnivall 1882: p. 68) of
women's shameless encroachment on male attitudes and fashions: 'Wherefore these
women may not improperly be called hermaphroditi, that is monsters of both kinds,
half women, half men.'

71. *grave*] Solemn and sober, befitting age rather than youth.

72. *autumnal*] Combining beauty and decay, a paradox as in the previous line's 'grave and
youthful', or the subsequent 'pieced [mended or botched] beauty'.

73. *ready*] Fully dressed and made up.

74. *painted and perfumed*] symptoms of female vanity that indicate household disorder
and unchastity.

76.2 **song**] A clever reworking of a poem found in a Leyden manuscript of the *Anthologia
Latina* (Codex Vossianus, Q 86), published by Scaliger in 1572; other versions of the
poem appeared in Pithou's *Epigrammata et Poemata Vetera* (Paris, 1590) and
Petronius's *Satyricon* (Paris, 1585 and 1587).

77. *Still*] Always. *neat*] Perfectly turned out.

Still to be powdered, still perfumed:
Lady, it is to be presumed,   80
Though art's hid causes are not found,
All is not sweet, all is not sound.
Give me a look, give me a face,
That makes simplicity a grace.
Robes loosely flowing, hair as free: 85
Such sweet neglect more taketh me
Than all th'adulteries of art.
They strike mine eyes, but not my heart.

TRUEWIT   And I am clearly o' the other side. I love a good dressing
before any beauty o' the world. O, a woman is then like a delicate   90
garden; nor is there one kind of it. She may vary every hour, take often
counsel of her glass, and choose the best. If she have good ears, show
'em; good hair, lay it out; good legs, wear short clothes; a good hand,
discover it often; practise any art – to mend breath, cleanse teeth,
repair eyebrows, paint – and profess it.   95
CLERIMONT   How? Publicly?
TRUEWIT   The doing of it, not the manner: that must be private.
Many things that seem foul, i' the doing, do please, done. A lady
should indeed study her face when we think she sleeps; nor when the
doors are shut should men be inquiring. All is sacred within then. Is   100
it for us to see their perukes put on, their false teeth, their complexion,
their eyebrows, their nails? You see gilders will not work but enclosed.
They must not discover how little serves with the help of art to adorn
a great deal. How long did the canvas hang afore Aldgate? Were the
people suffered to see the city's *Love* and *Charity* while they were   105
rude stone, before they were painted and burnished? No. No more
should servants approach their mistresses but when they are complete
and finished.
CLERIMONT   Well said, my Truewit.
TRUEWIT   And a wise lady will keep a guard always upon the place,   110

---

84. *simplicity*] Lack of ornament.
86. *taketh*] Captivates.
87. *adulteries*] Adulterations.
101. *complexion*] Punning on natural skin colour and texture; and application of cosmetics
    to the face. See *Volp* 4.2.6.
102. *gilders*] Craftsmen who apply gold leaf.
103. *discover*] Reveal.
104. *Aldgate*] The eastern entrance to the city through London Wall, demolished in 1604,
    and rebuilt by 1609. Within the new gate stood gilded statues of women, Peace on the
    south side carrying a dove in one hand and a garland in the other, and Charity on the
    north side holding a child in one arm and leading another by the hand.

that she may do things securely. I once followed a rude fellow into a
chamber where the poor madam, for haste and troubled, snatched at
her peruke to cover her baldness and put it on the wrong way.

CLERIMONT O prodigy!

TRUEWIT And the unconscionable knave held her in compliment an   115
hour with that reversed face, when I still looked when she should talk
from the t'other side.

CLERIMONT Why, thou shouldst ha' relieved her!

TRUEWIT No, faith, I let her alone, as we'll let this argument, if you
please, and pass to another. When saw you Dauphine Eugenie?   120

CLERIMONT Not these three days. Shall we go to him this morning?
He is very melancholic, I hear.

TRUEWIT Sick o' the uncle, is he? I met that stiff piece of formality,
his uncle, yesterday, with a huge turban of nightcaps on his head,
buckled over his ears.   125

CLERIMONT O, that's his custom when he walks abroad. He can
endure no noise, man.

TRUEWIT So I have heard. But is the disease so ridiculous in him as
it is made? They say he has been upon divers treaties with the
fishwives and orange-women, and articles propounded between them.   130
Marry, the chimney-sweepers will not be drawn in.

CLERIMONT No, nor the broom-men: they stand out stiffly. He cannot endure a costardmonger. He swoons if he hear one.

TRUEWIT Methinks a smith should be ominous.

CLERIMONT Or any hammerman. A brazier is not suffered to dwell   135
in the parish, nor an armourer. He would have hanged a pewterer's

---

114. *prodigy*] An amazing or marvellous thing, especially if abnormal or monstrous.

115. *compliment*] Fashionable small-talk.

122. *melancholic*] Depressed.

123. *Sick o' the uncle*] Playing on 'sick of the mother', denoting hysteria, originally thought
to be a woman's disease caused by a disturbance in the uterus.

130. *fishwives*] Known for their loud foul language while crying their wares (still called
'billingsgate' after the fish-market near that city gate). *orange-women*] Like fishwives, known for their piercing voices.

131. *chimney-sweepers*] Also cried their services in the streets. Sweeping out the soot
improved the 'draw' or upward draught of smoke through the chimney; hence
Truewit's pun on their refusal to be enticed into ('drawn in') peace treaties between
Morose and the street-women.

132. *broom-men*] Pedlars who either sold brooms or swapped them for other saleable
articles. *stand out*] Refuse to join; also quibbles on sexual erection, emphasising the
masculinity of men who reject being grouped with women.

133. *costardmonger*] Fruit-seller.

135. *hammerman*] Metal-worker, generally. *brazier*] Brass-worker.

136. *armourer*] Manufacturer of chain-mail. *pewterer*] Maker of pewter utensils.

'prentice once upon a Shrove-Tuesday's riot for being o' that trade, when the rest were quit.

TRUEWIT   A trumpet should fright him terribly, or the hau'boys.

CLERIMONT   Out of his senses. The waits of the city have a pension   140
of him not to come near that ward. This youth practised on him one night like the bellman, and never left till he had brought him down to the door with a longsword, and there left him flourishing with the air.

BOY   Why, sir, he hath chosen a street to lie in so narrow at both   145
ends that it will receive no coaches nor carts nor any of these common noises, and therefore we that love him devise to bring him in such as we may, now and then, for his exercise, to breathe him. He would grow resty else in his ease. His virtue would rust without action. I entreated a bearward one day to come down with the dogs of some   150
four parishes that way, and I thank him he did, and cried his games under Master Morose's window till he was sent crying away with his head made a most bleeding spectacle to the multitude. And another time a fencer marching to his prize had his drum most tragically run through for taking that street in his way, at my request.   155

TRUEWIT   A good wag. How does he for the bells?

CLERIMONT   O, i' the Queen's time, he was wont to go out of town every Saturday at ten o'clock, or on holiday eves. But now, by reason

---

137. *Shrove-Tuesday's riot*] The last Tuesday before Lent, a holiday for apprentices, whose rowdy celebrations traditionally included wrecking brothels and playhouses.

137–8. *for being ... quit*] That is, hanged simply for being a hammerman, when apprentices of other trades were acquitted for their share in the riots.

139. *hau'boys*] Oboes.

140. *waits*] Municipally supported street musicians.

141. *This youth*] Clerimont's boy.   *practised*] Played a trick.

142. *bellman*] Night-watchman who rang the hours and called out news. He also wakened people who did not keep a lantern burning at their doors to help maintain street safety.

148. *breathe*] Exercise briskly.

149. *resty*] Restive or peevish because of inactivity.   *virtue*] Manhood (Latin, *virtus*).   *action*] Exercise, implying substituted sexual activity.

150. *bearward*] Trainer of bears. He often attracted attention to announcements of bear-baitings by playing bagpipes.

154. *marching to his prize*] Parading through the street with drummers to advertise a fencing match.

156. *wag*] Mischief-maker.   *bells*] Church bells.

of the sickness, the perpetuity of ringing has made him devise a room
with double walls and treble ceilings, the windows close shut and   160
caulked, and there he lives by candlelight. He turned away a man last
week for having a pair of new shoes that creaked. And this fellow
waits on him now in tennis-court socks, or slippers soled with wool,
and they talk each to other in a trunk. See who comes here.

Act 1 scene 2*

[Enter] Dauphine

DAUPHINE   How now! What ail you sirs? Dumb?
TRUEWIT   Struck into stone almost, I am here, with tales o' thine uncle!
There was never such a prodigy heard of.
DAUPHINE   I would you would once lose this subject, my masters, for my
sake. They are such as you are that have brought me into that   5
predicament I am with him.
TRUEWIT   How is that?
DAUPHINE   Marry, that he will disinherit me, no more. He thinks I and my
company are authors of all the ridiculous acts and monuments are
told of him.   10
TRUEWIT   'Slid, I would be the author of more to vex him. That purpose
deserves it: it gives thee law of plaguing him. I'll tell thee what I would
do. I would make a false almanac, get it printed, and then ha' him

159. *sickness*] Plague, exceptionally virulent in 1609, when more deaths were recorded
than in any other year of James I's reign.   *perpetuity of ringing*] During severe
periods of plague, the passing-bells tolled parish death knells almost continuously. In
a city of 114 churches, the noise would be overwhelming.

161. *turned away a man*] Dismissed a servant.

162. *this fellow*] That is, the current employee.

164. *trunk*] Speaking-tube or ear-trumpet, into which servants may whisper when necessary.

*   The delayed entrance of the key plotter, Dauphine, sets off his secretiveness against the
chatter of the others. While Clerimont arouses Truewit's indignation with details of the
play's chief problem – Morose's intention of disinheriting his nephew Dauphine by
marrying and producing a son – Dauphine apparently resigns himself in silence to the
loss of a fortune.

3. *prodigy*] Monster.

9. *acts and monuments*] Anecdotes testifying to Morose's odd behaviour, enshrining him
in gossip as a comic martyr by referring to the original title of John Foxe's *The Book
of Martyrs* (1563, frequently reissued; the fifth edition was in 1596, and the sixth in
1610).

11. *'Slid*] A corruption of 'by God's eyelid', a popular oath.   *That purpose*] Morose's
intention of disinheriting Dauphine.

12. *gives thee law*] Entitles you.

drawn out on a coronation day to the Tower-wharf, and kill him with
the noise of the ordnance. Disinherit thee! He cannot, man. Art   15
not thou next of blood and his sister's son?

DAUPHINE   Ay, but he will thrust me out of it, he vows, and marry.

TRUEWIT   How! That's a more portent. Can he endure no noise, and will
venture on a wife?

CLERIMONT   Yes. Why, thou art a stranger, it seems, to his best trick   20
yet. He has employed a fellow this half year all over England to harken
him out a dumb woman, be she of any form or any quality, so she be
able to bear children. Her silence is dowry enough, he says.

TRUEWIT   But I trust to God he has found none.

CLERIMONT   No, but he has heard of one that's lodged i' the next   25
street to him who is exceedingly soft-spoken, thrifty of her speech,
that spends but six words a day. And her he's about now, and shall
have her.

TRUEWIT   Is't possible! Who is his agent i' the business?

CLERIMONT   Marry, a barber, one Cutbeard, an honest fellow, one   30
that tells Dauphine all here.

TRUEWIT   Why, you oppress me with wonder! A woman, and a barber,
and love no noise!

CLERIMONT   Yes, faith. The fellow trims him silently and has not the
knack with his shears or his fingers, and that continence in a barber   35
he thinks so eminent a virtue as it has made him chief of his counsel.

TRUEWIT   Is the barber to be seen? or the wench?

CLERIMONT   Yes, that they are.

TRUEWIT   I pray thee, Dauphine, let's go thither.

DAUPHINE   I have some business now. I cannot, i' faith.   40

TRUEWIT   You shall have no business shall make you neglect this, sir.
We'll make her talk, believe it, or if she will not, we can give out at
least so much as shall interrupt the treaty. We will break it. Thou art
bound in conscience, when he suspects thee without cause, to torment
him.   45

DAUPHINE   Not I, by any means. I'll give no suffrage to't. He shall never

---

14. *coronation day*] Anniversary of the king's coronation, 24 March, celebrated by salutes
of guns and cannons (*ordnance*, 15) at the Tower of London.

18. *a more portent*] A greater or more ominous portent, since Dauphine can legitimately
be disinherited if he is supplanted by a closer heir.

21-2. *harken ... out*] Search by inquiry.

22. *form ... quality*] Synonyms for rank or merit in learning, appearance, or social
standing.

32 *oppress*] Crush, weigh down. *woman ... barber*] Both proverbially loquacious.

35. *knack*] Clacking or snapping sound.

43. *interrupt the treaty*] Hinder the negotiation.

46. *suffrage*] Permission.

ha' that plea against me that I opposed the least fancy of his. Let it lie upon my stars to be guilty, I'll be innocent.

TRUEWIT   Yes, and be poor, and beg – do, innocent – when some groom of his has got him an heir, or this barber, if he himself cannot. 50 Innocent! [*To Clerimont*] I pray thee, Ned, where lies she? Let him be innocent still.

CLERIMONT   Why, right over against the barber's, in the house where Sir John Daw lies.

TRUEWIT   You do not mean to confound me! 55

CLERIMONT   Why?

TRUEWIT   Does he that would marry her know so much?

CLERIMONT   I cannot tell.

TRUEWIT   'Twere enough of imputation to her, with him.

CLERIMONT   Why? 60

TRUEWIT   The only talking sir i' th' town! Jack Daw! And he teach her not to speak – God b'w'you. I have some business too.

CLERIMONT   Will you not go thither then?

TRUEWIT   Not with the danger to meet Daw, for mine ears.

CLERIMONT   Why? I thought you two had been upon very good terms. 65

TRUEWIT   Yes, of keeping distance.

CLERIMONT   They say he is a very good scholar.

TRUEWIT   Ay, and he says it first. A pox on him, a fellow that pretends only to learning – buys titles, and nothing else of books in him.

CLERIMONT   The world reports him to be very learned. 70

TRUEWIT   I am sorry the world should so conspire to belie him.

CLERIMONT   Good faith, I have heard very good things come from him.

TRUEWIT   You may. There's none so desperately ignorant to deny that. Would they were his own. God b'w'you, gentlemen.

[*Exit Truewit*]

CLERIMONT   This is very abrupt! 75

47–8. *Let . . . stars*] Even if I am fated.

48, 49. *innocent*] Shifting the meaning from 'not guilty' to 'fool'.

53. *over against*] Opposite, across from.

55. *confound*] Perplex, astound.

59. *imputation to her*] Slur on her reputation.

61. *only talking sir*] Foremost blabbermouth.

62. *God b'w'you*] God be with you, corrupted eventually to 'good-bye'.

69. *buys titles*] Double-edged comment, implying that Daw knows only the titles, not the content, of books; and that his knighthood is purchased, not inherited. The latter is also apparently true of Dauphine (see Morose's final diatribe in 2.5).

74. *Would . . . own*] Implies Daw plagiarises his witty remarks.

Act 1 scene 3*

DAUPHINE   Come, you are a strange open man to tell everything thus.

CLERIMONT   Why, believe it, Dauphine, Truewit's a very honest fellow.

DAUPHINE   I think no other, but this frank nature of his is not for secrets.

CLERIMONT   Nay then, you are mistaken, Dauphine. I know where he
    has been well trusted and discharged the trust very truly and heartily.   5

DAUPHINE   I contend not, Ned, but with the fewer a business is carried,
    it is ever the safer. Now we are alone, if you'll go thither, I am for
    you.

CLERIMONT   When were you there?

DAUPHINE   Last night, and such a *Decameron* of sport fallen out! Boccace   10
    never thought of the like. Daw does nothing but court her, and the
    wrong way. He would lie with her, and praises her modesty; desires
    that she would talk and be free, and commends her silence in verses
    which he reads and swears are the best that ever man made. Then rails
    at his fortunes, stamps, and mutines why he is not made a councillor   15
    and called to affairs of state.

CLERIMONT   I pray thee, let's go. I would fain partake this. Some water,
    boy.

   [Exit Boy]

DAUPHINE   We are invited to dinner together, he and I, by one that came
    thither to him, Sir La Foole.   20

CLERIMONT   O, that's a precious manikin!

DAUPHINE   Do you know him?

CLERIMONT   Ay, and he will know you too, if ere he saw you but once,
    though you should meet him at church in the midst of prayers. He is
    one of the braveries, though he be none o' the wits. He will salute a   25
    judge upon the bench and a bishop in the pulpit, a lawyer when he is
    pleading at the bar, and a lady when she is dancing in a masque, and
    put her out. He does give plays and suppers, and invites his guests to

---

*   The relative degree of secrecy is what marks the difference between the two sets of
   gallants. Dauphine criticises Clerimont for being 'open' and Truewit for being 'frank',
   but mocks Daw's ludicrous indiscretion in courting the silent woman, just as Clerimont
   derides La Foole's disruptive greetings and invitations, issued to draw attention in
   public places.

 1. *open*] Unreserved.

 6. *contend not*] Do not dispute it.

10. *Decameron*] Using Boccaccio's title to suggest hyperbolically a hundred different
   comic follies.

15. *mutines why*] Complains rebelliously that.

21. *manikin*] Little man, often used contemptuously; puppet.

28. *put her out*] Make her lose her step by distracting her attention.

'em aloud out of his window as they ride by in coaches. He has a
lodging in the Strand for the purpose, or to watch when ladies are   30
gone to the china-houses or the Exchange, that he may meet 'em by
chance and give 'em presents, some two or three hundred pounds
worth of toys, to be laughed at. He is never without a spare banquet
or sweetmeats in his chamber for their women to alight at and come
up to, for a bait.   35

DAUPHINE   Excellent! He was a fine youth last night, but now he is much
finer! What is his Christian name? I ha' forgot.

[*Enter Boy*]

CLERIMONT   Sir Amorous La Foole.
BOY   The gentleman is here below that owns that name.
CLERIMONT   'Heart, he's come to invite me to dinner, I hold my life.   40
DAUPHINE   Like enough. Pray thee, let's ha' him up.
CLERIMONT   Boy, marshal him.
BOY   With a truncheon, sir?
CLERIMONT   Away, I beseech you.

[*Exit Boy*]

I'll make him tell us his pedigree now and what meat he has to   45
dinner, and who are his guests, and the whole course of his fortunes,
with a breath.

30. *Strand*] Fashionable residential and commercial street for gentry in the early seventeenth century, on the only road to Westminster.
31. *china-houses*] Shops for luxury goods imported from the Orient, and fashionable
meeting-places, especially for lovers. *Exchange*] The New Exchange in the Strand, a
fashionable shopping mall that had just opened in April 1609.
33. *toys*] Trifles, trinkets. *laughed at*] Either at the toys, or at La Foole. *spare banquet*] Snack of sweets, fruit, and wine.
34. *their*] Beaurline (1966) emends to 'there', arguing it is a doublet for 'their' in the days
of unstandardised spelling. The emendation eliminates the problem of 'their women',
which should refer to the women who frequent the china-houses and the Exchange, not
their womenservants. But see Truewit's advice on bribing the lady's maid, 4.1.101–7,
at which Clerimont seems appalled.
42. *marshal*] Conduct, or show in.
43. *truncheon*] Punning on a marshal's ceremonial staff and a cudgel.
45. *meat*] Food.

Act 1 scene 4*

[*Enter Sir Amorous*] *La Foole*

LA FOOLE   'Save, dear Sir Dauphine, honoured Master Clerimont.

CLERIMONT   Sir Amorous! You have very much honested my lodging
with your presence.

LA FOOLE   Good faith, it is a fine lodging! Almost as delicate a lodging as
mine.   5

CLERIMONT   Not so, sir.

LA FOOLE   Excuse me, sir, if it were i' the Strand, I assure you. I am come,
Master Clerimont, to entreat you wait upon two or three ladies to
dinner today.

CLERIMONT   How, sir! Wait upon 'em? Did you ever see me carry dishes?   10

LA FOOLE   No, sir, dispense with me. I meant to bear 'em company.

CLERIMONT   O, that I will, sir. The doubtfulness o' your phrase, believe
it, sir, would breed you a quarrel once an hour with the terrible boys,
if you should but keep 'em fellowship a day.

LA FOOLE   It should be extremely against my will, sir, if I contested with   15
any man.

CLERIMONT   I believe it, sir. Where hold you your feast?

LA FOOLE   At Tom Otter's, sir.

DAUPHINE   Tom Otter? What's he?

LA FOOLE   Captain Otter, sir. He is a kind of gamester, but he has had   20
command both by sea and by land.

DAUPHINE   O, then he is *animal amphibium*?

---

*   The satire on pedigree and ornate coats of arms attacks the faking of noble descent in
'mushroom' gentlemen like La Foole and Daw, who seem to spring up out of darkness
overnight. A more extended example appears in Act 3 of *EMO*: Sogliardo's coat depicts
a headless boar rampant, indicating his stupidity and social-climbing vulgarity. But
many new landowners, like Shakespeare, acquired coats of arms to symbolise their
achieved status. Jonson's friend, Edmond Bolton, wrote a manual of heraldry for do-it-
yourselfers (printed 1610); his mentor Camden served in the College of Heralds; and
Jonson himself devised impresas for his masques.

1.   *'Save*] Abbreviation of 'God save you'.

2.   *honested*] Honoured.

4.   *delicate*] Delightful, elegant: one of La Foole's trendy words.

11.   *dispense with me*] Affected for 'excuse me'.

13.   *terrible boys*] Street bullies or roughnecks, also called 'angry boys' (see Kastril in *Alch*)
or 'roarers' (like Val Cutting in *BF*).

15.   *contested*] Fought.

20.   *gamester*] Gambler.

22.   *animal amphibium*] That is, a creature of two contradictory natures.

LA FOOLE   Ay, sir. His wife was the rich china-woman that the courtiers
   visited so often, that gave the rare entertainment. She commands all
   at home.   25
CLERIMONT   Then she is Captain Otter?
LA FOOLE   You say very well, sir. She is my kinswoman, a La Foole by the
   mother side, and will invite any great ladies for my sake.
DAUPHINE   Not of the La Fooles of Essex?
LA FOOLE   No, sir, the La Fooles of London.   30
CLERIMONT   [*Aside to Dauphine*] Now he's in.
LA FOOLE   They all come out of our house, the La Fooles o' the north, the
   La Fooles of the west, the La Fooles of the east and south – we are as
   ancient a family as any is in Europe – but I myself am descended
   lineally of the French La Fooles – and we do bear for our coat yellow,   35
   or *or*, checkered *azure* and *gules*, and some three or four colours more,
   which is a very noted coat and has sometimes been solemnly worn by
   divers nobility of our house – but let that go, antiquity is not respected
   now – I had a brace of fat does sent me, gentlemen, and half a dozen
   of pheasants, a dozen or two of godwits, and some other fowl which   40
   I would have eaten while they are good, and in good company – there
   will be a great lady or two, my Lady Haughty, my Lady Centaur,
   Mistress Dol Mavis – and they come a' purpose to see the silent
   gentlewoman, Mistress Epicoene, that honest Sir John Daw has
   promised to bring thither – and then Mistress Trusty, my Lady's   45
   woman, will be there too, and this honourable knight, Sir Dauphine,
   with yourself, Master Clerimont – and we'll be very merry and have
   fiddlers and dance – I have been a mad wag in my time, and have spent

23. *china-woman*] Importer of luxury goods from the far east; also suggests she keeps a
   bawdy house, since china-houses were places of assignation.
24. *rare entertainment*] Splendid festivity. Jonson may refer to the East India Company's
   banquet of 1609 where guests received fine china to celebrate the launching of the new
   ship *Trade's Increase*; or perhaps the ceremonial opening of the New Exchange on the
   Strand, at which the royal family and the court were diverted with elaborate speeches,
   gifts, and spectacles.
28. *mother side*] Elides the possessive 's, as in 'river side'.
31. *in*] Theatrical term, meaning Dauphine has fed him the cue, and La Foole is now ready
   to deliver his set speech.
35. *coat*] Coat of arms. Jonson often jokes about heraldry, an obsessive hobby of the rising
   middle class who wish to associate with the gentry.
36. *or, azure, gules*] Heraldic colours, gold, blue, and red. Three colours on a coat of arms
   are honourable; six or more are ludicrous. La Foole's variegated coat suggests fool's
   motley, worn by court jesters.
38. *antiquity is not respected*] Because so many knighthoods were purchased for £30 or
   £40 during James's reign (see below, 50).
40. *godwits*] Marsh birds, fattened as expensive delicacies for London tables.

some crowns since I was a page in court to my Lord Lofty, and after
my Lady's gentleman-usher, who got me knighted in Ireland, since it   50
pleased my elder brother to die – I had as fair a gold jerkin on that day
as any was worn in the Island Voyage, or at Cadiz, none dispraised,
and I came over in it hither, showed myself to my friends in court, and
after went down to my tenants in the country and surveyed my lands,
let new leases, took their money, spent it in the eye o' the land here   55
upon ladies – and now I can take up at my pleasure.

DAUPHINE   Can you take up ladies, sir?

CLERIMONT   O, let him breathe. He has not recovered.

DAUPHINE   Would I were your half in that commodity –

LA FOOLE   No, sir, excuse me. I meant money, which can take up   60
anything. I have another guest or two to invite and say as much to,
gentlemen. I'll take my leave abruptly, in hope you will not fail – Your
servant.

[*Exit La Foole*]

DAUPHINE   We will not fail you, Sir precious La Foole, but she shall, that
your ladies come to see, if I have credit afore Sir Daw.   65

CLERIMONT   Did you ever hear such a wind-fucker as this?

50. *gentleman-usher*] An upper unliveried servant, often a younger son of good family,
employed as an escort for the lady of the house. *knighted in Ireland*] Elizabeth
chastised Essex for conferring knighthoods indiscriminately during his Irish campaign.
La Foole's scattered syntax makes it unclear whether his knighthood was the result of
Lord or Lady Lofty's influence, or of Essex's hope of obtaining funds from La Foole's
inheritance. La Foole may mean he came into money since (that is, after) he was
knighted.

51. *gold jerkin*] Snugly fitting jacket, usually made of leather, with or without sleeves, and
decorated with gold embroidery.

52. *Island Voyage*] A foolish boast of being in Essex's and Ralegh's unsuccessful raid on
the Spanish in the Azores, 1597. The elegant young men who joined the buccaneers
for the prospective booty deserted at Plymouth in face of violent storms at sea.
Cadiz] Essex took Cadiz in 1596, and English troops plundered it of considerable
riches.

56, 57, 60. *take up*] Possess and use. La Foole refers to his income; Dauphine plays on the
sexual meaning.

59. *half*] Partner. *commodity*] Dauphine is still playing on financial/sexual puns. To take
up commodity was to purchase something cheaply, on speculation, and resell it for
considerable profit; moneylenders used this tactic to take advantage of cash-poor
gentlemen with land or inherited goods either to sell or to offer as collateral for loans.

64. *she*] Epicoene.

66. *wind-fucker*] A windhover or kestrel, a small hawk that seems to hang in air in one
place, while briskly agitating its wings. Applied to La Foole, it suggests busy activity to
little purpose.

DAUPHINE   Or such a rook as the other, that will betray his mistress to be
     seen! Come, 'tis time we prevented it.
CLERIMONT   Go.

    [*Exeunt*]

ACT 2

Act 2 scene 1*

    [*Enter*] *Morose* [*carrying a speaking-tube, followed by*] *Mute*

MOROSE   Cannot I yet find out a more compendious method than by
     this trunk to save my servants the labour of speech and mine ears the
     discord of sounds? Let me see. All discourses but mine own afflict me;
     they seem harsh, impertinent, and irksome. Is it not possible that thou
     shouldst answer me by signs and I apprehend thee, fellow? Speak not,   5
     though I question you. You have taken the ring off from the street
     door as I bade you? Answer me not by speech but by silence, unless
     it be otherwise. – [*Mute makes a leg*] Very good. And you have
     fastened on a thick quilt or flockbed on the outside of the door, that
     if they knock with their daggers or with brickbats, they can make no   10

67. *rook*] A corvine, like the jackdaw, used figuratively for 'fool' or 'dupe'. Dauphine
     refers to Daw.
*   The scene shifts to Morose's house in a narrow alley near the Strand. The props have
     already been described in the last speech of 1.1: the servant wears socks, and is
     supposed to communicate with his master by whispering into the speaking-tube.
     Morose's humour of hating noise makes him try to model his household on the Turkish
     sultan's. The Islamic 'discipline' of unquestioning obedience was reportedly effective in
     maintaining order and silence even in vast ceremonial displays, when, according to the
     French ambassador to the Ottoman court in 1555, 'The men were so motionless that
     they seemed rooted to the ground on which they stood. There was no coughing, no
     clearing of the throat, and no voice to be heard, and no one looked behind him or
     moved his head' (*The Life and Letters of Ogier Ghiselin de Busbecq* [1881], trans.
     C. T. Forster and F. H. B. Daniell [London], vol. 1, p. 303; cited in H&S). The fact that
     Morose's mute speaks is a joke for the actors and the readers; the audience cannot
     appreciate its absurdity except as the servant's frustration at having to irritate Morose's
     humour.
1.   *compendious*] Time- or space-saving.
6.   *ring*] Circular knocker.
8.   *makes a leg*] Bows, here a sign of submission or agreement.
9.   *flockbed*] Quilt or mattress stuffed with flock, tufts of wool or cotton.
10. *brickbats*] Fragments of brick, used as missiles where stones are scarce.

noise? But with your leg, your answer, unless it be otherwise. –

At the breaches, still the fellow makes legs or signs

Very good. This is not only fit modesty in a servant, but good state and discretion in a master. And you have been with Cutbeard the barber to have him come to me? – Good. And he will come presently? Answer me not but with your leg, unless it be otherwise. If it be other- 15
wise,

shake your head or shrug. – [*Shrugs*] So. Your Italian and Spaniard are wise in these, and it is a frugal and comely gravity! How long will it be ere Cutbeard come? Stay, if an hour, hold up your whole hand; if half an hour, two fingers; if a quarter, one. – [*Holds up one finger bent*] Good: half a quarter? 'Tis well. And have you given him a key 20 to come in without knocking? – [*Makes a leg*] Good. And is the lock oiled, and the hinges, today? – Good. And the quilting of the stairs nowhere worn out and bare? – Very good. I see by much doctrine and impulsion it may be effected. Stand by. The Turk in this divine discipline is admirable, exceeding all the potentates of the earth, still 25 waited on by mutes, and all his commands so executed, yea, even in the war (as I have heard) and in his marches, most of his charges and directions given by signs and with silence: an exquisite art! And I am heartily ashamed and angry oftentimes that the princes of Christen- dom should suffer a barbarian to transcend 'em in so high a point of 30 felicity. I will practise it hereafter.

One winds a horn without

How now? Oh! Oh! What villain? What prodigy of mankind is that? Look.

[*Exit Mute. Horn sounds*] *again*

Oh! Cut his throat, cut his throat! What murderer, hell-hound, devil can this be? 35

[*Enter Mute*]

MUTE It is a post from the court –
MOROSE Out, rogue, and must thou blow thy horn too?

11.1 *breaches*] Interruptions in the text, marked with dashes.
12. *good state*] Appropriately dignified appearance.
17. *wise in these*] Prudent in using shrugs to replace words.
23. *doctrine*] Teaching.
24. *impulsion*] Coercion. *Stand by*] To Mute, who is to wait for further orders.
24–31. *Turk ... felicity*] The sultan of the Ottoman Empire was attended by mutes, and some of his troops or bodyguards were rendered mute to increase their secrecy and silence during surprise attacks.
36. *post*] Messenger.

MUTE   Alas, it is a post from the court, sir, that says he must speak with
you, pain of death –

MOROSE   Pain of thy life, be silent.   40

Act 2 scene 2*

[Enter] Truewit [carrying a post-horn and a halter]

TRUEWIT   *[To Morose]* By your leave, sir – I am a stranger here – is your
name Master Morose? *[To Mute]* Is your name Master Morose? –
Fishes! Pythagoreans all! This is strange! – *[To Morose]* What say
you, sir? Nothing? Has Harpocrates been here with his club among
you? Well, sir, I will believe you to be the man at this time. I will   5
venture upon you, sir. Your friends at court commend 'em to you,
sir –

MOROSE   *[Aside]* O men, O manners! Was there ever such an impudence?

TRUEWIT   – And are extremely solicitous for you, sir.   10

MOROSE   Whose knave are you?

---

*   Jonson modernised Juvenal's sixth *Satire* as the basis for Truewit's diatribe against
marriage in this scene. The speaker in Juvenal's text also laments the good old days
when wives were chaste, recommends suicide as an alternative to marriage, and warns
of the adulteries-to-come with actors, musicians, and circus performers, aside from the
expense of entertaining a wife's friends, clothing her fashionably, and supporting her
egocentric interests in politics, literature, or other more esoteric arts, while she herself
is so indifferent to her husband that she lets him see her covered in face-packs and
ointments.

0.1   *post-horn*] Usually blown by express messengers to signal their approach.
halter] Rope tied in a noose. The early audience would recognise it as an emblem of
suicidal despair, from morality plays like *Mankind* or *Magnificence*, or Spenser's *The
Faerie Queene* 1.9.

3.   *Fishes*] Proverbially, 'Mute as fishes'. *Pythagoreans*] A religious order following the
teachings of Pythagoras, whose members took vows of silence in order to examine
themselves through meditation, not to impose silence on others for egocentric vanity as
Morose does. See *Volp* 1.2.6, 26–8, 35, and notes.

4.   *Harpocrates*] The infant Horus, later the Egyptian god of the sun. The Greeks mistook
him for the god of silence because he was depicted as a boy with a finger in his mouth.
As the avenger of his father Osiris, the older Horus destroyed his enemies with a lance;
in Greek myth, the lance became the club of Hercules, with whom he was associated.

6.   *venture upon*] Dare approach, or run the risk of advancing upon a difficult or
dangerous person.

8.   *O men, O manners*] A variation of Cicero's 'O tempora, O mores' [What times! What
behaviour!] (*In Catilinam* 1.1.2).

11.   *knave*] Used to mean both menial manservant and unprincipled rogue.

TRUEWIT   Mine own knave and your compeer, sir.

MOROSE   [*To Mute*] Fetch me my sword –

TRUEWIT   [*To Mute*] You shall taste the one half of my dagger if you do,
groom, and [*To Morose*] you the other if you stir, sir. Be patient, I   15
    charge you in the king's name, and hear me without insurrection.
They say you are to marry! To marry! Do you mark, sir?

MOROSE   How then, rude companion!

TRUEWIT   Marry, your friends do wonder, sir, the Thames being so near
wherein you may drown so handsomely, or London Bridge at a low   20
    fall with a fine leap to hurry you down the stream, or such a delicate
steeple i' the town as Bow to vault from, or a braver height as Paul's, or, if
you affected to do it nearer home and a shorter way, an excellent garret
window into the street, or a beam in the said garret with this halter, which
they have sent –   25

He shows him a halter

    – and desire that you would sooner commit your grave head to this
knot than to the wedlock noose, or take a little sublimate and go out
of the world like a rat, or a fly (as one said) with a straw i' your arse.
Any way rather than to follow this goblin *matrimony*. Alas, sir, do you
ever think to find a chaste wife in these times? Now? When there are   30
so many masques, plays, puritan preachings, mad folks, and other
strange sights to be seen daily, private and public? If you had lived in

12. *compeer*] Equal; associate, used contemptuously. By asserting his equal rank, Truewit
    backhandedly returns Morose's insult.

14. *taste*] A common threat was to force someone to eat his antagonist's weapon.

18. *companion*] Fellow, a term of contempt.

20–1. *low fall*] Ebb-tide. London Bridge, constructed on a series of arches, turned the river
    into dangerous rapids at this point.

21–2. *delicate steeple … Bow*] The elegant church steeple of St Mary Le Bow in Cheapside,
    destroyed in the Great Fire of 1666, was square, with a pinnacle at each of the four
    corners, from which flying buttresses supported a central pinnacle, as though on a
    dome. See Wenceslas Hollar's *Long View of London from Bankside* (1647).

22. *braver height as Paul's*] The old St Paul's Cathedral, at 690 feet by 130 feet, was much
    bigger than Wren's structure which replaced it after the Great Fire (see Hollar). Paul's
    steeple, reportedly 520 feet high, had burned down in 1561, and had not been replaced,
    but the cathedral roof was probably still the highest vantage point in London, and could
    be reached by stairs.

27. *sublimate*] Mercuric chloride, a violent poison used to kill rats.

28. *fly*] Spider and fly fights were staged by gamblers, who impaled the fly with a straw to
    keep it from escaping.

31. *masques*] Court entertainments, usually mounted to celebrate an official court occa-
    sion, such as a royal birthday, marriage, state visit, or coronation day. Although

King Ethelred's time, sir, or Edward the Confessor's, you might
perhaps have found in some cold country hamlet then a dull frosty
wench would have been contented with one man. Now they will as   35
soon be pleased with one leg or one eye. I'll tell you, sir, the monstrous
hazards you shall run with a wife.

MOROSE   Good sir, have I ever cozened any friends of yours of their land?
Bought their possessions? Taken forfeit of their mortgage? Begged a
reversion from 'em? Bastarded their issue? What have I done that may   40
deserve this?

TRUEWIT   Nothing, sir, that I know, but your itch of marriage.

MOROSE   Why? If I had made an assassinate upon your father, vitiated
your mother, ravished your sisters –

TRUEWIT   I would kill you, sir, I would kill you if you had.   45

MOROSE   Why? You do more in this, sir. It were a vengeance centuple for
all facinorous acts that could be named, to do that you do –

intended as the highest form of artistic praise of king and court through poetry, music,
dance, elaborate costume and scenery, the actual performances often gave rise to
drunken or lascivious behaviour among the actors (court ladies and gentlemen, as well
as paid professionals) and their audience. *plays*] Puritan critics like Philip Stubbes (*An
Anatomy of Abuse*, 1583) and Stephen Gosson (*Quips for Upstart Newfangled
Gentlewomen: A Glass to view the Pride of vainglorious Women*, 1595) harshly
criticised playgoers, especially women, who, by showing themselves publicly and even
seeking attention with their fashionable dress, invited sexual advances. *puritan
preachings*] Public sermons at outdoor locations, like Paul's Cross or Charing Cross,
were popular entertainments, drawing large crowds. Renaissance argument, whether in
public speaking or in pamphlets, was colourful and histrionic, relying on example,
anecdote, appeal to authority, and analogy, well sprinkled with invective and jests.
mad folks] Asylums for the insane, like the Hospital of St Mary of Bethlehem, known
as Bedlam, allowed visitors, for a fee, to amuse themselves by watching the inmates.

33.   *King Ethelred's time ... or Edward the Confessor's*] Posited as an English golden age,
just before the Norman Conquest, when modesty was still possible. Ethelred the
Unready (968–1016), was the father of Edward (1003–66), whose piety was rewarded
with canonisation in 1161.

34.   *frosty*] Sexually cold.

38.   *cozened*] Cheated.

39.   *Taken forfeit*] Foreclosed.

40.   *reversion*] The transfer of, or right of succeeding to, an estate left ownerless after the
expiration of a grant, due to the death of the original grantor. *from*] Away from the
direct heirs.   *Bastarded their issue*] Had their offspring declared illegitimate to prevent
their inheriting property.

43.   *made an assassinate*] Murdered.

46.   *centuple*] Multiplied by one hundred.

47.   *facinorous acts*] Crimes, an elaborately elongated phrase for the then more common
synonym 'facts'.

TRUEWIT   Alas, sir, I am but a messenger. I but tell you what you must
hear. It seems your friends are careful after your soul's health, sir, and
would have you know the danger – but you may do your pleasure for   50
all them. I persuade not, sir. – If, after you are married, your wife do
run away with a vaulter, or the Frenchman that walks upon ropes, or
him that dances the jig, or a fencer for his skill at his weapon, why,
it is not their fault. They have discharged their consciences when you
know what may happen. Nay, suffer valiantly, sir, for I must tell you   55
all the perils that you are obnoxious to. If she be fair, young, and
vegetous, no sweetmeats ever drew more flies; all the yellow doublets
and great roses i' the town will be there. If foul and crooked, she'll be
with them and buy those doublets and roses, sir. If rich and that you
marry her dowry, not her, she'll reign in your house as imperious as   60
a widow. If noble, all her kindred will be your tyrants. If fruitful, as
proud as May and humorous as April, she must have her doctors, her
midwives, her nurses, her longings every hour, though it be for the
dearest morsel of man. If learned, there was never such a parrot; all
your patrimony will be too little for the guests that must be invited to   65
hear her speak Latin and Greek, and you must lie with her in those
languages too, if you will please her. If precise, you must feast all the
silenced brethren once in three days, salute the sisters, entertain the

52. *vaulter*] Gymnast, but suggesting sexual exercise. Brothels were known as 'vaulting
houses'. Amateur and professional acrobatic displays were popular at court for their
skill and daring as well as for the titillation provided by the performers' near-
nudity.   *Frenchman that walks upon ropes*] Elizabeth saw a French acrobat perform
on a tightrope in the Conduit Court, May 1600.

53. *jig*] A lively dance often acting out a bawdy ballad. Such performances appeared as
tavern entertainments or as intervals or afterpieces in the theatre. Dancing was a
euphemism for the motions of the sexual act.   *weapon*] Euphemism for penis.

56. *obnoxious*] Liable.

57. *vegetous*] Healthy and active.

57–8. *yellow doublets and great roses*] Epithets for the fashionable 'braveries' of the day,
with their bright colours and large rosettes on the toe or instep of their shoes.

59. *buy*] Bribe for sexual favours.

61. *fruitful*] Pregnant.

62. *proud*] Sexually excited, in heat; self-displaying, arrogant.   *humorous*] Changeable,
like weather in April.

63–4. *longings ... dearest morsel of man*] Equivocates cravings for expensive delicacies,
and insatiable sexual desires.

64. *parrot*] Like Lady Would-be, *Volp* 3.4.

66. *lie with*] Make love to.

67. *precise*] Puritanical.

68. *silenced brethren*] Excommunicated ministers who refused to accede to the High
Church canons, passed at the 1604 Hampton Court Conference, demanding acceptance

whole family or wood of 'em, and hear long-winded exercises,
singings, and catechisings, which you are not given to and yet must   70
give for, to please the zealous matron your wife, who for the holy
cause will cozen you over and above. You begin to sweat, sir? But this
is not half, i' faith. You may do your pleasure notwithstanding. As I
said before, I come not to persuade you.

The Mute is stealing away

Upon my faith, Master Servingman, if you do stir, I will beat you.   75
MOROSE   O, what is my sin! What is my sin?
TRUEWIT   Then, if you love your wife, or rather dote on her, sir, O, how
she'll torture you and take pleasure i' your torments! You shall lie with
her but when she lists – she will not hurt her beauty, her complexion;
or it must be for that jewel or that pearl when she does – every half-   80
hour's pleasure must be bought anew, and with the same pain and
charge you wooed her at first. Then, you must keep what servants she
please, what company she will; that friend must not visit you without
her licence, and him she loves most she will seem to hate eagerliest, to
decline your jealousy; or feign to be jealous of you first, and for that   85
cause go live with her she-friend or cousin at the college that can
instruct her in all the mysteries of writing letters, corrupting servants,
taming spies; where she must have that rich gown for such a great day,
a new one for the next, a richer for the third; be served in silver; have
the chamber filled with a succession of grooms, footmen, ushers, and   90

of the king's supremacy and endorsing the Prayer Book and the thirty-nine articles.
Since they were without official parishes, they depended on the charity of fellow-
puritans. *salute*] Greet with a kiss, customary at the time.
69. *family*] Perhaps a glance at the Family of Love, a puritan sect whose belief in religion
   as an exercise of love was misinterpreted by the general public as a belief in free love.
   wood] Crowd or collection; punning on 'mad'.
71. *zealous*] Fervently puritanical. See Zeal-of-the-Land Busy, the lay-preacher in *BF*.
72. *cozen*] Hoodwink, swindle. Jonson also depicts puritans as dishonest in *Alch* 3.2, and
   BF 1.3 and 5.2. *over and above*] Suggests sexual bribery beyond the other kinds of
   coercion already mentioned.
79. *but*] Only. *lists*] Wants.
84. *licence*] Permission, punning on licentious appeal. *eagerliest*] Most ardently or
   amorously.
85. *decline*] Avert, dismiss.
86. *she-friend*] Disparaging term for female friend. *cousin*] Relation or friend, but used
   contemptuously of a harlot. *college*] The residence of the Ladies Collegiate.
88. *spies*] Tell-tales.
90–91. *chamber filled … messengers*] Equivocal sexual allusion suggesting insatiability.

other messengers, besides embroiderers, jewellers, tire-women, sempsters, feathermen, perfumers; while she feels not how the land drops away, nor the acres melt, nor foresees the change when the mercer has your woods for her velvets; never weighs what her pride costs, sir, so she may kiss a page or a smooth chin that has the despair   95 of a beard; be a stateswoman, know all the news, what was done at Salisbury, what at the Bath, what at court, what in progress; or so she may censure poets and authors and styles, and compare 'em, Daniel with Spenser, Jonson with the t'other youth, and so forth; or be thought cunning in controversies or the very knots of divinity, and   100 have often in her mouth the state of the question, and then skip to the mathematics and demonstration, and answer in religion to one, in state to another, in bawdry to a third.

MOROSE   O, O!

TRUEWIT   All this is very true, sir. And then her going in disguise to that   105
    conjuror and this cunning-woman, where the first question is, how

91. *messengers*] Go-betweens. *tire-women*] Dressmakers; perhaps milliners, makers of head-tires.

92. *sempsters*] Tailors. *feathermen*] Dealers in feathers and plumes, and items made out of feathers, such as fans.

92–3. *land ... melt*] That is, her husband has to sell off some of his land to pay for her fashionable tastes.

94. *mercer*] Dealer in costly fabrics like silk and velvet.

95–6. *despair of a beard*] In Juvenal, referring to eunuchs; here possibly to lesbian seduction.

96. *stateswoman*] female politician – as unlikely in Jonson's day as a college for ladies. News of public affairs in this context refers only to the latest gossip.

97. *Salisbury*] location of prestigious horseraces held every March. *Bath*] Visitors to Bath only bathed in the springs; drinking the water became fashionable after the Restoration. *court*] Whitehall, the royal residence. *progress*] Royal tours of the country.

98. *censure*] Pass judgment on.

98–9. *Daniel with Spenser*] Contemporaries compared their sonnet sequences and epic poetry favourably, sometimes preferring Daniel's, but Jonson admired neither. Though he thought Daniel was 'no poet', according to William Drummond, Jonson had memorised some of Spenser's *Shepherd's Calendar*.

99. *t'other youth*] Never identified, but unlikely to be Shakespeare, who was about 9 years older than Jonson; however, neither man was a 'youth' in 1609. Jonson had at various times worked closely with Dekker, Chapman, and Marston.

100. *cunning*] Skilful, but hinting at female sexual skills. *controversies*] Debates. *knots*] Complicated problems; hinting at genitalia.

101. *state of the question*] The principal point or crux of an issue under debate; also equivocally sexual.

102. *demonstration*] Explication or proof, the reasoning behind a solution.

106. *conjuror, cunning-woman*] Fortune-tellers and quacks.

soon you shall die? next, if her present servant love her? next that, if she shall have a new servant? and how many? which of her family would make the best bawd, male or female? what precedence she shall have by her next match? and sets down the answers and believes 'em   110
above the scriptures. Nay, perhaps she'll study the art.

MOROSE   Gentle sir, ha' you done? Ha' you had your pleasure o' me? I'll think of these things.

TRUEWIT   Yes, sir. And then comes reeking home of vapour and sweat with going afoot, and lies in a month of a new face, all oil and   115
birdlime, and rinses in asses' milk, and is cleansed with a new *fucus*. God b'w'you, sir.

[*Begins to exit, then returns*]

One thing more (which I had almost forgot). This too, with whom you are to marry, may have made a conveyance of her virginity aforehand, as your wise widows do of their 'states, before they marry, in   120
trust to some friend, sir. Who can tell? Or if she have not done it yet, she may do upon the wedding day or the night before, and antedate you cuckold. The like has been heard of in nature. 'Tis no devised impossible thing, sir. God b'w'you. I'll be bold to leave this rope with you, sir, for a remembrance. Farewell, Mute.   125

[*Exit Truewit*]

MOROSE   Come, ha' me to my chamber. But first shut the door.

The horn again

O, shut the door, shut the door! Is he come again?

107. *servant*] Lover.

109. *precedence*] Rank, social superiority.

110. *match*] Marriage.

111. *art*] That is, astrology and other arcane lore.

115. *lies in ... face*] Stays in bed for a month undergoing facial treatments to improve her complexion, figuratively giving birth (literal sense of 'lying in') to a new face.

116. *birdlime*] Sticky substance spread on twigs to catch birds; Truewit's wording suggests his disgust at smearing any glutinous preparations on the skin, despite his earlier defence of cosmetic arts used by women. *rinses*] Although F1 has 'rises', most editors assume Jonson wrote 'rinses' in keeping with Juvenal's description of freshening the complexion with asses' milk (*Satires* 6.469–70), a habit attributed to Cleopatra, Poppaea, and Mary Queen of Scots. *fucus*] Cosmetic.

119. *conveyance*] Legal transfer of property.

120. *'states*] Estates. A widow could own property, but once she remarried, it became the property of her husband; she could retain control over it only by conveying it to a trusted friend (possibly a lover) before the wedding.

126. *ha' me*] Take me.

[*Enter Cutbeard*]

CUTBEARD   'Tis I, sir, your barber.

MOROSE   O, Cutbeard, Cutbeard, Cutbeard! Here has been a cutthroat
with me. Help me in to my bed, and give me physic with thy counsel.   130

[*Exeunt*]

Act 2 scene 3*

[*Enter*] *Daw, Clerimont, Dauphine, Epicoene*

DAW   Nay, and she will, let her refuse at her own charges. 'Tis nothing to
me, gentlemen. But she will not be invited to the like feasts or guests
every day.

CLERIMONT   O, by no means, she may not refuse –

[*Aside to her, with Dauphine:*] *they dissuade her privately*

to stay at home, if you love your reputation. 'Slight, you are   5
invited thither o' purpose to be seen and laughed at by the lady of the
college and her shadows. This trumpeter hath proclaimed you.

DAUPHINE   You shall not go. Let him be laughed at in your stead for not
bringing you, and put him to his extemporal faculty of fooling and   10
talking loud to satisfy the company.

CLERIMONT   He will suspect us. Talk aloud. – Pray, Mistress Epicoene,
let's see your verses. We have Sir John Daw's leave. Do not conceal
your servant's merit and your own glories.

EPICOENE   They'll prove my servant's glories, if you have his leave so   15
soon.

DAUPHINE   His vainglories, lady!

DAW   Show 'em, show 'em, mistress! I dare own 'em.

---

130. *physic*] Medicine. Barbers and surgeons belonged to the same guild and had much the
same training.

*   The scene moves to Daw's nearby lodgings, described in 1.2 as across the street from
Cutbeard's barbershop. The love-song, described first as 'a madrigal of modesty' but
finally as 'a madrigal of procreation', reveals Daw's crude banality. Jonson may have
intended, through Daw, to gibe at Sir John Harington's talents as a courtier and as a
poet whose translation of Ariosto and epigrams Jonson scorned. Harington was also
the author of *The Metamorphosis of Ajax* (1596), a history of a privy.

1. *at her own charges*] On her own responsibility, at her own expense or risk.

7. *shadows*] Parasitical companions.

7–8. *This trumpeter*] This loudmouth, i.e. Daw.

10. *fooling*] Making a fool of himself.

11. *satisfy*] Explain [Epicoene's absence] to.

15. *glories*] Splendours, triumphs. Epicoene and Dauphine shift the meaning to 'pretentious boasts'.

EPICOENE   [*Offers verses*] Judge you what glories!

DAW   [*Snatches them*] Nay, I'll read 'em myself, too. An author must   20
recite his own works. It is a madrigal of modesty:

> *Modest and fair, for fair and good are near*
> *Neighbours, howe'er –*

DAUPHINE   Very good.

CLERIMONT   Ay, is't not?   25

DAW   *No noble virtue ever was alone,*
> *But two in one.*

DAUPHINE   Excellent!

CLERIMONT   That again, I pray, Sir John.

DAUPHINE   It has something in't like rare wit and sense.   30

CLERIMONT   Peace.

DAW   *No noble virtue ever was alone,*
> *But two in one.*
> *Then, when I praise sweet modesty, I praise*
> *Bright beauty's rays;*   35
> *And having praised both beauty and modesty,*
> *I have praised thee.*

DAUPHIN   Admirable!

CLERIMONT   How it chimes and cries tink i' the close divinely!

DAUPHINE   Ay, 'tis Seneca.   40

CLERIMONT   No, I think 'tis Plutarch.

DAW   The dor on Plutarch and Seneca; I hate it. They are mine own
imaginations, by that light. I wonder those fellows have such credit
with gentlemen!

CLERIMONT   They are very grave authors.   45

---

21. *madrigal*] Love-song.

39. *chimes*] Jingles, a depreciating comment on the rhymes.   *cries tink*] Tinkles, also
depreciating, suggesting faint tinny echoes.   *close*] End of a musical phrase.

40. *Seneca*] Roman Stoic, essayist and playwright (4 BC to AD 65). Daw does not realise
that Seneca the essayist is the same man as Seneca the tragedian, mentioned at ll. 60–61.

41. *Plutarch*] Greek biographer and essayist (AD 45–120).

42. *The dor on*] Expression of contempt; a buzzing sound intended as a jeer. Daw's attack
on these highly reputed moral essayists reveals his own intellectual, artistic, and moral
inadequacies. Daw does not comprehend Clerimont's and Dauphine's mockery of his
attempt at high-sounding argument, or their implication that his poem is unmelodious
and prosaic, despite its form and rhyme.

DAW   Grave asses! Mere essayists! A few loose sentences, and that's all. A
man would talk so his whole age. I do utter as good things every hour,
if they were collected and observed, as either of 'em.

DAUPHINE   Indeed, Sir John?

CLERIMONT   He must needs, living among the wits and braveries too.   50

DAUPHINE   Ay, and being president of 'em, as he is.

DAW   There's Aristotle, a mere commonplace fellow; Plato, a discourser;
Thucydides and Livy, tedious and dry; Tacitus, an entire knot,
sometimes worth the untying, very seldom.

CLERIMONT   What do you think of the poets, Sir John?   55

DAW   Not worthy to be named for authors. Homer, an old tedious prolix
ass, talks of curriers and chines of beef. Virgil, of dunging of land and
bees. Horace, of I know not what.

CLERIMONT   I think so.

DAW   And so Pindarus, Lycophron, Anacreon, Catullus, Seneca the   60
tragedian, Lucan, Propertius, Tibullus, Martial, Juvenal, Ausonius,
Statius, Politian, Valerius Flaccus, and the rest –

CLERIMONT   What a sackful of their names he has got!

DAUPHINE   And how he pours 'em out! Politian with Valerius Flaccus!

46.   *mere essayists*] Jonson criticises essayists in *Disc* as shallow and inconsistent thinkers,
'even their master Montaigne. These, in all they write, confess still what books they
have read last; and therein their own folly, so much, that they bring it to the stake raw,
and undigested: not that the place did need it neither; but that they thought themselves
furnished, and would vent it.' See *Volp* 3.4.90 and note.   *sentences*] Maxims.

52–3.   *Aristotle ... Tacitus*] Daw's descriptions are in the tradition of learned wit: his
inanities suggest alternative meanings to the astute reader/listener. Aristotle is 'com
monplace', taken by Daw to mean 'trite', but understood by the educated to mean the
philosopher of the *locus communis* or universal truth; Plato is a 'discourser' not only
because he wrote dialogues, but also because his works illustrate 'discourse' or the
process of logical understanding. Daw pronounces 'Thucydides', the Greek historian of
the Peloponnesian War, as though the last two syllables echo or rhyme with 'tedious',
and describes Livy, the Roman historian of the Augustan period, as 'dry' because the
Latin *liveo*, to be black and blue, is the colour of melancholy, the dry humour. Tacitus
is a 'knot' because the Latin *tacitus* means tongue tied; in debate, a knot is a difficult
or tangled question.

56–8.   *Homer ... Horace*] Presumably Homer is 'prolix' because each of his epics is twenty-
four books long. The *Iliad* refers frequently to horses (hence the 'curriers', or grooms
who rub down horses) and to feasting on 'chines' or large roasts of beef. Daw's logic
here may be playing on 'curries', or the portions of the prey thrown to the hounds after
the hunt; hence, the 'chines'. Virgil's *Georgics* are in praise of rural life. Of Horace,
Jonson's favourite poet, Daw understands nothing.

60–64.   More indiscriminate name-dropping. *Pindarus*] Greek lyric poet, 518–438 BC, who
perfected the ode.   *Lycophron*] 300–250 BC, librarian at Alexandria, a minor poet and

CLERIMONT   Was not the character right of him?   65
DAUPHINE   As could be made, i' faith.
DAW   And Persius, a crabbed coxcomb, not to be endured.
DAUPHINE   Why? Whom do you account for authors, Sir John Daw?
DAW   *Syntagma Juris Civilis, Corpus Juris Civilis, Corpus Juris Canonici,*
    the King of Spain's Bible.   70
DAUPHINE   Is the King of Spain's Bible an author?
CLERIMONT   Yes, and *Syntagma*.
DAUPHINE   What was that *Syntagma*, sir?
DAW   A civil lawyer, a Spaniard.
DAUPHINE   Sure, *Corpus* was a Dutchman.   75
CLERIMONT   Ay, both the *Corpus*es, I knew 'em. They were very
    corpulent authors.
DAW   And then there's Vatablus, Pomponatius, Symancha; the other are

critic. *Anacreon*] *c.* 570 BC, lyric poet mostly writing about lighthearted pleasures. *Catullus*] 84–54 BC, witty and sophisticated lyric poet, contemporary of Horace and Virgil, and later acknowledged by Martial as the master of the epigram. *Lucan*] AD 39–65, author of the unfinished poem *Bellum Civile*, also called *Pharsalia*, on the civil war between Caesar and Pompey. *Propertius*] Born *c.* 50 BC, contemporary of Ovid; his elegies may have influenced John Donne. *Tibullus*] 55?–19 BC, an elegist praised by Quintillian for his refined style. *Martial*] AD 40–104, best known for his satiric epigrams, which influenced Jonson's own *Epigrams*, published in the 1616 folio. *Juvenal*] The last great Roman satiric poet, Martial's contemporary, and another profound influence on Jonson. *Ausonius*] Died *c.* AD 395, teacher and poet, best known for his *Mosella*, a laudatory poem describing river life. *Statius*] AD 45–96, fashionable court poet who wrote occasional and epic verse. *Politian*] Angelo Poliziano (1454–94), a humanist, poet, and critic, patronised by Lorenzo de' Medici. He is distinctly out of place in this list of classical poets. *Valerius Flaccus*] Died *c.* AD 92, a contemporary of Lucan and Statius, and author of the incomplete *Argonautica*.

65. *character*] The character sketch given of Daw earlier in 1.2 and 1.3.

67. *Persius*] AD 34–62, Stoic satirist praised by Lucan. He wrote in a vigorously colloquial, though difficult, style, which seems 'crabbed' or obscure to Daw; both Donne and Jonson imitated Persius's mockery of effete tastes, attacks on hypocrisy, and indictment of humankind generally for preferring vice to virtue.

69. *Syntagma ... Canonici*] Collections of Roman law, civil and canon. 'Syntagma' (Greek) and 'corpus' (Latin) both mean a general collection. Daw, however, believes these are proper names.

70. *King of Spain's Bible*] The Hebrew, Greek, and Latin Bible known as *Biblia Regia*, so called because Philip II of Spain paid for its publication in Antwerp, 1569–72.

75. *Dutchman*] Because the Dutch were reputedly corpulent, owing to their butter-and-cheese rich diet.

77. *corpulent*] Punning on 'weighty' or 'heavy' as 'difficult to understand'.

78. *Vatablus*] François Vatable (d. 1547?), authority on Hebrew, the Bible, and Aristotle at the Royal College of France. *Pomponatius*] Pietro Pomponazzi (1462–1524?),

not to be received within the thought of a scholar.

DAUPHINE   'Fore God, you have a simple learned servant, lady, in titles.   80

CLERIMONT   I wonder that he is not called to the helm and made a councillor!

DAUPHINE   He is one extraordinary.

CLERIMONT   Nay, but in ordinary! To say truth, the state wants such.

DAUPHINE   Why, that will follow.   85

CLERIMONT   I muse a mistress can be so silent to the dotes of such a servant.

DAW   'Tis her virtue, sir. I have written somewhat of her silence too.

DAUPHINE   In verse, Sir John?

CLERIMONT   What else?   90

DAUPHINE   Why, how can you justify your own being of a poet, that so slight all the old poets?

DAW   Why? Every man that writes in verse is not a poet; you have of the wits that write verses and yet are no poets. They are poets that live by it, the poor fellows that live by it.   95

DAUPHINE   Why, would not you live by your verses, Sir John?

CLERIMONT   No, 'twere pity he should. A knight live by his verses? He did not make 'em to that end, I hope.

DAUPHINE   And yet the noble Sidney lives by his, and the noble family not ashamed.   100

CLERIMONT   Ay, he professed himself, but Sir John Daw has more caution: he'll not hinder his own rising i' the state so much! Do you think he will? Your verses, good Sir John, and no poems.

DAW   *Silence in woman is like speech in man,*
               Deny't who can.   105

authority on Aristotle at the University of Padua, condemned as a heretic for his views on immortality. *Symancha*] Didacus de Simancas, sixteenth-century jurist and bishop, an authority on canon and civil law at the University of Salamanca.

82. *councillor*] Member of the Privy Council.

86. *dotes*] Talents, but implying 'dotage', or feeble-mindedness.

88. *'Tis her virtue*] That is, to be silent.

93–5. Daw thinks of himself as a wit, a gentleman who writes verse for the enjoyment of a closed circle of friends, not a mere poet who writes and publishes for a living. Such aristocratic snobbery stigmatised Jonson and other writers, including Shakespeare, as common, unless they published scholarly works. Jonson's publication of his own *Works* in the 1616 folio paved the way for greater acceptance of working poets as gentlemen and scholars.

99. *Sidney*] Sidney did not earn a living by writing. After circulating in manuscript during Sidney's lifetime, his works were published posthumously by his sister, the Countess of Pembroke, in 1598, with the approval of his family.

101. *professed*] Proclaimed openly.

DAUPHINE   Not I, believe it. Your reason, sir.

DAW   *Nor is't a tale*
                  That female vice should be a virtue male,
                  Or masculine vice a female virtue be.
                                  You shall it see   110
                                  Proved with increase:
                  I know to speak, and she to hold her peace.

         Do you conceive me, gentlemen?

DAUPHINE   No, faith, how mean you with increase, Sir John?

DAW   Why, with increase is when I court her for the common cause of   115
       mankind, and she says nothing but *consentire videtur*, and in time is
       gravida.

DAUPHINE   Then this is a ballad of procreation?

CLERIMONT   A *madrigal* of procreation, you mistake.

EPICOENE   'Pray give me my verses again, servant.   120

DAW   If you'll ask 'em aloud, you shall.

       [*They walk aside, Daw reciting*]

CLERIMONT   See, here's Truewit again!

Act 2 scene 4*

       [*Enter Truewit, still carrying the post-horn*]

CLERIMONT   Where hast thou been, in the name of madness, thus
       accoutred with thy horn?

TRUEWIT   Where the sound of it might have pierced your senses with
       gladness, had you been in ear-reach of it. Dauphine, fall down and
       worship me: I have forbid the banns, lad. I have been with thy virtuous   5
       uncle and have broke the match.

DAUPHINE   You ha' not, I hope.

TRUEWIT   Yes, faith, and thou shouldst hope otherwise, I should repent
       me. This horn got me entrance: kiss it. I had no other way to get in
       but by feigning to be a post, but when I got in once, I proved none,   10

107–13. *tale . . . vice . . . peace . . . conceive*] Sexual allusions.

116. *consentire videtur*] Seems to consent.

117. *gravida*] Pregnant.

* Inversion is a constant motif in *SW*. Truewit takes credit first for preventing Morose's
   wedding, and then for hastening it. Dauphine is first infuriated, then delighted. And the
   chatterbox Jack Daw, bereft of his mistress, vows 'melancholic' silence.

5. *worship*] The mock-religious celebration of Truewit's godly powers is continued in the
   offering of the relic for kissing, 9, and the command to 'adore', 15. *forbid the
   banns*] Formally objected to the intended marriage.

but rather the contrary, turned him into a post or a stone or what is stiffer, with thundering into him the incommodities of a wife and the miseries of marriage. If ever Gorgon were seen in the shape of a woman, he hath seen her in my description. I have put him off o' that scent forever. Why do you not applaud and adore me, sirs? Why stand   15

you mute? Are you stupid? You are not worthy o' the benefit.

DAUPHINE   [*To Clerimont*]   Did not I tell you? Mischief! –

CLERIMONT   [*To Truewit*]   I would you had placed this benefit somewhere else.

TRUEWIT   Why so?   20

CLERIMONT   'Slight, you have done the most inconsiderate, rash, weak thing that ever man did to his friend.

DAUPHINE   Friend! If the most malicious enemy I have had studied to inflict an injury upon me, it could not be a greater.

TRUEWIT   Wherein? For God's sake! Gentlemen, come to yourselves   25
again.

DAUPHINE   [*To Clerimont*]   But I presaged thus much afore to you.

CLERIMONT   Would my lips had been soldered when I spake on't. [*To Truewit*] 'Slight, what moved you to be thus impertinent?

TRUEWIT   My masters, do not put on this strange face to pay my courtesy.   30
Off with this visor. Have good turns done you, and thank 'em this way?

DAUPHINE   [*To Truewit*]   'Fore heaven, you have undone me. That which I have plotted for and been maturing now these four months, you have blasted in a minute. Now I am lost, I may speak. This gentlewoman   35
was lodged here by me o' purpose, and, to be put upon my uncle, hath professed this obstinate silence for my sake, being my entire friend, and one that for the requital of such a fortune as to marry him, would have made me very ample conditions – where now all my hopes are utterly miscarried by this unlucky accident.   40

CLERIMONT   Thus 'tis when a man will be ignorantly officious, do services and not know his why. I wonder what courteous itch

13. *Gorgon*] In Greek myth, one of three monstrous females, with serpents for hair, so horrifying that whoever dared look at them was turned to stone.

16. *stupid*] Stunned with amazement; rendered immobile.

17–29. Dauphine is so infuriated by Truewit's interference that, until 33, he speaks only to Clerimont, who acts as intermediary with Truewit.

27. *presaged*] Predicted.

30. *put on this strange face*] Act in such a hostile manner.

31. *visor*] Mask; here figurative for hostile facial expression.

36. *be put upon*] Trick, be imposed upon.

38. *requital*] Compensation for service rendered.

39. *conditions*] Settlement, allowance.

possessed you! You never did absurder part i' your life, nor a greater
trespass to friendship, to humanity.

DAUPHINE   Faith, you may forgive it best. 'Twas your cause principally.   45

CLERIMONT   I know it. Would it had not.

[Enter Cutbeard]

DAUPHINE   How now, Cutbeard? What news?

CUTBEARD   The best, the happiest that ever was, sir. There has been a
mad gentleman with your uncle this morning *[Notices Truewit]* – I
think this be the gentleman – that has almost talked him out of his wits   50
with threatening him from marriage –

DAUPHINE   On, I pray thee.

CUTBEARD   And your uncle, sir, he thinks 'twas done by your procure-
ment. Therefore he will see the party you wot of presently, and if he
like her, he says, and that she be so inclining to dumb as I have told   55
him, he swears he will marry her today, instantly, and not defer it a
minute longer.

DAUPHINE   Excellent! Beyond our expectation!

TRUEWIT   Beyond your expectation? By this light, I knew it would be
thus.   60

DAUPHINE   Nay, sweet Truewit, forgive me.

TRUEWIT   No, I was 'ignorantly officious', 'impertinent'. This was the
'absurd, weak part'.

CLERIMONT   Wilt thou ascribe that to merit now, was mere fortune?

TRUEWIT   Fortune? Mere Providence. Fortune had not a finger in't. I saw   65
it must necessarily in nature fall out so. My *genius* is never false to me
in these things. Show me how it could be otherwise.

DAUPHINE   Nay, gentlemen, contend not, 'tis well now.

TRUEWIT   Alas, I let him go on with 'inconsiderate' and 'rash' and what
he pleased.   70

CLERIMONT   Away, thou strange justifier of thyself, to be wiser than thou
wert by the event.

TRUEWIT   Event! By this light, thou shalt never persuade me but I foresaw
it as well as the stars themselves.

DAUPHINE   Nay, gentlemen, 'tis well now. Do you two entertain Sir John   75
Daw with discourse while I send her away with instructions.

TRUEWIT   I'll be acquainted with her first, by your favour.

---

45. *cause*] Fault.
54. *wot*] Know. *presently*] Immediately.
64. *was*] Which was.
65. *Fortune ... Providence*] Distinguishing between mere chance or luck, and divine
planning. *Mere*] Nothing but.
66. *genius*] Guardian angel.
72. *by the event*] After the fact, according to the outcome.

[*Epicoene approaches; Clerimont introduces Truewit*]

CLERIMONT   Master Truewit, lady, a friend of ours.

[*Epicoene curtseys*]

TRUEWIT   [*Bowing*] I am sorry I have not known you sooner, lady, to
celebrate this rare virtue of your silence.   80

[*Exeunt Dauphine, Epicoene, and Cutbeard*]

CLERIMONT   Faith, an' you had come sooner, you should ha' seen and
heard her well celebrated in Sir John Daw's *madrigals*.

[*Daw joins them*]

TRUEWIT   Jack Daw, God save you, when saw you La Foole?
DAW   Not since last night, Master Truewit.
TRUEWIT   That's a miracle! I thought you two had been inseparable.   85
DAW   He's gone to invite his guests.
TRUEWIT   Gods so! 'Tis true! What a false memory have I towards that
man! I am one. I met him e'en now upon that he calls his delicate fine
black horse, rid into a foam with posting from place to place and
person to person to give 'em the *cue* –   90
CLERIMONT   Lest they should forget?
TRUEWIT   Yes. There was never poor captain took more pains at a muster
to show men than he at this meal to show friends.
DAW   It is his quarter-feast, sir.
CLERIMONT   What! Do you say so, Sir John?   95
TRUEWIT   Nay, Jack Daw will not be out, at the best friends he has, to the
talent of his wit. Where's his mistress to hear and applaud him? Is she
gone?
DAW   Is Mistress Epicoene gone?
CLERIMONT   Gone afore with Sir Dauphine, I warrant, to the place.   100

---

87. *Gods so*] Exclamation of contempt, apparently a corruption of 'by God's soul', but
deriving from the Italian *cazzo*, penis.
88. *one*] One of the guests.   *delicate*] Elegant, mimicking La Foole's fashionable court-
vocabulary (see 1.4.4).
94. *quarter-feast*] A dinner-party celebrating the Quarter-day, when rents and other
quarterly charges were paid; as a landowner, La Foole would be receiving a quarter-
year's income. Daw may be ironically suggesting that, in giving his party, La Foole is
paying his dues to society, buying his way into the fashionable set with lavish
entertainment, the method used by La Foole's kinswoman, Mrs Otter (see 1.4. 23–8).
96. *out*] Stumped for words, silenced.
96–7. *to the talent of his wit*] To show off his cleverness; said ironically, since Daw has
merely given factual information, not scored a witticism at the expense of any friends.

TRUEWIT   Gone afore! That were a manifest injury, a disgrace and a half, to refuse him at such a festival time as this, being a *bravery* and a *wit* too.

CLERIMONT   Tut, he'll swallow it like cream. He's better read in *jure civili* than to esteem anything a disgrace is offered him from a mistress.   105

DAW   Nay, let her e'en go. She shall sit alone and be dumb in her chamber a week together, for John Daw, I warrant her. Does she refuse me?

CLERIMONT   No, sir, do not take it so to heart. She does not refuse you, but a little neglect you. Good faith, Truewit, you were to blame to put it into his head that she does refuse him.   110

TRUEWIT   She does refuse him, sir, palpably, however you mince it. An' I were as he, I would swear to speak ne'er a word to her today for 't.

DAW   By this light, no more I will not.

TRUEWIT   Nor to anybody else, sir.

DAW   Nay, I will not say so, gentlemen.   115

CLERIMONT   [*Aside to Truewit*] It had been an excellent happy condition for the company, if you could have drawn him to it.

DAW   I'll be very melancholic, i' faith.

CLERIMONT   As a dog, if I were as you, Sir John.

TRUEWIT   Or a snail, or a hog-louse. I would roll myself up for this day,   120
in troth; they should not unwind me.

DAW   By this picktooth, so I will.

CLERIMONT   [*Aside to Truewit*] 'Tis well done. He begins already to be angry with his teeth.

DAW   Will you go, gentlemen?   125

CLERIMONT   Nay, you must walk alone, if you be right melancholic, Sir John.

TRUEWIT   Yes, sir, we'll dog you, we'll follow you afar off.

[*Exit Daw melancholically*]

CLERIMONT   Was there ever such a two yards of knighthood, measured out by time to be sold to laughter?   130

TRUEWIT   A mere talking mole! Hang him. No mushroom was ever so

104. *jure civili*] Civil law, one of Daw's 'authors' at 2.3.69.

105. *is*] That is.

119. *As a dog*] Proverbially, 'Melancholy as a dog'.

120. *roll ... up*] As a beetle does, for self-protection. See *Volp* 5.2.91.

122. *picktooth*] Toothpick; among courtiers, a fashionable and publicly used accessory, often made of ivory and carried in an elaborately carved or jewelled case.

126. *right*] Thoroughly or convincingly. Victims of love-melancholy were conventionally represented as solitary drooping figures with their arms crossed over their chests.

131. *mole*] Mooncalf, or congenital idiot; a born fool. *mushroom*] Used contemptuously of new gentlemen, who spring up overnight, like fungi, from middle-class obscurity into purchased knighthood.

fresh. A fellow so utterly nothing as he knows not what he would be.

CLERIMONT   Let's follow him. But first let's go to Dauphine – he's hovering about the house – to hear what news.

TRUEWIT   Content.   135

[*Exeunt*]

Act 2 scene 5 *

[*Enter*] *Morose, Epicoene, Cutbeard, Mute*

MOROSE   Welcome, Cutbeard. Draw near with your fair charge, and in her ear softly entreat her to unmask.

[*Cutbeard whispers to Epicoene, who takes off her mask*]

So. Is the door shut?

[*Mute makes a leg*]

Enough. Now, Cutbeard, with the same discipline I use to my family, I will question you. As I conceive, Cutbeard, this gentlewoman is she   5
you have provided and brought in hope she will fit me in the place and person of a wife? Answer me not but with your leg, unless it be otherwise.

[*Cutbeard makes a leg*]

Very well done, Cutbeard. I conceive besides, Cutbeard, you have been pre-acquainted with her birth, education, and qualities, or else you   10
would not prefer her to my acceptance in the weighty consequence of marriage. – [*Cutbeard attempts to answer*] This I conceive, Cutbeard. Answer me not but with your leg, unless it be otherwise. – [*Makes a leg*] Very well done, Cutbeard. Give aside now a little and leave me to examine her condition and aptitude to my affection.   15

---

134. *hovering*] Used of a hawk ready to stoop on prey.

*   The scene returns to Morose's house for the interview with Epicoene, in which one major source of comedy is that, after finally locating a silent woman, Morose keeps asking her to speak up. Jonson exposes Morose's solitary fantasy in two unsavoury and indecorous postures: the old man sexually aroused by a young girl who will not reject him (1–83); and after 86, the old man crowing and jabbering in vindictive triumph over his young 'rival'. Contrary to the information Dauphine gives at 1.2.5–10, he has enraged his uncle by trying to intimidate him with the higher status of a knighthood (though purchased).

4. *family*] Household.

11. *prefer*] Nominate, recommend.

14. *Give aside*] Stand aside, give way.

15. *condition*] Shape.   *aptitude to*] Capacity to arouse.

He goes about her and views her

> She is exceeding fair and of a special good favour; a sweet composi-
> tion or harmony of limbs; her temper of beauty has the true height of
> my blood. The knave hath exceedingly well fitted me without. I will
> now try her within. Come near, fair gentlewoman. Let not my
> behaviour seem rude, though unto you, being rare, it may haply   20
> appear strange. –

She curtseys

> Nay, lady, you may speak, though Cutbeard and my man might not,
> for of all sounds only the sweet voice of a fair lady has the just length
> of mine ears. I beseech you, say, lady, out of the first fire of meeting
> eyes (they say) love is stricken: do you feel any such motion suddenly   25
> shot into you from any part you see in me? Ha, lady?

Curtsey

> Alas, lady, these answers by silent curtseys from you are too courtless
> and simple. I have ever had my breeding in court, and she that shall
> be my wife must be accomplished with courtly and audacious
> ornaments. Can you speak, lady?   30

She speaks softly

EPICOENE   Judge you, forsooth.
MOROSE   What say you, lady? Speak out, I beseech you.
EPICOENE   [*Louder*] Judge you, forsooth.
MOROSE   O' my judgment, a divine softness! But can you naturally, lady,
    as I enjoin these by doctrine and industry, refer yourself to the search   35
    of my judgment and (not taking pleasure in your tongue, which is a
    woman's chiefest pleasure) think it plausible to answer me by silent

16. *special good favour*] Particularly attractive appearance.   *sweet*] Well-tuned.
17. *temper*] Proportional arrangement of bodily parts; musically, tuning or adjusting the
    pitch of a key.   *height*] High pitch.
18. *blood*] Sexual desire.
19. *try her within*] Sexual quibble. Morose's courtly phrasing frequently slips into
    unconscious crudeness as he attempts to assess Epicoene's merits.
20. *rare*] Unaccustomed to his society.
23–4. *just length of*] Properly attuned pitch for.
25–6. *do you feel ... any part*] Morose asks if she has fallen in love at first sight, but his
    words suggest a bawdy subtext.
27. *courtless*] Uncourtly, unsophisticated.
29. *audacious*] Self-confident; usually, brazen or outrageous, the meaning that emerges
    later in the play.
35. *these*] Cutbeard and Mute.
37. *plausible*] Acceptable or workable.

gestures, so long as my speeches jump right with what you conceive? –

Curtsey

Excellent! Divine! If it were possible she should hold out thus!

[*Cutbeard attempts to speak*]

Peace, Cutbeard, thou art made forever, as thou hast made me, if this   40
felicity have lasting. But I will try her further. Dear lady, I am courtly,
I tell you, and I must have mine ears banqueted with pleasant and
witty conferences, pretty girds, scoffs, and dalliance in her that I
mean to choose for my bed-fere. The ladies in court think it a most
desperate impair to their quickness of wit and good carriage if they   45
cannot give occasion for a man to court 'em, and when an amorous
discourse is set on foot, minister as good matter to continue it as
himself. And do you alone so much differ from all them that, what
they (with so much circumstance) affect and toil for, to seem learned,
to seem judicious, to seem sharp and conceited, you can bury in   50
yourself with silence? And rather trust your graces to the fair
conscience of virtue than to the world's or your own proclamation?

EPICOENE   [*Very softly*] I should be sorry else.

MOROSE   What say you, lady? Good lady, speak out.

EPICOENE   [*Louder*] I should be sorry else.   55

MOROSE   That sorrow doth fill me with gladness! O, Morose! Thou art
happy above mankind! Pray that thou mayest contain thyself. I will
only put her to it once more, and it shall be with the utmost touch and
test of their sex. But hear me, fair lady: I do also love to see her whom
I shall choose for my heifer to be the first and principal in all fashions,   60
precede all the dames at court by a fortnight, have her counsel of
tailors, lineners, lace-women, embroiderers, and sit with 'em sometimes twice a day upon French intelligences, and then come forth
varied like Nature, or oftener than she, and better by the help of Art,

38. *jump right*] Agree.
43. *conferences*] Conversations. *girds*] Sharp or biting remarks.
44. *bed-fere*] Bedfellow, mate.
45. *carriage*] Deportment.
47. *on foot*] In motion. *minister*] Supply.
49. *circumstance*] Ceremony, archness. *affect*] Pretend.
52. *conscience*] Consciousness.
58–9. *put her to it, touch ... sex*] Sexual innuendo encumbers Morose's intended meaning
of 'test her', and 'trial of womankind'.
60. *heifer*] A young cow that has not calved, used fancifully here for 'wife', but
emphasising Morose's interest in her potential as a breeder.
62. *lineners*] Makers of shirts, collars, and smocks.
63. *French intelligences*] News of the latest French fashions.

her emulous servant. This do I affect. And how will you be able, lady,   65
with this frugality of speech, to give the manifold (but necessary)
instructions for that bodies, these sleeves, those skirts, this cut, that
stitch, this embroidery, that lace, this wire, those knots, that ruff,
those roses, this girdle, that fan, the t'other scarf, these gloves? Ha!
What say you, lady?   70

EPICOENE   [*Very softly*] I'll leave it to you, sir.

MOROSE   How, lady? Pray you, rise a note.

EPICOENE   [*Louder*] I leave it to wisdom and you, sir.

MOROSE   Admirable creature! I will trouble you no more. I will not sin
against so sweet a simplicity. Let me now be bold to print on those   75
divine lips the seal of being mine. [*Kisses her*] Cutbeard, I give thee
the lease of thy house free. Thank me not but with thy leg. –

[*Cutbeard makes a leg, and attempts to speak*]

I know what thou wouldst say, she's poor and her friends deceased.
She has brought a wealthy dowry in her silence, Cutbeard, and in
respect of her poverty, Cutbeard, I shall have her more loving and   80
obedient, Cutbeard. Go thy ways and get me a minister presently with
a soft low voice to marry us, and pray him he will not be impertinent,
but brief as he can. Away. Softly, Cutbeard.

[*Exit Cutbeard*]

Sirrah, conduct your mistress into the dining room, your now-
mistress.   85

---

65. *affect*] Enjoy, but suggesting a kinky sexual thrill in his attraction to an elaborately
dressed woman. Games of 'dress-up' figure in Volpone's sexual fantasies (3.7.220–34)
and Sir Epicure Mammon's (*Alch* 4.1.166–9).

67. *bodies*] Or 'pair of bodies', what we would now call a corset or bodice, stiffened with
whalebone; the back ended at the waist, but the front extended down over the stomach
in a long V. The centre front was strengthened with a long piece of wood, bone, or metal
which held the front of the bodies rigid, even when the wearer bent or sat. If worn from
an early age, the bodies, by restricting the growth of the rib-cage, gave women a very
narrow and fashionably flat figure. A bodies was not necessarily an undergarment: in
matching material, it might be worn over the shift as the upper part of a woman's dress,
like a waistcoat, to which ornamental sleeves and skirts would be fastened with laces.
cut] Slash in a sleeve or bodice through which the silk or linen undergarment would
show.

68. *wire*] Used to stiffen ruffs, coiffures, and head-dresses.   *knots*] Variously tied ribbons
used decoratively, often given by ladies as love-tokens to courtiers.

69. *roses*] Rosettes, worn on the shoes.   *girdle*] Belt.

82. *impertinent*] Padding the marriage service with irrelevant detail.

[Exit Mute with Epicoene]

O my felicity! How I shall be revenged on mine insolent kinsman and
his plots to fright me from marrying! This night I will get an heir and
thrust him out of my blood like a stranger. He would be knighted,
forsooth, and thought by that means to reign over me – his title must
do it. No, kinsman. I will now make you bring me the tenth lord's and   90
the sixteenth lady's letter, kinsman, and it shall do you no good,
kinsman. Your knighthood itself shall come on its knees and it shall
be rejected; it shall be sued for its fees to execution and not be
redeemed; it shall cheat at the twelvepenny ordinary, it knighthood,
for its diet all the term time and tell tales for it in the vacation to the   95
hostess; or it knighthood shall do worse: take sanctuary in Coleharbour and fast. It shall fright all it friends with borrowing letters,
and when one of the fourscore hath brought it knighthood ten
shillings, it knighthood shall go to the Cranes or the Bear at the
Bridge-foot and be drunk in fear; it shall not have money to discharge   100

88. *blood*] Lineage, direct line of inheritance. *would be knighted*] Insisted on purchasing a knighthood.

90-1. *tenth lord's ... sixteenth lady's letter*] A character reference from a series of titled
patrons?

92. *Your knighthood itself*] That is, even if Dauphine comes in person.

93. *sued ... execution*] Sued until all his goods are seized by the sheriff for defaulting on
payment of debts.

94. *twelvepenny ordinary*] Tavern serving fixed-price meals, often permitting gambling by
its patrons (hence 'cheat'). *it*] Archaic possessive, used affectedly and contemptuously; but may also indicate Morose's excitement and malice getting the better of his
tongue, reducing him to childish babble.

95. *term time*] One of the four annual periods when lawcourts were in session, filling
London with litigants and other visitors; hence, a lucrative time for gamesters preying
on unwary newcomers. *tell tales for it*] Get free meals by entertaining the hostess of
the ordinary and her guests; that is, perform the function of a parasite. *vacation*] re-
cess between legal terms.

96-7. *Coleharbour*] Or Cold Harbour, in Upper Thames Street near the present Cannon
Street Station, where the Earl of Shrewsbury built a block of tenements which
developed an unsavoury reputation as a sanctuary for debtors and vagrants; its
sanctuary privileges were abolished in 1608. A 'cold harbour' was a place providing
shelter but no food or fire.

97. *borrowing*] Begging for money.

99. *the Cranes*] Three Cranes in the Vintry, in Upper Thames Street just below Southwark
Bridge, a tavern considered the resort of thieves and whoremasters.

99-100. *the Bear at the Bridge-foot*] A tavern located in Southwark just below Old
London Bridge, a popular meeting-spot noted for its dinners.

one tavern reckoning to invite the old creditors to forbear it
knighthood, or the new that should be, to trust it knighthood. It shall
be the tenth name in the bond to take up the commodity of pipkins
and stone jugs, and the part thereof shall not furnish it knighthood
forth for the attempting of a baker's widow, a brown baker's widow.   105
It shall give it knighthood's name for a stallion to all gamesome
citizens' wives and be refused, when the master of a dancing school or
– How do you call him? – the worst reveller in the town is taken. It
shall want clothes and, by reason of that, wit to fool to lawyers. It
shall not have hope to repair itself by Constantinople, Ireland, or   110
Virginia. But the best and last fortune to it knighthood shall be to make
Dol Tearsheet or Kate Common a lady, and so it knighthood may eat.

[*Exit*]

101. *forbear*] Forgive debts of.

102. *trust*] Extend credit to.

103. *tenth name ... commodity*] In a bond with a moneylender, the tenth name in a list of
borrowers to receive a share of any profit from the sale of the commodity. Moneylenders
often increased their interest rate, legally set at 10 per cent, by forcing borrowers to accept
part of the loan in over-priced goods, which the borrowers must then sell back to the
moneylender or his designate, usually at a considerable loss, in order to get cash.
pipkins] Small pots or pans; not valuable items one could make a profit on.

104–5. *furnish ... forth*] Equip.

105. *attempting of*] Trying to seduce.   *brown baker*] Baker of wholemeal loaves, then
considered coarse and inferior, suitable only for the poor, and hence not very
profitable. Such a man's widow would not be financially secure.

106. *stallion*] Stud, gigolo.   *gamesome*] Lecherous.

108. *How do you call him?*] Perhaps referring to Edmund Howe, who continued Stow's
Chronicle, and reputedly led a dissipated life.   *taken*] Accepted as a lover.

109. *fool to*] Ingratiate himself with, perhaps to entice into giving legal aid; also, play the
buffoon with. Law-students at the Inns of Court were known as revellers; many of them
were chastised by the benchers for wearing frivolous and expensive clothing instead
of scholarly gowns, and for wasting their time on pranks and trendy pursuits instead of
sharpening their wits in study.

110–11. *Constantinople ... Virginia*] Places where poor gentlemen could try to recover
their fortunes. Constantinople and Jerusalem were popular destinations for travel
wagers: for a three-to-one or five-to-one bet, a traveller would undertake a dangerous
journey and hope to collect a fortune on his return; often, because of war or disease,
he did not return. Fynes Moryson, author of *Itinerary* (1616), lost £400 in a three-for-
one gamble when his brother Henry died in Aleppo. Wastrels and younger sons went
to Ireland to escape debts, or to Virginia to try their hands at plantation life.

111–12. *make ... a lady*] Marry a whore in order to live off her earnings; a knight's wife
becomes a lady. Dol Tearsheet was the prostitute in Shakespeare's *2 Henry IV*, and Kate
Common was a type name for a whore; Jonson combined the names for Dol Common in
Alch.

Act 2 scene 6*

> [*Enter*] *Truewit, Dauphine, Clerimont*

TRUEWIT   Are you sure he is not gone by?

DAUPHINE   No, I stayed in the shop ever since.

CLERIMONT   But he may take the other end of the lane.

DAUPHINE   No, I told him I would be here at this end. I appointed him
hither.   5

TRUEWIT   What a barbarian it is to stay then!

DAUPHINE   Yonder he comes.

> [*Enter Cutbeard*]

CLERIMONT   And his charge left behind him, which is a very good sign,
Dauphine.

DAUPHINE   How now, Cutbeard, succeeds it or no?   10

CUTBEARD   Past imagination, sir, *omnia secunda* – you could not have
prayed to have had it so well. *Saltat senex*, as it is i' the proverb. He
does triumph in his felicity, admires the party! He has given me the
lease of my house too! And I am now going for a silent minister to
marry 'em, and away.   15

TRUEWIT   'Slight, get one o' the silenced ministers, a zealous brother
would torment him purely.

CUTBEARD   *Cum privilegio*, sir.

DAUPHINE   O, by no means, let's do nothing to hinder it now! When 'tis
done and finished, I am for you, for any device of vexation.   20

CUTBEARD   And that shall be within this half hour, upon my dexterity,
gentlemen. Contrive what you can in the meantime, *bonis avibus*.

---

*   This scene takes place in the street near the barbershop, where Truewit hits on the first
'device of vexation': to move La Foole's quarter-feast to Morose's house as a wedding
banquet whose noises will afflict the groom

4–5. *appointed him hither*] Arranged to meet him here.

6. *barbarian*] Pun on barber.   *it*] Contemptuously for 'he'.   *stay*] Be late.

8. *charge*] Person left in his care, i.e. Epicoene.

11–12. *omnia secunda ... Saltat senex*] 'All's well, the old man is cutting capers.' The
Roman proverb referred to occasions when a religious rite was interrupted and the
returning worshippers discovered that one old man had preserved the rite unbroken by
continuing to dance in their absence.

16. *silenced ministers*] Puritan clergy who had lost their licence to preach. See 2.2.68 and
note.   *zealous*] Ardently puritanical.

17. *purely*] Both 'thoroughly' and 'puritanically'.

18. *Cum privilegio*] With the authority or right of one's profession; here the minister's
right to deliver uninterrupted a sermon on any religious occasion, including a wedding.

21. *upon my dexterity*] Oath suitable for a barber; see 1.2.34–5.

22. *bonis avibus*] The omens being favourable.

[*Exit Cutbeard*]

CLERIMONT   How the slave doth Latin it!

TRUEWIT   It would be made a jest to posterity, sirs, this day's mirth, if ye will.   25

CLERIMONT   Beshrew his heart that will not, I pronounce.

DAUPHINE   And for my part. What is't?

TRUEWIT   To translate all La Foole's company and his feast hither today to celebrate this bridal.

DAUPHINE   Ay, marry, but how will 't be done?   30

TRUEWIT   I'll undertake the directing of all the lady-guests thither, and then the meat must follow.

CLERIMONT   For God's sake, let's effect it. It will be an excellent comedy of affliction, so many several noises.

DAUPHINE   But are they not at the other place already, think you?   35

TRUEWIT   I'll warrant you for the college-honours: one o' their faces has not the priming colour laid on yet, nor the other her smock sleeked.

CLERIMONT   O, but they'll rise earlier than ordinary to a feast.

TRUEWIT   Best go see and assure ourselves.

CLERIMONT   Who knows the house?   40

TRUEWIT   I'll lead you. Were you never there yet?

DAUPHINE   Not I.

CLERIMONT   Nor I.

TRUEWIT   Where ha' you lived then? Not know Tom Otter!

CLERIMONT   No. For God's sake, what is he?   45

TRUEWIT   An excellent animal, equal with your Daw or La Foole, if not transcendent, and does Latin it as much as your barber. He is his wife's subject, he calls her Princess, and at such times as these follows her up and down the house like a page with his hat off, partly for heat, partly for reverence. At this instant, he is marshalling of his bull, bear,   50 and horse.

DAUPHINE   What be those, in the name of Sphinx?

TRUEWIT   Why, sir, he has been a great man at the Bear Garden in his time, and from that subtle sport has ta'en the witty denomination of

23. *Latin it*] Pepper his conversation with Latin tags; a reminder of the barber-surgeon's training (see 2.2.129–30).

28. *translate*] Transfer; transform, especially into monstrous shape.

34. *several*] Different, various.

35. *the other place*] The Otters' house.

36. *warrant you for*] Guarantee the condition of.

37. *priming colour*] As in house-painting, the undercoat.   *sleeked*] Smoothed or pressed.

49. *for heat*] Fanning himself with it.

52. *Sphinx*] The riddler of ancient legend.

53. *Bear Garden*] A bull- and bear-baiting pit near the Clink on the Bankside in

his chief carousing cups. One he calls his bull, another his bear, 55
another his horse. And then he has his lesser glasses that he calls his
deer and his ape, and several degrees of 'em too, and never is well nor
thinks any entertainment perfect till these be brought out and set o'
the cupboard.

CLERIMONT   For God's love! We should miss this if we should not go.   60

TRUEWIT   Nay, he has a thousand things as good that will speak him all
day. He will rail on his wife with certain commonplaces behind her
back, and to her face –

DAUPHINE   No more of him. Let's go see him, I petition you.

[*Exeunt*]

ACT 3

Act 3 scene 1*

[*Enter*] *Otter, Mistress Otter,* [*unaware they are followed by*] *Truewit,*
Clerimont, Dauphine

OTTER   Nay, good Princess, hear me *pauca verba*.

MRS OTTER   By that light, I'll ha' you chained up with your bull-dogs and
bear-dogs if you be not civil the sooner. I'll send you to kennel, i' faith.
You were best bait me with your bull, bear, and horse! Never a
time that the courtiers or collegiates come to the house but you   5

Southwark; often associated with the drinking and gambling resort at Paris Garden to
the west of the Bear Garden.

55. *cups*] The lids, hinged as on a stein, were shaped like animal heads.

57. *degrees*] Sizes. *well*] Happy.

58. *perfect*] Complete.

61. *speak*] Reveal.

*   The first three scenes take place at the Otter household. This scene illustrates a favourite
Jonsonian device: eavesdropping on a private and humiliating situation. Here, the
marital bickering, observed by the three wits, resembles a bear-baiting, with Tom as the
hapless bear and Mistress Otter as the vicious dog.

2. *pauca verba*] Few words. Otter uses this catch-phrase to get a word in, but the
expression comes aptly enough from the proverbial cry of tavern-drinkers, 'More drink
and less talk!'

4. *You were best bait me*] 'Just you try annoying me', with the unspoken threat of
imminent dire punishment.

make it a Shrove Tuesday! I would have you get your Whitsuntide
velvet cap and your staff i' your hand to entertain 'em. Yes, in troth,
do.

OTTER   Not so, Princess, neither, but under correction, sweet Princess, gi'
me leave – these things I am known to the courtiers by. It is reported   10
to them for my humour, and they receive it so, and do expect it. Tom
Otter's bull, bear, and horse is known all over England, in *rerum
natura*.

MRS OTTER   'Fore me, I will *na-ture* 'em over to Paris Garden, and
na-ture you thither too, if you pronounce 'em again. Is a bear a fit   15
beast, or a bull, to mix in society with great ladies? Think i' your
discretion, in any good polity?

OTTER   The horse then, good Princess.

MRS OTTER   Well, I am contented for the horse. They love to be well
horsed, I know. I love it myself.   20

OTTER   And it is a delicate fine horse, this. *Poetarum Pegasus*. Under
correction, Princess, Jupiter did turn himself into a – *Taurus*, or bull,
under correction, good Princess.

MRS OTTER   By my integrity, I'll send you over to the Bankside, I'll
commit you to the Master of the Garden, if I hear but a syllable more.   25
Must my house or my roof be polluted with the scent of bears and
bulls, when it is perfumed for great ladies? Is this according to the
instrument when I married you? That I would be Princess and reign
in mine own house, and you would be my subject and obey me? What

  7. *Shrove Tuesday*] The apprentices' holiday marked by riot and vandalism. *Whitsun-
     tide*] The week of festivities following Whitsunday (Pentecost).
  6–8. *I would have ... do*] Heavily sarcastic comment on Otter's inadequacies as an
     elegant host.
  8. *velvet cap*] Worn on Sundays and holidays. *staff*] A sneer at Otter's lower-class
     status; gentlemen carried swords.
  10. *under correction*] Subject to correction, an expression of deference to authority.
  12. *humour*] Distinguishing eccentricity, idiosyncrasy.
  13–14. *in rerum natura*] In the nature of things, in the physical universe; loosely, anywhere.
  17. *discretion*] Judgment. *good polity*] Respectable society.
  21. *Poetarum Pegasus*] The Pegasus of the poets. According to Pindar, Bellerophon tried to
     ride Pegasus, the winged horse, up to Olympus, and was thrown down by Zeus. Jonson
     refers to wine as the vehicle for poets' aspirations in 'Over the Door at the Entrance into
     the Apollo': 'Wine, it is the milk of Venus, / And the poet's horse accounted. / Ply it, and
     you all are mounted' (Parfitt 1975: p. 341).
  22. *Jupiter ... bull*] When he abducted and raped Europa.
  28. *instrument*] Legal document, their marriage contract from which Mrs Otter proceeds
     to cite clauses.

did you bring me, should make you thus peremptory? Do I allow you   30
your half-crown a day to spend where you will among your gamesters,
to vex and torment me at such times as these? Who gives you your
maintenance, I pray you? Who allows you your horse-meat and
man's-meat? Your three suits of apparel a year? Your four pair of
stockings, one silk, three worsted? Your clean linen, your bands and   35
cuffs, when I can get you to wear 'em? 'Tis mar'l you ha' 'em on now.
Who graces you with courtiers or great personages to speak to you out
of their coaches and come home to your house? Were you ever so
much as looked upon by a lord or a lady before I married you, but on
the Easter or Whitsun holidays? And then out at the Banqueting   40
House window, when Ned Whiting or George Stone were at the
stake?

TRUEWIT   [*Aside to his companions*] For God's sake, let's go stave her off
him.

MRS OTTER   Answer me to that. And did not I take you up from thence   45
in an old greasy buff-doublet with points, and green velvet sleeves out
at the elbows? You forget this.

TRUEWIT   [*Aside as before*] She'll worry him if we help not in time.

[*They approach the Otters*]

MRS OTTER   O, here are some o' the gallants! [*Hisses at Otter*] Go
to, behave yourself distinctly and with good morality, or, I protest, I'll   50
take away your exhibition.

---

30. *bring*] As financial contribution to the marriage. *peremptory*] Domineering, playing
on the legal phrase *peremptory challenge*, an objection without showing any cause.
33. *maintenance*] Domestic upkeep. *horse-meat*] Fodder.
34–5. *three suits ... worsted*] The standard outfit for domestic servants. The silk stockings
were for holidays.
35. *bands*] Collars
36. *mar'l*] Marvel.
40–41. *Banqueting House*] At Whitehall, where James was entertained with baitings at
Shrovetide and Easter, using the bulls and bears sent over from Southwark.
41. *Ned Whiting or George Stone*] Champion bears. George Stone was killed at court in
1606, in a baiting before the King of Denmark.
43. *stave ... off*] Drive off with a staff, a bear-baiting term.
46. *buff-doublet*] Leather jerkin, worn by common workers and soldiers. *points*] Laces.
48. *worry*] Injure by biting, another baiting term.
50. *distinctly*] In distinguished or orderly fashion.
51. *exhibition*] Allowance.

Act 3 scene 2

TRUEWIT   By your leave, fair Mistress Otter, I'll be bold to enter these
gentlemen in your acquaintance.

MRS OTTER   It shall not be obnoxious or difficil, sir.

TRUEWIT   How does my noble Captain? Is the bull, bear, and horse in
rerum natura still?   5

OTTER   Sir, *sic visum superis.*

MRS OTTER   I would you would but intimate 'em, do. Go your ways in,
and get toasts and butter made for the woodcocks. That's a fit
province for you.

[*Drives him out*]

CLERIMONT   [*Aside to Truewit and Dauphine*] Alas, what a tyranny   10
is this poor fellow married to.

TRUEWIT   O, but the sport will be anon, when we get him loose.

DAUPHINE   Dares he ever speak?

TRUEWIT   No Anabaptist ever railed with the like licence. But mark her
language in the meantime, I beseech you.   15

MRS OTTER   [*Returning to them*] Gentlemen, you are very aptly come.
My cousin, Sir Amorous, will be here briefly.

TRUEWIT   In good time, lady. Was not Sir John Daw here to ask for him
and the company?

MRS OTTER   I cannot assure you, Master Truewit. Here was a very   20
melancholy knight in a ruff that demanded my subject for somebody,
a gentleman, I think.

CLERIMONT   Ay, that was he, lady.

MRS OTTER   But he departed straight, I can resolve you.

DAUPHINE   What an excellent choice phrase this lady expresses in!   25

3. *obnoxious or difficil*] Offensive or troublesome. Mrs Otter affects pompous stilted
diction in order to seem courtly.

4–5. *in rerum natura*] In existence.

6. *sic visum superis*] As those above decree.

7. *intimate 'em*] Keep them out of sight (Latin, *intimus*, inmost).

8. *woodcocks*] A wildfowl savory, served on toast. Easily trapped, the birds became types
of gullibility; hence, fools.

14. *Anabaptist*] Loosely, puritan. Anabaptists were a radical and anarchic sect, satirised
more specifically in *Alch*, especially 2.5 and 3.3.   *railed*] Uttered abuse.   *licence*]
Punning on licence to preach, and lack of restraint.

17. *briefly*] Soon.

21. *demanded my subject*] Asked Otter.

24. *resolve*] Affected term for 'inform' or 'assure'.

TRUEWIT   O, sir! She is the only authentical courtier – that is not naturally
   bred one – in the city.
MRS OTTER   You have taken that report upon trust, gentlemen.
TRUEWIT   No, I assure you, the court governs it so, lady, in your behalf.
MRS OTTER   I am the servant of the court and courtiers, sir.   30
TRUEWIT   They are rather your idolaters.
MRS OTTER   Not so, sir.

[*Enter Cutbeard and talks to Dauphine privately*]

DAUPHINE   How now, Cutbeard? Any cross?
CUTBEARD   O, no, sir. *Omnia bene.* 'Twas never better o' the hinges, all's
   sure. I have so pleased him with a curate that he's gone to't almost   35
   with the delight he hopes for soon.
DAUPHINE   What is he for a vicar?
CUTBEARD   One that has catched a cold, sir, and can scarce be heard six
   inches off, as if he spoke out of a bulrush that were not picked, or his
   throat were full of pith: a fine quick fellow and an excellent barber of   40
   prayers. I came to tell you, sir, that you might *omnem movere lapidem*
   (as they say), be ready with your vexation.
DAUPHINE   Gramercy, honest Cutbeard. Be thereabouts with thy key to
   let us in.
CUTBEARD   I will not fail you, sir. *Ad manum.*   45

[*Exit Cutbeard*]

TRUEWIT   Well, I'll go watch my coaches.
CLERIMONT   Do, and we'll send Daw to you, if you meet him not.

[*Exit Truewit*]

MRS OTTER   Is Master Truewit gone?
DAUPHINE   Yes, lady, there is some unfortunate business fallen out.
MRS OTTER   So I judged by the physiognomy of the fellow that came in,   50

---

26. *authentical*] Genuine.
29. *governs*] Decides.
33. *Any cross?*] Has anything gone wrong?
34. *Omnia bene*] All is well.   *o' the hinges*] Working smoothly, like a well-hung door.
35–6. *gone to't . . . soon*] Proceeded with almost orgasmic pleasure.
37. *What . . . vicar?*] What kind of a parson is he?
39. *bulrush . . . picked*] Weak reedy voice.
40–41. *barber of prayers*] Because he has to cut them short.
41. *omnem movere lapidem*] Leave no stone unturned.
43. *Gramercy*] Thanks.
45. *Ad manum*] [I'll be] at hand, or ready.

and I had a dream last night too of the new pageant and my Lady
Mayoress, which is always very ominous to me. I told it my
Lady Haughty t'other day, when her honour came hither to see some
China stuffs, and she expounded it out of Artemidorus, and I have
found it since very true. It has done me many affronts.   55

CLERIMONT   Your dream, lady?

MRS OTTER   Yes, sir, anything I do but dream o' the city. It stained me a
damask tablecloth, cost me eighteen pound at one time, and burned
me a black satin gown as I stood by the fire at my Lady Centaur's
chamber in the college another time. A third time, at the Lords'   60
masque, it dropped all my wire and my ruff with wax candle, that I
could not go up to the banquet. A fourth time, as I was taking coach
to go to Ware to meet a friend, it dashed me a new suit all over (a
crimson satin doublet and black velvet skirts) with a brewer's horse,
that I was fain to go in and shift me, and kept my chamber a leash of   65
days for the anguish of it.

DAUPHINE   These were dire mischances, lady.

CLERIMONT   I would not dwell in the city and 'twere so fatal to me.

MRS OTTER   Yes, sir, but I do take advice of my doctor to dream of it as
little as I can.   70

DAUPHINE   You do well, Mistress Otter.

MRS OTTER   Will it please you to enter the house farther, gentlemen?

[*Enter Sir John Daw, melancholy as before; Clerimont takes him aside*]

DAUPHINE   And your favour, lady. But we stay to speak with a
knight, Sir John Daw, who is here come. We shall follow you, lady.

MRS OTTER   At your own time, sir. It is my cousin Sir Amorous his   75
feast –

DAUPHINE   I know it, lady.

51. *dream*] Considered prophetic by the superstitious.   *pageant*] Celebrating the installa-
tion of a new Lord Mayor.

51–2. *Lady Mayoress*] Wife of the Lord Mayor, perhaps an indication of Mrs Otter's social
aspirations.

54. *Artemidorus*] Second-century AD Greek physician who wrote a lengthy anecdotal
interpretation of dreams.

57. *anything . . . city*] Whenever I dream of the city.

63. *Ware*] Notorious rendezvous for assignations, a market town 24 miles north of
London; see also 5.1.53.   *friend*] Lover.

64. *doublet*] Mannish attire, the target of old-fashioned moralists from Stubbes to the
anonymous *Hic Mulier*, which accused women of wearing 'the loose, lascivious civil
embracement of a French doublet, being all unbuttoned to entice' (Henderson and
McManus 1985: p. 267), instead of the properly concealing gown worn by modest
women.

65. *shift me*] Change my clothes.   *a leash of*] Three; originally used of hounds or hawks.

MRS OTTER – and mine together. But it is for his honour, and therefore
     I take no name of it more than of the place.
DAUPHINE   You are a bounteous kinswoman.
MRS OTTER   Your servant, sir.   80

     [*Exit Mistress Otter*]

Act 3 scene 3*

CLERIMONT   Why, do not you know it, Sir John Daw?
DAW   No, I am a rook if I do.
CLERIMONT   I'll tell you then: she's married by this time! And whereas
     you were put i' the head that she was gone with Sir Dauphine, I assure
     you Sir Dauphine has been the noblest, honestest friend to you that   5
     ever gentleman of your quality could boast of. He has discovered the
     whole plot and made your mistress so acknowledging and indeed so
     ashamed of her injury to you that she desires you to forgive her and
     but grace her wedding with your presence today – She is to be married
     to a very good fortune, she says, his uncle, old Morose, and she willed   10
     me in private to tell you that she shall be able to do you more favours
     and with more security now than before.
DAW   Did she say so, i' faith?
CLERIMONT   Why, what do you think of me, Sir John! Ask Sir Dauphine.
DAW   Nay, I believe you. Good Sir Dauphine, did she desire me to forgive   15
     her?
CLERIMONT   I assure you, Sir John, she did.
DAW   Nay then, I do with all my heart, and I'll be jovial.
CLERIMONT   Yes, for look you, sir, this was the injury to you. La Foole
     intended this feast to honour her bridal day, and made you the   20
     property to invite the college ladies, and promise to bring her, and
     then at the time she should have appeared – as his friend – to have
     given you the dor. Whereas now, Sir Dauphine has brought her to a

78. *name of*] Credit for.   *place*] Location, the party being held at her house.
*   While Truewit is off-stage, ostensibly detouring the Ladies Collegiate's coaches to
     Morose's house, Clerimont and Dauphine set up Daw, La Foole, and Otter for later falls
     in 4.2 and 4.5. Daw and La Foole each believe the other has tried to disgrace him, and
     Otter finds classical support for the propriety of his drinking cups.
4.   *put i' the head*] Made to think.
6.   *your quality*] Ambiguously suggesting that Daw is getting the treatment he deserves.
8.   *injury*] Insult.
11. *favours*] Suggesting sexual favours.
12. *security*] Because any pregnancy would seem the logical outcome of marriage.
21. *property*] Tool.
23. *given … the dor*] Jeered.

feeling of it, with this kind of satisfaction, that you shall bring all the
ladies to the place where she is and be very jovial, and there she will   25
have a dinner which shall be in your name, and so disappoint La Foole
to make you good again and (as it were) a saver i' the main.

DAW   As I am a knight, I honour her and forgive her heartily.

CLERIMONT   About it then presently. Truewit is gone before to confront
the coaches and to acquaint you with so much, if he meet you. Join   30
with him and 'tis well.

[Enter La Foole]

See, here comes your antagonist, but take you no notice, but be very
jovial.

LA FOOLE   Are the ladies come, Sir John Daw, and your mistress?

[Exit Daw jovially]

Sir Dauphine! You are exceeding welcome, and honest Master   35
Clerimont. Where's my cousin! Did you see no collegiates, gentlemen?

DAUPHINE   Collegiates! Do you not hear, Sir Amorous, how you are
abused?

LA FOOLE   How, sir!   40

CLERIMONT   Will you speak so kindly to Sir John Daw, that has done you
such an affront?

LA FOOLE   Wherein, gentlemen? Let me be a suitor to you to know, I
beseech you!

CLERIMONT   Why, sir, his mistress is married today to Sir Dauphine's   45
uncle, your cousin's neighbour, and he has diverted all the ladies and
all your company thither to frustrate your provision and stick a

25. *jovial*] Merry; astrologically, anyone born under Jupiter (Jove) was regarded as a
source of joy and happiness. E. B. Partridge (1971) sees Daw as part of a larger
astrological joke in which he is under the influence of Truewit and Clerimont; earlier
their 'Saturnine' influence made him melancholy; and now their benign 'Jovial'
influence averts his melancholy by prescribing food, wine, music, and mirth as cures.

27. *saver i' the main*] Gambling terms in hazard, an early form of craps. The player throws
the dice to determine the 'main' (any number from 5 to 9), and throws again for the
'chance' (any number from 4 to 10). If he throws 'crabs' or 'craps' (a 2 or 3), he loses
his stake; if he throws his 'main', he 'nicks' (wins immediately). Otherwise, he continues
at the dice until either his 'chance' comes up (he wins), or his 'main' (he loses). A 'saver'
is a gambler who breaks even. Clerimont is advising Daw to compensate for the
humiliating loss of Epicoene by accepting her offer to have him as the guest of honour
at her wedding feast, thus humiliating La Foole, who hoped to crow over his former
rival. 'Main' is emended from *F1*'s 'man', possibly intended as a pun.

29. *confront*] Meet in order to redirect.

47. *provision*] Arrangements.

disgrace upon you. He was here, now, to have enticed us away from you too, but we told him his own, I think.

LA FOOLE   Has Sir John Daw wronged me so inhumanly?   50

DAUPHINE   He has done it, Sir Amorous, most maliciously and treacherously, but if you'll be ruled by us, you shall quit him, i' faith.

LA FOOLE   Good gentlemen! I'll make one, believe it. How, I pray?

DAUPHINE   Marry, sir, get me your pheasants, and your godwits, and your best meat, and dish it in silver dishes of your cousin's presently,   55
and say nothing, but clap me a clean towel about you, like a sewer, and bare-headed march afore it with a good confidence ('tis but over the way, hard by) and we'll second you, where you shall set it o' the board, and bid 'em welcome to 't, which shall show 'tis yours, and disgrace his preparation utterly. And for your cousin, whereas she   60
should be troubled here at home with care of making and giving welcome, she shall transfer all that labour thither and be a principal guest herself, sit ranked with the college-honours, and be honoured, and have her health drunk as often, as bare, and as loud as the best of 'em.   65

LA FOOLE   I'll go tell her presently. It shall be done, that's resolved.

[*Exit La Foole*]

CLERIMONT   I thought he would not hear it out, but 'twould take him.

DAUPHINE   Well, there be guests and meat now. How shall we do for music?   70

CLERIMONT   The smell of the venison going through the street will invite one noise of fiddlers or other.

DAUPHINE   I would it would call the trumpeters thither.

CLERIMONT   Faith, there is hope: they have intelligence of all feasts. There's good correspondence betwixt them and the London cooks.   75
'Tis twenty to one but we have 'em.

DAUPHINE   'Twill be a most solemn day for my uncle, and an excellent fit of mirth for us.

49   *his own*] What we thought of his behaviour.
52.   *quit*] Repay.
53.   *make one*] Join in.
56.   *sewer*] In great households, the servant who supervises the seating and serving of guests.
59.   *board*] Table.
64.   *bare*] Bare-headed, a sign of respect while toasting ladies.
72.   *noise*] Band.
75.   *correspondence*] Business relations.
77.   *solemn*] Punning on 'grave' and 'ceremonious', especially applied to the solemnising of a marriage. *fit*] Punning on a violent outburst, and a snatch of music.

CLERIMONT   Ay, if we can hold up the emulation betwixt Foole and Daw,
and never bring them to expostulate.   80
DAUPHINE   Tut, flatter 'em both (as Truewit says) and you may take their
understandings in a purse-net. They'll believe themselves to be just
such men as we make 'em, neither more nor less. They have nothing,
not the use of their senses, but by tradition.
CLERIMONT   See! Sir Amorous has his towel on already.   85

[*La Foole*] *enters like a sewer*

– Have you persuaded your cousin?
LA FOOLE   Yes, 'tis very feasible. She'll do anything, she says, rather than
the La Fooles shall be disgraced.
DAUPHINE   She is a noble kinswoman. It will be such a pestling device, Sir
Amorous! It will pound all your enemy's practices to powder and   90
blow him up with his own mine, his own train.
LA FOOLE   Nay, we'll give fire, I warrant you.
CLERIMONT   But you must carry it privately, without any noise, and take
no notice by any means –

[*Enter Otter*]

OTTER   Gentlemen, my Princess says you shall have all her silver   95
dishes *festinate*, and she's gone to alter her tire a little and go with
you –
CLERIMONT   And yourself too, Captain Otter.
DAUPHINE   By any means, sir.
OTTER   Yes, sir, I do mean it. But I would entreat my cousin Sir Amorous   100
and you gentlemen to be suitors to my Princess that I may carry my
bull and my bear, as well as my horse.
CLERIMONT   That you shall do, Captain Otter.
LA FOOLE   My cousin will never consent, gentlemen.

79. *emulation*] One-upmanship, rivalry.
80. *expostulate*] Face each other directly with their grievances.
82. *purse-net*] Bag-shaped net, the mouth of which can be drawn shut with a cord, used
for catching rabbits or 'conies'. 'Cony-catching' is a term for duping or cheating by
knaves.
84. *tradition*] What is handed to them.
89. *pestling*] Pounding or crushing with a pestle. The current pronunciation echoed
'pizzle' (= penis), with the same bawdy innuendo, as in Beaumont's *The Knight of the
Burning Pestle*, of sexual aggressiveness and the communication of VD, continued in
La Foole's 'fire' and Clerimont's warning to 'carry it privately'.
90. *practices*] Plots, tricks.
91. *mine*] Explosive.   *train*] Multiple punning on trick, party of followers, and military
supplies, especially artillery and fuses.
96. *festinate*] Quickly.   *tire*] Attire.

DAUPHINE   She must consent, Sir Amorous, to reason.   105
LA FOOLE   Why, she says they are no decorum among ladies.
OTTER   But they are *decora*, and that's better, sir.
CLERIMONT   Ay, she must hear argument. Did not Pasiphae, who was a
    queen, love a bull? And was not Callisto, the mother of Arcas, turned
    into a bear and made a star, Mistress Ursula, i' the heavens?   110
OTTER   O God! That I could ha' said as much! I will have these stories
    painted i' the Bear Garden, *ex Ovidii Metamorphosi.*
DAUPHINE   Where is your Princess, Captain? Pray be our leader.
OTTER   That I shall, sir.
CLERIMONT   Make haste, good Sir Amorous.   115

    [*Exeunt*]

Act 3 scene 4*

[*Enter*] *Morose, Epicoene, Parson, Cutbeard*

MOROSE   [*To Parson, paying him*] Sir, there's an angel for yourself
    and a brace of angels for your cold. Muse not at this manage of my
    bounty. It is fit we should thank fortune double to nature for any

---

106. *no decorum*] Not fitting or seemly behaviour.
107. *decora*] Latin plural, punning on *decorum* meaning 'handsome, ornamental', and
    making a grammatical joke on 'better' syntax, because La Foole's English noun
    decorum is also a Latin singular adjective, and does not agree with his plural
    antecedent 'they'.
108. *Pasiphae*] Queen of Crete as the wife of Minos, and mother of the Minotaur.
109. *Callisto*] Jupiter seduced Callisto, a companion of Diana sworn to chastity, and then
    transformed her for her own protection from the goddess's wrath first into a bear, and
    then into the constellation *Ursus Major*, 'Big Bear'; hence, 'Mistress Ursula'. Their son,
    Arcas, founded Arcadia.
112. *ex Ovidii Metamorphosi*] The story of Callisto appears in Ovid's *Metamorphoses*, but
    the Pasiphae legend is retold in his *Ars Amatoria*.
 *   From this point on, the setting is Morose's house, just 'over the way, hard by' (3.3.57–8)
    Mistress Otter's house. Morose's muffled household is gradually taken over by noise,
    while Morose keeps retreating off-stage. The post-marriage scene, the central scene of
    the play, inverts Morose's fantasy without a struggle. The prelude of the silenced
    parson's coughing gives way to the silent bride's volubility. Morose protests, but both
    inversions produce only more noise. Cowed, he does not even attempt to order his
    'regent' wife to be quiet.
1. *angel*] Gold coin, then worth about 10 shillings.
2. *manage*] Management.
3. *double to*] Twice as much as [we thank nature].

benefit she confers upon us. Besides, it is your imperfection, but my
solace.   5

The Parson speaks as having a cold

PARSON   I thank your worship, so is it mine now.
MOROSE   What says he, Cutbeard?
CUTBEARD   He says, *praesto*, sir, whensoever your worship needs him, he
    can be ready with the like. He got this cold with sitting up late and
    singing catches with cloth-workers.   10
MOROSE   No more. I thank him.
PARSON   God keep your worship, and give you much joy with your fair
    spouse.

He coughs

    Umh! Umh!
MOROSE   O, O, stay, Cutbeard! Let him give me five shillings of my
    money back. As it is bounty to reward benefits, so is it equity to mulct   15
    injuries. I will have it. What says he?
CUTBEARD   He cannot change it, sir.
MOROSE   It must be changed.
CUTBEARD   [*Aside to Parson*] Cough again.
MOROSE   What says he?   20
CUTBEARD   He will cough out the rest, sir.
PARSON   *Again* [*coughing*] Umh, umh, umh!
MOROSE   Away, away with him, stop his mouth, away. I forgive it –

    [*Exit Cutbeard with Parson*]

EPICOENE   Fie, Master Morose, that you will use this violence to a
    man of the church.   25
MOROSE   How!
EPICOENE   It does not become your gravity or breeding (as you pretend
    in court) to have offered this outrage on a waterman or any more
    boisterous creature, much less on a man of his civil coat.   30
MOROSE   You can speak then!
EPICOENE   Yes, sir.

4–5. *imperfection, solace*] That is, the parson's laryngitis.
8. *praesto*] At your service (Latin).
10. *catches*] Rounds. *cloth-workers*] Weavers proverbially sang at their craft, presum-
    ably to maintain the rhythm of the shuttle. The cloth-making industry was established
    in England by puritan émigrés from the Netherlands, who were given to hymn-singing.
15. *benefits*] Acts of kindness. *mulct*] Punish by fine.
27. *pretend*] Profess to have.
28. *waterman*] Thames boatmen were notoriously raucous in attracting customers or
    bickering over fares.
29. *civil coat*] Sober calling, referring to the black cloth worn by ministers.

MOROSE   Speak out, I mean.

EPICOENE   Ay, sir. Why, did you think you had married a statue? or a
motion only? one of the French puppets with the eyes turned with a
wire? or some innocent out of the hospital that would stand with her   35
hands thus, and a plaice-mouth, and look upon you?

MOROSE   O immodesty! A manifest woman! [*Calling*] What, Cutbeard!

EPICOENE   Nay, never quarrel with Cutbeard, sir; it is too late now. I
confess it doth bate somewhat of the modesty I had when I writ simply   40
maid, but I hope I shall make it a stock still competent to the estate
and dignity of your wife.

MOROSE   She can talk!

EPICOENE   Yes, indeed, sir.

MOROSE   [*Calling again*] What, sirrah! None of my knaves there?

[*Enter Mute*]

Where is this impostor, Cutbeard?   45

[*Mute makes signs to indicate Cutbeard has gone*]

EPICOENE   Speak to him, fellow, speak to him. I'll have none of this
coacted unnatural dumbness in my house, in a family where I govern.

[*Exit Mute*]

MOROSE   She is my regent already! I have married a Penthesilea, a
Semiramis, sold my liberty to a distaff!

34. *motion*] Puppet. *French puppets*] Marionettes.
35. *innocent*] Idiot. *hospital*] Bedlam.
36. *hands thus*] Crossed and hanging limply in front, a sign of placid obedience or
idiocy. *plaice-mouth*] Mouth gaping and puckering like a fish's.
39. *bate*] Lessen, diminish.
40. *stock*] Supply, as endowment or dowry; attribute complementary to her breeding.
still competent] Always appropriate. *estate*] Status.
47. *coacted*] Compulsory, enforced. *family*] Household.
48. *Penthesilea*] Queen of the Amazons, slain by Achilles at Troy.
49. *Semiramis*] Warrior queen of the Assyrians who, after the death of her husband Ninus
(perhaps executed through her plotting), ruled brilliantly, building cities, notably
Babylon, and subduing countries, reputedly wearing male attire and pretending to be
her own son until, after 42 years, she abdicated in his favour. *distaff*] A cleft stick
holding the wool or flax for spinning, hence representing woman's occupation, but also
a reference to female noise. In the working of the spinning wheel, the distaff clacks and
vibrates.

Act 3 scene 5*

[*Enter*] *Truewit*

TRUEWIT   Where's Master Morose?

MOROSE   Is he come again! Lord have mercy upon me.

TRUEWIT   [*Kisses the bride*] I wish you all joy, Mistress Epicoene, with
your grave and honourable match.

EPICOENE   [*Kisses him*] I return you the thanks, Master Truewit, so   5
friendly a wish deserves.

MOROSE   She has acquaintance too!

TRUEWIT   God save you, sir, and give you all contentment in your fair
choice here. Before I was the bird of night to you, the owl, but now
I am the messenger of peace, a dove, and bring you the glad wishes of   10
many friends to the celebration of this good hour.

MOROSE   What hour, sir?

TRUEWIT   Your marriage hour, sir. I commend your resolution that –
notwithstanding all the dangers I laid afore you in the voice of a night-
crow – would yet go on and be yourself. It shows you are a man   15
constant to your own ends and upright to your purposes, that would
not be put off with left-handed cries.

MOROSE   How should you arrive at the knowledge of so much?

TRUEWIT   Why, did you ever hope, sir, committing the secrecy of it to a
barber, that less than the whole town should know it? You might as   20
well ha' told it the conduit, or the bakehouse, or the infantry that
follow the court, and with more security. Could your gravity forget so
old and noted a remnant as *lippis et tonsoribus notum*? Well, sir,
forgive it yourself now, the fault, and be communicable with your

---

*   The object of this scene is to increase Morose's discomfort by anticipating the noisy
guests to come. Truewit's encounter with Morose ends in a burlesque cursing
competition which, as E. B. Partridge (1971) has suggested, parodies stichomythia, the
classical convention of alternating lines of dialogue between two speakers. In Senecan
tragedy, the convention expresses tension; here, the effect is of comic overkill as Truewit
continues to one-up Morose, despite the latter's pleas to desist.

9,14–15. *owl, night-crow*] Harbingers of ill omen, the latter bird non-specific.

17. *left-handed*] Sinister, inauspicious.

21. *conduit ... bakehouse*] Where common people gathered to collect water and bread;
hence, centres of gossip.

21–2. *infantry ... court*] The 'black guard', or menial servants who performed all the dirty
work at court, and hence were in a position to know the latest scandals.

22. *your gravity*] Variation on 'your worship' or 'your honour'.

23. *remnant*] Scrap of quotation. *lippis ... notum*] 'Known to the bleary-eyed [fre-
quenters of apothecary shops] and to barbers'; that is, to common retailers of gossip
(from Horace, *Satires* 1.7.3).

24. *communicable*] Communicative, sociable.

friends. Here will be three or four fashionable ladies from the college   25
to visit you presently, and their train of minions and followers.

MOROSE   Bar my doors! Bar my doors! Where are all my eaters? My
mouths now?

[*Enter Servants*]

Bar up my doors, you varlets.

EPICOENE   He is a varlet that stirs to such an office. Let 'em stand open.   30
I would see him that dares move his eyes toward it. Shall I have a
barricado made against my friends, to be barred of any pleasure they
can bring in to me with honourable visitation?

MOROSE   O Amazonian impudence!

TRUEWIT   Nay, faith, in this, sir, she speaks but reason, and methinks is   35
more continent than you. Would you go to bed so presently, sir, afore
noon? A man of your head and hair should owe more to that reverend
ceremony and not mount the marriage bed like a town bull or a
mountain goat, but stay the due season, and ascend it then with
religion and fear. Those delights are to be steeped in the humour and   40
silence of the night, and give the day to other open pleasures and
jollities of feast, of music, of revels, of discourse. We'll have all, sir,
that may make your hymen high and happy.

MOROSE   O my torment, my torment!

TRUEWIT   Nay, if you endure the first half hour, sir, so tediously and with   45
this irksomeness, what comfort or hope can this fair gentlewoman
make to herself hereafter in the consideration of so many years as are
to come –

MOROSE   Of my affliction. Good sir, depart, and let her do it alone.

TRUEWIT   I have done, sir.   50

MOROSE   That cursed barber!

TRUEWIT   Yes, faith, a cursed wretch indeed, sir.

27, 28. *eaters, mouths*] Servants, conventionally represented as greedy and lazy.

32. *barricado*] Barrier, hastily built obstruction using materials at hand.

33. *visitation*] Formal visit.

34. *Amazonian*] Morose compared Epicoene to Penthesilea at 3.4.48.

37. *head and hair*] Judgment and character, as befitting an elderly gentleman of experience.

38–9. *town bull ... goat*] Lecher, womaniser.

40. *religion and fear*] Piety and reverence, as in performing any sanctified act. *humour*] Moisture (see *steeped*); inclination or mood.

41. *open*] Public, liberal, but glancing at 'sexually available', especially in the context of 'other ... pleasures'.

43. *hymen*] Wedding, from the Roman god of marriage.

45. *tediously*] Irritatedly, hinting at 'fatiguingly', but *tedious* and *irksome* were synonyms.

47. *make*] Imagine.

MOROSE   I have married his cittern that's common to all men. Some
plague above the plague –

TRUEWIT   All Egypt's ten plagues.   55

MOROSE   – revenge me on him.

TRUEWIT   'Tis very well, sir. If you laid on a curse or two more, I'll assure
you he'll bear 'em. As that he may get the pox with seeking to cure it,
sir? Or that, while he is curling another man's hair, his own may drop
off? Or, for burning some male-bawd's lock, he may have his brain   60
beat out with the curling-iron?

MOROSE   No, let the wretch live wretched. May he get the itch and his
shop so lousy as no man dare come at him, nor he come at no man.

TRUEWIT   Ay, and if he would swallow all his balls for pills, let not them
purge him.   65

MOROSE   Let his warming pan be ever cold.

TRUEWIT   A perpetual frost underneath it, sir.

MOROSE   Let him never hope to see fire again.

TRUEWIT   But in hell, sir.

MOROSE   His chairs be always empty, his scissors rust, and his combs   70
mould in their cases.

TRUEWIT   Very dreadful, that! And may he lose the invention, sir, of
carving lanterns in paper.

MOROSE   Let there be no bawd carted that year to employ a basin of his,
but let him be glad to eat his sponge for bread.   75

TRUEWIT   And drink *lotium* to it, and much good do him.

MOROSE   Or, for want of bread –

---

53. *cittern*] Stringed instrument like a lute (see *lute-string*, 79), often with a woman's head
carved over the pegs, kept in barber shops for customers to play while waiting; hence,
'common to all'.

55. *ten plagues*] Sent by God to punish the Pharaoh in Exodus 7–12, an apt paradigm for
the catalogue of curses filling the rest of this scene.

58. *pox*] Syphilis. Barbers attempted to cure it by fumigating their clients with mercuric
sulphide in heated 'sweating-tubs' or pickling vats.

59–60. *drop off*] Hair loss is a symptom of syphilis.

60. *male-bawd*] Pimp.   *lock*] Love-lock, often decorated with ribbons.

62. *itch*] Lice (see *lousy*) or other infestation; but also suggesting sexual craving, and the
itch caused by venereal disease.

64. *balls*] Of soap.   *pills*] Cathartics or emetics.

73. *lanterns*] Cheap lanterns of oiled paper, commonly sold in barber shops.

74. *carted*] Paraded and whipped through the streets after sentencing.   *basin*] Metal
basins, rented from barbers, were beaten to attract crowds to witness the shame of
sexual offenders carted around town.

76. *lotium*] Stale urine, used as a cosmetic for hair.

TRUEWIT   Eat ear-wax, sir. I'll help you. Or draw his own teeth and add
them to the lute-string.

MOROSE   No, beat the old ones to powder and make bread of them.   80

TRUEWIT   Yes, make meal o' the millstones.

MOROSE   May all the botches and burns that he has cured on others break
out upon him.

TRUEWIT   And he now forget the cure of 'em in himself, sir. Or, if he do
remember it, let him ha' scraped all his linen into lint for 't and have   85
not a rag left him to set up with.

MOROSE   Let him never set up again, but have the gout in his hands for
ever. Now, no more, sir.

TRUEWIT   O, that last was too high set! You might go less with him, i'
faith, and be revenged enough. As, that he be never able to new-paint   90
his pole –

MOROSE   Good sir, no more. I forgot myself.

TRUEWIT   Or want credit to take up with a comb-maker –

MOROSE   No more, sir.

TRUEWIT   Or, having broken his glass in a former despair, fall now into   95
a much greater, of ever getting another –

MOROSE   I beseech you, no more.

TRUEWIT   Or that he never be trusted with trimming of any but chimney-
sweepers –

MOROSE   Sir –   100

TRUEWIT   Or may he cut a collier's throat with his razor by *chance
medley*, and yet hang for 't.

MOROSE   I will forgive him rather than hear any more. I beseech you, sir.

78. *ear-wax … teeth*] Barbers also cleaned ears and pulled teeth, which were then
displayed on strings as advertisements.

82. *botches*] Boils.

87. *set up*] Punning on 'set up business', and 'set hair'.

89. *high set, go less*] Gambling terms in primero, referring to high stakes. See *Volp* 3.5.37.

90–91. *new-paint his pole*] Ostensibly referring to the red and white stripes of the barber's
pole, but also quibbling on *paint* = prostitute or pander, and *pole* = penis.

93. *want*] Lack.   *take up with*] purchase supplies from. See also 1.4.57.

98. *trimming*] Clipping, with innuendo of sexual activity.

98–9. *chimney-sweepers*] Proverbially poor and professionally filthy.

101. *collier*] Coalman, not only dirty but also proverbially dishonest.

101–2. *chance medley*] Homicide by misadventure.

Act 3 scene 6*

[Enter] Daw [with] Haughty, [followed by] Centaur, Mavis, Trusty

DAW   *[To Haughty]* This way, madam.

MOROSE   O, the sea breaks in upon me! Another flood! An inundation!
I shall be o'erwhelmed with noise. It bears already at my shores. I feel
an earthquake in myself for 't.

DAW   *[Kisses the bride]* Give you joy, mistress.   5

MOROSE   Has she servants too!

DAW   I have brought some ladies here to see and know you.

She kisses them severally as he presents them

My Lady Haughty. This, my Lady Centaur. Mistress Dol Mavis.
Mistress Trusty, my Lady Haughty's woman. Where's your husband?
Let's see him. Can he endure no noise? Let me come to him.   10

MOROSE   What *nomenclator* is this!

TRUEWIT   Sir John Daw, sir, your wife's servant, this.

MOROSE   A Daw, and her servant! O, 'tis decreed, 'tis decreed of me, and
she have such servants.

[Tries to leave]

TRUEWIT   Nay, sir, you must kiss the ladies; you must not go away   15
now. They come toward you to seek you out.

HAUGHTY   I'faith, Master Morose, would you steal a marriage thus, in
the midst of so many friends, and not acquaint us? Well, I'll kiss you,
notwithstanding the justice of my quarrel. *[To Epicoene]* You shall
give me leave, mistress, to use a becoming familiarity with your   20
husband.

[Haughty kisses Morose]

EPICOENE   Your ladyship does me an honour in it, to let me know he

---

* The first appearance of the Ladies Collegiate justifies Truewit's earlier description of
their '*hermaphroditical* authority' (1.1.68–9): reversing the sexual stereotypes, they
stride in mannishly, exchange elaborate courtesies with the bride, kiss the groom, and
criticise Morose for breaking social custom with his hole-and-corner matrimonials.

6. *servants*] Lovers. Daw's salute is more informal, perhaps more intimate, than Truewit's
conventional kiss of greeting in 3.5.

11. *nomenclator*] Announcer of guests' names, punning on 'clatter'.

13. *'tis decreed of me*] Judgment is passed on me; I am a condemned man.   *and*] If.

17. *steal a marriage*] Get married secretly.

19–21. *You ... husband*] A conventional request for permission to salute a spouse, but
comically inverted as Lady Haughty assumes the traditional male role, addresses the
bride as the dominant marriage partner, and thrusts herself on the unwillingly
submissive husband.

is so worthy your favour, as you have done both him and me grace to
visit so unprepared a pair to entertain you.

MOROSE   Compliment! Compliment!   25

EPICOENE   But I must lay the burden of that upon my servant here.

HAUGHTY   It shall not need, Mistress Morose. We will all bear,
rather than one shall be oppressed.

MOROSE   I know it, and you will teach her the faculty, if she be to learn
it.   30

[*The collegiates confer privately*]

HAUGHTY   Is this the silent woman?

CENTAUR   Nay, she has found her tongue since she was married, Master
Truewit says.

[*Truewit joins them*]

HAUGHTY   O, Master Truewit! 'Save you. What kind of creature is
your bride here? She speaks, methinks!   35

TRUEWIT   Yes, madam, believe it, she is a gentlewoman of very absolute
behaviour and of a good race.

HAUGHTY   And Jack Daw told us she could not speak.

TRUEWIT   So it was carried in plot, madam, to put her upon this old
fellow, by Sir Dauphine, his nephew, and one or two more of us. But   40
she is a woman of an excellent assurance and an extraordinary happy
wit and tongue. You shall see her make rare sport with Daw, ere
night.

HAUGHTY   And he brought us to laugh at her!

TRUEWIT   That falls out often, madam, that he that thinks himself the   45
master-wit is the master-fool. I assure your ladyship, ye cannot laugh
at her.

HAUGHTY   No, we'll have her to the college. And she have wit, she shall
be one of us! Shall she not, Centaur? We'll make her a collegiate.

25. *Compliment!*] Expressing shock at Epicoene's courtly rhetoric; see 1.1.115n.

26. *must lay the burden*] Sexually equivocal, suggesting a superincumbent female during
coitus. Her verb indicates compulsion.

27, 8. *bear, oppressed*] Haughty continues the sexual equivocation by suggesting women
willingly *bear* or carry the weight of super-incumbent males, thus preventing anyone
from being *oppressed* or ravished. She also puns on 'bare', and adds a musical pun, *bear
the burden*, play the bass (or lower) part.

29–30. *faculty . . . it*] Ability to bear the sexual burden, if she is still a virgin.

36. *absolute*] Finished, perfect (Latin).

37. *race*] Family.

41. *assurance*] Self-confidence. *happy*] Ready, clever.

42. *with Daw*] At Daw's expense.

44. *And*] If.

CENTAUR   Yes, faith, madam, and Mavis and she will set up a side.   50
TRUEWIT   Believe it, madam, and, Mistress Mavis, she will sustain her
   part.
MAVIS   I'll tell you that when I have talked with her, and tried her.
HAUGHTY   Use her very civilly, Mavis.
MAVIS   So I will, madam.   55

   [Mavis walks aside with Epicoene]

MOROSE   Blessed minute, that they would whisper thus ever.
TRUEWIT   In the meantime, madam, would but your ladyship help to vex
   him a little. You know his disease: talk to him about the wedding
   ceremonies, or call for your gloves, or –
HAUGHTY   Let me alone. Centaur, help me. *[Loudly, looking around]*   60
   Master bridegroom, where are you?
MOROSE   O, it was too miraculously good to last!
HAUGHTY   We see no ensigns of a wedding here, no character of a bridal.
   Where be our scarfs and our gloves? I pray you, give 'em us. Let's
   know your bride's colours and yours at least.   65
CENTAUR   Alas, madam, he has provided none.
MOROSE   Had I known your ladyship's painter, I would.
HAUGHTY   He has given it you, Centaur, i' faith. But, do you hear, Master
   Morose, a jest will not absolve you in this manner. You that have
   sucked the milk of the court and from thence have been brought up   70
   to the very strong meats and wine of it, been a courtier from the biggin
   to the night-cap (as we may say), and you to offend in such a high
   point of ceremony as this! And let your nuptials want all marks of
   solemnity! How much plate have you lost today (if you had but

50. *side*] Partnership, as in a card game.
53. *tried*] Examined.
59. *gloves*] Usually presented to all the wedding guests.
60. *Let me alone*] Trust me.
63. *ensigns*] Tokens or signs that a wedding has taken place. Haughty proceeds to list such
   signs at length.
64. *scarfs*] Often presented to ladies as wedding favours.
65. *colours*] The bride and groom each usually selected colours which their respective
   friends then wore on the wedding day.
67. *painter*] Insulting remark directed at Centaur's cosmetician, with a glance at 'pander'.
71–2. *biggin ... night-cap*] Metaphorically, from youth to age, taken from headgear worn
   at the Inns of Court, where many courtiers were educated. The *biggin* is a lawyer's cap;
   the *night-cap* is worn only by serjeants-at-law, the senior men from among whom
   judges are selected.
73–4. *marks of solemnity*] See *ensigns*, 63 above.
74. *plate*] Gold or silver plate given as wedding gifts.

regarded your profit), what gifts, what friends, through your mere   75
rusticity?

MOROSE   Madam –

HAUGHTY   Pardon me, sir, I must insinuate your errors to you. No
gloves? No garters? No scarves? No *epithalamium*? No masque?

DAW   Yes, madam, I'll make an *epithalamium*, I promised my mistress. I   80
have begun it already. Will your ladyship hear it?

HAUGHTY   Ay, good Jack Daw.

MOROSE   Will it please your ladyship command a chamber and be private
with your friend? You shall have your choice of rooms to retire to
after. My whole house is yours. I know it hath been your ladyship's   85
errand into the city at other times, however now you have been
unhappily diverted upon me. But I shall be loath to break any
honourable custom of your ladyship's. And therefore, good madam –

EPICOENE   Come, you are a rude bridegroom to entertain ladies of
honour in this fashion.   90

CENTAUR   He is a rude groom indeed.

TRUEWIT   By that light, you deserve to be grafted and have your horns
reach from one side of the island to the other. – [*Aside to
Morose*] Do not mistake me, sir, I but speak this to give the ladies
some heart again, not for any malice to you.   95

MOROSE   Is this your *bravo*, ladies?

TRUEWIT   As God help me, if you utter such another word, I'll take
mistress bride in, and begin to you in a very sad cup, do you see? Go
to, know your friends and such as love you.

75–6. *mere rusticity*] Utter boorishness (as opposed to the urbanity expected of a courtier).

78. *insinuate*] Make known (Latin); hint obliquely (English sense), the latter made
ludicrous by Haughty's explicitness.

79. *garters*] After the ceremony, the bridesmaids and groomsmen would try to get
possession of the bride's garters.

80. *epithalamium*] Epithalamion or wedding song, sometimes commissioned for newly-
weds.

85. *it*] That is, commanding a chamber to be private with a friend. The tone of this whole
speech is openly insulting.

86. *errand*] Purpose of journeying (that is, to meet a lover).

91. *groom*] Punning on 'bridegroom' and 'lackey'.

92. *grafted*] Bound in a union intruded upon by a shoot of another stock; thus, made a
cuckold, and hence the growth of 'horns'.

96. *bravo*] Thug, often hired to protect prostitutes, or to help them rob customers (like
Pistol and Doll Tearsheet in *2 Henry IV*).

98. *begin ... cup*] Drink your health in a very painful way (a threat of violence).

Act 3 scene 7*

[Enter] Clerimont [with several groups of musicians]

CLERIMONT   By your leave, ladies. Do you want any music? I have brought you variety of noises. Play, sirs, all of you.

Music of all sorts

MOROSE   O, a plot, a plot, a plot, a plot upon me! This day, I shall be their anvil to work on. They will grate me asunder. 'Tis worse than the noise of a saw.   5

CLERIMONT   No, they are hair, rosin, and guts. I can give you the receipt.

TRUEWIT   Peace, boys.

CLERIMONT   Play, I say.

TRUEWIT   Peace, rascals. *[To Morose]* You see who's your friend now,   10
sir. Take courage. Put on a martyr's resolution. Mock down all their attemptings with patience. 'Tis but a day, and I would suffer heroically. Should an ass exceed me in fortitude? No. You betray your infirmity with your hanging dull ears, and make them insult. Bear up bravely and constantly.   15

La Foole passes over sewing the meat, [with servants, among them Dauphine, and followed by Mistress Otter]

Look you here, sir, what honour is done you unexpected by your nephew: a wedding dinner come, and a knight sewer before it, for the more reputation, and fine Mistress Otter, your neighbour, in the rump or tail of it.

---

*   At the high point of noise in the play, Jonson manages to cram thirteen characters and several musicians (at least two string bands, joined later by trumpets and drums) and servants (carrying La Foole's banquet) on to the stage. This most private of private houses has been turned into the equivalent of a busy public street. The discordant music and quarrelling guests suggest the folk-ritual of 'rough music', the rattling of pots and bones mixed with catcalls to serenade a May–December match, or comment upon a wife-dominated marriage, thus indicating the community's disapproval through ridicule.

  2.   *noises*] Bands; here, fiddlers (see 6 below).

  4.   *grate*] Make rasping noises; grind; irritate.

  6.   *hair, rosin, and guts*] For the stringed instruments making the noise; horsehair and rosin for the bow, sheep-gut for strings.

  7.   *receipt*] Recipe, account of the means by which an effect is produced.

  13.   *ass*] The type of fortitude, but also of stupidity.

  14.   *infirmity*] That is, hypersensitive hearing.   *insult*] Exult, brag scornfully.

  15.1.   *sewing the meat*] Directing the serving of the food.

MOROSE   Is that Gorgon, that Medusa, come? Hide me, hide me.   20
TRUEWIT   I warrant you, sir, she will not transform you. Look upon her
    with a good courage. Pray you entertain her and conduct your guests
    in. No? – Mistress Bride, will you entreat in the ladies? Your
    bridegroom is so shamefaced here –
EPICOENE   Will it please your ladyship, madam?   25
HAUGHTY   With the benefit of your company, mistress.
EPICOENE   Servant, pray you perform your duties.
DAW   And glad to be commanded, mistress.
CENTAUR   How like you her wit, Mavis?
MAVIS   Very prettily absolutely well.   30
MRS OTTER   [*Attempting to take precedence*]   'Tis my place.
MAVIS   You shall pardon me, Mistress Otter.
MRS OTTER   Why, I am a collegiate.
MAVIS   But not in ordinary.
MRS OTTER   But I am.   35
MAVIS   We'll dispute that within.

   [*Exeunt ladies, escorted by Daw*]

CLERIMONT   Would this had lasted a little longer.
TRUEWIT   And that they had sent for the heralds.

   [*Enter Otter*]

   Captain Otter, what news?
OTTER   I have brought my bull, bear, and horse in private, and yonder are   40
    the trumpeters without, and the drum, gentlemen.

   The drum and trumpets sound

MOROSE   O, O, O!

---

20. *Medusa*] The most appalling of the three Gorgons (cf. 2.4.13).
21. *transform*] Turn into stone.
22. *entertain*] Receive, converse or pass time with.
23. *entreat*] Invite.
24. *shamefaced*] Bashful.
30. *Very prettily*] Affected courtly compliment, grammatically unnecessary since 'abso-
    lutely' (= perfectly) is a superlative.
31. *place*] Meaning that she has higher rank than Mavis.
34. *in ordinary*] A regular member of the college, usually one who lives in the college, and
    hence the dispute. Mavis sees Mrs Otter as a collegiate *extraordinary* and thus of lower
    privilege.
38. *heralds*] Probably from the College of Heralds, who resolved questions of genealogy
    and precedence; possibly the heralds-at-arms, the royal trumpeters who played fanfares
    on ceremonious or momentous occasions.

OTTER   And we will have a rouse in each of 'em anon, for bold Britons, i' faith.

[*They sound again*]

MOROSE   O, O, O!   45

[*Exit Morose*]

ALL   Follow, follow, follow!

[*Exeunt*]

ACT 4

Act 4 scene 1*

[*Enter*] *Truewit, Clerimont*

TRUEWIT   Was there ever poor bridegroom so tormented? or man indeed?

CLERIMONT   I have not read of the like in the chronicles of the land.

TRUEWIT   Sure, he cannot but go to a place of rest after all this purgatory.

CLERIMONT   He may presume it, I think.   5

TRUEWIT   The spitting, the coughing, the laughter, the neezing, the farting, dancing, noise of the music, and her masculine and loud commanding and urging the whole family makes him think he has married a Fury.

CLERIMONT   And she carries it up bravely.   10

---

43. *rouse*] Full draught of liquor, often marked by fanfare.

46. *Follow … follow*] Stage shorthand for confused crowd-noises, or 'rhubarb'. See *Volp* 2.2.28.

*   In this scene, as in 1.1. and 2.2, Truewit holds forth on women, here on how women should dress to attract men and how men should behave in order to seduce them. Jonson draws on Ovid's *Ars Amatoria*, Bks 1 and 3, modernising particulars or adding contemporary details to create the effect of absurd, even grotesque vanity, and considerably lowering the tone of the original to emphasise the travesty of elegant behaviour that results. His discussion descends to a crude locker-room approval of date-rape at 61–107.

4. *place of rest*] Heaven.

6. *neezing*] Sneezing.

8. *urging*] Spurring on, inciting to disobedience.

9. *Fury*] One of the ferocious females of Greek myth, armed with whips and firebrands, sent from the Underworld to avenge crimes perpetrated by men.

10. *carries it up*] Carries it off, keeps it up.   *bravely*] Splendidly.

TRUEWIT   Ay, she takes any occasion to speak. That's the height on 't.

CLERIMONT   And how soberly Dauphine labours to satisfy him that it was none of his plot!

TRUEWIT   And has almost brought him to the faith i' the article. Here he comes.   15

[*Enter Dauphine*]

Where is he now? What's become of him, Dauphine?

DAUPHINE   O, hold me up a little. I shall go away i' the jest else. He has got on his whole nest of nightcaps, and locked himself up i' the top o' the house, as high as ever he can climb from the noise. I peeped in at a cranny and saw him sitting over a crossbeam o' the roof, like him   20 o' the saddler's horse in Fleet Street, upright. And he will sleep there.

CLERIMONT   But where are your collegiates?

DAUPHINE   Withdrawn with the bride in private.

TRUEWIT   O, they are instructing her i' the college-grammar. If she have grace with them, she knows all their secrets instantly.   25

CLERIMONT   Methinks the Lady Haughty looks well today, for all my dispraise of her i' the morning. I think I shall come about to thee again, Truewit.

TRUEWIT   Believe it, I told you right. Women ought to repair the losses time and years have made i' their features with dressings. And an   30 intelligent woman, if she know by herself the least defect, will be most curious to hide it, and it becomes her. If she be short, let her sit much, lest when she stands, she be thought to sit. If she have an ill foot, let her wear her gown the longer and her shoe the thinner. If a fat hand and scald nails, let her carve the less and act in gloves. If a sour breath,   35 let her never discourse fasting – and always talk at her distance. If she

---

11.   *height on 't*] Cream of the jest, the best part.

14.   *faith ... article*] Referring to the 39 Articles of Faith to which Church of England ministers had to subscribe, on penalty of being silenced or defrocked.

17.   *go away ... jest*] Die laughing.

17–21.   The description of Morose's retreat parallels that of the beleaguered husband in Proverbs 21:9: 'It is better to dwell in a corner of the housetop, Than in a house in common with a contentious woman.'

18.   *nest*] Stack of caps, each fitted into the next in order of diminishing size.

20–1.   *him ... horse*] Tradesman's sign of a mounted rider, outside a saddler's shop.

24.   *college-grammar*] Rules and practices of the college.

27.   *come ... thee*] Come around to your opinion.

30.   *dressings*] Personal adornments.

31.   *by*] About.

32.   *curious*] Careful, anxious (Latin).

35.   *scald*] Scaly; from a skin disease called 'scall'.   *carve*] Gesture affectedly and flirtatiously; also, carve meat at table.   *act*] Gesture.

have black and rugged teeth, let her offer the less at laughter,
especially if she laugh wide and open.

CLERIMONT   O, you shall have some women, when they laugh, you
would think they brayed, it is so rude and –   40

TRUEWIT   Ay, and others that will stalk i' their gait like an ostrich and take
huge strides. I cannot endure such a sight. I love measure i' the feet and
number i' the voice: they are gentlenesses that oft-times draw no less
than the face.

DAUPHINE   How camest thou to study these creatures so exactly? I would   45
thou wouldst make me a proficient.

TRUEWIT   Yes, but you must leave to live i' your chamber then a month
together upon *Amadis de Gaule* or *Don Quixote*, as you are wont,
and come abroad where the matter is frequent: to court, to tiltings,
public shows and feasts, to plays, and church sometimes. Thither they   50
come to show their new tires too, to see and to be seen. In these places
a man shall find whom to love, whom to play with, whom to touch
once, whom to hold ever. The variety arrests his judgment. A wench
to please a man comes not down dropping from the ceiling as he lies
on his back droning a tobacco pipe. He must go where she is.   55

DAUPHINE   Yes, and be never the near.

TRUEWIT   Out, heretic! That diffidence makes thee worthy it should be
so.

CLERIMONT   He says true to you, Dauphine.

37. *rugged*] Uneven.

42. *measure*] Grace and proportion in movement, as in dancing.

43. *number*] Musical rhythm, as in song or verse.   *gentlenesses*] Elegant graces, suitable
for gentlewomen.

46. *proficient*] Advanced student.

47. *leave*] Cease.

48. *Amadis de Gaule*] Popular romance of chivalry, first published in Spain in 1508, and
translated by Anthony Munday, 1590. Jonson held the romance and its translator in
contempt. *Don Quixote*] Cervantes' masterpiece was not published in English
translation until 1612, but may have circulated at court in manuscript, or may have
been read in Spanish before that date.

49. *matter is frequent*] Subject under discussion (i.e., women) turns up often.
tiltings] Mock-tournaments, often in semi-dramatic form, held as public spectacles in
the Tilt Yard at Whitehall.

51. *tires*] Outfits.

53. *arrests his judgment*] Legally, stays proceedings after a verdict, on the ground of error.

55. *droning ... pipe*] Smoking, a commonly made pun on bagpipes; possibly a male bee
analogy as well, to suggest a drone's dallying, or idling passively, waiting for a queen-
bee's attention.

56. *never the near*] No further ahead.

57–8. *That ... so*] Such lack of confidence deserves failure.

DAUPHINE   Why?   60
TRUEWIT   A man should not doubt to overcome any woman. Think he
   can vanquish 'em, and he shall, for though they deny, their desire is
   to be tempted. Penelope herself cannot hold out long. Ostend, you
   saw, was taken at last. You must persevere and hold to your purpose.
   They would solicit us, but that they are afraid. Howsoever, they wish   65
   in their hearts we should solicit them. Praise 'em, flatter 'em, you shall
   never want eloquence or trust. Even the chastest delight to feel
   themselves that way rubbed. With praises you must mix kisses too. If
   they take them, they'll take more. Though they strive, they would be
   overcome.   70
CLERIMONT   O, but a man must beware of force.
TRUEWIT   It is to them an acceptable violence and has oft-times the place
   of the greatest courtesy. She that might have been forced, and you let
   her go free without touching, though she then seem to thank you, will
   ever hate you after, and glad i' the face is assuredly sad at the heart.   75
CLERIMONT   But all women are not to be taken all ways.
TRUEWIT   'Tis true. No more than all birds or all fishes. If you appear
   learned to an ignorant wench, or jocund to a sad, or witty to a foolish,
   why, she presently begins to mistrust herself. You must approach them
   i' their own height, their own line, for the contrary makes many that   80
   fear to commit themselves to noble and worthy fellows run into the
   embraces of a rascal. If she love wit, give verses, though you borrow
   'em of a friend or buy 'em, to have good. If valour, talk of your sword
   and be frequent in the mention of quarrels, though you be staunch in
   fighting. If activity, be seen o' your barbary often, or leaping over   85

61. *doubt*] Mistrust his ability.
62. *deny*] Say no.
63. *Penelope*] Ancient model of the chaste wife. She put off her suitors for twenty years
   while waiting for the return of her husband Odysseus from Troy. *Ostend*] Modern
   example of resistance. The Belgian port fell to the Spanish in 1604 after a three-year
   siege.
67. *want*] Lack.
68. *rubbed*] Flattered; crudely, titillated.
69. *strive*] Struggle. *would be*] Desire to be.
72. *and*] If.
79. *presently*] At once.
80. *i' ... line*] At their own level; a fencing metaphor referring to 'high' and 'low' ward,
   and the angle of the sword.
84–5. *staunch in fighting*] Normally reserved or modest when referring to or participating
   in disputes.
85. *activity*] Physical exercise, especially sexual. *barbary*] Horse; transferring the idea of
   sexual 'riding'.
85–6. *leaping ... back*] A strong back implied sexual prowess.

stools for the credit of your back. If she love good clothes or dressing, have your learned counsel about you every morning, your French tailor, barber, linener, etc. Let your powder, your glass, and your comb be your dearest acquaintance. Take more care for the ornament of your head than the safety, and with the commonwealth rather   90
troubled than a hair about you. That will take her. Then if she be covetous and craving, do you promise anything and perform sparingly. So shall you keep her in appetite still. Seem as you would give, but be like a barren field that yields little, or unlucky dice to foolish and hoping gamesters. Let your gifts be slight and dainty rather than   95
precious. Let cunning be above cost. Give cherries at time of year, or apricots, and say they were sent you out o' the country, though you bought 'em in Cheapside. Admire her tires. Like her in all fashions. Compare her in every habit to some deity. Invent excellent dreams to flatter her and riddles, or, if she be a great one, perform always the   100
second parts to her: like what she likes, praise whom she praises, and fail not to make the household and servants yours, yea the whole family, and salute 'em by their names – 'Tis but light cost if you can purchase 'em so – and make her physician your pensioner, and her chief woman. Nor will it be out of your gain to make love to her too,   105
so she follow, not usher, her lady's pleasure. All blabbing is taken away when she comes to be a part of the crime.

DAUPHINE   On what courtly lap hast thou late slept, to come forth so sudden and absolute a courtling?

TRUEWIT   Good faith, I should rather question you that are so hearkening   110
after these mysteries. I begin to suspect your diligence, Dauphine. Speak, art thou in love in earnest?

DAUPHINE   Yes, by my troth, am I. 'Twere ill dissembling before thee.

TRUEWIT   With which of 'em, I pray thee?

DAUPHINE   With all the collegiates.   115

CLERIMONT   Out on thee. We'll keep you at home, believe it, i' the stable, and you be such a stallion.

TRUEWIT   No. I like him well. Men should love wisely, and all women: some one for the face, and let her please the eye; another for the skin, and let her please the touch; a third for the voice, and let her please   120

96. *cunning*] Ingenuity.   *at . . . year*] In season.
98. *Cheapside*] The chief commercial street of London; a market was held at the Cross opposite Wood Street.
103. *family*] All dependants supported by or within the household.
104. *pensioner*] Originally a gentleman-bodyguard maintained by the king; a dependant.
105. *woman*] Maidservant.   *out . . . gain*] Irrelevant to your purpose or interests.
109. *courtling*] Courtier, or perhaps 'little courtier', as contemptuous of Truewit's detailed knowledge for such petty ends.
119. *some one*] A certain one.

the ear; and where the objects mix, let the senses so too. Thou
wouldst think it strange if I should make 'em all in love with thee
afore night!

DAUPHINE   I would say thou hadst the best philtre i' the world and
couldst do more than Madam Medea or Doctor Forman.

TRUEWIT   If I do not, let me play the mountebank for my meat while I live,   125
and the bawd for my drink.

DAUPHINE   So be it, I say.

Act 4 scene 2*

[Enter] Otter [with his cups], Daw, La Foole

OTTER   O Lord, gentlemen, how my knights and I have missed you here!

CLERIMONT   Why, Captain, what service? What service?

OTTER   To see me bring up my bull, bear, and horse to fight.

DAW   Yes, faith, the Captain says we shall be his dogs to bait 'em.

DAUPHINE   A good employment.   5

TRUEWIT   Come on, let's see a course then.

LA FOOLE   I am afraid my cousin will be offended if she come.

OTTER   Be afraid of nothing. Gentlemen, I have placed the drum and the
trumpets and one to give 'em the sign when you are ready. [*Handing
out cups*] Here's my bull for myself, and my bear for Sir John Daw,   10
and my horse for Sir Amorous. Now set your foot to mine, [*Touching
cups in salute*] and yours to his, [*Another salute*] and –

123. *philtre*] Love potion.

124. *Medea*] The enchantress who helped Jason recover the golden fleece, and restored his
father Aeson to youth.   *Doctor Forman*] Simon Forman (1552–1611), astrologer and
quack, famous for supplying love potions to women at court.

*   Like 3.1, this scene combines bear-baiting with eavesdropping, but also fulfils Truewit's
promise at the end of 2.6. And like 3.7, it provides a crescendo of sounds. A parody of
manly contest, the baiting begins as the three drinkers doggedly attack the animal-
headed cups, urged on by the three wits. Otter is already drunk; La Foole is terrified of
Mrs Otter's catching him drinking with Otter; Daw is trying earnestly to impress La
Foole with his joviality. The baiting expands as the scene develops: Mrs Otter attacks
her husband for lying, and Morose assaults them all, including the musicians, for
making noise. As a result of this scene, Daw and La Foole remain more or less
intoxicated for the balance of the play.

2. *what service?*] 'What's up?', 'what's going on?'; 'how may I serve you?', an interroga-
tive variant of 'at your service'.

3. *to fight*] To participate as the victims in a baiting, the metaphor dominating this scene.
Horses were not baited for sport; Otter includes his horse-cup for symmetry.

6. *course*] Punning on a round of drinking, and an attack by dogs on the bull or bear
being baited. Here, the three drinkers attack the cups.

11. *set ... mine*] Toe to toe, the stance in drinking-bouts.

LA FOOLE   Pray God my cousin come not.

OTTER   Saint George and Saint Andrew, fear no cousins. Come, sound,
    sound! *Et rauco strepuerunt cornua cantu.*   15

    [*Drum and trumpets sound, and they drink*]

TRUEWIT   Well said, Captain, i' faith. Well fought at the bull.

CLERIMONT   Well held at the bear.

TRUEWIT   Low, low, Captain.

DAUPHINE   O, the horse has kicked off his dog already.

LA FOOLE   I cannot drink it, as I am a knight.   20

TRUEWIT   Gods so, off with his spurs, somebody.

LA FOOLE   It goes again' my conscience. My cousin will be angry with it.

DAW   I ha' done mine.

TRUEWIT   You fought high and fair, Sir John.

CLERIMONT   At the head.   25

DAUPHINE   Like an excellent bear-dog.

CLERIMONT   [*Aside to Daw*] You take no notice of the business, I hope.

DAW   [*Aside to Clerimont*] Not a word, sir. You see we are *jovial.*

OTTER   Sir Amorous, you must not equivocate. It must be pulled down,
    for all my cousin.   30

CLERIMONT   [*Aside to La Foole*] 'Sfoot, if you take not your drink,
    they'll think you are discontented with something. You'll betray all, if
    you take the least notice.

LA FOOLE   [*Aside to Clerimont*] Not I. I'll both drink and talk then.

    [*La Foole drinks*]

OTTER   You must pull the horse on his knees, Sir Amorous. Fear no   35
    cousins. *Jacta est alea.*

TRUEWIT   [*Aside to Clerimont and Dauphine*] O, now he's in his vein

---

14. *Saint George and Saint Andrew*] Patron saints of England and Scotland, appropriately
    nationalistic oath for the United Kingdom under the reign of James I of England and VI
    of Scotland. *fear no cousins*] Otter plays on the proverb 'Fear no colours' (= tricks).

15. *Et . . . cantu*] 'And the horns blared out with hoarse note' (Virgil, *Aeneid* 8.2).

16. *Well said*] Well done, from the original 'Well assayed'.

18. *Low, low*] Perhaps expressing disgust at some vulgar or unmannerly stage business,
    such as spewing from the mouth or belching. E. B. Partridge (1971) suggests Otter is not
    playing 'high and fair' (24). Holdsworth (1979) revises to ''Loo, 'loo', a cry to urge on
    dogs, the roles taken by the drinkers.

21. *off . . . spurs*] Deprive him of his knighthood.

27. *business*] The rivalry with La Foole, described in 3.3.

29. *pulled down*] Swallowed; in baiting, the baited animal dragged to the ground (see 29,
    35).

36. *Jacta est alea*] 'The die is cast', Caesar's words on crossing the Rubicon.

and bold. The least hint given him of his wife now will make him rail
desperately.

CLERIMONT   [*Aside to Truewit*] Speak to him of her.   40

TRUEWIT   [*Aside to Dauphine*] Do you, and I'll fetch her to the hearing
of it.

[*Exit Truewit*]

DAUPHINE   Captain he-Otter, your she-Otter is coming, your wife.

OTTER   Wife! Buzz! *Titivilitium*! There's no such thing in nature. I confess,
gentlemen, I have a cook, a laundress, a house-drudge, that serves my   45
necessary turns and goes under that title. But he's an ass that will be
so uxorious to tie his affections to one circle. Come, the name dulls
appetite. Here, replenish again. [*He fills the cups*] Another bout.
Wives are nasty sluttish animals.

DAUPHINE   O, Captain.   50

OTTER   As ever the earth bare, *tribus verbis*. Where's Master Truewit?

DAW   He's slipped aside, sir.

CLERIMONT   [*To Daw*] But you must drink and be *jovial*.

DAW   Yes, give it me.

LAFOOLE   And me too.   55

DAW   Let's be *jovial*.

LAFOOLE   As *jovial* as you will.

OTTER   Agreed. Now you shall ha' the bear, cousin, and Sir John Daw the
horse, and I'll ha' the bull still. Sound, Tritons o' the Thames! *Nunc
est bibendum, nunc pede libero –*   60

[*While they drink*] *Morose speaks from above, the trumpets sounding*

39. *desperately*] Recklessly.

44. *Buzz!*] Expression of contempt.   *Titivilitium!*] A worthless trifle (Plautus's coinage).
In *Mankind* (1470), an early Tudor interlude, Titivillus, a devil, drives Mankind to the
point of suicide; the name survives in later dramatic references. In that sense, Otter's
word may be translated as 'vile thing from Hell', or 'wife from Hell'.

47. *circle*] The metal ring on the stake to which baited animals were tied; also a quibble on
'cunt', a reductive term for a woman.

48. *appetite*] Sexual desire.

49. *sluttish*] Repulsively dirty or lewd; morally despicable.

51. *tribus verbis*] In three words; to put it bluntly.

52. *slipped*] Used of dogs in hunting or coursing.

59. *Tritons*] Sea-gods like mermen, half-man, half-fish, blowing shells for trumpets.

59–60. *Nunc ... libero*] 'Now is the time for drinking, now with free foot ...' (Horace,
Odes 1.37.1), celebrating the downfall of Cleopatra, the type of the man-destroying
woman; ironic, since his own 'Cleopatra' is about to fall on him.

MOROSE   Villains, murderers, sons of the earth, and traitors, what do
    you there?

CLERIMONT   O, now the trumpets have waked him, we shall have his
    company.

OTTER   A wife is a scurvy *clogdogdo*: an unlucky thing, a very foresaid   65
    bear-whelp, without any good fashion or breeding. *Mala bestia*.

    His wife is brought out [by Truewit] to hear him

DAUPHINE   Why did you marry one then, Captain?

OTTER   A pox – I married with six thousand pound, I. I was in love with
    that. I ha' not kissed my Fury these forty weeks.

CLERIMONT   The more to blame you, Captain.   70

TRUEWIT   [*Aside, holding Mrs Otter back*] Nay, Mistress Otter, hear him
    a little first.

OTTER   She has a breath worse than my grandmother's, *profecto*.

MRS OTTER   [*Aside to Truewit*] O treacherous liar! Kiss me, sweet
    Master Truewit, and prove him a slandering knave.   75

TRUEWIT   [*Releasing Mrs Otter*] I'll rather believe you, lady.

OTTER   And she has a peruke that's like a pound of hemp, made up in
    shoe-threads.

MRS OTTER   [*Aside*] O viper, mandrake!

OTTER   A most vile face! And yet she spends me forty pound a year in   80
    mercury and hogs' bones. All her teeth were made i' the Blackfriars,
    both her eyebrows i' the Strand, and her hair in Silver Street. Every
    part o' the town owns a piece of her.

MRS OTTER   [*Aside*] I cannot hold!

OTTER   She takes herself asunder still, when she goes to bed, into some   85
    twenty boxes, and about next day noon is put together again like a

61. *sons ... earth*] Bastards (Latin).

65. *clogdogdo*] Meaning uncertain; perhaps Bear Garden slang for a poorly trained dog,
    the 'bear-whelp' of the next line. A clog is a weight or *trash* attached to a dog's neck
    to impede motion during training.   *foresaid*] Aforesaid.

66. *Mala bestia*] Evil beast; expression used by Catullus (69.7–8) for a sexually repellent
    character.

69. *Fury*] Punishing female from hell; see 4.1.9.

73. *profecto*] Truly, indeed.

78. *shoe-threads*] Shoe-laces.

79. *mandrake*] Poisonous plant (mandragora) whose forked root resembles the human
    form; hence the term of abuse.

81–2. *Blackfriars ... Strand ... Silver Street*] Locations chosen to comment on her
    appearance, implying that her teeth are black, her eyebrows coarse 'strands' or bristles,
    and her hair grey.

81. *mercury and hogs' bones*] Cosmetic ingredients.

great German clock, and so comes forth and rings a tedious larum to the whole house, and then is quiet again for an hour, but for her quarters. [*To Daw and La Foole*] Ha' you done me right, gentle-   90
men?

MRS OTTER   No, sir, I'll do you right with my quarters, with my quarters!

She falls upon him and beats him

OTTER   O, hold, good Princess!

TRUEWIT   Sound, sound!

[*Musicians enter with drum and trumpets sounding*]

CLERIMONT   A battle, a battle!

MRS OTTER   You notorious stinkardly bearward, does my breath smell?   95

OTTER   Under correction, dear Princess. Look to my bear and my horse, gentlemen.

MRS OTTER   Do I want teeth and eyebrows, thou bull-dog!

TRUEWIT   Sound, sound still!

[*Drum and trumpets sound again*]

OTTER   No, I protest, under correction –   100

MRS OTTER   Ay, now you are under correction, you protest. But you did not protest before correction, sir. Thou Judas, to offer to betray thy Princess! I'll make thee an example –

Morose descends with a long sword

MOROSE   I will have no such examples in my house, Lady Otter.

MRS OTTER   Ah! –   105

MOROSE   Mistress Mary Ambree, your examples are dangerous.

[*She runs off shrieking; Daw and La Foole throw up their cups and follow her; Morose attacks the musicians and chases them out*]

Rogues, hell-hounds, *Stentors*, out of my doors, you sons of noise and tumult, begot on an ill May-day, or when the galley-foist is afloat to Westminster! A trumpeter could not be conceived but then!

87. *larum*] Chiming melody.
89. *quarters*] Quarter-hours; private living-quarters.   *done me right*] Matched me drink for drink.
91. *quarters*] Blows, strokes, as in fighting with staves or swords. In domestic conduct-books, the prerogative of spouse-beating belongs to the husband.
106. *Mary Ambree*] According to popular ballad, a transvestite female who became one of the English volunteer soldiers at the siege of Ghent in 1584.
107. *Stentors*] Noise-makers; from the Greek herald at Troy whose 'iron voice' was as loud as the shouts of fifty men (*Iliad* 5.785–6).
108. *ill May-day*] The expression comes from the 'Ill May-day' riots of 1517 when London

DAUPHINE   What ails you, sir?   110
MOROSE   They have rent my roof, walls, and all my windows asunder
    with their brazen throats.

   [Exit Morose, pursuing the musicians]

TRUEWIT   Best follow him, Dauphine.
DAUPHINE   So I will.

   [Exit Dauphine]

CLERIMONT   Where's Daw and La Foole?   115
OTTER   They are both run away, sir. *[Picks up their cups]* Good gentle-
    men, help to pacify my Princess and speak to the great ladies for me.
    Now must I go lie with the bears this fortnight and keep out o' the way
    till my peace be made, for this scandal she has taken. *[Looking for the*
    third cup] Did you not see my bull-head, gentlemen?   120
CLERIMONT   Is 't not on, Captain?
TRUEWIT   No – *[Aside to Clerimont]* but he may make a new one by
    that is on.
OTTER   O, here 'tis. *[Picks up cup]* And you come over, gentlemen, and
    ask for Tom Otter, we'll go down to Ratcliffe and have a course, i'   125
    faith, for all these disasters. There's *bona spes* left.
TRUEWIT   Away, Captain, get off while you are well.

   [Exit Otter]

CLERIMONT   I am glad we are rid of him.
TRUEWIT   You had never been, unless we had put his wife upon him. His
    humour is as tedious at last as it was ridiculous at first.   130

   [Noise of company approaching: Truewit and Clerimont withdraw to
    watch]

    apprentices attacked privileged foreign tradesmen; but Morose would think any May-
day ill, with its holiday dancing and serenading, simply because of the noise.   *galley-*
foist] State barge which carried the new Lord Mayor to be sworn in each year,
accompanied by drums, pipes, and trumpets and parades of other barges filled with
merrymakers.
119. *scandal]* Offence.
123. *on]* On the cup, and on his shoulders, as sign of the cuckold, deserved by a submissive
    husband. Clerimont and Truewit are commenting on the horn-like nubs Mrs Otter has
    raised on Otter's brow by beating him.
125. *Ratcliffe]* On the Thames below London, frequented by rogues looking for a hide-out
    or a quick get-away by sea (see *Alch* 4.7.125 and 5.4.76). *course]* Drinking-bout.
126. *bona spes]* Good hope; from Cicero, *In Catalinam* 2.25, 'Good hope strives against
    despair of all things' (Beaurline 1966).

Act 4 scene 3*

[*Enter*] *Haughty* [*comforting*] *Mistress Otter,* [*attended by*] *Mavis, Daw, La Foole, Centaur, Epicoene. Truewit* [*and*] *Clerimont* [*eaves-drop unobserved*]

HAUGHTY   We wondered why you shrieked so, Mistress Otter.

MRS OTTER   O God, madam, he came down with a huge long naked weapon in both his hands, and looked so dreadfully! Sure, he's beside himself.

MAVIS   Why, what made you there, Mistress Otter?   5

MRS OTTER   Alas, Mistress Mavis, I was chastising my subject, and thought nothing of him.

DAW   [*To Epicoene*] Faith, mistress, you must do so too. Learn to chastise. Mistress Otter corrects her husband so, he dares not speak but under correction.   10

LA FOOLE   And with his hat off to her. 'Twould do you good to see.

HAUGHTY   In sadness, 'tis good and mature counsel. Practise it, Morose. I'll call you Morose still now, as I call Centaur and Mavis. We four will be all one.

CENTAUR   And you'll come to the college and live with us?   15

HAUGHTY   Make him give milk and honey.

MAVIS   Look how you manage him at first, you shall have him ever after.

CENTAUR   Let him allow you your coach and four horses, your woman, your chambermaid, your page, your gentleman-usher, your French cook, and four grooms.   20

HAUGHTY   And go with us to Bedlam, to the China-houses, and to the Exchange.

---

*   The argument for female promiscuity, the topic of lines 29–52, comes from a compressed version of Ovid, *Ars Amatoria* 3.59–98. Ovid warns young women to enjoy sexual pleasures now, because no man will want them when they are wrinkled, grey, and worn out by childbirth. Ironically, the Ladies Collegiate are middle-aged. Ovid also compares the evanescence of time to ripples in a stream, and suggests that, despite losing their lovers, women gain much more in joys by loving many.

2–3. *huge . . . hands*] Unconscious sexual innuendo.

5. *made you*] Were you doing.

12. *In sadness*] Seriously.   *Morose*] That is, the masculine form of address.

13. *still*] Always.

16. *milk and honey*] Food of the Promised Land (Exodus 3:8). In other words, her husband will have to maintain her in the style to which she wants to become accustomed, if he hopes to enter the Promised Land, sexually speaking.

21. *Bedlam*] The insane asylum; see note at 2.2.31.

21–2. *China-houses, Exchange*] Fashionable shops and meeting-places for lovers; see note at 1.3.31.

CENTAUR   It will open the gate to your fame.

HAUGHTY   Here's Centaur has immortalised herself with taming of her
wild male.   25

MAVIS   Ay, she has done the miracle of the kingdom.

EPICOENE   But, ladies, do you count it lawful to have such plurality of
servants and do 'em all graces?

HAUGHTY   Why not? Why should women deny their favours to men? Are
they the poorer or the worse?   30

DAW   Is the Thames the less for the dyer's water, mistress?

LA FOOLE   Or a torch for lighting many torches?

TRUEWIT   [*Aside*] Well said, La Foole. What a new one he has got!

CENTAUR   They are empty losses women fear in this kind.

HAUGHTY   Besides, ladies should be mindful of the approach of age, and   35
let no time want his due use. The best of our days pass first.

MAVIS   We are rivers that cannot be called back, madam. She that now
excludes her lovers may live to lie a forsaken beldame in a frozen bed.

CENTAUR   'Tis true, Mavis. And who will wait on us to coach then? Or
write, or tell us the news then? Make anagrams of our names, and   40
invite us to the Cockpit and kiss our hands all the play-time, and draw
their weapons for our honours?

HAUGHTY   Not one.

DAW   Nay, my mistress is not altogether unintelligent of these things. Here
be in presence have tasted of her favours.   45

23. *open the gate ... fame*] Enhance your reputation, introduce you into society, but also
suggesting 'make you known as sexually available and receptive'. See 28.

28. *do ... graces*] Allow them sexual favours.

31. *dyer's water*] Industrial waste in the form of discoloured water, discharged into
the Thames; hence, a sexual metaphor for ejaculation. Proverbially, to cast water into the
Thames is to perform an insignificant action; Daw offers this commonplace as though
it were his own clever invention.

32. *torch ... torches*] Another borrowing from proverbial lore, 'One candle can light many
more', also with sexual connotations. A *torch* [= penis] may commmunicate venereal
disease by *lighting* others [= infecting with burning sores].

33. *new one*] Sarcastic comment on La Foole's triteness.

38. *beldame*] Ugly old hag.

39. *wait on*] Escort.

40. *anagrams*] Acrostics; riddle poems written as compliments, in which the letters of the
name become the first letter of each line of the poem. See 'The Argument' preceding
Volp for the form.

41. *Cockpit*] The Cockpit-in-court at Whitehall, a small cock-fighting arena also used as a
private theatre.

41–2. *draw their weapons*] Another sexually equivocal remark.

CLERIMONT   [*Aside*] What a neighing hobbyhorse is this?
EPICOENE   But not with intent to boast 'em again, servant. And have you
those excellent receipts, madame, to keep yourselves from bearing of
children?
HAUGHTY   O yes, Morose. How should we maintain our youth and   50
beauty else? Many births of a woman make her old, as many crops
make the earth barren.

Act 4 scene 4*

[*Enter*] *Morose, Dauphine*

MOROSE   O my cursed angel, that instructed me to this fate!
DAUPHINE   Why, sir?
MOROSE   That I should be seduced by so foolish a devil as a barber will
make!
DAUPHINE   I would I had been worthy, sir, to have partaken your counsel;   5
you should never have trusted it to such a minister.
MOROSE   Would I could redeem it with the loss of an eye, nephew, a hand,
or any other member.
DAUPHINE   Marry, God forbid, sir, that you should geld yourself to anger
your wife.   10
MOROSE   So it would rid me of her! And that I did supererogatory
penance in a belfry, at Westminster Hall, i' the cockpit, at the fall of
a stag, the Tower Wharf – what place is there else? – London Bridge,
Paris Garden, Billingsgate when the noises are at their height and
loudest. Nay, I would sit out a play that were nothing but fights at sea,   15

46. *neighing hobbyhorse*] Babbling fool. Clerimont plays on several meanings of the word:
a small Irish horse favoured by courtiers, especially ladies; a child's toy; a lustful antic
in morris dances; and hence anyone making a fool of himself.
48. *receipts*] Potions; here, prophylactic mixtures.
*   The diagnosis of Morose's 'mania' by learned women resembles Lady Would-be's
parody of medical prescription in *Volp* 3.4. The extreme to which Morose has been
pushed inspires him to mention divorce, and thus precipitates Truewit's plan in 1.7,
executed in 5.3–4.
1. *instructed*] Marshalled (Latin).
12–14. Morose gives a jumbled catalogue of noisy venues, mixing the general with the
specific. The belfry, the stag-hunt (one of James's favourite pastimes, aside from cock-
fighting), the cockpit (not necessarily the one at Whitehall), and the theatre invoke the
clamour of bells, the tumult of hounds, horses, and hunting-horns, the squawks of
fighting cocks and gamblers, and the din of mock-battles on stage. Westminster Hall,
reputedly one of the noisiest spots in London, held not only the Courts of Common
Law, but also crowded shops of booksellers, seamstresses, toy-vendors, and other small

drum, trumpet, and target!

DAUPHINE   I hope there shall be no such need, sir. Take patience, good
uncle. This is but a day, and 'tis well worn too, now.

MOROSE   O, 'twill be so for ever, nephew, I foresee it, for ever. Strife and
tumult are the dowry that comes with a wife.   20

TRUEWIT   I told you so, sir, and you would not believe me.

MOROSE   Alas, do not rub those wounds, Master Truewit, to blood again.
'Twas my negligence. Add not affliction to affliction. I have perceived
the effect of it too late in Madam Otter.

EPICOENE   [*Drawing near Morose*] How do you, sir?   25

MOROSE   Did you ever hear a more unnecessary question! As if she did
not see! Why, I do as you see, Empress, Empress.

EPICOENE   You are not well, sir! You look very ill! Something has
distempered you.

MOROSE   O horrible, monstrous impertinencies! Would not one of these   30
have served? Do you think, sir? Would not one of these have served?

TRUEWIT   Yes, sir, but these are but notes of female kindness, sir; certain
tokens that she has a voice, sir.

MOROSE   O, is 't so? Come, and 't be no otherwise – what say you?

EPICOENE   How do you feel yourself, sir?   35

MOROSE   Again, that!

TRUEWIT   Nay, look you, sir. You would be friends with your wife upon
unconscionable terms, her silence –

EPICOENE   They say you are run mad, sir.

MOROSE   Not for love, I assure you, of you, do you see?   40

EPICOENE   O lord, gentlemen! Lay hold on him, for God's sake.

tradesmen. At Tower Wharf, guns and cannon fired salutes on holidays and during state
visits (see 1.2.14–15). London Bridge was packed with houses and shops of several
stories, the commotion increased by calls from the watermen 'shooting the bridge', the
roar of the river rapids (see 2.2.20–21), the working of the watermills (installed in
1582), and the raising and lowering of the drawbridge to allow the passage of ships.
Paris Garden, across the river in Southwark, was a vulgar and dissolute area for public
gaming and drinking, close to theatres, brothels, and bear-baitings (see 3.1.14).
Billingsgate, the wharf just east of London Bridge, was the chief landing for commercial
and other travellers and site of the proverbially raucous fish-market.

16. *target*] Shield.

29. *distempered*] May mean anything from 'vexed' to 'physically diseased' or 'mentally
deranged'.

30. *impertinencies*] Irrelevances.   *one of these*] Epicoene has just made three synonymous
comments. Ironically, Morose repeats himself as well.

32. *notes*] Marks or signs.   *kindness*] Punning on 'behaviour according to kind'.

[*Truewit and Clerimont restrain Morose*]

What shall I do? Who's his physician – Can you tell? – that knows the
state of his body best, that I might send for him? Good sir, speak. I'll
send for one of my doctors else.

MOROSE   What, to poison me, that I might die intestate and leave you   45
possessed of all?

EPICOENE   Lord, how idly he talks, and how his eyes sparkle! He looks
green about the temples! Do you see what blue spots he has?

CLERIMONT   Ay, it's melancholy.

EPICOENE   Gentlemen, for heaven's sake, counsel me. Ladies! Servant,   50
you have read Pliny and Paracelsus. Ne'er a word now to comfort a
poor gentlewoman? Ay, me! What fortune had I to marry a distracted
man?

DAW   I'll tell you, mistress –

TRUEWIT   [*Aside to Clerimont*] How rarely she holds it up!   55

MOROSE   [*Struggling between them*] What mean you, gentlemen?

EPICOENE   [*To Daw*] What will you tell me, servant?

DAW   The disease in Greek is called *mania*, in Latin *insania, furor, vel
ecstasis melancholico*, that is, *egressio*, when a man *ex melancholica
evadit fanaticus*.   60

MOROSE   Shall I have a lecture read upon me alive?

DAW   But he may be but *phreneticus* yet, Mistress, and *phrenetis* is only
delirium or so –

EPICOENE   Ay, that is for the disease, servant, but what is this to the cure?
We are sure enough of the disease.   65

---

45. *intestate*] Legally, if a husband died without a will, leaving no child, his wife would
inherit only half the estate, the rest going to the next of kin.

49. *melancholy*] Depression; for a full description, see Burton's *Anatomy of Melancholy.*
H&S interpret it in the Greek sense of 'frenzy, aberration', based on Epicoene's
emphasis on his distraction and madly sparkling eyes. E. B. Partridge (1971) argues for
'love sickness', evidenced in Morose's denial of love as the cause of his rage, and in his
pallor, *green* (= sickly, pale) and *blue* (= livid).

51. *Pliny ... Paracelsus*] Ancient and modern authorities. Pliny the Elder, AD 24–79, wrote
Naturalis Historia, an encyclopaedia in 37 books, the last 9 dealing largely with
applications of botany, zoology, and metals to medicine. Paracelsus (Philippus von
Hohenheim), 1493–1541, the Swiss scientist who introduced chemistry to the study of
medicine, violently opposed classical and current scholastic authorities.

58. *mania*] Printed in Greek letters in *F1*.

58–60. *insania ... fanaticus*] Daw offers only a list of synonyms: 'insanity, madness, or
rather melancholic ecstasy ... a going out of one's mind, when a man turns crazy out
of melancholy'.

61. *lecture ... alive*] That is, be a live specimen for an anatomy class.

62–3. *phreneticus ... delirium*] More synonyms: 'frantic ... brain-sickness ... craziness'.

MOROSE   [*Struggling*] Let me go.

TRUEWIT   [*Kindly, as to a madman*] Why, we'll entreat her to hold her
peace, sir.

MOROSE   O, no. Labour not to stop her. She is like a conduit-pipe that
will gush out with more force when she opens again.   70

HAUGHTY   I'll tell you, Morose, you must talk divinity to him altogether,
or moral philosophy.

LA FOOLE   Ay, and there's an excellent book of moral philosophy, madam,
of Reynard the Fox and all the beasts, called *Doni's Philosophy*.

CLERIMONT   There is, indeed, Sir Amorous La Foole.   75

MOROSE   [*Still struggling*] O misery!

LA FOOLE   I have read it, my Lady Centaur, all over to my cousin here.

MRS OTTER   Ay, and 'tis a very good book as any is of the moderns.

DAW   Tut, he must have Seneca read to him, and Plutarch, and the
ancients; the moderns are not for this disease.   80

CLERIMONT   Why, you discommended them too today, Sir John.

DAW   Ay, in some cases. But in these they are best, and Aristotle's *Ethics*.

MAVIS   Say you so, Sir John? I think you are deceived. You took it upon
trust.

HAUGHTY   Where's Trusty, my woman? I'll end this difference. I prithee,   85
Otter, call her. Her father and mother were both mad when they put
her to me.

[*Exit Mistress Otter*]

MOROSE   I think so. Nay, gentlemen, I am tame. This is but an exercise,
I know, a marriage ceremony which I must endure.

[*They release him, but remain by him*]

HAUGHTY   And one of 'em – I know not which – was cured with *The*   90
Sick Man's Salve, and the other with Greene's *Groat's-worth of Wit*.

74. *Doni's Philosophy*] *The Moral Philosophy of Doni* (1601), North's English translation
of Doni's Latin version, a collection of oriental beast-fables now known as the fables of
Bidpai. Although several of the fables concern foxes, none is Reynard the Fox, whose
exploits were translated into English by William Caxton (1481), *The History of
Reynard the Fox*.

79, 82. *Seneca, Plutarch, Aristotle*] Daw takes the side of the ancients in this parody of the
battle between the ancients and the moderns.

88–9. *exercise . . . ceremony*] Custom, but not exact synonyms. 'Exercise' suggests not only
the performance of a ceremony, but also the training of an animal and the suffering of
a saint or martyr.

91. *Sick Man's Salve*] A Calvinist tract advocating patience and humility during sickness
and while awaiting death, written by Thomas Becon, first printed in 1561 and
frequently reissued.   *Greene's Groat's-worth of Wit*] Robert Greene's popular confes-
sional pamphlet, urging fellow playwrights to reject the low life of London; written on

TRUEWIT   A very cheap cure, madam.

HAUGHTY   Ay, 'tis very feasible.

   [*Enter Mistress Otter with Trusty*]

MRS OTTER   My lady called for you, Mistress Trusty. You must
   decide a controversy.   95

HAUGHTY   O Trusty, which was it you said, your father or your mother,
   that was cured with *The Sick Man's Salve*?

TRUSTY   My mother, madam, with the *Salve* –

TRUEWIT   Then it was *The Sick Woman's Salve*.

TRUSTY   – And my father with the *Groat's-worth of Wit*. But there was   100
   other means used: we had a preacher that would preach folk asleep
   still, and so they were prescribed to go to church, by an old woman
   that was their physician, thrice a week –

EPICOENE   To sleep?

TRUSTY   Yes, forsooth – and every night they read themselves asleep on   105
   those books.

EPICOENE   Good faith, it stands with great reason. I would I knew where
   to procure those books.

MOROSE   [*Groans*] O.

LA FOOLE   I can help you with one of 'em, Mistress Morose, the *Groat's-* 110
   worth of Wit.

EPICOENE   But I shall disfurnish you, Sir Amorous. Can you spare it?

LA FOOLE   O, yes, for a week or so. I'll read it myself to him.

EPICOENE   No, I must do that, sir. That must be my office.

MOROSE   O, O!   115

EPICOENE   Sure, he would do well enough if he could sleep.

MOROSE   No, I should do well enough if you could sleep. Have I no friend
   that will make her drunk? Or give her a little laudanum? Or opium?

TRUEWIT   Why, sir, she talks ten times worse in her sleep.

MOROSE   How!   120

CLERIMONT   Do you not know that, sir? never ceases all night.

TRUEWIT   And snores like a porpoise.

MOROSE   O, redeem me, fate, redeem me, fate! [*Turns to Dauphine*] For
   how many causes may a man be divorced, nephew?

DAUPHINE   I know not truly, sir.   125

TRUEWIT   Some divine must resolve you in that, sir, or canon lawyer.

MOROSE   I will not rest, I will not think of any other hope or comfort, till
   I know.

   [*Exit Morose with Dauphine*]

   his death-bed, published in 1592 and frequently reprinted.

112. *disfurnish*] Deprive (of the groat's-worth of wit he possesses).

126. *canon lawyer*] Specialist in ecclesiastical law.

CLERIMONT   Alas, poor man.
TRUEWIT   You'll make him mad indeed, ladies, if you pursue this.   130
HAUGHTY   No, we'll let him breathe now, a quarter of an hour or so.
CLERIMONT   By my faith, a large truce.
HAUGHTY   Is that his keeper that is gone with him?
DAW   It is his nephew, madam.
LAFOOLE   Sir Dauphine Eugenie.   135
CENTAUR   He looks like a very pitiful knight –
DAW   As can be. This marriage has put him out of all.
LAFOOLE   He has not a penny in his purse, madam –
DAW   He is ready to cry all this day.
LAFOOLE   A very shark, he set me i' the nick t'other night at primero.   140
TRUEWIT   [*Aside to Clerimont*] How these swabbers talk!
CLERIMONT   [*Aside to Truewit*] Ay, Otter's wine has swelled their
   humours above a spring tide.
HAUGHTY   Good Morose, let's go in again. I like your couches exceeding
   well. We'll go lie and talk there.   145
EPICOENE   I wait on you, madam.

   [*Exit Haughty, Centaur, Mavis, Trusty, Daw and La Foole*]

TRUEWIT   'Slight, I will have 'em as silent as signs, and their posts
   too, e'er I ha' done. Do you hear, lady bride? I pray thee now, as thou
   art a noble wench, continue this discourse of Dauphine within, but
   praise him exceedingly. Magnify him with all the height of affection   150
   thou canst – I have some purpose in't – and but beat off these two
   rooks, Jack Daw and his fellow, with any discontentment hither, and
   I'll honour thee for ever.
EPICOENE   I was about it here. It angered me to the soul to hear 'em begin
   to talk so malapert.   155
TRUEWIT   Pray thee perform it, and thou winn'st me an idolater to thee
   everlasting.
EPICOENE   Will you go in and hear me do it?

131. *let ... breathe*] Give a breathing-space or a cooling-down period, especially during
   horse- or dog-training, or brisk exercise.
136. *pitiful*] Sad.
140. *shark*] Cardsharp; rogue, petty cheat or gambler. *set ... nick*] Wiped me out, bet
   against me and won, implying dishonesty. La Foole uses the dicing term 'nick' from
   hazard (see note at 3.3.27), but refers to primero, a card-game like ombre or three-
   handed euchre.
141. *swabbers*] Louts.
147. *posts*] Poles on which signs are hung.
152. *discontentment*] Complaint.
154. *about it*] About to do so.
155. *malapert*] Impudently.

TRUEWIT   No, I'll stay here. Drive 'em out of your company, 'tis all I ask,
which cannot be any way better done than by extolling Dauphine,   160
whom they have so slighted.

EPICOENE   I warrant you, you shall expect one of 'em presently.

   [*Exit Epicoene*]

CLERIMONT   What a cast of kestrels are these to hawk after ladies
thus!

TRUEWIT   Ay, and strike at such an eagle as Dauphine.   165

CLERIMONT   He will be mad when we tell him. Here he comes.

Act 4 scene 5*

   [*Enter*] *Dauphine*

CLERIMONT   O sir, you are welcome.

TRUEWIT   Where's thine uncle?

DAUPHINE   Run out o' doors in's nightcaps to talk with a casuist about
his divorce. It works admirably.

TRUEWIT   Thou wouldst ha' said so, and thou hadst been here! The ladies   5
have laughed at thee most comically since thou wentst, Dauphine.

CLERIMONT   And asked if thou wert thine uncle's keeper?

TRUEWIT   And the brace of baboons answered yes, and said thou wert a
pitiful poor fellow and didst live upon posts, and hadst nothing but
three suits of apparel and some few benevolences that lords ga' thee   10
to fool to 'em and swagger.

---

163. *cast*] In hawking, a pair cast off at one time.   *kestrels*] Small hunting hawks; term of
abuse, as at 1.4.66, meaning 'busy fools'.

165. *strike*] Attack, a hawking term.

166. *mad*] Beside himself with rage, infuriated; suggests callous excitement at the prospect
of Dauphine's discomfiture.

*   Editors frequently compare this scene to *Twelfth Night* 3.4, in which two frightened
mock-men, Sir Andrew Aguecheek and Viola, disguised as Caesario, try to wriggle out
of a duel. But Jonson's 'closet scene' is far more cruel: the nose-tweaking and kicks are
degrading, deliberately prolonged, and potentially more humiliating in that both Daw
and La Foole need a chamber-pot. Truewit has to restrain Dauphine, who would have
lopped off Daw's arm 'for a jest'.

3. *casuist*] A priest or counsellor who resolves tricky questions of conscience or conduct
by means of hair-splitting analysis, often sophistical. Morose is following Truewit's
suggestion at 4.4.126.

9. *upon posts*] By running errands.

10. *three suits*] As allowed to servants; see 3.1.34.   *benevolences*] Charitable donations
of money to the poor.

11. *fool to 'em*] Play the fool for.

DAUPHINE   Let me not live, I'll beat 'em. I'll bind 'em both to grand
madam's bed-posts and have 'em baited with monkeys.

TRUEWIT   Thou shalt not need: they shall be beaten to thy hand,
Dauphine. I have an execution to serve upon 'em, I warrant thee shall   15
serve. Trust my plot.

DAUPHINE   Ay, you have many plots! So you had one to make all the
wenches in love with me.

TRUEWIT   Why, if I do not yet afore night, as near as 'tis, and that they do
not, every one, invite thee and be ready to scratch for thee, take the   20
mortgage of my wit.

CLERIMONT   'Fore God, I'll be his witness. Thou shalt have it, Dauphine.
[*To Truewit*] Thou shalt be his fool for ever, if thou dost not.

TRUEWIT   Agreed. Perhaps 'twill be the better estate. Do you observe this
gallery? Or rather lobby, indeed? Here are a couple of studies, at each   25
end one: here will I act such a tragicomedy between the Guelphs and

14. *beaten ... hand*] Driven into your power. The expression derives from hunting, when
bushes are struck in order to fright game out of hiding.

15. *execution to serve ... warrant*] Legal metaphors, implying Truewit, as sheriff, will
enforce the judgment of the 'court' (Dauphine) by arresting Daw and La Foole.

17. *So ... one*] You likewise claimed to have a plot.

20. *scratch*] Have a hen-fight; challenge one another.

23. *fool*] Butt of his jokes.

24. *better estate*] Playing on *mortgage*, 21, suggesting that Dauphine will have greater
profit taking Truewit as his fool than he will taking the ladies as his lovers.

25. *gallery*] The upper stage, perhaps only a large window off the musicians' alcove in the
private theatre. *Poet*, acted at the Blackfriars, mentions only one window in 4.9; but
DisA, also at the Blackfriars, directs: 'This scene is acted at two windows, as out of two
contiguous buildings' (2.6). For the Globe's gallery, see *Volp* 1.2.87, 3.7.13–14, and
notes.   *lobby*] Truewit designates the area beneath the upper stage, apparently large
enough to contain a recessed discovery-space with its own entrance door, as well as the
two stage doors found conventionally in early theatres. The opening stage direction for
EH!, a Blackfriars play, reads: 'Enter Master Touchstone and Quicksilver at several
doors. ... At the middle door, enter Golding, discovering a goldsmith's shop, and
walking short turns before it.'   *studies*] Possibly moveable properties, small booths
with doors. Their existence and location on stage are problematic: either the two stage
doors on either side represent the studies, in which case all other entrances or exits must
be from the middle door, or the booths are thrust on for the purpose, but whether they
appear from the middle door and stand on either side of the discovery-space, or from
the side doors to stand on either side of the stage, we can merely conjecture.

26. *tragicomedy*] A popular new genre introduced by Beaumont and Fletcher in 1608.
Truewit suggests that this bastard offshoot of two classical forms can only be played by
such undignified and unlettered puppets as Daw and La Foole. He offers it here as a
parodic play-within-the-play, and proceeds to allot roles.

the Ghibellines, Daw and La Foole – which of 'em comes out first will
I seize on. (You two shall be the chorus behind the arras, and whip out
between the acts and speak.) If I do not make 'em keep the peace for
this remnant of the day, if not of the year, I have failed once – I hear   30
Daw coming. Hide, and do not laugh, for God's sake.

[Clerimont and Dauphine hide behind the arras as Daw enters]

DAW   Which is the way into the garden, trow?
TRUEWIT   O, Jack Daw! I am glad I have met with you. In good faith, I
    must have this matter go no further between you. I must ha' it taken
    up.   35
DAW   What matter, sir? Between whom?
TRUEWIT   Come, you disguise it – Sir Amorous and you. If you love me,
    Jack, you shall make use of your philosophy now, for this once, and
    deliver me your sword. This is not the wedding the centaurs were at,
    though there be a she-one here. The bride has entreated me I will see   40
    no blood shed at her bridal – you saw her whisper me erewhile.
DAW   *[Giving his sword]* As I hope to finish Tacitus, I intend no murder.
TRUEWIT   Do you not wait for Sir Amorous?
DAW   Not I, by my knighthood.
TRUEWIT   And your scholarship too?   45
DAW   And my scholarship too.
TRUEWIT   Go to, then I return you your sword and ask you mercy, but put
    it not up, for you will be assaulted. I understood that you had
    apprehended it and walked here to brave him, and that you had held
    your life contemptible in regard of your honour.   50
DAW   No, no, no such thing, I assure you. He and I parted now as good
    friends as could be.
TRUEWIT   Trust not you to that visor. I saw him since dinner with another
    face. I have known many men in my time vexed with losses, with

26–7. *Guelphs ... Ghibellines*] Papal and imperial factions who contended for power in
    medieval Italy.
28. *chorus*] Witnesses of the action. *arras*] Tapestry acting as a backdrop over the
    discovery-space, a convenient cover for eavesdroppers.
32. *Which ... garden*] Presumably to urinate, La Foole's errand at 128. *trow?*] Do you
    think?
39. *wedding ... at*] The marriage of Pirithous and Hippodamia, at which a drunken
    centaur assaulted the bride and turned the wedding into a bloody brawl. See The
    Persons of the Play 12n., and Ovid's *Metamorphoses* 12.210ff.
42. *Tacitus*] Prolific Roman historian, *c.* AD 56–120.
47–8. *put ... up*] Do not sheathe it.
49. *brave*] Defy.
53. *visor*] False face.

deaths, and with abuses, but so offended a wight as Sir Amorous did   55
I never see or read of. For taking away his guests, sir, today, that's the
cause, and he declares it behind your back with such threatenings and
contempts – He said to Dauphine you were the arrantest ass –

DAW   Ay, he may say his pleasure.

TRUEWIT   – and swears you are so protested a coward that he knows you   60
will never do him any manly or single right, and therefore he will take
his course.

DAW   I'll give him any satisfaction, sir – but fighting.

TRUEWIT   Ay, sir, but who knows what satisfaction he'll take? Blood he
thirsts for, and blood he will have, and whereabouts on you he will   65
have it, who knows but himself?

DAW   I pray you, Master Truewit, be you a mediator.

TRUEWIT   Well, sir, conceal yourself then in this study till I return.

He puts him up [*inside a study, speaking through the door*]

Nay, you must be content to be locked in for, for mine own reputation,
I would not have you seen to receive a public disgrace while I have the   70
matter in managing. Gods so, here he comes! Keep your breath close,
that he do not hear you sigh. – [*Loudly, with suitable sound effects*]
In good faith, Sir Amorous, he is not this way. I pray you be merciful,
do not murder him. He is a Christian as good as you. You are armed
as if you sought a revenge on all his race. Good Dauphine, get him   75
away from this place. I never knew a man's choler so high but he
would speak to his friends, he would hear reason. – Jack Daw, Jack
Daw! Asleep?

DAW   Is he gone, Master Truewit?

TRUEWIT   Ay, did you hear him?   80

DAW   O God, yes.

TRUEWIT   What a quick ear fear has!

DAW   But is he so armed as you say?

TRUEWIT   Armed? Did you ever see a fellow set out to take possession?

DAW   Ay, sir.   85

TRUEWIT   That may give you some light to conceive of him, but 'tis
nothing to the principal. Some false brother i' the house has furnished
him strangely. Or, if it were out o' the house, it was Tom Otter.

---

55. *wight*] Person.

60. *protested*] Notorious, well-advertised.

68.1. *puts him up*] Locks him away.

84. *take possession*] Of his property. To complete the legal transfer of land, a purchaser
sometimes had to threaten or actually use physical violence to remove previous
occupants and establish his own residency.

87. *principal*] In law, one who is directly responsible for a crime; here referring to potential
murder by the heavily armed La Foole.

DAW   Indeed, he's a captain, and his wife is his kinswoman.

TRUEWIT   He has got somebody's old two-hand sword to mow you off at   90
the knees. And that sword hath spawned such a dagger! – But then he
is so hung with pikes, halberds, petronels, calivers, and muskets, that
he looks like a justice of peace's hall. A man of two thousand a year
is not 'sessed at so many weapons as he has on. There was never fencer
challenged at so many several foils. You would think he meant to   95
murder all Saint 'Pulchre's parish. If he could but victual himself for
half a year in his breeches, he is sufficiently armed to overrun a
country.

DAW   Good lord, what means he, sir! I pray you, Master Truewit, be you
a mediator.   100

TRUEWIT   Well, I'll try if he will be appeased with a leg or an arm. If not,
you must die once.

DAW   I would be loath to lose my right arm for writing madrigals.

TRUEWIT   Why, if he will be satisfied with a thumb or a little finger, all's
one to me. You must think I'll do my best.   105

DAW   Good sir, do.

He puts him up again, and then [Dauphine and Clerimont] come forth

CLERIMONT   What hast thou done?

TRUEWIT   He will let me do nothing, man: he does all afore me. He offers
his left arm.

CLERIMONT   His left wing, for a Jack Daw.   110

DAUPHINE   Take it, by all means.

TRUEWIT   How! Maim a man for ever for a jest? What a conscience hast
thou?

90. *two-hand sword*] Old-fashioned broadsword.

92. *pikes, halberds*] Infantry arms, not duelling weapons. The pike was a long (up to
16 feet) wooden shaft ending in a spear-point, and sometimes equipped with a
lateral hook for unhorsing the enemy. A halberd was a combination of spear and
battle-axe mounted on a handle 5 to 7 feet long.   *petronels*] Heavy pistols.
calivers] Light muskets.

93. *justice ... hall*] Used as both a modern armoury and a museum of ancient weapons.
man ... year] Gentlemen were required to keep a fixed number of weapons, horses,
and suits of armour. Truewit doubles the highest income mentioned in the Statute for
Arms and Armour, 1557, perhaps to terrify Daw further with the suggestion that La
Foole is carrying twice the maximum number of weapons required by law.

94. *'sessed*] Assessed.

95. *challenged ... foils*] Summoned to fight with so many different fencing weapons.

96. *Saint 'Pulchre's*] St Sepulchre's, a crowded parish near Newgate.   *victual himself*]
Store food for himself.

97. *breeches*] Probably the voluminously baggy fashion known as 'Dutch slops'.

102. *you ... once*] Proverbially, every man owes God a death.

DAUPHINE   'Tis no loss to him. He has no employment for his arms but
to eat spoon-meat. Beside, as good maim his body as his reputation.   115

TRUEWIT   He is a scholar and a wit, and yet he does not think so. But he
loses no reputation with us, for we all resolved him an ass before. To
your places again.

CLERIMONT   I pray thee, let me be in at the other a little.

TRUEWIT   Look, you'll spoil all. These be ever your tricks.   120

CLERIMONT   No, but I could hit of some things that thou wilt miss and
thou wilt say are good ones.

TRUEWIT   I warrant you. I pray forbear. I'll leave it off, else.

DAUPHINE   Come away, Clerimont.

[*They conceal themselves again, as La Foole enters*]

TRUEWIT   Sir Amorous!   125

LA FOOLE   Master Truewit.

TRUEWIT   Whither were you going?

LA FOOLE   Down into the court to make water.

TRUEWIT   By no means, sir, you shall rather tempt your breeches.

LA FOOLE   Why, sir?   130

TRUEWIT   [*Opening the other study*] Enter here, if you love your life.

LA FOOLE   Why! Why!

TRUEWIT   Question till your throat be cut, do. Dally till the enraged soul
find you.

LA FOOLE   Who's that?   135

TRUEWIT   Daw it is. Will you in?

LA FOOLE   Ay, ay, I'll in. What's the matter?

TRUEWIT   Nay, if he had been cool enough to tell us that, there had been
some hope to atone you, but he seems so implacably enraged.

LA FOOLE   'Slight, let him rage. I'll hide myself.   140

TRUEWIT   Do, good sir. But what have you done to him within that
should provoke him thus? You have broke some jest upon him afore
the ladies –

LA FOOLE   Not I, never in my life, broke jest upon any man. The bride was

---

115. *spoon-meat*] Custard dishes, considered unmanly compared to beef.

117. *resolved*] Considered.

121. *of*] Upon.

129. *tempt*] Risk soiling.

139. *atone*] Reconcile.

142. *broke . . . jest*] Cracked a joke.

144. The broken syntax of this line suggests La Foole's panic. Although H&S and E. B.
Partridge (1971) add the subject 'I' to regularise the sentence, Beaurline (1966) and
Holdsworth (1979) recognise that the omitted subject is common in Jonson's dialogue
as an indicator of distress. Retaining *F1*'s comma after 'life' increases the effect.

praising Sir Dauphine, and he went away in snuff, and I followed him   145
unless he took offence at me in his drink erewhile, that I would not
pledge all the horse full.

TRUEWIT   By my faith, and that may be, you remember well. But he walks
the round up and down, through every room o' the house, with a
towel in his hand, crying 'Where's La Foole? Who saw La Foole?', and   150
when Dauphine and I demanded the cause, we can force no answer
from him but 'O revenge, how sweet art thou! I will strangle him in
this towel!', which leads us to conjecture that the main cause of his
fury is for bringing your meat today, with a towel about you, to his
discredit.   155

LA FOOLE   Like enough. Why, and he be angry for that, I'll stay here till
his anger be blown over.

TRUEWIT   A good becoming resolution, sir. If you can put it on o' the
sudden.

LA FOOLE   Yes, I can put it on. Or I'll away into the country presently.   160

TRUEWIT   How will you get out o' the house, sir? He knows you are i' the
house, and he'll watch you this se'en-night but he'll have you. He'll
outwait a sergeant for you.

LA FOOLE   Why, then I'll stay here.

TRUEWIT   You must think how to victual yourself in time then.   165

LA FOOLE   Why, sweet Master Truewit, will you entreat my cousin Otter
to send me a cold venison pasty, a bottle or two of wine, and a
chamber pot?

TRUEWIT   A stool were better, sir, of Sir A-jax his invention.

LA FOOLE   Ay, that will be better indeed, and a pallet to lie on.   170

TRUEWIT   O, I would not advise you to sleep by any means.

LA FOOLE   Would you not, sir? Why, then, I will not.

TRUEWIT   Yet, there's another fear –

LA FOOLE   Is there, sir? What is 't?

TRUEWIT   [*Kicking the door*] No, he cannot break open this door with   175
his foot, sure.

LA FOOLE   I'll set my back against it, sir. I have a good back.

TRUEWIT   But then if he should batter.

---

145. *in snuff*] Offended, in a huff.

146. *unless*] In case.

147. *pledge ... full*] Recalling 4.2.19–33, when he had difficulty drinking all the ale in the horse-cup.

148–9. *walks the round*] Like a military patrol checking the security of a fortress.

158. *put it on*] Adopt or assume a character, echoing Truewit but missing the irony of 'resolution'.

163. *outwait a sergeant*] Proverbial. Sergeants served summonses and subpoenas.

169. *A-jax his invention*] A jakes or privy, repeating the popular pun from Sir John Harington's treatise on the flush-toilet, *The Metamorphosis of Ajax* (1596).

LA FOOLE   Batter! If he dare, I'll have an action of batt'ry against him.

TRUEWIT   Cast you the worst. He has sent for powder already, and what   180
he will do with it no man knows: perhaps blow up the corner o' the
house where he suspects you are. Here he comes – in quickly.

*He feigns as if one were present, to fright the other, who is run in to hide
himself*

I protest, Sir John Daw, he is not this way. What will you do? Before
God, you shall hang no petard here. I'll die rather. Will you not take
my word? I never knew one but would be satisfied. – [*Shouts through*   185
the door] Sir Amorous, there's no standing out. He has made a petard
of an old brass pot to force your door. Think upon some satisfaction
or terms to offer him.

LA FOOLE   [*Within*] Sir, I'll give him any satisfaction. I dare give any
terms.   190

TRUEWIT   You'll leave it to me then?

LA FOOLE   Ay, sir. I'll stand to any conditions.

[Truewit] calls forth Clerimont and Dauphine

TRUEWIT   How now, what think you, sirs? Were't not a difficult
thing to determine which of these two feared most?

CLERIMONT   Yes, but this [*Indicates La Foole's study*] fears the bravest;   195
the other [*Indicates Daw's study*] a whiniling dastard, Jack Daw!
But La Foole, a brave heroic coward! And is afraid in a great look and
a stout accent! I like him rarely.

TRUEWIT   Had it not been pity these two should ha' been concealed?

CLERIMONT   Shall I make a motion?   200

TRUEWIT   Briefly. For I must strike while 'tis hot.

CLERIMONT   Shall I go fetch the ladies to the catastrophe?

TRUEWIT   Umh? Ay, by my troth.

DAUPHINE   By no mortal means. Let them continue in the state of
ignorance and err still: think 'em wits and fine fellows, as they have   205
done. 'Twere sin to reform them.

TRUEWIT   Well, I will have 'em fetched, now I think on't, for a private

---

179. *action of battery*] In law, a charge for beating persons, not doors. The notion of
beating at or blowing up doors, as in the next lines, had sexual connotations.

180. *Cast*] Anticipate.   *powder*] Gunpowder.

184. *petard*] Bomb.

186. *no standing out*] No point in resisting.

192. *stand to*] Uphold, endorse; sexually, maintain an erection.

195. *the bravest*] With the most bravado.

196. *whiniling*] Whining, whimpering.

200. *motion*] Suggestion.

202. *catastrophe*] Finale, concluding the play-within-a-play motif.

purpose of mine. Do, Clerimont, fetch 'em, and discourse to 'em all
that's passed, and bring 'em into the gallery here.

DAUPHINE   This is thy extreme vanity now. Thou thinkst thou wert   210
undone if every jest thou mak'st were not published.

TRUEWIT   Thou shalt see how unjust thou art presently. Clerimont, say it
was Dauphine's plot.

[*Exit Clerimont*]

Trust me not, if the whole drift be not for thy good. There's a carpet
i' the next room: put it on with this scarf over thy face and a cushion   215
o' thy head, and be ready when I call Amorous. Away –

[*Exit Dauphine*]

John Daw!

DAW   [*Peeking out of his study*] What good news, sir?

TRUEWIT   Faith, I have followed and argued with him hard for you. I told
him you were a knight and a scholar, and that you knew fortitude did   220
consist *magis patiendo quam faciendo, magis ferendo quam feriendo.*

DAW   It doth so indeed, sir.

TRUEWIT   And that you would suffer, I told him. So at first he demanded,
by my troth, in my conceit, too much.

DAW   What was it, sir?   225

TRUEWIT   Your upper lip and six o' your fore-teeth.

DAW   'Twas unreasonable.

TRUEWIT   Nay, I told him plainly you could not spare 'em all. So after
long argument (*pro et con*, as you know) I brought him down to your
two butter-teeth and them he would have.   230

DAW   [*Coming forth*] O, did you so? Why, he shall have 'em.

[*Enter above Haughty, Centaur, Mavis, Mistress Otter, Epicoene, Trusty,
with Clerimont*]

TRUEWIT   But he shall not, sir, by your leave. The conclusion is this,
sir – because you shall be very good friends hereafter, and this never
to be remembered or upbraided, besides that he may not boast he has
done any such thing to you in his own person: he is to come here in   235
disguise, give you five kicks in private, sir, take your sword from you,
and lock you up in that study during pleasure. Which will be but a

214. *carpet*] Wool-tapestry tablecloth.
221. *magis ... feriendo*] More in suffering than in doing, more in enduring than in striking
    a blow.
224. *conceit*] Opinion.
230. *butter-teeth*] Front teeth.
236. *in private*] With the innuendo of 'private parts', hence rendering La Foole temporarily
    impotent; see the equivocations on 'sword' and 'pleasure' that follow.

little while – we'll get it released presently.

DAW   Five kicks? He shall have six, sir, to be friends.

TRUEWIT   Believe me, you shall not overshoot yourself to send him that   240
word by me.

DAW   Deliver it, sir. He shall have it with all my heart, to be friends.

TRUEWIT   Friends? Nay, and he should not be so, and heartily too, upon
these terms, he shall have me to enemy while I live. Come, sir, bear it
bravely.   245

DAW   O God, sir, 'tis nothing.

TRUEWIT   True. What's six kicks to a man that reads Seneca?

DAW   I have had a hundred, sir.

[Enter Dauphine in disguise, as Daw offers his posterior]

TRUEWIT   Sir Amorous. No speaking one to another, or rehearsing
old matters.   250

Dauphine comes forth, and kicks him

DAW   [*Counting the kicks*] One, two, three, four, five. I protest, Sir
Amorous, you shall have six.

TRUEWIT   Nay, I told you should not talk. Come, give him six, and he will
needs.

[Dauphine kicks him again]

Your sword. [*Takes his sword*] Now return to your safe custody. You   255
shall presently meet afore the ladies and be the dearest friends one to
another –

[Daw withdraws into his study again]

[*To Dauphine*] Give me the scarf now. Thou shalt beat the other
barefaced. Stand by.

[Exit Dauphine, removing rest of disguise]

– Sir Amorous!   260

[Enter La Foole]

LA FOOLE   What's here? [*Recoils*] A sword.

TRUEWIT   I cannot help it, without I should take the quarrel upon myself.
Here he has sent you his sword –

---

240. *overshoot*] Make any error, overreach; with an innuendo of premature ejaculation, or
even incontinent urination, depending on Daw's stage business during this sequence.
to send] If you send.

247. *Seneca*] The works of Stoic philosophy, not the tragedies.

249–50. *rehearsing old matters*] Rehashing former quarrels.

253. *told you should*] That is, told you [that you] should.

LA FOOLE   I'll receive none on 't.

TRUEWIT   – and he wills you to fasten it against a wall, and break your   265
head in some few several places against the hilts.

LA FOOLE   I will not. Tell him roundly. I cannot endure to shed my own
blood.

TRUEWIT   Will you not?

LA FOOLE   No. I'll beat it against a fair flat wall, if that will satisfy him.   270
If not, he shall beat it himself, for Amorous.

TRUEWIT   Why, this is strange starting off, when a man undertakes for
you! I offered him another condition. Will you stand to that?

LA FOOLE   Ay, what is 't?

TRUEWIT   That you will be beaten in private.   275

LA FOOLE   Yes. I am content, at the blunt.

TRUEWIT   Then you must submit yourself to be hoodwinked in this scarf
and be led to him, where he will take your sword from you and make
you bear a blow over the mouth, *gules*, and tweaks by the nose *sans
nombre*.   280

LA FOOLE   I am content. But why must I be blinded?

TRUEWIT   That's for your good, sir, because if he should grow insolent
upon this and publish it hereafter to your disgrace – which I hope he
will not do – you might swear safely and protest he never beat you,
to your knowledge.   285

LA FOOLE   O, I conceive.

TRUEWIT   I do not doubt but you'll be perfect good friends upon 't, and
not dare to utter an ill thought one of another in future.

LA FOOLE   Not I, as God help me, of him.

TRUEWIT   Nor he of you, sir. If he should – [*Blindfolds him*] Come,   290
sir. [*Leads him forward*] – All hid, Sir John.

Dauphine enters to [take his sword and] tweak him

LA FOOLE   O, Sir John, Sir John! O, O-O-O-O-O-O! –

TRUEWIT   Good Sir John, leave tweaking. You'll blow his nose off.

266. *hilts*] Sword-handle, used as a singular.

271. *for Amorous*] For all I care.

272. *undertakes*] Takes up a matter. The innuendo of sexual lure fits the context of
sadomasochistic titillation.

276. *at the blunt*] With a capped weapon.

277. *hoodwinked*] Blindfolded; punning on tricked.

279. *gules*] Blood-red, the heraldic colour giving a spuriously official knightly dignity to
this travesty of honourable procedure.   *nose*] Common euphemism for penis, possibly because a decayed nose was a sign of syphilis.

283. *publish it*] Make it known.

286. *conceive*] Understand.

291. *All hid*] The children's cry in hide-and-seek.

[*Exit Dauphine with the two swords*]

'Tis Sir John's pleasure you should retire into the study. Why, now you are friends. All bitterness between you, I hope, is buried. [*Removes*   295
blindfold and ushers him back into his study] You shall come forth by and by Damon and Pythias upon 't, and embrace with all the rankness of friendship that can be.

[*Enter Dauphine*]

I trust we shall have 'em tamer i' their language hereafter. Dauphine, I worship thee. – [*Looking up in mock astonishment at the collegiates*   300
above] God's will, the ladies have surprised us!

Act 4 scene 6*

[*Enter below*] Haughty, Centaur, Mavis, Mistress Otter, Epicoene, Trusty, Clerimont, *having discovered part of the past scene above*

HAUGHTY   Centaur, how our judgments were imposed on by these adulterate knights!
CENTAUR   Nay, madam, Mavis was more deceived than we. 'Twas her commendation uttered 'em in the college.
MAVIS   I commended but their wits, madam, and their braveries. I never   5
looked toward their valours.
HAUGHTY   Sir Dauphine is valiant, and a wit too, it seems?
MAVIS   And a bravery too.
HAUGHTY   Was this his project?
MRS OTTER   So Master Clerimont intimates, madam.   10

297. *Damon and Pythias*] The type of perfect friendship. Damon willingly became a hostage for his friend, who was condemned to death for plotting against the King of Syracuse, while Pythias made a farewell visit to his family. When Pythias returned at the last moment to liberate Damon, the King was so moved by their selflessness that he released them both.
298. *rankness*] Fulsomeness; also, sweaty warmth of sexual embraces.
* Truewit makes good his promise (4.1. 121–6) to make all the Ladies fall in love with Dauphine by allowing him to take credit for unbracing the 'brace of knights'. Jonson adapted the idea from Castiglione, *The Courtier*, Bk 2, which contains an anecdote about ladies who are made to fall in love with a gentleman from hearing another's good report of him. *Much Ado about Nothing* plays a variation on this theme in the Beatrice–Benedick plot.
2. *adulterate*] Counterfeit.
4. *uttered 'em*] Allowed them to circulate (like false coin).
5. *wits*] Cleverness. *braveries*] Fashionable clothing.
6. *valours*] Manliness, courage.
8. *bravery*] A trendy dresser; see 1.1.66.

HAUGHTY   Good Morose, when you come to the college, will you bring
   him with you? He seems a very perfect gentleman.
EPICOENE   He is so, madam, believe it.
CENTAUR   But when will you come, Morose?
EPICOENE   Three or four days hence, madam, when I have got me a coach   15
   and horses.
HAUGHTY   No, tomorrow, good Morose, Centaur shall send you her
   coach.
MAVIS   Yes, faith, do, and bring Sir Dauphine with you.
HAUGHTY   She has promised that, Mavis.   20
MAVIS   He is a very worthy gentleman in his exteriors, madam.
HAUGHTY   Ay, he shows he is judicial in his clothes.
CENTAUR   And yet not so superlatively neat as some, madam, that have
   their faces set in a brake!
HAUGHTY   Ay, and have every hair in form!   25
MAVIS   That wear purer linen than ourselves, and profess more neatness
   than the French hermaphrodite!
EPICOENE   Ay, ladies, they, what they tell one of us, have told a thousand,
   and are the only thieves of our fame, that think to take us with that
   perfume or with that lace, and laugh at us unconscionably when they   30
   have done.
HAUGHTY   But Sir Dauphine's carelessness becomes him.
CENTAUR   I could love a man for such a nose!
MAVIS   Or such a leg!
CENTAUR   He has an exceeding good eye, madam!   35
MAVIS   And a very good lock!
CENTAUR   Good Morose, bring him to my chamber first.
MRS OTTER   Please your honours, to meet at my house, madam?
TRUEWIT   [*Aside to Dauphine*] See how they eye thee, man! They are
   taken, I warrant thee.   40

23. *superlatively neat*] Exaggeratedly refined or elegant.
24. *faces ... brake*] Either metaphorical, 'fixed or frozen facial expressions' (see
   5.3.17–18), or physical, 'heads rigid as in a frame'. A brake is a framework intended to
   hold anything steady, such as a horse's hoof for shoeing. Here the framework might be
   the wires securing the hair-style and stiffening the clothing, thus forcing the wearers
   into an inflexible carriage.
27. *French hermaphrodite*] Possibly an allusion to Henri III, satirised for his transvestism
   in Thomas Arthus' play, *L'Isle des Hermaphrodites* (1605); or a reference to the
   hermaphrodite exhibited in London around 1607, mentioned in Beaumont's *The
   Knight of the Burning Pestle* (Revels) 3.279; or simply any effeminate gallant dressed
   in the French style.
29. *fame*] Reputation. *take*] Seduce.
36. *lock*] Love-lock.

[*The ladies approach them*]

HAUGHTY   You have unbraced our brace of knights here, Master Truewit.

TRUEWIT   Not I, madam. It was Sir Dauphine's engine, who, if he have disfurnished your ladyship of any guard or service by it, is able to make the place good again in himself.   45

HAUGHTY   [*Kisses Dauphine*] There's no suspicion of that, sir.

CENTAUR   [*Aside to Mavis*] God so, Mavis, Haughty is kissing.

MAVIS   [*Aside to Centaur*] Let us go too and take part.

HAUGHTY   But I am glad of the fortune (beside the discovery of two such empty caskets) to gain the knowledge of so rich a mine of virtue as Sir   50
Dauphine.

CENTAUR   We would be all glad to style him of our friendship and see him at the college.

MAVIS   He cannot mix with a sweeter society, I'll prophesy, and I hope he himself will think so.   55

DAUPHINE   I should be rude to imagine otherwise, lady.

TRUEWIT   [*Aside to Dauphine*] Did not I tell thee, Dauphine? Why, all their actions are governed by crude opinion, without reason or cause. They know not why they do anything, but as they are informed, believe, judge, praise, condemn, love, hate, and, in emulation one of   60
another, do all these things alike. Only they have a natural inclination sways 'em generally to the worst when they are left to themselves. But pursue it, now thou hast 'em.

HAUGHTY   Shall we go in again, Morose?

EPICOENE   Yes, madam.   65

CENTAUR   We'll entreat Sir Dauphine's company.

TRUEWIT   Stay, good madam, the interview of the two friends, Pylades and Orestes. I'll fetch 'em out to you straight.

HAUGHTY   Will you, Master Truewit?

DAUPHINE   Ay, but, noble ladies, do not confess in your countenance or   70
outward bearing to 'em any discovery of their follies, that we may see

---

41. *unbraced*] Exposed; disarmed, hence disgraced.

43. *engine*] Manly wit, glancing at sexual power.

44. *service*] Alluding to sexual service.

46. *suspicion*] Doubt.

52. *style him of*] Admit him to (affected rhetoric).

67. *Stay*] Wait for.

67–8. *Pylades and Orestes*] Pylades is the loyal friend who helped Orestes destroy the murderers of his father, Agamemnon. Later, like Damon and Pythias, each offered to be sacrificed to save the other when they were captured in the land of the Tauri, but both were rescued by the resident priestess, who turned out to be Iphigenia, Orestes' sister.

how they will bear up again, with what assurance and erection.

HAUGHTY   We will not, Sir Dauphine.

CENTAUR, MAVIS   Upon our honours, Sir Dauphine.

TRUEWIT   [*Calling at La Foole's door*] Sir Amorous, Sir Amorous! The   75
ladies are here.

LA FOOLE   [*Within*] Are they?

TRUEWIT   Yes, but slip out by and by as their backs are turned, and meet
Sir John here as by chance, when I call you. – [*Calls at Daw's
door*] Jack Daw!   80

DAW   [*Within*] What say you, sir?

TRUEWIT   Whip out behind me suddenly, and no anger i' your looks to
your adversary. – [*At La Foole's door*] Now, now.

[*Daw and La Foole enter*]

LA FOOLE   Noble Sir John Daw! Where ha' you been?

DAW   To seek you, Sir Amorous.   85

LA FOOLE   Me! [*Bowing*] I honour you.

DAW   [*Bowing more elaborately*] I prevent you, sir.

CLERIMONT   They have forgot their rapiers!

TRUEWIT   O, they meet in peace, man.

DAUPHINE   Where's your sword, Sir John?   90

CLERIMONT   And yours, Sir Amorous?

DAW   Mine! My boy had it forth to mend the handle e'en now.

LA FOOLE   And my gold handle was broke too, and my boy had it forth.

DAUPHINE   Indeed, sir? How their excuses meet!

CLERIMONT   What a consent there is i' the handles!   95

TRUEWIT   Nay, there is so i' the points too, I warrant you.

MRS OTTER   O me! Madam, he comes again, the madman! Away!

[*Exeunt the Ladies, Daw, and La Foole, in a panic*]

Act 4 scene 7*

[*Enter*] Morose: he had found the two swords drawn within

MOROSE   What make these naked weapons here, gentlemen?

---

72. *erection*] Cockiness, suggesting a sexual bravado to dispel the castrating effects of the
previous scene.

87. *prevent*] Am ahead of.

92. *had it forth*] Took it away.

95. *consent*] Agreement.

96. *points*] Sword-points, which both were afraid to use; and content of their excuses.

*   Unlike Morose's threat with his longsword in 4.2, his entrance here with two swords
only seems to escalate the violence. But these are the confiscated weapons belonging to

TRUEWIT   O, sir! Here hath like to have been murder since you went! A
couple of knights fallen out about the bride's favours. We were fain to
take away their weapons; your house had been begged by this time, else.

MOROSE   For what?   5

CLERIMONT   For manslaughter, sir, as being accessory.

MOROSE   And for her favours?

TRUEWIT   Ay, sir, heretofore, not present. Clerimont, carry 'em their
swords now. They have done all the hurt they will do.

[Exit Clerimont with the swords]

DAUPHINE   Ha' you spoke with a lawyer, sir?   10

MOROSE   O, no! There is such a noise i' the court that they have frighted
me home with more violence than I went! Such speaking, and counter-
speaking, with their several voices of *citations, appellations, allegations, certificates, attachments, intergatories, references, convictions,*
and *afflictions* indeed among the doctors and proctors, that the noise   15
here is silence to 't! A kind of calm midnight!

TRUEWIT   Why, sir, if you would be resolved indeed, I can bring you
hither a very sufficient lawyer and a learned divine that shall inquire
into every least scruple for you.

MOROSE   Can you, Master Truewit?   20

Daw and La Foole, retrieved by a puzzled Morose, who nevertheless has terrified the
company. That accident prepares for the other fortuitous event of the scene: Morose's
inability to withstand the noise of the lawcourts to inquire about divorce makes him
grateful for Truewit's suggestion to bring legal and religious specialists home for private
consultation. He thus sets himself up for the finale.

3. *fain*] Forced.

4. *begged*] The property of a criminal or accessory to a crime could be confiscated by the
Crown and *begged* or petitioned for in the courts.

8. *heretofore*] In the past, previous to the marriage.

13. *citations*] Summonings to court, cried by the clerks; or lawyers' quotations of
precedents in the common law.   *appellations*] Appeals to a higher court against the
decisions of an inferior one.

13–14. *allegations*] Making charges before a legal tribunal.

14. *certificates*] Giving of testimony, especially by reading out transcripts of facts, certified
by another court or authority, to decide the issue in the current trial.   *attachments*]
Judicial orders to seize property, usually for payment of debts.   *intergatories*]
Interrogatories; questions formally put to an accused or a witness.   *references*]
Submitting disputes for settlement in the Court of Chancery.   *convictions*] Proving or
finding a person guilty as charged, perhaps including the passing of sentence.

15. *afflictions*] Not a specifically legal term, here probably referring to expressions of
distress by those in court.   *doctors*] Barristers.   *proctors*] Attorneys, solicitors.

18. *sufficient*] Qualified, capable.

TRUEWIT   Yes, and are very sober grave persons that will dispatch it in a
chamber with a whisper or two.

MOROSE   Good sir, shall I hope this benefit from you and trust myself into
your hands?

TRUEWIT   Alas, sir! Your nephew and I have been ashamed and oft-times   25
mad since you went, to think how you are abused. Go in, good sir, and
lock yourself up till we call you. We'll tell you more anon, sir.

MOROSE   Do your pleasure with me, gentlemen. I believe in you, and that
deserves no delusion –

TRUEWIT   You shall find none, sir –   30

[*Exit Morose*]

– but heaped, heaped plenty of vexation.

DAUPHINE   What wilt thou do now, wit?

TRUEWIT   Recover me hither Otter and the barber, if you can by any
means, presently.

DAUPHINE   Why? To what purpose?   35

TRUEWIT   O, I'll make the deepest divine and gravest lawyer, out o' them
two for him –

DAUPHINE   Thou canst not, man. These are waking dreams.

TRUEWIT   Do not fear me. Clap but a civil gown with a welt o' the one,
and a canonical cloak with sleeves o' the other, and give 'em a few   40
terms i' their mouths. If there come not forth as able a doctor and
complete a parson, for this turn, as may be wished, trust not my
election. And, I hope, without wronging the dignity of either
profession, since they are but persons put on, and for mirth's sake, to
torment him. The barber smatters Latin, I remember.   45

DAUPHINE   Yes, and Otter too.

TRUEWIT   Well then, if I make 'em not wrangle out this case to his no
comfort, let me be thought a Jack Daw or La Foole or anything worse.
Go you to your ladies, but first send for them.

DAUPHINE   I will.   50

[*Exeunt*]

39–40. *civil gown ... canonical cloak*] Differences in dress between the civil lawyer, whose
gown had a *welt* or border of fur or velvet, and the canon lawyer, who wore a sleeved
cloak.

43. *election*] Judgment, discrimination.

43–4. *without ... sake*] A disclaimer to avoid charges of particular satire against lawyers
and divines; see Another [Prologue] 11–14.

44. *persons put on*] Impersonations.

49. *them*] Cutbeard and Otter.

ACT 5

Act 5 scene 1*

[*Enter*] *La Foole, Clerimont, Daw*

LA FOOLE   Where had you our swords, Master Clerimont?
CLERIMONT   Why, Dauphine took 'em from the madman.
LA FOOLE   And he took 'em from our boys, I warrant you?
CLERIMONT   Very like, sir.
LA FOOLE   Thank you, good Master Clerimont. Sir John Daw and I are   5
    both beholden to you.
CLERIMONT   Would I knew how to make you so, gentlemen.
DAW   Sir Amorous and I are your servants, sir.

[*Enter Mavis*]

MAVIS   Gentlemen, have any of you a pen and ink? I would fain
    write out a riddle in Italian for Sir Dauphine to translate.   10
CLERIMONT   Not I, in troth, lady. I am no scrivener.
DAW   I can furnish you, I think, lady.

[*Daw and Mavis walk aside*]

CLERIMONT   He has it in the haft of a knife, I believe!
LA FOOLE   No, he has his box of instruments.
CLERIMONT   Like a surgeon!   15
LA FOOLE   For the mathematics: his square, his compasses, his brass pens,

---

*   In a notorious instance of libellous 'application', *SW* was suppressed by the authorities
    early in 1610, shortly after its first performance, because of ll. 20–23 of this scene. Lady
    Arabella Stuart, James's cousin and next in line for the throne, complained that Jonson
    alluded to her as the Prince of Moldavia's mistress. Stephen Janiculo, representing
    himself as heir to the Romanian princedom of Moldavia, had visited England in 1607,
    and later in Venice announced, without the lady's consent, that he would marry her
    when he succeeded to his title. He did not indicate how he would dispose of his current
    wife. Arabella had been kept under house arrest since Elizabeth's reign, without access
    to her estates and fortune, primarily to prevent her marrying and producing heirs to
    oppose Elizabeth's choice. James continued this policy, and when Arabella eloped with
    William Seymour in 1611, James had her imprisoned. She died in the Tower in 1615.
    As for the Moldavian prince, he had himself been imprisoned in Turkey in 1606, and
    had escaped disguised as a woman. Jonson probably referred to him as yet another
    sexually inverted figure with pretensions to authority.
11. *scrivener*] Secretary.
13. *in the haft*] The physician and occult philosopher Cornelius Agrippa (1486–1535) was
    supposed to have carried alchemical formulas and medicines in the handle of his sword;
    Aubrey (1982: vol. 2, p. 334) mentions that Thomas Hobbes carried pen and ink in the
    handle of his walking stick.

and black lead, to draw maps of every place and person where he
comes.

CLERIMONT   How, maps of persons!

LA FOOLE   Yes, sir, of Nomentack, when he was here, and of the Prince   20
of Moldavia, and of his mistress, Mistress Epicoene.

CLERIMONT   Away! He has not found out her latitude, I hope.

LA FOOLE   You are a pleasant gentleman, sir.

[*Exit Mavis with pen and ink; Daw rejoins the gentlemen*]

CLERIMONT   Faith, now we are in private, let's wanton it a little, and talk
waggishly. Sir John, I am telling Sir Amorous here that you two   25
govern the ladies: where'er you come, you carry the feminine gender
afore you.

DAW   They shall rather carry us afore them, if they will, sir.

CLERIMONT   Nay, I believe that they do, withal – But that you are the
prime men in their affections and direct all their actions –   30

DAW   Not I. Sir Amorous is.

LA FOOLE   I protest, Sir John is.

DAW   As I hope to rise i' the state, Sir Amorous, you ha' the person.

LA FOOLE   Sir John, you ha' the person and the discourse too.

DAW   Not I, sir. I have no discourse – and then you have activity beside.   35

LA FOOLE   I protest, Sir John, you come as high from Tripoli as I do every
whit, and lift as many joint-stools and leap over 'em, if you would use
it

20. *Nomentack*] A Virginian Indian chief, adviser of Powhatan, brought as a hostage to
England in 1608/9, and murdered in Bermuda during the return voyage.

20–21. *Prince of Moldavia*] See the general note on this scene, above.

21. *his*] Daw's, not the Prince's. The grammatical ambiguity led to the premature closing
of the play, although it was not censored in the printed text.

22. *latitude*] Geographical and sexual quibble, suggesting laxity of conduct, freedom from
conventional restrictions.

23. *pleasant*] Full of jokes.

26. *ladies*] The collegiates.

26–7. *carry . . . you*] Punning glance at the knights' effeminacy.

28. *carry . . . them*] Punning boast on the sexual clasp of women bearing men's weight
during copulation.

29. *Nay . . . withal*] Because of their masculine aggressiveness.

30. *prime*] Multiple pun, meaning first, foremost; young; sexually exciting or excited,
derived from muskets readied for firing.

33. *person*] Attractive appearance.

34. *discourse*] Ease and wit in conversation.

35. *activity*] Athletic prowess, punning on the sexual.

36. *come . . . Tripoli*] Vault and tumble, first applied to apes imported from Tripoli;
perhaps denoting a particular gymnastic trick, but also implying sexual activity.

CLERIMONT   Well, agree on 't together, knights, for between you, you
    divide the kingdom or commonwealth of ladies' affections. I see it and   40
    can perceive a little how they observe you, and fear you, indeed. You
    could tell strange stories, my masters, if you would, I know.
DAW   Faith, we have seen somewhat, sir.
LA FOOLE   That we have – velvet petticoats, and wrought smocks, or so.
DAW   Ay, and –   45
CLERIMONT   Nay, out with it, Sir John. Do not envy your friend the
    pleasure of hearing, when you have had the delight of tasting.
DAW   Why – ah – do you speak, Sir Amorous.
LA FOOLE   No, do you, Sir John Daw.
DAW   I' faith, you shall.   50
LA FOOLE   I' faith, you shall.
DAW   Why, we have been –
LA FOOLE   In the Great Bed at Ware together in our time. On, Sir John.
DAW   Nay, do you, Sir Amorous.
CLERIMONT   And these ladies with you, knights?   55
LA FOOLE   No, excuse us, sir.
DAW   We must not wound reputation.
LA FOOLE   No matter – they were these, or others. Our bath cost us fifteen
    pound when we came home.
CLERIMONT   Do you hear, Sir John, you shall tell me but one thing truly,   60
    as you love me.
DAW   If I can, I will, sir.
CLERIMONT   You lay in the same house with the bride here?
DAW   Yes, and conversed with her hourly, sir.
CLERIMONT   And what humour is she of? Is she coming and open, free?   65
DAW   O, exceeding open, sir. I was her servant, and Sir Amorous was to
    be.
CLERIMONT   Come, you have both had favours from her? I know and
    have heard so much.
DAW   O, no, sir.   70

40. *commonwealth*] Because shared in common between the two men.
44. *velvet petticoats, wrought smocks*] Metonyms for wenches, or loose women.
    wrought] Embroidered.
53. *Great . . . Ware*] Giant-sized bed measuring nearly 11 feet square, kept at the Saracen's
    Head, Ware; built around 1580 for sleeping twelve people, now on view at the Victoria
    and Albert Museum.
58. *bath*] Presumably a hot medicinal bath to prevent venereal disease. The exorbitant cost
    is intended as a boast of sexual endurance.
63. *lay*] Lodged, but implying sexual experience.
64. *conversed*] Hinting at sexual conversation, or intercourse.
65. *coming, open, free*] Sexually eager and available.
66. *servant*] Lover.

LA FOOLE   You shall excuse us, sir. We must not wound reputation.

CLERIMONT   Tut, she is married now, and you cannot hurt her with any
report, and therefore speak plainly. How many times, i' faith? Which
of you led first? Ha?

LA FOOLE   Sir John had her maidenhead, indeed.   75

DAW   O, it pleases him to say so, sir, but Sir Amorous knows what's what
as well.

CLERIMONT   Dost thou, i' faith, Amorous?

LA FOOLE   In a manner, sir.

CLERIMONT   Why, I commend you lads. Little knows Don Bridegroom of   80
this. Nor shall he, for me.

DAW   Hang him, mad ox.

CLERIMONT   Speak softly. Here comes his nephew with the Lady
Haughty. He'll get the ladies from you, sirs, if you look not to him in
time.   85

LA FOOLE   Why, if he do, we'll fetch 'em home again, I warrant you.

   [*Exeunt*]

Act 5 scene 2*

   [*Enter*] *Haughty, Dauphine*

HAUGHTY   I assure you, Sir Dauphine, it is the price and estimation of
your virtue only that hath embarked me to this adventure, and I could
not but make out to tell you so, nor can I repent me of the act, since
it is always an argument of some virtue in ourselves that we love and
affect it so in others.   5

DAUPHINE   Your ladyship sets too high a price on my weakness.

HAUGHTY   Sir, I can distinguish gems from pebbles –

DAUPHINE   [*Aside*] Are you so skilful in stones?

HAUGHTY   And, howsoever I may suffer in such a judgment as yours by
admitting equality of rank or society with Centaur or Mavis –   10

80.   *Don*] Using the Spanish title as a term of contempt.

82.   *ox*] Suggesting a state of stupidity as well as of cuckoldry.

86.   *fetch … again*] Retrieve their interest.

*   The Ladies' courtship of Dauphine inverts the usually male prerogatives of gift-giving,
whispered assignations, and secret notes.

1.   *estimation*] Synonym for 'price'. Haughty's language, like her sex-life, is full of
redundant couplings. See ll.4–5, 'love and affect'; l.10, 'rank or society', and elsewhere.

2.   *virtue*] Merit, especially manliness, virility. See l.4.

3.   *make out*] Sally forth; inflated language, as in 'embarked'.

4.   *argument*] Token, proof.   *virtue*] Merit, but suggesting essence or power.

8.   *skilful in stones*] Knowledgeable or experienced in dealing with jewels, punning on
'testicles'.

DAUPHINE   You do not, madam. I perceive they are your mere foils.

HAUGHTY   Then are you a friend to truth, sir. It makes me love you the more. It is not the outward but the inward man that I affect. They are not apprehensive of an eminent perfection, but love flat and dully.

CENTAUR   [*Calling within*] Where are you, my Lady Haughty?   15

HAUGHTY   I come presently, Centaur. – My chamber, sir, my page shall show you, and Trusty, my woman, shall be ever awake for you. You need not fear to communicate anything with her, for she is a Fidelia. I pray you, wear this jewel [*Pressing it on him*] for my sake, Sir Dauphine.   20

[*Enter Centaur*]

Where's Mavis, Centaur?

CENTAUR   Within, madame, a-writing. I'll follow you presently. I'll but speak a word with Sir Dauphine.

[*Exit Haughty*]

DAUPHINE   With me, madam?

CENTAUR   Good Sir Dauphine, do not trust Haughty, nor make any credit   25
to her, whatever you do besides. Sir Dauphine, I give you this caution: she is a perfect courtier and loves nobody but for her uses, and for her uses she loves all. Besides, her physicians give her out to be none o' the clearest – whether she pay 'em or no, heaven knows – and she's above fifty too, and pargets! See her in a forenoon. Here comes Mavis, a   30
worse face than she! You would not like this by candlelight. If you'll come to my chamber one o' these mornings early, or late in an evening, I'll tell you more.

[*Enter Mavis with a paper in her hand*]

11. *foils*] Settings for a jewel; generally, contrasts that show one off to advantage.

13. *outward … inward*] Contrasting mere physical attractiveness to intellect or fine feeling.

14. *apprehensive of*] Capable of understanding.   *eminent*] Outstanding.   *flat and dully*] Synonyms for 'stupidly', 'without feeling or spirit'.

18. *Fidelia*] Latin punning on Trusty; faithful woman, like the heroines of that name in popular romances.

25–6. *make any credit to*] Put any faith in.

27. *courtier*] Politician, or Machiavel.   *uses*] Political and sexual employments.

29. *clearest*] Free of venereal disease.   *whether … no*] That is, whether the doctors say so out of spite for not being paid or because she really is diseased.

30. *pargets*] Plasters herself with cosmetics (a term usually used of whitewashing or mending walls).

31. *worse face*] Punning on the Italian *maviso* or *malviso*, a possible source for Mavis's name (Florio).   *by candlelight*] *Even* by candlelight, flattering to most women.

Where's Haughty, Mavis?

MAVIS   Within, Centaur.   35

CENTAUR   What ha' you there?

MAVIS   An Italian riddle for Sir Dauphine. [*Giving it to him*] – You shall
not see it, i' faith, Centaur.

[*Exit Centaur*]

Good Sir Dauphine, solve it for me. I'll call for it anon.

[*Exit Mavis*]
[*Enter Clerimont*]

CLERIMONT   How now, Dauphine? How dost thou 'quit thyself of   40
these females?

DAUPHINE   'Slight, they haunt me like fairies and give me jewels here. I
cannot be rid of 'em.

CLERIMONT   O, you must not tell though.

DAUPHINE   Mass, I forgot that. I was never so assaulted. One loves for   45
virtue, and bribes me with this. [*Shows jewel*] Another loves me with
caution, and so would possess me. A third brings me a riddle here, and
all are jealous, and rail each at other.

CLERIMONT   A riddle? Pray le' me see 't?

He reads the paper

'Sir Dauphine, I chose this way of intimation for privacy. The ladies   50
here, I know, have both hope and purpose to make a collegiate and
servant of you. If I might be so honoured as to appear at any end of
so noble a work, I would enter into a fame of taking physic tomorrow
and continue it four or five days, or longer, for your visitation. Mavis.'
By my faith, a subtle one! Call you this a riddle? What's their plain   55
dealing, trow?

DAUPHINE   We lack Truewit to tell us that.

---

40. *'quit ... of*] Acquit yourself with. At 43, Dauphine takes it to mean 'quit' (= rid
yourself of).

44. *not tell*] Revealing a gift from the fairies results in forfeiting the gift and provoking the
fairies' anger.

45. *Mass*] By the mass, a mild oath.

47. *caution*] Precaution; that is, Centaur's warnings about Haughty's shortcomings.

50. *intimation*] Secrecy.

52–3. *appear ... work*] Bizarre expression of sexual availability; 'serve any desire of so
worthy a creature as yourself', but also sounding like an offer of fellatio.

53. *enter ... fame*] Start a rumour.   *taking physic*] Undergoing medical treatment.

54. *visitation*] Visiting sick or distressed persons as an act of charity, usually a pastoral
duty.

CLERIMONT   We lack him for somewhat else too. His knights *reformados*
 are wound up as high and insolent as ever they were.

DAUPHINE   You jest.   60

CLERIMONT   No drunkards, either with wine or vanity, ever confessed
 such stories of themselves. I would not give a fly's leg in balance
 against all the women's reputations here, if they could be but thought
 to speak truth. And for the bride, they made their affidavit against her
 directly –   65

DAUPHINE   What, that they have lain with her?

CLERIMONT   Yes, and tell times and circumstances, with the cause why
 and the place where. I had almost brought 'em to affirm that they had
 done it today.

DAUPHINE   Not both of 'em.   70

CLERIMONT   Yes, faith. With a sooth or two more, I had effected it. They
 would ha' set it down under their hands.

DAUPHINE   Why, they will be our sport, I see, still – whether we will or
 no!

Act 5 scene 3*

[Enter] Truewit

TRUEWIT   O, are you here? Come, Dauphine. Go, call your uncle
 presently. I have fitted my divine and my canonist, dyed their beards
 and all. The knaves do not know themselves, they are so exalted and

58. *reformados*] Reformed in a military sense, as officers of disbanded companies who
 retain their rank; hence, spurious or pointless.

71. *sooth*] Exclamations of awe, indicating his flattering admiration and approval, such as
 'forsooth' (= really, indeed).

72. *set ... hands*] Made a written statement and signed it, as in 'affadavit', l.64 above.

*   The *twelve impediments* to marriage explored in the pseudo-judicial proceedings, as
 Cutbeard explains, do not strictly speaking grant divorce, but rather 'nullity' or
 annulment. The specifics elaborated here derive from the 'Supplementum ad Tertiam
 Partem' of Thomas Aquinas's *Summa Theologica*:

> Error, conditio, votum, cognatio, crimen,
> Cultus disparitas, vis, ordo, ligamen, honestas,
> Si sis affinis, si forte coire nequibis,
> Haec socianda vetant connubia, facta retractant.

Cutbeard quotes the third line at l.150; Otter quotes the last line at ll.178–9. The legal
 debate parodies moot-court practice-sessions for students at the Inns of Court.
 Truewit's schoolmasterly corrections of the Latin grammar are comic reminders of the
 boy-actors' ages.

2. *fitted*] Put into costume.

3. *exalted*] Raised in rank; proud of themselves.

altered. Preferment changes any man. Thou shalt keep one door, and
I another, and then Clerimont in the midst, that he may have no means   5
of escape from their cavilling when they grow hot once. And then the
women – as I have given the bride her instructions – to break in upon
him i' the *l'envoy*. O, 'twill be full and twanging! Away, fetch him.

[*Exit Dauphine*]
[*Enter Cutbeard disguised as a canon lawyer and Otter as a divine*]

Come, Master Doctor and Master Parson, look to your parts now and
discharge 'em bravely. You are well set forth; perform it as well.   10
If you chance to be out, do not confess it with standing still or
humming or gaping one at another, but go on and talk aloud and
eagerly, use vehement action, and only remember your terms, and you
are safe. Let the matter go where it will: you have many will do so. But
at first be very solemn and grave like your garments, though   15
you loose yourselves after and skip out like a brace of jugglers on a
table. Here he comes! Set your faces and look superciliously while I
present you.

[*Enter Morose with Dauphine*]

MOROSE   Are these the two learned men?
TRUEWIT   Yes, sir, please you salute 'em?   20
MOROSE   Salute 'em? I had rather do anything than wear out time so
   unfruitfully, sir. I wonder how these common forms as 'God save you'
   and 'You are welcome' are come to be a habit in our lives – or 'I am
   glad to see you' – when I cannot see what the profit can be of these
   words, so long as it is no whit better with him whose affairs are sad   25

4. *Preferment*] Advancement, promotion. *keep*] Guard.
5. *in the midst*] At the middle door on the Blackfriars stage; see notes at 1.5.25.
6. *cavilling*] Hair-splitting, bickering.
8. *l'envoy*] Conclusion of a poem, specifically the final stanza of an old ballad.
    twanging] Slang for 'wonderfully exciting'.
9. *Master Doctor, Master Parson*] 'Master' was a courtesy title for lawyers and parsons,
    but its superfluous use here with the professional titles seems rather a mockery of rank.
    E. B. Partridge (1971) points out further mockeries in the tone adopted by the two
    impersonators: Otter acts like a Puritan parson, debating by practical experience, and
    Cutbeard acts like a medieval Catholic, dogmatically citing canon law.
10. *well set forth*] Convincingly costumed.
11. *be out*] Forget your lines.
13. *action*] Rhetorical gestures. *terms*] Technical Latin terms.
14. *matter*] Content of the discussion.
16. *loose yourselves*] Let yourselves go.
20. *salute*] Greet courteously.
25. *so long as*] Since.

and grievous that he hears this salutation!

TRUEWIT   'Tis true, sir, we'll go to the matter then. Gentlemen, Master
Doctor and Master Parson, I have acquainted you sufficiently with the
business for which you are come hither. And you are not now to
inform yourselves in the state of the question, I know. This is the   30
gentleman who expects your resolution, and therefore, when you
please, begin.

OTTER   Please you, Master Doctor.

CUTBEARD   Please you, good Master Parson.

OTTER   I would hear the canon law speak first.   35

CUTBEARD   It must give place to positive divinity, sir.

MOROSE   Nay, good gentlemen, do not throw me into circumstances. Let
your comforts arrive quickly at me, those that are. Be swift in
affording me my peace, if so I shall hope any. I love not your
disputations, or your court tumults. And that it be not strange to you,   40
I will tell you. My father, in my education, was wont to advise me that
I should always collect and contain my mind, not suffering it to flow
loosely, that I should look to what things were necessary to the
carriage of my life and what not, embracing the one and eschewing the
other. In short, that I should endear myself to rest and avoid turmoil,   45
which now is grown to be another nature to me. So that I come not
to your public pleadings or your places of noise – not that I neglect
those things that make for the dignity of the commonwealth, but for
the mere avoiding of clamours and impertinencies of orators that
know not how to be silent. And for the cause of noise am I now a   50
suitor to you. You do not know in what a misery I have been exercised
this day, what a torrent of evil! My very house turns round with the
tumult! I dwell in a windmill! The perpetual motion is here and not
at Eltham.

TRUEWIT   Well, good Master Doctor, will you break the ice? Master   55
Parson will wade after.

CUTBEARD   Sir, though unworthy and the weaker, I will presume.

OTTER   'Tis no presumption, *Domine* Doctor.

MOROSE   Yet again!

36. *positive*] Practical, as opposed to theoretical or speculative.
37. *circumstances*] Circumstantialities.
47. *neglect*] Condemn, or overlook (Latin).
49. *impertinencies*] Irrelevances.
51. *exercised*] Harassed, afflicted.
53. *perpetual motion*] A hollow glass globe supposedly capable of perpetual motion,
invented by Cornelius Drebbel (1572–1634), the Dutch scientist patronised by James I;
in 1609–10, Drebbel was living at Eltham Palace in Kent, about 9 miles south east of
London, where the device was a popular public display.
58. *Domine*] Master (Latin).

CUTBEARD   Your question is for how many causes a man may have   60
    divortium legitimum, a lawful divorce. First, you must understand the
    nature of the word 'divorce': *a divertendo* –
MOROSE   No excursions upon words, good Doctor. To the question,
    briefly.
CUTBEARD   I answer then: the canon law affords divorce but in few cases,   65
    and the principal is in the common case, the adulterous case. But there
    are *duodecim impedimenta*, twelve impediments (as we call 'em), all
    which do not *dirimere contractum*, but *irritum reddere matrimonium*,
    as we say in the canon law, 'not take away the bond, but cause a
    nullity therein'.   70
MOROSE   I understood you before. Good sir, avoid your impertinency of
    translation.
OTTER   He cannot open this too much, sir, by your favour.
MOROSE   Yet more!
TRUEWIT   O, you must give the learned men leave, sir. To your impedi-   75
    ments, Master Doctor.
CUTBEARD   The first is *impedimentum erroris*.
OTTER   Of which there are several *species*.
CUTBEARD   Ay, as *error personae*.
OTTER   If you contract youself to one person, thinking her another.   80
CUTBEARD   Then, *error fortunae*.
OTTER   If she be a beggar, and you thought her rich.
CUTBEARD   Then, *error qualitatis*.
OTTER   If she prove stubborn or headstrong, that you thought obedient.
MOROSE   How? Is that, sir, a lawful impediment? One at once, I pray you,   85
    gentlemen.
OTTER   Ay, *ante copulam*, but not *post copulam*, sir.
CUTBEARD   Master Parson says right. *Nec post nuptiarum benedictio-*
    nem. It doth indeed but *irrita reddere sponsalia*, annul the contract.
    After marriage it is of no obstancy.   90
TRUEWIT   Alas, sir, what a hope are we fallen from by this time!

62. *a divertendo*] Derived from separating.
71. *impertinency*] Irrelevance. Nevertheless, Cutbeard and Otter continue to translate
    most of the Latin scraps.
73. *open*] Expound, expand on.
77. *impedimentum erroris*] The impediment of deception or mistaking, whether of person
    (*personae*), of property (*fortunae*), or of rank (*qualitatis*) – not personality flaws, as
    Otter suggests by his examples at l.84.
78. *species*] Kinds (Latin).
87. *ante copulam . . . post copulam*] Before the union, not after.
88–9. *Nec . . . benedictionem*] And not after the blessing of the marriage.
90. *obstancy*] Juridical opposition (medieval Latin).
91. *time*] Timing.

CUTBEARD   The next is *conditio*: if you thought her free-born and she prove a bondwoman, there is impediment of estate and condition.

OTTER   Ay, but Master Doctor, those servitudes are *sublatae* now among us Christians.   95

CUTBEARD   By your favour, Master Parson –

OTTER   You shall give me leave, Master Doctor.

MOROSE   Nay, gentlemen, quarrel not in that question; it concerns not my case. Pass to the third.

CUTBEARD   Well then, the third is *votum*. If either party have made a vow   100
of chastity. But that practice, as Master Parson said of the other, is taken away among us, thanks be to discipline. The fourth is *cognatio*: if the persons be of kin within the degrees.

OTTER   Ay. Do you know what the degrees are, sir?

MOROSE   No, nor I care not, sir. They offer me no comfort in the   105
question, I am sure.

CUTBEARD   But there is a branch of this impediment may, which is *cognatio spiritualis*. If you were her godfather, sir, then the marriage is incestuous.

OTTER   That 'comment' is absurd and superstitious, Master Doctor. I   110
cannot endure it. Are we not all brothers and sisters and as much a kin in that as godfathers and goddaughters?

MOROSE   O me! To end the controversy, I never was a godfather, I never was a godfather in my life, sir. Pass to the next.

CUTBEARD   The fifth is *crimen adulterii*: the known case. The sixth, *cultus*   115
disparitas, difference of religion. Have you ever examined her what religion she is of?

MOROSE   No, I would rather she were of none than be put to the trouble of it!

OTTER   You may have it done for you, sir.   120

MOROSE   By no means, good sir. On to the rest. Shall you ever come to an end, think you?

TRUEWIT   Yes, he has done half, sir. – [*To Cutbeard*] On to the rest. – [*To Morose*] Be patient and expect, sir.

CUTBEARD   The seventh is *vis*: if it were upon compulsion or force.   125

MOROSE   O no, it was too voluntary, mine, too voluntary.

CUTBEARD   The eighth is *ordo*: if ever she have taken holy orders.

---

94. *servitudes*] Otter misinterprets the term, which, in law, refers strictly to landed property, not personal relationships.   *sublatae*] Abolished.

102. *discipline*] Ecclesiastical regulations, Church government.

110. *superstitious*] That is, 'papist' or Roman Catholic thinking; Otter goes on to express an egalitarian puritan belief.

115. *crimen adulterii*] The accusation or crime of adultery.   *known case*] Legally proven instance; crudely, the sexually experienced vagina (a common joke).

124. *expect*] Wait.

OTTER   That's superstitious too.

MOROSE   No matter, Master Parson. Would she would go into a nunnery   130
  yet.

CUTBEARD   The ninth is *ligamen*: if you were bound, sir, to any other
  before.

MOROSE   I thrust myself too soon into these fetters.

CUTBEARD   The tenth is *publica honestas*: which is *inchoata quaedam*   135
  affinitas.

OTTER   Ay, or *affinitas orta ex sponsalibus*, and is but *leve impedi-*
  mentum.

MOROSE   I feel no air of comfort blowing to me in all this.

CUTBEARD   The eleventh is *affinitas ex fornicatione*.

OTTER   Which is no less *vera affinitas* than the other, Master Doctor.   140

CUTBEARD   True, *quae oritur ex legitimo matrimonio*.

OTTER   You say right, venerable Doctor. And *nascitur ex eo, quod per*
  conjugium duae personae efficiuntur una caro –

MOROSE   Heyday, now they begin.

CUTBEARD   I conceive you, Master Parson. *Ita per fornicationem aeque*   145
  est verus pater, qui sic generat –

OTTER   *Et vere filius qui sic generatur* –

MOROSE   What's all this to me?

CLERIMONT   [*Aside*] Now it grows warm.

CUTBEARD   The twelfth and last is *si forte coire nequibis*.   150

OTTER   Ay, that is *impedimentum gravissimum*. It doth utterly annul and
  annihilate, that. If you have *manifestam frigiditatem*, you are well,
  sir.

TRUEWIT   Why, there is comfort come at length, sir. Confess yourself but

---

134. *publica honestas*] Public integrity.

134–5. *inchoata quaedam affinitas*] Some immature or barely initiated relationship, such as
  a previous unconsummated marriage.

136. *affinitas ... sponsalibus*] Relationship arising out of a betrothal. *leve*] Slight.

139. *affinitas ex fornicatione*] Relationship from fornication; one person guilty of fornication could not marry or have legal issue with a near relative of the other sexual
  partner.

140. *vera affinitas*] True relationship, in that sexual intercourse, whether in or out of
  marriage, involves the same physical act.

141. *quae ... matrimonio*] Than that which arises from legal marriage.

142–3. *nascitur ... caro*] It proceeds from this, that through physical union in marriage,
  two people are made one flesh.

145–6. *Ita ... generat*] Thus he is equally a true father who begets through fornication.

147. *Et ... generatur*] And he truly a son who is thus begotten.

150. *si ... nequibis*] If by chance you are unable to copulate.

151. *gravissimum*] Most serious.

152. *manifestam frigiditatem*] Evident frigidity.

a man unable, and she will sue to be divorced first.   155

OTTER   Ay, or if there be *morbus perpetuus et insanabilis*, as *paralysis, elephantiasis*, or so –

DAUPHINE   O, but *frigiditas* is the fairer way, gentlemen.

OTTER   You say troth, sir, and as it is in the canon, Master Doctor.

CUTBEARD   I conceive you, sir.   160

CLERIMONT   [*Aside*] Before he speaks.

OTTER   That 'a boy or child, under years, is not fit for marriage, because he cannot *reddere debitum*'. So your *omnipotentes* –

TRUEWIT   [*Aside to Otter*] Your *impotentes*, you whoreson lobster.

OTTER   Your *impotentes*, I should say, are *minime apti ad contrahenda*   165
matrimonium.

TRUEWIT   [*Aside to Otter*] *Matrimonium*? We shall have most unmatrimonial Latin with you: *matrimonia*, and be hanged.

DAUPHINE   [*Aside to Truewit*] You put 'em out, man.

CUTBEARD   But then there will arise a doubt, Master Parson, in our case,   170
post matrimonium, that *frigiditate praeditus* – do you conceive me, sir?

OTTER   Very well, sir.

CUTBEARD   Who cannot *uti uxore pro uxore* may *habere eam pro sorore*.

OTTER   Absurd, absurd, absurd, and merely apostatical.   175

CUTBEARD   You shall pardon me, Master Parson, I can prove it.

OTTER   You can prove a will, Master Doctor, you can prove nothing else. Does not the verse of your own canon say *Haec socianda vetant conubia, facta retractant* –

CUTBEARD   I grant you, but how do they *retractare*, Master Parson?   180

MOROSE   [*Moaning to himself*] O, this was it I feared.

156. *morbus . . . insanabilis*] A continuous and incurable disorder.

163. *reddere debitum*] Pay his debt; fulfil his obligation.   *omnipotentes*] All-powerful.

164. *lobster*] From 'lob', a clownish dull-witted lout; unlikely to refer to a crustacean, or even a red-faced man (*OED*).

165–6. *minime . . . matrimonium*] Least suited to contracting marriages.

167–8. *unmatrimonial*] Because the grammatical inflections are not correctly 'married' (Holdsworth 1979); Otter should have used the plural *matrimonia* to agree with *contrahenda*.

169. *put 'em out*] Confuse them, make them forget their lines.

171. *frigitate praeditus*] One afflicted with frigidity.

174. *uti . . . sorore*] Use a wife as a wife, may keep her as a sister.

175. *merely apostatical*] Absolutely heretical.

177. *prove a will*] Establish a will as valid in law. Otter's point is that Cutbeard is a lawyer, not a theologian.

178. *verse*] See l.8n. above.

178–9. *Haec . . . retractant*] They prohibit these marriages from being joined, and annul those that are performed.

OTTER   *In aeternum*, sir.

CUTBEARD   That's false in divinity, by your favour.

OTTER   'Tis false in humanity, to say so. Is he not *prorsus inutilis ad thorum*? Can he *praestare fidem datam*? I would fain know.   185

CUTBEARD   Yes. How if he do *convalere*?

OTTER   He cannot *convalere*. It is impossible.

TRUEWIT   [*To Morose*] Nay, good sir, attend the learned men. They'll think you neglect 'em else.

CUTBEARD   Or, if he do *simulare* himself *frigidum*, *odio uxoris*, or so?   190

OTTER   I say he is *adulter manifestus*, then –

DAUPHINE   [*Aside*] They dispute it very learnedly, i'faith.

OTTER   – and *prostitutor uxoris*, and this is positive.

MOROSE   Good sir, let me escape.

TRUEWIT   You will not do me that wrong, sir?   195

OTTER   And therefore, if he be *manifeste frigidus*, sir –

CUTBEARD   Ay, if he be *manifeste frigidus*, I grant you –

OTTER   Why, that was my conclusion.

CUTBEARD   And mine too.

TRUEWIT   Nay, hear the conclusion, sir.   200

OTTER   Then *frigiditatis causa* –

CUTBEARD   Yes, *causa frigiditatis* –

MOROSE   O, mine ears!

OTTER   She may have *libellum divortii* against you.

CUTBEARD   Ay, *divortii libellum* she will sure have.   205

MOROSE   Good echoes, forbear.

OTTER   If you confess it.

CUTBEARD   Which I would do, sir –

MOROSE   I will do anything –

OTTER   And clear myself *in foro conscientiae* –   210

CUTBEARD   Because you want indeed

---

182. *In aeternum*] For ever.

184–5. *prorsus ... thorum*] Utterly useless in bed (correctly, *ad torum*; *thorum* means 'bull', an apt error for Otter).

185. *praestare ... datam*] To perform his given promise, but punning on 'stand before', that is, become sexually erect.

186. *convalere*] Recover.

190. *simulare ... uxoris*] Pretend to be frigid, out of hatred for his wife.

191. *adulter manifestus*] Plain adulterer.

193. *prostitutor uxoris*] The prostitutor of his wife.

196. *manifeste*] Palpably, clearly.

202. *causa*] On the grounds of, in a case of.

204. *libellum divortii*] A writ of divorce.

210. *in foro conscientiae*] At the bar of conscience (proverbial).

211. *want*] Lack.

MOROSE   Yet more?
OTTER   *Exercendi potestate.*

Act 5 scene 4*

[*Enter*] *Epicoene, Haughty, Centaur, Mavis, Mistress Otter, Daw, La Foole*

EPICOENE   I will not endure it any longer. Ladies, I beseech you help me. This is such a wrong as never was offered to poor bride before. Upon her marriage day, to have her husband conspire against her, and a couple of mercenary companions to be brought in for form's sake, to persuade a separation! If you had blood or virtue in you, gentlemen,   5
    you would not suffer such earwigs about a husband, or scorpions to creep between man and wife –
MOROSE   O, the variety and changes of my torment!
HAUGHTY   Let 'em be cudgelled out of doors by our grooms.
CENTAUR   I'll lend you my footman.   10
MAVIS   We'll have our men blanket 'em i' the hall.
MRS OTTER   As there was one at our house, madam, for peeping in at the door.
DAW   Content, i' faith.
TRUEWIT   Stay, ladies and gentlemen, you'll hear before you proceed?   15
MAVIS   I'd ha' the bridegroom blanketed too.
CENTAUR   Begin with him first.
HAUGHTY   Yes, by my troth.
MOROSE   O, mankind generation!
DAUPHINE   Ladies, for my sake forbear.   20
HAUGHTY   Yes, for Sir Dauphine's sake.
CENTAUR   He shall command us.
LA FOOLE   He is as fine a gentleman of his inches, madam, as any is about

---

213. *Exercendi potestate*] The power of wielding your weapon.
*   Usually comedies end in marriage, celebrating community, integrity, and perpetuity. Jonson's *catastrophe* lauds discomfiture, exclusion, and annulment. The next festive occasion Dauphine predicts is his uncle's funeral.
  4. *companions*] Fellows, term of contempt.
  6. *earwigs*] Insinuating slanderers; from a notion that the insects would penetrate the head through the ear. *scorpions*] Poisonous intruders.
11. *blanket*] Toss in a blanket.
19. *mankind*] Unnaturally masculine or virago-like; also a variant of 'mankeen', ferocious or cruel, said of animals prone to attack men.
23. *of his inches*] Valiant, a 'tall' man in the current slang; also a bawdy quibble on the length of the penis, as in *BF* 1.3.61–7.

the town, and wears as good colours when he list.

TRUEWIT   [*To Morose*] Be brief, sir, and confess your infirmity: she'll   25
be afire to be quit of you. If she but hear that named once, you shall
not entreat her to stay. She'll fly you like one that had the marks upon
him.

MOROSE   Ladies, I must crave all your pardons –

TRUEWIT   Silence, ladies.   30

MOROSE   – for a wrong I have done to your whole sex in marrying this fair
and virtuous gentlewoman –

CLERIMONT   Hear him, good ladies.

MOROSE   – being guilty of an infirmity which, before I conferred with
these learned men, I thought I might have concealed –   35

TRUEWIT   But now being better informed in his conscience by them, he is
to declare it and give satisfaction by asking your public forgiveness.

MOROSE   I am no man, ladies.

ALL   How!

MOROSE   Utterly unabled in nature, by reason of frigidity, to perform the   40
duties or any the least office of a husband.

MAVIS   Now, out upon him, prodigious creature!

CENTAUR   Bridegroom uncarnate!

HAUGHTY   And would you offer it to a young gentlewoman?

MRS OTTER   A lady of her longings?   45

EPICOENE   Tut, a device, a device, this! It smells rankly, ladies. A mere
comment of his own.

TRUEWIT   Why, if you suspect that, ladies, you may have him searched.

DAW   As the custom is, by a jury of physicians.

LA FOOLE   Yes, faith, 'twill be brave.   50

MOROSE   O me, must I undergo that!

MRS OTTER   No, let women search him, madam. We can do it ourselves.

MOROSE   Out on me, worse!

EPICOENE   No, ladies, you shall not need. I'll take him with all his faults.

MOROSE   Worst of all!   55

24. *wears … colours*] Keeps as good company, drawn from knightly 'colours' or military
ensigns; see Otter's variation on 'fear no colours', 4.2.14 and note.
27. *marks*] Plague-sores; possibly signs of venereal disease.
42. *prodigious*] Monstrous, unnatural.
43. *uncarnate*] Without flesh and blood, coined from 'incarnate'.
44. *offer it*] Ludicrously ambiguous, suggesting 'present your impotence' as though it were
either a positive inducement, as in 'propose marriage', or a kind of assault, as in
'perpetrate an insult'.
45. *longings*] Equally ambiguous, suggesting (a) belongings, (b) birth or background, and
(c) sexual desires.
46–7. *mere comment*] Complete fabrication.
50. *brave*] Excellent.

CLERIMONT   Why, then 'tis no divorce, Doctor, if she consent not?

CUTBEARD   No, if the man be *frigidus*, it is *de parte uxoris* that we grant *libellum divortii* in the law.

OTTER   Ay, it is the same in theology.

MOROSE   Worse, worse than worst!   60

TRUEWIT   Nay, sir, be not utterly disheartened. We have yet a small relic of hope left, as near as our comfort is blown out. – [*Aside to Clerimont*] Clerimont, produce your brace of knights. – [*Aloud*] What was that, Master Parson, you told me, *in errore qualitatis*, e'en now? – [*Aside to Dauphine*] Dauphine, whisper the bride that she   65 carry it as if she were guilty and ashamed.

OTTER   Marry, sir, *in errore qualitatis* – which Master Doctor did forbear to urge – if she be found *corrupta*, that is, vitiated or broken up, that was *pro virgine desponsa*, espoused for a maid –

MOROSE   What then, sir?   70

OTTER   It doth *dirimere contractum*, and *irritum reddere* too.

TRUEWIT   If this be true, we are happy again, sir, once more. Here are an honourable brace of knights that shall affirm so much.

DAW   Pardon us, good Master Clerimont.

LA FOOLE   You shall excuse us, Master Clerimont.   •   75

CLERIMONT   [*Threatening*] Nay, you must make it good now, knights. There is no remedy. I'll eat no words for you, nor no men. You know you spoke it to me?

DAW   Is this gentleman-like, sir?

TRUEWIT   [*Aside to Daw, as if fearful of Clerimont*] Jack Daw, he's worse   80 than Sir Amorous, fiercer a great deal. – [*Aside to La Foole*] Sir Amorous, beware: there be ten Daws in this Clerimont.

LA FOOLE   I'll confess it, sir.

DAW   Will you, Sir Amorous? Will you wound reputation?

LA FOOLE   I am resolved.   85

TRUEWIT   So should you be too, Jack Daw. What should keep you off? She is but a woman and in disgrace. He'll be glad on 't.

DAW   Will he? I thought he would ha' been angry.

CLERIMONT   You will dispatch, knights. It must be done, i' faith.

TRUEWIT   Why, an' it must, it shall, sir, they say. They'll ne'er go back.   90 – [*Aside to Daw and La Foole*] Do not tempt his patience.

DAW   It is true indeed, sir.

LA FOOLE   Yes, I assure you, sir.

MOROSE   What is true, gentlemen? What do you assure me?

DAW   That we have known your bride, sir –   95

LA FOOLE   In good fashion. She was our mistress, or so –

57. *de parte uxoris*] On the wife's behalf.
68. *vitiated*] Deflowered.
71. *dirimere … reddere*] Cancel the contract and render it null and void.

CLERIMONT   Nay, you must be plain, knights, as you were to me.

OTTER   Ay, the question is if you have *carnaliter*, or no.

LAFOOLE   *Carnaliter*? What else, sir?

OTTER   It is enough: a plain nullity.   100

EPICOENE   I am undone, I am undone!

MOROSE   O, let me worship and adore you, gentlemen!

EPICOENE   [*Collapsing*] I am undone!

MOROSE   Yes, to my hand, I thank these knights. Master Parson, let me
thank you otherwise. [*Gives money*]   105

CENTAUR   And ha' they confessed?

MAVIS   Now out upon 'em, informers!

TRUEWIT   You see what creatures you may bestow your favours on,
madams.

HAUGHTY   [*Consoling Epicoene*] I would except against 'em as beaten   110
knights, wench, and not good witnesses in law.

MRS OTTER   Poor gentlewoman, how she takes it!

HAUGHTY   Be comforted, Morose. I love you the better for't.

CENTAUR   So do I, I protest.

CUTBEARD   But gentlemen, you have not known her since *matrimonium*?   115

DAW   Not today, Master Doctor.

LAFOOLE   No, sir, not today.

CUTBEARD   Why, then I say, for any act before, the *matrimonium* is good
and perfect, unless the worshipful bridegroom did precisely, before
witness, demand if she were *virgo ante nuptias*.   120

EPICOENE   No, that he did not, I assure you, Master Doctor.

CUTBEARD   If he cannot prove that, it is *ratum conjugium*, notwithstanding the premises. And they do no way *impedire*. And this is my
sentence, this I pronounce.

OTTER   I am of Master Doctor's resolution too, sir. If you made not that   125
demand *ante nuptias*.

MOROSE   O my heart! Wilt thou break? Wilt thou break? This is worst of
all worst worsts that hell could have devised! Marry a whore! And
so much noise!

DAUPHINE   Come, I see now plain confederacy in this doctor and this   130
parson to abuse a gentleman. You study his affliction. I pray be gone,

---

98. *have carnaliter*] Have [known her] carnally.

100. *nullity*] Annulment.

104. *to my hand*] Fallen into my power; see 4.5.14.

110. *except against*] Lodge a formal objection to bar their testimony.

110–11. *beaten knights*] Recreant knights were considered to have lost their legal status,
and hence could not be empanelled on a jury or admitted as witnesses in court.

120. *virgo ... nuptias*] Virgin before the wedding.

122. *ratum conjugium*] Legal marriage.

131. *study*] Devise, contrive by erudite means.

companions. And, gentlemen, I begin to suspect you for having parts
with 'em. Sir, will it please you hear me?

MOROSE   O, do not talk to me. Take not from me the pleasure of dying
in silence, nephew.   135

DAUPHINE   Sir, I must speak to you. I have been long your poor despised
kinsman, and many a hard thought has strengthened you against me.
But now it shall appear if either I love you or your peace, and prefer
them to all the world beside. I will not be long or grievous to you, sir.
If I free you of this unhappy match absolutely and instantly after all   140
this trouble, and almost in your despair, now –

MOROSE   It cannot be.

DAUPHINE   – sir, that you be never troubled with a murmur of it more,
what shall I hope for or deserve of you?

MOROSE   O, what thou wilt, nephew! Thou shalt deserve me and have   145
me.

DAUPHINE   Shall I have your favour perfect to me, and love hereafter?

MOROSE   That and anything beside. Make thine own conditions. My
whole estate is thine. Manage it: I will become thy ward.

DAUPHINE   Nay, sir, I will not be so unreasonable.   150

EPICOENE   Will Sir Dauphine be mine enemy too?

DAUPHINE   You know I have been long a suitor to you, uncle, that out of
your estate, which is fifteen hundred a year, you would allow me but
five hundred during life and assure the rest upon me after, to which
I have often, by myself and friends, tendered you a writing to sign,   155
which you would never consent or incline to. If you please but to effect
it now –

MOROSE   Thou shalt have it, nephew. I will do it, and more.

DAUPHINE   If I quit you not presently and for ever of this cumber, you
shall have power instantly, afore all these, to revoke your act, and I   160
will become whose slave you will give me to, for ever.

MOROSE   Where is the writing? I will seal to it, that, or to a blank, and
write thine own conditions.

EPICOENE   O me, most unfortunate wretched gentlewoman!

HAUGHTY   Will Sir Dauphine do this?   165

EPICOENE   [*Sobbing*] Good sir, have some compassion on me.

MOROSE   O, my nephew knows you belike. Away, crocodile!

CENTAUR   He does it not, sure, without good ground.

---

132. *having parts*] Being on their side.
139. *grievous*] Complaining of injuries.
147. *perfect*] Wholly, absolutely.
152. *suitor*] Petitioner.
159. *cumber*] Encumbrance, distress.
167. *knows you belike*] Sees through your deceitful appearance.   *crocodile*] Thought to
weep before it devoured its prey.

DAUPHINE   [*Handing him document*]   Here, sir.

MOROSE   Come, nephew, give me the pen. I will subscribe to anything and   170
seal to what thou wilt for my deliverance. Thou art my restorer.
[*Signs, seals, and returns document*] Here I deliver it thee as my deed.
If there be a word in it lacking, or writ with false
orthography, I protest before – I will not take the advantage.

DAUPHINE   Then here is your release, sir.   175

He takes off Epicoene's peruke

You have married a boy, a gentleman's son that I have brought up this
half year at my great charges and for this composition which I have
now made with you. What say you, Master Doctor? This is
justum impedimentum, I hope, *error personae*?

OTTER   Yes, sir, *in primo gradu*.   180

CUTBEARD   *In primo gradu*.

DAUPHINE   I thank you, good Doctor Cutbeard and Parson Otter.

He pulls off their beards and disguise

You are beholden to 'em, sir, that have taken this pains for you, and
my friend Master Truewit who enabled 'em for the business. Now you
may go in and rest, be as private as you will, sir. I'll not trouble you   185
till you trouble me with your funeral, which I care not how soon it
come.

[*Exit Morose*]

Cutbeard, I'll make your lease good. Thank me not but with your leg,
Cutbeard. And Tom Otter, your Princess shall be reconciled to you.

[*Exeunt Cutbeard and Otter*]

[*To Clerimont and Truewit*] How now, gentlemen! Do you look at   190
me?

CLERIMONT   A boy.

DAUPHINE   Yes. Mistress Epicoene.

[*Epicoene bows*]

174. *protest before* –] Assert publicly beforehand. The dash seems to mark an emphatic
pause setting off the announcement that follows; as Holdsworth (1979) argues, it
cannot be an expunged oath, since blasphemies are frequent in the text.

177. *composition*] Contract; financial settlement based on some compromise, especially the
payment by agreement of a sum of money in lieu of discharging some other obligation.

180. *in primo gradu*] In the highest degree.

188. *make ... good*] Act on the promise given earlier by Morose at 2.5.76–7.

TRUEWIT Well, Dauphine, you have lurched your friends of the better half of the garland by concealing this part of the plot! But much   195
good do it thee. Thou deservest it, lad. – And Clerimont, for thy
unexpected bringing in these two to confession, wear my part of it
freely. – Nay, Sir Daw and Sir La Foole, you see the gentlewoman that
has done you the favours! We are all thankful to you, and so should
the womankind here, specially for lying on her, though not with her!   200
You meant so, I am sure? But that we have stuck it upon you today
in your own imagined persons and so lately, this Amazon, the
champion of the sex, should beat you now thriftily for the common
slanders which ladies receive from such cuckoos as you are. You are
they that, when no merit or fortune can make you hope to enjoy their   205
bodies, will yet lie with their reputations and make their fame suffer.
Away, you common moths of these and all ladies' honours. Go, travel
to make legs and faces, and come home with some new matter to be
laughed at. You deserve to live in an air as corrupted as that
wherewith you feed rumour.   210

[Exeunt Daw and La Foole]

Madams, you are mute upon this new metamorphosis! But here stands
she that has vindicated your fames. Take heed of such *insectae*
hereafter. And let it not trouble you that you have discovered any
mysteries to this young gentleman. He is – almost – of years, and will

---

194–5. *lurched ... garland*] Possibly a satiric echo of *Coriolanus* (1608): 'He lurch'd all
swords of the garland' (2.2.101).

194. *lurched*] Cheated, robbed; particularly by tricking others into doing most of the work,
and then leaping in to filch the profit; associated with 'lurchers', greyhounds bred by
poachers to hunt rabbits.

195. *garland*] Crown or wreath worn by a winner, the symbol of supreme achievement or
merit since classical times.

200. *lying on*] Lying about.

201. *stuck it*] Fastened the lie.

202. *this Amazon*] Mrs Otter.

204. *cuckoos*] Birds which take over other birds' nests.

207. *moths*] Pests that make holes in the ladies' reputations. *travel*] Originally *travail* in
F1, meaning 'work hard', the pun is lost in the modernisation. 'Travel' fits the context
of 'Go','come home', and 'live in an air as corrupted' – all of which imply a refresher
course in France to acquire more mannerisms, assumed to be ingrained in French
courtiers.

208. *make legs and faces*] Bow and simper.

212. *she*] That is, Epicoene. *insectae*] The moths, Daw and La Foole; perhaps Jonson
intended a final humiliating gibe at their effeminacy with the incorrect feminine plural
(instead of the neuter plural *insecta*).

make a good visitant within this twelvemonth. In the meantime, we'll   215
all undertake for his secrecy, that can speak so well of his silence.

[*Exeunt ladies*]

[*Turning to audience*] Spectators, if you like this comedy, rise cheerfully and, now Morose is gone in, clap your hands. It may
be that noise will cure him, at least please him.

[*Exeunt*]

THE END

[THE ACTORS]

This comedy was first

acted in the year

1609

By the Children of Her Majesty's

Revels   5

---

215. *visitant*] Formal visitor to the college as a lover.
216.1. Usually the actor speaking the epilogue has the stage to himself. Dauphine,
    Clerimont, and Epicoene may thus escort the Ladies Collegiate off-stage, in order to
    allow Truewit the last word, his share of the 'garland'.
219. *that noise*] Emphasising '*that* noise' of applause, as indicating approval.

The principal comedians were:

Nathan Field	William Barksted	
Giles Cary	William Penn	
Hugh Attawell	Richard Allin	
John Smith	John Blaney	10

With the allowance of the Master of Revels

7. *Nathan Field*] 1587–1620? or 1633? Jonson's 'Scholar', named in the cast lists of *CR*, *Poet*, and *BF*, in the last of which Cokes describes him as 'Your best actor. Your Field' (5.3.72). As poet, he prefixed commendatory verses to the 1607 quarto of *Volp* and the 1611 quarto of *Cat*; he became a playwright himself with *A Woman is a Weathercock* (1612) and *Amends for Ladies* (1618), and collaborated with Massinger on *The Fatal Dowry* and perhaps with Fletcher on an unspecified work. *William Barksted*] Poet (*Mirrha*, 1607; *Hiren*, 1611) and playwright (possibly finished Marston's last play, *The Insatiate Countess*, 1610), as well as actor at least since 1609. He played Morose. Later he joined the Lady Elizabeth's company in 1611, and the Prince's Men in 1616.
8. *Giles Cary*] Joined Lady Elizabeth's Men in 1611. *William Penn*] Later became a member of the Prince's Men.
9. *Hugh Attawell*] Died 1621. Thought to have played La Foole; with Cary and Penn, he is also recorded as a principal player in dramas by Beaumont and Fletcher. He joined the Lady Elizabeth's Men in 1613 with Richard Allin. *Richard Allin*] Or *Allen*. If the name were really *Alleyn*, conceivably he was related to the famous actor Edward Alleyn, whom Jonson praised in *Epigrams* 89, 'To Edward Allen'. But Queen Anne employed a tenor named John Allin (father? brother?) who performed some of the songs in Jonson's *The Masque of Queens*, also in 1609. Either or neither might be the 'M^r. Allin' whom Dekker praised for his fine performance ('delivered with excellent action, and a well tuned audible voice') in the *King's Entertainment*, 15 March 1603 (Henry 1906).
10. *John Smith*] Nothing further is known. *John Blaney*] A member of the Queen's Men from 1616 to 1619.
11. *Master of Revels*] The job of selecting and controlling entertainment for performance. Sir George Buc, formerly the deputy Master, was appointed in 1608 following the retirement of Edmund Tilney, who had held the post since 1579.

TEXTUAL NOTES

Selected Variants in the 1616 Folio of *Epicoene*

This list gives word-changes, additions, and omissions in the first folio or *F1* text. The line-references and words in the lemmas are from the modernised text. The variants are given in old spelling. Most of the changes occur on one reset sheet, Yy of the folio (from Prologue to 2.2.56). Press corrections are marked *F1a* for the original state, *F1 reset* for the reset state, and *F1b* for the corrected state; those marked *F1* represent all states of the folio.

Prologue

27.   *ord'naries*] *F1 reset*; ordinaries *F1a*.

Another

Occasioned . . . exception] *Marginal note in F1 reset*; *not in F1a*.

Act 1

1.1.31.   *Horses o' the time Marginal note in F1 reset*; *not in F1a*.
1.1.52.   *nor hear*] nor hearc *F1 reset*; not hearc *F1a*.
1.1.74.   *scoured*] scour'd *F1 reset*; sour'd *F1a*.
1.1.88.   *They*] *F1a*; Thy *F1 reset*. *not*] *F1 reset*; not, *F1a*.
1.1.92.   *choose*] *F1 reset*; chuse *F1a*.
1.1.137.   *upon*] vp on *F1 reset*; on *F1a*.
1.1.147.   *him in such*] *F1 reset*; him ouch *F1a*.
1.1.154.   *marching*] *F1 reset*; going *F1a*.
1.2.2.   *Struck* | Strooke *F1 reset*; Stroke *F1a*.
1.2.9.   *monuments*] moniments *F1 reset*; mon'ments *F1a*.
1.2.30.   *one Cutheard,*] *F1 reset*; not in *F1a*
1.2.62.   *speak –*] *F1 reset*; speak, *F1a*.
1.3.10.   *out!*] *F1 reset*; out, *F1a*.
1.3.21.   *manikin!*] mannikin! *F1 reset*; mannikin. *F1a*.
1.3.32.   *presents*] *F1 reset*; persents *F1a*.
1.3.35.   *for*] *F1 reset*; *not in F1a*.
1.3.38.   *Sir*] *F1 reset*; Sis *F1a*.
1.3.39.   *below*] *F1 reset*; *not in F1a*.   *owns*] *F1 reset*; owes *F1a*.
1.4.14.   *but*] *F1 reset*; *not in F1a*.
1.4.35.   *for*] *F1 reset*; *not in F1a*.
1.4.59.   *commodity –*] *F1 reset*; commodity. *F1a*.
1.4.60.   *LA FOOLE*] *F1 reset*; CLE. *F1a*.

Act 2

2.1.18.   *your*] *F1 reset*; you *F1a*.
2.1.38.   *with*] *F1 reset*; *not in F1a*.
2.2.3.   *all!*] *F1 reset*; all? *F1a.   strange!*] *F1 reset*; strange. *F1a.*
2.2.24.   *window*] *F1a*; windore *F1 reset.*
2.2.31.   *preachings*] *F1 reset*; parlee's *F1a.*
2.2.33.   *Ethelred's*] *F1 reset*; ETHELDRED'S *F1a.*
2.2.61.   *tyrants*] tyrannes *F1.*
2.2.116.   *rinses*] rises *F1.*
2.3.52.   *There's*] *F1b*; There is *F1a. commonplace fellow*] common place-fellow *F1.*
2.3.121.   *If you'll*] If you you'll *F1.*
2.4.14.   *have*] hane *F1.*
2.4.46.   *CLERIMONT*] DLE. *F1.*
2.4.47.   *DAUPHINE*] DAVP. *F1b*; CAVP. *F1a.*
2.5.1.   *your*] *F1b*; you *F1a.*
2.5.5.   *conceive*] concciue *F1.*
2.5.60.   *heifer*] heicfar *F1.*
2.5.82.   *soft low*] soft, low *F1b*; soft-low *F1a.*
2.5.84–5.   *now-mistress*] *F1b*; now – mistress *F1a.*

Act 3

3.1.46.   *velvet*] vellet *F1.*
3.3.15.   *DAW*] DAVP. *F1.*
3.3.17.   *John,*] JHON. *F1.*
3.3.27.   *main*] man *F1.*
3.4.32.   *Speak out*] *F1b*; Speake, out *F1a.*
3.5.37.   *reverend*] re-/ueuerend *F1.*
3.5.80.   *powder*] poulder *F1.*

Act 4

4.1.76.   *all ways*] alwaies *F1.*
4.4.12.   *i' the cockpit*] *F1b*; in a Cock-pit *F1a.*
4.4.122.   *porpoise*] porcpisce *F1.*
4.5.106.1.   *come*] came *F1.*

Act 5

5.1.16.   *square*] squire *F1.*
5.1.44.   *velvet*] vellet *F1.*
5.1.74.   *led*] lead *F1.*
5.3.49.   *impertinencies*] *F1b*; pertinencies *F1a.*
5.4.158.   *nephew*] *F1b*; nephew, *F1a.*
5.4.207.   *travel*] trauaile *F1.*

THE ALCHEMIST

INTRODUCTION

The setting: Blackfriars

Blackfriars was a London liberty, formerly a Dominican monastery, that retained the right of sanctuary and, though within the London city limits, certain exemptions from the jurisdiction of the sheriff. This freedom from the law was an advantage to many of its inhabitants who might otherwise be arrested for debt, dubious trade practices (since the City Guilds had no jurisdiction either), or various criminal and religious offences. Many former monastic buildings were converted into residences for the gentry, among them the Earl of Somerset and Jonson's patron Esmé Stuart, Lord Aubigny. They, like Lovewit, lived cheek-by-jowl with puritan feathermakers and shopkeepers, artisans and artists, foreigners, actors, and writers, including Jonson himself.

The area also attracted visitors to its alehouses, gambling dens, brothels, and theatre. Blackfriars Theatre, in which *The Alchemist* was first performed, was built by James Burbage in 1596 in the Upper Frater Hall of the former monastery, and was used by the Children of the Chapel Royal and the Children of the Queen's Revels between 1600 and 1608. The King's Men took over the space in 1609, performing there until 1642. The site, like *Epicoene*'s Whitefriars, reflected the play's setting, and the audience, having absorbed the milieu on the way to the theatre, was thus already seamlessly engaged in the performance even before it actually began.

Setting the play within the liberty has implications for the action of the comedy. Although Face is normally part of the Lovewit household, he finds himself at liberty to be his own master when the plague drives his employer out of town. With Subtle and Dol, also masterless and thus free to act as they choose, Face seizes the opportunity to follow his own ambitions without restraint, and signs a contract with his rogue-companions to form their own anarchic 'republic' (1.1.110), where they can be Sovereign, General, and Fairy Queen in a 'venture tripartite' (135) to dupe all comers. The licence to create a new world of wealth and exceptional power draws Mammon into the liberty as well: his private philanthropic fantasy eventually expands into a dream of 'a free state' of sensual excess, unhindered by king or country (4.1.147–69). The Anabaptists dream of another Münster Rising in London itself, with gold enough to buy military support, destroy the popish heretics, restore the silenced saints, and put the brethren in control of England – an ominous prevision of the Interregnum. Dapper aspires to the idle life of gentleman;

Drugger wants instant business success; Kastril wants to subdue his country neighbours with his urban prowess as a duelling Angry Boy. What they all have in common is the desire for easy attainment and absolute licence, freedom from the laws of necessity or of nature, even of fate.

But if the liberty of Blackfriars lets these dreams loose, it also regulates them. Lovewit's neighbours watch and listen, and when Lovewit returns they act. Their self-monitoring impulse, foolish, hestitant, but effective, provides the only brake that liberty allows. And the penalty for the abusers of liberty? Why, to go free, of course, and find the profit of the experience where they can.

Sources

The only specific source for *The Alchemist* is Jonson's prolific satiric imagination. Clearly, however, certain works lurk in the background. Jonson's devotion to Aristophanic structure dictated his scheme of the bizarre central fantasy-machine which sucks in believer after believer. *The Clouds* may have suggested Subtle's magic academy, where rhetoric displaces action and obsessive-compulsive dreamers hope to win a golden world for themselves through the delights of illogical experiment and false argument. *The Birds* provides a precedent for the Mammon plot as a satire on utopianism and capitalist expansion: the founder and champion of the birds' commonwealth soon becomes its tyrant, negotiates his marriage to a goddess, and becomes king of the universe. Possibly Lucian's *Alexander*, in which gullible visitors flock to a bogus oracle controlled by a false prophet, offered an early model of rogue-fiction. Plautus's *Mostellaria* (*The Haunted House*) helped Jonson handle Lovewit's return in 5.2.

For the satire on alchemy, Jonson may have been inspired by Chaucer's *The Canon's Yeoman's Tale*, in which the alchemist, a man of 'subtiltee', lurks in the alleys of the suburbs with other thieves, and stinks of the noxious fumes from experiments which blacken his face (and character) but delude his customers with promises of gold. Jonson certainly knew Erasmus's colloquy *Alchemy*, in which a corrupt priest supports his own vices by pretending to run alchemical experiments for a rich patron. Jonson's irony echoes Erasmus's when he demonstrates the symbiotic nurturing of dupe and rogue, the one needing and enjoying the delusions whereby the other makes his living. But much of Jonson's alchemical commentary is a product of his own serious reading of such authorities as Martin del Rio, Arnold of Villanova, Geber, Paracelsus, Vallensis, Sendivogius, and other German and English writers. Local contemporary knowledge of practitioners such as Dr John Dee or Simon Forman, and the general community belief in cunningfolk and witches, especially among puritans, rooted Jonson's views in the particular, as did current jokes which compared a conjuror's circle to a whore, and the raising of spirits to sexual acts.

Several plays of the period deal with scholar-magicians, like *Friar Bacon and Friar Bungay*, *John a Kent and John a Cumber*, or even *Doctor Faustus*; some represent a rogue-scholar, like *The Merry Devil of Edmonton*, or an ex-army trickster, like *The Merry Wives of Windsor*. But only one other play relies, like

Jonson's, on both a rogue-scholar and a trickster captain: *The Puritan; or The Widow of Watling Street* (1607), probably by Middleton. Although the scale and the performance of the trickery differ, the two plays overlap in concept and satirical targets. Both focus on a contest for the hand of a rich widow within a tangle of cony-catching plots staged by role-playing crooks who pass themselves off as cunningmen in order to swindle a specific London neighbourhood. After they burlesque magical feats reputedly performed by Forman and Dee, the scoundrels are foiled in the last act by the arrival of an influential landed gentleman. Although Jonson's treatment of these motifs is more complex than Middleton's, Jonson does seem to have used *The Puritan* at least as a point of departure. In both plays, a charlatan gains control of a bereaved household in the absence of the master. Both plays celebrate ingenious outlaw wit even while permitting stolid citizens to reassert their power at the end. And both revel in 'backstage' versions of magic tricks that had been carried out by such criminal pairs as John Darrell and his apprentice William Somers, tried in 1599 for faking demonic possession, or Sir Anthony Ashley and his brother, sued in chancery in 1609 for promising to help Thomas Rogers marry the Fairy Queen.

Stage history

The Alchemist was written for performance in Blackfriars, probably for the summer of 1610, but the first recorded performance seems to have been on tour in Oxford in September, where the King's Men also presented *Othello*. Dates given in the play (e.g., 3.2.129–32) suggest the action was designed to take place just in advance of contemporaneous time; however, because of plague, theatres had been closed in London since July and may not have reopened until October or November, thus frustrating Jonson's intention of setting the play a little in the future.

Nevertheless, the play was a resounding success, frequently revived in town, at court, and on tour. Even with the theatres closed between 1642 and 1660, the Drugger scenes continued to be performed as a 'droll' or comic sketch. After the Restoration, the play appeared regularly. Pepys records seeing at least two different actors playing Subtle, and after the turn of the century Steele termed it Jonson's masterpiece. Colley Cibber developed the part of Drugger with extra stage business in 1.3 and 4.7, and later in the eighteenth century David Garrick ripened the role into the quintessential booby. His popularity in this part led Francis Gentleman to write a series of farces about Drugger (*The Tobacconist*, 1770; *The Pantheonites*, 1773; and *Abel Drugger's Return from the Fête Champêtre at Marylebone Gardens*, 1774), the first of which was later revived by Edmund Kean. The last recorded early performance of *The Alchemist* was in 1815.

Modern performances began with William Poel's 1899 revival, and the play has been seen fairly frequently since. Sir Ralph Richardson was a notable Face in 1932 and again in 1947, when Sir Alec Guinness astonished the theatre world as Drugger. Leo McKern won acclaim as Subtle in 1962, as did William Hutt in 1969 for his superb Mammon at Ontario's Stratford Festival, a production noted for its rapid pacing and brilliant ensemble work. Trevor Nunn directed the play for the

Royal Shakespeare Company in 1977, with Ian McKellen as a dynamically manic Face, focusing the whole cast on the script's bizarre characterisations, whereas Griff Rhys Jones's production at the Lyric Hammersmith (1985) simplified character in order to increase the effects of farce.

Further reading

For more detail on the Blackfriars setting and how it localises the play, see R. L. Smallwood (1981); Cheryl Lynn Ross (1988) relates plague conditions in London to civic breakdown and social problems caused by 'masterless men'; and Jonathan Haynes (1989) discusses the new conception of criminality in the Jacobean period. For solid analysis of the dupes, see Wayne A. Rebhorn (1980) and G. D. Monsarrat (1983). On alchemy itself, Alvin Kernan's edition (1974) has an excellent appendix, 'Jonson's Use of Alchemy and a Glossary of Alchemical Terms', defining all the terms used in the play. On alchemy, Michael Flachmann (1977) discusses the metaphorical relations between alchemy and the role-playing; Gerard H. Cox (1983) explains the connection between alchemy and millenarianism, and John Mebane (1989) analyses the intellectual context. Keith Thomas (1971) is essential reading on witchcraft.

THE ALCHEMIST

A Comedy

Acted in the year 1610. By the

King's Majesty's

Servants.

THE AUTHOR B[EN] J[ONSON]

LUCRET[IUS]

– petere inde coronam,
Unde prius nulli velarint tempera Musa.

LONDON,

Printed by WILLIAM STANSBY

M. DC. XVI.

LUCRET[IUS] ... Musa] Lucretius, *On the Nature of the Universe* 4.1, 'To seek out the muses' garland where no one has won it before.'

[DEDICATION]

TO THE LADY MOST
DESERVING HER NAME
AND BLOOD:
MARY,
LADY WROTH

MADAM,

In the age of sacrifices, the truth of religion was not in the greatness and fat of the offerings, but in the devotion and zeal of the sacrificers. Else, what could a handful of gums have done in the sight of a hecatomb? Or how might I appear at this altar, except with those affections that no less love the   5
light and witness than they have the conscience of your virtue? If what I offer bear an acceptable odour and hold the first strength, it is your value of it which remembers where, when, and to whom it was kindled. Otherwise, as the times are, there comes rarely forth that thing so full of authority or example but by assiduity and custom grows less and loses. This,   10
yet, safe in your judgment (which is a Sidney's) is forbidden to speak more,

0.2. *DESERVING HER NAME*] Her name was also spelled, and probably pronounced, 'Worth'. Jonson wrote three poems praising her (*Epigrams* 103 and 105, and *Underwoods* 28), but expressed contempt for her husband, Sir Robert Wroth, of whom he told Drummond, 'My Lady Wroth is unworthily married on a jealous husband' (*Conv*, Parfitt 1975: p. 470). She was the mistress of her cousin the Earl of Pembroke, Jonson's patron, who gave him an annual book allowance of 20 pounds. The 1616 folio is dedicated to Pembroke and his brother, the Earl of Montgomery.

0.3. *AND BLOOD*] The niece of Sir Philip Sidney, she herself patronised, and participated in, the arts. She danced in *The Masque of Blackness* (1605), and published sonnets and songs with her pastoral romance *Urania* in 1621.

2–3. *In . . . sacrificers*] From Seneca, *De Beneficiis* 1.6.2.

4. *gums*] Incense made from the gums of various trees. *in the sight of*] Compared with.
hecatomb] Great public sacrifice, literally of a hundred oxen; loosely, any vast offering.

6. *light and witness*] Truth and acts of piety. *conscience*] Consciousness, awareness.

10. *assiduity*] Daily application; 'dailiness' in Q. *custom*] Familiarity, frequency. *This*] Jonson's dedication praising Lady Wroth.

lest it talk or look like one of the ambitious faces of the time who, the more they paint, are the less themselves.

Your Ladyship's
true honourer,   15
Ben Jonson

12. *faces*] Impudent rascals, hypocrites; perhaps playing on 'Face', the chief trickster and role-player of the comedy.
13. *paint*] Put on cosmetics.

THE PERSONS OF THE PLAY

SUBTLE, *the alchemist*
FACE, *the housekeeper*
DOL COMMON, *their colleague*
DAPPER, *a clerk*
[ABEL] DRUGGER, *a tobacco-man*   5
LOVEWIT, *master of the house*
[SIR] EPICURE MAMMON, *a knight*
[PERTINAX] SURLY, *a gamester*
TRIBULATION [WHOLESOME], *a pastor of Amsterdam*
ANANIAS, *a deacon there*   10
KASTRIL, *the angry boy*

1. *SUBTLE*] Crafty, wickedly cunning, insidiously sly, wily. The name implies abstruse and devious contrivances that can delude even the most observant or analytical of minds.
2. *FACE*] Impudence; brazen effrontery. *housekeeper*] Caretaker.
3. *DOL COMMON*] Type-name for a common plaything or whore.
4. *DAPPER*] Applied to a little person who is trim and smart in his ways and appearance (*OED*); a little ape of fashion.
5. *DRUGGER*] Druggist. *tobacco-man*] Tobacconist.
6. *LOVEWIT*] The name is never actually used in the play, but does prepare the reader for his appreciation of Face's cleverness.
7. *EPICURE*] Atheist and voluptuary, particularly given to the pleasures of eating (he is often described as fat); generally self-indulgent. *MAMMON*] Money, from the Aramaic word for 'riches', occurring in the Greek and Vulgate testaments, and used by medieval writers as the proper name for the devil of covetousness.
8. *PERTINAX*] Obstinate; also the name of a Roman emperor whose over-ambitious attempts at universal reform led to his own death (M. Butler 1989). *SURLY*] Supercilious, arrogant; aspiring to greatness (see *Epigrams* 28, 'On Don Surly'). Although *OED* claims that the idea of 'rude' or 'ill-humoured' dates from 1670, the context supports these meanings as well. *gamester*] Unscrupulous gambler; a gigolo (see *Epigrams* 69 and 82).
9. *TRIBULATION*] Puritan name, one of many advertising a family's godliness; see 3.2.92–7. *Amsterdam*] Where many English puritans took refuge, the Dutch being more tolerant of religious extremists.
10. *ANANIAS*] Another puritan name, based on the notion that, since all children are born in original sin, they might be named after any sinners in the Bible. At 2.5.72, Subtle refers to the Ananias of Acts 5:1–10 who greedily appropriated money owed to the community – the same crime Ananias tries to justify in the play.
11. *KASTRIL*] A small hawk, or windhover; figuratively, a busy fool (see *SW* 1.4.66 and 4.4.163). *angry boy*] A fashionable roisterer, of a set also known as roaring boys or terrible boys who entrapped victims into duels.

DAME PLIANT, *his sister, a widow*
NEIGHBOURS
OFFICERS
MUTES   15

The scene: London

12. *PLIANT*] Easily swayed to follow any particular course.
15. *MUTES*] The only mute given specific on-stage action is the Parson of the final scene.
    Possibly the 'Good wives' (1.3.1) and the fishwife and the bawd of Lambeth (1.4.1, 3)
    had walk-on parts.

THE ARGUMENT*

T he sickness hot, a master quit, for fear,
H is house in town, and left one servant there.
E ase him corrupted and gave means to know
A cheater and his punk who, now brought low
L eaving their narrow practice, were become   5
C ozeners at large and, only wanting some
H ouse to set up, with him they here contract,
E ach for a share, and all begin to act.
M uch company they draw, and much abuse
I n casting figures, telling fortunes, news,   10
S elling of flies, flat bawdry, with the *stone*,
T ill it and they and all in *fume* are gone.

*   The metaphor of lines 7–9, with its references to the 'house' (playhouse), the 'contract' and 'share' among those partners who 'act', and the 'company' (audience), makes explicit the connection among alchemical/magus scams, business practices, and theatrical performance.

1. *sickness hot*] The plague, virulent during 1609–10.
3. *Ease*] Indolence, lack of work.
4. *punk*] Prostitute.
5. *narrow practice*] Small-scale criminal dealings.
6. *Cozeners*] Confidence-tricksters. *at large*] At liberty, ready to engage in new (and bigger) business.
10. *casting figures*] Drawing up horoscopes. *news*] Ranging from local gossip to international events, in response to public demand for information in the pre-newspaper era.
11. *flies*] Personal spirits, or familiars; demons were supposed to materialise as flies. *flat bawdry*] Outright prostitution. *stone*] The philosopher's stone, but also punning on 'testicle'. The implication is that the quest for the philosopher's stone is only a cover for grosser titillation.
12. *in fume*] In vapour; referring both to the alchemical explosion of 4.5.65, and to the way the whole confidence-game vanished into thin air.

PROLOGUE*

Fortune, that favours fools, these two short hours
    We wish away, both for your sakes and ours,
Judging spectators, and desire in place
    To th' author justice, to ourselves but grace.
Our scene is London, 'cause we would make known   5
    No country's mirth is better than our own.
No clime breeds better matter for your whore,
    Bawd, squire, impostor, many persons more,
Whose manners, now call'd humours, feed the stage,
    And which have still been subject for the rage   10
Or spleen of comic writers. Though this pen
    Did never aim to grieve but better men,
Howe'er, the age he lives in doth endure
    The vices that she breeds above their cure.
But when the wholesome remedies are sweet   15
    And in their working gain and profit meet,
He hopes to find no spirit so much diseas'd
    But will with such fair correctives be pleas'd.
For here he doth not fear who can apply.
    If there be any that will sit so nigh   20
Unto the stream, to look what it doth run,
    They shall find things they'd think or wish were done:
They are so natural follies, but so shown
    As even the doers may see and yet not own.

---

*   The actor who delivers these lines speaks on behalf of Jonson ('th' author', 1) and the other players ('ourselves'). He wears a black cloak that both announces his function and hides his costume for his role within the play. Generally trumpets sounded to warn the audience, prior to the Prologue's entrance.

1. *Fortune*] Good luck. The actor compliments the audience, whose just opinion of the play will reward the company's skill; luck will have nothing to do with it. *two short hours*] Conventionally, the length of performance, but frequently three or more hours of actual stage-time.

8. *squire*] Pimp.

9. *humours*] Character-types, really caricatures, based on obsessive singlemindedness.

10. *still*] Always.

12. *grieve*] Afflict. *better*] Correct, or improve.

19. *here*] In this audience. *apply*] Twist general meaning into particular satire.

23. *natural*] Lifelike, recognisably part of all human nature.

24. *see ... not own*] Observe without feeling personally abused.

ACT 1

Act 1 scene 1*

[*Enter*] Face [*and*] Subtle [*quarrelling violently, followed by*]
   Dol Common [*attempting to quiet them*]

FACE [*Threatening with his sword*] Believe't, I will.
SUBTLE   Thy worst! I fart at thee!
DOL Ha' you your wits? Why, gentlemen! For love –
FACE Sirrah, I'll strip you –
SUBTLE   What to do? Lick figs
    Out at my –
FACE   Rogue, rogue, out of all your sleights!
DOL Nay, look ye! Sovereign, General, are you madmen?   5

  [*She holds Face back*]

SUBTLE O, let the wild sheep loose! I'll gum your silks
    With good strong water, an' you come.

  [*He threatens Face with a flask*]

DOL   Will you have
    The neighours hear you? Will you betray all?
    Hark, I hear somebody!

*   This bizarrely original opening scene defines the uneasy alliance among the three partners in crime: the atmosphere of distrust and malice, the competition for dominance, and the fear of discovery by outsiders create a peculiar tension of literalised vitriol and violence, rendered hilarious by the frustration at having to argue in whispers and mime. Subtle's complaint, 'I do not hear well' (24), may be related to the criminal/occultist career of Edward Kelly, or Kelley, whose ears were cropped in 1580 for coining. He apparently wore a turban to hide the disfigurement; contemporary staging might have taken advantage of this costuming trick. Face accuses Subtle of 'barbing' at 114; Subtle represents himself to the Anabaptists as a forger of Dutch coins at 3.2.140–58, and they try to hire him at 4.7.75–8. Mammon refers to Kelly at 4.1.90.
1. *Thy worst!*] Do thy worst.
3. *figs*] Slang for piles. Refers to Rabelais's tale of Frederic Barbarossa's revenge on the Milanese rebels who chased his empress out of town tied backwards on a mule; those who removed a fig from the mule's posteriors with their teeth might be saved, but all others were to be executed immediately (*Pantagruel* 4.45).
4. *sleights*] Tricks.
5. *Sovereign, General*] Elevated titles intended to restore them to dignified behaviour. Face wears a Captain's uniform.
6. *wild sheep*] Blabbermouth. A sheep's head is all jaw; hence the term of abuse for a ranting opponent.   *gum your silks*] Spoil the fine uniform Face is wearing.
7. *strong water*] Acid, in the flask with which Subtle is armed.

[*Pause. The quarrel continues in hoarse whispers*]

FACE   Sirrah –
SUBTLE   I shall mar
    All that the tailor has made if you approach.   10
FACE   You most notorious whelp, you insolent slave!
    Dare you do this?
SUBTLE   Yes, faith, yes, faith!
FACE   Why! Who
    Am I, my mongrel? Who am I?
SUBTLE   I'll tell you,
    Since you know not yourself –
FACE   Speak lower, rogue.
SUBTLE   Yes. You were once (time's not long past) the good,   15
    Honest, plain, livery-three-pound-thrum that kept
    Your master's worship's house here in the Friars
    For the vacations –
FACE   Will you be so loud?
SUBTLE   – Since, by my means, translated suburb-captain.
FACE   By your means, Doctor Dog?   20
SUBTLE   Within man's memory,
    All this I speak of.
FACE   Why, I pray you, have I
    Been countenanced by you? or you by me?
    Do but collect, sir, where I met you first.

9–10. *mar ... made*] Reversing the proverb, 'The tailor makes the man': will destroy Face's new uniform, and possibly his manhood too.

11. *whelp*] Common term of abuse for impertinence; see 13, 20.

16. *livery-three-pound-thrum*] Cheap shabby servant. *Thrum*, coarse material used for servants' livery, contrasts vividly with the elaborate uniform Face wears now; also slang for 'beat up' and 'fornicate', the term suggests Face is a crude bully. *Three-pound* gibes at his wages as a caretaker, when he was a 'good, Honest, plain' fellow – implying 'not too bright'. Subtle considers himself the brains of the operation, and Face a mere thug.

17. *Friars*] Blackfriars, the liberty between St Paul's and the Thames, which retained its old monastic right of sanctuary and thus had a mixed population of thieves, artists, and puritans living among the aristocrats who had converted disestablished church buildings into residences; also the location of the theatre for which the play was written.

18. *vacations*] Intervals between legal terms when court was in session.

19. *translated*] Transformed into; promoted to. *suburb-*] Bogus; suburbs were associated with petty crime and prostitution.

20. *Doctor*] A sneer at Subtle's masquerade as a scholar.

22. *countenanced*] Supported by a patron; given a front.

23. *collect*] Recollect.

SUBTLE   I do not hear well.

FACE   Not of this, I think it.
    But I shall put you in mind, sir: at Pie Corner,   25
    Taking your meal of steam in from cooks' stalls
    Where, like the father of hunger, you did walk
    Piteously costive, with your pinched-horn-nose
    And your complexion of the Roman wash,
    Stuck full of black and melancholic worms   30
    Like powder corns shot at th'Artillery Yard.

SUBTLE   I wish you would advance your voice a little.

FACE   When you went pinned up in the several rags
    You'd raked and picked from dunghills before day,
    Your feet in mouldy slippers for your kibes,   35
    A felt of rug and a thin threaden cloak
    That scarce would cover your no-buttocks –

SUBTLE   So, sir!

FACE   When all your *alchemy* and your *algebra*,
    Your *minerals*, *vegetals*, and *animals*,
    Your conjuring, cozening, and your dozen of trades   40
    Could not relieve your corpse with so much linen
    Would make you tinder but to see a fire,
    I ga' you count'nance, credit for your coals,

25. *Pie-Corner*] Formerly the site of an inn south of Smithfield with the sign of a magpie; later an area of cookshops, popular as a meeting-place for ruffians and indigents.

28. *costive*] Constipated; slow-moving. *pinched-horn-nose*] Syphilitic condition, referring to the sores (pinches) caused by syphilis, the disease obviously advanced because of the decayed nose and deterioration of the skin. 'Nose' and 'horn' were common colloquialisms for 'penis'.

29. *Roman wash*] Face-paint or herbal remedy to cover sores; perhaps simply a swarthy complexion.

30. *worms*] Blackheads; perhaps ringworm or similar infestation.

31. *powder-corns*] Unexploded grains of gunpowder. *Artillery Yard*] A practice range east of Bishopsgate used by the Honourable Artillery Company, a militia newly reorganised in 1610, and by other amateur bodies; often satirised as evidence of a degenerate society whose noblemen reject their responsibility to defend.

32. *advance your voice*] Speak up.

35. *kibes*] Chilblains.

36. *felt of rug*] Hat of coarse woollen cloth. *thin threaden*] Threadbare.

38–9. The italics emphasise Face's mimicry of Subtle's alchemical jargon.

38. *algebra*] Mistakenly associated by sound with the Arab alchemist Al-Djaber (Mares 1967). But mathematics had been associated with alchemy since Pythagoras.

41. *linen*] Underclothes; graveclothes. Linen scraps were twisted with other flammable waste for use as spills or tinder.

Your stills, your glasses, your *materials*,
Built you a furnace, drew you customers,   45
Advanced all your black arts; lent you, beside,
A house to practise in –
SUBTLE   Your master's house?
FACE   Where you have studied the more thriving skill
Of bawdry, since.
SUBTLE   Yes, in your master's house.
You and the rats here kept possession.   50
Make it not strange. I know y'were one could keep
The buttery-hatch still locked and save the chippings,
Sell the dole-beer to *aqua-vitae* men,
The which, together with your Christmas vails,
At 'post and pair' your letting out of counters,   55
Made you a pretty stock, some twenty marks,
And gave you credit to converse with cobwebs
Here since your mistress' death hath broke up house.
FACE   You might talk softlier, rascal.
SUBTLE   [*His voice gradually rising*] No, you scarab,
I'll thunder you in pieces. I will teach you   60
How to beware to tempt a fury again
That carries tempest in his hand and voice.
FACE   The place has made you valiant.
SUBTLE   [*Becoming louder*]   No, your clothes.

44. *stills*] Alembics, retorts used to distil liquids. *glasses*] Flasks or vials. *materials*]
Basic ingredients for making the philosopher's stone, especially sulphur and mercury.
45. *furnace*] For the constant heat needed to distil the elixir, the final product of alchemy
that turns base metal into gold.
49. *bawdry*] Running a brothel.
51. *Make it not strange*] Don't pretend not to understand.
51–3. *I know ... men*] Subtle accuses Face of taking for his own profit food and drink
normally distributed as dole to the poor at the kitchen-door (*buttery-hatch*) of any
comfortable household; *chippings* (dole-bread) were crusts of bread; *dole-beer*, leftover
wine and beer, could be sold to *aqua-vitae men*, who distilled and resold it as hard
liquor.
54. *vails*] Tips given to servants.
55. *post and pair*] Card game in which the winning hand was three of a kind. *letting out
of counters*] Supplying gambling chips to the players for a fee.
56. *twenty marks*] About 14 pounds, a measly profit compared to their illicit gains during
the play.
59. *scarab*] Dung-beetle.
61. *fury*] Avenging spirit. The folio text has '*furie*'againe', the apostrophe indicating that,
in the interests of exact poetic metre, the vowels should be elided to 'fury 'gain'.
63. *your clothes*] A gibe at Face's false bravery as 'Captain'.

Thou vermin, have I ta'en thee out of dung,
So poor, so wretched, when no living thing   65
Would keep thee company but a spider or worse?
Raised thee from brooms and dust and watering pots?
Sublimed thee and *exalted* thee and *fixed* thee
I'the *third region*, called our *state of grace*?
Wrought thee to *spirit*, to *quintessence*, with pains   70
Would twice have won me the *philosopher's work*?
Put thee in words and fashion? Made thee fit
For more than ordinary fellowships?
Giv'n thee thy oaths, thy quarrelling dimensions?
Thy rules to cheat at horse-race, cockpit, cards,   75
Dice, or whatever gallant tincture else?
Made thee a second in mine own great art?
And have I this for thanks? Do you rebel?
Do you fly out i' the *projection*?
Would you be gone now?   80

DOL   Gentlemen, what mean you?
   Will you mar all?

SUBTLE   Slave, thou hadst had no name –
DOL Will you undo yourselves with civil war?
SUBTLE – Never been known, past *equi clibanum*,
   The heat of horse-dung, underground, in cellars,

68–71. Alchemical jargon by which Subtle claims his transmutation of Face from a base
butler into a higher class of being.

68. *Sublimed*] Vaporised. *exalted*] Concentrated or purified. *fixed*] Stabilised, solidi-
fied.

69. *third region*] Air is divided into lower, middle, and upper regions, of which the third
is the purest.

70. *spirit*] The essence informing matter, associated with mercury. *quintessence*] The
fifth essence, a heavenly element refined from sulphur and quicksilver that can
transform the other four (earth, air, fire, water) into the philosopher's stone.

71. *philosopher's work*] The elixir, or stone.

72. *Put thee in words and fashion*] Taught you fashionable patter and behaviour.

73. *ordinary*] Punning on 'commonplace', and 'eating-house', where a small-time crook
might find a dupe to fleece.

74. *oaths ... quarrelling dimensions*] Swearing and rules for picking fights (see 3.4.25–41)
that would establish Face as a trendy roisterer or angry boy.

76. *tincture*] Another alchemical term, a spiritual quality or colour that infuses and
transforms material bodies.

79. *fly out*] Explode, like a spoiled alchemical experiment. *projection*] Final stage of the
alchemical process: adding the powdered stone to the molten metal to turn it into gold.

83. *equi clibanum*] Translated in the next line, 'heat of horse-dung'. Manure was used as
a fuel for the gentle heat required in the initial phase of the alchemical process.

Or an alehouse, darker than Deaf John's, been lost   85
To all mankind but laundresses and tapsters,
Had not I been.
DOL   D'you know who hears you, Sovereign?
FACE   Sirrah –
DOL   Nay, General, I thought you were civil –
FACE   I shall turn desperate if you grow thus loud.
SUBTLE   And hang thyself, I care not.   90
FACE   [*Also becoming louder*]   Hang thee, collier,
And all thy pots and pans in picture, I will,
Since thou hast moved me –
DOL   [*Aside*]   O, this'll o'erthrow all!
FACE   Write thee up bawd in Paul's; have all thy tricks
Of cozening with a hollow coal, dust, scrapings,
Searching for things lost with a sieve and shears,   95
Erecting *figures* in your rows of *houses*,
And taking in of shadows with a glass,
Told in red letters. And a face cut for thee
Worse than Gamaliel Ratsey's.
DOL   Are you sound?
Ha' you your senses, masters?   100
FACE   I will have
A book but barely reckoning thy impostures

85. *Deaf John's*] An unidentified alehouse.
90. *collier*] Coal-carrier; a filthy job assumed to be fit only for a blackguard. Proverbially,
  'Like will to like, quoth the devil to the collier'.
91. *in picture*] In a drawing. Face threatens (93–9) to post an illustrated notice in St Paul's
  (the west doors were used for messages and advertisements) giving public warning
  against Subtle and his fraudulent schemes.
94. *hollow coal, dust, scrapings*] The trick is to fill and seal a hollow coal with silver or
  gold filings, so that when the coal is heated, the nugget spills out, thus producing
  alchemical results for the gullible.
95. *sieve and shears*] 'Divining' with a pair of open scissors stuck in a wooden sieve held
  in the air, first chanting biblical verses, and then naming possible thieves, or places
  where lost items might be found, until the sieve spins at the right answer.
96. *figures*] Horoscopes.   *houses*] Signs of the zodiac.
97. *shadows ... glass*] Spirits raised in a magic mirror or crystal ball.
98. *red letters ... face cut*] Face is describing the broadside sheet of his advertisement,
  complete with special type and woodcut.
99. *Gamaliel Ratsey*] A highwayman, executed in 1605, who wore an ugly mask when
  committing robberies.   *sound*] Sane.
101–2. *book ... printers*] Face expands the single sheet exposing Subtle as a fraud into a
  book that, as a best-seller, will produce as much gold for the printers as any
  philosopher's stone.

Shall prove a true *philosopher's stone* to printers.
SUBTLE   Away, you trencher-rascal.
FACE   Out, you dog-leech,
    The vomit of all prisons –
DOL   Will you be
    Your own destructions, gentlemen?   105
FACE   – still spewed out
    For lying too heavy o'the basket.
SUBTLE   Cheater!
FACE   Bawd!
SUBTLE   Cowherd!
FACE   Conjuror!
SUBTLE   Cutpurse!
FACE   Witch!
DOL   O me!
    We are ruined! Lost! Ha'you no more regard
    To your reputations? Where's your judgment? 'Slight,
    Have yet some care of me, o'your *republic* –   110
FACE   Away this brach. [*Pushes Dol aside*] I'll bring thee, rogue, within
    The statute of sorcery, *tricesimo tertio.*
    Of Harry the eight. Ay, and perhaps thy neck
    Within a noose for laundering gold and barbing it.
DOL   You'll bring your head within a coxcomb, will you?   115

She catcheth out Face his sword, and breaks Subtle's glass

    And you, sir, with your *menstrue*, gather it up.
    'Sdeath, you abominable pair of stinkards,
    Leave off your barking and grow one again

103. *trencher-rascal*] A 'trencher-knight' is a servant at table; Subtle's substitution of 'rascal' suggests inferior, unreliable service.   *dog-leech*] A variation of 'Doctor Dog' (20).
106. *lying ... basket*] Overeating from the basket of scraps sent by the sheriff for prisoners who could not buy their own food.
110. *republic*] In the political analogy Dol has pursued since 83, she refers to their 'commonwealth of joint interests', but also to herself as the literal *res publica*, 'common thing', they share.
111. *brach*] Bitch.
112–13. *statute ... Harry the eight*] Forbidding the practice of witchcraft and conjuring, passed in 1541, the thirty-third year of Henry's reign; it was passed again in 1604 under James I, and finally repealed in 1689.
114. *laundering gold*] Washing it in acid to dissolve and reuse some of the gold.
    barbing] Clipping the edges. Defacing the coinage was a capital offence.
115. *coxcomb*] A fool's headgear. Dol means Face is making a fool of himself.
116. *menstrue*] Solvent.

Or, by the light that shines, I'll cut your throats.
I'll not be made a prey unto the marshal   120
For ne'er a snarling dog-bolt o' you both.
Ha' you together cozened all this while
And all the world, and shall it now be said
You've made most courteous shift to cozen yourselves?
[*To Face*] You will accuse him? You will bring him in   125
Within the statute? Who shall take your word?
A whoreson upstart apocryphal captain,
Whom not a puritan in Blackfriars will trust
So much as for a feather! [*To Subtle*] And you too
Will give the cause, forsooth? You will insult   130
And claim a primacy in the divisions?
You must be chief? As if you only had
The powder to project with? And the work
Were not begun out of equality?
The venture tripartite? All things in common?   135
Without priority? 'Sdeath, you perpetual curs,
Fall to your couples again and cozen kindly,
And heartily, and lovingly as you should,
And lose not the beginning of a term,
Or by this hand I shall grow factious too,   140
And take my part, and quit you.
FACE   'Tis his fault.
He ever murmurs and objects his pains,
And says the weight of all lies upon him.
SUBTLE Why so it does.
DOL   How does it? Do not we
Sustain our parts?   145

120. *marshal*] The provost-marshal charged offenders, heard cases, gave sentence, and maintained a prison in Southwark.
121. *dog-bolt*] Blunt arrow, noisy but not dangerous.
127. *apocryphal*] Phoney.
129. *feather*] The trade in feathers for fashion accessories was largely managed by puritans in Blackfriars.
131. *claim ... divisions*] Be the leader of the pack.
133. *powder*] Powdered stone used in alchemical transmutations; but Dol refers metaphorically to the power to dazzle their dupes.
137. *couples*] Hunting-dogs worked in pairs.
139. *term*] When the lawcourts sat, and many people (potential dupes) came to town for business or pleasure. If the play takes place in late October, 1610, Michaelmas Term would be in session.
140. *factious*] Quarrelsome, divisive.
141. *part*] Share.

SUBTLE   Yes, but they are not equal.
DOL   Why, if your part exceed today, I hope
       Ours may tomorrow match it.
SUBTLE   Ay, they may.
DOL   'May', murmuring mastiff? Ay, and do. Death on me!
       [*To Face*] Help me to throttle him!

       [*Dol begins to strangle Subtle, who wrestles with her*]

SUBTLE   Dorothy, Mistress Dorothy,
       'Ods precious, I'll do anything. What do you mean?   150
DOL   Because o' your *fermentation* and *cibation*?
SUBTLE   Not I, by heaven –
DOL   Your *Sol* and *Luna* – [*To Face*] Help me!
SUBTLE   Would I were hanged then. [*Gagging*] I'll conform myself.
DOL   Will you, sir? Do so, then, and quickly. Swear!
SUBTLE   What should I swear?   155
DOL   To leave your faction, sir.
       And labour kindly in the common work.
SUBTLE   [*Gasping*] Let me not breathe if I meant aught beside.
       I only used those speeches as a spur
       To him.
DOL   I hope we need no spurs, sir. Do we?
FACE   'Slid, prove today who shall shark best.   160
SUBTLE   Agreed.
DOL   Yes, and work close and friendly.
SUBTLE   'Slight, the knot
       Shall grow the stronger for this breach with me.

       [*Dol releases him*]

DOL   Why so, my good baboons! Shall we go make
       A sort of sober, scurvy, precise neighbours,
       That scarce have smiled twice sin' the king came in,   165
       A feast of laughter at our follies? Rascals,
       Would run themselves from breath to see me ride

150. *'Ods precious*] By God's precious body (or blood).
151. *fermentation and cibation*] Alchemical processes, infusing with air (sixth stage) and
      then with liquid (seventh stage).
152. *Sol and Luna*] Sun and moon, representing gold and siver, and the parents of all
      metals, sulphur and mercury.
160. *shark*] Cheat. Face's challenge and Subtle's agreement shape their rivalry and one-
      upmanship throughout the rest of the play.
164. *sort*] Group. *precise*] Puritan.
167. *ride*] Be carted as a whore.

Or you t'have but a hole to thrust your heads in,
For which you should pay ear-rent? No, agree.
And may Don Provost ride a-feasting long   170
In his old velvet jerkin and stained scarves,
My noble Sovereign and worthy General,
Ere we contribute a new crewel garter
To his most worsted worship.

SUBTLE   Royal Dol!
Spoken like Claridiana, and thyself!   175

FACE   For which, at supper, thou shalt sit in triumph
And be not styled Dol Common, but Dol Proper,
Dol Singular. The longest cut at night
Shall draw thee for his Dol Particular.

[*Bell rings*]

SUBTLE   Who's that? One rings. To the window, Dol.   180

[*Exit Dol*]

                                              Pray heaven
The master do not trouble us this quarter.

FACE   O fear not him. While there dies one a week
O'the plague, he's safe from thinking toward London.
Beside, he's busy at his hopyards now.
I had a letter from him. If he do,   185
He'll send such word for airing o'the house
As you shall have sufficient time to quit it.
Though we break up a fortnight, 'tis no matter.

[*Enter Dol*]

SUBTLE   Who is it, Dol?
DOL   A fine young quodling.
FACE   O,

168–9. *have ... ear-rent*] Be pilloried and have your ears clipped. If Subtle is being played as a Kelly whose ears have already been clipped, Dol would address these lines to Face, perhaps indicating Subtle as a case in point.

170. *Don Provost*] The provost-marshal, but here referring to his hangman, entitled to the victims' clothes.

173. *crewel*] Worsted yarn, punning on the 'cruel garter', the hangman's rope.

174. *worsted*] Continues the 'crewel' pun; also punning on 'defeated' or 'thwarted'.

175. *Claridiana*] Heroine of a popular Spanish romance, *The Mirror of Knighthood*.

178–9. *longest cut ... Dol Particular*] That is, Subtle and Face shall draw straws to see who sleeps with Dol that night.

189. *quodling*] An unripe apple, a raw youth; perhaps joking on legal-Latin phrasing (*quod*) to describe the junior law-clerk.

My lawyer's clerk I lighted on last night   190
In Holborn at the Dagger. He would have
(I told you of him) a *familiar*
To rifle with at horses and win cups.
DOL   O, let him in.
SUBTLE   Stay. Who shall do't?
FACE   Get you
Your robes on. I will meet him, as going out.   195
DOL   And what shall I do?
FACE   Not be seen. Away.

   [*Exit Dol*]

Seem you very reserved.
SUBTLE   Enough.

   [*Exit Subtle by one stage door; Face opens the other door, as though
   he were a departing guest*]

FACE   God b'w'you, sir.
I pray you, let him know that I was here.
His name is Dapper. I would gladly have stayed, but –

   Act 1 scene 2*

DAPPER   [*Within*] Captain, I am here.
FACE   Who's that? He's come, I think, Doctor.

   [*Enter*] *Dapper*

Good faith, sir, I was going away.
DAPPER   In truth,
I'm very sorry, Captain.
FACE   But I thought
Sure I should meet you.
DAPPER   Ay, I'm very glad.
I'd a scurvy writ or two to make,   5

191. *the Dagger*] A tavern famous for its pies.
192. *familiar*] Spirit to assist him at gambling.
193. *rifle*] Gamble.
199. *stayed*] Waited.
*   Like *Volp*, the first act of this play is filled with visits from various dupes. Dapper's
     request here for a gambling fly was not uncommon. In the 1570s, Adam Squire was
     almost expelled as Master of Balliol College, Oxford, for selling gambling flies. Like Dr
     Read (l. 17), Dr Elkes, a conjurer, supplied a client with a gambling ring that contained
     a spirit and a Hebrew spell (Thomas 1971: p. 231).

And I had lent my watch last night to one
That dines today at the sheriff's, and so was robbed
Of my pass-time.

[*Enter Subtle in his alchemist's robes, remaining aloof*]

                           Is this the cunning-man?

FACE   This is his worship.

DAPPER   Is he a doctor?

FACE   Yes.

DAPPER   And ha' you broke with him, Captain?   10

FACE   Ay.

DAPPER   And how?

FACE   Faith, he does make the matter, sir, so dainty,
     I know not what to say –

DAPPER   Not so, good Captain.

FACE   Would I were fairly rid on't, believe me.

DAPPER   Nay, now you grieve me, sir. Why should you wish so?
     I dare assure you. I'll not be ungrateful.   15

FACE   I cannot think you will, sir. But the law
     Is such a thing – And then, he says, Read's matter
     Falling so lately –

DAPPER   Read? He was an ass
     And dealt, sir, with a fool.

FACE   It was a clerk, sir.

DAPPER   A clerk?   20

FACE   Nay, hear me, sir, you know the law
     Better, I think –

DAPPER   I should, sir, and the danger.
     You know I showed the statute to you?

FACE   You did so.

DAPPER   And will I tell, then? By this hand of flesh,
     Would it might never write good court-hand more,
     If I discover. What do you think of me,   25

---

6. *lent my watch*] A watch was an expensive and prestigious item; hence, sought after by the upwardly mobile.

7. *sheriff's*] The metre is better served by F's obsolete one-syllable *shrieffs* (= shrieve's).

8. *pass-time*] Because showing how time passes. *cunning-man*] One learned in esoteric arts; witch.

10. *broke with him*] Told him what I want.

11. *make . . . dainty*] Fret over the difficulties, feel leery about it.

17. *Read's matter*] Dr Simon Read of Southwark was charged and pardoned in 1608 for successfully raising spirits who gave information leading to the recovery of money stolen from Toby Matthews (the 'fool' of l. 19).

24. *court-hand*] The handwriting used in the court records.

                    That I am a *chiaus*?
FACE   What's that?
DAPPER   The Turk was here –
        As one would say, do you think I am a Turk?
FACE   I'll tell the Doctor so.
DAPPER   Do, good sweet Captain.

        [*Face approaches Subtle, Dapper trailing behind*]

FACE   Come, noble Doctor, pray thee, let's prevail.
        This is the gentleman, and he is no *chiaus*.   30
SUBTLE   Captain, I have returned you all my answer.
        I would do much, sir, for your love – But this
        I neither may nor can.
FACE   Tut, do not say so.
        You deal now with a noble fellow, Doctor,
        One that will thank you richly, and he's no *chiaus*.   35
        Let that, sir, move you. [*Offers money*]
SUBTLE   [*Refuses it*]   Pray you, forbear –
FACE   [*Offering it again*]   He has
        Four angels here –
SUBTLE   [*Refusing*]   You do me wrong, good sir.
FACE   Doctor, wherein? To tempt you with these spirits?
SUBTLE   To tempt my art and love, sir, to my peril.
        'Fore heaven, I scarce can think you are my friend,   40
        That so would draw me to apparent danger.
FACE   I draw you? A horse draw you, and a halter,
        You and your flies together –
DAPPER   Nay, good Captain.
FACE   – That know no difference of men.
SUBTLE   Good words, sir.
FACE   Good deeds, sir, Doctor Dogs-meat. 'Slight, I bring you   45
        No cheating Clim-o'the-Cloughs or Claribels

26. *chiaus*] Cheat, from the Turkish word for 'messenger'. *The Turk was here*] From
    July to November 1607, a Turk posing as the Sultan's ambassador (though only using
    the title *Chaush*) had all his expenses in England paid by the Levant Company, even
    though his credentials were disputed. The swindle was exposed after the fact.
36. *angels*] Gold coins engraved with the figure of the Archangel Michael fighting a
    dragon.
38. *spirits*] Punning on the angels.
42. *horse . . . halter*] May a horse draw you in a cart to your own hanging.
43. *flies*] Familiar spirits.
45. *Dog's-meat*] Offal.
46. *Clim-o'the-Cloughs*] Outlaw in 'The Ballad of Adam Bell', reprinted by William
    Jaggard in 1610.   *Claribel*] The lewd knight in *The Faerie Queene* 4.9.

That look as big as *five-and-fifty* and *flush*,
And spit out secrets like hot custard –
DAPPER   Captain!
FACE – Nor any melancholic under-scribe
     Shall tell the vicar, but a special gentle   50
     That is the heir to forty marks a year,
     Consorts with the small poets of the time,
     Is the sole hope of his old grandmother,
     That knows the law and writes you six fair hands,
     Is a fine clerk and has his ciphering perfect,   55
     Will take his oath o'the Greek Xenophon,
     If need be, in his pocket, and can court
     His mistress out of Ovid.
DAPPER   Nay, dear Captain.
FACE Did you not tell me so?
DAPPER   Yes, but I'd ha' you
     Use Master Doctor with some more respect.   60
FACE Hang him, proud stag, with his broad velvet head.
     But for your sake, I'd choke ere I would change
     An article of breath with such a puckfist –
     Come, let's be gone.

     [*Going*]

SUBTLE   Pray you, le'me speak with you.
DAPPER His worship calls you, Captain.   65
FACE   I am sorry
     I e'er embarked myself in such a business.
DAPPER Nay, good sir. He did call you.
FACE [*Waving the money*]   Will he take, then?
SUBTLE First, hear me –

47. *five-and-fifty and flush*] The 'prime' or winning hand in primero, holding ace (1 point), seven, six, and five (added and trebled, 54 points) for a total of 55, all in one suit.
50. *vicar*] Vicar-general, bishop's deputy in the ecclesiastical court, acting on sorcery cases.
55. *six fair hands*] The six styles of penmanship used for various documents: court-hand, English and French secretary, Italic, Roman, and chancery.
55. *ciphering*] Book-keeping.
56. *Xenophon*] 'Testament' in Q. The conveniently pocketed Greek book suggests that Dapper wants to appear scholarly, and swearing on it suggests either that no one could tell the difference between that and a bible, or that oaths taken on a political text cannot be expected to be other than self-serving.
58. *Ovid*] Probably from *Amores* and *Ars Amatoria*, but perhaps, like Volpone's fantasy at 3.7.20, play-acting the 'changed shapes' of the *Metamorphoses*.
61. *velvet head*] Doctors wore velvet caps.
63. *puckfist*] Empty boaster.

FACE   Not a syllable, 'less you take.
SUBTLE   Pray y', sir –
FACE   Upon no terms but an *assumpsit*.
SUBTLE   Your humour must be law.   70

    He takes the money

FACE   Why now, sir, talk.
    Now I dare hear you with mine honour. Speak.
    So may this gentleman too.
SUBTLE   [*To Face as if aside*] Why, sir –
FACE   No whispering.
SUBTLE   'Fore heaven, you do not apprehend the loss
    You do yourself in this.
FACE   Wherein? For what?
SUBTLE   Marry, to be so importunate for one   75
    That, when he has it, will undo you all.
    He'll win up all the money i'the town.
FACE   How!
SUBTLE   Yes. And blow up gamester after gamester
    As they do crackers in a puppet-play.
    If I do give him a familiar,   80
    Give you him all you play for. Never set him,
    For he will have it.
FACE   You're mistaken, Doctor.
    Why, he does ask one but for cups and horses,
    A rifling fly. None o' your great familiars.
DAPPER   Yes, Captain, I would have it for all games.   85
SUBTLE   I told you so.
FACE   [*Taking Dapper aside*]   'Slight, that's a new business!
    I understood you, a tame bird, to fly
    Twice in a term or so, on Friday nights
    When you had left the office. For a nag
    Of forty or fifty shillings.   90
DAPPER   Ay, 'tis true, sir,
    But I do think now I shall leave the law,
    And therefore –
FACE   Why, this changes quite the case!
    D'you think that I dare move him?

69. *assumpsit*] Legal term for voluntary verbal promise, confirmed by a fee.
78. *blow up*] Wipe out.
79. *crackers*] Fire-crackers, as in *BF* 5.4.
81. *set*] Bet against.
84. *great familiars*] Powerful demons, like Dr Faustus's Mephistophilis.
90. *Of*] Worth.

DAPPER   If you please, sir.
 All's one to him, I see.
FACE   What! For that money?
 I cannot with my conscience. Nor should you   95
 Make the request, methinks.
DAPPER   No, sir, I mean
 To add consideration.
FACE   Why then, sir,
 I'll try. [*Returns to Subtle*] Say that it were for all games, Doctor?
SUBTLE   I say, then, not a mouth shall eat for him
 At any ordinary but o'the score.   100
 That is a gaming mouth, conceive me.
FACE   Indeed!
SUBTLE   He'll draw you all the treasure of the realm,
 If it be set him.
FACE   Speak you this from art?
SUBTLE   Ay, sir, and reason too: the ground of art.
 He's o'the only best complexion   105
 The Queen of Fairy loves.
FACE   What! Is he!
SUBTLE   Peace.
 He'll overhear you. Sir, should she but see him –
FACE   What?
SUBTLE   Do not you tell him.
FACE   Will he win at cards too?
SUBTLE   The spirits of dead Holland, living Isaac,
 You'd swear were in him: such a vigorous luck   110
 As cannot be resisted. 'Slight, he'll put
 Six o' your gallants to a cloak, indeed.
FACE   A strange success that some man shall be born to!
SUBTLE   He hears you, man –
DAPPER   Sir, I'll not be ingrateful.
FACE   Faith, I have a confidence in his good nature.   115
 You hear, he says he will not be ingrateful.
SUBTLE   Why, as you please. My venture follows yours.
FACE   Troth, do it, Doctor. Think him trusty, and make him.
 He may make us both happy in an hour:

97. *consideration*] Further compensation.
99. *for*] Because of.
100. *o'the score*] On credit, having lost his cash to Dapper.
109. *of*] Conjured by. *dead Holland, living Isaac*] John and Isaac Holland, Dutch alchemists of the fifteenth century whose works were first printed between 1600 and 1608, thus giving rise to confusion about one being still alive.
118. *make him*] Make his fortune; make him a new man.

Win some five thousand pound and send us two on't.   120
DAPPER   Believe it, and I will, sir.
FACE   And you shall, sir.

Face takes him aside

You have heard all?
DAPPER   No, what was't? Nothing, I, sir.
FACE   Nothing?
DAPPER   A little, sir.
FACE   Well, a rare star
Reigned at your birth.
DAPPER   At mine, sir? No.
FACE   The Doctor
Swears that you are –   125
SUBTLE   Nay, Captain, you'll tell all now.
FACE   – Allied to the Queen of Fairy.
DAPPER   Who? That I am?
Believe it, no such matter –
FACE   Yes, and that
Y'were born with a caul o'your head.
DAPPER   Who says so?
FACE   Come.
You know it well enough, though you dissemble it.
DAPPER   I'fac, I do not. You are mistaken.   130
FACE   How!
Swear by your fac? And in a thing so known
Unto the Doctor? How shall we, sir, trust you
I'the other matter? Can we ever think,
When you have won five or six thousand pound,
You'll send us shares in't, by this rate?   135
DAPPER   By Jove, sir,
I'll win ten thousand pound and send you half.
I'fac's no oath.
SUBTLE   No, no, he did but jest.
FACE   Go to. Go, thank the Doctor. He's your friend
To take it so.
DAPPER   I thank his worship.
FACE   [*To Dapper aside*]   So?

126. *Allied*] Related.
128. *caul*] Considered a good omen, if a child is born with a portion of membrane from the
     foetal sac capping its head.
130. *I'fac*] 'In faith', so mild an oath that Dapper claims at 138 it does not even count as
     swearing.
138. *Go to*] A comment, not a directive, as in 'Go on', or 'Come off it'.

    Another angel.   140

DAPPER   Must I?

FACE   Must you? 'Slight,

    What else is thanks? Will you be trivial?

    [*Dapper gives Subtle another coin*]

                                      Doctor,

    When must he come for his familiar?

DAPPER   Shall I not ha'it with me?

SUBTLE   O, good sir!

    There must a world of ceremonies pass.

    You must be bathed and fumigated first;   145

    Besides, the Queen of Fairy does not rise

    Till it be noon.

FACE   Not if she danced tonight.

SUBTLE   And she must bless it.

FACE   Did you never see

    Her royal Grace yet?

DAPPER   Whom?

FACE   Your aunt of Fairy?

SUBTLE   Not since she kissed him in the cradle, Captain,   150

    I can resolve you that.

FACE   Well, see her Grace,

    Whate'er it cost you, for a thing that I know!

    It will be somewhat hard to compass. But,

    However, see her. You are made, believe it,

    If you can see her. Her Grace is a lone woman,   155

    And very rich, and if she take a fancy,

    She will do strange things. See her, at any hand.

    'Slid, she may hap to leave you all she has!

    It is the Doctor's fear.

DAPPER   How will't be done then?

FACE   Let me alone, take you no thought. Do you   160

    But say to me, 'Captain, I'll see her Grace.'

DAPPER   Captain, I'll see her Grace.

FACE   Enough.

---

143. *ha'it*] Take it.

147. *tonight*] Last night.

151. *resolve*] Answer.

152. *for a thing that I know*] To find out something I know to be worth your while.

153. *compass*] Arrange.

155. *lone*] Unmarried.

One knocks without

SUBTLE   [*Calling through door*]   Who's there?
          Anon! [*Aside to Face*] Conduct him forth by the back way.
          [*To Dapper*] Sir, against one o'clock, prepare yourself.
          Till when you must be fasting. Only take   165
          Three drops of vinegar in at your nose,
          Two at your mouth, and one at either ear,
          Then bathe your fingers' ends, and wash your eyes,
          To sharpen your five senses, and cry *hum*
          Thrice, and then *buzz* as often, and then come.   170
FACE   Can you remember this?
DAPPER   I warrant you.
FACE   Well then, away. 'Tis but your bestowing
          Some twenty nobles 'mong her Grace's servants,
          And put on a clean shirt. You do not know
          What grace her Grace may do you in clean linen.   175

[*Exeunt Face and Dapper*]

Act 1 scene 3*

[*Subtle opening door, enter*] Drugger

SUBTLE   Come in.

[*Calling back through still open door*]

                    – Good wives, I pray you forbear me now.
          Troth, I can do you no good till afternoon. –

[*Closes door*]

173. *twenty nobles*] Almost 7 pounds, about one-quarter of Dapper's annual income of
     'forty marks' (51), or 26 pounds.
175. *clean linen*] The emphasis is on cleaning Dapper out physically (see the directions for
     the purification of the senses at ll. 165–70), as well as financially.
*   The role of Drugger has been a crowd-pleaser since its first performance by Robert
     Armin, the clown employed by the King's Men. David Garrick revived the role to great
     acclaim in the eighteenth century, and inspired farcical sequels to capitalise on his
     popular rendition of the part. Hazlitt described Edmund Kean's similar success. Alec
     Guinness triumphed as Drugger in the Old Vic production of 1947, with a droll blend
     of pathos and what one critic called 'asininity and halitosis' (Jensen 1985: pp. 89–90).
  1. *Good wives*] Perhaps played briefly on stage by the mutes mentioned in The Persons
     of the Play, although the roles, presumably the 'fishwife' and 'The bawd of Lambeth'
     (1.4.1–3), suggest vituperatively noisy extras.

What is your name, say you, Abel Drugger?
DRUGGER   Yes, sir.
SUBTLE   A seller of tobacco?
DRUGGER   Yes, sir.
SUBTLE   'Umh.
   Free of the Grocers?   5
DRUGGER   Ay, and't please you.
SUBTLE   Well –
   Your business, Abel?
DRUGGER   This, and't please your worship,
   I'm a young beginner and am building
   Of a new shop, and't like your worship, just
   At corner of a street. [*Shows a ground-plan*] Here's the plot on't.
   And I would know by art, sir, of your worship   10
   Which way I should make my door, by necromancy.
   And where my shelves. And which should be for boxes.
   And which for pots. I would be glad to thrive, sir.
   And I was wished to your worship by a gentleman,
   One Captain Face, that says you know men's planets   15
   And their good angels and their bad.
SUBTLE   I do,
   If I do see 'em –

   [*Enter Face*]

FACE   What! My honest Abel?
   Thou art well met here!
DRUGGER   Troth, sir, I was speaking,
   Just as your worship came here, of your worship.
   I pray you, speak for me to Master Doctor.   20
FACE   He shall do anything. Doctor, do you hear?
   This is my friend Abel, an honest fellow.
   He lets me have good tobacco and he does not
   Sophisticate it with sack-lees or oil,

---

5. *Free ... Grocers*] A full member of the Grocers' Company, the guild regulating trade
   in foreign produce like tobacco.
9. *plot*] Ground-plan.
11. *necromancy*] Magic, the 'art' of the previous line.
14. *wished*] Recommended.
15. *know men's planets*] Can cast horoscopes.
16. *angels*] Attendant spirits.
24. *Sophisticate*] Adulterate. Uncured tobacco deteriorated during the journey from
   America, and mouldiness and dryness were disguised by the various means Face
   lists.   *sack-lees*] Dregs of wine.

Nor washes it in muscadel and grains,   25
Nor buries it in gravel underground
Wrapped up in greasy leather or pissed clouts,
But keeps it in fine lily-pots that, opened,
Smell like conserve of roses or French beans.
He has his maple block, his silver tongs,   30
Winchester pipes, and fire of juniper.
A neat spruce-honest-fellow, and no goldsmith.

SUBTLE   He's a fortunate fellow, that I am sure on –
FACE   Already, sir, ha'you found it? Lo' thee Abel!
SUBTLE   And in right way t'ward riches –   35
FACE   Sir!
SUBTLE   This summer
He will be of the clothing of his company,
And next spring called to the scarlet. Spend what he can.
FACE   What, and so little beard?
SUBTLE   Sir, you must think
He may have a receipt to make hair come.
But he'll be wise, preserve his youth, and fine for't.   40
His fortune looks for him another way.
FACE   'Slid, Doctor, how canst thou know this so soon?
I'm amused at that!
SUBTLE   By a rule, Captain,

25. *muscadel*] Sweet Spanish wine. *grains*] Spices.
27. *clouts*] Rags, strips of cloth.
28. *lily-pots*] Ornamental vases.
29. *conserve of roses*] Medicinal cordial. *French beans*] Sweet-smelling flowers of the broad-bean plant.
30. *maple block*] On which tobacco was shredded. *tongs*] For holding the ember to light the pipe.
31. *Winchester*] Where the best pipes were made. *juniper*] A slow-burning sweet-smelling wood.
32. *goldsmith*] Usurer; that is, he does not charge extortionate prices for tobacco, or for teaching the art of smoking it. An in-joke: Robert Armin, who played Drugger, was apprenticed to a goldsmith before he became an actor (M. Butler 1989).
34. *Already ... it?*] Have you read his future so quickly? *Lo' thee*] Interjection, responding positively to the immediate situation. See 2.3.224.
36. *of the clothing*] Promoted from freeman (ordinary member) to liveryman (privileged member) in the Grocers' Company.
37. *called to the scarlet*] Elected sheriff.
38. *so little beard*] That is, so young.
39. Subtle implies Drugger has the power to look old and distinguished, if he so chooses.
40. *fine for't*] Pay the fine for refusing the office.
43. *amused*] Amazed, puzzled.

In metaposcopy, which I do work by,
A certain star i'the forehead, which you see not.   45
Your chestnut or your olive-coloured face
Does never fail, and your long ear doth promise.
I knew't by certain spots too in his teeth
And on the nail of his mercurial finger.
FACE   Which finger's that?   50
SUBTLE   His little finger. Look.
[*To Drugger*] Y'were born upon a Wednesday?
DRUGGER   Yes, indeed, sir.
SUBTLE   The thumb, in chiromancy, we give Venus,
The forefinger to Jove, the midst to Saturn,
The ring to Sol, the least to Mercury,
Who was the lord, sir, of his horoscope,   55
His house of life being Libra, which foreshowed
He should be a merchant and should trade with balance.
FACE   Why, this is strange! Is't not, honest Nab?
SUBTLE   There is a ship now, coming from Ormuz,
That shall yield him such a commodity   60
Of drugs – [*Examining the plan*] This is the west, and this the south?
DRUGGER   Yes, sir.
SUBTLE   And those are your two sides?
DRUGGER   Ay, sir.
SUBTLE   Make me your door then south; your broad side west;
And on the east side of your shop, aloft,
Write *Mathlai*, *Tarmiel*, and *Baraborat*;   65
Upon the north part, *Rael*, *Velel*, *Thiel*.
They are the names of those mercurial spirits
That do fright flies from boxes.

44. *metaposcopy*] Fortune-telling by inspecting the face.
46. *chestnut ... olive-coloured*] Indications of good nature and honesty (H&S).
47. *long ear*] According to Paracelsus, a sign of competence and diligence (H&S).
52. *chiromancy*] Palmistry.
55. *lord ... horoscope*] If Drugger were born under Libra (the sign of the scale, apt for merchants), then the ruling planet would have been Venus, not Mercury. But Subtle tells Drugger what he wants to hear: that the dominant influence is Mercury, the god of business success – also, ironically, the god of thieves and rogues.
57. *balance*] Scale.
59. *Ormuz*] Hormuz, a port for the spice trade at the entrance to the Persian Gulf.
65-6. *Mathlai ... Thiel*] Names of good spirits governing east and north, when Mercury is dominant.
68. *flies*] Either demons associated with Beelzebub, the lord of flies, or simply parasites that might contaminate the supplies.

DRUGGER   Yes, sir.
SUBTLE   And
    Beneath your threshold bury me a loadstone
    To draw in gallants that wear spurs. The rest,   70
    They'll seem to follow.
FACE   That's a secret, Nab!
SUBTLE   And on your stall a puppet with a vice,
    And a court-fucus to call city-dames.
    You shall deal much with minerals.
DRUGGER   Sir, I have
    At home already –   75
SUBTLE   Ay, I know, you've ars'nic,
    Vitriol, sal-tartar, argaile, alkali,
    Cinoper. I know all. This fellow, Captain,
    Will come in time to be a great distiller,
    And give a say (I will not say directly,
    But very fair) at the philosopher's stone.   80
FACE   Why, how now, Abel! Is this true?
DRUGGER   Good Captain,
    What must I give?
FACE   Nay, I'll not counsel thee.
    Thou hear'st what wealth (he says 'Spend what thou canst')
    Th'art like to come to.
DRUGGER   I would gi'him a crown.
FACE   A crown! 'nd toward such a fortune? Heart,   85
    Thou shalt rather gi'him thy shop. No gold about thee?
DRUGGER   Yes, I have a portague I ha' kept this half year.
FACE   Out on thee, Nab. 'Slight, there was such an offer –
    Shalt keep't no longer. I'll gi'it him for thee?

    [*Gives Subtle the portague*]

69. *loadstone*] Magnet.
71. *seem*] Be seen.
72. *stall*] Outdoor display-table. *vice*] Mechanism or device moving the eyes and lips of
    the figure, perhaps with a pipe to simulate smoking, as an attention-getter.
73. *court-fucus*] Makeup used by ladies at court, whom city wives emulated. Such
    preparations often contained dangerous chemicals.
76. *vitriol*] Sulphuric acid. *sal-tartar*] Carbonate of potash. *argaile*] Tartar deposited
    by wine on the sides of casks. *alkali*] Soda-ash.
77. *Cinoper*] Cinnabar, a crystalline form of mercuric sulphide.
79. *give a say*] Give assay; 'have a shot at' (Mares 1967).
79–80. *not . . . fair*] Perhaps not successfully, but creditably.
84. *crown*] Worth about 25 pence.
87. *portague*] Portuguese gold coin, worth about 4 pounds.

Doctor, Nab prays your worship to drink this, and swears   90
He will appear more grateful as your skill
Does raise him in the world.
DRUGGER   I would entreat
Another favour of his worship.
FACE   What is't, Nab?
DRUGGER   But to look over, sir, my almanac,
And cross out my ill-days, that I may neither   95
Bargain nor trust upon them.
FACE   That he shall, Nab.
Leave it, it shall be done 'gainst afternoon.
SUBTLE   And a direction for his shelves.
FACE   Now, Nab?
Art thou well pleased, Nab?
DRUGGER   Thank, sir, both your worships.
FACE   Away.

[*Exit Drugger*]

Why, now, you smoky persecutor of nature!   100
Now do you see that something's to be done,
Beside your beech-coal and your cor'sive waters,
Your crosslets, crucibles, and cucurbites?
You must have stuff brought home to you to work on?
And yet you think I am at no expense   105
In searching out these veins, then following 'em,
Then trying 'em out. 'Fore God, my intelligence
Costs me more money than my share oft comes to
In these rare works.
SUBTLE   You're pleasant, sir. How now?

---

95. *ill-days*] Unlucky days, according to his horoscope.
96. *trust*] Deal on credit.
100. *persecutor of nature*] Both 'follower' and 'tormenter' of nature, whether con-man or
    alchemist. As follower, the alchemist follows through on the premise that all metals, if
    perfected, would be gold; and torments the metals in his furnace to force the change.
    The con-man follows human 'nature' or folly, and squeezes his profits out of their
    fantasies.
102. *beech-coal*] The best charcoal, made from beech-wood.   *cor'sive*] Corrosive.
103. *crosslets*] Melting-pots.   *cucurbites*] Gourd-shaped retorts.
104. *stuff*] Raw material; that is, dupes.
107. *intelligence*] Information.

Act 1 scene 4*

[*Enter*] *Dol*

FACE   What says my dainty Dolkin?
DOL   Yonder fish-wife
    Will not away. And there's your giantess,
    The bawd of Lambeth.
SUBTLE   Heart, I cannot speak with 'em.
DOL   Not afore night, I have told 'em in a voice
    Through the trunk, like one of your familiars.   5
    But I have spied Sir Epicure Mammon –
SUBTLE   Where?
DOL   Coming along at far end of the lane,
    Slow of his feet, but earnest of his tongue
    To one that's with him.
SUBTLE   Face, go you and shift.

[*Exit Face*]

    Dol, you must presently make ready too –   10
DOL   Why, what's the matter?
SUBTLE   O, I did look for him
    With the sun's rising. Marvel he could sleep!
    This is the day I am to perfect for him
    The *magisterium*, our great work, the stone;
    And yield it, made, into his hands, of which   15
    He has this month talked as he were possessed.
    And now he's dealing pieces on't away.
    Methinks I see him ent'ring ordinaries,

---

*   Where earlier scenes introduce minor dupes drawn to Subtle for his white witchcraft,
    this scene establishes Subtle as a pseudo-practitioner of the higher craft of alchemy,
    spurred on by the greedy fantasies of his favourite dupe, Sir Epicure Mammon.
1–3. *Yonder ... Lambeth*] See 1.3.1 and note. If these figures did appear on stage, they
    would have been played, not by boys, but by men, as suggested by 'giantess'.
  3. *Lambeth*] The marshy area on the south bank of the Thames opposite Westminster, the
    haunt of whores and pickpockets, despite the Archbishop of Canterbury's Palace
    located near the ferry landing.
  5. *trunk*] Speaking-tube.
  9. *shift*] Change clothes.
10. *presently*] At once.
14. *magisterium*] The master-work.
16. *possessed*] Punning on 'already in possession' and 'mad'.
17. *dealing ... away*] Giving away portions of his anticipated wealth.

Dispensing for the pox, and plaguy-houses,
Reaching his dose; walking Moorfields for lepers;   20
And offering citizens' wives pomander-bracelets
As his preservative, made of the elixir;
Searching the spital to make old bawds young;
And the highways for beggars to make rich.
I see no end of his labours. He will make   25
Nature ashamed of her long sleep, when art,
Who's but a stepdame, shall do more than she,
In her best love to mankind, ever could.
If his dream last, he'll turn the age to gold.

[*Exeunt*]

ACT 2

Act 2 scene 1*

[*Enter*] *Mammon, Surly*

MAMMON   Come on, sir. Now you set your foot on shore

19–23. *Dispensing ... young*] The philosopher's stone, in a liquid for medicinal use, was
  called the *elixir*, and could alter man's condition from sick to healthy or old to young,
  just as it altered base metals to gold.
19. *pox*] Syphilis. *plaguy-houses*] Pesthouses, for those sick of plague.
20. *Reaching his dose*] Handing out his cure. *Moorfields*] A notorious beggars' quarter
  north of the city walls between Bishopsgate and Cripplegate (now the area of Finsbury
  Square), where the indigents included lepers and licensed mad-folk from nearby
  hospitals.
21. *pomander-bracelets*] Bracelets decorated with balls of perfumed herbs and spices,
  thought to ward off infection.
23. *Spittle*] Unsavoury district of prostitutes and thieves; specifically, the Hospital of St
  Mary, founded in 1471 on what is now the south side of Spital Square, just east of
  Bishopsgate St.
27. *stepdame*] Stepmother. Despite tales of unkind stepmothers, Art, mankind's stepmother, manages to relieve diseases that Nature, mankind's mother, cannot cure even
  with mother-love.
*   The first three scenes of this act focus on Sir Epicure Mammon's self-centred utopian
  dreams of becoming the new Solomon, possessor of the philosopher's stone and all that
  it implies for the acquisition of boundless wealth and power – intellectual, political,
  spiritual, and sexual. Jonson counterpoints Mammon's delusions with Surly's scepti-
  cism. In this scene, Mammon, like Marlowe's Faustus, envisions enriching his friends,
  curing disease, especially the plague, abolishing old age, and learning the secrets of the
  universe.

In *novo orbe*. Here's the rich Peru,
And there within, sir, are the golden mines,
Great Solomon's Ophir! He was sailing to't
Three years, but we have reached it in ten months.   5
This is the day wherein, to all my friends,
I will pronounce the happy word, 'Be rich.'
This day, you shall be *spectatissimi*.
You shall no more deal with the hollow die,
Or the frail card. No more be at charge of keeping   10
The livery-punk for the young heir that must
Seal at all hours in his shirt. No more
If he deny, ha'him beaten to't, as he is
That brings him the commodity. No more
Shall thirst of satin or the covetous hunger   15
Of velvet entrails for a rude-spun cloak,
To be displayed at Madam Augusta's, make

2. *novo orbe*] The New World, America, an analogy for Lovewit's house. The exhilaration and anticipation aroused by early explorers is extended to the alchemical researchers.   *Peru*] Conquered by Pizarro in 1532, the source of Spanish gold; fabled as El Dorado.

4. *Solomon's Ophir*] Solomon was thought to have possessed the philosopher's stone, with which he secretly made gold in Ophir, Arabia; treasure was shipped to Jerusalem every three years, giving rise to speculation that three years was the time required for alchemical projection (1 Kings 10:22).

8. *spectatissimi*] Very much looked up to, highly respected.

9. *hollow die*] Loaded dice.

10. *frail*] Possibly marked, or simply unreliable, unlucky.

10–14. *charge ... commodity*] Mammon refers to complicated money-making schemes to which Surly might have been reduced: pandering for young gentlemen to encourage them to waste their money in dissipation, and then bullying them into commodity swindles – forcing them to take out loans, part of which was given in goods instead of cash; the goods were resold at a loss, but the loan had to be repaid at the inflated rate assigned by the moneylender. The bully's job was to threaten or beat up those who refused to pay.

11. *livery-punk*] Whore in collusion with the usurer to seduce young heirs. 'Livery' usually refers to freemen of a city company or guild, but here suggests a full member of a gang of swindlers.

12. *Seal*] Sign and seal a contract or promissory note; punning on sexual bonding.

16. *entrails*] Lining.

17. *Madam Augusta's*] A brothel-cum-gambling-den. The name suggests an upper-class resort whose clientele can afford high stakes.

The sons of sword and hazard fall before
The golden calf and on their knees, whole nights,
Commit idolatry with wine and trumpets,   20
Or go a-feasting after drum and ensign.
No more of this. You shall start up young viceroys
And have your punks and punketees, my Surly.
And unto thee, I speak it first, 'Be rich.'
[*Calling*] Where is my Subtle there? Within, ho?   25
[FACE] *Within*   Sir!
He'll come to you by and by.
MAMMON   That's his fire-drake,
His lungs, his Zephyrus, he that puffs his coals
Till he firk nature up in her own centre.
You are not faithful, sir. This night, I'll change
All that is metal in thy house to gold.   30
And early in the morning will I send
To all the plumbers and the pewterers
And buy their tin and lead up, and to Lothbury
For all the copper.
SURLY   What, and turn that too?
MAMMON   Yes, and I'll purchase Devonshire and Cornwall   35
And make them perfect Indies! You admire now?
SURLY   No, faith.

18. *sons of sword and hazard*] Adventurers; bullies and gamblers.
18–20. *fall ... trumpets*] Gamble and carouse. 'Commit idolatry', a play on 'commit
    adultery', and the reference to the 'golden calf', false god of the Phoenicians, condemn
    the hedonism of the scene in Old Testament terms.
21. For down-and-out gamblers, the way to recoup losses was to join the army.
22. *start up*] Beget
23. *punketees*] Jonson's coinage for little punks.
25. *Within, ho*] The conventional call for service. *Q* and *F* have 'Within hough', offering
    an alternative meaning: 'Within spitting distance'.
26. *fire-drake*] A fire-breathing dragon, or salamander (thought able to live in fire),
    humorously applied to the alchemist's assistant, whose job was chiefly to keep the
    furnaces at the right temperature.
27. *lungs*] Bellows, another nickname for the laboratory assistant. *Zephyrus*] West
    wind, generally represented on maps as a boy with his cheeks puffed out.
28. *firk ... up*] Stir up, with sexual connotations.
29. *faithful*] A believer.
33. *Lothbury*] A street of copper and brass foundries.
35. *Devonshire and Cornwall*] For their tin and copper mines.
36. *Indies*] West Indies, indeed all the New World, popularly thought to be flowing with
    gold.   *admire*] Are impressed, or convinced.

MAMMON   But when you see th'effects of the great med'cine,
                Of which one part projected on a hundred
                Of Mercury, or Venus, or the Moon
                Shall turn it to as many of the Sun,   40
                Nay, to a thousand, so *ad infinitum*,
                You will believe me!
SURLY   Yes, when I see't, I will.
                But if my eyes do cozen me so (and I
                Giving'em no occasion) sure I'll have
                A whore shall piss'em out next day.   45
MAMMON   Ha! Why?
                Do you think I fable with you? I assure you,
                He that has once the flower of the sun,
                The perfect ruby which we call elixir,
                Not only can do that, but by its virtue
                Can confer honour, love, respect, long life,   50
                Give safety, valour, yea, and victory
                To whom he will. In eight-and-twenty days
                I'll make an old man of fourscore a child.
SURLY   No doubt he's that already.
MAMMON   Nay, I mean
                Restore his years, renew him like an eagle   55
                To the fifth age, make him get sons and daughters,
                Young giants, as our philosophers have done
                (The ancient patriarchs afore the flood)
                But taking, once a week on a knife's point,
                The quantity of a grain of mustard of it: 60
                Become stout Marses and beget young Cupids.

37. *great med'cine*] The elixir, or philosopher's stone.
39. *Mercury*] Quicksilver. *Venus*] Copper. *Moon*] Silver.
40. *Sun*] Gold.
45. *piss*] Another form of golden shower.
47. *flower ... ruby ... elixir*] Synonyms for the philosopher's stone.
55. *renew ... eagle*] According to Psalms 103:5, a gift of God, not of Mammon.
56. *fifth age*] Mature manhood, from 42 to 56 years old, as opposed to the second
     childhood Surly sneers at (Mares 1967); a time of middle-aged wisdom (*As You Like It*
     2.7.153–7).
57–8. *philosophers ... patriarchs*] Mammon refers to the vigorous old ages of Noah,
     Abraham, and others who, alchemists believed, possessed the philosopher's stone. Abra-
     ham and Sarah had a son in advanced old age.
61. *Marses*] Plural of Mars, god of war and father of Cupid.

SURLY   The decayed vestals of Pict Hatch would thank you,
　That keep the fire alive there.
MAMMON   'Tis the secret
　Of nature, naturized 'gainst all infections!
　Cures all diseases coming of all causes: 65
　A month's grief in a day, a year's in twelve,
　And of what age soever in a month –
　Past all the doses of your drugging doctors.
　I'll undertake withal to fright the plague
　Out o'the kingdom in three months.   70
SURLY   And I'll
　Be bound, the players shall sing your praises then
　Without their poets.
MAMMON   Sir, I'll do't. Meantime,
　I'll give away so much unto my man,
　Shall serve th' whole city with preservative,
　Weekly, each house his dose, and at the rate –   75
SURLY   As he that built the waterwork does with water?
MAMMON   You are incredulous.
SURLY   Faith, I have a humour,
　I would not willingly be gulled. Your stone
　Cannot transmute me.
MAMMON   Pertinax Surly,
　Will you believe antiquity? Records?   80
　I'll show you a book where Moses and his sister
　And Solomon have written of the art,
　Ay, and a treatise penned by Adam.
SURLY   How!

62. *decayed*] Syphilitic. *vestals*] Virgin priestesses who tended the sacred fire in the Temple of Vesta in ancient Rome, used ironically here for whores. *Pict Hatch*] An other district of brothels south of Old Street and Goswell Road.
63. *fire*] The burning sensation of venereal disease.
64. *naturized*] Endowed with a specific nature (scholastic jargon).
66. *grief*] Illness.
68. *doses*] Cures.
71. *players*] Actors, because theatres were closed when deaths from plague reached forty a week, as they did in 1610, perhaps delaying the London opening of *Alch*.
72. *poets*] Playwrights.
76. *waterwork*] London had two pumps supplying piped water to private homes, one at London Bridge, built in 1582, and the other near Broken Wharf, built in 1594. The New River aqueduct was under construction in 1610 for the same purpose.
81–3. *Moses ... Adam*] More than one book claimed to be alchemical treatises by Old Testament figures. Adam was believed to have learned the secret of the stone in Eden; the Song of Solomon was understood as an alchemical allegory of Sun and Moon.

MAMMON   O'the philosopher's stone, and in High Dutch.
SURLY   Did Adam write, sir, in High Dutch?   85
MAMMON   He did,
    Which proves it was the primitive tongue.
SURLY   What paper?
MAMMON   On cedar board.
SURLY   O that, indeed (they say)
    Will last 'gainst worms.
MAMMON   'Tis like your Irish wood
    'Gainst cobwebs. I have a piece of Jason's fleece too,
    Which was no other than a book of alchemy,   90
    Writ in large sheepskin, a good fat ram-vellum.
    Such was Pythagoras' thigh, Pandora's tub,
    And all that fable of Medea's charms,
    The manner of our work. The bulls, our furnace,
    Still breathing fire; our *argent-vive*, the dragon;   95
    The dragon's teeth, mercury sublimate,
    That keeps the whiteness, hardness, and the biting;
    And they are gathered into Jason's helm
    (Th'alembic) and then sowed in Mars his field,
    And thence sublimed so often till they are fixed.   100
    Both this, th'Hesperian garden, Cadmus' story,

84. *High Dutch*] High German.
86. *primitive tongue*] Original language, an argument published in Antwerp in 1569 by Johannes Goropius Becanus (H&S).
88. *Irish wood*] Thought to repel spiders.
89. *Jason's fleece*] The story of the Golden Fleece, which Jason recovered after great hardship, becomes an allegory of the alchemical quest.
91. *ram-vellum*] Parchment.
92. *Pythagoras' thigh*] Reputedly made of gold.   *Pandora's tub*] Her box; assumed to be gold because given by the gods.
93. *charms*] Magic.
94. *bulls*] The fire-breathing, brass-footed bulls with which Jason ploughed and sowed a field with dragon's teeth; following Medea's instructions, he then destroyed the warriors who sprang up.
95. *argent-vive*] Quicksilver, or mercury, one alchemical symbol of which is the dragon.
96. *mercury sublimate*] Chloride of mercury, corrosive sublimate.
98–9. *Jason's helm ... alembic*] Distilling-flask, the cap or helm of which had a long beak to carry off the vapour into the condenser.
99. *Mars his field*] Iron vessel within which the vapour could be refined and fixed in its perfect state as the stone. Mars is the astrological sign for iron.
101. *Hesperian garden*] Where the golden apples grew, guarded by a dragon.   *Cadmus*] The original sower of dragon's teeth, from which sprang up armed men who fought until only five remained; they helped Cadmus found Thebes.

Jove's shower, the boon of Midas, Argus' eyes,
Boccace his Demogorgon, thousands more,
All abstract riddles of our stone. How now?

Act 2 scene 2*

[*Enter*] *Face*

MAMMON   Do we succeed? Is our day come? And holds it?
FACE   The evening will set red upon you, sir;
    You have colour for it, crimson. The red ferment
    Has done his office. Three hours hence, prepare you
    To see projection.   5
MAMMON   Pertinax, my Surly,
    Again I say to thee aloud, 'Be rich.'
    This day thou shalt have ingots, and tomorrow
    Give lords th'affront. Is it, my Zephyrus, right?
    Blushes the bolt's head?
FACE   Like a wench with child, sir,
    That were but now discovered to her master.   10
MAMMON   Excellent witty Lungs! My only care is
    Where to get stuff enough now to project on.
    This town will not half serve me.
FACE   No, sir? Buy
    The covering off o'churches.
MAMMON   That's true.

102. *Jove's shower*] Jupiter pierced through Danae's brass prison in a shower of gold to
    become her lover; the result was her son Perseus.   *boon of Midas*] The golden touch,
    which turned everything he handled to gold, including his daughter.   *Argus' eyes*]
    Guard with a hundred eyes, set to watch Io by the jealous Juno; Mercury charmed him
    to sleep. His eyes were set in the peacock's tail, an alchemical symbol (2.2.27).
103. *Demogorgon*] In Boccaccio's *De Genealogia Deorum*, the primal god or origin of all
    things; he represents the knowledge that the alchemist seeks.
104. *abstract riddles*] Allegories.
*   While Mammon indulges himself in sensual fantasy, Surly quietly points out the essential
    difference between a greedy hypocrite and a true seeker of the philosopher's stone, the
    homo frugi (97–9). Mammon argues that *funding* the experiments does not demand the
    probity required of the alchemist *doing* the experiments. This quibble resembles the later
    Anabaptist distinction between 'coining' and 'casting' (3.2.140–58 and 4.7.75–8).
2–3. *set red ... red ferment*] Indicating the successful progress of the experiment.
  5. *projection*] Initiating the final transmutation into gold.
  8. *Give ... th'affront*] Snub.
  9. *bolt's head*] Globular flask with a long cylindrical neck.
14. *covering ... churches*] Lead roofs.

FACE   Yes.
    Let 'em stand bare as do their auditory.   15
    Or cap 'em new with shingles.
MAMMON   No, good thatch:
    Thatch will lie light upo' the rafters, Lungs.
    Lungs, I will manumit thee from the furnace.
    I will restore thee thy complexion, Puff,
    Lost in the embers, and repair this brain,   20
    Hurt wi'the fume o'the metals.
FACE   I have blown, sir,
    Hard for your worship, thrown by many a coal
    When 'twas not beech, weighed those I put in just
    To keep your heat still even. These bleared eyes
    Have waked to read your several colours, sir,   25
    Of the pale citron, the green lion, the crow,
    The peacock's tail, the plumed swan.
MAMMON   And lastly
    Thou hast descried the flower, the *sanguis agni*?
FACE   Yes, sir.
MAMMON   Where's master?
FACE   At's prayers, sir, he,
    Good man, he's doing his devotions   30
    For the success.
MAMMON   Lungs, I will set a period
    To all thy labours. Thou shalt be the master
    Of my seraglio.
FACE   Good, sir.
MAMMON   But do you hear?
    I'll geld you, Lungs.
FACE   Yes, sir.
MAMMON   For I do mean

16. *shingles*] Wooden roofing tiles.
18. *manumit*] Release; free a slave.
19. *complexion*] Burnt and sooty from blowing on the coals.
23. *just*] Exactly.
24. *still*] Always.
26–7. *pale citron … swan*] The sequence of colours preceding the final perfect red,
    described by George Ripley in *The Compound of Alchymy* (London, 1591), K4: yellow,
    green, blue-grey or blue-black, multicoloured, and white.
28. *sanguis agni*] Blood of the lamb (equivocal analogy to Christ), the perfect red that
    flowers in the last stage of a successful transmutation.
29. *At's prayers*] A successful alchemist had to be morally pure (see Surly's comment at
    ll. 95–7).
31. *period*] Full stop.

To have a list of wives and concubines   35
Equal with Solomon, who had the stone
Alike with me, and I will make me a back
With the elixir that shall be as tough
As Hercules', to encounter fifty a night. –
Th'art sure thou saw'st it blood?   40
FACE   Both blood and spirit, sir.
MAMMON   I will have all my beds blown up, not stuffed.
Down is too hard. And then, mine oval room
Filled with such pictures as Tiberius took
From Elephantis, and dull Aretine
But coldly imitated. Then, my glasses   45
Cut in more subtle angles to disperse
And multiply the figures as I walk
Naked between my *succubae*. My mists
I'll have of perfume, vapoured 'bout the room
To lose ourselves in, and my baths like pits   50
To fall into, from whence we will come forth
And roll us dry in gossamer and roses. –

[*He pauses for reassurance from Face*]

Is it arrived at ruby? –

[*Face nods*]

                    Where I spy
A wealthy citizen or rich lawyer
Have a sublimed pure wife, unto that fellow   55
I'll send a thousand pound to be my cuckold.

36. *stone*] Still identifying with Solomon for his wealth and his rich sexual life, Mammon
puns on the philosopher's stone and the slang term for testicles.

37. *back*] A strong back was a sign of sexual potency.

39. *Hercules'*] As a youth, the hero deflowered and impregnated all but one of the fifty
daughters of King Thespius.

40. *blood and spirit*] The right colour and quality.

43–4. *Tiberius ... Elephantis*] According to Suetonius, Tiberius's palace at Capri was
decorated with pornographic pictures, some executed by the Egyptian Elephantis.

44. *Aretine*] Pietro Aretino, Italian satirist, whose erotic poems, *Sonnetti Lussorioso*
(1523), were illustrated by Giulio Romano's pornographic drawings of 'Postures'. See
Volp 3.4.80, 96–7.

45. *glasses*] Mirrors.

48. *succubae*] Female demons who had sexual intercourse with men; but here simply the
concubines in his harem.   *mists*] Devices spraying perfume, like those described in
Suetonius, *Nero* 31.

55. *sublimed*] Borrowing the alchemical term, intensely refined.

FACE   And I shall carry it?

MAMMON   No. I'll ha' no bawds
　　　But fathers and mothers. They will do it best,
　　　Best of all others. And my flatterers
　　　Shall be the pure and gravest of divines   60
　　　That I can get for money. My mere fools,
　　　Eloquent burgesses, and then my poets
　　　The same that writ so subtly of the fart,
　　　Whom I will entertain still for that subject.
　　　The few that would give out themselves to be   65
　　　Court and town stallions, and each-where belie
　　　Ladies who are known most innocent for them,
　　　Those will I beg to make me eunuchs of.
　　　And they shall fan me with ten ostrich tails
　　　Apiece, made in a plume to gather wind.   70
　　　We will be brave, Puff, now we ha' the med'cine.
　　　My meat shall all come in in Indian shells,
　　　Dishes of agate set in gold and studded
　　　With emeralds, sapphires, hyacinths, and rubies.
　　　The tongues of carps, dormice, and camels' heels   75
　　　Boiled i' the spirit of sol and dissolved pearl
　　　(Apicius' diet 'gainst the epilepsy)
　　　And I will eat these broths with spoons of amber,
　　　Headed with diamond and carbuncle.
　　　My foot-boy shall eat pheasants, calvered salmons,   80

60. *divines*] Clergymen.

61. *mere*] Pure.

62. *burgesses*] Members of parliament.

63. *fart*] Subject of an anonymous poem, 'The Fart Censured in the Parliament House', in which forty MPs comment on Henry Ludlow's 'peculiar' reply to the House of Lords in 1607. See *Epigrams* 133.

66. *stallions*] Studs, sexual athletes.

67. *for them*] Of any contact with these braggarts.

68. *beg*] Ask for custody of them, as wards.

71. *brave*] Ostentatiously stylish.

74. *hyacinths*] Originally, precious blue stones like sapphires; now, zircons.

75. *dormice*] A Roman delicacy, stuffed and roasted.   *camels' heels*] From Apicius's list of bizarre foods that prevent plague.

76. *spirit of sol*] Distillate of gold.   *dissolved pearl*] A classical extravagance (see *Volp* 3.7.191–3).

77. *Apicius*] Roman glutton, Marcus Gavius Apicius (*c.* AD 30), who ate up most of his fortune and then killed himself for fear of starving in poverty.

80. *calvered*] Cut up very fresh, or while still alive, and marinated; a delicacy something like gravlax.

Knots, godwits, lampreys. I myself will have
The beards of barbels served instead of salads,
Oiled mushrooms, and the swelling unctuous paps
Of a fat pregnant sow, newly cut off,
Dressed with an exquisite and poignant sauce,   85
For which I'll say unto my cook, 'There's gold.
Go forth and be a knight.'
FACE   Sir, I'll go look
A little how it heightens.
MAMMON   Do.

[*Exit Face*]

                          My shirts
I'll have of taffeta-sarsnet, soft and light
As cobwebs, and for all my other raiment,   90
It shall be such as might provoke the Persian,
Were he to teach the world riot anew.
My gloves of fishes' and birds' skins, perfumed
With gums of paradise and eastern air –
SURLY   And d'you think to have the stone with this?   95
MAMMON   No, I do think t'have all this with the stone.
SURLY   Why, I have heard he must be *homo frugi*,
A pious, holy, and religious man,
One free from mortal sin, a very virgin.
MAMMON   That makes it, sir, he is so. But I buy it.   100
My venture brings it me. He, honest wretch,
A notable, superstitious, good soul,
Has worn his knees bare and his slippers bald
With prayer, and fasting for it, and, sir, let him
Do't alone, for me, still. Here he comes.   105
Not a profane word afore him. 'Tis poison.

---

81. *Knots*] Wildfowl of the snipe family, named after King Canute who favoured them.
    godwits] Marsh birds like curlews (see *SW* 1.4.40).   *lampreys*] Eel-like boneless fish.
82. *beards of barbels*] The fleshy filaments hanging from the mouth of a species of carp.
83–4. *paps … sow*] Considered a delicacy if prepared after the sow has farrowed but
    before it has suckled.
87. *be a knight*] Under James I, knighthoods could be purchased for 30 or 40 pounds.
88. *how it heightens*] How the experiment is progressing.
89. *taffeta-sarsnet*] Fine silk from the Middle East.
91. *the Persian*] Sardanapalus, king of ninth-century BC Nineveh, notorious for his luxury.
94. *gums of paradise*] Oriental essences; Eden was thought to be in the east.
97. *homo frugi*] An abstemious man.
105. *for me*] As far as I'm concerned.

Act 2 scene 3*

[Enter] Subtle

MAMMON   Good morrow, father.
SUBTLE   Gentle son, good morrow,
    And to your friend there. What is he is with you?
MAMMON   An heretic that I did bring along
    In hope, sir, to convert him.
SUBTLE   Son, I doubt
    You're covetous that thus you meet your time   5
    I'the just point, prevent your day at morning.
    This argues something worthy of a fear
    Of importune and carnal appetite.
    Take heed you do not cause the blessing leave you
    With your ungoverned haste. I should be sorry   10
    To see my labours now, e'en at perfection,
    Got by long watching and large patience,
    Not prosper where my love and zeal hath placed 'em.
    Which (heaven I call to witness with yourself,
    To whom I have poured my thoughts) in all my ends   15
    Have looked no way but unto public good,
    To pious uses, and dear charity,
    Now grown a prodigy with men. Wherein
    If you, my son, should now prevaricate
    And to your own particular lusts employ   20
    So great and catholic a bliss, be sure
    A curse will follow, yea, and overtake
    Your subtle and most secret ways.
MAMMON   I know, sir,

---

*   The object of this scene is to introduce the ingredient which will ultimately jeopardise
    the experiments Mammon is funding. Jonson balances the mating of the elements in
    alchemy against the mating of couples in a brothel, a concept reinforced by the designs
    on alchemical flasks showing copulating lovers (see 72n.). Mammon is first aroused by
    alchemical foreplay (43–210) and then by Dol's brief appearance (210–12); the
    alchemical descriptions of Dol's erotic behaviour (253–7) confirm the association
    between greed and lust.
 4. *doubt*] Suspect.
 5. *I' ... point*] So exactly.   *prevent*] Anticipate, by coming early for results that will not
    be available till late in the day.
12. *watching*] Working late at night.
18. *prodigy*] Rare practice.
19. *prevaricate*] Deviate from the path of righteousness.
20. *particular*] Private, personal.
21. *catholic*] Universal (as opposed to 'particular').

You shall not need to fear me. I but come
To ha'you confute this gentleman.   25
SURLY   Who is,
Indeed, sir, somewhat costive of belief
Toward your stone; would not be gulled.
SUBTLE   Well, son,
All that I can convince him in is this:
The work is done. Bright Sol is in his robe.
We have a med'cine of the triple soul,   30
The glorified spirit. Thanks be to heaven
And make us worthy of it. Ulen Spiegel!
FACE   [*Within*] Anon, sir!

[*Enter Face*]

SUBTLE   Look well to the register
And let your heat still lessen by degrees
To the aludels.   35
FACE   Yes, sir.
SUBTLE   Did you look
O'the bolt's head yet?
FACE   Which? On D, sir?
SUBTLE   Ay.
What's the complexion?
FACE   Whitish.
SUBTLE   Infuse vinegar
To draw his volatile substance and his tincture.
And let the water in glass E be filtered
And put into the gripe's egg. Lute him well,   40

26. *costive*] Slow-moving, impacted.
29. *in his robe*] Ready to work projection.
30–31. *med'cine ... spirit*] The transcendent power of gold, as found in the philosopher's
    stone.
30. *triple soul*] The three spirits linking soul to body: vital (heart), natural (liver), and
    animal (brain).
32. *Ulen Spiegel*] Till Eulenspiegel (or Owl-glass, a mirror), the trickster and practical
    joker of German folk-tales. The foreign name is intended to impress Mammon, but also
    places Face and Subtle as heirs to a long tradition of hoodwinking and nosethumbing
    comic heroes.
33. *register*] Damper in the flue, controlling the heat.
35. *aludels*] Pear-shaped pots, open at both ends, fitted together and sealed to form a
    condenser.
37. *complexion*] Alchemical colour, 'tincture'.
40. *gripe's egg*] Egg-shaped vessel used for boiling (*gripe* = vulture).   *Lute*] Enclose in
    clay, seal shut.

And leave him closed *in balneo*.

FACE   I will, sir.

SURLY   [*Aside*] What a brave language here is! Next to canting!

SUBTLE   I've another work you never saw, son,
That three days since passed the philosopher's wheel
In the lent heat of athanor, and's become   45
Sulphur o'nature.

MAMMON   But 'tis for me?

SUBTLE   What need you?
You have enough in that is perfect.

MAMMON   O, but –

SUBTLE   Why, this is covetise!

MAMMON   No, I assure you
I shall employ it all in pious uses:
Founding of colleges and grammar schools,   50
Marrying young virgins, building hospitals
And, now and then, a church.

   [*Enter Face*]

SUBTLE   How now?

FACE   Sir, please you,
Shall I not change the filter?

SUBTLE   Marry, yes!
And bring me the complexion of glass B.

   [*Exit Face*]

MAMMON   Ha' you another?   55

SUBTLE   Yes, son. Were I assured
Your piety were firm, we would not want
The means to glorify it. But I hope the best.
I mean to tinct C in sand-heat tomorrow,
And give him imbibition.

41. *in balneo*] In a bath of sand or water, to diffuse the heat.

42. *canting*] The jargon used by thieves and beggars.

44. *philosopher's wheel*] Various stages of the alchemical cycle of experiments, sometimes depicted as a wheel, as on the last page of Ripley's *Compound of Alchemy* (1591).

45. *lent*] Slow. *athanor*] Furnace to maintain slow heat.

46. *Sulphur o' nature*] Very pure form of sulphur.

47. *perfect*] Completed. So too at l. 69.

48. *covetise*] Greed, one of the seven deadly sins that would disqualify Mammon as a recipient of the stone.

51. *Marrying*] Giving dowries.

58. *sand-heat*] In the bath as at 41.

59. *imbibition*] Saturation and supersaturation.

MAMMON   Of white oil?

SUBTLE   No, sir, of red. F is come over the helm too,   60
    I thank my Maker, in St Mary's bath,
    And shows *lac virginis*. Blessed be heaven.
    I sent you of his *faeces* there, calcined.
    Out of that calx I ha' won the salt of mercury.

MAMMON   By pouring on your rectified water?   65

SUBTLE   Yes, and reverberating in athanor.

   [*Enter Face*]

    How now? What colour says it?

FACE   The ground black, sir.

MAMMON   That's your crow's head?

SURLY   [*Aside*]   Your coxcomb's, is't not?

SUBTLE   No, 'tis not perfect. Would it were the crow.
    That work wants something.   70

SURLY   [*Aside*]   O, I looked for this.
    The hay is a-pitching.

SUBTLE   Are you sure you loosed'em
    I'their own menstrue?

FACE   Yes, sir, and then married'em,
    And put'em in a bolt's head, nipped to digestion,
    According as you bade me, when I set
    The liquor of Mars to circulation   75
    In the same heat.

59–60. *white oil ... red*] Fluid derived from mercury (white) or sulphur (red). See l. 192
    below.
61. *St Mary's bath*] Specific kind of sand or water bath.
62. *lac virginis*] Mercury.
63. *faeces*] Sediment. *calcined*] Reduced to a fine powder by heating and drying.
64. *calx*] Powder. *salt of mercury*] Mercuric oxide.
65. *rectified*] Distilled. *reverberating*] Heating with indirect or reflected heat.
68. *crow's head*] Blue-grey or blue-black, one of the expected sequence of colours.
    coxcomb's] Fool's.
71. *hay is a-pitching*] The trap is being set. In snaring rabbits, or cony-catching, the *hay* or
    net is cast, or pitched, over the rabbit-hole; when the rabbits are started or 'bolted' (see
    88) from the hole, they are snagged in the net. In thieves' cant, the 'cony' or rabbit is
    the dupe in a swindle.
72. *menstrue*] Solvent. *married*] Combined in a flask. Bolt's head flasks were often
    decorated with pictures of copulating couples to illustrate union. See van Lennep 1984:
    pp. 135–6.
73. *nipped to digestion*] Sealed and placed in a slow furnace to permit the extraction of
    soluble substances.
75. *liquor of Mars*] Molten iron.

SUBTLE   The process, then, was right.
FACE   Yes, by the token, sir, the retort brake,
    And what was saved was put into the pelican
    And signed with Hermes' seal.
SUBTLE   I think 'twas so.
    We should have a new amalgama.   80
SURLY   [*Aside*]   O, this ferret
    Is rank as any polecat.
SUBTLE   But I care not.
    Let him e'en die. We have enough beside,
    In embrion. H has his white shirt on?
FACE   Yes, sir,
    He's ripe for inceration. He stands warm
    In his ash-fire. I would not you should let   85
    Any die now, if I might counsel, sir,
    For luck's sake to the rest. It is not good.
MAMMON   He says right.
SURLY   [*Aside*]   Ay, are you bolted?
FACE   Nay, I know't, sir.
    I've seen th'ill fortune. What is some three ounces
    Of fresh materials?   . 90
MAMMON   Is't no more?
FACE   No more, sir,
    Of gold, t'amalgam, with some six of mercury.
MAMMON   Away, here's money. What will serve?
FACE   [*Indicating Subtle*]   Ask him, sir.
MAMMON   How much?
SUBTLE   Give him nine pound – you may gi' him ten.
SURLY   [*Aside*] Yes, twenty, and be cozened, do.
MAMMON   [*Gives Face money*]   There 'tis.
SUBTLE   This needs not. But that you will have it so,   95

---

77. *token*] Outward appearance. *retort*] Glass vessel with a long curved neck for distilling.
78. *pelican*] Distilling flask with a neck that curves down to the bottom, permitting continuous refinement and recirculation. The vessel imitates the shape of the emblematic pelican pecking her own heart to feed her children.
79. *Hermes' seal*] Hermetically sealing a tube by heating and twisting it closed.
80. *amalgama*] Union of metals effected with mercury.
81. *ferret*] In cony-catching, a ferret digs down one rabbit-hole, forcing the rabbits to try to escape by the bolt-hole where the net has been stretched.
83. *In embrion*] In the early stage of the process.
84. *inceration*] Mixing a fluid and a powder until they unite as a waxlike substance. Face's double-talk at 84–7 implies that Mammon is ready to be cozened further – by Dol's appearance.

To see conclusions of all. For two
Of our inferior works are at fixation.
A third is in ascension. Go your ways.
Ha' you set the oil of Luna in kemia?

FACE   Yes, sir.   100
SUBTLE   And the philosopher's vinegar?
FACE   Ay.
SURLY   [*Aside*] We shall have a salad.

    [*Exit Face*]

MAMMON   When do you make projection?
SUBTLE   Son, be not hasty. I exalt our med'cine
    By hanging him in *balneo vaporoso*
    And giving him solution, then congeal him,
    And then dissolve him, then again congeal him;   105
    For look, how oft I iterate the work,
    So many times I add unto his virtue.
    As, if at first one ounce convert a hundred,
    After his second loose he'll turn a thousand;
    His third solution, ten; his fourth, a hundred.   110
    After his fifth, a thousand thousand ounces
    Of any imperfect metal into pure
    Silver or gold, in all examinations
    As good as any of the natural mine.
    Get you your stuff here against afternoon: 115
    Your brass, your pewter, and your andirons.
MAMMON   Not those of iron?
SUBTLE '   Yes. You may bring them too.
    We'll change all metals.
SURLY   [*Aside*]   I believe you in that.
MAMMON   Then I may send my spits?
SUBTLE   Yes, and your racks.
SURLY   And dripping-pans, and pot-hangers, and hooks?   120

  97. *fixation*] Solidification.
  98. *ascension*] Distillation, evaporation.
  99. *oil of Luna*] White or silver elixir.   *in kemia*] In the retort for chemical analysis.
 101. *philosopher's vinegar*] The universal solvent for dissolving metals. The 'vinegar' may
       be a mercury, or a mild acid made from mead.
 102. *exalt*] Refine.
 103. *balneo vaporoso*] Steam bath in which the flask is suspended.
 104. *giving him solution*] Dissolving it.
 109. *loose*] Solution.
 110. *ten, hundred*] That is, ten thousand, hundred thousand.
 119. *racks*] Bars which supported the spits in front of the fire.

    Shall he not?

SUBTLE   If he please.

SURLY   To be an ass.

SUBTLE How, sir!

MAMMON   This gent'man you must bear withal.
    I told you he had no faith.

SURLY   And little hope, sir,
    But much less charity, should I gull myself.

SUBTLE Why, what have you observed, sir, in our art   125
    Seems so impossible?

SURLY   But your whole work, no more.
    That you should hatch gold in a furnace, sir,
    As they do eggs in Egypt!

SUBTLE   Sir, do you
    Believe that eggs are hatched so?

SURLY   If I should?

SUBTLE Why, I think that the greater miracle.   130
    No egg but differs from a chicken more
    Than metals in themselves.

SURLY   That cannot be.
    The egg's ordained by nature to that end,
    And is a chicken in *potentia*.

SUBTLE The same we say of lead and other metals,   135
    Which would be gold if they had time.

MAMMON   And that
    Our art doth further.

SUBTLE   Ay, for 'twere absurd
    To think that nature in the earth bred gold
    Perfect, i'the instant. Something went before.
    There must be remote matter.   140

SURLY   Ay, what is that?

SUBTLE Marry, we say –

MAMMON   Ay, now it heats. Stand, father.
    Pound him to dust –

SUBTLE   It is, of the one part,
    A humid exhalation which we call

---

128. *eggs in Egypt*] Eggs had been incubated in dung-heated ovens in Egypt since classical times (H&S).

131–207. The alchemical arguments are taken mostly from vol. 1 of Martin Del Rio, *Disquisitiones Magicae* (H&S).

140. *remote matter*] The original indeterminate matter or essence from which all particular things grew recognisable forms.

141. *father*] Title of respect.

Materia liquida, or the unctuous water,
On th'other part, a certain crass and viscous   145
Portion of earth, both which, concorporate,
Do make the elementary matter of gold –
Which is not yet *propria materia*,
But common to all metals and all stones.
For where it is forsaken of that moisture   150
And hath more dryness, it becomes a stone;
Where it retains more of the humid fatness,
It turns to sulphur or to quicksilver,
Who are the parents of all other metals.
Nor can this remote matter suddenly   155
Progress so from extreme unto extreme
As to grow gold and leap o'er all the means.
Nature doth first beget th'imperfect; then
Proceeds she to the perfect. Of that airy
And oily water, mercury is engendered;   160
Sulphur o' the fat and earthy part, the one
(Which is the last) supplying the place of male,
The other of the female, in all metals.
Some do believe hermaphrodeity,
That both do act and suffer. But these two   165
Make the rest ductile, malleable, extensive.
And even in gold they are, for we do find
Seeds of them by our fire, and gold in them,
And can produce the *species* of each metal
More perfect thence than nature doth in earth.   170
Beside, who doth not see in daily practice
Art can beget bees, hornets, beetles, wasps,
Out of the carcasses and dung of creatures,
Yea, scorpions of an herb, being rightly placed!

144. *Materia liquida*] Liquid matter. *unctuous*] Oily.
145. *crass*] Dense. *viscous*] Imperfectly fluid; adhesively soft.
146. *concorporate*] United into one substance.
148. *propria materia*] A specific substance.
157. *means*] Intermediate stages.
162. *the last*] The latter.
164. *hermaphrodeity*] Seeing chemical union as having characteristics of both sexes. Alternatively, chemical unions might be seen as 'married', as at l. 72 above.
165. *both ... suffer*] Are both active and passive.
166. *extensive*] Capable of being drawn out.
171–4. Incorrect deduction from observing decayed animal matter suggested that insects were generated spontaneously out of carrion.
174. *herb*] Basil, according to Pliny. *rightly*] As prescribed by ritual; 'ritely' in Q and F.

And these are living creatures, far more perfect   175
And excellent than metals!

MAMMON   Well said, father!
Nay, if he take you in hand, sir, with an argument,
He'll bray you in a mortar.

SURLY   Pray you, sir, stay.
Rather than I'll be brayed, sir, I'll believe
That alchemy is a pretty kind of game,   180
Somewhat like tricks o'the cards, to cheat a man
With charming.

SUBTLE   Sir?

SURLY   What else are all your terms,
Whereon no one o'your writers 'grees with other?
Of your *elixir*, your *lac virginis*,
Your *stone*, your *med'cine*, and your *chrysosperm*,   185
Your *sal*, your *sulphur*, and your *mercury*,
Your *oil of height*, your *tree of life*, your *blood*,
Your *marchesite*, your *tutty*, your *magnesia*,
Your *toad*, your *crow*, your *dragon*, and your *panther*,
Your *sun*, your *moon*, your *firmament*, your *adrop*,   190
Your *lato*, *azoch*, *zernich*, *chibrit*, *heautarit*,
And then your *red man*, and your *white woman*,
With all your broths, your *menstrues*, and *materials*,

178. *bray*] Pound with a pestle.

182. *charming*] Magic, beguiling.

185. *chrysosperm*] Seed of gold.

186. *sal*] Salt, according to Paracelsian alchemists, the third basic metal, along with sulphur and mercury. Its purpose was to fix the gold colour in the transformed material.

187. *oil of height*] Oil derived from mercury or sulphur; see 59–60.   *tree of life*] Emblem of the seven basic metals.   *blood*] The red colour indicating successful near-completion of an alchemical experiment.

188. *marchesite*] White iron pyrites.   *tutty*] Impure zinc oxide.   *magnesia*] Thick salty water.

189. Colours in the alchemical process, virtually synonymous tinctures of blackness: earth-black, blue-black, silver- or grey-black, and mottled black.

190. *firmament*] Philosophers' heaven, in the sphere of the fixed stars.   *adrop*] Lead, a source of mercury.

191. *lato*] A mixed metal like brass.   *azoch*] Mercury.   *zernich*] Trisulphide of arsenic.   *chibrit*] Sulphur.   *heautarit*] Mercury.

192. *red man*] Sulphur, male because of its penetrating principle.   *white woman*] Mercury, female because it receives the sulphur in the alchemical union.

193. *broths ... menstrues*] Synonyms for solvents.

Of piss and egg-shells, women's terms, man's blood,
Hair o' the head, burnt clouts, chalk, merds, and clay,   195
Powder of bones, scalings of iron, glass,
And worlds of other strange *ingredients*
Would burst a man to name?

SUBTLE   And all these, named,
Intending but one thing, which art our writers
Used to obscure their art.   200

MAMMON   Sir, so I told him,
Because the simple idiot should not learn it
And make it vulgar.

SUBTLE   Was not all the knowledge
Of the Egyptians writ in mystic symbols?
Speak not the scriptures oft in parables?
Are not the choicest fables of the poets,   205
That were the fountains and first springs of wisdom,
Wrapped in perplexèd allegories?

MAMMON   I urged that,
And cleared to him that Sisyphus was damned
To roll the ceaseless stone only because
He would have made ours common. – Who is this?   210

Dol is seen

SUBTLE   God's precious – What do you mean? Go in, good lady,
Let me entreat you.

[*Exit Dol*]

                          Where's this varlet?

[*Enter Face*]

FACE   Sir?
SUBTLE   You very knave! Do you use me thus?
FACE   Wherein, sir?

194. *piss*] A common ingredient either alone, or mixed with wine or vinegar. *egg-shells*] Dr John Dee used to distil eggshells, according to Aubrey, who assumed that Jonson parodied Dee in Subtle (Mares 1967). *women's terms*] menstrual blood.
195. *clouts*] Clods of earth. *merds*] Excrement.
208. *Sisyphus*] For defrauding the gods, condemned to roll a huge rock uphill in Hades. The task was perpetual since, just at the top, the rock rolled downhill again.
210. *common*] Dol's cue. Dol's brief but tantalising appearance parodies the vision of Helen of Troy in Marlowe's *Doctor Faustus*.

SUBTLE   Go in and see, you traitor. Go.

   [*Exit Face*]

MAMMON   Who is it, sir?
SUBTLE   Nothing, sir. Nothing.   215
MAMMON   What's the matter? Good sir,
   I have not seen you thus distempered! Who is't?
SUBTLE   All arts have still had, sir, their adversaries,
   But ours the most ignorant.

   Face returns

                              What now?
FACE   'Twas not my fault, sir. She would speak with you.
SUBTLE   Would she, sir? Follow me.   220

   [*Exit Subtle*]

MAMMON   Stay, Lungs.
FACE   [*Going*]   I dare not, sir.

MAMMON   Stay, man. What is she?
FACE   [*Still going*]   A lord's sister, sir.
MAMMON   How! Pray thee stay!
FACE   She's mad, sir, and sent hither –
   He'll be mad too.
MAMMON   I warrant thee! Why sent hither?
FACE   Sir, to be cured.
SUBTLE   [*Calling within*] Why, rascal!
FACE   [*Calling*]   Lo you! Here, sir!

   [*Exit Face*]

MAMMON   'Fore God, a Bradamante, a brave piece!   225
SURLY   Heart, this is a bawdy-house! I'll be burnt else.
MAMMON   O, by this light, no! Do not wrong him. He's
   Too scrupulous that way. It is his vice.
   No, he's a rare physician, do him right.
   An excellent Paracelsian! And has done   230

---

224. *Lo you!*] Either indicating to Mammon, 'See what I mean?'; or responding to Subtle's
   call.
225. *Bradamante*] The lady warrior in Ariosto's *Orlando Furioso*. *brave piece*] Attractively 'tough' female.
230. *Paracelsian*] Follower of the revolutionary physician and alchemist Paracelsus,
   1493–1541, who first applied chemistry to medicine (the 'mineral physic' of 231),
   seeking to eliminate disease by restoring the body's healthy balance of salt, mercury,
   and sulphur, the universal constituents of matter. Fantastic stories about his radical

Strange cures with mineral physic. He deals all
With spirits, he. He will not hear a word
Of Galen or his tedious recipes.

Face again

How now, Lungs!
FACE   [*Taking him aside*] Softly, sir, speak softly. I meant
  To ha' told your worship all. This [*Indicating Surly*] must not hear. 235
MAMMON   No, he will not be gulled. Let him alone.
FACE   You're very right, sir, she is a most rare scholar,
  And is gone mad with studying Broughton's works.
  If you but name a word touching the Hebrew,
  She falls into her fit and will discourse 240
  So learnedly of genealogies
  As you would run mad too to hear her, sir.
MAMMON   How might one do t'have conference with her, Lungs?
FACE   O, divers have run mad upon the conference.
  I do not know, sir. I am sent in haste 245
  To fetch a vial.

[*While Face finds the vial, Surly rejoins Mammon*]

SURLY   Be not gulled, Sir Mammon.
MAMMON   Wherein? Pray ye be patient.
SURLY   Yes, as you are.
  And trust confederate knaves and bawds and whores.
MAMMON   You are too foul, believe it. Come here, Ulen.
  One word. 250
FACE   [*Going*] I dare not, in good faith.
MAMMON   Stay, knave.
FACE   He's extreme angry that you saw her, sir.
MAMMON   Drink that. [*Gives money*] What is she when she's
  out of her fit?
FACE   O, the most affablest creature, sir! So merry!

practice made him into a quack or magician. See *Volp* 2.2.122 and note.
232. *spirits*] Chemical distillations, but also supernatural spirits.
233. *Galen*] Classical physician (AD 130–210) whose medical writings were studied and
  followed in the Middle Ages and later. His prescriptions for disease ('tedious recipes')
  were traditional herbal and animal remedies approved by conservative doctors.
236. *gulled*] Ironical repetition from 27.
238. *Broughton's works*] Hugh Broughton (1549–1612), puritan minister and scholar
  whose many monographs and pamphlets explain obscure biblical points.
241. *genealogies*] Broughton attempted to rationalise biblical chronology (parodied in
  4.5).
243. *t'have conference*] To meet, but also suggesting a sexual 'bringing together'.

So pleasant! She'll mount you up like quicksilver
Over the helm, and circulate like oil,   255
A very vegetal; discourse of state,
Of mathematics, bawdry, anything –
MAMMON   Is she no way accessible? No means,
No trick, to give a man a taste of her – wit –
Or so? – Ulen?   260
FACE   I'll come to you again, sir.

   [*Exit Face*]

MAMMON   Surly, I did not think one o' your breeding
Would traduce personages of worth.
SURLY   Sir Epicure,
Your friend to use, yet still loath to be gulled.
I do not like your philosophical bawds.
Their stone is lechery enough to pay for   265
Without this bait.
MAMMON   Heart, you abuse yourself.
I know the lady, and her friends and means,
The original of this disaster. Her brother
Has told me all.
SURLY   And yet you ne'er saw her
Till now?   270
MAMMON   O, yes, but I forgot. I have (believe it)
One o' the treacherous't memories, I do think,
Of all mankind.
SURLY   What call you her brother?
MAMMON   My lord –
He wi'not have his name known, now I think on't.
SURLY   A very treacherous memory!
MAMMON   O' my faith –
SURLY   Tut, if you ha'it not about you, pass it   275
Till we meet next.
MAMMON   Nay, by this hand, 'tis true.

254. *mount up ... circulate*] Describing the reaction of mercury in an alembic, but also
    suggesting sexual activity.
256. *vegetal*] Healthy and active; sexually attractive, like 'vegetous' in *SW* 2.2.57.   *state*]
    Politics.
258. *accessible*] Capable of being reached or entered. The wording here and in the
    following lines is equivocally sexual.
259. *wit*] Or 'whit', euphemistic term for pudendum; see 4.7.45 and note.
263. *to use*] At your service.
265. *lechery*] Illicit or immoderate desire, derived from 'stone' = testicle.
275. *pass it*] Forget it.

He's one I honour, and my noble friend,
And I respect his house.

SURLY   Heart! Can it be
That a grave sir, a rich, that has no need,
A wise sir, too, at other times, should thus   280
With his own oaths and arguments make hard means
To gull himself? And this be your *elixir*,
Your *lapis mineralis*, and your *lunary*,
Give me your honest trick yet at primero
Or gleek, and take your *lutum sapientis*,   285
Your *menstruum simplex*. I'll have gold before you
And with less danger of the quicksilver
Or the hot sulphur.

[Enter Face delivering a message] to Surly

FACE   Here's one from Captain Face, sir,
Desires you meet him i' the Temple Church
Some half-hour hence and upon earnest business.   290

He whispers [to] Mammon

Sir, if you please to quit us now, and come
Again within two hours, you shall have
My master busy examining o' the works,
And I will steal you in unto the party,

---

282. *And*] If.
283. *lapis mineralis*] The mineral (or philosopher's) stone. *lunary*] A herb, moonwort, commonly called 'honesty', used in alchemy to produce silver.
284. *honest trick*] Either winning cards dealt honestly during play, or straightforward card-sharping (as opposed to Subtle's devious alchemy game), playing on *lunary*. *primero*] Popular card-game in which the best hand is a four-card flush worth 55 points (see 1.2.47).
285. *gleek*] A three-handed game in which the winning hand is three face-cards of the same rank. *lutum sapientis*] A paste used to make plugs or seals for flasks.
286. *menstruum simplex*] Plain solvent derived from mercury, used to dissolve gold.
287–8. *quicksilver . . . sulphur*] Used to treat venereal disease.
289. *Temple Church*] Official church for lawyers at the Inner and Middle Temples, and a common meeting-place for lawyers and clients. St Paul's, an even more popular rendezvous, was closer to Face's house in Blackfriars, but not as prestigious or as safe from recognition by other rogues.
293. *busy . . . works*] Working on his experiments in the lab.

That you may see her converse.   295
        [*To Surly*]   Sir, shall I say
You'll meet the Captain's worship?
SURLY   Sir, I will.
        [*Aside*] But by attorney and to a second purpose.
        Now I am sure it is a bawdy-house.
        I'll swear it, were the Marshal here to thank me.
        The naming this commander doth confirm it.   300
        Don Face! Why, he's the most authentic dealer
        I'these commodities! The superintendent
        To all the quainter traffickers in town.
        He is their visitor and does appoint
        Who lies with whom, and at what hour, what price,   305
        Which gown, and in what smock, what fall, what tire.
        Him will I prove, by a third person, to find
        The subtleties of this dark labyrinth.
        Which, if I do discover, dear Sir Mammon,
        You'll give your poor friend leave, though no philosopher, 310
        To laugh. For you that are, 'tis thought, shall weep.
FACE   Sir. He does pray you'll not forget.
SURLY   I will not, sir.
        Sir Epicure, I shall leave you.
MAMMON   I follow you, straight.

        [*Exit Surly*]

FACE   But do so, good sir, to avoid suspicion.
        This gent'man has a parlous head.   315
MAMMON   But wilt thou, Ulen,
        Be constant to thy promise?
FACE   As my life, sir.
MAMMON   And wilt thou insinuate what I am? And praise me?
        And say I am a noble fellow?
FACE   O, what else, sir?
        And that you'll make her royal with the stone,

295. *converse*] Talking, and engaging in sexual intercourse.
297. *by attorney*] By proxy, appearing as the Spaniard rather than in his own person. Refer to 307 below.
299. *marshal*] Administrator of the law (see 1.1.120).
303. *quainter traffickers*] The more cunning class of dealers in prostitution and knavery; punning on *quaint*, 'cunt'.
304. *visitor*] Official inspector or supervisor.
306. *fall*] Falling band, a flat collar as distinct from the starched ruff. *tire*] Clothing accessory, probably 'head-tire' or head-dress.
315. *parlous head*] Perilous, or dangerously clever, mind.

An empress, and yourself king of Bantam.   320
MAMMON   Wilt thou do this?
FACE   Will I, sir?
MAMMON   Lungs, my Lungs!
    I love thee.
FACE   Send your stuff, sir, that my master
    May busy himself about projection.
MAMMON   Th'hast witched me, rogue. [*Gives money*] Take, go.
FACE   Your jack and all, sir.
MAMMON   Thou art a villain – I will send my jack,   325
    And the weights too. Slave, I could bite thine ear.
    Away, thou dost not care for me.
FACE   Not I, sir?
MAMMON   Come, I was born to make thee, my good weasel,
    Set thee on a bench, and ha' thee twirl a chain
    With the best lords vermin of 'em all.   330
FACE   Away, sir.
MAMMON   A count, nay a count-palatine –
FACE   Good sir, go.
MAMMON   – Shall not advance thee better. No, nor faster.

    [*Exit Mammon*]

320 *Bantam*] Javanese capital of a Mohammedan empire in Indonesia. Drake described its
    fabulous wealth when he stopped there in 1580; a former English resident, Edmund
    Scott, described its customs and on-going commerce with the English and Dutch in a
    book published in 1606 (H&S).
324. *jack*] Mechanism for turning a spit.
326. *weights*] In the clockwork mechanism turning the jack.   *Slave . . . ear*] Expression of
    rough affection, like 'villain' above.
328. *make thee*] Give you professional and social prestige.   *weasel*] Epithet prais-
    ing Face's quick wits; ironic, in view of the cony-catching game (see 71 and 81
    above).
330. *vermin*] Punning on 'ermine'. Mammon's references to 'bench', 'chain', and 'lords'
    seem to promise Face an important office as judge, member of parliament, or
    alderman.
332. *count-palatine*] Vice-regent, having in his county supreme judicial power equal to the
    monarch's. The Dukes of Chester and Lancaster and the Bishop of Durham had this
    power, allowing them to quell uprisings along the Welsh or Scottish borders.

Act 2 scene 4*

[*Enter*] *Subtle, Dol*

SUBTLE   Has he bit? Has he bit?

FACE   And swallowed too, my Subtle.
    I ha' giv'n him line, and now he plays, i'faith.

SUBTLE   And shall we twitch him?

FACE   Through both the gills.
    A wench is a rare bait with which a man
    No sooner's taken but he straight firks mad.   5

SUBTLE   Dol, my Lord What's'hum's sister, you must now
    Bear yourself *statelich*.

DOL   O, let me alone.
    I'll not forget my race, I warrant you.
    I'll keep my distance, laugh, and talk aloud;
    Have all the tricks of a proud scurvy lady,   10
    And be as rude's her woman.

FACE   Well said, Sanguine.

SUBTLE   But will he send his andirons?

FACE   His jack too,
    And's iron shoeing-horn. I ha' spoke to him. Well,
    I must not lose my wary gamester yonder.

SUBTLE   O, Monsieur Caution that will not be gulled?   15

FACE   Ay, if I can strike a fine hook into him now!
    The Temple Church, there I have cast mine angle.
    Well, pray for me. I'll about it.

    One knocks

SUBTLE   What, more gudgeons!
    Dol, scout, scout.

    [*Dol peeps out*]

        Stay, Face, you must go to the door.

---

*   This scene, like the congratulatory moments in *Volp* in which Mosca and Volpone
    chortle over their dupes, or the 'locker-room' chat in 4.1 of *SW*, gives us a backstage
    look at role-playing, from the successful rogues' point of view.

1–5. Extended fishing metaphor, retrieved at ll. 16–18.

  5. *firks mad*] Is aroused to violent madness.

  7. *statelich*] Aristocratically (Dutch).

11. *woman*] Maidservant.   *Sanguine*] The 'blood' humour, signifying sexual passion.

17. *angle*] Fishing line.

18. *gudgeons*] Fish that swallow any bait; hence, gullible persons.

Pray God it be my Anabaptist. Who is't Dol?   20
DOL   I know him not. He looks like a gold-end-man.
SUBTLE   Gods so! 'Tis he, he said he would send. What call you him?
    The sanctified elder that should deal
    For Mammon's jack and andirons! Let him in.
    Stay, help me off, first, with my gown.   25

    [*Face assists him, and exit*]

                           Away,
Madam, to your withdrawing chamber.

    [*Exit Dol*]

                           Now,
In a new tune, new gesture, but old language!
This fellow is sent from one negotiates with me
About the stone too, for the holy brethren
Of Amsterdam, the exiled saints, that hope   30
To raise their discipline by it. I must use him
In some strange fashion, now, to make him admire me.

Act 2 scene 5*

SUBTLE   Where is my drudge?

    [*Enter*] *Face* [*with*] *Ananias*

FACE   Sir.

20. *Anabaptist*] Member of a puritan sect advocating such heresies as adult baptism, total immersion, and communal ownership of goods.
21. *gold-end-man*] Itinerant jeweller buying up odd or broken bits of jewellery.
30. *exiled saints*] Among the group of outspoken puritans expelled after 1604 for refusing to accept the 39 Articles of the Church of England; perhaps referring to the earlier zealots who fled to England in the 1530s, following John of Leyden's failure to maintain his brief rule in Münster or to gain control of Amsterdam and other Dutch towns.
31. *raise their discipline*] Increase the power of their sect.
*   Anabaptists were radical dissenters whose faith in direct revelation from God made them believe themselves above established church and state; nevertheless, Anabaptists were largely pacifists. The splinter group and leaders under attack here are violent revolutionary millenarians, the most famous of whom were those involved in the Münster Uprising (see l. 13 below, and Mebane 1989: ch. 7, esp. pp. 140–41). Radical reformers espoused Hermetic philosophy and alchemy because occultist theories of spiritual perfectibility complemented their sectarian beliefs. In Ananias and Subtle, Jonson balances the canting fanaticism of the Anabaptist against that of the alchemist, brothers in spiritual swindle.

SUBTLE   Take away the recipient,
    And rectify your menstrue from the phlegma.
    Then pour it o' the sol in the cucurbite,
    And let 'em macerate together.
FACE   Yes, sir.
    And save the ground?   5
SUBTLE   No. *Terra damnata*
    Must not have entrance in the work. – Who are you?
ANANIAS   A faithful brother, if it please you.
SUBTLE   What's that?
    A Lullianist? A Ripley? *Filius artis*?
    Can you sublime and dulcify? Calcine?
    Know you the *sapor pontic*? *Sapor styptic*?   10
    Or what is homogene or heterogene?
ANANIAS   I understand no heathen language, truly.
SUBTLE   'Heathen', you Knipper-Doling? Is *ars sacra*,
    Or *chrysopoeia*, or *spagyrica*,
    Or the pamphysic or panarchic knowledge   15
    A 'heathen' language?

1. *recipient*] Vessel for receiving and condensing distilled matter.
2. *rectify*] Refine to raise to its required strength. *phlegma*] Watery distillate.
3. *cucurbite*] Gourd-shaped retort flask.
4. *mascerate*] Soften by soaking.
5. *ground ... Terra damnata*] Synonyms; sediment left after all the volatile substances have been distilled.
7. *faithful brother*] Anabaptist. Subtle deliberately mistakes him for a member of an alchemical society, and proceeds to question him on that basis.
8. *Lullianist*] Follower of Raymond Lull, 1235–1315, Spanish scientist and logician. *Ripley*] Follower of George Ripley, Canon of Bridlington (d. 1490?), who popularised Lull's work in *Medulla Alchemiae* (1476), and the posthumously published *The Compound of Alchemy* (1591). *Filius artis*] Son of the art, an alchemist.
9. *sublime*] Distil. *dulcify*] Refine the salts from a substance. *calcine*] Reduce to a powder by heating and drying.
10. *sapor pontic ... styptic*] Two of the nine classifications of taste, sour (*pontic*) and somewhat less sour (*styptic*).
11. *homogene or heterogene*] Of one kind, or of various kinds.
13. *Knipper-Doling*] Bernt Knipperdollinck, one of the Anabaptist leaders of the Münster uprising under 'King' John (Jan Bockelson) of Leyden, 1534–6, whose brief rule was notorious for its tyranny and debauchery. *ars sacra*] The sacred art, another synonym for alchemy, like those of the next lines.
14. *chrysopoeia*] Gold-making. *spagyrica*] A Paracelsian term for alchemy, indicating the method of repeatedly separating and uniting ingedients.
15. *pamphysic or panarchic*] Pertaining to the nature or ruling power of the universe, words coined by Jonson from Greek.

ANANIAS   Heathen Greek, I take it.
SUBTLE   How? 'Heathen Greek'?
ANANIAS   All's heathen but the Hebrew.
SUBTLE   Sirrah, my varlet, stand you forth and speak to him
    Like a philosopher. Answer i'the language.
    Name the vexations and the martyrisations   20
    Of metals in the work.
FACE   Sir, putrefaction,
    Solution, ablution, sublimation,
    Cohobation, calcination, ceration, and
    Fixation.
SUBTLE   [*To Ananias*] This is 'heathen Greek' to you now?
    [*To Face*] And when comes vivification?   25
FACE   After mortification.
SUBTLE   What's cohobation?
FACE   'Tis the pouring on
    Your *aqua regis*, and then drawing him off
    To the trine circle of the seven spheres.
SUBTLE   What's the proper passion of metals?
FACE   Malleation.

17. *Hebrew*] Puritans tried to enforce Hebrew as the universal language, based on the
    widely accepted theory (except by those mentioned at 2.1.84) that Adam spoke it in
    Eden. Anabaptist extremists in Münster proposed burning all books except the Old
    Testament; less zealous puritans merely condemned classical learning as heathen.
19. *language*] Alchemical jargon, which Subtle mockingly opposes to puritan cant in the
    following catechism.
20. *vexations ... martyrisations*] Trials and sufferings. Subtle uses the puritan language of
    Foxe's *Acts and Monuments* to describe alchemical processes.
21. *putrefaction*] Breaking down compounds and reducing the materials.
22. *Solution*] Transforming a solid to a liquid by the use of a solvent. *ablution*] Washing
    away impurities. *sublimation*] Distillation.
23. *Cohobation*] Repeated distillation of the distillate. *calcination*] Reducing to a fine
    powder. *ceration*] Mixing fluid and powder into a waxlike substance.
24. *Fixation*] stabilising a volatile substance into a solid compound.
25. *vivification*] Refinement to extract pure metal from a compound. *mortification*]
    Breaking down materials into chemical components.
27. *aqua regis*] 'Supreme water', acid capable of dissolving gold.
28. *trine ... spheres*] When three of the seven planets form a trine (positioned in a circle
    divided into segments of 120° each), the configuration was thought to indicate
    astrologically favourable conditions for an alchemical experiment.
29. *particular passion*] Distinguishing condition to which a thing may be subjected. *Mal-
    leation*] Hammering, which makes metals expand.

SUBTLE   What's your *ultimum supplicium auri*?   30
FACE   Antimonium.
SUBTLE   [*To Ananias*] This's 'heathen Greek' to you? [*To Face*] And
   what's your mercury?
FACE   A very fugitive. He will be gone, sir.
SUBTLE   How know you him?
FACE   By his viscosity,
   His oleosity, and his suscitability.
SUBTLE   How do you sublime him?   35
FACE   With the calce of egg-shells,
   White marble, talc.
SUBTLE   Your *magisterium*, now?
   What's that?
FACE   Shifting, sir, your elements:
   Dry into cold, cold into moist, moist in-
   To hot, hot into dry.
SUBTLE   [*To Ananias*] This's 'heathen Greek' to you still?
   [*To Face*] Your *lapis philosophicus*?   40
FACE   'Tis a stone, and not
   A stone: a spirit, a soul, and a body,
   Which, if you do dissolve, it is dissolved,
   If you coagulate, it is coagulated,
   If you make it to fly, it flieth.
SUBTLE   Enough.

  [*Exit Face*]

   This's 'heathen Greek' to you? What are you, sir?   45
ANANIAS   Please you, a servant of the exiled brethren
   That deal with widows' and with orphans' goods,
   And make a just account unto the saints.
   A deacon.
SUBTLE   O, you are sent from Master Wholesome,
   Your teacher?   50

30. *ultimum supplicium auri*] The final punishment of gold. Antimony makes gold
  immalleable.
33. *viscosity*] State of being neither liquid nor solid.
34. *oleosity*] Oiliness. *suscitability*] Volatility; hence 'fugitive', l. 32 above.
35. *calce*] Calx or powder.
36. *magisterium*] Master-work, the philosopher's stone.
37–9. *Shifting … dry*] Face defines alchemy as the understanding of how to change the four
  elements until the fifth essence, or quintessence, emerges – otherwise called the
  philosopher's stone.
40–44. Face defines the philosopher's stone paradoxically as essentially undefinable,
  infinitely mutable and indestructible.

ANANIAS   From Tribulation Wholesome,
    Our very zealous pastor.
SUBTLE   Good. I have
    Some orphans' goods to come here.
ANANIAS   Of what kind, sir?
SUBTLE   Pewter and brass, andirons and kitchen ware,
    Metals that we must use our med'cine on –
    Wherein the brethren may have a penn'orth.   55
    For ready money.
ANANIAS   Were the orphans' parents
    Sincere professors?
SUBTLE   Why do you ask?
ANANIAS   Because
    We then are to deal justly and give (in truth)
    Their utmost value.
SUBTLE   'Slid, you'd cozen else,
    And if their parents were not of the faithful?   60
    I will not trust you, now I think on't,
    Till I ha' talked with your pastor. Ha' you brought money
    To buy more coals?
ANANIAS   No, surely.
SUBTLE   No? How so?
ANANIAS   The brethren bid me say unto you, sir,
    Surely they will not venture any more   65
    Till they may see projection.
SUBTLE   How!
ANANIAS   You've had
    For the instuments, as bricks and loam and glasses,
    Already thirty pound, and for materials,
    They say, some ninety more. And they have heard since
    That one at Heidelberg made it of an egg   70
    And a small paper of pin-dust.
SUBTLE   What's your name?
ANANIAS   My name is Ananias.
SUBTLE   Out, the varlet
    That cozened the apostles! Hence, away!

57. *sincere professors*] True practising believers.
70. *Heidelberg*] University town dominated by Protestant reformers. The Heidelberg
    Catechism, a key document of the Reformation, was authorised by eminent Lutherans.
    Puritans were more likely to cite alchemical success stories from this town than from
    more 'heathen' centres.
71. *pin-dust*] Metal filings, waste matter in pin manufacturing.
72–3. Ananias and his wife Sapphira stole from their community, and were exposed by St
    Peter (Acts 5:1–11). See The Persons of the Play 10 and note.

Flee, Mischief! Had your holy consistory
No name to send me of another sound   75
Than wicked Ananias? Send your elders
Hither to make atonement for you quickly.
And gi'me satisfaction, or out goes
The fire, and down the alembics and the furnace,
Piger Henricus or what not. Thou wretch,   80
Both sericon and bufo shall be lost,
Tell 'em. All hope of rooting out the bishops
Or th'antichristian hierarchy shall perish,
If they stay threescore minutes. The aqueity,
Terreity, and sulphureity   85
Shall run together again, and all be annulled,
Thou wicked Ananias.

[*Exit Ananias*]

             This will fetch 'em,
And make 'em haste towards their gulling more.
A man must deal like a rough nurse and fright
Those that are froward to an appetite.   90

---

74. *consistory*] Governing body of the church, usually the pastor, the elders, and the deacons.
80. *Piger Henricus*] 'Lazy Henry', a multiple furnace with one fire in the central compartment, from which heat wafts through openings into side furnaces: both efficient and easily maintained.
81. *sericon and bufo*] Red tincture and black (literally, toad).
82. *rooting out the bishops*] Radical reformers opposed the retention of bishops in the Church of England as a vestige of popish or 'antichristian hierarchy' which biblical precedent did not justify.
84–6. *aqueity ... annulled*] The clarified mercury, the sediment (as at l. 5 above), and the sulphur will mix and spoil the experiment.

Act 2 scene 6*

[*Enter*] *Face, Drugger*

FACE [*To Drugger*] He's busy with his spirits, but we'll upon him.
SUBTLE How now! What mates? What Bayards ha' we here?
FACE [*To Drugger*] I told you he would be furious. – Sir, here's Nab
    Has brought y'another piece of gold to look on –
    [*Aside to Drugger*] We must appease him. Give it me. [*To Subtle,*   5
      handing him the coin] – and prays you,
    You would devise – What is it, Nab?
DRUGGER   A sign, sir.
FACE Ay, a good lucky one, a thriving sign, Doctor.
SUBTLE I was devising now.
FACE [*Aside to Subtle*]   'Slight, do not say so.
    He will repent he ga'you any more. –
    [*Aloud*] What say you to his constellation, Doctor?   10
    The balance?
SUBTLE   No, that way is stale and common.
    A townsman, born in Taurus, gives the bull
    Or the bull's head. In Aries, the ram.
    A poor device. No, I will have his name
    Formed in some mystic character, whose radii,   15
    Striking the senses of the passers-by,
    Shall, by a virtual influence, breed affections
    That may result upon the party owns it,
    As thus – [*Shows his design*]

    The first snag in the rogues' plot occurs when the over-eager Drugger arrives early for his appointment. To overcome the problem, they send Drugger to fetch the final pair of dupes, the young heir Kastril and his wealthy widowed sister Pliant. Here also begins the private contest between Face and Subtle, one that breaks the tripartite agreement with Dol by going well beyond the earlier contest to 'prove today who shall shark best' (1.1.160).

1. *spirits*] Either distilled essences, or supernatural beings, with the same ambiguity as at 2.3.232.
2. *mates*] Low persons. *Bayards*] Common name for a horse, after Charlemagne's steed. Proverbially, 'as bold as blind Bayard' implies foolhardiness.
10. *constellation*] Sign of the zodiac.
11. *balance*] Libra (see 1.3.55–6).
12. *Taurus*] Sign of the Bull.
13. *Aries*] Sign of the Ram.
15. *radii*] Emanations.
17. *virtual*] Capable of producing a certain effect or result; powerful. *affections*] Feelings, inclinations (that is, for tobacco).
18. *result upon*] Return upon by reflex; benefit.

FACE   Nab!
SUBTLE   He first shall have a bell, that's 'A-bel'.
　　　　And by it standing one whose name is Dee,   20
　　　　In a rug gown; there's 'D' and *rug*, that's 'Drug'.
　　　　And right anenst him a dog snarling 'Er';
　　　　There's 'Drugg-er', 'Abel Drugger'. That's his sign.
　　　　And here's now mystery and hieroglyphic!
FACE   Abel, thou art made!   25
DRUGGER   [*Bowing*]   Sir, I do thank his worship.
FACE   Six o' thy legs more will not do it, Nab.
　　　　He has brought you a pipe of tobacco, Doctor.
DRUGGER   [*Gives the tobacco*]   Yes, sir.
　　　　I have another thing I would impart –
FACE   Out with it, Nab!
DRUGGER   Sir, there is lodged, hard by me,
　　　　A rich young widow –   30
FACE   Good! A *bona roba*?
DRUGGER   But nineteen, at the most.
FACE   Very good, Abel.
DRUGGER   Marry, she's not in fashion yet. She wears
　　　　A hood, but 't stands a-cop.
FACE   No matter, Abel.
DRUGGER   And I do now and then give her a *fucus* –
FACE   What! Dost thou deal, Nab?   35
SUBTLE   I did tell you, Captain.
DRUGGER   And physic too sometime, sir, for which she trusts me
　　　　With all her mind. She's come up here of purpose
　　　　To learn the fashion.

20. *Dee*] Dr John Dee, 1527–1608, mathematician, astronomer, and occult scientist. Elizabeth I consulted him as an astrologer.
21. *rug*] Coarse wool worn by academics.
22. *anenst*] Opposite, facing.
24. *hieroglyphic*] Egyptian writing was believed to be esoteric symbols preserving ancient magical and alchemical knowledge, and thus was frequently imitated in Renaissance emblems.
27. *legs*] Bows.
31. *bona roba*] Fashionable woman, presumed to be free and easy sexually, especially if widowed.
33. *hood … a-cop*] Hats were the fashionable head-wear. Dame Pliant tries to make her French hood (usually worn on the back of the head) look more in fashion by wearing it on top of her head.
34. *fucus*] Makeup.
35. *deal*] Transact business; crudely, have intercourse.

FACE   Good – [*Aside*] His match too! – On, Nab!
DRUGGER   And she does strangely long to know her fortune.
FACE   God's lid, Nab, send her to the Doctor hither.   40
DRUGGER   Yes, I have spoke to her of his worship already.
      But she's afraid it will be blown abroad
      And hurt her marriage.
FACE   Hurt it? 'Tis the way
      To heal it, if 'twere hurt, to make it more
      Followed and sought. Nab, thou shalt tell her this.   45
      She'll be more known, more talked of, and your widows
      Are ne'er of any price till they be famous;
      Their honour is their multitude of suitors.
      Send her. It may be thy good fortune. What?
      Thou dost not know.   50
DRUGGER   No, sir, she'll never marry
      Under a knight. Her brother has made a vow.
FACE   What, and dost thou despair, my little Nab,
      Knowing what the Doctor has set down for thee,
      And seeing so many o'the city dubbed?
      One glass o'thy water with a madam I know   55
      Will have it done, Nab. What's her brother? A knight?
DRUGGER   No, sir, a gentleman newly warm in's land, sir,
      Scarce cold in his one-and-twenty, that does govern
      His sister here, and is a man himself
      Of some three thousand a year, and is come up   60
      To learn to quarrel and to live by his wits,
      And will go down again and die i' the country.
FACE   How! To quarrel?
DRUGGER   Yes, sir, to carry quarrels
      As gallants do, and manage 'em by line.
FACE   'Slid, Nab! The Doctor is the only man   65
      In Christendom for him. He has made a table
      With mathematical demonstrations
      Touching the art of quarrels. He will give him
      An instrument to quarrel by. Go, bring 'em both,

38. *His match*] His equal in stupidity.
43. *hurt her marriage*] Ruin her chances for remarriage.
54. *so ... dubbed*] Wealthy citizens paid 30 or 40 pounds for knighthoods; see 2.2.87.
55. *water*] Urine.   *madam*] A cunningwoman who might make a spell or charm with it,
      in order to bring the marriage about.
57. *newly warm in*] Just inherited.
64. *by line*] According to the rules.
66. *table*] Diagram.
69. *instrument*] Written instructions.

Him and his sister. And for thee with her   70
The Doctor happ'ly may persuade. Go to.
Shalt give his worship a new damask suit
Upon the premises.
SUBTLE   O, good Captain.
FACE   He shall.
He is the honestest fellow, Doctor. Stay not.
No offers! Bring the damask and the parties.   75
DRUGGER   I'll try my power, sir.
FACE   And thy will too, Nab.
SUBTLE   [*Testing the tobacco*] 'Tis good tobacco, this! What
        is't an ounce?
FACE   He'll send you a pound, Doctor.
SUBTLE   O, no.
FACE   He will do't.
It is the goodest soul. Abel, about it.
[*To Drugger aside*] Thou shalt know more anon. Away, be gone!   80

   [*Exit Drugger*]

A miserable rogue, and lives with cheese,
And has the worms. That was the cause indeed
Why he came now. He dealt with me in private
To get a med'cine for 'em.
SUBTLE   And shall, sir. This works.
FACE   A wife, a wife for one on's, my dear Subtle.   85
We'll e'en draw lots and he that fails shall have
The more in goods the other has in tail.
SUBTLE   Rather the less. For she may be so light
She may want grains.
FACE   Ay, or be such a burden,
A man would scarce endure her for the whole.   90
SUBTLE   Faith, best let's see her first, and then determine.
FACE   Content. But Dol must ha' no breath on't.
SUBTLE   Mum.
Away you to your Surly yonder. Catch him.

71. *happ'ly*] Luckily.
73. *premises*] Prospect.
81. *miserable*] Cheap.
87. *in tail*] Sexual pleasure, but punning on the legal sense, the settlement of succession of
    a landed estate so that it cannot be bequeathed elsewhere. When an estate was entailed
    on the eldest male, the other heirs might receive more in moveable property or money.
88. *light*] Morally loose.
89. *grains*] Some weight added to compensate for her moral lightness.
90. *whole*] The whole estate might not compensate for the ordeal of being married to her.

FACE   Pray God I ha' not stayed too long.
SUBTLE   I fear it.

   [*Exeunt*]

ACT 3

Act 3 scene 1*

   [*Enter*] *Tribulation, Ananias*

TRIBULATION   These chastisements are common to the saints,
      And such rebukes we of the separation
      Must bear with willing shoulders as the trials
      Sent forth to tempt our frailties.
ANANIAS   In pure zeal,
      I do not like the man. He is a heathen,   5
      And speaks the language of Canaan, truly.
TRIBULATION   I think him a profane person indeed.
ANANIAS   He bears
      The visible mark of the beast in his forehead.
      And for his stone, it is a work of darkness,
      And with philosophy blinds the eyes of man.   10
TRIBULATION   Good brother, we must bend unto all means
      That may give furtherance to the holy cause.
ANANIAS   Which his cannot. The sanctified cause
      Should have a sanctified course.
TRIBULATION   Not always necessary.
      The children of perdition are oft-times   15
      Made instruments even of the greatest works.

* The first two scenes of Act 3, similar in structure to the Mammon scenes of Act 2, expose the hypocrisy of the Anabaptist project by contrasting two of the expelled brethren: the fanatically zealous Ananias and the more practical and venal Tribulation, who insists that rigid doctrine 'must bend' to profit (see ll. 11–14 below).

1. *saints*] The elect, predestined by God for heaven; members of the Anabaptist sect. See 2.4.29–30 and 2.5.46–8.

2. *separation*] Temporally, the exile imposed on extremist puritan sects; spiritually, the gulf God created between his new elect or 'chosen people' (Anabaptists) and the reprobate (everyone else).

4. *In pure zeal*] From a religious point of view; that is, without personal malice. Satirists mocked 'zeal' as a puritan cant-word.

6. *language of Canaan*] Ungodly conversation (Isaiah 19:18).

8. *mark of the beast*] Sign of the irrevocably damned (Revelation 16:2, 19:20).

11. *bend*] Yield, conform.

Beside, we should give somewhat to man's nature,
The place he lives in, still about the fire
And fume of metals that intoxicate
The brain of man and make him prone to passion.   20
Where have you greater atheists than your cooks?
Or more profane or choleric than your glass-men?
More antichristian than your bell-founders?
What makes the devil so devilish, I would ask you,
Satan, our common enemy, but his being   25
Perpetually about the fire and boiling
Brimstone and ars'nic? We must give, I say,
Unto the motives and the stirrers up
Of humours in the blood. It may be so.
When as the work is done, the stone is made,   30
This heat of his may turn into a zeal
And stand up for the beauteous discipline
Against the menstruous cloth and rag of Rome.
We must await his calling and the coming
Of the good spirit. You did fault t'upbraid him   35
With the brethren's blessing of Heidelberg, weighing
What need we have to hasten on the work
For the restoring of the silenced saints,
Which ne'er will be but by the philosopher's stone.

17. *give*] Concede, allow (for); so too at l. 27.   *nature*] Disposition.
20. *prone to passion*] Liable to be affected by external conditions; liable to feel violent emotion.
21–3. A series of examples of the fiery environment, the image of hell, producing the ungodly: *cooks*, who cannot see beyond their bellies and fires; *glass-men* or glass-blowers, whose fires make them foul-mouthed and angry; and *bell-founders*, who become antagonistic to religion by casting molten metal for bells.
28. *motives*] Stimulations.
29. *humours*] Affections and passions, strong feelings.   *It may be so*] The preceding analysis of conditions may be accurate, or the following situation may occur.
30. *When as*] Once.
32. *beauteous discipline*] Puritanism (a pious catch-phrase).
33. *menstruous ... Rome*] Referring to priestly vestments worn by Roman Catholic clergy, and hence to what puritans thought were heathen rituals and displays prostituting the true church. The Church of Rome was metaphorically the Whore of Babylon and the Scarlet Woman, as indicated by the contemptuous reference to menstrual discharge.
36. *blessing*] The alchemical success mentioned at 2.5.70.   *weighing*] Considering.
38. *silenced saints*] Excommunicated ministers who refused to adopt High Church canons. Anglican doctrine, ratified at the 1604 Hampton Court Conference, demanded acceptance of the king's supremacy, the Prayer Book, and the 39 Articles.

And so a learned elder, one of Scotland,   40
Assured me, *aurum potabile* being
The only med'cine for the civil magistrate,
T'incline him to a feeling of the cause,
And must be daily used in the disease.

ANANIAS   I have not edified more, truly, by man,   45
Not since the beautiful light first shone on me,
And I am sad my zeal hath so offended.

TRIBULATION   Let us call on him then.

ANANIAS   The motion's good,
And of the spirit. I will knock first. [*Knocks, calling*]   Peace be within!

[*The door opens*]

Act 3 scene 2*

[*Enter*] *Subtle*

SUBTLE   O, are you come? 'Twas time. Your threescore minutes
Were at the last thread, you see, and down had gone
Furnus acediae, turris circulatorius:
'Lembic, bolt's head, retort, and pelican
Had all been cinders. Wicked Ananias!   5
Art thou returned? Nay then, it goes down yet.

TRIBULATION   Sir, be appeased. He is come to humble
Himself in spirit and to ask your patience,
If too much zeal hath carried him aside
From the due path.   10

SUBTLE   Why, this doth qualify!

TRIBULATION   The brethren had no purpose, verily,

40. *Scotland*] Where puritanism had already reformed the church.
41. *aurum potabile*] Drinkable gold used in medicine, but here a metaphor for bribery.
45. *edified*] Been enlightened.
46. *beautiful light*] Of puritanism. Compare to l. 32 above.
48. *motion*] Inward prompting or stirring of the soul (puritan cant).
*   Like Volpone's mountebank speeches praising Scoto's oil, Subtle's promotion of the 'medicine' (esp. ll. 20–51) entices his purchasers with visions of military and political success based on the restoration of health, youth, beauty, and sexual prowess.
2. *down had gone*] Would have ruined. See l. 6.
3. *Furnus acediae*] Furnace of sloth, a synonym for 'lazy Henry', noted at 2.5.80.   *turris circulatorius*] Circulating tower, or pelican (see note at 2.3.78); a distilling flask for continuous sublimation, condensation, and resublimation of contents.
4. All synonyms for distilling apparatus.
6. *it goes down yet*] It is still going to be ruined.
10. *qualify*] Mollify Subtle's rage; alchemically, dilute.

To give you the least grievance, but are ready
To lend their willing hands to any project
The spirit and you direct.

SUBTLE   This qualifies more!

TRIBULATION   And, for the orphans' goods, let them be valued,   15
Or what is needful else to the holy work,
It shall be numbered. Here by me, the saints
Throw down their purse before you. [*Shows money*]

SUBTLE   This qualifies most!
Why, thus it should be. Now you understand.
Have I discoursed so unto you of our stone?   20
And of the good that it shall bring your cause?
Showed you (beside the main of hiring forces
Abroad, drawing the Hollanders, your friends,
From th' Indies to serve you with all their fleet)
That even the med'cinal use shall make you a faction   25
And party in the realm? As, put the case
That some great man in state he have the gout,
Why, you but send three drops of your elixir,
You help him straight. There you have made a friend.
Another has the palsy or the dropsy,   30
He takes of your incombustible stuff,
He's young again. There you have made a friend.
A lady that is past the feat of body,
Though not of mind, and hath her face decayed
Beyond all cure of paintings, you restore   35
With the oil of talc. There you have made a friend,

---

14. *spirit*] The holy spirit moving within the elect.

22. *main*] Chief purpose.

23. *Hollanders*] 'Friends' of Anabaptists, giving them refuge after their flights from Germany after 1536 and England since 1604 (see 2.4.30n.). The Dutch navy served mostly to protect the East Indian trade; Subtle speculates that, with gold produced by the philosopher's stone, the exiled brethren could hire mercenaries and establish themselves as a force to be reckoned with in England.

27. *in state*] In high office.

30. *palsy*] Degeneration of the nervous system, usually due to age, varying from involuntary tremors to paralysis.   *dropsy*] Medically, a morbid condition of the elderly, characterised by water retention; figuratively, an insatiable craving, especially for riches or power.

31. *incombustible*] Impervious to fire, because it has been refined to a quintessence.

33. *feat of body*] Sexual intercourse.

34. *not of mind*] Not past thinking about sex.

36. *oil of talc*] A white face-powder; alchemically, white elixir.

And all her friends. A lord that is a leper,
A knight that has the bone-ache, or a squire
That hath both these, you make 'em smooth and sound
With a bare fricace of your med'cine. Still,   40
You increase your friends.

TRIBULATION   Ay, 'tis very pregnant.

SUBTLE   And then the turning of this lawyer's pewter
To plate at Christmas –

ANANIAS   Christ-tide, I pray you.

SUBTLE   Yet, Ananias?

ANANIAS   I have done.

SUBTLE   Or changing
His parcel gilt to massy gold. You cannot   45
But raise your friends. With all, to be of power
To pay an army in the field, to buy
The king of France out of his realms, or Spain
Out of his Indies: what can you not do
Against lords spiritual or temporal   50
That shall oppone you?

TRIBULATION   Verily, 'tis true.
We may be temporal lords ourselves, I take it.

SUBTLE   You may be anything, and leave off to make
Long-winded exercises. Or suck up
Your ha and hum in a tune. I not deny   55
But such as are not graced in a state
May for their ends be adverse in religion,
And get a tune to call the flock together.
For, to say sooth, a tune does much with women

---

37. *her friends*] Her lovers.

38. *bone-ache*] Syphilis.

40. *bare fricace*] Mere rubbing.

41. *pregnant*] Full of promise or lively ideas; of an argument, compelling or convincing.

43. *Christ-tide*] Puritans repudiated any 'popish' terms such as '-mas' (= mass); *-tide* simply means 'time'.

45. *parcel gilt*] Gilded (gold-plated) silver.   *massy*] Solid.

51. *oppone*] Oppose.

54. *Long-winded exercises*] Puritans were known for their long prayers and sermons. *suck up*] Swallow.

55. *ha and hum*] The peculiar whining pitch affected by puritan preachers; see *BF* 1.3.75ff.   *tune*] Hymn-singing. The redeeming effect of such singing is mocked in the last act of *EH!*, where Quicksilver and Security 'sit you up all night singing of psalms and edifying the whole prison'. Subtle goes on to argue that the politically powerless may gain a following by leading a religious cause.

And other phlegmatic people: it is your bell.   60
ANANIAS   Bells are profane. A tune may be religious.
SUBTLE   No warning with you? Then farewell my patience.
      'Slight, it shall down. I will not be thus tortured.
TRIBULATION   I pray you, sir!
SUBTLE   All shall perish. I have spoke it.
TRIBULATION   Let me find grace, sir, in your eyes! The man   65
      He stands corrected. Neither did his zeal,
      But as yourself, allow a tune somewhere!
      Which now being to'ard the stone, we shall not need.
SUBTLE   No, nor your holy vizard to win widows
      To give you legacies, or make zealous wives   70
      To rob their husbands for the common cause.
      Nor take the start of bonds broke but one day
      And say, 'They were forfeited by providence.'
      Nor shall you need o'ernight to eat huge meals
      To celebrate your next day's fast the better,   75
      The whilst the brethren and the sisters, humbled,
      Abate the stiffness of the flesh. Nor cast
      Before your hungry hearers scrupulous bones,
      As whether a Christian may hawk or hunt,
      Or whether matrons of the holy assembly   80

60. *phlegmatic*] Affected by the watery humour, hence lacking enthusiasm, sluggish.
61. *Bells are profane*] Because associated with Catholic practice.
62. *No warning with you?*] Can you not take a warning?   *it shall down*] The alchemical experiment (see 2 and 6 above).
66–8. *Neither ... need*] That is, there is no reason to argue. Ananias agrees that tunes are politically useful, only making a minor and now irrelevant objection to Subtle's comparison of tunes to church bells, since with the philosopher's stone they will not need to sing.
68. *to'ard*] Near to (producing).
69–73. The pretence of piety as a front for extortion appears also in Truewit's warnings against marriage (*SW* 2.2.67–74) and Dame Purecraft's confession (*BF* 5.2.47–63).
73. *take the start of*] Take advantage of (by foreclosing on bonds only technically overdue).
77. *stiffness*] Pride, with sexual innuendo. Some puritan sects (notably, the Family of Love) were thought to practise communal wife-swapping, as well as communal sharing of goods.
78. *scrupulous bones*] Petty points of contention concerning appropriate puritan behaviour.
79. *hawk or hunt*] Aristocratic sports spurned by the largely middle-class and work-oriented puritans.

May lay their hair out, or wear doublets,
Or have that idol Starch about their linen.
ANANIAS It is indeed an idol.
TRIBULATION   Mind him not, sir.
[*Praying over Ananias*] I do command thee, spirit of zeal but trouble,
To peace within him. [*To Subtle*] Pray you, sir, go on.   85
SUBTLE Nor shall you need to libel 'gainst the prelates
And shorten so your ears against the hearing
Of the next wire-drawn grace. Nor, of necessity,
Rail against plays to please the alderman
Whose daily custard you devour. Nor lie   90
With zealous rage till you are hoarse. Not one
Of these so singular arts. Nor call yourselves
By names of Tribulation, Persecution,
Restraint, Long-Patience, and such like, affected
By the whole family or wood of you   95
Only for glory and to catch the ear
Of the disciple.
TRIBULATION   Truly, sir, they are
Ways that the godly brethren have invented
For propagation of the glorious cause
As very notable means, and whereby also   100
Themselves grow soon and profitably famous.
SUBTLE   O, but the stone, all's idle to it! Nothing!
The art of angels, nature's miracle,
The divine secret that doth fly in clouds
From east to west, and whose tradition   105

81. *lay their hair out*] Wear fashionable coiffures imitating court ladies, and thus waste time in frivolous vanities. *wear doublets*] Wear mannish attire, thus disobeying biblical injunctions about sexual propriety (Deuteronomy 22:5). Puritans objected similarly to actors for wearing women's clothing on stage; for the full absurdity of this argument, see *BF* 5.5.

82. *idol Starch*] Thought an invention of the devil to promote vanity.

87. *shorten ... ears*] Have your ears cropped; associated with the pillory at 1.1.168–9.

88. *wire-drawn grace*] Long-drawn-out prayer at table.

89. *please the alderman*] Middle-class citizens tended to be puritan, and objected to the theatre for biblical reasons (as at l. 80 above) as well as practical reasons of public order.

90. *custard*] Custard tart traditionally appeared at official city receptions like the Lord Mayor's feast, sometimes as an excuse for clowning ('like him that leaped into the custard' in *All's Well that Ends Well* 2.5.41). Jonson's satirical assumption is that city councilmen gave their private tables official status by serving it daily. See *BF* 3.3.25–6.

95. *wood*] *Silva*, Latin, a miscellaneous collection; also a colloquialism for 'crazy'.

103–6. More synonyms for the philosopher's stone.

Is not from men, but spirits.

ANANIAS   I hate traditions.

I do not trust them –

TRIBULATION   Peace!

ANANIAS   They are popish all.

I will not peace. I will not –

TRIBULATION   Ananias!

ANANIAS   – Please the profane to grieve the godly. I may not.

SUBTLE   Well, Ananias, thou shalt overcome.   110

TRIBULATION   It is an ignorant zeal that haunts him, sir.

But truly, else, a very faithful brother,

A botcher, and a man, by revelation,

That hath a competent knowledge of the truth.

SUBTLE   Has he a competent sum there i'the bag   115

To buy the goods within? I am made guardian

And must, for charity and conscience sake,

Now see the most be made for my poor orphan,

Though I desire the brethren, too, good gainers.

There they are within. When you have viewed and bought 'em,   120

And ta'en the inventory of what they are,

They are ready for projection. There's no more

To do. Cast on the med'cine, so much silver

As there is tin there, so much gold as brass,

I'll gi'it you in by weight.   125

TRIBULATION   But how long time

Sir, must the saints expect yet?

SUBTLE   Let me see,

How's the moon now? Eight, nine, ten days hence,

He will be silver potate; then three days

---

106. *traditions*] Puritans rejected all tradition and ritual as Roman Catholic error, preferring to base their daily lives on strictly literal readings of the Bible.

113. *botcher*] Tailor who does repairs and alterations, or makes one new garment out of
remnants of worn-out clothing; by convention a puritan job, since it illustrates the
ethic of hard work and frugal habits.   *by revelation*] That is, guided subjectively by
the intuition exercised by each individual who studies the Bible, which itself contains
the direct word of God. Such a philosophy of knowledge eliminates scholarly
humanism or socio-religious tradition.

118. *orphan*] Singular in F and Q, as in H&S; plural in Mares (1967), Kernan (1974), and
M. Butler (1989), conforming to the sense of other references.

125. *gi'it ... weight*] Transmute it for you, weight for weight.

126. *expect*] Wait.

128. *silver potate*] Silver in liquid form.

Before he citronise; some fifteen days,
The *magisterium* will be perfected.   130

ANANIAS   About the second day of the third week
In the ninth month?

SUBTLE   Yes, my good Ananias.

TRIBULATION   What will the orphans' goods arise to, think you?

SUBTLE   Some hundred marks, as much as filled three cars
Unladed now. You'll make six millions of 'em.   135
But I must ha' more coals laid in.

TRIBULATION   How!

SUBTLE   Another load,
And then we ha' finished. We must now increase
Our fire to *ignis ardens*; we are passed
Fimus equinus, balnei, cineris,
And all those lenter heats. If the holy purse   140
Should with this draught fall low, and that the saints
Do need a present sum, I have trick
To melt the pewter you shall buy now, instantly,
And with a tincture make you as good Dutch dollars
As any are in Holland.   145

TRIBULATION   Can you so?

SUBTLE   Ay, and shall bide the third examination.

ANANIAS   It will be joyful tidings to the brethren.

SUBTLE   But you must carry it secret.

---

129. *citronise*] Turns yellow, a colour part-way between white and the perfect red that
signals the successful elixir.

130. *magisterium*] The master work.

131–2. *second ... month*] That is, 16 November, fixing the date on which the play takes
place as 1 November. But at 5.5.102–3 Ananias gives the play's date as 23 October.
The calculation is based on the old-style English calendar in which March is the first
month (Puritans also believed that God created the world in March), although Ananias
names no months because they derive from the Roman calendar, which he considers
either 'popish' or pagan.

134. *hundred marks*] Slightly less than 100 pounds.

138. *ignis ardens*] The hottest fire.

139. *Fimus equinus*] The fire of horse dung, the mildest heat. *balnei*] The slow heat
baths, of which the milder is of ashes, and next of sand. *cineris*] The first heat bath,
the ash-fire (2.3.85).

140. *lenter*] Slower, gentler.

144. *tincture*] Either a chemical additive to make the pewter look more like silver, or a
synonym for 'colour', meaning 'trick', a word already used at 142. For 'colour' in this
sense, see 3.3.17, and *Volp* 1.4.96.   *Dutch dollars*] Large silver coins worth about 5
shillings.

146. *bide ... examination*] Counterfeits so good that they pass repeated inspection.

TRIBULATION   Ay, but stay –
   This act of coining, is it lawful?
ANANIAS   Lawful?
   We know no magistrate. Or, if we did,   150
   This's foreign coin.
SUBTLE   It is no coining, sir.
   It is but casting.
TRIBULATION   Ha? You distinguish well.
   Casting of money may be lawful.
ANANIAS   'Tis, sir.
TRIBULATION   Truly, I take it so.
SUBTLE   There is no scruple,
   Sir, to be made of it. Believe Ananias.   155
   This case of conscience he is studied in.
TRIBULATION   I'll make a question of it to the brethren.
ANANIAS   The brethren shall approve it lawful, doubt not.
   Where shall't be done?
SUBTLE   For that we'll talk anon.

   Knock without

   There's some to speak with me. Go in, I pray you,   160
   And view the parcels. That's the inventory.
   I'll come to you straight.

   [*Exeunt Tribulation and Ananias*]

         Who is it? Face! Appear!

150. *no magistrate*] Puritans denied civil jurisdiction in matters of religion or conscience, because God is the only lawgiver.

151. *foreign coin*] Not an actual legal loophole. Coining, whether foreign or domestic, was an indictable offence.

151–2. *coining … casting*] A clever quibble, similar to the 'scrupulous bones' and letter-legal practices Subtle described earlier among puritans. Only at this point does Ananias stop being obstructive or belligerent, and agree unreservedly to Subtle's plan.

152. *distinguish*] Make distinctions.

157. *question*] Problem suitable for doctrinal analysis.

161. *parcels*] Portions into which the inventory has been divided.

Act 3 scene 3*

[*Enter*] *Face*

SUBTLE How now? Good prize?
FACE   Good pox! Yond costive cheater
    Never came on.
SUBTLE   How then?
FACE   I ha' walked the round
    Till now, and no such thing.
SUBTLE   And ha' you quit him?
FACE Quit him? And hell would quit him too, he were happy.
    'Slight, would you have me stalk like a mill-jade   5
    All day for one that will not yield us grains?
    I know him of old.
SUBTLE   O, but to ha' gulled him
    Had been a mastery.
FACE   Let him go, black boy,
    And turn thee, that some fresh news may possess thee.
    A noble count, a don of Spain, my dear   10
    Delicious compere and my party-bawd,
    Who is come hither private for his conscience

---

*   Another snag in the plot: Surly has failed to meet Face at the Temple Church (see 2.3.288–312), so that he can infiltrate the house disguised as a customer. The 'Spanish Don' double-game begins in this 'backstage' scene, with Face, Subtle, and Dol preparing to cozen the Spaniard, unaware that Surly means to prove that they are running a brothel, not an alchemical laboratory. The 'Spanish Don' cycles through several transformations by Act 5, with Drugger, Face, and finally Lovewit vying for the part.

1. *Good prize?*] A soldier's question about booty. The comparison of the con-men with mercenaries continues at ll. 17–19 and 34–45. *Yond . . . cheater*] Surly.
2. *came on*] Showed up for their appointment. *the round*] The rotunda at the rear of the congregational area in Temple Church (see 2.3.289), a meeting-place for lawyers and clients.
3. *no such thing*] No Surly appeared. *quit him*] Given up on him
5. *mill-jade*] Horse which walked in a circle harnessed to the arm that drove the grindstone of a mill.
6. *grains*] Continuing the mill metaphor, but meaning 'profit'.
8. *black boy*] Problematic reference. If addressing Subtle, the phrase refers to his black rug gown and sooty appearance, the by-product of alchemical furnaces. If referring to Surly, the expression dismisses him as a 'blackguard' or menace.
9. *turn thee*] Change the topic of conversation.
11. *party-bawd*] Fellow pimp.
12. *his conscience*] Implying that the Spaniard is a Protestant.

And brought munition with him, six great slops
Bigger than three Dutch hoys, beside round trunks
Furnished with pistolets and pieces of eight,   15
Will straight be here, my rogue, to have thy bath
(That is the colour), and to make his batt'ry
Upon our Dol, our castle, our Cinque Port,
Our Dover pier, our what-thou-wilt. Where is she?
She must prepare perfumes, delicate linen,   20
The bath in chief, a banquet, and her wit,
For she must milk his *epididymis*.
Where is the doxy?
SUBTLE   I'll send her to thee,
And but dispatch my brace of little John Leydens
And come again myself.   25
FACE   Are they within then?
SUBTLE   Numb'ring the sum.
FACE   How much?
SUBTLE   A hundred marks, boy.

   [*Exit Subtle*]

FACE   Why, this's a lucky day! Ten pounds of Mammon!
       Three o' my clerk! A portague o' my grocer!
       This o' the brethren! Beside reversions
       And states to come i' the widow and my count!   30
       My share today will not be bought for forty –

13. *munition*] Provisions of money and clothing.   *slops*] Or Dutch slops, voluminously baggy breeches.
14. *Dutch hoys*] Small coastal vessels for transporting goods and passengers.   *round trunks*] Trunk-hose, full bag-like breeches covering the hips and upper thighs, sometimes stuffed to define the shape.
15. *pistolets*] Spanish gold coins.   *pieces of eight*] Spanish dollars worth 8 *reales*.
16. *bath*] The bath-house and the whorehouse were synonymous. See *Epigrams* 7.
17. *colour*] Trick, pretence.   *make his batt'ry*] Military metaphor for 'copulate'.
18. *Cinque Port*] One of five ports (*Dover* was another) on the SE coast of England designated as privileged fortresses for defence against continental invasion.
21. *in chief*] Especially.   *wit*] Punning on 'whit', pudendum.
22. *milk his epididymis*] Cause him to ejaculate during orgasm.
23. *doxy*] Thieves' cant for wench, whore.
24. *John Leydens*] Ananias and Tribulation, referring dismissively to the Anabaptist leader of the Münster rising (see 2.5.13).
28. *portague*] Portuguese gold coin (see 1.3.87).
29. *reversions*] Future benefits; the rights to something after the present owner dies or gives it up.
30. *states*] Estates, whether money or property.   *count*] The 'Spaniard'.

[*Enter Dol*]

DOL   What?
FACE   Pounds, dainty Dorothy. Art thou so near?
DOL   Yes. Say, Lord General, how fares our camp?
FACE   As with the few that had entrenched themselves
    Safe by their discipline against a world, Dol,   35
    And laughed within those trenches and grew fat
    With thinking on the booties, Dol, brought in
    Daily by their small parties. This dear hour,
    A doughty don is taken with my Dol,
    And thou may'st make his ransom what thou wilt,   40
    My Dousabel. He shall be brought here fettered
    With thy fair looks before he sees thee, and thrown
    In a down-bed as dark as any dungeon,
    Where thou shalt keep him waking with thy drum,
    Thy drum, my Dol, thy drum, till he be tame   45
    As the poor blackbirds were i' the great frost,
    Or bees are with a basin, and so hive him
    I'the swan-skin coverlid and cambric sheets
    Till he work honey and wax, my little God's-gift.
DOL   What is he, General?   50
FACE   An *adalantado*,
    A grandee, girl. Was not my Dapper here yet?
DOL   No.
FACE   Nor my Drugger?
DOL   Neither.
FACE   A pox on 'em.

---

33. *Say … camp*] From the opening line, after the Induction, of Kyd's *The Spanish Tragedy* (1588), frequently quoted mockingly by the later playwrights, including Shakespeare.

36. *laughed … and grew fat*] 'Laughed themselves sweaty', proverbial expression for hearty enjoyment.

39. *taken with*] Captured, or captivated, by.

41. *Dousabel*] *Douce et belle*, sweet and pretty.

44–5. *drum … drum*] Imitating the thrumming sound of the military drum, to indicate the pounding sexual rhythms of vigorous intercourse.

45. *tame*] Sexually worn out, impotent.

46. *great frost*] When the Thames froze over in 1607/8.

47. *bees … basin*] Swarms were supposed to settle at the sound of banging pots.

47–8. *hive him … sheets*] Keep him hard at work between the sheets.

49. *work honey*] Ejaculate, have an orgasm. *wax*] Sexual secretion; surge in potency or intensity. *God's-gift*] Translation of 'Dorothea'.

50. *adalantado*] Spanish governor; loosely, member of the ruling class.

They are so long a-furnishing! Such stinkards
Would not be seen upon these festival days.

[*Enter Subtle*]

How now! Ha' you done?   55

SUBTLE   Done. They are gone. The sum
Is here in bank, my Face. I would we knew
Another chapman now would buy 'em outright.

FACE   'Slid, Nab shall do't, against he ha' the widow,
To furnish household.

SUBTLE   Excellent, well thought on!
Pray God he come.   60

FACE   I pray he keep away
Till our new business be o'er-passed.

SUBTLE   But, Face,
How cam'st thou by this secret don?

FACE   A spirit
Brought me th'intelligence in a paper here,
As I was conjuring yonder in my circle
For Surly. I ha' my flies abroad. Your bath   65
Is famous, Subtle, by my means. Sweet Dol,
You must go tune your virginal, no losing
O' the least time. And – do you hear? – good action!
Firk like a flounder. Kiss like a scallop, close.
And tickle him with thy mother-tongue. His great   70

53. *a-furnishing*] Getting ready, or finding ready cash.
54. *Would*] Should.
56. *in bank*] Securely locked up.
57. *chapman*] Wholesale dealer.   *'em*] Mammon's ironware, which the Anabaptists have
     purchased. Subtle is hoping for a third party to dupe with the same goods.
64. *conjuring ... in my circle*] Scouting in the round at Temple Church. The expression,
     borrowed from necromancy and alchemy (the mystic symbol of the pentagram, or five-
     pointed star within a circle, is common to both), also described sexual foreplay, or
     sexual congress, based on the idea of the raising of spirits.
67. *tune your virginal*] Prepare to give a sexual performance, not a keyboard enter-
     tainment.
68. *action*] Continuing the virginal metaphor, the finger movement at the keyboard, as
     well as the sexual play.
69. *Firk*] Arouse, stir up; used alchemically at 2.1.28.   *like a flounder*] Imitating the fish's
     undulations.   *like a scallop*] With her lips sealing his, using suction like a bivalve
     mollusc.
70. *tickle ... mother-tongue*] Arouse him with erotic language; penetrate his mouth with
     your tongue.

Verdugoship has not a jot of language:
So much the easier to be cozened, my Dolly.
He will come here in a hired coach, obscure,
And our own coachman, whom I have sent as guide,
No creature else.   75

One knocks

                Who's that?
SUBTLE   It i'not he?
FACE O no, not yet this hour.
SUBTLE   Who is't?
DOL [*Peeping out*]   Dapper,
Your clerk.
FACE   God's will, then, Queen of Fairy,
On with your tire, and, Doctor, with your robes.
Let's dispatch him, for God's sake.

[*Exit Dol*]

SUBTLE   'Twill be long.
FACE I warrant you, take but the cues I give you,   80
It shall be brief enough. [*Peeping out*] 'Slight, here are more!
Abel and, I think, the angry boy, the heir
That fain would quarrel.
SUBTLE   And the widow?
FACE   No,
Not that I see. Away.

[*Exit Subtle, as Face opens the door*]

          O sir, you are welcome.

71. *Verdugoship*] Coined title of mock-respect, from the Spanish *verdugo*, either 'young
shoot of a tree', apt for one who is too green to catch on to rogues' tricks, or 'hangman
or very cruel person', for the lingering torments of the Spanish Inquisition. *has* ...
language] Cannot speak any English.
78. *On* ... *tire*] Into your costume.
82. *angry boy*] Kastril, the would-be swaggerer (see The Persons of the Play 11 and note).

Act 3 scene 4*

[*Enter*] *Dapper*

FACE   The Doctor is within, a-moving for you.
    I have had the most ado to win him to it.
    He swears you'll be the darling o' the dice.
    He never heard her highness dote till now, he says.
    Your aunt has giv'n you the most gracious words   5
    That can be thought on.
DAPPER   Shall I see her grace?
FACE   See her, and kiss her too.

    [*Enter Drugger and Kastril*]   What? Honest Nab!
    Hast brought the damask?
‹DRUGGER›   No, sir. Here's tobacco.
FACE   'Tis well done, Nab. Thou'lt bring the damask too?
DRUGGER   Yes. Here's the gentleman, Captain, Master Kastril,   10
    I have brought to see the Doctor.
FACE   [*To Drugger aside*]   Where's the widow?
DRUGGER   Sir, as he likes, his sister (he says) shall come.
FACE   O, is it so? [*Greets Kastril*] 'Good time. Is your name Kastril, sir?
KASTRIL   Ay, and the best o' the Kastrils. I'd be sorry else
    By fifteen hundred a year. Where is this Doctor?   15
    My mad tobacco-boy here tells me of one
    That can do things. Has he any skill?
FACE   Wherein, sir?
KASTRIL   To carry a business, manage a quarrel fairly,
    Upon fit terms.

*   The *duello* (25) or Italian duel was by 1610 defunct in Italy but at its acme in France: Henri IV (1589–1610) commuted the punishment of 7,000 duellists, despite the fact that one-third of the French nobles had perished in duels between 1574 and 1610. In England, where the duel was not tolerated, would-be quarrellers studied such rule-books as *Vincentio Saviolo his Practise. In two Bookes. The first intreating of the use of the Rapier and Dagger. The second, of Honor and honorable Quarrels* (1595) in order to escalate a quarrel that stopped just short of mortal violence. See Shakespeare's parody of this practice in *As You Like It* 5.4.65–102; and compare Kastril's lack of skill at 4.2.18–28.

1. *a-moving*] Conjuring (to raise the promised fly).
2. *ado*] Difficulty.
13. *'Good time*] 'In good time', sometimes 'In fair time', commonly a moderately formal greeting or farewell, like 'Good day'. See *EMO* 4.4.7 and 2.3.282.
14. *sorry*] That is, poorer.
18. *carry a business*] The sense is repeated in the next phrase: manage a duel properly, according to the rules.

FACE   It seems, sir, you're but young
    About the town that can make that a question!   20
KASTRIL   Sir, not so young but I have heard some speech
    Of the angry boys, and seen 'em take tobacco,
    And in his shop; and I can take it too.
    And I would fain be one of 'em, and go down
    And practise i' the country.   25
FACE   Sir, for the *duello*,
    The Doctor, I assure you, shall inform you
    To the least shadow of a hair, and show you
    An instrument he has, of his own making,
    Wherewith, no sooner shall you make report
    Of any quarrel, but he will take the height on't   30
    Most instantly, and tell in what degree
    Of safety it lies in, or mortality.
    And how it may be borne, whether in a right line
    Or a half-circle, or may else be cast
    Into an angle blunt, if not acute.   35
    All this he will demonstrate. And then, rules
    To give and take the lie by.
KASTRIL   How? To take it?
FACE   Yes, in oblique he'll show you, or in circle,
    But never in diameter. The whole town
    Study his theorems, and dispute them ordinarily   40
    At the eating academies.
KASTRIL   But does he teach
    Living by the wits too?
FACE   Anything whatever.
    You cannot think that subtlety but he reads it.
    He made me a captain. I was a stark pimp,

---

25. *practise ... country*] A modest ambition to become a rustic 'roarer' instead of the more sophisticated urban rowdy.

28. *instrument*] Text on measuring insults (ll. 30–35, 38–9), to be used like an astrolabe as a navigational tool for the duellist.

37. *give ... lie*] Call your adversary a liar, or be so called by him.

39. *never in diameter*] Directly opposing the adversary. The 'lie direct', flat and unequivocal accusation, is the most serious insult, and must end in a challenge. Indirect (*in oblique*) or roundabout (*in circle*) accusation may be denied or apologised for.

40–41. *ordinarily ... eating academies*] Punning on 'ordinary' or eating-house, where people found occasions to quarrel while dining, drinking, or gambling.

43. 'The Doctor [Subtle] can lecture on any subject, no matter how complicated', punning on 'subtlety'.

44. *stark pimp*] Penniless ne'er-do-well.

Just o' your standing, 'fore I met with him.   45
It i'not two months since. I'll tell you his method.
First, he will enter you at some ordinary.
KASTRIL   No, I'll not come there. You shall pardon me.
FACE   For why, sir?
KASTRIL   There's gaming there, and tricks.
FACE   Why, would you be
A gallant, and not game?   50
KASTRIL   Ay, 'twill spend a man.
FACE   Spend you? It will repair you when you are spent.
How do they live by their wits there that have vented
Six times your fortunes?
KASTRIL   What, three thousand a year!
FACE   Ay, forty thousand.
KASTRIL   Are there such?
FACE   Ay, sir.
And gallants yet. Here's a young gentleman   [*Points out Dapper*]   55
Is born to nothing, forty marks a year,
Which I count nothing. He's to be initiated
And have a fly o' the Doctor. He will win you
By unresistable luck, within this fortnight,
Enough to buy a barony. They will set him   60
Upmost at the Groom-porter's all the Christmas!
And for the whole year through, at every place
Where there is play, present him with the chair,
The best attendance, the best drink, sometimes
Two glasses of canary, and pay nothing,   65
The purest linen and the sharpest knife,
The partridge next his trencher – and somewhere
The dainty bed, in private with the dainty.
You shall ha' your ordinaries bid for him
As playhouses for a poet, and the master   70
Pray him aloud to name what dish he affects,

45. *o'your standing*] That is, a novice in the art of quarrelling.
47. *enter*] Introduce, as a student.
50. *spend a man*] Waste a man's fortune.
52. *vented*] Blown away.
53. *three thousand a year*] Kastril's own income (see 2.6.60).
58. *fly*] Familiar spirit.
60. *barony*] Presumably far more costly than merely purchasing a knighthood (see 2.2.87).
61. *Upmost*] In the seat of honour; varied at 63.   *Groom-porter*] Court officer of the
     Lord Chamberlain, in charge of gambling and disputes arising from play.
65. *canary*] Light sweet wine from the Canary Islands.
68. *dainty*] Strumpet.   *in private*] Secluded; in sexual congress.

Which must be buttered shrimps. And those that drink
To no mouth else will drink to his, as being
The goodly president mouth of all the board.

KASTRIL   Do you not gull one?   75

FACE   'Od's my life! Do you think it?
You shall have a cast commander, can but get
In credit with a glover or a spurrier
For some two pair of either's ware aforehand,
Will, by most swift posts, dealing with him,
Arrive at competent means to keep himself,   80
His punk, and naked boy in excellent fashion.
And be admired for't.

KASTRIL   Will the Doctor teach this?

FACE   He will do more, sir. When your land is gone
(As men of spirit hate to keep earth long),
In a vacation when small money is stirring   85
And ordinaries suspended till the term,
He'll show a perspective, where on one side
You shall behold the faces and the persons
Of all sufficient young heirs in town
Whose bonds are current for commodity;   90
On th'other side, the merchants' forms and others
That, without help of any second broker
(Who would expect a share) will trust such parcels;
In the third square, the very street and sign
Where the commodity dwells and does but wait   95
To be delivered, be it pepper, soap,
Hops, or tobacco, oatmeal, woad, or cheeses.
All which you may so handle to enjoy

---

72. *buttered shrimps*] Probably an allusion to wanton women. Used contemptuously,
      'shrimps' meant puny or insignificant people. Shrimps were also very common on the
      coasts of Great Britain, and seafood buttered or oiled usually represented sexual tastes,
      or at least aphrodisiacs, as at 4.1.159–60.

76. *cast commander*] Out-of-work officer.

79. *by ... posts*] Very rapidly.

81. *naked boy*] Equivocal; either infant, or catamite.

84. Because 'spirit' is volatile essence, and 'earth' is base.

85. *vacation*] Between law-terms, when there was little business.

87. *perspective*] An optical device, such as a three-panel hinged mirror reflecting different
      angles; here suggesting either a magic mirror, or simply a metaphor for a prospectus,
      with separate listings for heirs, moneylenders, and wholesale dealers available to
      participate in a commodity swindle (see 2.1.10–14n.).

93. *parcels*] Of goods.

97. *woad*] Either the herb for making blue dye, or the dye itself.

To your own use, and never stand obliged.
KASTRIL   I' faith! Is he such a fellow?   100
FACE   Why, Nab here knows him.
And then for making matches for rich widows,
Young gentlewomen, heirs, the fortunat'st man!
He's sent to, far and near, all over England,
To have his counsel and to know their fortunes.
KASTRIL   God's will, my suster shall see him.   105
FACE   I'll tell you, sir,
What he did tell me of Nab. It's a strange thing!
– By the way, you must eat no cheese, Nab. It breeds melancholy,
And that same melancholy breeds worms – but pass it.
He told me honest Nab here was ne'er at tavern
But once in's life!   110
DRUGGER   Truth, and no more I was not.
FACE   And then he was so sick –
DRUGGER   Could he tell you that too?
FACE   How should I know it?
DRUGGER   In troth we had been a-shooting,
And had a piece of fat ram-mutton to supper
That lay so heavy o' my stomach –
FACE   And he has no head
To bear any wine, for what with the noise o' the fiddlers   115
And care of his shop, for he dares keep no servants –
DRUGGER   My head did so ache –
FACE   As he was fain to be brought home,
The Doctor told me. And then a good old woman –
DRUGGER   Yes, faith, she dwells in Seacoal Lane – did cure me
With sodden ale and pellitory o' the wall.   120
Cost me but two pence. I had another sickness
Was worse than that.
FACE   Ay, that was with the grief
Thou took'st for being 'sessed at eighteen pence

105. *suster*] Rustic dialect.
108. *pass it*] Forget it.
119. *Seacoal Lane*] A narrow alley, now called Old Seacoal Lane, running to Fleet Lane
     from Farringdon St, formerly the Fleet Ditch; hence its reputation as 'stinking' and
     disease-ridden. Named after its boat-landing for coal deliveries, the street was poor
     and overcrowded, the kind of neighbourhood where one might expect to find an old
     woman dealing in cheap remedies.
120. *sodden*] Boiled. *pellitory o' the wall*] Bushy plant with greenish flowers, readily
     found growing at the foot of walls, and usually boiled for cough medicine, or relief
     from kidney stones, not for hangovers.
123. *'sessed*] Assessed.

For the waterwork.
DRUGGER   In truth, and it was like
    T'have cost me almost my life.   125
FACE   Thy hair went off?
DRUGGER   Yes, sir, 'twas done for spite.
FACE   Nay, so says the Doctor.
KASTRIL   Pray thee, tobacco-boy, go fetch my suster.
    I'll see this learnèd boy before I go.
    And so shall she.
FACE   Sir, he is busy now.
    But if you have a sister to fetch hither,   130
    Perhaps your own pains may command her sooner,
    And he by that time will be free.
KASTRIL   I go.

    [*Exit Kastril*]

FACE   Drugger, she's thine. The damask!

    [*Exit Drugger*]

                    [*Aside*]   Subtle and I
    Must wrestle for her. – Come on, Master Dapper.
    You see how I turn clients here away,   135
    To give your cause dispatch. Ha' you performed
    The ceremonies were enjoined you?
DAPPER   Yes, o' the vinegar
    And the clean shirt.
FACE   'Tis well. That shirt may do you
    More worship than you think. Your aunt's afire,
    But that she will not show it, t'have a sight on you.   140
    Ha' you provided for her Grace's servants?
DAPPER   Yes, here are six score Edward shillings.
FACE   Good.
DAPPER   And an old Harry's sovereign.

124. *waterwork*] Either to pay for piped water from the London Bridge pump-house, or to pay for the New River pump-house, under construction between 1609 and 1613.

126. *'twas ... spite*] The high assessment. *Nay*] An expression of disapproval; Face is agreeing with Drugger that spite caused the high rate.

142. *Edward shillings*] Silver coins minted in Edward VI's reign (1547–53), when the Lord Protector debased them to about one-quarter of their original value during Henry VII's reign. The monarch's name signals the coins' value, which shifted with each reign according to the amount of silver used to mint them.

143. *old Harry's sovereign*] Gold coin worth about 10 shillings in the reign of Henry VIII (1509–47), who debased the coinage in 1526 and again in 1544–46. The earlier Henry VII sovereigns were worth more than 22 shillings.

FACE   Very good.
DAPPER   And three James shillings and an Elizabeth groat:
    Just twenty nobles.   145
FACE   O, you are too just.
    I would you had had the other noble in Mary's.
DAPPER   I have some Philip and Mary's.
FACE   Ay, those same
    Are best of all. Where are they? – Hark, the Doctor.

Act 3 scene 5*

[Enter] Subtle disguised like a priest of Fairy

SUBTLE   Is yet her Grace's cousin come?
FACE   He is come.
SUBTLE   And is he fasting?
FACE   Yes.
SUBTLE   And hath cried *hum*?
FACE   [*To Dapper*] Thrice, you must answer.
DAPPER   Thrice.
SUBTLE   And as oft *buzz*?
FACE   If you have, say.
DAPPER   I have.
SUBTLE   Then to her coz,
    Hoping that he hath vinegared his senses   5
    As he was bid, the Fairy Queen dispenses

144. *groat*] Small coin worth fourpence.

145. *nobles*] Each worth 6 shillings and eightpence.   *just*] Exact, implying tight-fisted.

146–7. *Mary's ... Philip and Mary's*] In an effort to squeeze more money out of Dapper, Face pretends to have an interest in filling the gap in the successive reigns with shillings minted by Mary I, who insisted on including her husband Philip of Spain, by name at least, in her rule (1553–58).

*   The 'Queen of Fairy' scam was popular with tricksters. Judith Philips, the Bankside cunningwoman, was whipped in 1595 for gulling clients into paying hugely to meet the Queen of Fairies. In 1609, Sir Anthony Ashley and his brother were sued in Chancery for the recovery of money paid them by a dupe, Thomas Rogers, who thought himself betrothed to the Fairy Queen. Even after *Alch* was staged, Alice and John West, convicted in 1613, posed as the King and Queen of Fairies to squeeze clients who hoped to acquire fairy gold. Subtle enhances his disguise as a priest of Fairy by adopting a foreign sound: he speaks in stilted rhyming couplets in ll. 1–18, even when the lines are broken (see 1 and 2, 'come' and '*hum*'; 3 and 4, '*buzz*' and 'coz').

1, 4. *cousin, coz*] The latter a diminutive of 'cousin', used loosely for any family relationship, such as the aunt/nephew kinship advanced here.

By me this robe, the petticoat of Fortune,
Which that he straight put on, she doth importune.

[Dapper puts on the petticoat]

And though to Fortune near be her petticoat,
Yet nearer is her smock, the Queen doth note.   10
And therefore even of that a piece she hath sent,
Which, being a child, to wrap him in was rent,
And prays him for a scarf he now will wear it
(With as much love as then her Grace did tear it)
About his eyes, to show he is fortunate.   15

They blind him with a rag

And trusting unto her to make his state,
He'll throw away all worldly pelf about him,
Which that he will perform she doth not doubt him.
FACE   She need not doubt him, sir. Alas, he has nothing
But what he will part withal as willingly   20
Upon her Grace's word – *[To Dapper]* Throw away your purse! –
As she would ask it – *[To Dapper]* Handkerchiefs and all! –
She cannot bid that thing but he'll obey.

He throws away as they bid him

If you have a ring about you, cast it off,
Or a silver seal at your wrist. Her Grace will send   25
Her fairies here to search you. Therefore deal
Directly with her Highness. If they find
That you conceal a mite, you are undone.
DAPPER   Truly, there's all.
FACE   All what?
DAPPER   My money, truly.

---

7. *petticoat*] Ornamental underskirt or kirtle worn exposed at the front by the opening in
    the gown.
10 *smock*] Shift, then a woman's only undergarment; worn also for sleeping. The smock
    is 'nearer' because more intimate, closer to her private parts, than a petticoat.
    Proverbially, 'Though nigh be my kirtle, yet near is my smock'.
12. *to wrap him in*] Fortune's favoured 'child' was proverbially swaddled in her smock.
    rent] Torn (from her smock).
16. *state*] Estate or fortune.
17. *worldly pelf*] Material goods or money.
27. *Directly*] Honestly.
28. *mite*] Originally a Flemish copper coin; in England, a half-farthing, the lowest
    denomination of money (in 1600, 24 mites = 1 penny).

FACE   Keep nothing that is transitory about you.   30
    [*Aside to Subtle*] Bid Dol play music. [*To Dapper*] Look,
        the elves are come
    To pinch you if you tell not truth. Advise you.

    Dol enters with a cittern: they pinch him

DAPPER   O, I have a paper with a spur-rial in't.
FACE   *Ti, ti!*
    They knew't, they say.
SUBTLE   *Ti, ti, ti, ti!* He has more yet.
FACE   *Ti, ti-ti-ti!* I'the t'other pocket?   35
SUBTLE   *Titi, titi, titi, titi.*
    They must pinch him, or he will never confess, they say.
DAPPER   O! O!
FACE   Nay, pray you hold. He is her Grace's nephew.
    Ti, ti, ti? What care you? Good faith, you shall care.
    Deal plainly, sir, and shame the fairies. Show
    You are an innocent.   40
DAPPER   By this good light, I ha' nothing.
SUBTLE   *Titi, titi to ta.* He does equivocate, she says.
    Ti, ti do ti, ti ti do, ti da. And swears by the light when he is blinded.
DAPPER   By this good dark, I ha' nothing but a half-crown
    Of gold about my wrist that my love gave me,
    And a leaden heart I wore sin' she forsook me.   45
FACE   I thought 'twas something. And would you incur
    Your aunt's displeasure for these trifles? Come,
    I had rather you had thrown away twenty half-crowns.
    You may wear your leaden heart still. [*Takes the money*]

    [*Noises off-stage. Doll peeps out*]

                  How now?
    [*Dol, Subtle, and Face whisper aside*]

SUBTLE   What news, Dol?   50

---

30. *transitory*] That is, belonging to this material world.
32.1. *cittern*] Cheap stringed instrument like a guitar, commonly left out for customers to
    entertain themselves in barbershops; associated with prostitutes, because available for
    anyone's use.
33. *spur-rial*] Or spur-royal, gold coin first struck by Edward IV in 1465 and then chiefly
    coined by James I, with a blazing sun on the reverse that resembled the rowel of a spur;
    worth about 15 shillings.   *Ti, ti*] Elves' jabber, followed by 'translation'.
39. *Deal ... fairies*] Ludicrous variation of 'Tell truth and shame the devil'.
40. *innocent*] Guiltless man; also, fool.
43–4. *half-crown Of gold*] First coined by Henry VIII.

DOL   Yonder's your knight, Sir Mammon.
FACE   God's lid, we never thought of him till now.
    Where is he?
DOL   Here, hard by. He's at the door.
SUBTLE   And you are not ready now? Dol, get his suit.
    He must not be sent back.
FACE   O, by no means.
    What shall we do with this same puffin here,   55
    Now he's o' the spit?
SUBTLE   Why, lay him back awhile
    With some device. – *Ti, ti ti, tititi*. Would her Grace speak with me?
    I come. – Help, Dol.

    [*Dol helps Face remove his Captain's costume while*] *he speaks
    through the keyhole, the other knocking*

FACE   Who's there? Sir Epicure,
    My master's i'the way. Please you to walk
    Three or four turns, but till his back be turned,   60
    And I am for you. – Quickly, Dol!
SUBTLE   [*To Dapper*]   Her Grace
    Commends her kindly to you, Master Dapper.
DAPPER   I long to see her Grace.
SUBTLE   She now is set
    At dinner in her bed, and she has sent you,
    From her own private trencher, a dead mouse   65
    And a piece of gingerbread to be merry withal,
    And stay your stomach lest you faint with fasting.
    Yet, if you could hold out till she saw you (she says),
    It would be better for you.
FACE   Sir, he shall
    Hold out, and 'twere this two hours, for her Highness.   70
    I can assure you that. We will not lose
    All we ha' done –

---

53. *suit*] Uniform; Face must do a rapid quick-change into his costume as Lungs, the
    alchemical assistant.
55. *puffin*] Sea bird abundant on N Atlantic coasts, 'having a very large curiously shaped
    furrowed and parti-coloured bill' (*OED*), perhaps a comment on the blindfold Dapper
    is currently wearing. Young puffins appear plump because of their puffed-out feathers,
    and were considered a delicacy; Face speaks of Dapper as ready for roasting *o' the spit*.
    The term was used contemptuously for a person puffed up with vanity or pride.
56. *lay him back*] A kitchen expression: take the spit from the fire to delay the roasting for
    the time being.
67. *stay your stomach*] Appease your hunger.
70. *and ... hours*] If he had to wait two hours.

SUBTLE   He must nor see nor speak
    To anybody till then.
FACE   For that, we'll put, sir,
    A stay in's mouth.
SUBTLE   Of what?
FACE   Of gingerbread.
    Make you it fit. He that hath pleased her Grace   75
    Thus far shall not now crinkle for a little.
    Gape, sir, and let him fit you.

    [*Dapper opens his mouth wide, and Subtle gags him with gingerbread*]

SUBTLE   [*Whispering aside*]   Where shall we now
    Bestow him?
DOL   I' the privy.
SUBTLE   [*Aloud*]   Come along, sir,
    I now must show you Fortune's privy lodgings.
FACE   Are they perfumed? And his bath ready?   80
SUBTLE   All.
    Only the fumigation's somewhat strong.

    [*Exeunt Subtle leading Dapper, and Dol carrying off the Captain's
    uniform; Face completes his quick-change into Lungs's costume*]

FACE   [*Calling*] Sir Epicure, I am yours, sir, by and by.

ACT 4

Act 4 scene 1*

    [*Enter*] Mammon

FACE   O, sir, you're come i' the only finest time –
MAMMON   Where's Master?

74. *stay*] Gag.
75. *Make ... fit*] You put it in.
76. *crinkle*] Cringe, shrink from the purpose. *little*] Trifle.
79. *privy*] Private, punning on latrine. The joke continues with references to odour.
82. *by and by*] Right away.
*   In the assignation between Mammon and Dol (as the mad rabbinic scholar), Jonson
    creates another satiric balance: Mammon's torrid fantasies of high romance ignore
    Dol's 'Irish costermonger' (57) responses (and Face's deflating asides). Aroused,
    Mammon confuses a 'free state' (156) with anarchy in which the humanitarian impulse
    yields to sensual excess and imperialist exhibitionism.
  1. *only finest time*] Absolutely the best time.

FACE   Now preparing for projection, sir.
    Your stuff will be all changed shortly.
MAMMON   Into gold?
FACE   To gold and silver, sir.
MAMMON   Silver I care not for.
FACE   Yes, sir, a little to give beggars.   5
MAMMON   Where's the lady?
FACE   At hand, here. I ha' told her such brave things o' you,
    Touching your bounty and your noble spirit –
MAMMON   Hast thou?
FACE   As she is almost in her fit to see you.
    But, good sir, no divinity i' your conference,
    For fear of putting her in rage –   10
MAMMON   I warrant thee.
FACE   Six men will not hold her down. And then,
    If the old man should hear or see you –
MAMMON   Fear not.
FACE   The very house, sir, would run mad. You know it
    How scrupulous he is, and violent
    'Gainst the least act of sin. Physic or mathematics,   15
    Poetry, state, or bawdry (as I told you)
    She will endure, and never startle. But
    No word of controversy.
MAMMON   I am schooled, good Ulen.
FACE   And you must praise her house, remember that,
    And her nobility.   20
MAMMON   Let me alone.
    No herald, no, nor antiquary, Lungo,
    Shall do it better. Go.
FACE *[Aside]*   Why, this is yet

---

  4. *Silver I care not for*] Another aping of Solomon in rejecting silver as inferior even for household use (1 Kings 10:21).

  9. *no ... conference*] No talking about theology.

10. *rage*] Madness.

14. *scrupulous*] Over-meticulous in matters of right and wrong; suspicious or fearful of wrong-doing. See 2.2.97–8.

15. *Physic*] Medicine.

16. *state*] Politics.

17. *startle*] Be startled. The active form is still used to describe an infant's reflexive response to noise.

18. *controversy*] Religious debates.

21. *herald*] Genealogist at the College of Heralds, where records of lineage and coats of arms were kept. *antiquary*] Historian.

A kind of modern happiness, to have
Dol Common for a great lady.

[*Exit Face*]

MAMMON   Now, Epicure,
Heighten thyself. Talk to her all in gold.   25
Rain her as many showers as Jove did drops
Unto his Danae. Show the god a miser
Compared with Mammon. What? The stone will do't.
She shall feel gold, taste gold, hear gold, sleep gold.
Nay, we will *concumbere* gold. I will be puissant   30
And mighty in my talk to her! Here she comes.

[*Enter Dol with Face*]

FACE   [*Aside to Dol*] To him, Dol, suckle him. [*Aloud*] This is the
    noble knight
    I told your ladyship –
MAMMON   Madam, with your pardon,
    I kiss your vesture.
DOL   Sir, I were uncivil
    If I would suffer that. My lip to you, sir.   35

[*She kisses him*]

MAMMON   I hope my lord your brother be in health, lady?
DOL   My lord my brother is, though I no lady, sir.
FACE   [*Aside*] Well said, my guinea-bird.
MAMMON ·   Right noble madam –
FACE   [*Aside*] O, we shall have most fierce idolatry!
MAMMON   'Tis your prerogative.   40
DOL   Rather your courtesy.
MAMMON   Were there nought else t'enlarge your virtues to me,

23. *modern*] Common (punning on Dol's name) or trivial, as well as current. *happiness*] Aptness; good fortune. The ambiguity comments ironically on status-seeking and the erosion of values in Jacobean London.
25. *Heighten*] Equivocal, implying both elevated rhetoric and sexual arousal.
26. *showers*] Jupiter, disguised as a shower of gold, pierced the walls of Danae's prison and became her lover (see 2.2.102).
30. *concumbere gold*] Lie together sexually, *gold* because the union will be perfectly satisfying once the lovers have drunk the elixir.
32. *suckle*] Figuratively, nurse him along, baby him.
34. *vesture*] Clothing, an example of heightened rhetoric.
38. *guinea-bird*] Prostitute.
40. *prerogative*] Right to be called 'lady'.
41. *enlarge*] Make known.

These answers speak your breeding and your blood.
DOL   Blood we boast none, sir: a poor baron's daughter.
MAMMON   Poor! And gat you? Profane not. Had your father
    Slept all the happy remnant of his life   45
    After that act, lain but there still, and panted,
    He'd done enough to make himself, his issue,
    And his posterity noble.
DOL   Sir, although
    We may be said to want the gilt and trappings,
    The dress of honour, yet we strive to keep   50
    The seeds and the materials.
MAMMON   I do see
    The old ingredient, virtue, was not lost,
    Nor the drug money, used to make your compound.
    There is a strange nobility i'your eye,
    This lip, that chin! Methinks you do resemble   55
    One o' the Austriac princes.
FACE   [*Aside*]   Very like!
    Her father was an Irish costermonger.
MAMMON   The house of Valois, just, had such a nose.
    And such a forehead yet the Medici
    Of Florence boast.   60
DOL   Troth, and I have been likened
    To all these princes.
FACE   [*Aside*]   I'll be sworn I heard it.
MAMMON   I know not how! It is not any one,
    But e'en the very choice of all their features.
FACE   [*Aside*] I'll in and laugh.

    [*Exit Face*]

MAMMON   A certain touch or air
    That sparkles a divinity, beyond   65
    An earthly beauty!
DOL   O, you play the courtier.
MAMMON   Good lady, gi'me leave –
DOL   In faith, I may not,

---

51. *seeds ... materials*] Alchemical metaphor for essential elements. Mammon continues
    the metaphor to l. 53.
54. *strange*] Foreign, as from another country; exceptional or rare.
56. *Austriac*] Austrian. The 'Hapsburg lip' is a prominently thick lower lip, frequently
    accompanied by receding chin and somewhat protruding eyes. The Valois nose (58) and
    the Medici forehead (59), however, are not distinctive features.
57. *Irish costermonger*] A puncturing class reference.
63. *the very choice*] The best or ideal composition.

       To mock me, sir.

MAMMON   To burn i' this sweet flame.

       The phoenix never knew a nobler death.

DOL   Nay, now you court the courtier and destroy   70

       What you would build. This art, sir, i' your words

       Calls your whole faith in question.

MAMMON   By my soul –

DOL   Nay, oaths are made o' the same air, sir.

MAMMON   Nature

       Never bestowed upon mortality

       A more unblamed, a more harmonious feature.   75

       She played the step-dame in all faces else.

       Sweet madam, le'me be particular –

DOL   Particular, sir? I pray you, know your distance.

MAMMON   In no ill sense, sweet lady, but to ask

       How your fair graces pass the hours? I see   80

       You're lodged here, i' the house of a rare man,

       An excellent artist. But what's that to you?

DOL   Yes, sir. I study here the mathematics

       And distillation.

MAMMON   O, I cry your pardon.

       He's a divine instructor! Can extract   85

       The souls of all things by his art; call all

       The virtues and the miracles of the sun

       Into a temperate furnace. Teach dull nature

       What her own forces are. A man the Emp'ror

       Has courted above Kelly. Sent his medals   90

---

69. *phoenix*] Unique mythical bird that self-destructs in flames, and is reborn from its own ashes.

70. *court the courtier*] Over-play the role of courtier; that is, speak in too affectedly elaborate a rhetoric, so as to defy belief.

75. *feature*] Physical appearance.

77, 78. *particular*] Mammon asks equivocal permission to speak to her about her personal interests. Dol understands him to mean that he wishes to become physically intimate.

83. *mathematics*] Astrology, but also the Pythagorean concepts of number and harmony pertinent to alchemy.

84. *distillation*] Chemistry, alchemical procedures.

88. *temperate*] Regulated.

89. *Emp'ror*] Rudolph II of Germany.

90. *Kelly*] Colleague of Dr John Dee, Edward Kelly (alias Talbot), 1555–95, a disbarred lawyer who boasted of having the philosopher's stone. After welcoming him to Prague, Rudolph imprisoned him in 1593 and again in 1595 when he failed to produce gold; Kelly broke his leg trying to escape, and died as a result.

And chains t'invite him.
DOL   Ay, and for his physic, sir –
MAMMON   Above the art of Aesculapius,
         That drew the envy of the Thunderer!
         I know all this and more.
DOL   Troth, I am taken, sir,
         Whole with these studies that contemplate nature.   95
MAMMON   It is a noble humour. But this form
         Was not intended to so dark a use!
         Had you been crooked, foul, of some coarse mould,
         A cloister had done well. But such a feature,
         That might stand up the glory of a kingdom,   100
         To live recluse is a mere solecism,
         Though in a nunnery! It must not be.
         I muse my lord your brother will permit it!
         You should spend half my land first, were I he.
         Does not this diamant better on my finger   105
         Than i' the quarry?
DOL   Yes.
MAMMON   Why, you are like it.
         You were created, lady, for the light!
         Here, you shall wear it. Take it, the first pledge
         Of what I speak, to bind you to believe me.

         [*He gives her the ring*]

DOL   In chains of adamant?   110
MAMMON   Yes, the strongest bands.
         And take a secret too. Here by your side
         Doth stand this hour the happiest man in Europe.
DOL   You are contented, sir?
MAMMON   Nay, in true being:
         The envy of princes and the fear of states.
DOL   Say you so, Sir Epicure!   115
MAMMON   Yes, and thou shalt prove it,

 91. *chains*] Punning on gifts of jewellery and prison chains.
 92. *Aesculapius*] The god-physician, capable of restoring men to life; he was killed by
     Zeus the 'Thunderer' (whose weapon was the thunderbolt) lest men should escape
     death altogether (H&S).
101. *recluse*] As a recluse.   *mere solecism*] Absolute incongruity.
105. *diamant*] Diamond. See note at 110.
110. *adamant*] Indestructible metal, probably steel, sometimes indicating an equally hard
     crystalline gem, punning on 'a diamant', the old form for diamond.   *bands*] Continu-
     ing the pun, 'rings' and 'bonds'.
112. *happiest*] Wealthiest, luckiest.

Daughter of honour. I have cast mine eye
Upon thy form, and I will rear this beauty
Above all styles.

DOL   You mean no treason, sir!

MAMMON   No, I will take away that jealousy.
I am the lord of the philosopher's stone,   120
And thou the lady.

DOL   How, sir! Ha' you that?

MAMMON   I am the master of the mastery.
This day, the good old wretch here o' the house
Has made it for us. Now he's at projection.
Think therefore thy first wish now. Let me hear it,   125
And it shall rain into thy lap, no shower,
But floods of gold, whole cataracts, a deluge,
To get a nation on thee!

DOL   You are pleased, sir,
To work on the ambition of our sex.

MAMMON   I'm pleased the glory of her sex should know   130
This nook here of the Friars is no climate
For her to live obscurely in, to learn
Physic and surgery for the constable's wife
Of some odd hundred in Essex. But come forth
And taste the air of palaces. Eat, drink   135
The toils of emp'rics and their boasted practice,
Tincture of pearl, and coral, gold, and amber.
Be seen at feasts and triumphs. Have it asked
What miracle she is. Set all the eyes

118. *styles*] Fashions, types.

119. *jealousy*] Suspicion.

121. *mastery*] Masterwork, the stone.

126. *no shower*] Mammon is preoccupied with outdoing Jove in sexualised power (refer to ll. 25–7).

128. *get*] Beget.

131. *Friars*] Blackfriars.

134. *hundred*] Subdivision of a county, with its own court.

136. *emp'rics*] Physicians who practise medicine learned through experience, not formal study; quacks.

137. Common herbal and alchemical remedies also mentioned by Lady Would-be (*Volp* 3.4.52–3, 56): *Tincture of pearl*] Prepared in a cordial to stimulate the heart (see also 2.2.76). *coral*] Coralline, a sea-moss used pharmaceutically to renew strength. *gold*] Aurum potabile, a drinkable form of gold considered a potent medicine. *amber*] Fossil resin worn as an amulet or burned as incense to attract lovers; perhaps ambergris, used to disguise the scent of medications.

Of court afire like a burning glass,   140
And work 'em into cinders, when the jewels
Of twenty states adorn thee and the light
Strikes out the stars, that, when thy name is mentioned,
Queens may look pale, and, we but showing our love,
Nero's Poppaea may be lost in story!   145
Thus will we have it.

DOL   I could well consent, sir.
But in a monarchy how will this be?
The prince will soon take notice, and both seize
You and your stone, it being a wealth unfit
For any private subject.   150

MAMMON   If he knew it.

DOL   Yourself do boast it, sir.

MAMMON   To thee, my life.

DOL   O, but beware, sir! You may come to end
The remnant of your days in a loathed prison
By speaking of it.

MAMMON   'Tis no idle fear!
We'll therefore go with all, my girl, and live   155
In a free state, where we will eat our mullets
Soused in high-country wines, sup pheasants' eggs,
And have our cockles boiled in silver shells,
Our shrimps to swim again, as when they lived,
In a rare butter made of dolphin's milk,   160
Whose cream does look like opals, and with these
Delicate meats set ourselves high for pleasure,
And take up down again, and then renew
Our youth and strength with drinking the elixir,
And so enjoy a perpetuity   165

140. *burning*] Magnifying.

141–3. *when ... stars*] Referring to Caligula's bride (AD 38, divorced 39), decked from head to foot with jewels looted from the provinces; see *Volp* 3.7.94–7 and note.

145. *Nero's Poppaea*] Nero's mistress, later his wife, for whom Nero murdered his first wife and his mother. Their passion was ill-fated: she died while pregnant as a result of his kicking her in a fit of temper. Nero deified her (by way of apology?) after the funeral.

153. *loathed prison*] Like Kelly, 90 above. Alchemical texts cautioned secrecy because of anti-sorcery laws (see 1.1.112) and because of economic fears for the state, should easy gold flood the country, causing inflation or political upset (see 4.7.81–2).

156. *free state*] Republic.   *mullets*] Fish that was an expensive delicacy at Roman feasts.

160. *dolphin's milk*] Another wild extravagance.

162. *high for pleasure*] Sexually excited, ready for any sensual experience.

Of life and lust. And thou shalt ha' thy wardrobe
Richer than Nature's, still to change thyself
And vary oft'ner for thy pride than she
Or Art, her wife and almost-equal servant.

[*Enter Face*]

FACE   Sir, you are too loud. I hear you, every word,   170
    Into the laboratory. Some fitter place.
    The garden, or great chamber above. How like you her?
MAMMON   Excellent! Lungs, there's for thee. [*Gives money*]
FACE   But do you hear?
    Good sir, beware: no mention of the Rabbins.
MAMMON   We think not on 'em.   175
FACE   O, it is well, sir.

    [*Exeunt Mammon and Dol*]

                                          Subtle!

Act 4 scene 2*

[*Enter*] *Subtle*

FACE   Dost thou not laugh?
SUBTLE   Yes. Are they gone?
FACE   All's clear.
SUBTLE   The widow is come.
FACE   And your quarrelling disciple?
SUBTLE   Ay.
FACE   I must to my captainship again then.
SUBTLE   Stay, bring'em in first.
FACE   So I meant. What is she?
    A bonnibel?   5
SUBTLE   I know not.
FACE   We'll draw lots.
    You'll stand to that?

166–9. *wardrobe ... servant*] The idea of art stimulating nature with erotic dress-up games
    is a common fantasy in Jonson, as in *Volp* 3.7.220–34.
174. *Rabbins*] Rabbis, especially the talmudic scholars whose hairsplitting theological
    debates resemble those in Broughton, the cause of Dol's fits of madness (see 2.3.238).
*   The introduction of the luscious Dame Pliant accelerates the decay of relations between
    Face and Subtle. This scene replicates the Dol–Mammon infatuation at a more realistic
    level.
3. *captainship*] Captain's uniform.
5. *bonnibel*] Attractive girl (*bonne et belle*, French).

SUBTLE   What else?
FACE   O, for a suit
   To fall now like a curtain, flap!
SUBTLE   To th' door, man.
FACE   You'll ha' the first kiss, 'cause I am not ready.

   [*Face goes to the door*]

SUBTLE   [*Aside*] Yes, and perhaps hit you through both the nostrils.

   [*Enter Kastril and Dame Pliant in the doorway*]

FACE   Who would you speak with?   10
KASTRIL   Where's the Captain?
FACE   Gone, sir,
   About some business.
KASTRIL   Gone?
FACE   He'll return straight.
   But Master Doctor, his Lieutenant, is here.
SUBTLE   [*Aside*] Come near, my worshipful boy, my *terrae fili*,
   That is, my boy of land. Make thy approaches.

   [*Face introduces Kastril and Dame Pliant, and exit*]

   Welcome. I know thy lusts and thy desires,   15
   And I will serve and satisfy 'em. Begin.
   Charge me from thence, or thence, or in this line.
   Here is my centre. Ground thy quarrel.
KASTRIL   You lie.
SUBTLE   How, child of wrath and anger! The loud lie?

---

7. *curtain*] Perhaps the drop-cloth of painted scenery used to effect immediate transformations in court masques. Face is praying for an instant quick-change of costume.
   As it is, Face has only 36 lines to complete his quick-change, but he managed an
   on-stage change in only 30 lines at the end of Act 3.

9. *hit . . . nostrils*] Put your nose out of joint. The expression may derive from the custom
   of controlling dangerous male animals (bulls, boars) by putting rings in their noses
   (Mares 1967).

10. *terrae fili*] Son of earth, which Subtle translates to mean a young man with a landed
   estate, though in Latin the phrase meant the opposite: a bastard, one without family or
   property rights. In alchemical or occult science, the phrase refers to spirits guiding
   divination by signs derived from earth, as in tossing a handful of dirt on a surface and
   reading a message in the resulting random shape.

15. *lusts*] Used generally as a synonym of 'desires'.

17. *Charge*] Attack. *line*] Direction.

18. *centre*] The stance of the adversary. *Ground*] Give reasons for. *You lie*] Too
   blatant and general a challenge. The rules of duelling demanded specific and careful
   reasoning; otherwise, the opponent had the advantage of choosing the weapon.

For what, my sudden boy?   20
KASTRIL   Nay, that look you to.
I am aforehand.
SUBTLE   O, this's no true grammar
And as ill logic! You must render causes, child,
Your first and second intentions, know your canons,
And your divisions, moods, degrees, and differences,
Your predicaments, substance and accident,   25
Series extern and intern, with their causes
Efficient, material, formal, final,
And ha' your elements perfect –
KASTRIL   What is this!
The angry tongue he talks in?
SUBTLE   That false precept
Of being aforehand has deceived a number,   30
And made 'em enter quarrels, oftentimes
Before they were aware, and afterward
Against their wills.
KASTRIL   How must I do then, sir?
SUBTLE   I cry this lady mercy. She should first
Have been saluted. I do call you lady   35
Because you are to be one ere't be long,
My soft and buxom widow.

   He kisses her

KASTRIL   Is she, i'faith?
SUBTLE   Yes, or my art is an egregious liar.
KASTRIL   How know you?
SUBTLE   By inspection on her forehead
And subtlety of her lip, which must be tasted   40

20. *sudden*] Impetuous.
21. *am aforehand*] Have made the first move.   *grammar*] The 'science' of duelling. Subtle
    teaches his lesson in the vocabulary of scholastic logic.
23. *canons*] Standards set by duelling authorities.
25. *predicaments*] Assertions in argument.
28. *elements*] Basic principles.
38. *egregious*] Flagrant, infamous.
40. *subtlety*] A complicated pun, suggesting primarily the sweetness associated with
    elaborate sugar confections devised for table ornaments. Beyond 'skill' and 'delicacy',
    the word also meant 'whorishness', from its aural association with 'sutler', a tradesman
    who follows an army and sells provisions; hence, a subtle woman is a whore who serves
    thousands. Dame Pliant's kiss, in other words, conveys erotic experience.

Often to make a judgment.

He kisses her again

                    [*Aside*] 'Slight, she melts
Like a myrobalane! [*Aloud*] Here is yet a line
In *rivo frontis* tells me he is no knight.

PLIANT What is he then, sir?

SUBTLE   Let me see your hand.

O, your *linea fortunae* makes it plain,   45
And *stella* here in *monte veneris*,
But most of all *junctura annularis*.
He is a soldier or a man of art, lady,
But shall have some great honour shortly.

PLIANT   Brother,
He's a rare man, believe me!   50

KASTRIL   Hold your peace.

[*Enter Face in the captain's uniform*]

Here comes the t'other rare man. – 'Save you, Captain.

FACE Good Master Kastril. Is this your sister?

KASTRIL   Ay, sir.
Please you to kuss her and be proud to know her?

[*Face kisses Dame Pliant*]

FACE I shall be proud to know you, lady.

PLIANT   Brother,
He calls me lady too.   55

KASTRIL   Ay, peace. I heard it.

[*Face confers with Subtle aside*]

FACE The Count is come.

SUBTLE   Where is he?

FACE   At the door.

SUBTLE Why, you must entertain him.

---

42. *myrobalane*] Plum-like fruit imported from the East, usually dried or candied, thus continuing the sweetmeat metaphor.
43. *rivo frontis*] In phrenology, the frontal vein. *no knight*] That is, no mere knight. Her husband will be of higher rank.
45. *linea fortunae*] In palmistry, the line of fortune running from the little finger towards the index finger.
46. *stella ... veneris*] Star on the mount of Venus at the base of the thumb, supposed to indicate an amorous disposition.
47. *junctura annularis*] Joint of the ring-finger, which Subtle claims foretells her imminent marriage to a distinguished man. Ironically, this sham forecast turns out to be correct.

FACE   What'll you do
    With these the while?
SUBTLE   Why, have 'em up and show 'em
    Some fustian book or the dark glass.
FACE   'Fore God,
    She is a delicate dabchick! I must have her.   60

    [*Exit Face*]

SUBTLE Must you? Ay, if your fortune will, you must.

    [*Turning to Kastril and Dame Pliant*]

    Come, sir, the Captain will come to us presently.
    I'll ha' you to my chamber of demonstrations,
    Where I'll show you both the grammar and logic
    And rhetoric of quarrelling, my whole method   65
    Drawn out in tables, and my instrument
    That hath the several scale upon't shall make you
    Able to quarrel at a straw's breadth by moonlight.
    And, lady, I'll have you look in a glass
    Some half an hour, but to clear your eyesight   70
    Against you see your fortune, which is greater
    Than I may judge upon the sudden, trust me.

    [*Exeunt*]

Act 4 scene 3*

    [*Enter Face, calling*]

FACE Where are you, Doctor?
SUBTLE [*Off-stage*]   I'll come to you presently.
FACE I will ha' this same widow, now I ha' seen her,
    On any composition.

59. *fustian*] Worthless, pretentious. *dark glass*] Fortune-teller's crystal ball or mirror.
60. *delicate*] Voluptuous, wanton. *dabchick*] Small bird, colloquial for an attractive girl.
66. *tables*] Diagrams.
67. *several scale*] A way of measuring each different situation.
69. *glass*] Crystal (see 59 above).
71. *Against*] Until, preparing for the time that.
72. *upon the sudden*] In so short a time.
*   A 'cross-talk' scene: Face and Subtle assume that the 'Spanish Don' cannot understand their insults, but Surly enjoys the irony of his Spanish replies, which they cannot translate: see '*Entiendo*' (40). The misinterpretations of manner and meaning add to the confusion of the double-game in progress.
 3. *composition*] Mutually beneficial arrangement.

[*Enter Subtle*]

SUBTLE   What do you say?
FACE   Ha' you disposed of them?
SUBTLE   I ha' sent 'em up.
FACE   Subtle, in troth, I needs must have this widow.   5
SUBTLE   Is that the matter?
FACE   Nay, but hear me.
SUBTLE   Go to,
   If you rebel once, Dol shall know it all.
   Therefore, be quiet and obey your chance.
FACE   Nay, thou art so violent now – Do but conceive.
   Thou art old and canst not serve –   10
SUBTLE   Who, cannot I?
   'Slight, I will serve her with thee, for a –
FACE   Nay,
   But understand. I'll gi'you composition.
SUBTLE   I will not treat with thee. What, sell my fortune?
   'Tis better than my birthright. Do not murmur.
   Win her and carry her. If you grumble, Dol   15
   Knows it directly.
FACE   Well, sir, I am silent.
   Will you go help to fetch in Don, in state?
SUBTLE   I follow you, sir.

[*Exit Face*]

   We must keep Face in awe,
   Or he will overlook us like a tyrant.
   Brain of a tailor! Who comes here? Don John?   20

[*Enter*] *Surly like a Spaniard,* [*ushered in by Face*]

SURLY   *Señores, beso las manos a vuestas mercedes.*
SUBTLE   Would you had stooped a little, and kissed our *anos.*
FACE   Peace, Subtle.
SUBTLE   Stab me, I shall never hold, man.

---

10. *serve*] Perform sexually.
13. *treat*] Bargain.
17. *in state*] Ceremoniously, formally.
20. *Brain of a tailor!*] Oath prompted by Surly's elaborate costume. *Don John*] Don Juan, a common Spanish name, perhaps recalling the legendary Spanish libertine. Face calls him a 'travelled punk-master' at l. 56.
21. 'Sirs, I kiss your honours' hands.'
22. *anos*] Arses.

He looks in that deep ruff like a head in a platter,
Served in by a short cloak upon two trestles!   25
FACE   Or what do you say to a collar of brawn, cut down
Beneath the souse and wriggled with a knife.
SUBTLE   'Slud, he does look too fat to be a Spaniard.
FACE   Perhaps some Fleming or some Hollander got him
In D'Alva's time: Count Egmont's bastard.   30
SUBTLE   [*Bowing to Surly*]   Don,
Your scurvy yellow Madrid face is welcome.
SURLY   *Gracias.*
SUBTLE   He speaks out of a fortification.
Pray God he ha'no squibs in those deep sets.
SURLY   *Por dios, Señores, muy linda casa!*
SUBTLE   What says he?   35
FACE   Praises the house, I think.
I know no more but's action.
SUBTLE   Yes, the *casa*,
My precious Diego, will prove fair enough
To cozen you in. Do you mark? You shall
Be cozened, Diego.
FACE   Cozened, do you see?
My worthy Donzel, cozened.   40
SURLY   *Entiendo.*
SUBTLE   Do you intend it? So do we, dear Don.
Have you brought pistolets? or portagues?

24. *deep ruff*] Starched collar composed of several layers of pleated linen.
26. *collar of brawn*] Pig's neck.
27. *souse*] Pig's ear.   *wriggled with a knife*] The fat scored in ripples to look like a ruff.
28. *too fat*] Spaniards were thought to be ascetically thin, like those in El Greco's paintings.
29. *Fleming ... Hollander*] Proverbially fat from eating butter and drinking beer.
30. *D'Alva's time*] Fernando Alvarez, Duke of Alva, was governor-general of the Netherlands, 1567–73.   *Count Egmont*] Dutch patriot executed by Alva in 1568.
33. *squibs*] Rockets or grenades.   *deep sets*] Thick folds of the ruff.
34. 'By God, sirs, a very handsome house!'
36. *action*] Gestures.
37. *Diego*] James in Spanish; the forerunner of 'dago' as a term of abuse.
40. *Donzel*] Mocking diminutive for 'Don', perhaps borrowed from the Italian *donzello* (= squire).   *Entiendo*] 'I understand'; in fact, Surly does.
42. *pistolets*] Spanish gold coins worth about 6 shillings.   *portagues*] Portuguese gold coins worth about 4 pounds.

My solemn Don?

[*Face*] *feels his pockets*

                    Dost thou feel any?
FACE   Full.
SUBTLE   You shall be emptied, Don, pumped and drawn
    Dry, as they say.   45
FACE   Milked, in troth, sweet Don.
SUBTLE   See all the monsters, the great lion of all, Don.
SURLY   *Con licencia, se puede ver a esta Señora?*
SUBTLE   What talks he now?
FACE   O' the *Señora*.
SUBTLE   O, Don,
    That is the lioness, which you shall see
    Also, my Don.   50
FACE   'Slid, Subtle, how shall we do?
SUBTLE   For what?
FACE   Why, Dol's employed, you know.
SUBTLE   That's true!
    'Fore heaven I know not. He must stay, that's all.
FACE   Stay? That he must not by no means.
SUBTLE   No? Why?
FACE   Unless you'll mar all. 'Slight, he'll suspect it.
    And then he will not pay, not half so well.   55
    This is a travelled punk-master, and does know
    All the delays – a notable hot rascal,
    And looks already rampant.
SUBTLE   'Sdeath, and Mammon
    Must not be troubled.
FACE   Mammon, in no case!
SUBTLE   What shall we do then?   60
FACE   Think. You must be sudden.
SURLY   *Entiendo que la Señora es tan hermosa que codicio tan*

44–5. *Pumped … Dry*] Sexually and financially.
45. *Milked*] Caused to ejaculate (see 3.3.22).
46. *monsters … lion*] Metaphorically, show him all the sights in town. The lions kept at
    the Tower were a popular attraction (see *Volp* 2.1.34–5).
47. 'With your permission, may one see this lady?'
52. *stay*] Wait.
56. *travelled punk-master*] Experienced whoremaster.
57. *notable*] Notorious.   *hot*] Sexually eager.
58. *rampant*] Heraldic term for an animal rearing up on its hind legs; used to describe the
    vulgarly wanton.

> *A verla, como la bien aventuranza de mi vida.*

FACE   *Mi vida?* 'Slid, Subtle, he puts me in mind o' the widow.
What dost thou say to draw her to't? Ha?
And tell her it is her fortune. All our venture   65
Now lies upon't. It is but one man more,
Which on's chance to have her. And beside
There is no maidenhead to be feared or lost.
What dost thou think on't, Subtle?

SUBTLE   Who, I? Why –

FACE   The credit of our house too is engaged.   70

SUBTLE   You made me an offer for my share erewhile.
What wilt thou gi' me, i' faith?

FACE   O, by that light,
I'll not buy now. You know your doom to me.
E'en take your lot, obey your chance, sir. Win her
And wear her out, for me.   75

SUBTLE   'Slight, I'll not work her then.

FACE   It is the common cause; therefore, bethink you.
Dol else must know it, as you said.

SUBTLE   I care not.

SURLY   *Señores, por qué se tarda tanto?*

SUBTLE   Faith, I am not fit. I am old.

FACE   That's now no reason, sir.

SURLY   *Puede ser de hazer burla de mi amor?*   80

FACE   You hear the Don too? By this air, I call.
And loose the hinges. [*Calls*] Dol!

SUBTLE   A plague of hell –

FACE   Will you then do?

SUBTLE   You're a terrible rogue.
I'll think of this. Will you, sir, call the widow?

FACE   Yes, and I'll take her too, with all her faults,   85
Now I do think on't better.

62–3. 'I understand that the lady is so beautiful that I fervently desire as much to see her as the great good fortune of my life.'

63. *Mi vida?*] Face's echo should sound more like 'widow' than Surly's Castilian pronunciation.

67. *Which on's*] Whichever one of us.

74–5. *Win . . . out*] Proverbial expression given a vigorous sexual twist with Face's addition of 'out'. *for me*] For all I care.

75. *work her*] Set her to work as a whore.

78. 'Sirs, why is there so much delay?'

80. 'Can it be that you are making fun of my love?'

82. *loose the hinges*] Let it all go; break the agreement.

84. *think of*] Remember (vengefully).

SUBTLE   With all my heart, sir.
    Am I discharged o' the lot?
FACE   As you please.
SUBTLE   Hands.

   [*They shake hands*]

FACE Remember now that upon any change
    You never claim her.
SUBTLE   Much good joy and health to you, sir.
    Marry a whore? Fate, let me wed a witch first.   90
SURLY *Por estas honradas barbas* –
SUBTLE   He swears by his beard.
    Dispatch, and call the brother too.

   [*Exit Face*]

SURLY   *Tengo duda, Señores,*
    Que no me hagan alguna traición.
SUBTLE How, issue on? Yes, *presto, Señor*. Please you
    Entratha the *chambratha*, worthy Don,   95
    Where, if it please the Fates, in your *bathada*
    You shall be soaked and stroked and tubbed and rubbed
    And scrubbed and fubbed, dear don, before you go.
    You shall, in faith, my scurvy baboon Don,
    Be curried, clawed, and flawed and tawed indeed.   100
    I will the heartilier go about it now,
    And make the widow a punk so much the sooner,
    To be revenged on this impetuous Face.
    The quickly doing of it is the grace.

   [*Exeunt*]

87. *discharged*] Freed from obligation.
91. *Por ... barbas*] 'By this honourable beard'.
92–3. *Tengo ... traición*] 'I suspect, sirs, that you are tricking me.'
94. *presto*] Soon, quickly.
95–6. *Entratha the chambratha ... bathada*] Mock-Spanish lisp, taking off Surly's Castilian accent. The 'bath' may be literal, as well as sexual and financial, assuming Dol offers the usual hot-house treatments of bath and massage.
98. *fubbed*] Cheated.
100. Subtle describes the curing of leather: *curried*] Rubbed and beaten. *clawed*] Scraped. *flawed*] Skinned. *tawed*] tanned.

Act 4 scene 4*

[Enter] Face, Kastril, Dame Pliant

FACE   Come, lady. I knew the Doctor would not leave
    Till he had found the very nick of her fortune.
KASTRIL   To be a countess, say you?
FACE   A Spanish countess, sir.
PLIANT   Why? Is that better than an English countess?
FACE   Better? 'Slight, make you that a question, lady?   5
KASTRIL   Nay, she is a fool, Captain. You must pardon her.
FACE   Ask from your courtier to your Inns of Court man
    To your mere milliner. They will tell you all
    Your Spanish jennet is the best horse. Your Spanish
    Stoop is the best garb. Your Spanish beard   10
    Is the best cut. Your Spanish ruffs are the best
    Wear. Your Spanish pavan is the best dance.
    Your Spanish titillation in a glove
    The best perfume. And, for your Spanish pike
    And Spanish blade, let your poor Captain speak.   15
    Here comes the Doctor.

*   In order to con Dame Pliant into giving herself to the 'Spanish Don', Face defends
    Spanish accomplishments; his irony (esp. ll. 7–15) is not entirely a praise–blame
    inversion, but the tone is scoffing. Spain was associated with the bloody Catholic reign
    of Mary I, wife of Philip of Spain, with growing English naval power challenging
    Spanish control of the sea, best illustrated by the destruction of the Spanish Armada in
    1588, and with English military support of the Netherlands in their battle to free
    themselves from Spanish domination. James I's efforts to bring Spanish fashion to court
    and to encourage closer diplomatic relations with Spain had no popular support. Anti-
    Spanish sentiment was still rife in 1624, as the long run of Middleton's *A Game at
    Chess* indicates.
2. *nick*] Critical moment, turning point; crudely, vagina.
3, 4. *countess*] Punning on 'cunt-ess', whore, as at ll. 22, 40, and 87 below. The debate on
    the relative merits of Spanish and English permits the comical repetition of 'countess'.
9. *jennet*] Small Spanish horse; frequently associated with sexual 'riding' and, like 'jenny',
    the term for any female animal, with female sexual voracity.
10. *Stoop*] Bow; lower oneself for or submit to the sexual act. See similar equivocation at
    ll. 44–5, 'Is served / Upon the knee!'   *garb*] Fashion.
12. *pavan*] Stately dance.
13. *titillation . . . glove*] Perfuming process in which gloves were soaked in perfumed oils to
    fix the scent; also equivocally sexual.
14. *pike*] A weapon consisting of a long wooden shaft with a pointed iron head; crudely,
    penis.
15. *blade*] The Toledo blade was the best sword; like any weapon, the term has a sexual
    edge.

[*Enter Subtle with a horoscope*]

SUBTLE   My most honoured lady –
 For so I am now to style you, having found
 By this my scheme you are to undergo
 An honourable fortune very shortly –
 What will you say now, if some –   20
FACE   I ha' told her all, sir,
 And her right worshipful brother here, that she shall be
 A countess. Do not delay 'em, sir. A Spanish countess.
SUBTLE   Still, my scarce-worshipful Captain, you can keep
 No secret. Well, since he has told you, madam,
 Do you forgive him, and I do.   25
KASTRIL   She shall do that, sir.
 I'll look to't. 'Tis my charge.
SUBTLE   Well then. Nought rests
 But that she fit her love, now, to her fortune.
PLIANT   Truly, I shall never brook a Spaniard.
SUBTLE   No?
PLIANT   Never sin' eighty-eight could I abide 'em,
 And that was some three year afore I was born, in truth.   30
SUBTLE   Come, you must love him, or be miserable.
 Choose which you will.
FACE   [*To Kastril*]   By this good rush, persuade her.
 She will cry strawberries else within this twelvemonth.
SUBTLE   Nay, shads and mackerel, which is worse.
FACE   Indeed, sir!

[*Kastril threatens Dame Pliant*]

KASTRIL   God's lid, you shall love him, or I'll kick you   35
PLIANT   Why?
 I'll do as you will ha' me, brother.
KASTRIL   Do,
 Or by this hand, I'll maul you.
FACE   Nay, good sir,
 Be not so fierce.
SUBTLE   No, my enragèd child,

18. *scheme*] The horoscope.
29. *eighty-eight*] The year of the Armada.
32. *rush*] Presumably picked up from the floor, where green rushes were strewn in lieu of
 carpets, then used only as table- or wall-coverings.
33. *cry strawberries*] As a street-hawker.
· 34. *shads and mackerel*] Fish-hawkers, especially at Billingsgate, were cruder in language
 and odour than fruit-sellers, by reputation at least.

She will be ruled. What, when she comes to taste
The pleasures of a countess! To be courted –   40
FACE   And kissed and ruffled!
SUBTLE   Ay, behind the hangings.
FACE   And then come forth in pomp!
SUBTLE   And know her state!
FACE   Of keeping all th'idolaters o' the chamber
Barer to her than at their prayers!
SUBTLE   Is served
Upon the knee!   45
FACE   And has her pages, ushers,
Footmen and coaches –
SUBTLE   Her six mares –
FACE   Nay, eight!
SUBTLE   To hurry her through London to th'Exchange,
Bedlam, the china-houses –
FACE   Yes, and have
The citizens gape at her and praise her tires!
And my lord's goose-turd bands, that rides with her!   50
KASTRIL   Most brave! By this hand, you are not my suster
If you refuse.
PLIANT   I will not refuse, brother.

   [*Enter Surly*]

SURLY   *Qué es esto, Señores, que no se venga?*
Esta tardanza me mata!
FACE   It is the Count come!
The Doctor knew he would be here, by his art.   55
SUBTLE   *En galanta madama, Don! Galantissima!*

41. *ruffled*] Fondled. *hangings*] Wall-coverings, tapestries.
42. *know her state*] Demand what is due to one of her social rank.
43. *idolaters*] Playing on 'adulterers'. *chamber*] Presence-chamber or reception room in the palace, but equivocating on 'bed-chamber' and 'vagina', sexual chamber.
44. *barer to her*] In taking off their hats, but with sexual innuendo of other baring. Hats were worn indoors, but were doffed as a sign of respect.
47–8. *Exchange ... china-houses*] Fashionable meeting-places for shopping and assignations. The New Exchange, a mall in the Strand opened in 1609, had shops for dressmakers and milliners. The china-houses sold luxury items imported from the orient. Bedlam, the hospital for the insane, offered entertaining glimpses of madmen for a small fee.
49. *tires*] Clothes.
50. *goose-turd bands*] Collars of fashionable yellowish-green.
53–4. 'Why is it, sirs, that she does not come? This delay is killing me!'
56. Mock-Spanish: 'A gallant lady, Don! Most gallant!'

SURLY   *Por todos los dioses, la más acabada*
       Hermosura que he visto en mi vida!
FACE   Is't not a gallant language that they speak?
KASTRIL   An admirable language! Is't not French?   60
FACE   No, Spanish, sir.
KASTRIL   It goes like law-French,
       And that, they say, is the courtliest language.
FACE   List, sir.
SURLY   *El sol ha perdido su lumbre con el*
       Resplandor que trae esta dama. Válgame dios!
FACE   H'admires your sister.   65
KASTRIL   Must not she make curtsey?
SUBTLE   'Ods will, she must go to him, man, and kiss him!
       It is the Spanish fashion for the women
       To make first court.
FACE   'Tis true he tells you, sir.
       His art knows all.
SURLY   *Por qué no se acude?*
KASTRIL   He speaks to her, I think?   70
FACE   That he does, sir.
SURLY   *Por el amor de dios, qué es esto que se tarda?*
KASTRIL   Nay, see. She will not understand him! Gull!
       Noddy!
PLIANT   What say you, brother?
KASTRIL   Ass, my suster,
       Go kuss him as the cunning-man would ha' you.
       I'll thrust a pin i' your buttocks else.   75
FACE   O, no, sir!

       [*Dame Pliant kisses Surly*]

SURLY   *Señora mía, mi persona muy indigna está*
       A llegar a tanta hermosura.
FACE   Does he not use her bravely?
KASTRIL   Bravely, i' faith!
FACE   Nay, he will use her better.

57–8. 'By all the gods, the most perfect beauty that I have seen in my life!'
61. *law-French*] Corrupt form of Norman French used in the lawcourts up to the
    seventeenth century.
63–4. 'The sun has lost its light, with the brilliance which this lady brings. So help me God!'
69. *Por . . . acude*] 'Why does she not approach?'
72. 'For the love of God, what is she waiting for?'
76–7. 'Lady, my person is very unworthy of attaining so much beauty.'
78. *use*] A comment on Surly's eagerness in returning Pliant's kiss. At 79, Face implies
    fuller sexual service.

KASTRIL   Do you think so?

SURLY   *Señora, si sera servida, entremos.*   80

[*Exit Surly with Dame Pliant*]

KASTRIL   Where does he carry her?

FACE   Into the garden, sir.
Take you no thought. I must interpret for her.

[*Face starts to exit*]

SUBTLE   [*Aside to Face*] Give Dol the word.

[*Exit Face*]

                              Come, my fierce child, advance.
We'll to our quarrelling lesson again.

KASTRIL   Agreed.
I love a Spanish boy with all my heart.   85

SUBTLE   Nay, and by this means, sir, you shall be brother
To a great count.

KASTRIL   Ay, I knew that at first.
This match will advance the house of the Kastrils.

SUBTLE   Pray God your sister prove but pliant.

KASTRIL   Why,
Her name is so, by her other husband.   90

SUBTLE   How!

KASTRIL   The Widow Pliant. Knew you not that?

SUBTLE   No, faith, sir.
Yet by erection of her figure I guessed it.
Come, let's go practise.

KASTRIL   Yes, but do you think, Doctor,
I e'er shall quarrel well?

SUBTLE   I warrant you.

[*Exeunt*]

80. 'Lady, if it would please you, let us go in.' Surly's words, especially *servida*, continue the
expectation of sexual use.

83. *the word*] The signal to begin her mad fit.

92. *by ... figure*] By casting her horoscope, but also commenting on her sexually
provocative appearance.

Act 4 scene 5*

[Enter] Dol in her fit of talking [with] Mammon

DOL   *For after Alexander's death –*
MAMMON   Good lady –
DOL   *That Perdiccas and Antigonus were slain,*
      The two that stood, Seleuc' and Ptolemy –
MAMMON   Madam –
DOL   *Made up the two legs, and the fourth Beast.*
      That was Gog-north, and Egypt-south, which after   5
      Was called Gog Iron-leg and South Iron-leg –
MAMMON   Lady –
DOL   *And then Gog-hornèd. So was Egypt too.*
      Then Egypt clay-leg and Gog clay-leg –
MAMMON   Sweet madam –
DOL   *And last Gog-dust and Egypt-dust, which fall*
      In the last link of the fourth chain. And these   10
      Be stars in story, which none see or look at –
MAMMON   What shall I do?
DOL   *For, as he says, except*
      We call the Rabbins and the heathen Greeks –
MAMMON   Dear lady –
DOL   *To come from Salem and from Athens,*

---

*   The cue for Dol's performance is at 4.4.82. Dol's mad chatter (1–32) comes from Hugh
     Broughton *A Concent of Scripture* (1590) (see 2.3.238), an eccentric puritan millenar-
     ianist treatise which demonstrates God's scheme of predestination by rationalising the
     historical chronology of the Bible as well as its accuracy in foretelling the future, and
     predicting on that basis the fall of papist Rome (see 25–32) and the founding of the
     New Jerusalem. In ll. 1–16, Dol burbles scraps of Broughton's analysis of Daniel 2,
     interpreting Nebuchadnezzar's dream of a great image with a golden head, silver body,
     brass thighs, and iron and clay legs: a stone smashes the image, and then grows into a
     mountain. According to Daniel, the image represents successive pagan empires
     crumbling before the power of the God of Israel, the stone mountain. Broughton
     identifies Egypt and Syria as the last 'link' in the four periods or 'chains' of pagan
     empires, with whose destruction comes the apocalypse and the fifth empire, the
     kingdom of God.

2–3. *Perdiccas ... Ptolemy*] Alexander the Great's generals, who divided the empire among
     themselves in squabbling after his death. Ptolemy and Selucas eventually destroyed the
     other two generals, and founded their own empires in Egypt and Syria.

5–9. *Gog-north ... Egypt-dust*] From the headlines to the three columns of Broughton's
     biblical chronology.

10. *fourth chain*] The final period of historical decline before the apocalypse.

11. *stars in story*] Jews and Greeks who bore witness to Christ.

14. *Salem*] Jerusalem.

    And teach the people of Great Britain –   15

[*Enter Face*]

FACE   What's the matter, sir?
DOL   *To speak the tongue of Eber and Javan –*
MAMMON   O,
    She's in her fit.
DOL   *We shall know nothing –*
FACE   Death, sir,
    We are undone.
DOL   *Where then a learnèd linguist*
    Shall see the ancient used communion
    Of vowels and consonants –   20
FACE   My master will hear!
DOL   *A wisdom which Pythagoras held most high –*
MAMMON   Sweet honourable lady –
DOL   *To comprise*
    All sounds of voices in few marks of letters –
FACE   Nay, you must never hope to lay her now.

   They speak together [*Face and Mammon talking over Dol's recitation*]

DOL *And so we may arrive by*	FACE How did you put her into't? 25
Talmud skill	MAMMON Alas, I talk'd
And profane Greek to raise the	Of a fifth monarchy I would
building up	erect
Of Helen's house against the	With the philosopher's stone, by
Ismaelite,	chance, and she
King of Thogarma and his	Falls on the other four straight.
Habergeons	FACE Out of Broughton!

16. *tongue ... Javan*] Hebrew and Greek. Eber and Javan, descendants of Noah, were the ancestors of the Jews and Gentiles respectively.

18–23. *linguist ... letters*] From Broughton's 'Preface', referring to the primal language spoken in Eden, which, if recovered, would be the key to all knowledge (see 2.1.83–6).

24. *lay*] Allay, punning on 'bed'.

24–32. The verbal explosion into farcical polyphony sets up the chemical explosion that follows.

26. *profane*] Because pagan. *fifth monarchy*] The millennium of Revelation 20, when Jesus would return to earth and reign. But Mammon uses the expression metaphorically for his own utopia of gold and sensuality.

27. *Helen's*] In Broughton, Heber's. Dol is confusing her mythologies. *Ishmaelite*] Non-believer.

28. *Thogarma*] Togarmah, the armed supporters of Ezekiel against Gog in Ezekiel 38:6. *habergeons*] Sleeveless mailed armour, not biblical. *the other four*] Assyria, Persia, Greece, and Rome.

Brimstony, blue and fiery, and
the force
Of King Abaddon and the
beast of Cittim,
Which Rabbi David Kimchi,
Onkelos,
And Aben-Ezra do interpret
Rome.

Upon Subtle's entry they disperse

MAMMON   Where shall I hide me?
SUBTLE   How! What sight is here!
Close deeds of darkness and that shun the light!
Bring him again. Who is he?   35

[*Subtle discovers Mammon as Dol exits*]

                                    What, my son!
O, I have lived too long.
MAMMON   Nay, good dear father,
There was n'unchaste purpose.
SUBTLE   Not? And flee me
When I come in?
MAMMON   That was my error.
SUBTLE   Error?
Guilt, guilt, my son. Give it the right name. No marvel
If I found check in our great work within,   40
When such affairs as these were managing!
MAMMON   Why, have you so?
SUBTLE   It has stood still this half-hour,
And all the rest of our less works gone back.
Where is the instrument of wickedness,

I told you so. 'Slid, stop her mouth.
MAMMON   Is't best?
FACE   She'll never leave else. If   30
the old man hear her,
We are but faeces, ashes.
SUBTLE [*Off-stage*] What's to do there?
FACE   O, we are lost! Now she
hears him, she is quiet.

---

29. *Brimstony ... fiery*] Garbling Wyclif's version of the horsemen of the apocalypse in Revelation 9:17.
30. *Abaddon ... Cittim*] Names Broughton uses for the Pope.
31. *David Kimchi*] 1160–1235, Jewish grammarian and biblical commentator at Narbonne. *Onkelos*] First century translator and commentator on the Old Testament in Aramaic. *faeces*] Literally, excrement; alchemically, sediment or ashes left after refinement.
32. *Aben-Ezra*] Abraham ben Meir Ibn Ezra, 1092–1167, poet and pioneering biblical commentator who made Arab learning available to his fellow Jews in Europe.
34. *Close*] Hidden.
35. *again*] Back.
41. *managing*] Going on.

My lewd false drudge?   45

[*Exit Face unobserved*]

MAMMON   Nay, good sir, blame not him.
   Believe me, 'twas against his will or knowledge.
   I saw her by chance.
SUBTLE   Will you commit more sin
   T'excuse a varlet?
MAMMON   By my hope, 'tis true, sir.
SUBTLE Nay, then I wonder less if you, for whom
   The blessing was prepared, would so tempt heaven,   50
   And lose your fortunes.
MAMMON   Why, sir?
SUBTLE   This'll retard
   The work a month at least.
MAMMON   Why, if it do,
   What remedy? But think it not, good father.
   Our purposes were honest.
SUBTLE   As they were,
   So the reward will prove.   55

  A great crack and noise within

                How now! Ay me!
   God and all saints be good to us. What's that?

[*Enter Face*]

FACE   O, sir, we are defeated! All the works
   Are flown *in fumo*. Every glass is burst.
   Furnace and all rent down! As if a bolt
   Of thunder had been driven through the house.   60
   Retorts, receivers, pelicans, bolt-heads,
   All struck in shivers!

  Subtle falls down as in a swoon

                Help, good sir! Alas,
   Coldness and death invades him. Nay, Sir Mammon,
   Do the fair offices of a man! You stand
   As you were readier to depart than he.   65

  One knocks

   Who's there? [*Looking out*] My lord her brother is come.
MAMMON   Ha, Lungs?

58. *in fumo*] Up in smoke, vaporised.
61. *receivers*] Vessels receiving the products of distillation.

FACE His coach is at the door. Avoid his sight,
　For he's as furious as his sister is mad.
MAMMON Alas!
FACE 　　　　　My brain is quite undone with the fume, sir.
　I ne'er must hope to be mine own man again. 　　　　70
MAMMON Is all lost, Lungs? Will nothing be preserved
　Of all our cost?
FACE 　　　　　Faith, very little, sir.
　A peck of coals or so, which is cold comfort, sir.
MAMMON O, my voluptuous mind! I am justly punished.
FACE And so am I, sir. 　　　　75
MAMMON 　　　　Cast from all my hopes –
FACE Nay, certainties, sir.
MAMMON 　　　　By mine own base affections.

Subtle seems come to himself

SUBTLE O, the curst fruits of vice and lust!
MAMMON 　　　　　　Good father,
　It was my sin. Forgive it.
SUBTLE 　　　　Hangs my roof
　Over us still, and will not fall? O, justice
　Upon us for this wicked man! 　　　　80
FACE [*To Mammon*] 　　　Nay, look, sir,
　You grieve him now with staying in his sight.
　Good sir, the nobleman will come too and take you,
　And that may breed a tragedy.
MAMMON 　　　　I'll go.
FACE Ay, and repent at home, sir. It may be,
　For some good penance, you may ha' it yet: 　　　　85
　A hundred pound to the box at Bedlam –
MAMMON 　　　　Yes.
FACE For the restoring such as ha' their wits.
MAMMON 　　　　I'll do't.
FACE I'll send one to you to receive it.
MAMMON 　　　　Do.
　Is no projection left?
FACE 　　　All flown, or stinks, sir.
MAMMON Will nought be saved that's good for med'cine, thinkst thou? 90
FACE I cannot tell, sir. There will be, perhaps,

68. *furious*] Hot-tempered.
70. *mine own man*] Myself, in my right senses.
76. *affections*] Passions, lusts.
86. *box at Bedlam*] For charitable donations to help patients at the hospital for the insane.
90. *med'cine*] The elixir.

Something about the scraping of the shards
Will cure the itch, though not your itch of mind, sir.
It shall be saved for you and sent home. Good sir,
This way, for fear the lord should meet you.   95

[*Exit Mammon, as Face holds door*]

SUBTLE   Face?
FACE   Ay.
SUBTLE   Is he gone?
FACE   Yes, and as heavily
As all the gold he hoped for were in his blood.
Let us be light, though.
SUBTLE   Ay, as balls, and bound
And hit our heads against the roof for joy.
There's so much of our care now cast away!   100
FACE   Now to our Don.
SUBTLE   Yes, your young widow, by this time,
Is made a countess, Face. She's been in travail
Of a young heir for you.
FACE   Good, sir.
SUBTLE   Off with your case,
And greet her kindly, as a bridegroom should
After these common hazards.   105
FACE   Very well, sir.
Will you go fetch Don Diego off the while?
SUBTLE   And fetch him over too, if you'll be pleased, sir.
Would Dol were in her place to pick his pockets now.
FACE   Why, you can do it as well, if you would set to't.
I pray you prove your virtue.   110
SUBTLE   For your sake, sir.

[*Exeunt*]

93. *though ... sir*] Possibly spoken as an aside, but Face does not need to repress his
    criticism, since Mammon has been reproving himself openly for greed and sensuality.
98. *light*] Joyful.
103. *case*] Costume as Lungs.
107. *fetch him over*] Get the better of him.
110. *virtue*] Special ability or strength.

Act 4 scene 6*

[Enter] Surly [with] Dame Pliant

SURLY   Lady, you see into what hands you are fall'n,
    'Mongst what a nest of villains! And how near
    Your honour was t'have catched a certain clap,
    Through your credulity, had I but been
    So punctually forward as place, time,   5
    And other circumstance would ha' made a man.
    For you're a handsome woman. Would y'were wise too.
    I am a gentleman, come here disguised
    Only to find the knaveries of this citadel,
    And where I might have wronged your honour, and have not,   10
    I claim some interest in your love. You are,
    They say, a widow, rich, and I am a bachelor,
    Worth nought. Your fortunes may make me a man,
    As mine ha' preserved you a woman. Think upon it,
    And whether I have deserved you or no.   15
PLIANT   I will, sir.
SURLY   And for these household rogues, let me alone
    To treat with them.

[Enter Subtle]

SUBTLE   How doth my noble Diego?
    And my dear madam Countess? Hath the Count
    Been courteous, lady? Liberal? And open?
    Donzel, methinks you look melancholic   20
    After your *coitum*, and scurvy! Truly,
    I do not like the dulness of your eye.
    It hath a heavy cast. 'Tis upsee Dutch,

---

*   The success of Surly's 'Spanish Don' caper seems to cause a major reversal for the rogues. The 'exploding' of Subtle's fraud parallels the previous scene's explosions: Dol's mad verbal eruption, the alchemical detonation, Subtle's burst of rage, and Mammon's blasted dreams and guilty flight.

3.   *clap*] Colloquially, gonorrhoea; generally, harm or disgrace.

5.   *punctually forward*] Ready to take advantage.

19.   *Liberal ... open*] Sexually forthcoming and available; but ambiguously addressed. Subtle may still be questioning Dame Pliant about her lover, or about her own behaviour, or he may be nudging the 'Spaniard' for indications of Dame Pliant's performance.

21.   *coitum*] Sexual intercourse.

23.   *upsee Dutch*] 'In the manner of the Dutch', from the Dutch *op zijn*, usually applied to drinking, not post-coital, behaviour.

And says you are a lumpish whoremaster.
Be lighter. I will make your pockets so.   25

He falls to picking of them

SURLY   Will you, Don bawd and pickpurse? How now? Reel you?
Stand up, sir. You shall find, since I am so heavy,
I'll gi'you equal weight.
SUBTLE   Help! Murder!
SURLY   No, sir.
There's no such thing intended. A good cart
And a clean whip shall ease you of that fear.   30
I am the Spanish Don that should be cozened,
Do you see? Cozened? Where's your Captain Face?
That parcel-broker and whole-bawd, all rascal?

[*Enter Face*]

FACE   How, Surly!
SURLY   O, make your approach, good Captain.
I've found from whence your copper rings and spoons   35
Come now, wherewith you cheat abroad in taverns.
'Twas here you learned t'anoint your boot with brimstone,
Then rub men's gold on't for a kind of touch,
And say 'twas naught, when you had changed the colour,
That you might ha't for nothing! And this Doctor,   40
Your sooty, smoky-bearded compeer, he
Will close you so much gold in a bolt's-head
And, on a turn, convey i' the stead another
With sublimed mercury, that shall burst i' the heat
And fly out all *in fumo*! Then weeps Mammon.   45

24. *lumpish*] Dull and heavy.

29–30. *cart ... whip*] Public punishment for whores and pimps, to be whipped through town tied to the end of a cart.

33. *parcel-broker*] Middle-man in a goods fraud; Surly suspects Mammon's household metal goods are being sold in parcels or lots elsewhere – to the Anabaptists, as we know.

35. *copper rings*] Treated to look like gold.

37–9. Apparently a black boot could be used as a rough touchstone to test gold; when rubbed on the leather, the gold would leave a mark which would indicate its quality. If Face blacked his boot with brimstone, he could change the colour of the gold rubbed on it, making the item appear worthless; Face could then pocket it for nothing or a fraction of its real value.

42–5. Surly describes the trick just played on Mammon: the alchemist deliberately sets an explosion so that he cannot produce the gold his client has paid for; but since all the experiments were faked, the alchemist still makes a profit.

Then swoons his worship.

[*Face sneaks out*]

               Or he is the Faustus
That casteth figures and can conjure, cures
Plague, piles, and pox by the *ephemerides*,
And holds intelligence with all the bawds
And midwives of three shires! While you send in –   50
Captain? What, is he gone? – damsels with child,
Wives that are barren, or the waiting-maid
With the green-sickness! Nay, sir, you must tarry
Though he be 'scaped, and answer by the ears, sir.

Act 4 scene 7*

[*Enter*] *Face, Kastril*

FACE Why, now's the time, if ever you will quarrel
     Well, as they say, and be a true-born child.
     The Doctor and your sister both are abused.
KASTRIL Where is he? Which is he? He is a slave,
     Whate'er he is, and the son of a whore. – Are you   5
     The man, sir, I would know?
SURLY   I should be loath, sir,
     To confess so much.
KASTRIL   Then you lie i' your throat.
SURLY   How?

46. *Faustus*] Magician, familiar to Jonson's audience not only from Marlowe's play, but also from the *Faustbook*, a collection of tales about Faustus's conjuring tricks.
48. *ephemerides*] Astronomical almanacs.
49–51. These hints at medical consultations for sex-related problems suggest that Subtle is practising witchcraft, probably by supplying herbal or chemical potions, to bring on abortions, cure infertility, and relieve anaemia in young virgins (green-sickness, or chlorosis, was thought to affect girls at puberty).
54. *by the ears*] That is, being sentenced to have them clipped, like Edward Kelly (see the note on 1.1, and 1.1.169).
*   In a counterblast to the previous scene, Face choreographs the expulsion of Surly by drawing on the new confidence of the dupes. Kastril believes himself a quarrelling expert; Drugger believes himself destined to marry Dame Pliant; and Ananias believes he has had divine revelation that Spaniards are unclean idolaters. But the victory over Surly heralds yet another reversal in the arrival of Lovewit.
7. *lie i'your throat*] Exactly the kind of downright challenge that Subtle has been cautioning him against. Kastril actually refuses to give reasons (12), or to listen to extenuations (14).

FACE   A very errant rogue, sir, and a cheater,
  Employed here by another conjurer
  That does not love the Doctor and would cross him   10
  If he knew how –
SURLY   [*To Kastril*]   Sir, you are abused.
KASTRIL   You lie.
  And 'tis no matter.
FACE   · Well said, sir. He is
  The impudent'st rascal –
SURLY   You are indeed. Will you hear me, sir?
FACE   By no means. Bid him be gone.
KASTRIL   Be gone, sir, quickly.
SURLY   This's strange! Lady, do you inform your brother. 15
FACE   There is not such a foist in all the town.
  The Doctor had him presently, and finds yet
  The Spanish Count will come here. [*Aside to Subtle*] Bear up, Subtle.
SUBTLE   Yes, sir, he must appear within this hour.
FACE   And yet this rogue would come in a disguise,   20
  By the temptation of another spirit,
  To trouble our art, though he could not hurt it.
KASTRIL   Ay,
  I know –

  [*Dame Pliant tries to whisper in his ear*]

    Away, you talk like a foolish mauther!

  [*Exit Dame Pliant*]

SURLY   Sir, all is truth she says.
FACE   Do not believe him, sir.

---

16. *foist*] Cheater who palms dice or cards; an unwelcome intruder; also, a foul unannounced smell or noiseless fart.
17. *had him presently*] Saw through his pretence immediately.
18. *Spanish Count*] Implying the *real* Count is on his way. Face still intends to take this role at l. 100.   *Bear up*] Play along, improvise.
21–2. An alchemist works through white magic, like Shakespeare's Prospero, using good spirits or angels. Sometimes evil spirits or demons try to spoil his contacts with the heavenly spheres, but in a Christian universe evil has no lasting power to do harm; evil may interrupt or 'trouble', but cannot 'hurt'.
23. *mauther*] Young girl (dialect).

He is the lying'st swabber! Come your ways, sir.   25
SURLY   You are valiant out of company.
KASTRIL   Yes, how then, sir?

[*Enter Drugger with a roll of damask*]

FACE   Nay, here's an honest fellow too that knows him
And all his tricks. [*Aside to Drugger*] – Make good what I say, Abel.
This cheater would ha' cozened thee o' the widow. –
[*Aloud*] He owes this honest Drugger here seven pound   30
He has had on him in two-penny'orths of tobacco.
DRUGGER   Yes, sir. And he's damned himself three terms to pay me.
FACE   And what does he owe for lotium?
DRUGGER   Thirty shillings, sir,
And for six syringes.
SURLY   Hydra of villainy!
FACE   Nay, sir, you must quarrel him out o' the house.   35
KASTRIL   I will.
Sir, if you get not out o'doors, you lie,
And you are a pimp.
SURLY   Why, this is madness, sir,
Not valour in you. I must laugh at this.
KASTRIL   It is my humour. You are a pimp, and a trig,
And an Amadis de Gaule, or a Don Quixote.   40
DRUGGER   Or a knight o' the curious coxcomb. Do you see?

25. *swabber*] Lout; a menial sailor or deck-swabber. The term also refers to certain hands
  in the game of whist, entitling the player to a share of the stakes. Although *OED* cites
  the first use of this sense in 1700, the idea of the cheating gamester fits in with Face's
  other terms of abuse (see *foist*, 16) and with Surly's activity: he did briefly hold, by
  secret means (his disguise), a winning hand (Dame Pliant's) that would entitle him to
  part of the rogues' profits (her estate as a rich widow).
26. *out of company*] In front of a supportive audience.
32. *damned . . . terms*] Sworn falsely over three law-terms, or about nine months.
33. *lotium*] Stale urine, used as a hair-dressing.
34. *syringes*] For squirting lotium or medicines, perhaps enemas.   *Hydra*] The many-
  headed snake of Lerna, killed by Hercules as his seventh labour. As one head was cut
  off, two grew in its place, an apt image for the multiplying enemies facing Surly.
39. *humour*] Whim, inclination.   *trig*] Dandy, coxcomb, commenting on the elaborate
  Spanish dress; perhaps 'trug', male whore or catamite.
40. *Amadis . . . Quixote*] Heroes of Spanish romances, deplored by Jonson; Kastril uses the
  names because they are foreign and hence deplorable.
41. *knight . . . coxcomb*] A reference to Surly's Spanish hat (see 55 below); playing on
  Beaumont and Fletcher's *The Coxcomb*, based on *The Curious Impertinent* from *Don
  Quixote* (H&S), and perhaps Beaumont's parodic *The Knight of the Burning Pestle* as
  well.

[*Enter Ananias*]

ANANIAS   Peace to the household.
KASTRIL   I'll keep peace for no man.
ANANIAS   Casting of dollars is concluded lawful.
KASTRIL   Is he the constable?
SUBTLE   Peace, Ananias.
FACE   No, sir.
KASTRIL   Then you are an otter, and a shad, a whit,   45
   A very tim.
SURLY   You'll hear me, sir?
KASTRIL   I will not.
ANANIAS   What is the motive?
SUBTLE   Zeal in the young gentleman
   Against his Spanish slops –
ANANIAS   They are profane,
   Lewd, superstitious, and idolatrous breeches.
SURLY   New rascals!   50
KASTRIL   Will you be gone, sir?
ANANIAS   Avoid, Satan!
   Thou art not of the light. That ruff of pride
   About thy neck betrays thee, and is the same
   With that which the unclean birds, in seventy-seven,

43. *keep ... man*] Hearing the conventional puritan greeting only as a comment on his own waspishness.

45–6. Kastril's abuse suggests sexual perversity or inversion.

45. *otter*] An unclassifiable animal, neither fish nor fowl; Surly talks like an Englishman, but looks like a Spaniard. That is, he sounds manly, but looks effeminate. *shad*] A herring; usually 'shotten herring' was the insult applied to one who is worthless or destitute of resources, having made his play and lost. Jonson may be punning on 'shade' or 'shadow', a euphemism for an effeminate homosexual. *whit*] Good-for-nothing. Literally something small and insignificant, it was euphemistically applied to sexual organs, dainty if female (see 2.3.259), puny if male. Captain Whit in *BF* is a bawd.

46. *tim*] Untraced term of abuse, perhaps from 'timid', another slam at Surly's foppish dress and unmanly refusal to fight.

47. *Zeal*] Puritanical fervour.

48. *slops*] Baggy breeches.

53. *unclean ... seventy-seven*] Spain invaded the Netherlands in 1567, and the 'Spanish Fury' devastated Antwerp in 1576; Jonson either muddled his dates, or meant the renewed repression of Dutch Protestants that followed under Don John of Austria, 1577–78. The reference to birds may be biblical, as at 5.3.47, referring to 'the habitation of devils, and the hold of every foul spirit, and a cage of every unclean and hateful bird' (Revelation 18:2); or it may be otherwise historical, referring wittily to the

Were seen to prank it with on divers coasts.
Thou look'st like Antichrist in that lewd hat.   55
SURLY   I must give way.
KASTRIL   Be gone, sir.
SURLY   But I'll take
A course with you –
ANANIAS   Depart, proud Spanish fiend.
SURLY   Captain and Doctor –
ANANIAS   Child of perdition.
KASTRIL   Hence, sir.

    [Exit Surly]

Did I not quarrel bravely?
FACE   Yes, indeed, sir.
KASTRIL   Nay, and I give my mind to't, I shall do't.   60
FACE   O, you must follow, sir, and threaten him tame.
He'll turn again else.
KASTRIL   I'll re-turn him then.

    [Exit Kastril]

FACE   Drugger, this rogue prevented us for thee.
We'd determined that thou shouldst ha' come
In a Spanish suit and ha' carried her so, and he,   65
A brokerly slave, goes, puts it on himself.
Hast brought the damask?
DRUGGER   *[Giving it]*   Yes, sir.
FACE   Thou must borrow
A Spanish suit. Hast thou no credit with the players?
DRUGGER   Yes, sir. Did you never see me play the fool?
FACE   I know not, Nab. Thou shalt, if I can help it.   70

pirates, Hawkins and Drake, who helped defeat Spain by plundering and sinking
Spanish ships around the world (Drake set off for the Pacific in 1577, skimming
treasure from Spanish-American coasts, and later patrolled the Spanish coast in 1587,
delaying the launch of the Armada); or the reference may be simply ornithological: in
Lincolnshire, strange birds with ruffled necks, according to a 1586 pamphlet, were
interpreted as fearful signs of Spanish power.

54. *prank it with*] Play tricks; show off their fancy plumage.
63. *prevented us*] Thwarted our plans.
66. *brokerly*] Fraudulent middle-man (see 4.6.33).
69. *play the fool*] Theatrical in-joke for Robert Armin, leading clown with the King's Men,
who played Drugger.

Hieronimo's old cloak, ruff, and hat will serve.
I'll tell thee more when thou bringst 'em.

[*Exit Drugger*]
Subtle hath whispered with [*Ananias*] *this while*

ANANIAS   Sir, I know
     The Spaniard hates the brethren, and hath spies
     Upon their actions, and that this was one
     I make no scruple. But the holy Synod   75
     Have been in prayer and meditation for it.
     And 'tis revealed no less to them than me
     That casting of money is most lawful.
SUBTLE   True.
     But here I cannot do it. If the house
     Should chance to be suspected, all would out,   80
     And we be locked up in the Tower for ever
     To make gold there for the state, never come out,
     And then are you defeated.
ANANIAS   I will tell
     This to the elders and the weaker brethren,
     That the whole company of the separation   85
     May join in humble prayer again.
SUBTLE   And fasting.
ANANIAS   Yea, for some fitter place. The peace of mind
     Rest with these walls.
SUBTLE   Thanks, courteous Ananias.

     [*Exit Ananias*]

FACE   What did he come for?
SUBTLE   About casting dollars
     Presently, out of hand. And so I told him   90
     A Spanish minister came here to spy
     Against the faithful –
FACE   I conceive. Come, Subtle,

71. *Hieronimo*] In Kyd's *The Spanish Tragedy*, a play which Jonson frequently derided,
     perhaps because as a young actor he performed the part unsuccessfully with a touring
     company. Henslowe paid him in 1602 to expand the play for a revival, but whether the
     surviving additions are Jonson's is moot.
75. *holy Synod*] Ecclesiastical assembly.
81–2. *locked ... state*] For challenging the economy and the balance of power with easy
     money; a state must control its funds (see 4.1.90n. and 153n.). Fear of sedition
     presumably lay behind Edward II's imprisonment of Raymond Lull, and Elizabeth's
     imprisonment of Cornelius Lannoy.
85. *separation*] Exiled puritans (see 3.1.2).

Thou art so down upon the least disaster!
How wouldst thou ha' done, if I had not helped thee out?

SUBTLE I thank thee, Face, for the angry boy, i' faith.   95

FACE Who would ha' looked it should ha' been that rascal?
Surly? He had dyed his beard and all. Well, sir,
Here's damask come to make you a suit.

SUBTLE   Where's Drugger?

FACE He is gone to borrow me a Spanish habit.
I'll be the Count now.   100

SUBTLE   But where's the widow?

FACE Within, with my lord's sister. Madam Dol
Is entertaining her.

SUBTLE   By your favour, Face,
Now she is honest, I will stand again.

FACE You will not offer it?

SUBTLE   Why?

FACE   Stand to your word,
Or – Here comes Dol. She knows –   105

SUBTLE   You're tyrannous still.

FACE Strict for my right.

   [*Enter Dol*]

                        How now, Dol? Hast told her
The Spanish Count will come?

DOL   Yes, but another is come
You little looked for!

FACE   Who's that?

DOL   Your master.
The master of the house.

SUBTLE   How, Dol!

FACE   She lies!
This is some trick. Come, leave your quiblins, Dorothy.   110

DOL Look out and see.

   [*Face looks out*]

SUBTLE   Art thou in earnest?

DOL   'Slight,
Forty o' the neighbours are about him, talking.

FACE 'Tis he, by this good day.

DOL   'Twill prove ill day

93. *down upon*] Depressed or defeated by.
103. *honest*] Chaste. *stand again*] Return to their former agreement, broken at 4.3.87, of
the better man winning the widow.
110. *quiblins*] Teasing.

For some on us.

FACE   We are undone and taken.

DOL   Lost, I'm afraid.   115

SUBTLE   You said he would not come
While there died one a week within the liberties.

FACE   No. 'Twas within the walls.

SUBTLE   Was't so? Cry you mercy.
I thought the liberties. What shall we do now, Face?

FACE   Be silent. Not a word. If he call or knock.
I'll into mine old shape again, and meet him,   120
Of Jeremy the butler. I' the meantime,
Do you two pack up all the goods and purchase
That we can carry i' the two trunks. I'll keep him
Off for today, if I cannot longer, and then
At night I'll ship you both away to Ratcliffe,   125
Where we'll meet tomorrow, and there we'll share.
Let Mammon's brass and pewter keep the cellar.
We'll have another time for that. But, Dol,
'Pray thee, go heat a little water quickly.
Subtle must shave me. All my Captain's beard   130
Must off, to make me appear smooth Jeremy.
You'll do't?

SUBTLE   Yes, I'll shave you as well as I can.

FACE   And not cut my throat, but trim me?

SUBTLE   You shall see, sir.

[*Exeunt*]

114. *taken*] Caught in the act.

116. *liberties*] Whitefriars and Blackfriars, London areas formerly controlled by the church, subsequently placed under the jurisdiction of the Crown.

117. *walls*] London wall, marking off the square mile of City of London. *Cry you mercy*] I beg your pardon.

120. *old shape*] Former appearance.

122. *purchase*] Winnings.

125. *Ratcliffe*] A hamlet about a mile E of London on the N bank of the Thames, dominated by prostitutes, victuallers, and taverns catering for sailors (see *SW* 4.2.125).

127. *keep*] Remain in.

131. *smooth*] Clean-shaven; also, glib and guilelessly effeminate.

132–3. *shave . . . trim*] Playing on 'trick' or 'defraud'.

ACT 5

Act 5 scene 1*

[Enter] Lovewit, Neighbours

LOVEWIT	Has there been such resort, say you?
NEIGHBOUR 1	Daily, sir.
NEIGHBOUR 2	And nightly, too.
NEIGHBOUR 3	Ay, some as brave as lords.
NEIGHBOUR 4	Ladies and gentlewomen.
NEIGHBOUR 5	Citizens' wives.
NEIGHBOUR 1	And knights.
NEIGHBOUR 6	In coaches.
NEIGHBOUR 2	Yes, and oyster-women.
NEIGHBOUR 1	Beside other gallants.
NEIGHBOUR 3	Sailors' wives.
NEIGHBOUR 4	Tobacco-men.
NEIGHBOUR 5	Another Pimlico!
LOVEWIT	What should my knave advance

LOVEWIT   What should my knave advance
  To draw this company? He hung out no banners
  Of a strange calf with five legs to be seen?
  Or a huge lobster with six claws?
NEIGHBOUR 6   No, sir.
NEIGHBOUR 3   We had gone in then, sir.   10
LOVEWIT   He has no gift
  Of teaching i' the nose that ere I knew of!
  You saw no bills set up that promised cure

---

*   Jonson accompanies the arrival of Lovewit with gossiping puritan neighbours, naive, conventional, and curious (see Dol's references to these neighbours at 1.1.126–9 and 163–6). Their presence on stage in 5.1, 2, and 3 (and their possible return with the officers in 5.5) adds to the speed and confusion of the final scenes, and marks out the gradations of difference between rogues and dupes, insiders and outsiders, winners and losers. But those who have been acting out their fantasies in Lovewit's house do have something in common with the neighbours whose perception of reality blurs when challenged.

2. *brave*] Finely dressed.
6. *Pimlico*] A public house famed for its cakes and ale in Hoxton (Hogsden), near the sites of the Theatre, Curtain, and Fortune playhouses north of the City, an apt comparison for a house full of play-actors and their audiences.
7. *banners*] Advertisements.
8. *calf ... legs*] A freak shown at Uxbridge Fair, mentioned in *BF* 3.6.6–7 and 5.4.74–6.
11. *teaching ... nose*] The nasal intonation of puritan preaching.
12. *bills*] Advertising posters.

Of agues or the tooth-ache?
NEIGHBOUR 2   No such thing, sir.
LOVEWIT   Nor heard a drum struck for baboons or puppets?
NEIGHBOUR 5   Neither, sir.   15
LOVEWIT   What device should he bring forth now!
I love a teeming wit as I love my nourishment.
Pray God he ha' not kept such open house
That he hath sold my hangings and my bedding.
I left him nothing else. If he have eat 'em,
A plague o' the moth, say I. Sure he has got   20
Some bawdy pictures, to call all this ging:
The friar and the nun; or the new motion
Of the knight's courser covering the parson's mare;
The boy of six year old with the great thing;
Or't may be he has the fleas that run at tilt   25
Upon a table, or some dog to dance?
When saw you him?
NEIGHBOUR 1   Who, sir? Jeremy?
NEIGHBOUR 2   Jeremy butler?
We saw him not this month.
LOVEWIT   How!
NEIGHBOUR 4   Not these five weeks, sir.
NEIGHBOUR 1   These six weeks, at the least.
LOVEWIT   Y'amaze me, neighbours!
NEIGHBOUR 5   Sure, if your worship know not where he is,   30
He's slipped away.
NEIGHBOUR 6   'Pray God he be not made away!

13. *agues ... tooth-ache*] Conditions cured by mountebanks and itinerant barbers at fairs and markets (see *Volp* 2.2).
14. *drum*] Another form of advertisement, drumming through the streets for attention and then calling out the attraction to be seen.   *baboons*] Shown at Southwark more or less permanently, and elsewhere on tour.
21. *ging*] Contemptuously, gang or crew.
22–4. Pornographic displays catering to lower-class tastes, broadly attacking Roman Catholic celibates (such as a picture of 'the friar whipping the nun's arse' on display near the Windmill Tavern, according to Heywood, *If You Know Not Me*, 1606), the gentry, and Church of England parish authority, as well as more general freaks.
22. *motion*] Puppet-show; sexual movement.
23. *covering*] Used of copulation between horses.
24. *great thing*] Enlarged penis, mentioned in Beaumont's *The Knight of the Burning Pestle* 3.278–9 (Revels).
25. *fleas*] The flea circus is also mentioned in *DisA* 5.2.10–13.   *run at tilt*] Joust.
26. *dog to dance*] 'Dogs that dance the morris', mentioned in *BF* 5.4.76.
31. *made away*] Murdered.

LOVEWIT   Ha? It's no time to question then.

He knocks

NEIGHBOUR 6   About
   Some three weeks since, I heard a doleful cry
   As I sat up a-mending my wife's stockings.
LOVEWIT   This's strange! That none will answer! Didst thou hear   35
   A cry, say'st thou?
NEIGHBOUR 6   Yes, sir, like unto a man
   That had been strangled an hour, and could not speak.
NEIGHBOUR 2   I heard it too, just this day three weeks, at two o'clock
   Next morning.
LOVEWIT   These be miracles, or you make 'em so!
   A man an hour strangled and could not speak,   40
   And both you heard him cry?
NEIGHBOUR 3   Yes, downward, sir.
LOVEWIT   Thou art a wise fellow. Give me thy hand, I pray thee.
   What trade art thou on?
NEIGHBOUR 3   A smith, and't please your worship.
LOVEWIT   A smith? Then lend me thy help to get this door open.
NEIGHBOUR 3   That I will presently, sir, but fetch my tools –   45

   [*Exit Neighbour 3*]

NEIGHBOUR 1   Sir, best to knock again afore you break it.

Act 5 scene 2*

LOVEWIT   I will.

|*He knocks again; Face, as the butler, opens the door*|

FACE   What mean you, sir?
NEIGHBOURS 1, 2, 4   O, here's Jeremy!
FACE   Good sir, come from the door.
LOVEWIT   Why! What's the matter?

   [*Face urges him away from the door*]

FACE   Yet farther. You are too near yet.
LOVEWIT   I'the name of wonder!
   What means the fellow?

39. *Next*] In the.
*   Face's trick of claiming the house is contaminated by plague echoes Plautus's
    Mostellaria (*The Ghost-Story*), in which the tricky slave, claiming the house is haunted,
    prevents the unexpectedly returned master from entering and discovering the roguery
    that has gone on in his absence.

FACE   [*Still urging*]   The house, sir, has been visited.
LOVEWIT   What? With the plague? Stand thou then farther!   5

[*Lovewit leaps away from him*]

FACE   No, sir,
    I had it not.
LOVEWIT   Who had it then? I left
    None else but thee i' the house!
FACE   Yes, sir. My fellow,
    The cat that kept the buttery, had it on her
    A week before I spied it. But I got her
    Conveyed away i' the night. And so I shut   10
    The house up for a month –
LOVEWIT   How!
FACE   Purposing then, sir,
    T'have burnt rose-vinegar, treacle, and tar,
    And ha' made it sweet, that you should ne'er ha' known it,
    Because I knew the news would but afflict you, sir.
LOVEWIT   Breathe less and farther off. Why, this is stranger!   15
    The neighbours tell me all here that the doors
    Have still been open –
FACE   How, sir!
LOVEWIT   Gallants, men, and women,
    And of all sorts, tag-rag, been seen to flock here
    In threaves these ten weeks, as to a second Hogsden
    In days of Pimlico and Eye-bright!   20
FACE   Sir,
    Their wisdoms will not say so!
LOVEWIT   Today they speak
    Of coaches and gallants. One in a French hood
    Went in, they tell me. And another was seen
    In a velvet gown at the window! Divers more
    Pass in and out!   25
FACE   They did pass through the doors then,
    Or walls, I assure their eyesights and their spectacles,
    For here, sir, are the keys, and here have been
    In this my pocket now above twenty days!

4. *visited*] By plague.
12. To fumigate.
19. *threaves*] Droves.   *Hogsden*] Hoxton, a favourite resort for holiday-makers.
20. *Pimlico*] Popular tavern (see 5.1.6n.).   *Eye-bright*] Another tavern in Hoxton, once
    famed for its beer, but forsaken by the trendy in favour of Pimlico.
22. *One ... hood*] Dame Pliant (cf. 2.6.33).
23–4. *another ... velvet gown*] Dol (cf. 5.4.134).

And for before, I kept the fort alone there.
But that 'tis yet not deep i'the afternoon,   30
I should believe my neighbours had seen double
Through the black-pot and made these apparitions!
For, on my faith to your worship, for these three weeks
And upwards, the door has not been opened.

LOVEWIT   Strange!

NEIGHBOUR 1   Good faith, I think I saw a coach!   35

NEIGHBOUR 2   And I too,
I'd ha' been sworn!

LOVEWIT   Do you but think it now?
And but one coach?

NEIGHBOUR 4   We cannot tell, sir. Jeremy
Is a very honest fellow.

FACE   Did you see me at all?

NEIGHBOUR 1   No. That we are sure on.

NEIGHBOUR 2   I'll be sworn o'that.

LOVEWIT   Fine rogues to have your testimonies built on!   40

[Enter Neighbour 3 with tools]

NEIGHBOUR 3   Is Jeremy come?

NEIGHBOUR 1   O, yes, you may leave your tools.
We were deceived, he says.

NEIGHBOUR 2   He's had the keys,
And the door has been shut these three weeks.

NEIGHBOUR 3   Like enough.

LOVEWIT   Peace and get hence, you changelings.

[Enter Surly and Mammon]

FACE   [*Aside*]   Surly come!
And Mammon made acquainted? They'll tell all. –   45
How shall I beat them off? What shall I do? –
Nothing's more wretched than a guilty conscience.

---

32.   *black-pot*] Beer tankard.

44.   *changelings*] People of inconstant opinions; also, mischievous imps exchanged for
      human children at birth; mooncalves or idiots (see 5.3.30).

Act 5 scene 3*

SURLY [*Mocking*] No, sir, he was a great physician. This,
    It was no bawdy-house, but a mere chancel.
    You knew the lord and his sister.
MAMMON   Nay, good Surly –
SURLY The happy word, 'Be rich' –
MAMMON   Play not the tyrant –
SURLY – Should be today pronounced to all your friends.   5
    And where be your andirons now? And your brass pots?
    That should ha' been golden flagons and great wedges?
MAMMON Let me but breathe.

   Mammon and Surly knock

                      What! They ha' shut their doors,
    Methinks!
SURLY   Ay, now 'tis holiday with them.
MAMMON [*Knocking and shouting*]   Rogues,
    Cozeners, impostors, bawds!   10
FACE   What mean you, sir?
MAMMON To enter if we can.
FACE   Another man's house?
    Here is the owner, sir. Turn you to him,
    And speak your business.
MAMMON   Are you, sir, the owner?
LOVEWIT Yes, sir.
MAMMON   And are those knaves within your cheaters?
LOVEWIT What knaves? What cheaters?   15
MAMMON   Subtle and his Lungs.
FACE The gentleman is distracted, sir! No lungs
    Nor lights ha'been seen here these three weeks, sir,
    Within these doors, upon my word!
SURLY   Your word,
    Groom arrogant?
FACE   Yes, sir, I am the housekeeper,

---

*   Jonson's love for the ebb and flow of crowd scenes sets up the play's finale. Characters move on and off the stage with farcical rapidity, watched by the bemused neighbours: first Surly and Mammon, then Kastril, then Ananias and Tribulation, all enraged, pounding at Lovewit's door, threatening to 'come with warrant' (25), 'fetch the marshal' (35), and 'raise the street' (52); from the other side of the door we hear Dapper's cry and Subtle's rebuke, finally echoed on stage by Face's. 'I am catched', says Face – or is he? Alone with Lovewit, his confession is not exactly frank and full.

2. *mere chancel*] Absolute church (specifically, where the officiating clergy stand).

7. *wedges*] Ingots of gold and silver.

17–18. *lungs . . . lights*] Livestock lungs, sold by butchers, are called lights.

And know the keys ha'not been out o'my hands.   20

SURLY   This's a new Face?

FACE   You do mistake the house, sir!

What sign was't at?

SURLY   You rascal! This is one

O' the confederacy. Come, let's get officers

And force the door.

LOVEWIT   'Pray you stay, gentlemen.

SURLY   No, sir, we'll come with warrant.   25

MAMMON   Ay, and then

We shall ha' your doors open.

   [Exeunt Mammon and Surly]

LOVEWIT   What means this?

FACE   I cannot tell, sir!

NEIGHBOUR 1   These are two o'the gallants

That we do think we saw.

FACE   Two o' the fools?

You talk as idly as they. Good faith, sir,

I think the moon has crazed 'em all!   30

   [Enter Kastril]

                [Aside] O me,

The angry boy come too? He'll make a noise,

And ne'er away till he have betrayed us all.

   Kastril knocks

KASTRIL   What, rogues, bawds, slaves! You'll open the door anon!

Punk, cocatrice, my suster! By this light,

I'll fetch the marshal to you. You are a whore   35

To keep your castle –

FACE   Who would you speak with, sir?

KASTRIL   The bawdy Doctor and the cozening Captain

And Puss my suster.

LOVEWIT   This is something, sure!

---

21. *a new Face*] 'Another impudent rogue like Face'. Surly has recognised a rogue, not Face personally.

22. *sign*] Implying Surly was looking for a brothel, which, like other commercial establishments, would have hung out a sign to attract customers.

30. *moon has crazed*] The full moon was thought to make men lunatics or mooncalves (idiots) – a good cue for the entrance of the 'furious' fool, Kastril.

34. *cockatrice*] Basilisk, a mythical serpent that could kill with its glance; slang for whore.

38. *Puss*] Contemptuous diminutive for young girl, implying slyness and probably indecency as well.

FACE   Upon my trust, the doors were never open, sir.
KASTRIL   I have heard all their tricks told me twice over   40
    By the fat knight and the lean gentleman.

    [*Enter Ananias and Tribulation*]

LOVEWIT   Here comes another.
FACE   Ananias too?
    And his pastor?

    They beat too at the door

TRIBULATION   The doors are shut against us.
ANANIAS   Come forth, you seed of sulphur, sons of fire,
    Your stench it is broke forth. Abomination   45
        Is in the house.
KASTRIL   Ay, my suster's there.
ANANIAS   The place,
    It is become a cage of unclean birds.
KASTRIL   Yes, I will fetch the scavenger and the constable.
TRIBULATION   You shall do well.
ANANIAS   We'll join to weed them out.
KASTRIL   You will not come then? Punk device, my suster!   50
ANANIAS   Call her not sister. She is a harlot, verily.
KASTRIL   I'll raise the street.
LOVEWIT   Good gentlemen, a word.
ANANIAS   Satan, avoid, and hinder not our zeal.
LOVEWIT   The world's turned Bedlam.
FACE   These are all broke loose
    Out of St Kather'ne's, where they use to keep   55
    The better sort of mad-folks.
NEIGHBOUR 1   All these persons

---

41. *fat knight*] Mammon. *lean gentleman*] Surly, who must have padded his Spanish costume to appear 'fat' at 4.3.28.

44. *sulphur . . . fire*] Associated with hell and, aptly, with alchemy.

47. *unclean birds*] Referring to the fallen, or those that feed on them like vultures, in Revelation 18:2; see 4.7.53n.

48. *scavenger*] Parish officer who employed workers to clean the streets.

50. *punk device*] Arrant whore, 'device' intensifying meaning on analogy with 'point device' (= perfectly dressed).

51. *not sister*] Puritans called each other brother and sister to affirm integrity within the larger 'family' or religious community.

52. *raise the street*] Apparently for a 'hue and cry' after the wrongdoers.

55. *St Kather'ne's*] The old hospital, founded in 1148, razed to make way for St Katherine's Docks. The area, largely populated by Dutch and Flemish immigrants, was considered a resort of 'drunkards' (l. 58 below).

We saw go in and out here.

NEIGHBOUR 2   Yes, indeed, sir.

NEIGHBOUR 3   These were the parties.

FACE   Peace, you drunkards. Sir,
 I wonder at it! Please you to give me leave
 To touch the door, I'll try an' the lock be changed.   60

LOVEWIT   It mazes me!

FACE   Good faith, sir, I believe
 There's no such thing. 'Tis all *deceptio visus*.
 [*Aside*] Would I could get him away.

 Dapper cries out within

DAPPER   Master Captain! Master Doctor!

LOVEWIT   Who's that?

FACE   [*Aside*]   Our clerk within, that I forgot! – [*To Lovewit*] I
 know not, sir.

DAPPER   For God's sake, when will her Grace be at leisure?   65

FACE   Ha!
 Illusions, some spirit o' the air. [*Aside*] His gag is melted,
 And now he sets out the throat.

DAPPER   I am almost stifled –

FACE   [*Aside*] Would you were altogether.

LOVEWIT   'Tis i'the house.
 Ha! List.

FACE   Believe it, sir, i'the air!

LOVEWIT   Peace, you –

DAPPER   Mine aunt's Grace does not use me well.   70

SUBTLE   [*Within*]   You fool,
 Peace! You'll mar all.

FACE   [*Exasperated*]   Or you will else, you rogue.

LOVEWIT   O, is it so? Then you converse with spirits!
 Come, sir. No more o' your tricks, good Jeremy.
 The truth, the shortest way.

FACE   Dismiss this rabble, sir.
 What shall I do? I am catched.   75

LOVEWIT   Good neighbours,

---

62. *deceptio visus*] Hallucination.

67. *sets ... throat*] Raises his voice, shouts.

74. *the shortest way*] Speedily and directly.

75. *What ... catched*] Face has no need to say this aside, as indicated by most modern
 editors. His complete frankness earns him salvation at Lovewit's hands.

    I thank you all. You may depart.

[Exit Neighbours]

                                    Come, sir,
    You know that I am an indulgent master,
    And therefore conceal nothing. What's your med'cine
    To draw so many several sorts of wild-fowl?
FACE   Sir, you were wont to affect mirth and wit –   80
    But here's no place to talk on't i'the street –
    Give me but leave to make the best of my fortune,
    And only pardon me th'abuse of your house.
    It's all I beg. I'll help you to a widow
    In recompense, that you shall gi' me thanks for,   85
    Will make you seven years younger, and a rich one.
    'Tis but your putting on a Spanish cloak.
    I have her within. You need not fear the house.
    It was not visited.
LOVEWIT   But by me, who came
    Sooner than you expected.   90
FACE   It is true, sir.
    'Pray you forgive me.
LOVEWIT   Well, let's see your widow.

    [Exeunt]

Act 5 scene 4*

[Enter] Subtle, Dapper

SUBTLE   How! Ha' you eaten your gag?
DAPPER   Yes, faith, it crumbled
    Away i'my mouth.
SUBTLE   You ha' spoiled all then.
DAPPER   No,
    I hope my aunt of Fairy will forgive me.
SUBTLE   Your aunt's a gracious lady, but in troth
    You were to blame.   5
DAPPER   The fume did overcome me,

---

80. *wont to affect*] Used to appreciate.
89. *visited*] By plague.
*   The Fairy Queen interlude with Dapper allows Face time off-stage to co-ordinate his latest plot matching Lovewit with Dame Pliant; he retrieves the Spanish Don costume (68–9), secures the chaplain (99–100), and expels his former partners while officers knock at the door.

And I did do't to stay my stomach. Pray you
So satisfy her Grace.

[*Enter Face in his uniform*]

                              Here comes the Captain.
FACE   How now! Is his mouth down?
SUBTLE   Ay! He has spoken!
FACE   [*Aside to Subtle*] A pox, I heard him, and you too. – [*Aloud*]
He's undone then.

[*Face and Subtle talk aside*]

I have been fain to say the house is haunted   10
With spirits to keep churl back.
SUBTLE   And hast thou done it?
FACE   Sure, for this night.
SUBTLE   Why, then triumph, and sing
Of Face so famous, the precious king
Of present wits.
FACE   Did you not hear the coil
About the door?   15
SUBTLE   Yes, and I dwindled with it.
FACE   Show him his aunt, and let him be dispatched.
I'll send her to you.

[*Exit Face*]

SUBTLE   [*To Dapper*]   Well, sir, your aunt her Grace
Will give you audience presently, on my suit
And the Captain's word, that you did not eat your gag
In any contempt of her Highness.   20
DAPPER   Not I, in troth, sir.

[*Enter*] *Dol like the Queen of Fairy*

SUBTLE   Here she is come. Down o' your knees and wriggle.
She has a stately presence.

[*Dapper grovels and crawls to Dol's feet*]

                              Good. Yet nearer,
And bid 'God save you'.
DAPPER   Madam.

---

 8. *down*] Open.
11. *churl*] The 'rustic' Lovewit, who has been living in the country at his hop-yards
     (1.1.184). Face assumes a deprecating tone to match Subtle's.
14. *coil*] Turmoil, commotion.
18. *suit*] Request.

SUBTLE   [*Prompting him*]   And your aunt.
DAPPER   And my most gracious aunt, God save your Grace.
DOL   Nephew, we thought to have been angry with you,   25
    But that sweet face of yours hath turned the tide
    And made it flow with joy, that ebbed of love.
    Arise, and touch our velvet gown.
SUBTLE   The skirts,
    And kiss 'em. So!

    [*Dapper rises to his knees and kisses Dol's hems*]

DOL   Let me now stroke that head.

    [*Dol strokes his head and chants*]

    Much, nephew, shalt thou win; much shalt thou spend;   30
    Much shalt thou give away; much shalt thou lend.
SUBTLE   [*Aside*] Ay, much indeed. – Why do you not thank her Grace?
DAPPER   I cannot speak for joy.
SUBTLE   See, the kind wretch!
    Your Grace's kinsman right.
DOL   Give me the bird.

    [*Subtle hands her a tiny bag, which Dol gives Dapper*]

    Here is your fly in a purse about your neck, cousin.   35
    Wear it and feed it about this day sennight
    On your right wrist –
SUBTLE   Open a vein with a pin,
    And let it suck but once a week. Till then,
    You must not look on't.
DOL   No. And, kinsman,
    Bear yourself worthy of the blood you come on.   40
SUBTLE   Her grace would ha' you eat no more Woolsack pies,
    Nor Dagger furmety.
DOL   Nor break his fast
    In Heaven and Hell.
SUBTLE   She's with you everywhere!

33. *kind*] Full of natural feeling.
34–5. *bird . . . fly*] Familiar spirit.
36. *sennight*] Week.
40. *come on*] Spring from.
41–2. *Woolsack . . . Dagger*] Neighbouring taverns in Cheapside, famous for their pies,
    linked similarly in *DisA* 1.1.66.
42. *furmety*] Wheat cakes boiled in milk, heavily spiced.
43. *Heaven and Hell*] Taverns near Westminster Hall, popular with law clerks.

Nor play with costermongers at mumchance, tray-trip,
God-make-you-rich (whenas your aunt has done it), but keep   45
The gallant'st company and the best games –
DAPPER   Yes, sir.
SUBTLE   Gleek and primero – and what you get, be true to us.
DAPPER   By this hand, I will.
SUBTLE   You may bring's a thousand pound
Before tomorrow night (if but three thousand
Be stirring), an' you will.   50
DAPPER   I swear I will then.
SUBTLE   Your fly will learn you all games.
FACE   [*Within*]   Ha' you done there?
SUBTLE   Your Grace will command him no more duties?
DOL   No.
But come and see me often. I may chance
To leave him three or four hundred chests of treasure
And some twelve thousand acres of Fairyland,   55
If he game well and comely with good gamesters.
SUBTLE   There's a kind aunt! Kiss her departing part.

[*Dol turns, and Dapper kisses her train*]

But you must sell you forty mark a year now.
DAPPER   Ay, sir, I mean.
SUBTLE   Or gi't away. Pox on't.
DAPPER   I'll gi't mine aunt. I'll go and fetch the writings.   60
SUBTLE   'Tis well. Away.

[*Exit Dapper by one door, and enter Face by another*]

FACE   Where's Subtle?
SUBTLE   Here. What news?
FACE   Drugger is at the door. Go take his suit,
And bid him fetch a parson presently.
Say he shall marry the widow. Thou shalt spend
A hundred pound by the service!   65

44. *mumchance, tray-trip*] Dice-games.
45. *God-make-you-rich*] A variety of backgammon.
47. *Gleek, primero*] 'High-class' card-games (see 2.3.284–5).   *be true to us*] Remember
      to give us a share of your winnings.
50. *Be stirring*] Be available as stakes.
52. *learn*] Teach.
56. *comely*] Handsomely, decorously.
57. *departing part*] Equivocating on 'arse'.
64. *spend*] Earn, and therefore have to spend.

[*Exit Subtle*]

Now, Queen Dol,
Ha' you packed up all?

DOL   Yes.

FACE   And how do you like
The lady Pliant?

DOL   A good dull innocent.

[*Enter Subtle with Spanish costume*]

SUBTLE   Here's your Hieronimo's cloak and hat.

FACE   Give me 'em.

SUBTLE   And the ruff too?

FACE   Yes. I'll come to you presently.

[*Exit Face with costume*]

SUBTLE   Now he is gone about his project, Dol,   70
I told you of, for the widow.

DOL   'Tis direct
Against our articles.

SUBTLE   Well, we'll fit him, wench.
Hast thou gulled her of her jewels or her bracelets?

DOL   No, but I will do't.

SUBTLE   Soon at night, my Dolly,
When we are shipped and all our goods aboard   75
Eastward for Ratcliffe, we will turn our course
To Brainford, westward, if thou sayst the word,
And take our leaves of this o'erweaning rascal,
This peremptory Face.

DOL   Content, I'm weary of him.

SUBTLE   Thou'st cause, when the slave will run a-wiving, Dol,   80
Against the instrument that was drawn between us.

DOL   I'll pluck his bird as bare as I can.

SUBTLE   Yes, tell her
She must by any means address some present
To th' cunning-man, make him amends for wronging
His art with her suspicion, send a ring,   85
Or chain of pearl. She will be tortured else
Extremely in her sleep, say, and ha' strange things

67. *innocent*] Naive girl, without wiles; ignoramus.

72. *our articles*] The agreement by which all three should profit, described at
1.1.132–6.   *fit*] Fix or punish.

77. *Brainford*] Now Brentford, a village at the junction of the Brent and Thames rivers,
west of London; often mentioned as a place of assignation.

81. *instrument*] Formal legal document recording an agreement.

Come to her. Wilt thou?

DOL   Yes.

SUBTLE   My fine flittermouse,
My bird o' the night, we'll tickle it at the Pigeons
When we have all, and may unlock the trunks   90
And say, 'This's mine, and thine, and thine, and mine' –

They kiss. [Enter Face]

FACE   What now, a-billing?

SUBTLE   Yes, a little exalted
In the good passage of our stock-affairs.

FACE   Drugger has brought his parson. Take him in, Subtle,
And send Nab back again to wash his face.   95

SUBTLE   I will, and shave himself?

FACE   If you can get him.

[Exit Subtle]

DOL   You are hot upon it, Face, whate'er it is!

FACE   A trick that Dol shall spend ten pound a month by.

[Enter Subtle]

Is he gone?

SUBTLE   The chaplain waits you i' the hall, sir.

FACE   I'll go bestow him.   100

[Exit Face]

DOL   He'll now marry her instantly.

SUBTLE   He cannot yet. He is not ready. Dear Dol,
Cozen her of all thou canst. To deceive him
Is no deceit but justice, that would break
Such an inextricable tie as ours was.

DOL   Let me alone to fit him.   105

[Enter Face]

FACE   Come, my venturers,

88. *flittermouse*] Bat.
89. *tickle it*] Bring our business to a satisfactory end; but with an innuendo of 'gratify ourselves sexually'. *the Pigeons*] The Three Pigeons, in Brentford market-place, closed January 1916. The actor John Lowin, who played Mammon, was the innkeeper under the Commonwealth until his death in 1653 (H&S).
92. *exalted*] Raised up, an alchemical term referring to the refinement of materials, but Subtle uses it to mean 'high-spirited' and 'sexually aroused'.
93. *passage*] Progress. *stock-affairs*] Joint capital in a business venture.
100. *bestow him*] Settle him in an appropriate place.

You ha' packed up all? Where be the trunks? Bring forth.

SUBTLE   Here.

FACE   Let's see'em. Where's the money?

SUBTLE   Here,
In this.

FACE   [*Counting*] Mammon's ten pound, eight-score before.
The brethren's money, this. Drugger's, and Dapper's.
What paper's that?   110

DOL   The jewel of the waiting-maid's,
That stole it from her lady to know certain –

FACE   If she should have precedence of her mistress?

DOL   Yes.

FACE   What box is that?

SUBTLE   The fishwives' rings, I think,
And th'alewives' single money. Is't not, Dol?

DOL   Yes, and the whistle that the sailor's wife   115
Brought you, to know and her husband were with Ward.

FACE   We'll wet it tomorrow, and our silver beakers
And tavern cups. Where be the French petticoats
And girdles and hangers?

SUBTLE   Here, i' the trunk,
And the bolts of lawn.   120

FACE   Is Drugger's damask there?
And the tobacco?

SUBTLE   Yes.

FACE   Give me the keys.

DOL   Why you the keys?

SUBTLE   No matter, Dol, because
We shall not open'em before he comes.

FACE   'Tis true, you shall not open them indeed,
Nor have 'em forth. Do you see? Not forth, Dol.   125

DOL   No!

FACE   No, my smock-rampant. The right is, my master
Knows all, has pardoned me, and he will keep 'em.
Doctor, 'tis true – You look! – for all your figures.

114. *single money*] Small change.

116. *and*] If.   *Ward*] A famous pirate in the Mediterranean about whom a pamphlet and
     a play had been written during 1609–12.

117. *wet it*] To 'wet one's whistle' = to drink.

119. *hangers*] Ornamental loops to slip on a belt for holding a sword.

120. *lawn*] Fine linen.

126. *smock-rampant*] Whore who is a 'roaring girl' as well, like Doll Tearsheet in
     2 Henry 4.

128. *for ... figures*] Despite your casting of horoscopes to know the future.

I sent for him, indeed. Wherefore, good partners,
Both he and she, be satisfied. For here   130
Determines the indenture tripartite
'Twixt Subtle, Dol, and Face. All I can do
Is to help you over the wall o' the back side,
Or lend you a sheet to save your velvet gown, Dol.
Here will be officers presently. Bethink you   135
Of some course suddenly to scape the dock,
For thither you'll come else.

Some knock

        Hark you, thunder.
SUBTLE You are a precious fiend!
OFFICER [*Within*]   Open the door.
FACE Dol, I am sorry for thee, i' faith. But hear'st thou?
 It shall go hard, but I will place thee somewhere.   140
 Thou shalt ha' my letter to Mistress Amo.
DOL   Hang you –
FACE Or Madam Caesarean.
DOL   Pox upon you, rogue!
 Would I had but time to beat thee.
FACE   Subtle,
 Let's know where you set up next. I'll send you
 A customer now and then, for old acquaintance.   145
 What new course ha' you?
SUBTLE   Rogue, I'll hang myself,
 That I may walk a greater devil than thou,
 And haunt thee i'the flock-bed and the buttery.

[*Exeunt*]

---

133. *the back side*] The rear of the premises.

136. *dock*] Where prisoners stand in a court of law.

141–2. *Amo ... Caesarean*] Brothel-keepers.

145. *old acquaintance*] Old times' sake, former friendship.

148. *flock-bed ... buttery*] That is, night and day. The butler is in charge of the buttery, or service from the kitchen.

Act 5 scene 5*

> [*More knocking at the door: enter*] Lovewit [*in the Spanish costume,*
> *followed by the Parson*]

LOVEWIT   What do you mean, my masters?

> [*Mammon, Officers, Surly, Kastril, Ananias, and Tribulation shout*
> *from without*]

MAMMON   Open your door!
    Cheaters, bawds, conjurers!
OFFICER   Or we'll break it open.
LOVEWIT   What warrant have you?
OFFICER   Warrant enough, sir, doubt not,
    If you'll not open it.
LOVEWIT   Is there an officer there?
OFFICER   Yes, two or three for failing.   5
LOVEWIT   Have but patience,
    And I will open it straight.

> [*Enter Face*]

FACE   Sir, ha' you done?
    Is it a marriage? Perfect?
LOVEWIT   Yes, my brain.
FACE   Off with your ruff and cloak then. Be yourself, sir.
SURLY   Down with the door!
KASTRIL   'Slight, ding it open!
LOVEWIT   [*Opening the door*]   Hold!
    Hold, gentlemen! What means this violence?   10

> [*Enter Mammon, Surly, Kastril, Ananias, Tribulation, and Officers*]

MAMMON   Where is this collier?
SURLY   And my Captain Face?
MAMMON   These day-owls.
SURLY   That are birding in men's purses.

---

*   The final scene of the play is filled with almost the entire cast of characters (except for
Subtle and Dol), plus extras as officers and neighbours. Puffed up with their own self-
importance, they swarm on stage, flow off again apparently to search Lovewit's house,
and re-enter in manageable groups only to be deflated and dispersed once more. The
final tripartite partnership in the house is at least legal, if not more honest: the house-
owner Lovewit displaces Subtle, the bride Dame Pliant displaces Dol, and the butler
Jeremy displaces his own criminal guise as Face.
5.   *for failing*]   As insurance against failure.
9.   *ding*]   Beat, batter.
12.   *birding*]   Hunting for birds; that is, preying (on).

MAMMON   Madam Suppository.
KASTRIL   Doxy, my suster.
ANANIAS   Locusts
    Of the foul pit.
TRIBULATION   Profane as Bel and the dragon.
ANANIAS   Worse than the grasshoppers or the lice of Egypt.   15
LOVEWIT   Good gentlemen, hear me. Are you officers,
    And cannot stay this violence?
OFFICER 1   Keep the peace.
LOVEWIT   Gentlemen, what is the matter? Whom do you seek?
MAMMON   The chemical cozener.
SURLY   And the Captain Pander.
KASTRIL   The nun my suster.   20
MAMMON   Madam Rabbi.
ANANIAS   Scorpions
    And caterpillars.
LOVEWIT   Fewer at once, I pray you.
OFFICER 1   One after another, gentlemen, I charge you,
    By virtue of my staff –
ANANIAS   They are the vessels
    Of pride, lust, and the cart.
LOVEWIT   Good zeal, lie still
    A little while.   25
TRIBULATION   Peace, Deacon Ananias.
LOVEWIT   The house is mine here, and the doors are open.
    If there be any such persons as you seek for,
    Use your authority: search on o' God's name.
    I am but newly come to town, and finding
    This tumult 'bout my door, to tell you true,   30
    It somewhat mazed me, till my man here, fearing

13. *Madam Suppository*] Punning on 'the supposed lady' and a whore, one who allows
herself to be plugged into, vaginally or rectally; possibly alluding to Dol's claim of
studying medicine. *Doxy*] Whore, mistress of a rogue (thieves' cant). *Locusts*]
Symbols of those who maintain false doctrines, according to the Geneva Bible's gloss on
Revelation 9:2–3.
14. *Bel . . . Dragon*] In the Apocrypha, two idols worshipped in Babylon and destroyed by
Daniel: a brazen image called Baal, and a dragon, respectively the false gods of money
and alchemy/science.
15. *grasshoppers . . . Egypt*] Two of the plagues sent to punish the Egyptians in Exodus
7–12.
20. *nun*] Slang for whore. *Madam Rabbi*] Referring to the Broughton-based fit of
madness.
24. *cart*] Deserving punishment at the cart, as at 4.6.29–30.
31. *mazed*] Confused, astonished.

My more displeasure, told me had done
Somewhat an insolent part, let out my house –
Belike, presuming on my known aversion
From any air o' the town while there was sickness –   35
To a Doctor and a Captain, who, what they are,
Or where they be, he knows not.

MAMMON   Are they gone?

LOVEWIT   You may go in and search, sir.

They enter [the house]

                                        Here I find
The empty walls, worse than I left 'em, smoked,
A few cracked pots and glasses, and a furnace,   40
The ceiling filled with poesies of the candle,
And 'Madam with a Dildo' writ o'the walls.
Only one gentlewoman I met here,
That is within, that said she was a widow –

KASTRIL   Ay, that's my suster. I'll go thump her. Where is she?   45

[Exit Kastril, following the others]

LOVEWIT   And should ha' married a Spanish count, but he,
When he came to't, neglected her so grossly
That I, a widower, am gone through with her.

SURLY   How! Have I lost her then?

LOVEWIT   Were you the Don, sir?
Good faith, now she does blame y'extremely, and says   50
You swore and told her you had ta'en the pains
To dye your beard, and umber o'er your face,
Borrowed a suit and ruff, all for her love,
And then did nothing. What an oversight
And want of putting forward, sir, was this!   55
Well fare an old harquebusier yet
Could prime his powder and give fire and hit,

35. *sickness*] Plague.
41. *poesies ... candle*] Smoke and grease marks on the ceiling, perhaps spelling out words
     or charms.
42. *'Madam ... writ*] Either a scatalogical poem or an obscene sketch of a woman using
     an artificial penis.
48. *gone ... her*] Performed the marriage ceremony with her; with innuendo of sexual
     achievement, as at ll. 56–8.
56. *harquebusier*] Musketeer; one armed with a harquebus, an early rifle.

All in a twinkling.

Mammon comes forth

MAMMON   The whole nest are fled!
LOVEWIT   What sort of birds were they?
MAMMON   A kind of choughs,
   Or thievish daws, sir, that have picked my purse   60
   Of eight-score and ten pounds within these five weeks,
   Beside my first materials, and my goods
   That lie i'the cellar, which I am glad they ha'left.
   I may have home yet.
LOVEWIT   Think you so, sir?
MAMMON   Ay.
LOVEWIT   By order of law, sir, but not otherwise.   65
MAMMON   Not mine own stuff?
LOVEWIT   Sir, I can take no knowledge
   That they are yours but by public means.
   If you can bring certificate that you were gulled of 'em,
   Or any formal writ out of a court
   That you did cozen yourself, I will not hold them.   70
MAMMON   I'll rather lose 'em.
LOVEWIT   That you shall not, sir,
   By me, in troth. Upon these terms they're yours.
   What should they ha' been, sir? Turned into gold all?
MAMMON   No.
   I cannot tell. It may be they should. What then?
LOVEWIT   What a great loss in hope have you sustained!   75
MAMMON   Not I. The commonwealth has.
FACE   Ay, he would ha' built
   The city new, and made a ditch about it
   Of silver, should have run with cream from Hogsden,
   That every Sunday in Moorfields the younkers
   And tits and tom-boys should have fed on, *gratis*.   80
MAMMON   I will go mount a turnip-cart and preach
   The end o' the world within these two months. Surly,
   What! In a dream?

59. *choughs*] Corvines, similar to jackdaws.
62. *first materials*] The chemicals and coal needed to start the experiments.
67. *public means*] Course of law.
79. *Moorfields*] Beggars' area north of the City (see 1.4.20n.) that had been newly converted into a civic recreational ground.   *younkers*] Young men.
80. *tits*] Young women, usually deprecatingly as minxes or hussies.   *tom-boys*] Bold or immodest women; hoydens, or roaring girls.
81. *turnip-cart*] Farm-cart used by itinerant preachers.

SURLY   Must I needs cheat myself
　　With that same foolish vice of honesty!
　　Come, let us go, and harken out the rogues.   85
　　That Face I'll mark for mine, if e'er I meet him.
FACE   If I can hear of him, sir, I'll bring you word
　　Unto your lodging, for in troth, they were strangers
　　To me. I thought 'em honest as myself, sir.

[Exeunt Surly and Mammon, as Tribulation and Ananias] come forth

TRIBULATION   'Tis well the saints shall not lose all yet. Go   90
　　And get some carts –
LOVEWIT   For what, my zealous friends?
ANANIAS   To bear away the portion of the righteous
　　Out of this den of thieves.
LOVEWIT   What is that portion?
ANANIAS   The goods, sometimes the orphans', that the brethren
　　Bought with their silver pence.   95
LOVEWIT   What, those i'the cellar
　　The knight Sir Mammon claims?
ANANIAS   I do defy
　　The wicked Mammon. So do all the brethren,
　　Thou profane man. I ask thee with what conscience
　　Thou canst advance that idol against us,
　　That have the seal? Were not the shillings numbered   100
　　That made the pounds? were not the pounds told out
　　Upon the second day of the fourth week
　　In the eighth month upon the table dormant,
　　The year of the last patience of the saints,
　　Six hundred and ten.   105
LOVEWIT   Mine earnest vehement botcher
　　And deacon also, I cannot dispute with you,
　　But, if you get you not away the sooner,
　　I shall confute you with a cudgel.
ANANIAS   Sir –
TRIBULATION   Be patient, Ananias.

85. *harken out*] Find out by enquiry.
86. *mark for mine*] Set aside for my personal vengeance; scar with the beating I shall give
　　him.
100. *seal*] The mark of God on their foreheads exempting them from the harm caused by
　　others (Revelation 9:4).
102–3. 23 October; but see 3.2.132.
103. *table dormant*] Fixed table, as opposed to moveable furniture.
104–5. *last ... ten*] 1610. The 'last patience' is the last thousand years before the end of the
　　world and the Second Coming.

ANANIAS   I am strong,
    And will stand up, well girt, against an host   110
    That threaten Gad in exile.
LOVEWIT   I shall send you
    To Amsterdam to your cellar.
ANANIAS   I will pray there
    Against thy house. May dogs defile thy walls,
    And wasps and hornets breed beneath thy roof,
    This seat of falsehood and this cave of coz'nage.   115

[Exeunt Tribulation and Ananias, as] Drugger enters

LOVEWIT   Another too?

And he beats him away

DRUGGER   Not I, sir, I am no brother.
LOVEWIT   Away, you Harry Nicholas! Do you talk?

[Exit Drugger, as Face restrains Lovewit]

FACE   No, this was Abel Drugger.

To the Parson

                           Good sir, go
    And satisfy him. Tell him all is done.
    He stayed too long a-washing of his face.   120
    The Doctor, he shall hear of him at Westchester,
    And of the Captain, tell him, at Yarmouth, or
    Some good port-town else, lying for a wind.

[Exit Parson]

    If you get off the angry child, now, sir –

[Enter Kastril hauling and berating] his sister

KASTRIL   Come on, you ewe, you have matched most sweetly,   125
      ha' you not?

111. *Gad in exile*] Alluding to Jacob's prophecy of Gad's defeat by enemy troops, and his
    ultimate victory over them in Genesis 49:19.
117. *Harry Nicholas*] Henrick Niclaes, Anabaptist mystic and leader of 'The Family of
    Love', a sect banned by Elizabeth in 1580. Lovewit mistakes Drugger for one of the
    brethren.
121. *Westchester*] Chester, associated with magic at least since 1594, when *The Wise Man
    of Westchester* was first performed at the Rose. The then-popular play has been
    tentatively identified with Anthony Munday's *John A Kent and John A Cumber*.
122. *Yarmouth*] A port in the north east, too far from London, as is Chester, for Drugger
    to seek him out.

Did not I say I would never ha' you tupped
But by a dubbed boy, to make you a lady-tom?
'Slight, you are a mammet! O, I could touse you, now.
Death, mun' you marry, with a pox?

LOVEWIT   You lie, boy!
As sound as you, and I am aforehand with you.   130

KASTRIL   Anon?

LOVEWIT   Come, will you quarrel? I will feeze you, sirrah.
Why do you not buckle to your tools?

KASTRIL   God's light!
This is a fine old boy as e'er I saw!

LOVEWIT   What, do you change your copy now? Proceed.
Here stands my dove. Stoop at her if you dare.   135

KASTRIL   'Slight, I must love him! I cannot choose, i'faith,
And I should be hanged for't! Suster, I protest,
I honour thee for this match.

LOVEWIT   O, do you so, sir?

KASTRIL   Yes, and thou canst take tobacco and drink, old boy,
I'll give her five hundred pound more to her marriage   140
Than her own 'state.

LOVEWIT   Fill a pipe-full, Jeremy.

FACE   Yes, but go in and take it, sir.

LOVEWIT   We will.
I will be ruled by thee in anything, Jeremy.

KASTRIL   'Slight, thou art not hide-bound! Thou art a Jovy boy!
Come, let's in, I pray thee, and take our whiffs.   145

LOVEWIT   Whiff in with your sister, brother boy.

[Exeunt Kastril and Dame Pliant]
[Lovewit comes forward and addresses the audience]

                                              That master
That had received such happiness by a servant,

126. *tupped*] Mated, the ewe mounted by the ram.
127. *dubbed boy*] Knight.   *lady-tom*] Knight's wife; a misnomer for Dame Pliant, who is
    not a 'tom' or aggressive roaring girl (see l. 80 above).
128. *mammet*] Doll, puppet.   *touse*] Beat.
129. *mun'*] Dialect for 'must'.
130. *sound*] Fit or healthy, not pox-ridden.
131. *feeze*] Settle your business; put some fear into you.
132. *buckle . . . tools*] Draw your weapons.
134. *change your copy*] Alter your behaviour; reject your angry-boy role-model.
135. *dove*] Dame Pliant.   *Stoop at*] Attack, used of hawks swooping down on prey.
141. *'state*] Estate.
144. *Jovy*] Jovial, merry.

In such a widow and with so much wealth,
Were very ungrateful if he would not be
A little indulgent to that servant's wit,   150
And help his fortune, though with some small strain
Of his own candour. Therefore, gentlemen
And kind spectators, if I have outstripped
An old man's gravity or strict canon, think
What a young wife and a good brain may do: 155
Stretch age's truth sometimes, and crack it too.
[*To Face*] Speak for thyself, knave.

FACE   So I will, sir.

[*Coming forward*]   Gentlemen,

My part a little fell in this last scene,
Yet 'twas decorum. And though I am clean
Got off from Subtle, Surly, Mammon, Dol,   160
Hot Ananias, Dapper, Drugger, all
With whom I traded, yet I put myself
On you, that are my country, and this pelf
Which I have got, if you do 'quit me, rests
To feast you often and invite new guests.   165

[*Exeunt*]

THE END

152. *candour*] Unspotted reputation, honour.
154. *canon*] Standard of behaviour.
159. *decorum*] Well within the laws of propriety for the plausible development of dramatic
    character.
162–3. *put ... you*] Submit to your judgment.
163. *that ... country*] Appealing to the audience as an accused prisoner entreats a jury of
    his peers. *pelf*] Loot.
164. *'quit*] Acquit.

[THE ACTORS]

This comedy was first

acted in the year

1610

By the King's Majesty's

Servants.   5

The principal comedians were:

Richard Burbage	John Hemminges
John Lowin	William Ostler
Henry Condel	John Underwood
Alexander Cooke	Nicholas Tooley 10
Robert Armin	William Eglestone

With the allowance of the Master of Revels.

4–5. *King's Majesty's Servants*] King's Men, the company at the Globe, and Blackfriars since 1609.

7–10. Burbage, Hemminges, Lowin, Condel, and Cooke have brief biographies at the end of *Volp*. Burbage probably played Mammon.

8. *William Ostler*] Trained as a child-actor with the Children of the Chapel, with whom he performed in *Poet*. As an adult with the King's Men, he is also on the cast list for *Cat*, 1611. He married John Hemminges's daughter in 1611, became a housekeeper in the Globe and Blackfriars, and died in 1614.

9. *John Underwood*] Also trained with the Children of the Chapel, listed in *CR*; later joined the King's Men, appearing also in *Cat*. He eventually became a shareholder in the Globe, Blackfriars, and Curtain theatres, and died 1624.

10. *Nicholas Tooley*] Also on the cast list for *Cat*; d. 1623.

11. *Robert Armin*] Comic actor and author who joined the Lord Chamberlain's Company (later the King's Men) in 1599. He is best known for roles believed to have been created for him by Shakespeare, including Touchstone, Feste, and Lear's fool. He wrote several jest-books and one play, *Two Maids of Moreclacke*, 1609, performed by the King's Men.   *William Eglestone*] Or Ecclestone, who also played in *Cat*; subsequently joined the Lady Elizabeth's company, 1611–13, and then rejoined the King's Men as a principal player.

TEXTUAL NOTES

Selected Variants between the 1616 Folio and the 1612 Quarto

Texts of *The Alchemist*

This list gives word-changes, additions, and omissions where *Q* differs substantively from the *F* text. Different states of *Q* are indicated as *Qa* and *Qb*. Since *Q* has only one marginal stage direction (*Dol is seen*, 2.3.210), the other omitted stage directions are not indicated here. Variations in the use of dashes and parentheses are likewise not indicated. The line-references and words in the lemmas are from the modernised text based on the folio. The variants are given in old spelling, except for *Q*'s epistle 'To the Reader', omitted in *F* and modernised below.

Dedication

0.2–3. *DESERVING ... BLOOD*] *F*; aequall with vertue, *and her Blood*: The Grace, and Glory of women. *Q*.

4–6. *Or ... virtue?*] *F*; Or how, yet, might a gratefull minde be furnish'd against the iniquitie of *Fortune*; except, when she fail'd it, it had power to impart it selfe? A way found out, to ouercome euen those, whom *Fortune* hath enabled to returne most, since they, yet leaue themselues more. In this assurance am I planted; and stand with those affections at this Altar, as shall no more auoide the light and witnesse, then they doe the conscience of your vertue. *Q*.

7–8. *value of it, which*] *F*; valew, that *Q*.

9. *as the times are*] *F*; in these times *Q*.

10. *assiduity*] *F*; daylinesse *Q*.

10–11. *This yet*] *F*; But this *Q*.

Following the Dedication in Q:

TO THE READER.

If thou beest more, thou art an understander, and then I trust thee. If thou art one that takest up, and but a pretender, beware at what hands thou receivest thy commodity; for thou wert never more fair in the way to be cozened (than in this age) in poetry, especially in plays, wherein now the concupiscence of jigs and

1. *understander*] (a) One who comprehends; (b) spectator in the pit of the theatre, one who stood under the level of the stage.

2. *takest up*] Accept goods as an equivalent to a specified sum of money, but lose the value because of the extortionate rate of exchange or the shoddiness of the commodity. In this context, the swindle is a metaphor for the reader's purchase of a printed play. *pretender*] One pretending to understand; here, a naive victim of both a commodity swindle and a literary fraud.

4. *concupiscence*] Cheap thrill.

4–5. *jigs and dances*] *Qa*; dances and antics *Qb*.

534 *The Alchemist*

dances so reigneth, as to run away from Nature and be afraid of her, is the only   5
point of art that tickles the spectators. But how out of purpose and place do I
name art? When the professors are grown so obstinate contemners of it and
presumers on their own naturals, as they are deriders of all diligence that way,
and, by simple mocking at the terms when they understand not the things, think
to get off wittily with their ignorance. Nay, they are esteemed the more learned   10
and sufficient for this by the multitude, through their excellent vice of judgment.
For they commend writers as they do fencers or wrestlers, who, if they come in
robustiously and put for it with a great deal of violence, are received for the
braver fellows, when many times their own rudeness is the cause of their
disgrace, and a little touch of their adversary gives all that boisterous force the   15
foil. I deny not but that these men, who always seek to do more than enough,
may some time happen on some thing that is good and great, but very seldom.
And when it comes it doth not recompence the rest of their ill. It sticks out
perhaps and is more eminent because all is sordid and vile about it, as lights are
more discerned in a thick darkness than a faint shadow. I speak not this out   20
of a hope to do good on any man against his will, for I know if it were put to
the question of theirs and mine, the worse would find more suffrages, because
the most favour common errors. But I give thee this warning, that there is a great
difference between those that (to gain the opinion of copy) utter all they can,
however unfitly, and those that use election and a mean. For it is   25
only the disease of the unskilful to think rude things greater than polished, or
scattered more numerous than composed.

Following this epistle is a commendatory poem by George Lacy; not in F.

The Persons of the Play

  0.   *Play*] F; Comoedie Q.
 16.   *THE SCENE: LONDON*] F; *not in Q.*

Prologue

  0.   *PROLOGUE*] F; THE PROLOGUE Q.
10.   *for*] F; to Q.

Act 1

1.1.51.   *y'were*] yo' were F; you were Q. *Also at 1.2.128; 1.3.51; and 4.6.7.*
1.1.69.   *called our*] F; call'd the high Q*a*; the high Q*b*.

  7. *professors*] Those who claim to produce literature.
  8. *naturals*] Natural talents, but punning on innate folly.
 11. *sufficient*] Qualified and capable. *multitude*] Q*a*; many Q*b*. *excellent vice*] Unsurpassed viciousness.
 13. *robustiously*] Rambunctiously. *put for it*] Engage in a bout.
 14. *braver*] Suggests bravado more than courage. *rudeness*] Crudeness, lack of skill.
 16. *foil*] Overthrow.
21–2. *put to the question*] Put to the vote.
 24. *copy*] Copiousness.
 25. *election*] Discrimination. *mean*] moderation.
 27. *numerous*] Harmoniously measured (of poetic lines).

1.1.114.	it] F; not in Q.
1.1.148.	Death on me] F; Gods will Q.
1.2.3.	I'm] I'am F; I am Q. So too at 4 et passim.
1.2.45.	Dog's-meat] F; Dogges-mouth Q.
1.2.56.	Xenophon] F; Testament Q.
1.2.135.	Jove] F; Gad Q.
1.2.137.	I'fac's] I-fac's F; I fac is Q.
1.2.138.	He's] F; He is Q.
1.3.67.	mercurial] F; Mercurian Q.
1.4.16.	possessed] F; possess'd on't Q.

Act 2

2.1.11.	the] F; my Q.
2.1.30.	thy] F; my Q, perhaps correctly.
2.2.13.	Buy] F; Take Q.
2.2.21.	wi'the] F; with the Q.
2.2.58–9.	They ... others] F; not in Q.
2.2.60.	pure] F; best Q.
2.2.67.	who are] F; who'are Q.
2.3.25.	SURLY] SVR. F; SVB. Q.
2.3.176.	metals] F; Mettall Q.
2.3.215.	What's] F; What is Q.
2.3.221 2]	Q; transposed in F. Q has a better logical flow, although F is not impossible.
2.3.246.	vial] Q; violl F.
2.3.249.	Ulen] F; Zephyrus Q.
2.3.260.	– Ulen] F; not in Q; SUBTLE Ulen! conj. Gifford.
2.3.272.	SURLY] conj. Gifford, H&S; SVB. F, Q.
2.3.315.	Ulen] F; not in Q.
2.4.6.	What's'hum's] F; Whachums Q.
2.5.10.	styptic] stipstick F, Q.
2.5.18.	Sirrah] F; S'rah Q.
2.6.25.	FACE] F; not in Q.
2.6.74.	Stay] F, Qb; Say Qa.

Act 3

3.1.2–4.	we ... forth] F; th'Elect must beare, with patience; / They are the exercises of the Spirit, / And sent Q.
3.2.35.	paintings] F, painting Q.
3.2.36.	talc] Q; Talek F.
3.2.72.	bonds] F; Bandes Q.
3.2.99.	glorious] F; holy Q.
3.2.107.	them] F; 'hem Q.
3.2.122.	They are] F; They'are Q.
3.2.135.	you'll] F; you shall Q.
3.3.22.	milk] F; feele Q.
3.3.62.	FACE] not in F or Q.
3.3.79.	Let's] F; Lett's 'vs Q.
3.4.4.	he says] F; not in Q.

3.4.8.   ⟨DRUGGER⟩] NAB Q, F.
3.4.9.   *Nab*] F; *not in* Q.
3.4.60.   *barony*] F; baronry Q.
3.4.75.   *'Od's*] F; God's Q.
3.4.123.   *'sessed*] F; seast Q.
3.4.132.   *go*] F; goe, Sir Q.

Act 4

4.1.6.   *o'*] F; on Q.
4.1.18.   *Ulen*] F; Lungs Q.
4.1.107.   *the light*] F; light Q.
4.1.112.   *in*] F; of Q.
4.3.11.   *'Slight*] F; 'Sblood Q.
4.3.12.   *gi'*] F; giue Q.
4.3.89.   *to you*] F; to'you Q.
4.4.3.   FACE] Q; *not in* F.
4.5.27.   *With*] F; Which Q.
4.5.42.   *stood still*] F; gone back Q.
4.5.43.   *gone back*] F; stand still Q.
4.5.51.   *This'll retard*] F; This will hinder Q.
4.6.16.   SURLY] SVR. Q; SVB. F.
4.7.32.   *he's*] h'has F; he hath Q.
4.7.126.   *there*] F; then Q.

Act 5

5.3.44.   *sulphur, sons of fire*] F; Vipers, Sonnes of Belial Q.
5.3.45.   *stench, it*] F; wickednesse Q.
5.3.46.   *Ay*] F; *not in* Q.
5.3.48.   *Yes*] F; I Q.
5.4.23.   *you*] F; her Q.
5.4.50.   *an'*] F; if Q.
5.4.55.   *twelve*] F; fiue Q.
5.4.58.   *sell you*] F; sell your Q.
5.4.59.   *pox*] F; A poxe Q.
5.4.60.   DAPPER] FAC. Q, F.
5.4.95.   *Nab*] F; him Q.
5.4.142.   *Caesarean*] F; Imperiall Q.
5.5.13.   *suster*] Q; sister F.
5.5.24.   *pride, lust, and the cart*] F; shame, and of dishonour Q.
5.5.63.   *ha'left*] F; haue left Q.
5.5.99.   *idol*] F; Nemrod Q.
5.5.145.   *I*] F; *not in* Q.
After THE END] *The statement of the first performance and actors appears in*
F; *not in* Q.

BARTHOLOMEW FAIR

INTRODUCTION

The setting: Smithfield

Bartholomew Fair was an annual event in West Smithfield between 1120 and 1855, opening on the feast of St Bartholomew, 24 August, and lasting from three days to a week or more. According to the fair's historian, Henry Morley, the fair's founder was Rayer, or Rahere, once Henry I's jester, who during a visit to Rome had a sickbed vision of St Bartholomew ordering him to establish a church in Smithfield to help the poor. The result was the Priory (later, the Hospital) of St Bartholomew, whose churchyard housed the fair. This fair is particularly appropriate for Jonson's play because of its tradition of cheating and sleight of hand. Rayer, himself a juggler, was denounced as an impostor for creating 'miracles' to improve fair attendance and profits; he may have cared for the poor, but he apparently fleeced everyone else. The symbols on the Priory rent-rolls suggest the guile for which the fair and its founder were known: a pike swallowing a gudgeon (the latter a small fish, easily caught, and thus a type of the dupe), and a fox-preacher giving a pastoral kiss to the goose he has grasped by the neck (emblematic of self-serving hypocrisy taking advantage of the silly) (Morley 1880; rpt 1968: pp. 20, 21). Even the saint was associated with greed: one popular legend tells how the spirit of St Bartholomew pursued thieves and extortionists of the parish in order to demand his share of the take.

Originally, clothiers from all over England and drapers from London had booths and stands within the walls of the Priory, where gates secured the goods overnight, and the Pie-Powders court judged disputes over debts and contracts during the day. To improve trade at the fair, at one time city tradesmen had to close their shops not only during the fair, but also as much as two weeks beforehand. Eventually, however, after the 1540s, urban sprawl took over much of the fairground, houses were built in the churchyard, and the north wall at Long Lane was razed, to be replaced by tenements. Of the small field that remained, a triangular open space of about five acres, the northern end known as The Elms was used for horse- and cattle-markets. Although the cloth-fair continued to be held in the shrunken churchyard, with the rents going to the Priory's new owner Lord Rich, the pleasure-fair licensed by the London Corporation spread out over a large area ranging from Newgate, where vendors of food and small wares temporarily set up in the nearby Cloisters of Christ Church, to Clerkenwell, where the Lord Mayor and Sheriffs of London presided over wrestling competitions in a large tent. The disorderly behaviour aroused by the scope and density of the occasion may be guessed at from the proclamations officially declaimed during the opening procession of the Lord Mayor, sheriffs, and aldermen. In 1604, crowds were warned against breaking the peace by brawling, selling short measures of drink, making unwholesome bread, falsely measuring any goods for sale, and breaching any law whatsoever within the fair precincts (Morley, pp. 110–12). The play incorporates evidence for these complaints in Ursula's habitual adulterations of ale or tobacco and her shifting pork prices, the bickering among stall-holders and customers, the corrupt policing practices, and the many thefts and deceptions.

Bartholomew Fair actually has a double setting. Jonson re-creates the rollicking carnival festivity and its sordidly commercialised dissipations in the newly built Hope Theatre, erected on Bankside by Henslowe and Alleyn as an entertainment site that would alternate playing with bull- and bear-baiting. The festive play time of St Bartholomew's Day parallels the festive occasion of its first performance on Halloween, with its tradition of trickstering, treating, and disguising. Jonson deliberately draws many parallels between the fairground and the theatre. Both are 'dirty' and 'stinking'. Both use temporary structures to house their diversions, the Hope platform being a removable trestle stage over the baiting pit. The bears kept at the Hope have their parallel in the 'she-bear' Ursula, baited by the 'lion-chap' Knockem (King James introduced the sport of lions baiting bears) and 'dog's-head' Quarlous. The baiting associated with Ursula's booth – including the game of vapours and the cat-fight between Ramping Alice and Mistress Overdo – shares space with the puppet show at the fair, just as bear-baiting coexists with theatrical playing at the Hope. Both places accommodate similar 'enormities' of social disorder in pickpockets and prostitutes, creating an atmosphere of corruption that infects citizens and their families. At the very least, both fair and theatre incite the waste of money and time with shoddy goods and trifling pleasures. But to those who enter their precincts, both hold up a mirror that reflects, somewhat distortedly, the uncomfortable truths behind the proprieties and practices that seem to divide the legitimate community from criminal gangs, thus levelling some of their differences.

Sources

With this play, Jonson seems, even more thoroughly than in the earlier comedies of this volume, to have invented his own plots and to have kept his dialogue free of classical importation and reference. At the same time, he demonstrates his skills as an acute observer of the social groupings and interactions that give this play its realistic edge. In Wasp, for example, Jonson was clearly drawing on Aristophanes' *The Wasps* in creating a 'governor' whose salient feature is his hyperbolic urge to pass judgment, often in defiance of evidence and based simply on the desire to have the last truculent word. But this same waspish judgmentality reappears in Zeal-of-the-land Busy and Adam Overdo as sharply differentiated extrapolations from the Aristophanic originals. Similarly, the vapours that rule all the characters in the play vary the concept of the Clouds in Aristophanes' play of that name. In Busy,

Jonson lampoons the career of William Whately, the puritan preacher known as the Roaring Boy of Banbury; Busy's speech is a rabble-rousing parody of puritan cant, resonating with what Jonas Barish calls its 'distinctive incantational hum', bracing its hypocrisies with high-sounding sophistical nonsense (1960: p. 198). In Overdo, Jonson travesties such disguised-ruler dramas as Shakespeare's *Measure for Measure*, Marston's *The Malcontent*, Day's *Law Tricks*, and Middleton's *The Phoenix*, all from about 1604, along with jabs at Thomas Middleton (no relation to the playwright), who, as the then Lord Mayor of London (1613–14), played detective to discover infractions of standards (see Induction 120n.). He may also be borrowing from Aristophanes' *The Frogs* for the beating Overdo stoically decides to accept rather than reveal his true function, just as Dionysius accepts a drubbing rather than reveal he is really a god. Overdo's language melds the rhetorical strategies of Cicero with the earnestness of George Whetstone (*A Mirror for Magistrates of Cities*, 1584) and the ardour of Richard Johnson (*Look on me London*, 1613). But all of these influences, like the debt to Erasmus's *The Praise of Folly*, merely provide broad satirical strokes for Jonson's caricatures of puritanical repressiveness, rather than sources for detailed and particular attacks.

In the same way, the fairground characters owe some of their local flavour to the pamphlets of Robert Greene, especially *A Notable Discovery of Cosenage* (1591) and *The Third and Last Part of Cony-Catching* (1592), as well as to other rogue-tales and jest-books. Troubleall seems to be a debased variation of the martyred St Bartholomew, a victim of bigotry and harsh sentencing. Whereas the original saint was flayed alive, Troubleall is pared of his sanity and peeled of his clothes, the stripped-down spirit of the fair, seeking out Overdo as the god who warrants all. Jonson inverts the moral of other prodigal-plays (for example, Wager's *The Longer Thou Livest*, 1559, Fulwell's *Like Will to Like*, 1587, the anonymous *The Contention between Liberality and Prodigality*, 1601, or even Heywood's *The Wise-Woman of Hogsden*, 1604) by reforming the father-figures (Wasp, Overdo, Busy) and ironically celebrating the prodigal sons, Cokes and Quarlous. In Beaumont's *The Knight of the Burning Pestle* (1608) the prodigal father, Merri-thought, plays a similarly inverted role by forcing his sober son and sour wife to spend, sing, and play. The lovers' competition for Grace parodies romantic heroes in Sidney's *Arcadia* and Shakespeare and Fletcher's *Two Noble Kinsmen*. Littlewit's playwriting activities owe a debt to Marlowe's *Hero and Leander* (1593) completed by Chapman in 1598, and Richard Edwardes's *Damon and Pythias* (1565). But the bulk of the characters and plots spring from the prolifically satiric imagination of Ben Jonson, whose eclectic vision of the grotesque and the symbolic rivals that of Bosch or Brueghel.

Stage history

After the opening performances of *Bartholomew Fair* at the Hope, 31 October 1614, and the following evening at court, 1 November, no record of further performances appears until the Restoration. Pepys remarks in his diary for 7 September 1661 that he had seen a performance of the play including the puppet show 'which had not been these forty years' – but whether he meant the play in its entirety, or merely the puppet-show scenes is not clear. Apparently the puppet show had been omitted when he saw the play on 8 June and 27 June 1661, and Pepys preferred it that way. In the following years, the play tended to be revived during the actual fair season in August. The early eighteenth century started the tradition of playing Ursula as a dame-role for a male actor, and the play continued to enjoy regular performances up to 1735, at which point it vanished from the stage for almost two hundred years.

The modern history of *Bartholomew Fair* begins on 26 June 1921, when the Phoenix Society of the New Oxford Theatre revived it. Since then it has been popular for university productions (particularly in the 1950s and 1970s) and increasingly for professional companies. The Old Vic Company (dir. George Devine) performed it at the Edinburgh Festival in 1949, and again at the Old Vic in 1950, receiving mixed or entirely negative reviews, as did the Bristol Old Vic in 1966. The Royal Shakespeare Company (dir. Terry Hands) performed it at the Aldwych in 1969, with Ben Kingsley as Winwife and Patrick Stewart as Leather-head. This production, criticised for its raucous horseplay and gimmickry, also suffered from antagonistic reviews, despite praise for individual actors – Helen Mirren as Win, Alan Howard as Cokes, and Lila Kaye as Ursula – but the most enthusiastic praise went to the puppets. The 1976 production for the Nottingham Playhouse (dir. Richard Eyre) set the scene in Victorian times and updated the fair-visitors' roles to suit. The Roundhouse period production of 1978 (dir. Peter Barnes) stressed the carnival festivity, the stage packed with stalls, gamblers, and morris dancers. The Young Vic (dir. Michael Bogdanov), also in 1978 but in modern dress, played up the darker implications of the fairground in a circus atmosphere of the big top, with a puppet having the last laugh in a final spotlight.

Further reading

For the Smithfield milieu, Henry Morley (1880; rpt 1968) is the sole historian of the fair. On the structure of the play, see Richard Levin (1965); both Leo Salingar (1986), in his chapter on 'Crowd and Public in *Bartholomew Fair*', and G. R. Hibbard (1977) in his edition's introduction, offer thoughtful correctives to Levin's work, while agreeing with much of it. Gail Kern Paster (1987) examines the women of the play in terms of ideological constructions of urinary and sexual incontinence. Calvin C. Smith (1972) and Guy Hamel (1973) both give positive readings of Grace and her suitors. Neil Rhodes (1980), in the second half of chapter 7, 'The Fatness of the Fair', focuses on Ursula's role, as does Joel H. Kaplan (1970). On the puppets, George Speaight (1955) gives excellent background material, and Jonas A. Barish (1959) still offers the best interpretation of the play's puppets in action. Several fine articles examine legalism and judgment, including those by Richard A. Burt (1987), Jackson I. Cope (1965), and Ray L. Heffner (1961). Finally, Fran Teague (1985) assesses the play's history of performance, and R. B. Parker (1970) discusses the physical staging in relation to medieval mansions of heaven and hell.

BARTHOLOMEW FAIR

A COMEDY

ACTED IN THE
YEAR 1614
By the Lady Elizabeth's
Servants
And then dedicated to King James of
most Blessed Memory

By the author, Benjamin Jonson

Si foret in terris, rideret Democritus: *nam*
Spectaret populum ludis attentius ipsis,
Ut sibi praebentem, mimo spectacula plura.
Scriptores autem narrare putaret assello
Fabellam surdo.
Hor[atius], lib[er] 2, epist[ula] 1

LONDON
Printed by John Beale for Robert Allot and are
to be sold at the sign of the Bear in Paul's
Churchyard, 1631

BARTHOLOMEW FAIR] A fair in Smithfield held annually, from 1120 to 1855, on 24–26 August, the feast of St Bartholomew. A common spelling of the name, 'Bartholomew', as in F, accorded with the usual pronunciation, 'Bartle-mee' or 'Battle-mee'. In the original text, the only modern spelling, 'Bartholomew', occurs at 1.3.3, when Littlewit cites Cokes's full name as it appears on the licence. This text uses the modern spelling throughout, but reminds the reader to pronounce the name in the old style.

Lady Elizabeth's Servants] A company founded in 1611, and later, in 1614, established at

THE PROLOGUE TO THE KING'S MAJESTY*

Your Majesty is welcome to a fair.
Such place, such men, such language, and such ware
You must expect; with these, the zealous noise
Of your land's faction, scandalised at toys,
As babies, hobbyhorses, puppet-plays,   5
And such like rage, whereof the petulant ways
Yourself have known and have been vexed with long.
These for your sport, without particular wrong,
Or just complaint of any private man

the newly built Hope Theatre, erected on the Bankside by Henslowe and Alleyn as an entertainment site that would alternate playing with bull- and bear-baiting. The building had a removeable trestle stage to accommodate the baiting, but was otherwise similar in structure to other theatres, except that the roof over the stage area was not supported by stage posts.

Si foret ... surdo] In the epigraph on the 1631 title-page, from Horace's *Epistles*, 2.1.194, 197–200, Jonson adapted Horace to suit the context; he omitted two lines (195–6) of the original, and at the end of the first line, changed *seu* (= or rather) to *nam* (= for). He also incorrectly doubled the *s* in *asello*:

> If Democritus were still on earth, he'd laugh. Why?
> He would watch the audience more attentively than the play,
> Since the audience offers a much more interesting spectacle.
> However, he would think the writers were telling an ass
> Their plots – and a deaf one, at that!

*   This prologue, like the epilogue, was written for the performance at court, 1 November 1614, as a replacement for the induction, which was created with the Hope Theatre in mind. The prologue succinctly sums up the induction's argument by defending the *decorum* of the play and disclaiming particular satire. Unlike the induction, the prologue uses courtly language to introduce its courtly audience to the vernacular and manners of the fair. It also directs the king's attention to those elements in the play which in real life exercised his own zeal: the puritan 'faction'; the watchfulness of justices of peace as representations of the king's authority; his abhorrence of tobacco and pork; and the final spirit of comradeship and toleration.

3.   *zealous*] Puritanically fervent. 'Zeal' was associated with the religious enthusiasm of the puritans; cf. 'Zeal-of-the-land Busy', the aptly named puritan lay-preacher in the play.

4.   *faction*] The puritans, with whom James had ideological differences ever since the Hampton Court Conference of 1604 silenced or expelled unruly nonconformists.

5.   *As babies*] Such as dolls.

6.   *rage*] Foolish vehemence.

8.   *sport*] Entertainment.   *particular wrong*] Satirising a specific individual.

Who of himself or shall think well or can,   10
The maker doth present, and hopes tonight
To give you, for a fairing, true delight.

10. Who either over-estimates his own importance, or twists the play's meaning for some
    ulterior motive. Jonson is criticising, somewhat ambiguously, the foolishly over-
    sensitive or manipulative members of the audience. See the Scrivener's first article of
    agreement [*Imprimus . . . themselves*] in the induction, ll.62–72.
11. *maker*] Author.
12. *fairing*] A gift given or purchased at a fair.

THE PERSONS OF THE PLAY*

JOHN LITTLEWIT, *a proctor*
[SOLOMON, *his man-servant*]
WIN LITTLEWIT, *his wife*
DAME PURECRAFT, *her mother and a widow*
ZEAL-OF-THE-LAND BUSY, *her suitor, a Banbury man*   5
[NED] WINWIFE, *his rival, a gentleman*
[TOM] QUARLOUS, *his companion, a gamester*
BARTHOLOMEW COKES, *an esquire of Harrow*
HUMPHREY ['NUMPS'] WASP, *his man*
ADAM OVERDO, *a Justice of Peace*   10

* With the largest cast of any Jonsonian drama, the play has thirty-six speaking parts, as well as porters, passers-by, boys, and six puppets (whose voices are rendered by Lantern/Leatherhead). Only about one-half of the speaking parts are capable of being doubled; the cast requires at least twenty-six actors, or twice the usual number. Jonson was able to populate the play so variously because he wrote it for the combined companies at the Hope Theatre, the Children of the Queen's Revels and Lady Elizabeth's Men.

1. *proctor*] Attorney in the ecclesiastical courts.

4. *PURECRAFT*] Ambiguous, suggesting either 'unmitigated guile', or paradoxically 'virtuous deceit'.

5. *ZEAL-OF-THE-LAND*] 'Zeal' is associated with puritan religious enthusiasm. Such naming was considered the pious alternative to the 'popish' practice of naming children after saints. See *Alch* Persons 9–10, 3.1.4, and 3.2 for details of contemporary attitudes towards puritan zeal.   *BUSY*] Implies both 'diligent' and 'officiously meddling'; when used of prayers, 'earnest, eager, importunate'. The name suggests that mere activity or occupation replaces intellection.   *Banbury*] In Oxfordshire, proverbially renowned for its cheese, cakes, and ale, and by the early seventeenth century a hotbed of puritanism. Both a glutton and a puritan, Busy was a baker before he became a preacher (see 1.3.100).

7. *QUARLOUS*] Suggests 'quarrelsome' and, by analogy with *parlous*, 'dangerously clever'.   *gamester*] Unscrupulous gambler; but also suggests 'lecher', clear from his manhandling of Win in 1.3, and 'actor', as in his impersonation of Trouble-all in Act 5.

8. *COKES*] Fool, simpleton. The name would have been pronounced 'Cox', as in coxcomb, a comment on his silliness.   *Harrow*] then a village in Middlesex 12 miles NW of London.

9. *'NUMPS'*] Diminutive for Humphrey, but also used jocularly of a silly or stupid person. Nashe dedicated his *Lenten Stuff* (1599) to 'Lusty Humphrey, according as the townsmen do christen him, little Numps, as the nobility and courtiers do name him, and Honest Humphrey, as all his friends and acquaintance esteem him'. Wasp seems to be held in the same affectionate, if patronising, regard, despite his 'waspish' temper.   *WASP*] An irascible person; probably derived from Aristophanes' *The Wasps*, in

DAME [ALICE] OVERDO, *his wife*
GRACE WELBORN, *his ward*
LANTERN LEATHERHEAD, *a hobbyhorse-seller* [*and puppet-master*]
JOAN TRASH, *a gingerbread-woman*
EZEKIEL EDGWORTH, *a cutpurse*   15
NIGHTINGALE, *a ballad-singer*
URSULA, *a pig-woman*
MOONCALF, *her tapster*
JORDAN KNOCKEM, *A horse-courser and ranger o' Turnbull*
VAL CUTTING, *a roarer*   20
CAPTAIN WHIT, *a bawd*
PUNK ALICE, *mistress o' the game*
TROUBLE-ALL, *a madman*
[TOBY HAGGIS]
[OLIVER 'DAVY' BRISTLE]   }   *watchmen, three*   25
[POCHER, *a beadle*]
COSTARDMONGER
MOUSETRAP- [OR TINDERBOX-] MAN

     which the eponymous chorus of grumpy middle-aged men thrives on jury duty, condemning the crimes and follies of their fellow-citizens.

13.   *LANTERN*] Associated with special lighting and shadow effects used in puppet-plays, but also suggesting the unsavoury job of the lantern-man who emptied privies during the night.

17.   *URSULA*] 'Little she-bear' (Latin); cf. 2.3.1. Her name appears in F as 'Ursla', indicating the pronunciation.

18.   *MOONCALF*] Born fool.

19.   *JORDAN*] Chamber-pot; figuratively, term of abuse for a fool. *horse-courser*] Dealer in riding-horses, assumed to be dishonest, rather like a used-car salesman. Horse-dealing was a principal feature of the Smithfield fair; see Dekker's *Lanthorne and Candle-light* for details of sharp practices among dealers. *ranger o' Turnbull*] Gamekeeper of Turnbull (a corruption of 'Turnmill') St, notorious for brothels in London. The 'game' is prostitution, and a 'ranger' is a pimp and libertine.

20.   *CUTTING*] Attribute of the cut-throat. *roarer*] Rowdy, bully, associated with the sword-and-buckler brawlers who met near the horse-market at Smithfield in the area known as Ruffians' Hall. A roarer often worked with a prostitute, either to make sure her customers paid her, or to beat and rob reluctant customers, tactics Pistol and Doll Tearsheet used in Shakespeare's *2 Henry IV* (cf. 5.4).

21.   *WHIT*] 'A little something', euphemism for genitals.

22.   *PUNK*] Prostitute. *mistress o' the game*] Prostitute. She is another denizen of Turnbull St (see 4.5.54, 68).

26.   *beadle*] Parish constable. His official function is at odds with his name, which suggests 'poacher', a thief who steals game.

27.   *COSTARDMONGER*] Fruit-vendor, originally an apple-seller.

28.   Maker of small traps or containers; figuratively, a trickster or brawler.

[CORNCUTTER]
[NORTHERN, *a*] *clothier*   30
[PUPPY, *a*] *wrestler*
[FILCHER,
SHARKWELL,]   } *doorkeepers* [*at the puppet-show*]
PORTERS
PUPPETS   35
[PASSENGERS]
[BOYS]
[STAGE-KEEPER]
[BOOK-HOLDER]
[SCRIVENER]   40

[The scene: Smithfield]

30. *clothier*] Maker or seller of woollen cloth, the key trade at the Smithfield fair.
36. *PASSENGERS*] Passers-by.
40. *BOOK-HOLDER*] Prompter, and manager responsible for the play-scripts.
41. *Smithfield*] In Jonson's day, a triangular open space of five or six acres just NW of the city. The Fair itself actually sprawled over a large area ranging from Newgate to the north-west suburbs.

THE INDUCTION ON THE STAGE*

[Enter] Stage-keeper

STAGE-KEEPER   Gentlemen, have a little patience: they are e'en upon
coming, instantly. He that should begin the play, Master Littlewit, the
proctor, has a stitch new fallen in his black silk stocking; 'twill be
drawn up ere you can tell twenty. He plays one o' the Arches that
dwells about the Hospital, and he has a very pretty part. But for the   5
whole play, will you ha' the truth on't? – I am looking, lest the poet
hear me, or his man, Master Brome, behind the arras – it is like to be
a very conceited scurvy one, in plain English. When't comes to the Fair
once, you were e'en as good go to Virginia for anything there is of

---

*   This stage-conscious induction disrupts whatever preconceptions the audience may
have by pointing out what Jonson has *not* intended or included in the play: it is not a
rehash of twenty- or thirty-year-old sex-and-violence melodramas, circus acts, or Inns
of Court pranks. The disappointment expressed by the old stage-keeper, who wanted to
re-experience those old-fashioned entertainments, is echoed by the disdainful book-
holder (the custodian of the full prompt copy of the script – actors would simply be
given their own lines and cues), who thinks Jonson has written just such a low comedy
aimed at viewers in the pit. To prevent the audience in the theatre from behaving as
riotously as the fair-going crowd in the play, the scrivener (or professional scribe) reads
out the contract which Jonson proposes as the conditions of performance. The articles
demand that the spectators watch the whole play patiently; that they criticise only in
proportion to what they paid for their tickets; that they use their own judgments instead
of aping their neighbours'; that they not anticipate fantastic action, except among the
puppets; and that they not particularise the satire nor complain about the earthiness of
the milieu. The contract as the official prelude to the play corresponds to the
proclamations uttered during the Lord Mayor's procession which formally opened the
fair. See the Introduction to *BF*, pp. 537–8. The legal metaphor, a favourite of Jonson's,
also appears in the epilogues of *Volp* and *Alch*.
3.   *has a stitch new fallen*] Just broke a thread, laddered.
4.   *drawn up*] Mended.   *one o' the Arches*] A lawyer in the Court of Arches, the court of
appeal from the diocesan courts; held in Bow Church on Cheapside, the first London
church built on stone arches or 'bows'.
5.   *Hospital*] Either St Bartholomew's, just east of Smithfield, the earliest hospital in
London, founded 1123, and operated by the city of London since 1547; or Christ's, a
school for foundlings near Newgate in the Christ Church parish, a location closer to
Bow Church, Littlewit's place of employment.
7.   *Brome*] Richard Brome, Jonson's assistant and later a dramatist in the Jonsonian style.
See Jonson's prefatory poem to Brome's *The Northern Lass* (1632), 'To My Old
Faithful Servant: And (by His Continued Virtue) My Loving Friend: the Author of this
Work, Mr Rich. Brome' (H&S 8:409).   *behind the arras*] Backstage. Tapestries were
hung over the tiring-house wall beneath the gallery.

Smithfield. He has not hit the humours, he does not know 'em; he has   10
not conversed with the Bartholomew-birds, as they say; he has ne'er
a sword-and-buckler man in his Fair, nor a little Davy to take toll o'
the bawds there, as in my time, nor a Kindheart, if anybody's teeth
should chance to ache in his play. Nor a juggler with a well-educated
ape to come over the chain for the King of England and back again for   15
the Prince, and sit still on his arse for the Pope and the King of Spain!
None o' these fine sights! Nor has he the canvas-cut i' the night, for
a hobbyhorse-man to creep in to his she-neighbour and take his leap
there! Nothing! No, and some writer that I know had had but the
penning o' this matter, he would ha' made you such a jig-a-jog i' the   20
booths, you should ha' thought an earthquake had been i' the Fair!
But these master-poets, they will ha' their own absurd courses; they
will be informed of nothing! He has (sir-reverence) kicked me three or
four times about the tiring-house, I thank him, for but offering to put
in with my experience. I'll be judged by you, gentlemen, now but for   25
one conceit of mine! Would not a fine pump upon the stage ha' done
well for a property now? And a punk set under upon her head, with
her stern upward, and ha' been soused by my witty young masters o'
the Inns o' Court? What think you o' this for a show now? He will not

10. *hit the humours*] Captured the distinctive mood and manners in the dialogue.
11. *Bartholomew-birds*] Underworld characters of the fair.
12. *sword-and-buckler man*] Old-fashioned ruffian, swashbuckler from the 1580s, when
     men still fought with sword and shield instead of the more modern rapier and dagger
     of 1614. *little Davy*] Dekker, among others, mentions him, in *News from Hell*
     (1606), as a professional bully. The original Davy, according to Stow, falsely accused his
     master of treason, and then killed him in a duel.
13. *Kindheart*] Itinerant tooth-drawer commemorated in Chettle's pamphlet *Kindheart's
     Dream* (1593).
17. *canvas-cut*] Slit in a tent for illicit entry; crude term for woman who solicits for sexual
     purposes (= canvass-cunt).
18. *hobbyhorse-man*] Both seller of hobbyhorses (children's toys) and patron of prosti-
     tutes, called 'hobbyhorses' because of the riding motion of sexual intercourse. *take his
     leap*] Fornicate; usually used of horses.
20. *jig-a-jog*] The rocking or riding of sexual intercourse.
23. *sir-reverence*] Corruption of 'save your reverence' (= with all due respect).
24. *tiring-house*] Backstage area with dressing-rooms.
24–5. *put in*] Advise, correct.
27. *punk*] Prostitute.
29. *the Inns o' Court*] The law societies and schools, considered the Third University,
     whose students frequently engaged in rowdy or crudely satirical activity.

hear o' this! I am an ass! I! And yet I kept the stage in Master Tarlton's   30
time, I thank my stars. Ho! And that man had lived to have played in
Bartholomew Fair, you should ha' seen him ha' come in, and ha' been
cozened i' the cloth-quarter so finely! And Adams, the rogue, ha'
leaped and capered upon him, and ha' dealt his vermin about as
though they had cost him nothing. And then a substantial watch to ha'   35
stolen in upon 'em and taken 'em away with mistaking words, as the
fashion is in the stage-practice.

[Enter] Book-holder, Scrivener to him

BOOK-HOLDER   How now? What rare discourse are you fallen upon?
Ha? Ha' you found any familiars here, that you are so free? What's
the business?   40
STAGE-KEEPER   Nothing, but the understanding gentlemen o' the ground
here asked my judgment.
BOOK-HOLDER   Your judgment, rascal? For what? Sweeping the stage?
Or gathering up the broken apples for the bears within? Away, rogue!
It's come to a fine degree in these spectacles when such a youth as you   45
pretend to a judgment.

[Exit Stage-keeper]

And yet he may i' the most o' this matter, i' faith. For the author hath

30–31. *Master Tarlton's time*] Richard Tarlton, the famous clown who ended his career as
a member of the Queen's Men from 1583 until his death in 1588, invented stories, jigs,
and ballads perpetuated in anecdotes and jest-books.
31. *And*] If.
33. *cozened*] Tricked. *the cloth-quarter*] Along the north wall of St Bartholomew's
Church, commercially the most important site at the fair. *Tarlton's Jests* (1611) records
how thieves stole Tarlton's clothes while he was absorbed in listening to the fiddlers
there; when a heckler at the Curtain subsequently asked him to improvise on this theme,
he did so, in verse. *Adams*] John Adams, another comedian in the Queen's Men.
34. *dealt his vermin*] Scattered his fleas.
35. *watch*] Constables.
36. *mistaking words*] Malapropisms, such as Dogberry and Verges use in *Much Ado
About Nothing*.
39. *free*] Outspoken.
41. *understanding . . . ground*] Punning on the spectators standing under or below the stage
in the pit. See 48, 'grounded judgments'.
44. *bears within*] A reminder that the Hope was also a bear-baiting pit at least once every
two weeks.
45. *youth*] Alluding sarcastically to second childhood, since the Stage-keeper is old enough
to remember Tarlton. The role may have been performed by a boy-actor adept at
playing old men, like Salomon Pavy, whose death at 'scarce thirteen' Jonson commemorated in *Epigrams* 120, 'Epitaph on S. P., a Child of Queen Elizabeth's Chapel'.

writ it just to his meridian and the scale of the grounded judgments
here, his play-fellows in wit. Gentlemen, not for want of a prologue,
but by way of a new one, I am sent out to you here with a scrivener   50
and certain articles drawn out in haste between our author and you,
which if you please to hear and, as they appear reasonable, to approve
of, the play will follow presently. Read, scribe; gi' me the counterpane.

SCRIVENER   Articles of agreement, indented, between the spectators or   55
hearers at the Hope on the Bankside, in the County of Surrey on the
one party; and the author of *Bartholomew Fair* in the said place and
County on the other party: the one-and-thirtieth day of October,
1614, and in the twelfth year of the reign of our Sovereign Lord,
James, by the grace of God King of England, France, and Ireland,   60
Defender of the faith. And of Scotland the seven-and-fortieth.

    Inprimis, It is covenanted and agreed by and between the parties
abovesaid, [that] and the said spectators and hearers, as well the
curious and envious as the favouring and judicious, as also the
grounded judgments and understandings, do for themselves severally   65
covenant and agree to remain in the places their money or friends have
put them in, with patience, for the space of two hours and an half, and
somewhat more. In which time the author promiseth to present them
by us with a new sufficient play called *Bartholomew Fair*, merry and
as full of noise as sport, made to delight all and to offend none.   70
Provided they have either the wit or the honesty to think well of
themselves.

    It is further agreed that every person here have his or their free will
of censure, to like or dislike at their own charge, the author having

48. *just to his meridian*] Keeping within his audience's limited intellectual range.

53–4. *counterpane*] Duplicate.

56. *Bankside*] On the south bank of the Thames in Southwark.

62. *Inprimis*] In the first place.

63. *[that]*] The first sentence of the agreement seems to have a missing 'that'-clause after 'abovesaid'; subsequent paragraphs all include the words 'agreed that', completed by a clause. *and ... as well*] Both ... and.

64. *curious*] Finicky or disparaging. *envious*] Spiteful, grudging.

69. *sufficient*] Legal term, said of a document that is complete, sound, and effective for the designated purpose.

70. *noise*] Expected by an audience accustomed to bear-baiting.

71–2. *Provided ... themselves*] That is, provided they have a healthy enough self-esteem not to see personal injury where none exists. A similar proviso appears in *Poet*'s 'Apological Dialogue', 144–5, referring to the over-sensitivity of actors who assume that criticism of one player applies to all the players.

74. *censure*] Critical opinion, judgment.

now departed with his right. It shall be lawful for any man to judge   75
his six penn'orth, his twelve penn'orth, so to his eighteen pence, two
shillings, half a crown, to the value of his place. Provided always his
place get not above his wit. And if he pay for half a dozen, he may
censure for all them too, so that he will undertake that they shall be
silent. He shall put in for censures here as they do for lots at the   80
lottery. Marry, if he drop but sixpence at the door and will censure a
crown's worth, it is thought there is no conscience or justice in that.

It is also agreed that every man here exercise his own judgment and
not censure by contagion or upon trust from another's voice or face
that sits by him, be he never so first in the Commission of Wit. As also   85
that he be fixed and settled in his censure, that what he approves or
not approves today, he will do the same tomorrow, and if tomorrow,
the next day, and so the next week (if need be), and not to be brought
about by any that sits on the bench with him, though they indict and
arraign plays daily. He that will swear *Jeronimo* or *Andronicus* are the   90
best plays yet shall pass unexcepted at here as a man whose judgment
shows it is constant and hath stood still these five-and-twenty or thirty
years. Though it be an ignorance, it is a virtuous and stayed ignorance,
and next to truth a confirmed error does well. Such a one the author
knows where to find him.   95

It is further covenanted, concluded, and agreed that how great
soever the expectation be, no person here is to expect more than he
knows, or better ware than a fair will afford, neither to look back to
the sword-and-buckler age of Smithfield, but content himself with the
present. Instead of a little Davy to take toll o' the bawds, the author   100
doth promise a strutting horse-courser with a leer drunkard, two or
three to attend him, in as good equipage as you would wish. And then

---

75. *departed with*] Given up.
76–7. These admission prices are high, perhaps because this was a new play at a new
house. The best location in the gallery usually cost 12 pence at other public theatres,
although indoor theatres charged double the price of open-air theatre admissions.
81. *lottery*] Instituted under royal patronage in 1612 to raise money for colonising
Virginia.
85. *Commission of Wit*] Tongue-in-cheek metaphor comparing a group of casual theatre
critics to a panel of judges in a courtroom; cf 'bench', and 'indict and arraign',
ll.89–90.
90. *Jeronimo ... Andronicus*] Kyd's *The Spanish Tragedy* (*c.* 1587), and Shakespeare's
Titus Andronicus (*c.* 1593), two popular but old-fashioned tragedies.
91. *unexcepted at*] Allowed to serve as a juror without the objection that his prejudice
jeopardises the court action (legal term).
93. *stayed*] Arrested or halted in its course.
101. *leer*] Sly, underhand.
102. *equipage*] Retinue, escort.

for Kindheart, the tooth-drawer, a fine oily pig-woman with her
tapster to bid you welcome, and a consort of roarers for music. A wise
Justice of Peace *meditant*, instead of a juggler with an ape. A civil   105
cutpurse *searchant*. A sweet singer of new ballads *allurant*, and as
fresh an hypocrite as ever was broached *rampant*. 'If there be never a
servant-monster i' the Fair, who can help it?' he says, 'nor a nest of
antics?' He is loath to make nature afraid in his plays, like those that
beget *Tales*, *Tempests*, and such like drolleries, to mix his head with   110
other men's heels. Let the concupiscence of jigs and dances reign as
strong as it will amongst you. Yet if the puppets will please anybody,
they shall be entreated to come in.

In consideration of which, it is finally agreed by the foresaid
hearers and spectators that they neither in themselves conceal, nor   115
suffer by them to be concealed, any state-decipherer or politic
picklock of the scene, so solemnly ridiculous as to search out who was
meant by the gingerbread-woman, who by the hobbyhorse-man, who
by the costardmonger, nay, who by their wares. Or that will pretend
to affirm (on his own inspired ignorance) what *Mirror of Magistrates*   120

105–6. *meditant* ... *searchant* ... *allurant*] Mock-heraldic terms, modelled on *rampant*, a
genuine heraldic description of a four-legged animal rearing up on its hind legs.

108. *servant-monster*] The term used by Stephano and Trinculo to address Caliban in *The
Tempest* 3.2.

108–9. *nest of antics*] Either a group of clowns, or dancing grotesques like the satyrs in *The
Winter's Tale* 4.4.

110. *Tales, Tempests*] Referring to romantic or fantastic elements in Shakespeare's final
plays, *The Winter's Tale* and *The Tempest*. *drolleries*] Entertainments like the 'living
drollery' of 'several strange shapes' that appear in *The Tempest* 3.3.

110–11. *mix his head with other men's heels*] Mingle serious ideas with music and dance,
thereby trivialising the intellectual content.

112. *puppets*] Jonson permits puppets because he uses them to satirise popular taste, not
pander to it.

116–17. *state-decipherer ... picklock*] Professional informers who interpret Jonson's satire
as sedition or slander. Jonson had been imprisoned for his share in *The Isle of Dogs*
(1597), and *EH!* (1605), and had been questioned by the Privy Council about elements
in *Sej* (1603), and *SW* (1609).

120. *Mirror of Magistrates*] Probably referring to *A Mirror for Magistrates of Cities*
(1584), by George Whetstone, which encouraged magistrates to tour places of
entertainment in disguise in order to witness and root out vice. Thomas Middleton (no
relation to the playwright) had successfully followed this method in shutting down
many brothels during his terms as sheriff in 1603–4 and as Lord Mayor of London in
1613–14, and was still, in the month of this play's first performance, pursuing his
investigation of false weights and measures in the food and beer industry. Whetstone's
work had recently been recycled in Richard Johnson's systematically plagiarised *Look
on me, London* (1613), a pamphlet dedicated to Mayor Middleton.

is meant by the Justice, what great lady by the pig-woman, what concealed statesman by the seller of mousetraps, and so of the rest. But that such person or persons so found be left discovered to the mercy of the author as a forfeiture to the stage and your laughter aforesaid. As also, such as shall so desperately or ambitiously play the   125
fool by his place aforesaid to challenge the author of scurrility because the language somewhere savours of Smithfield, the booth, and the pig-broth, or of profaneness, because a madman cries 'God quit you' or 'bless you'. In witness whereof, as you have preposterously put to your seals already (which is your money) you will now add the other   130
part of suffrage, your hands. The play shall presently begin. And though the Fair be not kept in the same region that some here, perhaps, would have it, yet think that therein the author hath observed a special decorum, the place being as dirty as Smithfield and as stinking every whit.   135

Howsoever, he prays you to believe his ware is still the same, else you will make him justly suspect that he that is so loath to look on a baby or an hobbyhorse here would be glad to take up a commodity of them at any laughter or loss in another place.

[*Exeunt*]

122. *concealed statesman*] Secret agent.
123. *discovered*] Revealed.
128. '*God quit you*'] Trouble all actually says only 'quit you' or 'multiply you', thus avoiding profanity charges stemming from the statute of January 1606, which levied a fine of 10 pounds for blasphemy.
129. *preposterously*] In reversed order, back-to-front.
131. *suffrage*] Approval. *hands*] Signatures, as on a legal document, but punning on applause.
134. *decorum*] Fitness.
136–9. Jonson concludes with the warning that people should not confuse the play's low subject-matter with inferior intellectual and moral worth. Those who refuse to laugh at this excellent play will be easily duped by second-rate offerings elsewhere – at Smithfield, for example – thus exposing themselves as inadequate judges.
138. *take up a commodity*] A usurer's trick to earn more interest than the officially allowed 10 per cent: the desperate borrower would receive part of his loan in cash, and part in shoddy goods, which he then would sell at an unfavourable rate to a merchant colluding with the usurer. Any borrower tricked into this scheme clearly had little discretion.

ACT 1

Act 1 scene 1*

[Enter] Littlewit

LITTLEWIT   A pretty conceit, and worth the finding! I ha' such luck to spin
   out these fine things still and like a silkworm, out of myself. Here's
   Master Bartholomew Cokes of Harrow o' th' Hill, i' th' County of
   Middlesex, Esquire, takes forth his licence to marry Mistress Grace
   Welborn of the said place and county. And when does he take it forth?   5
   Today! The four-and-twentieth of August! Bartholomew day! Bartholomew upon Bartholomew! There's the device! Who would have
   marked such a leap-frog chance now? A very less than ames-ace on
   two dice! Well, go thy ways, John Littlewit, Proctor John Littlewit.
   One o' the pretty wits o'Paul's, the Little Wit of London (so thou art   10
   called) and something beside. When a quirk or a quiblin does scape
   thee, and thou dost not watch, and apprehend it, and bring it afore the
   constable of conceit – there now, I speak quib too – let 'em carry thee
   out o' the Archdeacon's court into his kitchen and make a Jack of
   thee instead of a John. – There I am again, la! –   15

   [Enter] to him Win

   Win! Good morrow, Win. Ay, marry, Win! Now you look finely

---

*   Act 1 takes place at the Littlewit house, probably located near Christ's Hospital, just
   east of Newgate, and thus on the edge of the Christ Church parish within which
   Bartholomew Fair was held. This location was also adjacent to the puritan community
   in Blackfriars, which ran south of Newgate within the City walls to the river. Littlewit
   demonstrates Jonson's maxim, 'Language most shows a man: speak that I may see thee'
   (*Disc*, Parfitt 1975: p. 435). He is 'conceited' in that he is both arrogant and as foolishly
   elaborate in his metaphors and puns as he is in dictating his wife's dress. The
   superficiality of both pursuits prepares us for his skill as a puppet-playwright.
   1.   *conceit*] Witty turn of phrase, or ingenious fancy.
   7.   *device*] Clever contrivance.
   8.   *leap-frog chance*] One thing fortuitously popping up on the back of another:
       'Bartholomew upon Bartholomew!'   *A very less*] That is, a [chance] considerably
       slighter.   *ames-ace*] Double ace, the lowest throw with two dice.
   10.   *Paul's*] St Paul's Cathedral, just south west of Newgate below Cheapside. The middle
       aisle of Paul's was a fashionable strolling area and meeting-place for merchants and
       lawyers. See *EMO* 3.1.
   11.   *quirk*] Quip.   *quiblin*] Pun.
   13.   *quib*] Punningly.
   14.   *Arch-deacon's court*] Court of Arches, where Littlewit works.   *Jack*] Rogue; mecha-
       nism for turning the spit when roasting meat; common nickname for John.

indeed, Win! This cap does convince! You'd not ha' worn it, Win, nor
ha' had it velvet, but a rough country beaver with a copper band, like
the coney-skin woman of Budge Row? Sweet Win, let me kiss it! And
her fine high shoes, like the Spanish lady! Good Win, go a little. I   20
would fain see thee pace, pretty Win! By this fine cap, I could never
leave kissing on't.

WIN   Come, indeed la, you are such a fool still!

LITTLEWIT   No, but half a one, Win. You are the t'other half: man and
wife make one fool, Win. – Good! – Is there the proctor or doctor   25
indeed i'the diocese that ever had the fortune to win him such a Win!
– There I am again! – I do feel conceits coming upon me, more than
I am able to turn tongue to. A pox o' these pretenders to wit! Your
Three Cranes, Mitre, and Mermaid men! Not a corn of true salt nor
a grain of right mustard amongst them all. They may stand for places   30
or so, again' the next witfall, and pay twopence in a quart more for
their canary than other men. But gi' me the man can start up a Justice
of Wit out of six-shillings beer, and give the law to all the poets and

17.   *does convince*]   Is stunning, smashing.

18.   *beaver*]   Hat made of beaver fur.

19.   *coney-skin woman*]   Seller of rabbit skins.   *Budge Row*]   City street named for the
furriers and skinners who worked there. Budge is lambskin dressed with the fur
outward.   *kiss it*]   Baby-talk for 'kiss you'. Jonson frequently satirised men who were
aroused by games of dress-up, like Volpone in 3.7.220–38, or Clerimont's and
Dauphine's attraction to the seductive artifice of the Ladies Collegiate in *SW*,
Mammon's fantasy of Dol at 4.2.166–9, or Nick Stuff and his wife's masquerade in *NI*
4.3.

20.   *the Spanish lady*]   Also mentioned in *DisA* 2.8.23ff., as an English widow who travelled
widely and dressed in the Spanish style, including chopines, or high cork-heeled shoes
fashionable in Italy and Spain.

22.   *on't*]   That is, kissing Win; see above, *kiss it*.

29.   *Three Cranes*]   A tavern upriver from London Bridge, on Upper Thames Street at the
Vintry wharf, where three wooden cranes stood to unload wine at the landing. The
tavern catered for rivermen and other low company; see *SW* 2.5.99.   *Mitre*]   Several
taverns of this name existed in Jacobean London, but the one in Bread Street between
the river landings at Queenhithe and Three Cranes seems the likeliest because of its
proximity to the other two taverns mentioned here. Jonson celebrated this tavern, noted
for fine dining, in *EMO*, especially 5.4–7.   *Mermaid*]   A famous tavern also on lower
Bread Street, not far from the Thames. The Mermaid, renowned for its seafood dinners,
had many theatrical patrons, thanks to its convenient location near Blackfriars and the
stairs for river crossings to Bankside. The patrons included Jonson, Shakespeare,
Beaumont, and Donne.   *corn*]   Grain.

31.   *again' the next witfall*]   In anticipation of the next joke or witticism.

32.   *canary*]   A popular light sweet wine from the Canary Islands.

33.   *six-shillings beer*]   Small beer at 6 shillings a barrel, a cheap drink.

poet-suckers i' town, because they are the players' gossips? 'Slid, other
men have wives as fine as the players, and as well dressed. Come   35
hither, Win. [*Kisses her*]

Act 1 scene 2*

[*Enter*] *Winwife*

WINWIFE   Why, how now, Master Littlewit! Measuring of lips? Or
moulding of kisses? Which is it?

LITTLEWIT   Troth, I am a little taken with my Win's dressing here! Does't
not fine, Master Winwife? How do you apprehend, sir? She would not
ha' worn this habit. I challenge all Cheapside to show such   5
another: Moorfields, Pimlico Path, or the Exchange in a summer
evening, with a lace to boot as this has. Dear Win, let Master Winwife
kiss you. He comes a-wooing to our mother, Win, and may be our
father perhaps, Win. There's no harm in him, Win.

WINWIFE   None i' the earth, Master Littlewit.   10

LITTLEWIT   I envy no man my delicates, sir.

[*Winwife kisses Win*]

WINWIFE   Alas, you ha' the garden where they grow still! A wife here with
a strawberry-breath, cherry-lips, apricot-cheeks, and a soft velvet
head like a melicotton.

LITTLEWIT   Good, i' faith! – [*Aside*] Now dullness upon me, that I had   15
not that before him, that I should not light on 't as well as he! Velvet
head!

34. *poet-suckers*] Young poets, an analogy to infant rabbits = rabbitsuckers. *gossips*]
Close companions.

* This scene introduces the madness motif: the widow Dame Purecraft seeks a mad
husband, but whether he is to be a Bedlamite, a zealot, or a madcap is the question, not
resolved until Acts 4 and 5.

3. *Does't*] Doesn't she look.

4. *How do you apprehend*] Can you imagine.

5. *habit*] Outfit.   *Cheapside*] Main shopping street in London, especially for fine fabrics.

6. *Moorfields*] A former marsh just north of the city wall, reclaimed as parkland in 1606.
By 1614, it was a popular pleasure-ground for the fashionably dressed.   *Pimlico
Path*] A resort in Hoxton (Hogsden), near the sites of the Theatre, Curtain, and
Fortune playhouses north of the City.   *Exchange*] The New Exchange in the Strand,
a fashionable shopping mall that had just opened in April 1609.

7. *lace*] Trimming on the seams of a gown.   *to boot*] As well.

11. *envy*] Grudge.   *delicates*] Delights, tasty treats or sexual pleasures.

14. *melicotton*] Peach grafted on a quince.

WINWIFE   But my taste, Master Littlewit, tends to fruit of a later kind: the
  sober Matron, your wife's mother.

LITTLEWIT   Ay! We know you are a suitor, sir. Win and I both wish you   20
  well. By this licence here, would you had her, that your two names
  were as fast in it as here are a couple. Win would fain have a fine
  young father-i'-law with a feather, that her mother might hood it and
  chain it with Mistress Overdo. But you do not take the right course,
  Master Winwife.   25

WINWIFE   No? Master Littlewit, why?

LITTLEWIT   You are not mad enough.

WINWIFE   How? Is madness a right course?

LITTLEWIT   I say nothing, but I wink upon Win. You have a friend, one
  Master Quarlous, comes here sometimes?   30

WINWIFE   Why? He makes no love to her, does he?

LITTLEWIT   Not a tokenworth that ever I saw, I assure you, but –

WINWIFE   What?

LITTLEWIT   He is the more madcap o' the two. You do not apprehend
  me.   35

WIN   You have a hot coal i' your mouth, now, you cannot hold.

LITTLEWIT   Let me out with it, dear Win.

WIN   I'll tell him myself.

LITTLEWIT   Do, and take all the thanks, and much do good thy pretty
  heart, Win.   40

WIN   Sir, my mother has had her nativity-water cast lately by the
  cunningmen in Cow Lane, and they ha' told her her fortune, and do
  ensure her she shall never have happy hour unless she marry within
  this sennight, and when it is, it must be a madman, they say.

LITTLEWIT   Ay, but it must be a gentleman madman.   45

WIN   Yes, so the t'other man of Moorfields says.

WINWIFE   But does she believe 'em?

LITTLEWIT   Yes, and has been at Bedlam twice since, every day, to enquire
  if any gentleman be there, or to come there, mad!

WINWIFE   Why, this is a confederacy, a mere piece of practice upon her by   50

---

23. *feather*] A sign of rank, like Mistress Overdo's French hood and Justice Overdo's chain
  of office, of which his wife boasts.

32. *tokenworth*] Tokens of non-negotiable metal were issued to merchants in lieu of small
  change, which was in short supply. A tokenworth means the least possible amount.

41. *nativity-water*] Win confuses two activities of cunningmen (witches): casting nativities
  (= horoscopes), and casting water (= diagnosing from a urine specimen). Puritans were
  notoriously superstitious.

42. *Cow Lane*] Curving from West Smithfield towards Holborn.

44. *sennight*] Week.

48. *Bedlam*] Hospital of St Mary of Bethlehem in Bishopsgate, a lunatic asylum.

50. *confederacy*] Conspiracy.   *mere*] Sheer.   *practice*] Trickery.

these impostors!

LITTLEWIT   I tell her so; or else, say I, that they mean some young madcap
gentleman (for the devil can equivocate as well as a shopkeeper), and
therefore would I advise you to be a little madder than Master
Quarlous hereafter.   55

WIN[WIFE]   Where is she? Stirring yet?

LITTLEWIT   Stirring! Yes, and studying an old elder, come from Banbury,
a suitor that puts in here at meal-tide to praise the painful brethren,
or pray that the sweet singers may be restored, says a grace as long as
his breath lasts him! Sometime the spirit is so strong with him, it gets   60
quite out of him, and then my mother or Win are fain to fetch it again
with malmsey or *aqua coelestis*.

WIN   Yes indeed, we have such a tedious life with him for his diet and his
clothes too: he breaks his buttons and cracks seams at every saying he
sobs out.   65

LITTLEWIT   He cannot abide my vocation, he says.

WIN   No, he told my mother a proctor was a claw of the Beast, and that
she had little less than committed abomination in marrying me so as
she has done.

LITTLEWIT   Every line, he says, that a proctor writes, when it comes to be   70
read in the Bishop's court, is a long black hair combed out of the tail
of Antichrist.

WINWIFE   When came this proselyte?

LITTLEWIT   Some three days since.

53. *equivocate*] Quibble, trick with ambiguous wording.
56. *WIN[WIFE]*] The usual speech-heading for Winwife in the folio was 'WIN-W', but the
compositor frequently confused Winwife's speech-heading with 'WIN', the speech-
heading for Win Littlewit. In this instance, Win would know her mother's whereabouts,
but the visitor Winwife would have to ask.
58. *meal-tide*] Mocking the puritan habit of substituting 'mass' in such words as 'Christmas' with 'tide', meaning 'time'. *painful*] Taking pains, diligent.
59. *sweet singers*] Exiled or silenced puritan ministers, deprived of their livings because
they refused to conform to the Church of England according to the rules set down at
Hampton Court in 1604.
61. *fetch it again*] Restore him to his senses, revive him.
62. *aqua coelestis*] A brandy, or distilled wine.
64. *breaks his buttons*] Bursting or popping one's buttons was a conventional sign of
excessively powerful emotion.
67–8. *a claw of the Beast . . . abomination*] Puritans considered the Beast of the Apocalypse,
described in Revelation 13, as the Antichrist, identified with the Pope and Roman
Catholicism. As a proctor, Littlewit is an official of the Bishop's court in the Church of
England, which puritans argued was merely the Church of Rome in an English disguise.

Act 1 scene 3*

[Enter] Quarlous

QUARLOUS   [*Greeting Winwife*]   O sir, ha' you ta'en soil here? It's well a
man may reach you after three hours running yet! What an unmerciful
companion art thou, to quit thy lodging at such ungentlemanly hours?
None but a scattered covey of fiddlers, or one of these rag-rakers in
dunghills, or some marrow-bone man at most, would have been up   5
when thou wert gone abroad, by all description. I pray thee what ailest
thou, thou canst not sleep? Hast thou thorns i' thy eyelids or thistles
i' thy bed?

WINWIFE   I cannot tell. It seems you had neither i' your feet, that took this
pain to find me.   10

QUARLOUS   No, and I had, all the lyam-hounds o' the City should have
drawn after you by the scent rather. – Master John Littlewit! God save
you, sir. 'Twas a hot night with some of us last night, John. Shall we
pluck a hair o' the same wolf today, Proctor John?

LITTLEWIT   Do you remember, Master Quarlous, what we discoursed on   15
last night?

QUARLOUS   Not I, John: nothing that I either discourse or do at those
times. I forfeit all to forgetfulness.

LITTLEWIT   No? Not concerning Win? Look you: there she is, and dressed
as I told you she should be. Hark you, sir, had you forgot?   20

QUARLOUS   By this head, I'll beware how I keep you company, John,
when I drunk, and you have this dangerous memory! That's certain.

LITTLEWIT   Why, sir?

QUARLOUS   Why? [*To the others*]   We were all a little stained last night,
sprinkled with a cup or two, and I agreed with Proctor John here to   25
come and do somewhat with Win (I know not what 'twas) today; and
he puts me in mind on 't now. He says he was coming to fetch me. –

"   Quarlous expresses his misogyny first in his physical assault on Win, who attempts to
reject his embraces, and then in his verbal assault on Dame Purecraft, who gives him an
excuse to vent his contempt for widows, widow-hunters, and puritans. His 'sermon'
here has ironic implications for his marriage in Act 5.

1. *ta'en soil*] Taken refuge, a hunting term for a stag that takes to water to elude pursuit.
3. *companion*] Fellow.
4. *covey of fiddlers*] Musicians seeking employment.   *rag-rakers*] Scavengers who pick
through trash for saleable items; dealers in old clothes.
5. *marrow-bone man*] Dealer in junk; possibly, hired bully who uses his fists as weapons;
or one who falls to his knees for prayers.
11. *and*] If.   *lyam-hounds*] Bloodhounds held on a lyam (= leash).
13. *hot*] Hectic, thirst-provoking.
14. *hair o' the same wolf*] Hair of the dog that bit us; i.e., more drink.
24. *stained*] Drunk.

Before truth, if you have that fearful quality, John, to remember when
you are sober, John, what you promise drunk, John, I shall take heed
of you, John. For this once, I am content to wink at you. Where's your   30
wife? Come hither, Win.

He kisseth her

WIN   Why, John! Do you see this, John? Look you! Help me, John.

LITTLEWIT   O Win, fie, what do you mean, Win! Be womanly, Win. Make
an outcry to your mother, Win? Master Quarlous is an honest
gentleman and our worshipful good friend, Win, and he is Master   35
Winwife's friends too. And Master Winwife comes a suitor to your
mother, Win, as I told you before, Win, and may perhaps be our
father, Win. They'll do you no harm, Win. They are both our
worshipful good friends. Master Quarlous! You must know Master
Quarlous, Win; you must not quarrel with Master Quarlous, Win.   40

QUARLOUS   No, we'll kiss again and fall in.

LITTLEWIT   Yes, do, good Win.

WIN   I' faith, you are a fool, John.

LITTLEWIT   A fool-John, she calls me. Do you mark that, gentlemen?
Pretty littlewit of velvet! A fool-John!   45

QUARLOUS   She may call you an apple-John, if you use this.

WINWIFE   Pray thee forbear for my respect somewhat.

[Quarlous argues with Winwife, apart from the Littlewits]

QUARLOUS   Hoy-day! How respective you are become o' the sudden! I
fear this family will turn you reformed too; pray you come about
again. Because she is in possibility to be your daughter-in-law, and   50

---

30. *wink at you*] Overlook your indiscretion.
36. *friends*] Colloquial use of plural; cf. 'I am good friends with my father, and may do
   anything' (*1 Henry IV* 3.3.203).
39. *know*] Be acquainted with; have carnal intercourse with.
41. *fall in*] Be reconciled; fornicate.
44. *fool-John*] Instead of hearing her annoyance at his stupidity, Littlewit hears either an
   endearment, or a pun now lost, perhaps an analogy to a fruit-dessert, or a man who
   loves stewed fruit (thus facilitating Quarlous's 'apple-John'). Littlewit described Win
   earlier as a delicacy, 1.2.11; Winwife sees her as luscious fruit, 1.2.13–14; and Wasp
   describes her as a custard tart, 1.4.49.
46. *apple-John*] A pander. *use this*] Employ your wife sexually.
47. *respect*] Sake.
48. *respective*] Concerned about good manners.
49. *reformed*] Puritan.

may ask you blessing hereafter when she courts it to Tottenham to eat cream! Well, I will forbear, sir, but, i' faith, would thou wouldst leave thy exercise of widow-hunting once! This drawing after an old reverend smock by the splay-foot! There cannot be an ancient tripe or trillibub i' the town but thou art straight nosing it, and 'tis a fine   55 occupation thou'lt confine thyself to when thou hast got one: scrubbing a piece of buff as if thou hadst the perpetuity of Pannier Alley to stink in, or perhaps, worse, currying a carcass that thou hast bound thyself to alive. I'll be sworn some of them that thou art or hast been a suitor to are so old as no chaste or married pleasure can ever   60 become 'em. The honest instrument of procreation has, forty years since, left to belong to 'em. Thou must visit 'em as thou wouldst do a tomb, with a torch or three handfuls of link, flaming hot, and so thou mayst hap to make 'em feel thee, and after, come to inherit according to thy inches. A sweet course for a man to waste the brand   65 of life for, to be still raking himself a fortune in an old woman's embers. We shall ha' thee, after thou hast been but a month married

---

51. *ask you blessing*] Conventional request by a child of a parent upon greeting or leave-taking.

51–2. *Tottenham to eat cream*] A popular place of entertainment, opposite Tottenham Court on Hampstead Road, where visitors came to eat cakes and cream.

53. *widow-hunting*] This part of Quarlous's diatribe is loosely based on Martial, *Epigrams*, 3.93, and Juvenal, 1.41. *drawing after*] Tracking, usually by scent, but Quarlous goes on to suggest that Winwife is following foot-prints.

54. *smock*] Disrespectful term for a woman. *splay-foot*] Turned-out feet, suggesting an old woman's hobble, but also crudely hinting that the feet turn out with the legs in sexual readiness.

54–5. *tripe or trillibub*] Entrails, bag of guts.

56. *occupation*] Copulation.

57, 58. *scrubbing, currying*] Part of the process of tanning leather, but sexually suggestive and demeaning variations of 'rubbing'.

57. *buff*] Heavy leather; bare skin. *perpetuity*] Tenure for life.

57–8. *Pannier Alley*] A narrow street running north from Paternoster Row to Newgate Street, where buff leather, the material for catchpoles' jerkins, was sold.

63. *link*] Tow and pitch, torch material. The 'three handfuls' suggests an especially large head on the torch. *flaming hot*] Sexually aroused, alluding to the torch as a penis; cf. 'the brand of life', ll.65–6.

64–5. *inherit according to thy inches*] Acquire a fortune depending on the size of your penis.

65. *brand*] Torch.

66. *raking*] Crude term for penetrating sexually; covering embers with ashes in order to keep a fire without active burning.

to one of 'em, look like the quartan ague and the black jaundice met
in a face, and walk as if thou hadst borrowed legs of a spinner and
voice of a cricket. I would endure to hear fifteen sermons a week for   70
her, and such coarse and loud ones as some of 'em must be. I would
e'en desire of fate I might dwell in a drum and take in my sustenance
with an old broken tobacco-pipe and a straw. Dost thou ever think to
bring thine ears or stomach to the patience of a dry grace as long as
thy tablecloth? And droned out by thy son here (that might be thy   75
father) till all the meat o' thy board has forgot it was that day i' the
kitchen? Or to brook the noise made in a question of predestination
by the good labourers and painful eaters assembled together, put to
'em by the matron, your spouse, who moderates with a cup of wine,
ever and anon, and a sentence out of Knox between? Or the perpetual   80
spitting before and after a sober drawn exhortation of six hours,
whose better part was the *hum-ha-hum*? Or to hear prayers groaned
out over thy iron chests, as if they were charms to break 'em? And all
this, for the hope of two apostle-spoons, to suffer! And a cup to eat
a caudle in! For that will be thy legacy. She'll ha' conveyed her state   85
safe enough from thee, an' she be a right widow.

WINWIFE   Alas, I am quite off that scent now.

QUARLOUS   How so?

WINWIFE   Put off by a brother of Banbury, one that, they say, is come here
and governs all already.   90

QUARLOUS   What do you call him? I knew divers of those Banburians
when I was in Oxford.

WINWIFE   Master Littlewit can tell us.

---

68. *quartan ague*] Fever with recurrent paroxysms every fourth day. *black*] Discolora-
tion of tissues with bile pigment, caused by jaundice, a liver ailment.

69. *spinner*] Spider.

70–71. *for her*] Rather than marry her.

74. *patience*] Tolerating, enduring. *dry*] Boring; rigorous; unpalatable. *grace*] On the
length of puritan prayers at table, see *Alch* 3.2.86–8.

77. *question*] Controversial argument.

78. *painful*] Painstaking, earnest.

79. *moderates*] Arbitrates, conducts the assembly like a Presbyterian moderator.

80. *sentence*] Pithy quotation, maxim. *Knox*] John Knox, 1505–72, founder of Scottish
Presbyterianism whose works were much read by puritans.

82. *hum-ha-hum*] The peculiar whining pitch affected by puritan preachers; see *Alch*
3.2.53–5.

84. *apostle-spoons*] Customarily presented by the sponsors at a baptism. The set of silver
spoons, each with the figure of an apostle on the handle, was not a particularly
appropriate gift among puritans.

85. *caudle*] Warm drink, like an egg-nog, concocted for invalids. *conveyed her state*]
Made her estate over to a trustee, in order not to lose control of it to her husband.

LITTLEWIT   Sir! – Good Win, go in, and if Master Bartholomew Cokes his
man come for the licence – the little old fellow – let him speak with   95
me.

[*Exit Win*]

What say you, gentlemen?

WINWIFE   What call you the reverend elder you told me of? Your Banbury
man?

LITTLEWIT   Rabbi Busy, sir. He is more than an elder, he is a prophet, sir.   100

QUARLOUS   O, I know him! A baker, is he not?

LITTLEWIT   He was a baker, sir, but he does dream now, and see visions.
He has given over his trade.

QUARLOUS   I remember that too: out of a scruple he took that (in spiced
conscience) those cakes he made were served to bridals, maypoles,   105
morrises, and such profane feasts and meetings. His Christian name
is Zeal-of-the-land.

LITTLEWIT   Yes, sir, Zeal-of-the-land Busy.

WINWIFE   How, what a name's there!

LITTLEWIT   O, they have all such names, sir. He was witness for Win here   110
– they will not be called godfathers – and named her Win-the-fight.
You thought her name had been Winifred, did you not?

WINWIFE   I did indeed.

LITTLEWIT   He would ha' thought himself a stark reprobate if it had.

QUARLOUS   Ay, for there was a blue-starch-woman o' the name at the   115
same time. A notable hypocritical vermin it is: I know him. One that
stands upon his face more than his faith at all times. Ever in seditious
motion and reproving for vainglory; of a most lunatic conscience and
spleen, and affects the violence of singularity in all he does. – He has

100. *prophet*] Puritan given to prophetic visions

104. *spiced*] Rigidly principled.

105. *bridals*] Wedding feasts.

105–6. *bridals ... meetings*] Non-conformist Protestants considered such celebrations to be
pagan survivals.   *maypoles, morrises*] Dancing that originated in fertility rites.

110. *witness*] Puritan term for godfather.

114. *reprobate*] One of the ungodly.

115. *blue-starch-woman*] Laudress adept at bleaching and starching, a skill imported from
Holland during the 1580s. Puritans condemned both the starched ruffs and the starch-
women as wanton and vain.

117. *stands upon his face*] Depends upon his effrontery or outward appearance of
piety.   *seditious*] Fractious, unruly.

119. *singularity*] Judgment independent of social norms or rational education; private
standards produced (wrongly, in Jonson's view) by the puritan reliance on direct
inspiration.

undone a grocer here in Newgate market that broke with him, trusted   120
him with currants, as errant a zeal as he. That's by the way. – By his
profession, he will ever be i' the state of innocence, though, and
childhood; derides all antiquity; defies any other learning than
inspiration; and what discretion soever years should afford him, it is
all prevented in his original ignorance. Ha' not to do with him, for he   125
is a fellow of a most arrogant and invincible dullness, I assure you. –
Who is this?

Act 1 scene 4*

[Enter] Wasp [with Win]

WASP   By your leave, gentlemen, with all my heart to you and God you
    good morrow. Master Littlewit, my business is to you. Is this licence
    ready?
LITTLEWIT   Here, I ha'it for you in my hand, Master Humphrey.
WASP   That's well. Nay, never open or read it to me. It's labour in vain, you   5
    know. I am no clerk. I scorn to be saved by my book. I' faith, I'll hang
    first. Fold it up o' your word and gi'it me. What must you ha' for 't?
LITTLEWIT   We'll talk of that anon, Master Humphrey.
WASP   Now, or not at all, good Master Proctor. I am for no anons, I assure
    you.   10
LITTLEWIT   Sweet Win, bid Solomon send me the little black box within,
    in my study.

120. *undone*] Ruined. *Newgate market*] On Newgate Street just west of St Paul's,
    primarily selling grain. *broke*] Traded as a middleman in a special market, here
    currants. Apparently the broker, a fellow-puritan, trusted Busy, then a baker, with
    shipments of currants for which Busy did not pay.
121. *zeal*] Zealot.
122. *profession*] Declaration of faith.
122–3. *state of innocence ... childhood*] Puritans believed that once baptised they con-
    tinued free of sin as children of God.
123. *antiquity*] Classical learning, derided because it is pagan.
*   Wasp introduces the spirit of contrariness in his gratuitous verbal hostility. His
    waspishness seems to be set off by his young master's 'head full of bees'. Both
    symptoms are related to the game of vapours, played in 4.4, and other murky-brained
    activities in the fair.
1. *God you*] God give you.
6. *clerk*] Cleric. *saved by my book*] Wasp refers to his 'neck-verse'; if a convicted felon
    demonstrated his ability to read biblical verse in Latin, he was exempted from the
    penalty of hanging for his crime. This loophole in the law, repealed in 1827, was known

WASP   Ay, quickly, good mistress, I pray you, for I have both eggs o' the
spit and iron i' the fire.

[*Exit Win*]

    Say what you must have, good Master Littlewit.   15
LITTLEWIT   Why, you know the price, Master Numps.
WASP   I know? I know nothing. I? What tell you me of knowing? – Now
I am in haste – Sir, I do not know, and I will not know, and I scorn
to know, and yet – now I think on 't – I will and do know as well as
another. You must have a mark for your thing here, and eight pence   20
for the box. I could ha' saved two pence i' that, an' I had bought it
myself, but here's fourteen shillings for you. Good Lord! How long
your little wife stays! Pray God, Solomon your clerk be not looking i'
the wrong box, Master Proctor.
LITTLEWIT   Good, i' faith! No, I warrant you, Solomon is wiser than so,   25
sir.
WASP   Fie, fie, fie, by your leave, Master Littlewit, this is scurvy, idle,
foolish, and abominable! With all my heart, I do not like it.
WINWIFE   Do you hear? Jack Littlewit, what business does thy pretty head
think this fellow may have, that he keeps such a coil with?   30
QUARLOUS   More than buying of gingerbread i' the Cloister here (for that
we allow him), or a gilt pouch i' the Fair?
LITTLEWIT   Master Quarlous, do not mistake him. He is his master's
both-hands, I assure you.
QUARLOUS   What? To pull on his boots a-mornings, or his stockings,   35
does he?
LITTLEWIT   Sir, if you have a mind to mock him, mock him softly and
look t'other way, for if he apprehend you flout him once, he will fly
at you presently. A terrible testy old fellow, and his name is Wasp too.
QUARLOUS   Pretty insect! Make much on him.   40

---

as 'benefit of clergy'; originally it permitted clerics to escape trial in a secular court. Jonson
himself benefited from this law when he escaped hanging for the murder of Gabriel
Spencer, an actor, in 1598.
13–14. *eggs . . . fire*] Proverbially, no time to waste.
20. *mark*] 13 shillings, 4 pence.
20, 21. *thing, box*] Equivocally sexual, setting up the insult that Littlewit's clerk has caused
a delay by 'looking i' the wrong box', ll.23–4. Littlewit, however, is amused, because
Wasp gives him the opportunity to make a joke about the wisdom of Solomon, l.25.
30. *keeps such a coil with*] Makes such a fuss about.
31. *Cloister*] The Cloisters of Christ Church were taken over by vendors of food and small
wares during the Fair.
34. *both-hands*] Jonson's coinage for a factotum more essential than simply a 'right-hand
man'.
39. *presently*] Immediately.

WASP   A plague o' this box, and the pox too, and on him that made it, and
her that went for't, and all that should ha' sought it, sent it, or brought
it! Do you see, sir?

LITTLEWIT   Nay, good Master Wasp.

WASP   Good Master Hornet, turd i'your teeth, hold you your tongue. Do   45
not I know you? Your father was a pothecary, and sold glisters, more
than he gave, I wusse.

   [*Enter Win with the box*]

And turd i' your little wife's teeth too – here she comes – 'twill
make her spit as fine as she is, for all her velvet-custard on her head,
sir.   50

LITTLEWIT   O! Be civil, Master Numps.

WASP   Why, say I have a humour not to be civil, how then? Who shall
compel me? You?

LITTLEWIT   Here is the box now.

WASP   Why a pox o' your box once again. Let your little wife stale in it,   55
and she will. Sir, I would have you to understand, and these gentlemen
too, if they please –

WINWIFE   With all our hearts, sir.

WASP   – that I have a charge, gentlemen.

LITTLEWIT   They do apprehend, sir.   60

WASP   Pardon me, sir, neither they nor you can apprehend me yet. You are
an ass. I have a young master, he is now upon his making and marring:
the whole care of his well-doing is now mine. His foolish school-
masters have done nothing but run up and down the country with him
to beg puddings and cake-bread of his tenants, and almost spoiled   65
him. He has learned nothing but to sing catches and repeat *Rattle,
Bladder, Rattle* and *O, Madge*. I dare not let him walk alone for fear
of learning of vile tunes which he will sing at supper and in the
sermon-times! If he meet but a carman i' the street, and I find him not
talk to keep him off on him, he will whistle him and all his tunes over   70

45. *Hornet*] Implies that Littlewit is a cuckold.
46. *glisters*] Enemas.
47. *I wusse*] Iwis, truly, certainly.
49. *velvet-custard*] Pie-shaped velvet hat. A custard was an open pie of meat or fruit,
     covered with thickened broth or cream.
52. *humour*] Whim, inclination.
55. *stale*] Urinate (used of animals).
66. *catches*] Round-songs.
66–7. *Rattle ... Rattle*] A tongue-twister: 'Three blue beans in a blue bladder, rattle bladder
     rattle'.
67. *O, Madge*] A ballad about a barn-owl.
69. *carman*] Carter, notorious for whistling.

at night in his sleep! He has a head full of bees! I am fain now, for this
little time I am absent, to leave him in charge with a gentlewoman. 'Tis
true, she is a Justice of Peace his wife, and a gentlewoman o' the hood,
and his natural sister. But what may happen under a woman's
government, there's the doubt. Gentlemen, you do not know him. He   75
is another manner of piece than you think for! But nineteen year old,
and yet he is taller than either of you by the head, God bless him.
QUARLOUS   Well, methinks this is a fine fellow!
WINWIFE   He has made his master a finer by this description, I should
  think.   80
QUARLOUS   'Faith, much about one: it's cross and pile whether for a new
  farthing.
WASP   I'll tell you gentlemen –
LITTLEWIT   Will't please you drink, Master Wasp?
WASP   Why, I ha' not talked so long to be dry, sir. You see no dust or   85
  cobwebs come out o' my mouth, do you? You'd ha' me gone, would
  you?
LITTLEWIT   No, but you were in haste e'en now, Master Numps.
WASP   What an' I were? So I am still, and yet I will stay too. Meddle you
  with your match, your Win there; she has as little wit as her husband,   90
  it seems. I have others to talk to.
LITTLEWIT   She's my match indeed, and as little wit as I – Good!
WASP   We ha' been but a day and a half in town, gentlemen, 'tis true, and
  yesterday i' the afternoon we walked London to show the City to the
  gentlewoman he shall marry, Mistress Grace, but afore I will endure   95
  such another half-day with him, I'll be drawn with a good gib-cat
  through the great pond at home, as his uncle Hodge was! Why, we
  could not meet that heathen thing all day but stayed him: he would
  name you all the signs over, as he went, aloud, and where he spied a
  parrot or a monkey, there he was pitched with all the little long-coats   100
  about him, male and female. No getting him away! I thought he would

71. *head full of bees*] Proverbially, full of crazy notions.
73. *hood*] Sign of her consequence as a justice's wife.
74. *natural*] Begotten by the same parents; punning on foolish.
76. *another manner of piece*] Different type of fellow.
81. *cross and pile*] Heads or tails, from the emblems on the two sides of a French coin
  (*croix et pile*).
81–2. *whether for a new farthing*] No matter which you choose, there's not a farthings-
  worth of difference between them.
96–7. *drawn ... pond*] A rustic practical joke. The dupe makes a bet that a gib-cat
  (= tomcat) will draw him through a pond. The rope is tied around the dupe's waist, and
  the loose end thrown across the pond and apparently attached to a cat; actually those
  who pretend to guide the cat haul the victim across the water.
100. *little long-coats*] Children dressed in petticoats.

ha' run mad o' The Black Boy in Bucklersbury that takes the scurvy
roguy tobacco there.

LITTLEWIT   You say true, Master Numps. There's such a one indeed.

WASP   It's no matter whether there be or no. What's that to you?   105

QUARLOUS   He will not allow of John's reading at any hand.

Act 1 scene 5*

[Enter] Cokes, Mistress Overdo, Grace

COKES   O Numps! Are you here, Numps? Look where I am, Numps! And
    Mistress Grace, too! Nay, do not look angerly, Numps! My sister is
    here and all. I do not come without her.

WASP   What the mischief! Do you come with her? Or she with you?   5

COKES   We came all to seek you, Numps.

WASP   To seek me? Why, did you all think I was lost? Or run away with
    your fourteen shillingsworth of small ware here? Or that I had
    changed it i' the Fair for hobbyhorses? 'Sprecious – to seek me!

MISTRESS OVERDO   Nay, good Master Numps, do you show discretion,
    though he be exorbitant (as Master Overdo says) and't be but for   10
    conservation of the peace.

WASP   Marry, gip, Goody She-Justice, Mistress French-hood! Turd i' your
    teeth, and turd i' your French hood's teeth too, to do you service, do

102. *The Black Boy*] A common London apothecary and tobacconist sign, depicting a
    Native American, an African, or an Indian, depending on the geographical origin of
    the products sold in the shop. *Bucklersbury*] A street running south east from
    Cheapside, full of apothecary shops selling imported pharmaceutical products and
    tobacco, then thought to have medicinal properties.

106. *reading*] Commentary. *at any hand*] On any account.

*   With this scene, the movement of all the city visitors to the fair begins: Cokes, Mistress
    Overdo, Grace, and Wasp go first; Quarlous and Winwife follow; and the Littlewits
    decide to attend as well, if they can fool Dame Purecraft into permitting the excursion.
    The Littlewits' plot links acting punningly with hypocrisy as a feature of puritanism,
    but the association of the two expands beyond the sectarian throughout the play.

8. *changed*] Exchanged. *hobbyhorses*] Toys, or prostitutes. *'Sprecious*] By God's
    precious (blood or body).

10. *exorbitant*] Outrageous, deviating from normal behaviour. Master Overdo's use of the
    word may derive from the Roman legal term *exorbitans*, used of cases or offences that
    do not come within the intended scope of the law.

12. *Marry, gip*] An exclamation that confuses the oath 'by Mary Gipsy' ('by St Mary of
    Egypt'), with 'gee-up' (to a horse) and 'get away with you' (to a person). *Goody*] Ab-
    breviated from Goodwife, old-fashioned address to a married woman in humble life,
    here used sarcastically to put down Mistress Overdo's fine airs. *French-
    hood*] Fashionable among citizens' wives; made of softly pleated silk or velvet draping

you see? Must you quote your Adam to me! You think you are
Madam Regent still, Mistress Overdo, when I am in place? No such   15
matter, I assure you. Your reign is out when I am in, dame.

MISTRESS OVERDO   I am content to be in abeyance, sir, and be governed
    by you; so should he too, if he did well; but 'twill be expected you
    should also govern your passions.

WASP   Will 't so, forsooth? Good Lord! How sharp you are! With being at   20
    Bedlam yesterday? Whetstone has set an edge upon you, has he?

MISTRESS OVERDO   Nay, if you know not what belongs to your dignity,
    I do yet to mine.

WASP   Very well, then.

COKES   Is this the licence, Numps? For love's sake, let me see 't. I never   25
    saw a licence.

WASP   Did you not so? Why, you shall not see 't then.

COKES   An' you love me, good Numps.

WASP   Sir, I love you, and yet I do not love you i' these fooleries. Set your
    heart at rest. There's nothing in 't but hard words, and what would   30
    you see 't for?

COKES   I would see the length and the breadth on 't, that's all, and I will
    see 't now, so I will.

WASP   You sha' not see it here.

COKES   Then I'll see 't at home, and I'll look upo' the case here.   35

WASP   Why, do so. – A man must give way to him a little in trifles,
    gentlemen. These are errors, diseases of youth, which he will mend
    when he comes to judgment and knowledge of matters. I pray you
    conceive so, and I thank you. And I pray you pardon him, and I thank
    you again.   40

QUARLOUS   Well, this dry-nurse, I say still, is a delicate man.

---

the back of the head, with a round stiff band curving upright over the head above the ears,
    exposing a frame of hair around the face.

15. *Regent*] Governor ruling in place of the real authority; at Oxford and Cambridge, one
    who presides over academic disputations.

18. *if he did well*] If he behaved himself properly.

21. *Bedlam*] Lunatic asylum where visitors, for a fee, were entertained by the antics of the
    inmates.   *Whetstone*] Punning on the dull stone used to sharpen blades. Other editors
    suggest the man may have been a keeper or an inmate at the asylum; Hibbard cites *As
    You Like It* 1.2.49–50: 'the dullness of the fool is the whetstone of the wits'. But
    Mistress Overdo's sententious remarks may simply echo the style of the puritan
    pamphleteer George Whetstone, whose *Mirror for Magistrates of Cities* Jonson
    mentions twice (Induction 120, 5.6.29) as a tongue-in-cheek exemplar of civic duty.

41. *dry-nurse*] A nanny, as opposed to a wet-nurse who breast-feeds the infant in her
    care.   *delicate*] Courteous, used sarcastically in response to Wasp's heavy-handed
    apology.

WINWIFE   And I am for the cosset, his charge! Did you ever see a fellow's face more accuse him for an ass?

QUARLOUS   Accuse him? It confesses him one without accusing. What pity 'tis yonder wench should marry such a cokes.   45

WINWIFE   'Tis true.

QUARLOUS   She seems to be discreet, and as sober as she is handsome.

WINWIFE   Ay, and if you mark her, what a restrained scorn she casts upon all his behaviour and speeches!

COKES   Well, Numps, I am now for another piece of business more, the   50
Fair, Numps, and then –

WASP   Bless me! Deliver me! Help! Hold me! The Fair!

COKES   Nay, never fidge up and down, Numps, and vex itself. I am resolute Bartholomew in this. I'll make no suit on 't to you. 'Twas all the end of my journey, indeed, to show Mistress Grace my Fair. I call   55
't my Fair because of Bartholomew. You know my name is Bartholomew, and Bartholomew Fair.

LITTLEWIT   [*Aside to Quarlous and Winwife*] That was mine afore, gentlemen. This morning, I had that, i' faith, upon his licence, believe me. There he comes after me.   60

QUARLOUS   Come, John, this ambitious wit of yours, I am afraid, will do you no good i'the end.

LITTLEWIT   No? Why, sir?

QUARLOUS   You grow so insolent with it, and overdoing, John, that if you look not to it and tie it up, it will bring you to some obscure place in   65
time, and there 'twill leave you.

WINWIFE   Do not trust it too much, John. Be more sparing and use it but now and then. A wit is a dangerous thing in this age. Do not overbuy it.

LITTLEWIT   Think you so, gentlemen? I'll take heed on 't hereafter.   70

WIN   Yes, do, John.

COKES   A pretty little soul, this same Mistress Littlewit! Would I might marry her.

GRACE   [*Aside*] So would I, or anybody else, so I might scape you.

COKES   Numps, I will see it, Numps, 'tis decreed. Never be melancholy for   75
the matter.

WASP   Why, see it, sir, see it, do see it! Who hinders you? Why do you not go see it? 'Slid, see it.

42. *cosset*] Pampered child; literally, a lamb raised by hand.
45. *cokes*] Fool.
53. *fidge*] Pace nervously, fidget.   *itself*] Yourself.
64. *insolent*] Immoderate, beyond the bounds of propriety.
69. *overbuy*] Pay too much for (by getting into trouble).
71. *WIN*] Another possibly confused speech-heading. Winwife is as likely as Win to make this remark.

COKES   The Fair, Numps, the Fair.

WASP   Would the Fair and all the drums and rattles in 't were i' your belly,   80
for me. They are already i' your brain. He that had the means to travel
your head now should meet finer sights than any are i' the Fair, and
make a finer voyage on 't, to see it all hung with cockle-shells, pebbles,
fine wheat-straws, and here and there a chicken's feather and a
cobweb.   85

QUARLOUS   Good faith, he looks, methinks, an' you mark him, like one
that were made to catch flies, with his Sir Cranion legs.

WINWIFE   And his Numps to flap 'em away.

WASP   God be w'you, sir, there's your bee in a box, and much good do't
you.   90

[Wasp gives Cokes the box and starts to leave]

COKES   [*Bowing*] Why, your friend and Bartholomew, an' you be so
contumacious.

QUARLOUS   What mean you, Numps?

WASP   I'll not be guilty, I, gentlemen.

MISTRESS OVERDO   You will not let him go, brother, and lose him?   95

COKES   Who can hold that will away? I had rather lose him than the Fair,
I wusse.

WASP   You do not know the inconvenience, gentlemen, you persuade to,
nor what trouble I have with him in these humours. If he go to the
Fair, he will buy of everything to a baby there, and household stuff for   100
that too. If a leg or an arm on him did not grow on, he would lose it
i' the press. Pray heaven I bring him off with one stone! And then he
is such a ravener after fruit! You will not believe what a coil I had
t'other day to compound a business between a Kat'er'ne-pear-woman
and him about snatching! 'Tis intolerable, gentlemen.   105

WINWIFE   O! But you must not leave him now to these hazards, Numps.

WASP   Nay, he knows too well I will not leave him, and that makes him
presume. – Well, sir, will you go now? If you have such an itch i' your
feet to foot it to the Fair, why do you stop? Am I your tarriers? Go!
Will you go? Sir, why do you not go?   110

87. *Sir Cranion*] Daddy-long-legs.

89. *God be w'you*] God be with you (in the process of being corrupted into 'goodbye').

91. *your friend and Bartholomew*] Taking formal farewell, as at the end of a letter.

92. *contumacious*] Stubbornly contemptuous of your employer.

96. *that*] Him who.

100. *baby*] Doll.

102. *press*] Thick of the crowd.   *stone*] Testicle.

104. *Kat'er'ne-pear-woman*] Vendor of Catherine pears, a small early variety.

109. *tarriers*] Hinderers.

COKES   O Numps! Have I brought you about? Come, Mistress Grace and
    sister, I am resolute Bat, i' faith, still.
GRACE   Truly, I have no such fancy to the Fair, nor ambition to see it.
    There's none goes thither of any quality or fashion.
COKES   O Lord, sir! You shall pardon me, Mistress Grace, we are enow of   115
    ourselves to make it a fashion, and for qualities, let Numps alone.
    He'll find qualities.

   [Exeunt Cokes, Grace, Mistress Overdo, Wasp]

QUARLOUS   What a rogue in apprehension is this! To understand her
    language no better!
WINWIFE   Ay, and offer to marry to her? Well, I will leave the chase of my   120
    widow for today, and directly to the Fair. These flies cannot, this hot
    season, but engender us excellent creeping sport.
QUARLOUS   A man that has but a spoonful of brain would think so.
    Farewell, John.

   [Exeunt Quarlous, Winwife]

LITTLEWIT   Win, you see 'tis in fashion to go to the Fair, Win. We must   125
    to the Fair too, you and I, Win. I have an affair i' the Fair, Win, a
    puppet-play of mine own making – say nothing – that I writ for the
    motion-man, which you must see, Win.
WIN   I would I might, John, but my mother will never consent to such a
    'profane motion', she will call it.   130
LITTLEWIT   Tut, we'll have a device, a dainty one. – Now, wit, help at a
    pinch, good wit come, come, good wit, and 't be thy will. – I have it,
    Win, I have it, i' faith, and 'tis a fine one. Win, long to eat of a pig,
    sweet Win, i'the Fair, do you see? I' the heart o' the Fair, not at Pie
    Corner. Your mother will do anything, Win, to satisfy your longing,   135

111. *brought you about*] Changed your mind.
112. *Bat*] Short for Bartholomew; also, a lump of earth or stone.
114. *quality*] Social standing.
116. *qualities*] Character traits.   *let Numps alone*] Leave it to Numps.
118. *rogue in apprehension*] Fellow of inferior intelligence.
121–2. *flies ... creeping*] Contemptuous metaphor based on the belief that insects propa-
    gated spontaneously in the heat of the sun; 'flies' places Cokes and Wasp as petty
    minds whose behaviour in the heat of the Fair will generate low or 'creeping' comedy
    for their observers.
123. *A man ... so*] Even an idiot would agree with you.
128. *motion-man*] Puppet-master.
130. *motion*] Proposal.
131. *dainty*] In exquisite taste, an apt term for the device of craving roast pig.
134–5. *Pie Corner*] Formerly the site of an inn south of Smithfield with the sign of a
    magpie; later an area of cookshops. See *Alch* 1.1.15.

you know. Pray thee, long presently, and be sick o' the sudden, good
Win. I'll go in and tell her. Cut thy lace i' the mean time, and play the
hypocrite, sweet Win.

WIN   No, I'll not make me unready for it. I can be hypocrite enough,
though I were never so straitlaced.   140

LITTLEWIT   You say true. You have been bred i' the family, and brought
up to 't. Our mother is a most elect hypocrite, and has maintained us
all this seven year with it like gentlefolks.

WIN   Ay, let her alone, John. She is not a wise wilful widow for nothing,
nor a sanctified sister for a song. And let me alone too. I ha' somewhat   145
o' the mother in me, you shall see. Fetch her, fetch her! Ah! Ah!

[Exit Littlewit as Win continues to moan]

Act 1 scene 6*

[Enter] Purecraft, John [Littlewit]

PURECRAFT   Now, the blaze of the beauteous discipline fright away
this evil from our house! How now, Win-the-fight, child, how do you?
Sweet child, speak to me.

WIN   Yes, forsooth.

138. *hypocrite*] Actor; fraud, especially a religious person who pretends to virtue in order
to dissimulate real inclinations.

139. *make me unready*] Get undressed.

140. *straitlaced*] Bodice tightly laced; puritanically moral.

141. *family*] Puritan sect in which the members are spiritual brethren and sisters; especially
the Family of Love or Familists, who went to fanatical lengths to teach the love of God
and were considered particularly hypocritical by non puritans.

142. *elect*] Predestined by God for heaven; the opposite is *reprobate* (cf. 1.3.114).

143. *this seven year*] See Dame Purecraft's confession at 5.2.44 ff.

145. *sanctified sister*] An official in the sect's governing body.

146. *mother*] (1) Inherited traits of her parent; (2) hysteria.

*   The introduction of Dame Purecraft and Rabbi Busy sets up the satire against puritans,
especially by mocking their vocabulary and rhythms of speech. The puritan faith is the
'discipline', the 'cause', or any synonym for 'light', described as 'sanctified' or 'holy'. At
prayer-meetings, the 'assembly' is 'edified' and thus kept 'pure' in face of assaults by the
'foul', 'polluted', or 'profane' agents of the devil ('enemy', 'Tempter', 'adversary').
Many puritan cant-words are drawn from the Old Testament with its emphasis on sins
of the flesh and its repetitive epithets ('verily', 'exceeding'). Busy's rhetoric derives from
the long-winded nit-picking of puritan sermons.

1   *blaze*] Fervent religious belief, a cant-word. *beauteous discipline*] Faith pleasing in
God's sight. Tribulation Wholesome uses the same canting expression in *Alch* 3.1.32.

PURECRAFT   Look up, sweet Win-the-fight, and suffer not the enemy to   5
  enter you at this door. Remember that your education has been with
  the purest. What polluted one was it that named first the unclean
  beast, pig, to you, child?
WIN   Uh! Uh!
LITTLEWIT   Not I, o' my sincerity, mother. She longed above three hours   10
  ere she would let me know it. Who was it, Win?
WIN   A profane black thing with a beard, John.
PURECRAFT   O! Resist it, Win-the-fight, it is the Tempter, the wicked
  Tempter. You may know it by the fleshly motion of pig. Be strong
  against it and its foul temptations in these assaults, whereby it   15
  broacheth flesh and blood, as it were, on the weaker side, and pray
  against its carnal provocations, good child, sweet child, pray.
LITTLEWIT   Good mother, I pray you that she may eat some pig, and her
  bellyful too, and do not you cast away your own child, and perhaps
  one of mine, with your tale of the Tempter. – How do you, Win? Are   20
  you not sick?
WIN   Yes, a great deal, John. Uh! Uh!
PURECRAFT   What shall we do? Call our zealous brother Busy hither for
  his faithful fortification in this charge of the adversary.

  [*Exit Littlewit*]

  Child, my dear child, you shall eat pig, be comforted, my sweet child.   25
WIN   Ay, but i' the Fair, mother.
PURECRAFT   I mean i' the Fair, if it can be any way made or found
  lawful.

  [*Enter Littlewit*]

 5. *suffer*] Permit.   *enemy*] Devil. Puritan cant often uses metaphors based on warfare, as
    at ll.15, 24.
 6. *at this door*] Through the belly, with sexual implications.   *education*] Religious
    enlightenment.
 7. *purest*] Puritans.   *polluted one*] Non-puritan.   *unclean*] According to the kosher
    laws in the Old Testament (Leviticus 11:7).
12. According to testimony given at witch-trials, women became witches after they were
    seduced by an incubus who appeared as a black figure in their beds. See, for example,
    John Stearne, *A Confirmation and Discovery of Witch Craft* (1648), which relays Mrs
    Bush of Barton's testimony about her demon-lover (p. 29).
14. *motion*] Urging, appetite.
16. *weaker*] Female. Women were perceived as instinctive and emotional, unable to resist
    carnal desires.
19–20. *perhaps one of mine*] Win is pregnant. Her condition need not be heavily apparent
    in her costume, since other characters do not remark on it. But the more obviously
    pregnant she is, the more shocking her later behaviour appears to the audience, and the
    more culpable her husband's neglect.
24. *adversary*] Devil.

Where is our brother Busy? Will he not come? Look up, child.

LITTLEWIT   Presently, mother, as soon as he has cleansed his beard. I   30
found him fast by the teeth i' the cold turkey pie i' the cupboard with
a great white loaf on his left hand and a glass of malmsey on his right.

PURECRAFT   Slander not the brethren, wicked one.

[*Enter Busy*]

LITTLEWIT   Here he is now, purified, Mother.

PURECRAFT   O Brother Busy! Your help here to edify and raise us up in   35
a scruple. My daughter Win-the-fight is visited with a natural disease
of women called 'a longing to eat pig'.

LITTLEWIT   Ay, sir, a Bartholomew-pig, and in the Fair.

PURECRAFT   And I would be satisfied from you, religiously-wise, whether
a widow of the sanctified assembly, or a widow's daughter, may   40
commit the act without offence to the weaker sisters.

BUSY   Verily, for the disease of longing, it is a disease, a carnal disease, or
appetite, incident to women, and as it is carnal, and incident, it is
natural, very natural. Now pig, it is a meat, and a meat that is
nourishing, and may be longed for, and so consequently eaten. It   45
may be eaten, very exceeding well eaten. But in the Fair, and as
a Bartholomew-pig, it cannot be eaten, for the very calling
it a Bartholomew-pig, and to eat it so, is a spice of idolatry, and you
make the Fair no better than one of the high places. This, I take it, is
the state of the question. A high place.   50

LITTLEWIT   Ay, but in state of necessity, place should give place, Master
Busy. – [*Aside*] I have a conceit left yet.

PURECRAFT   Good Brother Zeal-of-the-land, think to make it as lawful as
you can.

LITTLEWIT   Yes, sir, and as soon as you can, for it must be, sir. You see   55
the danger my little wife is in, sir.

PURECRAFT   Truly, I do love my child dearly, and I would not have her

31. *fast*] Fastened.

34. *purified*] Cant-word, used ironically of Busy's washed face.

35. *edify*] Enlighten, a cant-word.   *raise us up*] Assist us.

36. *scruple*] Crisis of conscience.

40–41. *widow ... weaker sisters*] Purecraft distinguishes between her independence as a
'wise wilful widow' (1.5.144) of official standing in her sect and other women whose
behaviour is regulated by husbands or fathers.

48. *spice*] species.

49. *high places*] Places of idolatrous worship and sacrifice (cf. Leviticus 26:30; Jeremiah
19:5).

51. *place ... place*] Quibble on high rank or position yielding precedence to even higher
status.

miscarry or hazard her first fruits, if it might be otherwise.

BUSY   Surely it may be otherwise, but it is subject to construction, subject, and hath a face of offence with the weak, a great face, a foul face, but 60
that face may have a veil put over it, and be shadowed, as it were. It may be eaten, and in the Fair, I take it, in a booth, the tents of the wicked. The place is not much, not very much. We may be religious in midst of the profane, so it be eaten with a reformed mouth, with sobriety, and humbleness, not gorged in with gluttony or greediness. 65
There's the fear, for, should she go there as taking pride in the place or delight in the unclean dressing, to feed the vanity of the eye or the lust of the palate, it were not well, it were not fit, it were abominable, and not good.

LITTLEWIT   Nay, I knew that afore, and told her on 't, but courage, Win, 70
we'll be humble enough. We'll seek out the homeliest booth i' the Fair, that's certain. Rather than fail, we'll eat it o' the ground.

PURECRAFT   Ay, and I'll go with you myself, Win-the-fight, and my brother, Zeal-of-the-land, shall go with us too, for our better consolation. 75

WIN   [*More distressed than before*] Uh, uh!

LITTLEWIT   Ay, and Solomon too. [*Aside to Win*] Win – the more, the merrier! – Win, we'll leave Rabbi Busy in a booth. – [*Calling*] Solomon, my cloak.

[*Enter Solomon*]

SOLOMON   Here, sir. 80

BUSY   In the way of comfort to the weak, I will go and eat. I will eat exceedingly, and prophesy. There may be a good use made of it too, now I think on 't: by the public eating of swine's flesh, to profess our hate and loathing of Judaism, whereof the brethren stand taxed. I will therefore eat, yea, I will eat exceedingly. 85

LITTLEWIT   Good, i' faith, I will eat heartily too, because I will be no Jew. I could never away with that stiffnecked generation, and truly I hope

58. *her first fruits*] The child of her first pregnancy.
60. *face*] Outward appearance.
64. *reformed*] Converted to puritan belief.
66. *fear*] Thing to be feared.
67. *dressing*] Preparation of the meat.
68–9. *abominable and not good*] Anti-climax borrowed from Proverbs 20:23.
82. *prophesy*] Have religious visions.
84. *Judaism ... taxed*] Because of the puritan adherence to the Old Testament. In fact, puritans were more tolerant of Jews than were other Christian sects; expelled from England in the thirteenth century, Jews were allowed to return under Cromwell during the Puritan Republic.
87. *stiffnecked*] Stubborn and proud because they would not convert to Christianity.

my little one will be like me, that cries for pig so i' the mother's belly.

BUSY   Very likely, exceeding likely, very exceeding likely.

[*Exeunt*]

ACT 2

Act 2 scene 1 *

[*Enter*] *Justice Overdo* [*disguised*]

OVERDO   Well, in justice' name, and the king's, and for the commonwealth! Defy all the world, Adam Overdo, for a disguise and all
story, for thou hast fitted thyself, I swear. Fain would I meet the
Linceus now, that eagle's eye, that piercing Epidaurian serpent, as my

---

*   The stage set for the fair remains constant from Act 2 to Act 5. According to Whitehall
records, the performance at court (based, presumably, on the staging at the Hope)
required the building of booths which localise and focus the shifts in the plot, as the
action moves from one booth to another. Like medieval mansion staging, the booths
provide parameters and create simultaneity while characters drift around Ursula's pig-
booth, Leatherhead's toy stall and puppet-theatre, and the stocks. Perhaps, as R. B.
Parker (1970) suggests, the locations form a triangular emblematic design on stage,
with Ursula's booth stage-left as a secular hell, Leatherhead's stall and puppet-theatre
stage-right as a relative paradise of order and forgiveness, and the stocks at centre-stage
front as summary justice. Symbolically the three represent appetite, art, and law, all in
crude or debased form. The main actions at these sites are put into perspective by the
bustle and chatter of nameless street-sellers and passers-by, of whom the stage is never
quite empty.

    Justice Overdo's zeal for public reform, placed by his fool disguise, blends several
classical and contemporary allusions. Jonson undercuts Overdo's pose as the Cicer-
onian guardian of public welfare with references (ll.4–6) to Horace's ridicule of those
who claim to judge others accurately, but are blind to their own faults. Similarly, the
fool-disguise, like Junius Brutus's (see 40 n.), masks the rigid severity of his opinions.
Jonson also satirises the civic pamphlets of George Whetstone and Richard Johnson,
and the political activity of Mayor Thomas Middleton, as well as the disguised-ruler
comedies of Marston, Middleton, and Shakespeare. See W. D. Kay (1976) and
D. McPherson (1976) for fuller discussion.

1–2. *commonwealth*] Public welfare.

2–3. *all story*] Complete fabrication, based on the legend or folk-tale from which Overdo
drew his disguise.

3. *fitted*] Furnished.

4. *Linceus*] The keen-eyed Argonaut.   *Epidaurian serpent*] The snake coiled around the
staff of Asclepius, the god of healing, whose chief shrine was at Epidaurus. The serpent
assisted the healer in his diagnoses and cures.

Quintus Horace calls him, that could discover a Justice of Peace, and   5
lately of the quorum, under this covering. They may have seen many
a fool in the habit of a Justice, but never till now a Justice in the habit
of a fool. Thus must we do, though, that wake for the public good,
and thus hath the wise magistrate done in all ages. There is a doing of
right out of wrong, if the way be found. Never shall I enough   10
commend a worthy worshipful man, sometime a capital member of
this city, for his high wisdom in this point, who would take you now
the habit of a porter, now of a carman, now of the dog-killer in this
month of August, and in the winter of a seller of tinder-boxes, and
what would he do in all these shapes? Marry, go you into every   15
alehouse and down into every cellar, measure the length of puddings,
take the gauge of black pots and cans, ay, and custards with a stick,
and their circumference with a thread, weigh the loaves of bread on
his middle-finger. Then would he send for 'em home, give the
puddings to the poor, the bread to the hungry, the custards to his   20
children, break the pots, and burn the cans himself. He would not
trust his corrupt officers; he would do 't himself. Would all men in
authority would follow this worthy precedent! For, alas, as we are
public persons, what do we know? Nay, what can we know? We hear
with other men's ears; we see with other men's eyes! A foolish   25
constable or a sleepy watchman is all our information. He slanders a
gentleman by the virtue of his place, as he calls it, and we, by the vice
of ours, must believe him. As, a while agone, they made me, yea me,
to mistake an honest zealous pursuivant for a seminary, and a proper

5. *Quintus Horace*] In *Satires* 1.3.26–7.
6. *quorum*] Certain justices of eminent learning or ability whose presence was necessary
    to constitute a bench of magistrates.
7–8. *in the habit of a fool*] Either motley, or some costume, later identified as Arthur of
    Bradley's, probably associated with a well-known clown-act of the time.
8. *wake*] Are vigilant, keep watch.
11. *worthy worshipful man*] Thomas Middleton, Lord Mayor of London in 1613–14, who
    disguised himself in order to investigate abuses of weights and measures by brewers,
    bakers, and other victuallers. See note at Induction 120. *capital*] Leading.
13. *dog-killer*] The city hired exterminators to destroy stray dogs as a plague-preventative
    during the dog-days, the hot and unwholesome peak period of summer; ironically, these
    killings had the opposite effect, since the dogs used to keep down the black rat
    population, whose fleas carried the infection.
16. *puddings*] Sausages.
17. *take the gauge*] Calculate the volume. *pots and cans*] Used for serving measures of
    ale. *custards*] Pies. *stick*] For measuring the depth.
27. *by the virtue of his place*] By the authority of his office.
29. *pursuivant*] State messenger having power to execute warrants for arrest. *semi-
    nary*] A Roman Catholic priest trained at a European seminary.

young Bachelor of Music for a bawd. This we are subject to, that live   30
in high place: all our intelligence is idle and most of our intelligencers
knaves, and, by your leave, ourselves thought little better, if not
arrant fools, for believing 'em. I, Adam Overdo, am resolved
therefore to spare spy-money hereafter, and make mine own discoveries. Many are the yearly enormities of this Fair, in whose courts of   35
Pie-Powders I have had the honour during the three days sometimes
to sit as judge. But this is the special day for detection of those
foresaid enormities. Here is my black book for the purpose, this the
cloud that hides me. Under this covert I shall see and not be seen. On,
Junius Brutus! And as I began, so I'll end: in justice' name, and the   40
king's, and for the commonwealth.

[*Stands aside*]

Act 2 scene 2*

[*Enter*] *Leatherhead, Trash*

LEATHERHEAD The Fair's pest'lence dead, methinks. People come not
abroad today, whatever the matter is. Do you hear, Sister Trash, Lady
o' the Basket? Sit farther with your gingerbread-progeny there and
hinder not the prospect of my shop, or I'll ha' it proclaimed i' the Fair
what stuff they are made on.   5
TRASH Why, what stuff are they made on, Brother Leatherhead? Nothing
but what's wholesome, I assure you.

31. *high place*] Position of authority, not Busy's specifically scriptural phrase at 1.6.49 and
elsewhere. *intelligence*] Information. *intelligencers*] Spies, informants.
35. *enormities*] Irregularities, crimes; a key-word in Overdo's vocabulary, recurring at least
23 times in the play, and in Mayor Middleton's as well (McPherson 1976: p. 224)
35–6. *courts of Pie-Powders*] Summary courts held at fairs and markets to administer
justice among itinerant vendors and their customers; from the French *pied-poudreux*,
dusty-feet, or wayfarers.
38. *black book*] Record book. *this*] Overdo's costume.
40. *Junius Brutus*] Founder of the Roman Republic. According to legend, he preserved his
inexorable moral views during the Tarquin regime by pretending to be a fool; he
subsequently demonstrated his rigour as a judge by sentencing his own sons to death for
conspiring to restore the Tarquin monarchy.
* Jonson defines Ursula's pig-booth as a variation on a medieval hell-mouth, accompanied by trivial temptations of Joan Trash's cakes and Leatherhead's toys. Ursula
describes her kitchen as hotter than hell (41), and herself as 'all fire and fat' (47), a gross
Eve seducing the unwary with the devil's food, reeking of tobacco smoke and the fumes
of roasting flesh. Her tapster is a 'changeling' (60) or an 'incubee' (76).
1. *pest'lence*] Plaguily.
2. *Sister*] Mock-puritan address.

LEATHERHEAD   Yes, stale bread, rotten eggs, musty ginger, and dead
honey, you know.

OVERDO   [*Aside, writing in his black book*] Ay! Have I met with   10
enormity so soon?

LEATHERHEAD   I shall mar your market, old Joan.

TRASH   Mar my market, thou too-proud pedlar? Do thy worst. I defy thee,
I, and thy stable of hobbyhorses. I pay for my ground as well as thou
dost, and thou wrong'st me, for all thou art parcel-poet and an   15
inginer. I'll find a friend shall right me and make a ballad of thee and
thy cattle all over. Are you puffed up with the pride of your wares?
Your arsedine?

LEATHERHEAD   Go to, old Joan, I'll talk with you anon, and take you
down too afore Justice Overdo. He is the man must charm you. I'll ha'   20
you i' the Pie-Powders.

TRASH   Charm me? I'll meet thee face to face afore his worship when thou
dar'st, and though I be a little crooked o' my body, I'll be found as
upright in my dealing as any woman in Smithfield, I! Charm me?

OVERDO   [*Aside*] I am glad to hear my name is their terror yet. This is   25
doing of justice.

   [*Enter*] *passengers*

LEATHERHEAD   What do you lack? What is 't you buy? What do
you lack? Rattles, drums, halberts, horses, babies o' the best? Fiddles
o' th' finest?

   Enter Costardmonger

COSTARDMONGER   Buy any pears, pears, fine, very fine pears!   30
TRASH   Buy any gingerbread, gilt gingerbread!

10–11. Overdo's credulousness marks him from the start as incapable of detecting crime
accurately.

15. *parcel-*] Part-time.

16. *inginer*] Designer of shows.

17. *cattle*] Chattels, stock.

18. *arsedine*] Imitation gold leaf, used for embellishing inferior goods.

20. *charm*] Silence, as though by magic. The implication is that Joan Trash is a witch, a
characterisation supported by the unruly aggressiveness of her replies to Leatherhead's
baiting, and by her physical appearance, 'a little crooked o' my body'. Any bent old
woman with a shrewish tongue was liable to such charges.

26.1 *passengers*] Passers-by.

27. *What do you lack?*] Conventional street-vendor's cry.

28. *halberts*] Toy soldiers carrying halberts, spears mounted with a battle-axe.
babies] Dolls.

31. *gilt*] Decorated with gold leaf.

[Enter] Nightingale, [singing]

NIGHTINGALE　*Hey, now the Fair's a-filling!*
O, for a tune to startle
The birds o'the booths here billing
Yearly with old Saint Barthle!　35
The drunkards they are wading,
The punks and chapmen trading.
Who'd see the Fair without his lading?
Buy any ballads, new ballads?

[Enter] Ursula [from the back of the pig-booth]

URSULA　Fie upon 't. Who would wear out their youth and prime thus in　40
roasting of pigs, that had any cooler vocation? Hell's a kind of cold
cellar to 't, a very fine vault, o' my conscience! What, Mooncalf!
MOONCALF　*[Within]* Here, mistress.
NIGHTINGALE　How now, Ursula? In a heat, in a heat?
URSULA　*[Calling to Mooncalf]* My chair, you false faucet, you, and my　45
morning's draught quickly, a bottle of ale to quench me, rascal! – I am
all fire and fat, Nightingale. I shall e'en melt away to the first woman,
a rib again, I am afraid. I do water the ground in knots as I go like a
great garden-pot. You may follow me by the S's I make.
NIGHTINGALE　Alas, good Urs! Was 'Zekiel here this morning?　50
URSULA　'Zekiel? What 'Zekiel?
NIGHTINGALE　'Zekiel Edgworth, the civil cutpurse. You know him well
enough, he that talks bawdy to you still. I call him my Secretary.
URSULA　He promised to be here this morning. I remember.
NIGHTINGALE　When he comes, bid him stay. I'll be back again pres-　55
ently.
URSULA　Best take your morning's dew in your belly, Nightingale.

Mooncalf brings in the chair

Come, sir, set it here. Did not I bid you should get this chair let out
o' the sides for me, that my hips might play? You'll never think of
anything till your dame be rump-galled. 'Tis well, changeling: because　60
it can take in your grasshopper's thighs, you care for no more. Now

36. *wading*] Awash with drink.
37. *chapmen*] Hawkers and pedlars.
38. *without his lading*] Without making purchases.
45. *faucet*] Tap for a barrel.
48. *knots*] Intricate designs of criss-cross lines used in heraldry and embroidery.
53. *Secretary*] Confidant and confederate.
60. *rump-galled*] Injured on the buttocks by rubbing or chafing. *changeling*] Ugly or
stupid child left by fairies in exchange for a better one they have stolen.

you look as you had been i' the corner o' the booth fleaing your breech with a candle's end, and set fire o' the Fair. Fill, stoat, fill!

[Mooncalf serves ale to Ursula and Nightingale]

OVERDO   *[Aside]* This pig-woman do I know, and I will put her in for my second enormity. *[Writes]* She hath been before me, punk, pinnace, 65 and bawd, any time these two-and-twenty years, upon record i' the Pie-Powders.

URSULA   Fill again, you unlucky vermin.

MOONCALF   *[Filling]* 'Pray you be not angry, mistress. I'll ha' it widened anon. 70

URSULA   No, no, I shall e'en dwindle away to 't ere the Fair be done, you think, now you ha' heated me! A poor vexed thing I am. I feel myself dropping already, as fast as I can: two stone o' suet a day is my proportion. I can but hold life and soul together with this – Here's to you, Nightingale – and a whiff of tobacco, at most. Where's my pipe 75 now? Not filled? Thou arrant incubee!

NIGHTINGALE   Nay, Ursula, thou'lt gall between the tongue and the teeth with fretting now.

URSULA   How can I hope that ever he'll discharge his place of trust, tapster, a man of reckoning under me, that remembers nothing I say 80 to him?

[Exit Nightingale]

But look to 't, sirrah, you were best. Threepence a pipeful I will ha' made of all my whole half pound of tobacco, and a quarter of a pound of coltsfoot mixed with it too, to itch it out. I that have dealt so long in the fire will not be to seek in smoke now. Then six-and-twenty 85 shillings a barrel I will advance o' my beer, and fifty shillings a hundred o' my bottle-ale. I ha' told you the ways how to raise it. Froth your cans well i' the filling at length, rogue, and jog your bottles o' the buttock, sirrah. Then skink out the first glass ever, and drink with all companies, though you be sure to be drunk. You'll misreckon the 90

62. *fleaing*] Removing fleas from.
63. *stoat*] Weasel, a comment on Mooncalf's long thin body (cf. 'grasshopper's thighs', 61, 'vermin', 68, and 'weasel', 2.5.57); possibly *stot*, young castrated ox, a term of contempt for a stupid clumsy person.
65. *pinnace*] Go-between.
74. *proportion*] Estimate (of weight loss).
76. *incubee*] Corruption of 'incubus' = demon.
84. *coltsfoot*] Leaves of a herb used for smoking as a cure for asthma.   *itch*] Eke.
86. *advance*] Raise.
87. *raise*] Increase.
88. *at length*] Holding the can as far as possible from the tap.
89. *skink*] Pour.

better, and be less ashamed on 't. But your true trick, rascal, must be
to be ever busy, and mistake away the bottles and cans in haste before
they be half drunk off, and never hear anybody call – if they should
chance to mark you – till you ha' brought fresh, and be able to
forswear 'em. Give me a drink of ale.   95

OVERDO [*Aside*] This is the very womb and bed of enormity! Gross as
herself! [*Writes again*] This must all down for enormity, all, every
whit on 't.

One knocks

URSULA Look who's there, sirrah! Five shillings a pig is my price, at least.
If it be a sow-pig, sixpence more. If she be a great-bellied wife and long   100
for 't, sixpence more for that.

OVERDO [*Aside*] O *tempora!* O *mores!* I would not ha' lost my
discovery of this one grievance for my place and worship o' the bench.
How is the poor subject abused here! Well, I will fall in with her and
with her Mooncalf, and win out wonders of enormity.   105

[*Approaches Ursula*]

By thy leave, goodly woman, and the fatness of the Fair, oily as the
king's constable's lamp, and shining as his shoeing-horn! Hath thy ale
virtue, or thy beer strength? That the tongue of man may be tickled?
And his palate pleased in the morning? Let thy pretty nephew here go
search and see.   110

URSULA What new roarer is this?

MOONCALF O Lord! Do you not know him, Mistress? 'Tis mad Arthur
of Bradley that makes the orations. – Brave Master, old Arthur of
Bradley, how do you? Welcome to the Fair. When shall we hear you
again to handle your matters? With your back again' a booth, ha? I   115
ha' been one o' your little disciples i' my days!

OVERDO Let me drink, boy, with my love, thy aunt, here, that I may be
eloquent – but of thy best, lest it be bitter in my mouth and my words
fall foul on the Fair.

102. *O tempora! O mores!*] What times! What behaviour! (Cicero, *In Catilinam* 1.1.2).
103. *grievance*] Wrong, transgression. *worship*] Honour, dignity.
104. *subject*] Citizen.
105. *win out*] Extract.
112–13. *Arthur of Bradley*] The clown-hero of a sixteenth-century song, 'A Merry
    Wedding; or, O Brave Arthur of Bradley' in Joseph Ritson, *Robin Hood* (London:
    William Pickering, 1832) 2.210–16. The ballad describes Arthur's country wedding
    and the antics of his rustic guests; the refrain, 'Oh fine Arthur of Bradley', refers to his
    wedding clothes, as does the 'brave' of the title. The connection to Overdo seems to lie
    in the heavily trimmed coat, perhaps the livery of a fool, and the provincial diction.
    The ballad hero did not make orations; Jonson's source for this trait may have been a
    contemporary clown's act.

URSULA   Why dost thou not fetch him drink? And offer him to sit?   120
MOONCALF   Is 't ale or beer, Master Arthur?
OVERDO   Thy best, pretty stripling, thy best. The same thy dove drinketh, and thou drawest on holy-days.
URSULA   Bring him a six-penny bottle of ale. They say a fool's handsel is lucky.   125
OVERDO   Bring both, child. Ale for Arthur, and beer for Bradley. Ale for thine aunt, boy.

[*Exit Mooncalf*]

[*Aside*]   My disguise takes to the very wish and reach of it. I shall, by the benefit of this, discover enough and more, and yet get off with the reputation of what I would be: a certain middling thing between a fool   130 and a madman.

Act 2 scene 3*

[*Enter*] *to them Knockem*

KNOCKEM   What! My little lean Ursula! My she-bear! Art thou alive yet? With thy litter of pigs to grunt out another Bartholomew Fair? Ha!
URSULA   Yes, and to amble afoot, when the Fair is done, to hear you groan out of a cart up the heavy hill.
KNOCKEM   Of Holborn, Ursula, meanst thou so? For what? For what,   5 pretty Urs?
URSULA   For cutting halfpenny purses, or stealing little penny dogs out o'the Fair.
KNOCKEM   O! Good words, good words, Urs.
OVERDO   [*Aside*] Another special enormity. A cutpurse of the sword, the   10 boot, and the feather! Those are his marks.
URSULA   You are one of those horse-leeches that gave out I was dead in Turnbull Street of a surfeit of bottle-ale and tripes?
KNOCKEM   No, 'twas better meat, Urs: cows' udders, cows' udders!

---

122. *dove*] Darling.
124–5. *a fool's handsel is lucky*] Proverb. A 'handsel' is the first money taken in a day.
*   The term *vapours*, first used here, is a key-word for Knockem, apparently meaning whatever he wants it to mean: nonsense, fantastic notions, or ludicrous urges to boast and quarrel over trifles. *Motion* breeds them (38), whether physical bustle, carnal craving, emotional or spiritual hubbub, propositions of all kinds.
  4. *out ... heavy hill*] On his way to his own hanging. Holborn Hill was on the route between Newgate Prison and Tyburn, where the gallows stood.
12. *horse-leeches*] Veterinarians; large bloodsucking parasites (fig. and lit.).
13. *Turnbull Street*] Red-light district (see The Persons of the Play, 19).

URSULA   Well, I shall be meet with your mumbling mouth one day.   15

KNOCKEM   What? Thou'lt poison me with a newt in a bottle of ale, wilt
thou? Or a spider in a tobacco-pipe, Urs? Come, there's no malice in
these fat folks. I never fear thee, and I can scape thy lean Mooncalf
here. Let's drink it out, good Urs, and no vapours!

[*Exit Ursula*]

OVERDO   [*Aside to Mooncalf, paying him*] Dost thou hear, boy? –   20
There's for thy ale, and the remnant for thee. – Speak in thy faith of
a faucet, now. Is this goodly person before us here, this vapours, a
knight of the knife?

MOONCALF   What mean you by that, Master Arthur?

OVERDO   I mean, a child of the horn-thumb, a babe of booty, boy, a   25
cutpurse.

MOONCALF   O Lord, sir! Far from it. This is Master Dan Knockem:
Jordan, the Ranger of Turnbull. He is a horse-courser, sir.

OVERDO   Thy dainty dame, though, called him cutpurse.

MOONCALF   Like enough, sir. She'll do forty such things in an hour, an   30
you listen to her, for her recreation, if the toy take her i' the greasy
kerchief: it makes her fat, you see. She battens with it.

OVERDO   [*Aside*] Here might I ha' been deceived now, and ha' put a
fool's blot upon myself, if I had not played an after-game o'
discretion.   35

Ursula comes in again dropping

KNOCKEM   Alas, poor Urs, this 's an ill season for thee.

URSULA   Hang yourself, hackney-man.

KNOCKEM   How? How? Urs, vapours! Motion breed vapours?

URSULA   Vapours? Never tusk nor twirl your dibble, good Jordan. I know
what you'll take to a very drop. Though you be captain o' the roarers   40

---

15. *meet with*] Even with, revenged on.

16. *newt*] The word appears as 'neuft' in F (also at 2.6.11).

25. *horn-thumb*] Thimble worn by cutpurses to protect the thumb from the edge of the
knife while cutting purses.

28. *Jordan*] Chamber-pot, derisively used of a person; cf. 'piss-pots', l.41.

31. *toy*] Whim.

32. *kerchief*] Head; literally, a fine veil covering the head, sides of the face, and neck, worn
by women of the lower classes.   *battens with*] Grows fat or feeds on.

34. *after-game*] Second game played to reverse the issue of the first.

35.1 *dropping*] Exhausted and sweating.

37. *hackney-man*] Keeper of riding-horses for hire.

38. *Motion breed vapours?*] An aggressive threat: 'Is your exertion making you quarrelsome?'

39. *Never tusk nor twirl your dibble*] 'Don't sneer and finger your beard', suggesting

and fight well at the case of piss-pots, you shall not fright me with your lion-chap, sir, nor your tusks. You angry? You are hungry. Come, a pig's head will stop your mouth and stay your stomach at all times.

KNOCKEM   Thou art such another mad merry Urs still! Troth, I do make conscience of vexing thee now i' the dog-days, this hot weather, for 45 fear of found'ring thee i' the body and melting down a pillar of the Fair. Pray thee take thy chair again and keep state, and let's have a fresh bottle of ale and a pipe of tobacco, and no vapours. I'll ha' this belly o' thine taken up and thy grass scoured, wench. Look! Here's Ezekiel Edgworth, a fine boy of his inches as any is i' the Fair! Has still 50 money in his purse and will pay all with a kind heart, and good vapours.

Act 2 scene 4*

[*Enter*] *to them Edgworth*

EDGWORTH   That I will, indeed, willingly, Master Knockem. [*To Mooncalf*] Fetch some ale and tobacco.

[*Exit Mooncalf*]
[*Enter*] *Corncutter, Tinderbox-man, Passengers*

LEATHERHEAD   What do you lack, gentlemen? Maid, see a fine hobby-horse for your young Master, cost you but a token a week his provender.   5
CORNCUTTER   Ha' you any corns i' your feet and toes?

provocative jeering behaviour consistent with a roarer. To 'tusk' is to show one's teeth; a 'dibble' is a spade-shaped beard worn by soldiers.
41. *case of piss-pots*] Deliberate revising of 'case of pistols' as a counter-jeer to Knockem's attempted intimidation.
42. *lion-chap*] Lion-jaw, referring to the beard; also, belittling Knockem's roaring.
46. *found'ring*] Causing a horse to collapse or go lame through over-work.
47. *keep state*] Preside like a queen. The expression usually describes the formal sitting of a monarch.
49. *taken up*] Reduced.   *scoured*] Purged.
50. *fine boy of his inches*] Splendid fellow for his size.
*   Jonson represents the fair-folk as a kind of anti-society of criminals who conduct their business meeting according to the same social conventions that bind legitimate partners in commerce. Edgworth, the Secretary and master pickpocket, invites Nightingale his side-kick to 'Leave your mart a little' and join the gang for a drink, sign of their contractual 'indenture' and 'covenant'. They have a reciprocal arrangement: Edgworth acts as the accountant/manager of 'the purses and purchase'; Knockem and Whit provide the 'smocks' and 'whimsies'; and Ursula stores their stock, to be shared at the day's end.

TINDERBOX-MAN   Buy a mousetrap, a mousetrap, or a tormentor for a
    flea!
TRASH   Buy some gingerbread!

    [Enter] Nightingale

NIGHTINGALE   Ballads, ballads! Fine new ballads!   10

    [Sings]

> Hear for your love and buy for your money
> A delicate ballad o' 'The Ferret and the Cony',
> 'A Preservative again' the Punk's Evil',
> Another of 'Goose-green-starch and the Devil',
> 'A Dozen of Divine Points' and 'The Godly Garters',   15
> 'The Fairing of Good Counsel', of an ell and three quarters.
  What is 't you buy?
> 'The Windmill blown down by the Witch's Fart!'
> Or 'Saint George that O! did break the Dragon's heart!'

EDGWORTH   Master Nightingale, come hither. Leave your mart a little.   20
NIGHTINGALE   O, my Secretary! What says my Secretary?

    [Enter Mooncalf with ale and tobacco]

OVERDO   *[To Mooncalf, indicating Edgworth]* Child o' the bottles,
    what's he? What's he?
MOONCALF   A civil young gentleman, Master Arthur, that keeps com-
    pany with the roarers and disburses all still. He has ever money in his   25
    purse. He pays for them, and they roar for him: one does good offices
    for another. They call him the Secretary, but he serves nobody. A great

---

7. *tormentor*] Flea-trap.
12. *'The Ferret and the Cony'*] The weasel (= swindler) and the rabbit (= dupe), thieves'
    cant.
13. *Punk's Evil*] Venereal disease.
14. *'Goose-green-starch and the Devil'*] A ballad about a vain woman of Antwerp who,
    when her servants failed to starch her ruffs to her satisfaction, swore the devil might
    take her before she wore any of them; the devil, materialising as a handsome youth,
    starched her ruffs perfectly, then seduced and strangled her. See 'blue starch woman'
    and note at 1.3.115 for moral attitudes to starch.   *Goose-green*] Usually 'gooseturd-
    green', a yellow-green.
15. *'A Dozen of Divine Points'*] A ballad of twelve moral maxims sent by a gentlewoman
    to her lover as a new year's gift. 'Points' were also laces used to fasten clothes.   *'The
    Godly Garters'*] The full title in the Stationers' Register for John Charlwood's ballad
    was 'A pair of garters for young men to wear that serve the Lord God and live in his
    fear'.
16. *ell*] 45 inches.
26. *roar*] Riot.

friend of the ballad-man's, they are never asunder.

OVERDO   What pity 'tis so civil a young man should haunt this debauched
    company! Here's the bane of the youth of our time apparent. A proper   30
    penman, I see 't in his countenance. He has a good clerk's look with
    him, and I warrant him a quick hand.

MOONCALF   A very quick hand, sir.

    [Exit Mooncalf]
    This they whisper, that Overdo hears it not

EDGWORTH   All the purses and purchase I give you today by conveyance,
    bring hither to Ursula's presently. Here we will meet at night in her   35
    lodge and share. Look you choose good places for your standing i' the
    Fair when you sing, Nightingale.

URSULA   Ay, near the fullest passages, and shift 'em often.

EDGWORTH   And i' your singing, you must use your hawk's-eye nimbly,
    and fly the purse to a mark still – where 'tis worn, and o'which side   40
    – that you may gi' me the sign with your beak, or hang your head that
    way i' the tune.

URSULA   Enough, talk no more on 't. Your friendship, masters, is not now
    to begin. Drink your draught of indenture, your sup of covenant, and
    away. The Fair fills apace, company begins to come in, and I ha' ne'er   45
    a pig ready yet.

KNOCKEM   Well said! Fill the cups, and light the tobacco. Let's give fire
    i' th' works, and noble vapours!

EDGWORTH   And shall we ha' smocks, Ursula, and good whimsies, ha?

URSULA   Come, you are i' your bawdy vein! The best the Fair will afford,   50
    'Zekiel, if bawd Whit keep his word.

    [Enter Mooncalf]

    How do the pigs, Mooncalf?

MOONCALF   Very passionate, mistress, one on 'em has wept out an eye.

---

32.   *hand*] Scribe.
33.   *hand*] Cutpurse, thief.
34.   *purchase*] Booty.   *conveyance*] Sleight of hand.
38.   *fullest passages*] Most crowded thoroughfares.
40.   *fly … to a mark*] In hawking, said of a goshawk which stands over the spot where a
    covey of partridges disappeared, waiting for the falconer to start them; here, 'mark the
    location of a purse'.
41.   *beak*] Nose.
43–4.   *Your friendship … is not now to begin*] 'You are old hands in this partnership.'
44.   *draught of indenture*] Punning on the drink that celebrates the signing of an agreement
    (draft).
49.   *smocks, whimsies*] Women's undergarments, female genitalia; metonymically, whores.
53.   *passionate*] Sorrowful.   *wept out an eye*] Sign that the roasting pig is nearly ready.

Master Arthur o'Bradley is melancholy here. Nobody talks to him.
Will you any tobacco, Master Arthur?   55
OVERDO   No, boy, let my meditations alone.
MOONCALF   He's studying for an oration now.
OVERDO   [*Aside*] If I can, with this day's travail and all my policy, but
rescue this youth here out of the hands of the lewd man and the
strange woman, I will sit down at night and say with my friend Ovid,   60
'*Iamque opus exegi, quod nec Jovis ira, nec ignis, etc.*'
KNOCKEM   Here, 'Zekiel, here's a health to Ursula, and a kind vapour!
Thou hast money i'thy purse still, and store! How dost thou come by
it? Pray thee vapour thy friends some in a courteous vapour.
EDGWORTH   Half I have, Master Dan Knockem, is always at your   65
service.
OVERDO   [*Aside*] Ha, sweet nature! What goshawk would prey upon
such a lamb?
KNOCKEM   Let's see what 'tis, 'Zekiel! Count it. [*To Mooncalf*] Come,
fill him to pledge me.   70

Act 2 scene 5*

[*Enter*] *Winwife, Quarlous, to them*

WINWIFE   We are here before 'em, methinks.
QUARLOUS   All the better. We shall see 'em come in now.
LEATHERHEAD   What do you lack, gentlemen, what is 't you lack? A fine

58. *policy*] Shrewdness.
60. *strange woman*] Whore.
61. *Iamque ... etc.*] From the first two of the concluding nine lines of *Metamorphoses*] 'And now I have finished a work which neither the wrath of Jove, nor fire, [nor
sword, nor devouring time will ever destroy.]'
63. *store*] Plenty.
*   The quarrel and the hellish confusion that take over Ursula's booth achieve mock-
heroic status through the Greek myths associated with Hades. Leatherhead amid his
toys is an 'Orpheus among the beasts', a trivial version of the musician who soothed
wild animals and charmed his way into the underworld to rescue his wife; Joan Trash
is a Ceres who commodifies her daughter's image in cake; Knockem is a Neptune who
roars to cover for a pickpocket (l.24). Ursula herself takes the form of Demeter Erinnys,
a Fury enraged after being violated by Neptune. She is also the Demeter of the
Thesmophoria, or Eleusinian Mysteries: the Sow-goddess, goddess of women. Her
worshippers, like the Thesmophoriazusae in Aristophanes' play, celebrated the return of
Persephone from Hades by purifying and sacrificing pigs, roasting and devouring them
as a kind of sacrament. By the end of this scene, Ursula is associated with a figure in
Ripa's *Iconologia*, a popular Renaissance emblem book: Discordia is a female
embodiment of noisy irrational conflict, armed with a firebrand and lame in one leg.

horse? A lion? A bull? A bear? A dog or a cat? An excellent fine
Bartholomew-bird? Or an instrument? What is 't you lack?   5

QUARLOUS 'Slid! Here's Orpheus among the beasts, with his fiddle and
all!

TRASH Will you buy any comfortable bread, gentlemen?

QUARLOUS And Ceres selling her daughter's picture in ginger-work!

WINWIFE That these people should be so ignorant to think us chapmen   10
for 'em! Do we look as if we would buy gingerbread? Or hobbyhorses?

QUARLOUS Why, they know no better ware than they have, nor better
customers than come. And our very being here makes us fit to be
demanded, as well as others. Would Cokes would come! There were   15
a true customer for 'em.

KNOCKEM [*To Edgworth*] How much is 't? Thirty shillings? Who's
yonder! Ned Winwife? And Tom Quarlous, I think! Yes – Gi' me it all,
gi' me it all – Master Winwife! Master Quarlous! Will you take a pipe
of tobacco with us? – Do not discredit me now, 'Zekiel.   20

WINWIFE Do not see him! He is the roaring horse-courser. Pray thee let's
avoid him. Turn down this way.

QUARLOUS 'Slud, I'll see him and roar with him too, and he roared as
loud as Neptune. Pray thee go with me.

WINWIFE You may draw me to as likely an inconvenience, when you   25
please, as this.

QUARLOUS Go to, then, come along. We ha' nothing to do, man, but to
see sights now.

KNOCKEM Welcome, Master Quarlous and Master Winwife! Will you
take any froth and smoke with us?   30

QUARLOUS Yes, sir, but you'll pardon us if we knew not of so much
familiarity between us afore.

KNOCKEM As what, sir?

QUARLOUS To be so lightly invited to smoke and froth.

6. *Orpheus*] In Greek myth, the greatest musician who ever lived, able to calm wild beasts
with his lyre.

8. *comfortable*] Strengthening or refreshing to the bodily organs.

9. *Ceres ... ginger-work*] Ceres, the Roman Demeter, goddess of grain, lost her daughter
Persephone to Hades, god of the underworld, who abducted her for his bride. On
special pleading, Demeter recovered her for the spring and summer seasons; the rest of
the year the girl spent as queen of Hades.

10. *chapmen*] Customers.

23. *'Slud*] By God's blood.

24. *Neptune*] God of the sea, associated with horses and wild tempests.

25–6. *You ... this*] Similar to Laurel and Hardy's 'This is another fine mess you've gotten
me into'; an 'inconvenience' means impropriety, or trouble generally. Winwife expresses
distaste and reluctance.

KNOCKEM   A good vapour! Will you sit down, sir? This is old Ursula's   35
   mansion. How like you her bower? Here you may ha' your punk and
   your pig in state, sir, both piping hot.
QUARLOUS   I had rather ha' my punk cold, sir.
OVERDO   [*Aside, writing*] There's for me: punk! and pig!

   [*Ursula*] *calls within*

URSULA   What, Mooncalf! You rogue!   40
MOONCALF   By and by. The bottle is almost off, mistress. – Here, Master
   Arthur.
URSULA   [*Within*] I'll part you and your play-fellow there i' the guarded
   coat, an' you sunder not the sooner.
KNOCKEM   Master Winwife, you are proud, methinks. You do not talk   45
   nor drink. Are you proud?
WINWIFE   Not of the company I am in, sir, nor the place, I assure you.
KNOCKEM   You do not except at the company! Do you? Are you in
   vapours, sir?
MOONCALF   Nay, good Master Dan Knockem, respect my mistress'   50
   bower, as you call it. For the honour of our booth, none o' your
   vapours here.
URSULA   [*Within*] Why, you thin lean polecat you, and they have a mind
   to be i' their vapours, must you hinder 'em?

   She comes out with a fire-brand

   What did you know, vermin, if they would ha' lost a cloak or such a   55
   trifle? Must you be drawing the air of pacification here? While I am
   tormented within i' the fire, you weasel?
MOONCALF   Good mistress, 'twas in the behalf of your booth's credit that
   I spoke.
URSULA   Why? Would my booth ha' broke if they had fallen out in 't? Sir?   60
   Or would their heat ha' fired it? In, you rogue, and wipe the pigs and
   mend the fire, that they fall not, or I'll both baste and roast you till
   your eyes drop out like 'em. – Leave the bottle behind you and be
   cursed a while.

   [*Exit Mooncalf*]
   She drinks this while [as the men goad her]

QUARLOUS   Body o' the Fair! what's this? Mother o' the bawds?   65
KNOCKEM   No, she's mother o' the pigs, sir, mother o' the pigs!

38. *cold*] Because a 'hot' punk has venereal disease.
43. *guarded*] Trimmed with braid or embroidery.
60. *broke*] Fallen to pieces; gone bankrupt.
61. *wipe*] Baste.
62. *baste and roast*] Culinary puns for 'beat', 'thrash'.

WINWIFE Mother o' the Furies, I think, by her fire-brand.

QUARLOUS Nay, she is too fat to be a Fury. Sure, some walking sow of tallow!

WINWIFE An inspired vessel of kitchen-stuff! 70

QUARLOUS She'll make excellent gear for the coach-makers here in Smithfield to anoint wheels and axle-trees with.

URSULA Ay, ay, gamesters, mock a plain plump soft wench o' the suburbs, do, because she's juicy and wholesome. You must ha' your thin pinched ware, pent up i' the compass of a dog-collar – or 'twill not do 75
– that looks like a long laced conger set upright, and a green feather like fennel i' the joll on 't.

KNOCKEM Well said, Urs, my good Urs. To 'em, Urs.

QUARLOUS Is she your quagmire, Dan Knockem? Is this your bog?

NIGHTINGALE We shall have a quarrel presently. 80

KNOCKEM How? Bog? Quagmire? Foul vapours! Hum'h!

QUARLOUS Yes, he that would venture for 't, I assure him, might sink into her and be drowned a week ere any friend he had could find where he were.

WINWIFE And then he would be a fortnight weighing up again. 85

QUARLOUS 'Twere like falling into a whole shire of butter. They had need be a team of Dutchmen should draw him out.

KNOCKEM Answer 'em, Urs. Where's thy Bartholomew-wit now? Urs, thy Bartholomew-wit?

URSULA Hang 'em, rotten roguy cheaters! I hope to see 'em plagued one 90
day – poxed they are already, I am sure – with lean playhouse poultry that has the bony rump sticking out like the ace of spades, or the point of a partizan, that every rib of 'em is like the tooth of a saw, and will so grate 'em with their hips and shoulders as – take 'em altogether –
they were as good lie with a hurdle. 95

67. *Furies*] Avenging goddesses from the underworld, armed with firebrands.

68. *sow*] Female pig; drain or channel, usually of water, but here of *tallow*, liquid pork fat.

70. *inspired*] Inflated; animated by supernatural power. *vessel of kitchen-stuff*] Container of grease.

71. *gear*] Matter.

76. *laced*] Streaked. *conger*] Eel.

77. *joll*] Jowl, fish-head.

79. *quagmire ... bog*] Horse-dealers kept a corner of their yards where unsound horses could stand up to their knees in soft wet clay to disguise their deficiencies. These references also cast Ursula as an unsavoury sexual object.

85. *weighing up*] Raising, as an anchor.

87. *team*] Used of horses. *Dutchmen*] Proverbially lovers of butter.

91. *playhouse poultry*] Whores who frequented the theatre for customers.

93. *partizan*] Long-handled spear.

QUARLOUS   Out upon her, how she drips! She's able to give a man the
    sweating sickness with looking on her.

URSULA   Marry, look off, with a patch o' your face, and a dozen i' your
    breech, though they be o' scarlet, sir. I ha' seen as fine outsides as
    either o' yours bring lousy linings to the brokers ere now, twice a   100
    week!

QUARLOUS   Do you think there may be a fine new cucking-stool i' the Fair
    to be purchased? One large enough, I mean. I know there is a pond
    of capacity for her.

URSULA   For your mother, you rascal! Out, you rogue, you hedge-bird,   105
    you pimp, you pannier-man's bastard you!

QUARLOUS   Ha, ha, ha.

URSULA   Do you sneer, you dog's-head, you trendle-tail! You look as you
    were begotten atop of a cart in harvest-time, when the whelp was hot
    and eager. Go snuff after your brother's bitch, Mistress Commodity.   110
    That's the livery you wear. 'Twill be out at the elbows shortly. It's time
    you went to 't for the t'other remnant.

KNOCKEM   Peace, Urs, peace, Urs! – They'll kill the poor whale and make
    oil of her. – Pray thee go in.

URSULA   I'll see 'em poxed first, and piled and double piled.   115

WINWIFE   Let's away. Her language grows greasier than her pigs.

URSULA   Does 't so, snotty-nose? Good Lord! Are you snivelling? You
    were engendered on a she-beggar in a barn when the bald thrasher,
    your sire, was scarce warm.

WINWIFE   Pray thee, let's go.   120

QUARLOUS   No, faith. I'll stay the end of her now. I know she cannot last
    long. I find by her similes she wanes apace.

---

97. *sweating sickness*] Intense fever characterised by profuse sweating; epidemics of this
    disease in fifteenth- and sixteenth-century England were widespread and rapidly fatal.

98–9. *patch … breech*] Scabs indicating venereal disease (pox).

100. *lousy linings to the brokers*] Lice-infested underclothes to the second-hand clothing
    dealers.

102. *cucking-stool*] Close-stool on which unruly women and fraudulent tradespeople were
    tied, conveyed to a pond, and ducked, a punishment that exposed them to the jeers of
    their community.

103. *pond*] Probably Smithfield Pond, formerly used for bathing horses, but by the end of
    the sixteenth century silted up and foul through misuse.

105. *hedge-bird*] Vagrant.

106. *pannier-man*] Hawker.

108. *trendle-tail*] Mongrel with a curly tail.

110. *Commodity*] Shoddy goods sold for more than they are worth (see the note at
    Induction 138); hence, any unscrupulous business, especially prostitution.

115. *piled*] Bald, a symptom of pox (cf. 98–9); suffering from piles; threadbare, reduced to
    beggary.

URSULA   Does she so? I'll set you gone. – [*Calling to kitchen*] Gi' me my
pig-pan hither a little. – I'll scald you hence, and you will not go.

[*Exit Ursula*]

KNOCKEM   Gentlemen, these are very strange vapours! And very idle   125
vapours! I assure you.

QUARLOUS   You are a very serious ass, we assure you.

KNOCKEM   Humh! Ass? And serious? Nay, then pardon me my vapour.
I have a foolish vapour, gentlemen: any man that does vapour me the
ass, Master Quarlous –   130

QUARLOUS   What then, Master Jordan?

KNOCKEM   I do vapour him the lie.

QUARLOUS   Faith, and to any man that vapours me the lie, I do vapour
that. [*Strikes him*]

KNOCKEM   [*Striking back*] Nay then, vapours upon vapours.   135

EDGWORTH, NIGHTINGALE   'Ware the pan, the pan, the pan! She comes
with the pan, gentlemen!

Ursula comes in with the scalding-pan [*while*] *they fight. She falls
with it*

God bless the woman!

URSULA   Oh!

[*Enter Mooncalf*]

TRASH   What's the matter?   140

OVERDO   Goodly woman!

MOONCALF   Mistress!

[*Exeunt Quarlous and Winwife*]

URSULA   Curse of hell, that ever I saw these fiends. Oh! I ha' scalded my
leg, my leg, my leg, my leg! I ha' lost a limb in the service! Run for
some cream and salad oil quickly!   145

[*Mooncalf kneels to see the wound*]

Are you underpeering, you baboon? – Rip off my hose, an' you be
men, men, men!

MOONCALF   Run you for some cream, good Mother Joan. I'll look to
your basket.

123. *set you gone*] Get you going.
132. *vapour him the lie*] To give someone the lie, or call him a liar, was a sure prelude to
a *duello* (see *Alch* 3.4.25) or a brawl.
146. *underpeering*] Looking up my skirts.

[*Exit Trash*]

LEATHERHEAD   Best sit up i' your chair, Ursula. Help, gentlemen.   150

[*They lift her into her chair*]

KNOCKEM   Be of good cheer, Urs. Thou hast hindered me the currying
of a couple of stallions here that abused the good race-bawd o'
Smithfield. 'Twas time for 'em to go.

NIGHTINGALE   I'faith, when the pan came, they had made you run else.
– [*To Edgworth*] This had been a fine time for purchase, if you had   155
ventured.

EDGWORTH   Not a whit. These fellows were too fine to carry money.

KNOCKEM   Nightingale, get some help to carry her leg out o'the air. Take
off her shoes. – Body o'me, she has the mallanders, the scratches, the
crown scab, and the quitter bone i' the t'other leg.   160

URSULA   Oh! The pox, why do you put me in mind o' my leg thus, to make
it prick and shoot? Would you ha' me i' the hospital afore my time?

KNOCKEM   Patience, Urs, take a good heart. 'Tis but a blister as big as a
windgall. I'll take it away with the white of an egg, a little honey, and
hog's grease, ha' thy pasterns well rolled, and thou shalt pace again by   165
tomorrow. I'll tend thy booth and look to thy affairs the while. Thou
shalt sit i' thy chair and give directions, and shine Ursa Major.

[*Exeunt Knockem and Mooncalf with Ursula in her chair*]

---

151. *currying*] Thrashing the hide, dressing-down.
152. *race-bawd*] Mother of all bawds.
155. *purchase*] Theft.
157. *fine*] Smart.
159–60. *mallanders ... quitter bone*] Diseases afflicting horses' legs: *mallanders*, dry hard
scabs with ingrown hairs behind the knee; *scratches*, scabby rifts on the pastern
(ankle); *crown scab*, running sore in the hoof; *quitter bone*, hard swelling on the inside
of the foot.
162. *hospital*] St Bartholomew's, just east of Smithfield. Going to the hospital in those days
meant certain death.
164. *windgall*] Soft tumour on a horse's leg.
164–5. *white ... grease*] A professional farrier's remedy.
165. *rolled*] Bandaged.
167. *Ursa Major*] Constellation, the Great Bear.

Act 2 scene 6*

OVERDO   These are the fruits of bottle-ale and tobacco! The foam of the one and the fumes of the other! Stay, young man, and despise not the wisdom of these few hairs that are grown grey in care of thee.

EDGWORTH   Nightingale, stay a little. Indeed I'll hear some o' this!

[Enter] Cokes [first, then] Wasp, Mistress Overdo, Grace

COKES   Come, Numps, come. Where are you? Welcome into the Fair,   5
    Mistress Grace.

EDGWORTH   *[To Nightingale]* 'Slight, he will call company, you shall
    see, and put us into doings presently.

OVERDO   Thirst not after that frothy liquor, ale, for who knows, when he
    openeth the stopple, what may be in the bottle? Hath not a snail, a   10
    spider, yea, a newt, been found there? Thirst not after it, youth. Thirst
    not after it.

COKES   This is a brave fellow, Numps. Let's hear him.

WASP   'Sblood, how brave is he? In a guarded coat? You were best truck
    with him, e'en strip and truck presently. It will become you. Why will   15
    you hear him – because he is an ass and may be akin to the Cokeses?

COKES   O, good Numps!

OVERDO   Neither do thou lust after that tawny weed, tobacco.

COKES   Brave words!

OVERDO   Whose complexion is like the Indian's that vents it!   20

COKES   Are they not brave words, sister?

OVERDO   And who can tell if, before the gathering and making up thereof,
    the alligator hath not pissed thereon?

WASP   'Heart, let 'em be brave words, as brave as they will! And they were
    all the brave words in a country, how then? Will you away yet? Ha'   25
    you enough on him? Mistress Grace, come you away, I pray you, be
    not you accessory. If you do lose your licence or somewhat else, sir,

---

*   Overdo's 'sermon' against tobacco, aside from supporting one of King James's pet peeves, connects several strands of plot. It illustrates Cokes's complete immersion in the entertainment of the moment (repeated again in 3.5, 4.2, and 5.4); Edgworth's skill in theft (repeated in 3.5, 4.2, and 4.4); Overdo's tendency to suffer the consequence (3.5 and 4.1); and Wasp's violent irascibility (3.5 and 4.4).

  8. *doings*]   Business.

13. *brave*]   Loosely a term of praise, 'capital' or 'excellent'.

14. *brave*]   Finely dressed. Wasp is sarcastic.   *guarded*]   Trimmed with braid or embroidery.

15. *truck*]   Make an exchange or deal, usually for something unworthy, like Overdo's coat.

20. *vents*]   Vends, sells.

23. *alligator*]   'Alligarta' in F.

with list'ning to his fables, say Numps is a witch, with all my heart,
do, say so.

COKES   Avoid i' your satin doublet, Numps.   30

OVERDO   The creeping venom of which subtle serpent, as some late
writers affirm, neither the cutting of the perilous plant, nor the drying
of it, nor the lighting or burning, can any way persway or assuage.

COKES   Good, i' faith! Is 't not, sister?

OVERDO   Hence it is that the lungs of the tobacconist are rotted, the liver   35
spotted, the brain smoked like the backside of the pig-woman's booth
here, and the whole body within black as her pan you saw e'en now
without.

COKES   [*To Edgworth*]   A fine similitude, that, sir! Did you see the pan?

EDGWORTH   Yes, sir.   40

OVERDO   Nay, the hole in the nose here of some tobacco-takers, or the
third nostril (if I may so call it) which makes that they can vent the
tobacco out like the ace of clubs, or rather the flower-de-lys, is caused
from the tobacco, the mere tobacco! When the poor innocent pox,
having nothing to do there, is miserably and most unconscionably   45
slandered.

COKES   Who would ha' missed this, sister?

MISTRESS OVERDO   Not anybody but Numps.

COKES   He does not understand.

EDGWORTH   [*Aside*]   Nor you feel.   50

   He picketh his purse

COKES   What would you have, sister, of a fellow that knows nothing
but a basket-hilt and an old fox in 't? The best music i' the Fair will
not move a log.

EDGWORTH   [*Slipping purse to Nightingale*]   In to Ursula, Nightingale,
and carry her comfort. See it told. This fellow was sent to us by   55
fortune for our first fairing.

28. *witch*]   Because he foresaw the future.
30. *Avoid*]   Go away, clear out.
31–2. *late writers*]   Recent authors of anti-smoking pamphlets, such as James I, whose
   Counterblast to Tobacco was printed in 1604.
33. *persway*]   Diminish.
35. *tobacconist*]   Smoker.
39. *similitude*]   Comparison made for a moral purpose.
41–2. *hole ... third nostril*]   An effect of syphilis.
42. *vent*]   Exhale.
52. *basket-hilt*]   Handle of a sword, with a basket-like protection for the hand.   *fox*]
   Blade of a sword.
55. *told*]   Counted.

[*Exit Nightingale*]

OVERDO   But what speak I of the diseases of the body, children of the
Fair?

COKES   That's to us, sister. Brave, i'faith!

OVERDO   Hark, O you sons and daughters of Smithfield! And hear what   60
malady it doth the mind. It causeth swearing, it causeth swaggering,
it causeth snuffling and snarling, and now and then a hurt.

MISTRESS OVERDO   He hath something of Master Overdo, methinks,
brother.

COKES   So methought, sister, very much of my brother Overdo. And 'tis   65
when he speaks.

OVERDO   Look into any angle o' the town – the Straits or the Bermudas
– where the quarrelling lesson is read, and how do they entertain the
time but with bottle-ale and tobacco? The lecturer is o' one side and
his pupils o' the other, but the seconds are still bottle-ale and tobacco,   70
for which the lecturer reads and the novices pay. Thirty pound a week
in bottle-ale! Forty in tobacco! And ten more in ale again. Then for a
suit to drink in, so much, and – that being slavered – so much for
another suit, and then a third suit, and a fourth suit! And still the
bottle-ale slavereth and the tobacco stinketh!   75

WASP   Heart of a madman! Are you rooted here? Will you never away?
What can any man find out in this bawling fellow to grow here for?
He is a full handful higher sin' he heard him. Will you fix here? and
set up a booth? Sir?

OVERDO   I will conclude briefly –   80

WASP   Hold your peace, you roaring rascal. I'll run my head i' your chaps
else. [*To Cokes*] You were best build a booth and entertain him,
make your will, and you say the word, and him your heir! Heart, I

62. *snuffling*] Sniffing with contempt.

67. *angle*] Corner.   *Straits*] Triangle of alleys and courts at the east end of the Strand,
then full of disreputable tenements and thieves.   *Bermudas*] Popular name for a
warren of courts and lanes just north of the west end of the Strand near the bottom of
St Martin's Lane. Once the haunt of whores, bullies, and vagrants, the site was cleared
in 1829 to create Trafalgar Square.

68. *the quarrelling lesson*] Another 'similitude', ludicrously comparing the duelling academies popular among the gentry with the brawling that erupts among the riff-raff in
slums.   *read*] Taught.   *entertain*] While away.

70. *seconds*] Supports for an activity.

75. *slavereth*] Soils with spittle and sweat.

81. *chaps*] Mouth.

82. *entertain*] Maintain, retain or hire.

never knew one taken with a mouth of a peck afore. By this light, I'll
carry you away o' my back, and you will not come.   85

He gets him up on pickaback

COKES   Stay, Numps, stay! Set me down! I ha' lost my purse, Numps! O,
my purse! One o' my fine purses is gone.

MISTRESS OVERDO   Is 't indeed, brother?

COKES   Ay, as I am an honest man, would I were an arrant rogue else! A
plague of all roguy damned cutpurses for me!   90

WASP   Bless 'em with all my heart, with all my heart, do you see! Now, as
I am no infidel that I know of, I am glad on 't. Ay, I am – here's my
witness! – do you see, sir? I did not tell you of his fables, I? No, no,
I am a dull malt-horse, I, I know nothing. Are you not justly served
i' your conscience now? Speak i' your conscience. Much good do you   95
with all my heart, and his good heart that has it, with all my heart
again.

EDGWORTH   [*Aside*] This fellow is very charitable. Would he had a purse
too! But I must not be too bold all at a time.

COKES   Nay, Numps, it is not my best purse.   100

WASP   Not your best! Death! Why should it be your worst? Why should
it be any, indeed, at all? Answer me to that. Gi'me a reason from you
why it should be any!

COKES   Nor my gold, Numps. I ha' that yet. Look here else, sister. [*Shows
Mistress Overdo his other purse*]

WASP   Why so, there's all the feeling he has!   105

MISTRESS OVERDO   I pray you, have a better care of that, brother.

COKES   Nay, so I will, I warrant you. Let him catch this that catch can. I
would fain see him get this, look you here.

WASP   So, so, so, so, so, so, so, so! Very good.

COKES   I would ha' him come again, now, and but offer at it. Sister, will   110
you take notice of a good jest? I will put it just where th' other was,
and if we ha' good luck, you shall see a delicate fine trap to catch the
cutpurse nibbling.

EDGWORTH   [*Aside*] Faith, and he'll try ere you be out o' the Fair.

COKES   Come, Mistress Grace, prithee be not melancholy for my mis-   115
chance. Sorrow wi' not keep it, sweetheart.

GRACE   I do not think on 't, sir.

COKES   'Twas but a little scurvy white money, hang it. It may hang the

84. *of a peck*] Of two gallons' capacity.
85.1 *pickaback*] *Pick-packe* in F.
94. *malt-horse*] Heavy horse that pulls a brewer's dray.
110. *offer*] Make an attempt.
116. *wi' not keep it*] Proverbially, will not bring it back.
118. *white money*] Silver.

cutpurse one day. I ha' gold left to gi' thee a fairing yet, as hard as the
world goes. Nothing angers me but that nobody here looked like a   120
cutpurse, unless 'twere Numps.

WASP   How? I? I look like a cutpurse? Death! Your sister's a cutpurse! And
your mother and father and all your kin were cutpurses! And here is
a rogue is the bawd o' the cutpurses, whom I will beat to begin with.

They speak all together, and Wasp beats the Justice

COKES   Numps, Numps!   125
MISTRESS OVERDO   Good Master Humphrey!
OVERDO   Hold thy hand, child of wrath and heir of anger. Make it not
Childermas Day in thy fury, or the feast of the French Bartholomew,
parent of the Massacre.

WASP   You are the patrico! Are you? The patriarch of the cutpurses? You   130
share, sir, they say. Let them share this with you. Are you i' your hot
fit of preaching again? I'll cool you.

OVERDO   Murder, murder, murder!

[*Exeunt*]

ACT 3

Act 3 scene 1*

[*Enter*] *Whit, Haggis, Bristle; Leatherhead* [*in his booth, and*] *Trash*
[*with her basket nearby*]

WHIT   Nay, 'tish all gone now! Dish 'tish phen tou vilt not be phitin call,
Master Offisher! Phat ish a man te better to lishen out noyshes for tee,

---

128.   *Childermas Day*] 28 December, Holy Innocents' Day, commemorating the Slaughter
of the Innocents.   *French Bartholomew*] The massacre of the Huguenots in France on
St Bartholomew's Day, 1572.

130.   *patrico*] Thieves' cant for a hedge-priest, an illiterate or vagabond parson of uncertain
official standing.

*   Whit speaks in Elizabethan stage-Irish, a broader treatment of dialect than that
suggested by the watchmen's names. Haggis's Scottish burr and Davy Bristle's Welsh lilt
add to the cacophony of street cries and the range of London and suburban accents of
various classes already on stage. Shakespeare created a similar effect in the voices of his
captains – the Welsh Fluellen, Irish MacMorris, and Scot Jamy – among various English
and French accents in *Henry V.* Whit's opening complaint about the tardiness of the
watchmen relates to his sideline as a spy and police informer. See also 4.4.134.1–2 and
151–9.

1.   *'tish*] 'Tis.   *phitin*] Within.

and tou art in anoder 'orld, being very shuffishient noyshes and
gallantsh too? One o' their brabblesh would have fed ush all dish
fortnight, but tou art so bushy about beggersh still, tou hast no   5
leishure to intend shentlemen, and 't be.

HAGGIS   Why, I told you, Davy Bristle.

BRISTLE   Come, come, you told me a pudding, Toby Haggis. A matter of
nothing, I am sure it came to nothing! You said, 'Let's go to Ursula's',
indeed, but then you met the man with the monsters, and I could not   10
get you from him. An old fool, not leave seeing yet?

HAGGIS   Why, who would ha' thought anybody would ha' quarrelled so
early? Or that the ale o' the Fair would ha' been up so soon.

WHIT   Phy? Phat o'clock tost tou tink it ish, man?

HAGGIS   I cannot tell.   15

WHIT   Tou art a vishe vatchman i' te mean teeme.

HAGGIS   Why? Should the watch go by the clock, or the clock by the
watch, I pray?

BRISTLE   One should go by another, if they did well.

WHIT   Tou art right now! Phen didst tou ever know or hear of a   20
shuffishient vatchman, but he did tell the clock, phat bushiness soever
he had?

BRISTLE   Nay, that's most true, a sufficient watchman knows what
o'clock it is.

WHIT   Shleeping or vaking! Ash well as te clock himshelf or te jack dat 25
shtrikes him!

BRISTLE   Let's inquire of Master Leatherhead or Joan Trash here.
– [*Calling across the stage*] Master Leatherhead, do you hear,
Master Leatherhead?

WHIT   If it be a Ledderhead, tish a very tick Ledderhead, tat sho mush   30
noish vill not piersh him.

LEATHERHEAD   I have a little business now. Good friends, do not trouble
me.

WHIT   Phat? Because o' ty wrought neetcap and ty phelvet sherkin, man?
Phy? I have sheen tee in ty ledder sherkin ere now, Mashter o' de   35
hobbyhorses, as bushy and as stately as tou sheem'st to be.

TRASH   Why, what an' you have, Captain Whit? He has his choice of

4. *brabblesh*] Brabbles, brawls.
5. *bushy*] Busy.
6. *intend*] Pay attention to.
8. *pudding*] A load of tripe, punning on 'haggis'.
10. *monsters*] Deformed creatures such as the five-legged bull mentioned at 3.6.6–7 and
5.4.75, and in *Alch* 5.1.7–9.
16. *vishe*] Wise.
25. *jack*] Mechanical striking figure on a clock.
34. *wrought neetcap*] Wrought or embroidered nightcap.

jerkins, you may see by that, and his caps too, I assure you, when he
pleases to be either sick or employed.

LEATHERHEAD   God a mercy, Joan, answer for me.   40

WHIT   [*To the watchmen*] Away, be not sheen i'my company. Here be
shentlemen and men of vorship.

[*Exeunt Haggis, Bristle*]

Act 3 scene 2*

[*Enter*] Quarlous, Winwife

QUARLOUS   We had wonderful ill luck to miss this prologue o' the purse,
but the best is, we shall have five acts of him ere night: he'll be
spectacle enough! I'll answer for't.

WHIT   O Creesh! Duke Quarlous, how dosht tou? Tou dosht not know
me, I fear? I am te vishesht man, but Justish Overdo, in all   5
Bartholomew Fair, now. Gi' me twelvepence from tee, I vill help tee
to a vife vorth forty marks for't, and 't be.

QUARLOUS   Away, rogue, pimp, away!

WHIT   And she shall show tee as fine cut-'ork for't in her shmock too, as
tou cansht vish, i' faith. Vilt tou have her, vorshipful Vinvife? I vill   10
help tee to her here, be an't be, in te pig-quarter, gi' me ty twel'pence
from tee.

WINWIFE   Why, there's twel'pence. Pray thee wilt thou be gone?

WHIT   Tou art a vorthy man and a vorshipful man still.

QUARLOUS   Get you gone, rascal.   15

WHIT   I do mean it, man. Prinsh Quarlous, if tou hasht need on me, tou
shalt find me here at Ursula's. I vill see phat ale and punk ish i' te
pigshty for tee, bless ty good vorship!

41.   *Away ... company*] Whit is anxious to preserve his cover.

*   Class warfare underlies relations between hucksters and their customers. Whit
addresses the gentlemen by name, and unctuously offers his services as the best pimp in
the fair. Quarlous rejects him rudely, and Winwife bribes him to disappear; these face-
saving tactics mean neither has to admit knowing the man. Knockem plays the hearty
host welcoming the puritan party to the pig-booth with sham solicitousness; Whit
characteristically attempts to seduce Win into satisfying her appetite. Busy pompously
ignores their words, seduced more directly by the smell of roast pork. When Ursula
objects to having only puritan guests who she assumes will not consume enough for
profit, Knockem drops his *bonhomie* and coldly sums them up as 'right hypocrites,
good gluttons'.

4.   *Creesh*] Christ.

5.   *vishest*] Wisest, most knowing.   *but*] Excepting.

9.   *cut-'ork*] Cut-work, openwork embroidery or lace; also crudely punning on 'cunt-
work', the whore's expertise.

[*Whit lounges by the pig-booth*]

QUARLOUS   Look! Who comes here! John Littlewit!
WINWIFE   And his wife and my widow, her mother: the whole family.   20

[*Enter*] *Busy, John* [*Littlewit*], *Purecraft, Win*

QUARLOUS   'Slight, you must gi' 'em all fairings now!
WINWIFE   Not I, I'll not see 'em.
QUARLOUS   They are going a-feasting. What schoolmaster's that is with
   'em?
WINWIFE   That's my rival, I believe, the baker!   25
BUSY   So, walk on in the middle way, fore-right. Turn neither to the right
   hand nor to the left. Let not your eyes be drawn aside with vanity, nor
   your ear with noises.
QUARLOUS   O, I know him by that start!
LEATHERHEAD   What do you lack? What do you buy, pretty mistress! A   30
   fine hobbyhorse to make your son a tilter? A drum to make him a
   soldier? A fiddle to make him a reveller? What is 't you lack? Little
   dogs for your daughters! Or babies, male or female?
BUSY   Look not toward them, harken not. The place is Smithfield, or the
   field of smiths, the grove of hobbyhorses and trinkets: the wares are   35
   the wares of devils. And the whole Fair is the shop of Satan! They are
   hooks and baits, very baits, that are hung out on every side to catch
   you and to hold you, as it were, by the gills and by the nostrils as the
   fisher doth. Therefore, you must not look, nor turn toward them –
   The heathen man could stop his ears with wax against the harlot o'   40
   the sea. Do you the like with your fingers against the bells of the
   Beast.
WINWIFE   What flashes comes from him!
QUARLOUS   O, he has those of his oven! A notable hot baker 'twas, when
   he plied the peel. He is leading his flock into the Fair now.   45
WINWIFE   Rather driving 'em to the pens, for he will let 'em look upon
   nothing.

26.   *fore-right*] Straight ahead.
31.   *tilter*] Jouster; fornicator (from 'tilth', ploughing).
32.   *reveller*] Law student at the Inns of Court.
35.   *field of smiths*] Incorrect etymology. The real derivation is from 'Smoothfield', an open
   area in front of St Bartholomew's Church, paved over in 1614.
40–41.   *The heathen man ... sea*] Ulysses stopped his men's ears with wax and had himself
   tied to the mast so that he could hear the lure of the sirens' song without sailing closer
   and thus perishing on the rocks. Busy has confused the details.
41.   *bells*] Puritans opposed church bells as papist.
45.   *peel*] Long-handled baker's shovel for moving food in and out of the oven.

[Enter] Knockem

KNOCKEM   Gentlewomen, the weather's hot! Whither walk you? Have a
care o' your fine velvet caps. The Fair is dusty. Take a sweet delicate
booth with boughs here i' the way, and cool yourselves i' the shade,   50
you and your friends.

Littlewit is gazing at the sign, which is The Pig's Head with a large
writing under it

The best pig and bottle-ale i' the Fair, sir. Old Ursula is cook, there
you may read: the pig's head speaks it. Poor soul, she has had a
stringhalt, the maryhinchco, but she's prettily amended.

WHIT   A delicate show-pig, little mistress, with shweet sauce and crack-   55
ling, like de bay-leaf i' de fire, la! Tou shalt ha' de clean side o' de
table-clot and dy glass vashed with phatersh of Dame Annessh Clear.

LITTLEWIT   This's fine, verily: 'Here be the best pigs, and she does roast
'em as well as ever she did,' the pig's head says.

KNOCKEM   Excellent, excellent, mistress, with fire o' juniper and rose-   60
mary branches! The oracle of The Pig's Head, that, sir.

PURECRAFT   Son, were you not warned of the vanity of the eye? Have you
forgot the wholesome admonition so soon?

LITTLEWIT   Good mother, how shall we find a pig if we do not look about
for't? Will it run off o' the spit into our mouths, think you? As in   65
Lubberland? And cry 'Wee, wee'?

BUSY   No, but your mother, religiously wise, conceiveth it may offer itself
by other means to the sense, as by way of steam, which I think it doth
here in this place –

Busy scents after it like a hound

Huh, huh! – yes, it doth. And it were a sin of obstinacy, great   70
obstinacy, high and horrible obstinacy, to decline or resist the good
titillation of the famelic sense, which is the smell. Therefore, be bold

49. *delicate*] Delightful, beautiful.
54. *stringhalt, the maryhinchco*] Synonyms for sudden painful twitching in a horse's hind
legs, making them unable to bear weight.
55. *delicate*] Succulent. *show-pig*] Sow-pig.
57. *phatersh of Dame Annessh Clear*] A spring in Hoxton named after a rich widow, Annis
(Agnes) Clare, who drowned herself there, *c.* 1300, after a disastrous second marriage
to a courtier who wasted her fortune and left her in poverty.
66. *Lubberland*] Mythical land of luxury and leisure, also known as Cockaigne.
70. *Huh, huh*] Aristophanes has the sycophant in *Wealth* also snort loudly as he sniffs out
a dinner.
72. *famelic*] Exciting hunger (Latin, *famelicus*).

– huh, huh, huh! – follow the scent. Enter the tents of the unclean for
once, and satisy your wife's frailty. Let your frail wife be satisfied.   75
Your zealous mother and my suffering self will also be satisfied.

LITTLEWIT   Come, Win, as good winny here as go farther and see
nothing.

BUSY   We scape so much of the other vanities by our early ent'ring.

PURECRAFT   It is an edifying consideration.   80

WIN   This is scurvy that we must come into the Fair and not look on 't.

LITTLEWIT   Win, have patience, Win. I'll tell you more anon.

KNOCKEM   [*Calling into the booth*] Mooncalf, entertain within there the
best pig i' the booth, a porklike pig. These are Banbury bloods o' the
sincere stud come a-pig-hunting. – Whit, wait, Whit, look to your   85
charge.

BUSY   A pig prepare presently, let a pig be prepared to us.

[*Exeunt Busy, Purecraft, Littlewit, Win into the pig-booth, escorted by
   Whit*]
[*Enter*] *Mooncalf, Ursula*

MOONCALF   'Slight, who be these?

URSULA   Is this the good service, Jordan, you'd do me?

KNOCKEM   Why, Urs? Why, Urs? Thou'lt ha' vapours i' thy leg again   90
presently. Pray thee go in. 'T may turn to the scratches else.

URSULA   Hang your vapours – they are stale and stink like you. Are these
the guests o' the game you promised to fill my pit withal today?

KNOCKEM   Ay, what ail they, Urs?

URSULA   Ail they? They are all sippers, sippers o' the City. They look as   95
they would not drink off two penn'orth of bottle-ale amongst 'em.

MOONCALF   A body may read that i' their small printed ruffs.

KNOCKEM   Away, thou art a fool, Urs, and thy Mooncalf too, i' your
ignorant vapours now! Hence! Good guests, I say, right hypocrites,
good gluttons. In, and set a couple o' pigs o' the board, and half a   100
dozen of the biggest bottles afore 'em, and call Whit. I do not love to

---

74–5. *Enter ... satisfied*] Busy's lines are inadvertently equivocal, but ironically suited to
   Ursula's double function of serving both pig and punk (cf. 2.5.36 7).
76. *suffering*] Enduring hardship for the sake of religion (puritan cant).
77. *winny*] Stay.
80. *edifying*] Morally enlightening (puritan cant).
85. *sincere stud*] Morally uncorrupted breed; that is, puritans.
91. *scratches*] Scabby rifts on the pastern (ankle).
94. *what ail they?*] What's wrong with them?
95. *sippers*] Fastidious types.
97. *small printed ruffs*] Puritans wore very modest collars pressed into precise upright folds
   without the aid of starch or wires.

hear innocents abused. Fine ambling hypocrites! And a stone-puritan with a sorrel head and beard! Good-mouthed gluttons, two to a pig! Away!

[*Exit Mooncalf*]

URSULA   Are you sure they are such?   105
KNOCKEM   O' the right breed. Thou shalt try 'em by the teeth, Urs. Where's this Whit?

[*Enter Whit*]

WHIT   *Behold, man, and see what a worthy man am ee!*
    With the fury of my sword and the shaking of my beard,
    I will make ten thousand men afeard.   110
KNOCKEM   Well said, brave Whit! In, and fear the ale out o'the bottles into the bellies of the brethren and the sisters, drink to the cause, and pure vapours.

[*Exeunt Whit, Knockem, Ursula*]

QUARLOUS   My roarer is turned tapster, methinks. Now were a fine time for thee, Winwife, to lay aboard thy widow. Thou'lt never be master   115
of a better season or place. She that will venture herself into the Fair and a pig-box will admit any assault, be assured of that.
WINWIFE   I love not enterprises of that suddenness, though.
QUARLOUS   I'll warrant thee, then, no wife out o' the widow's hundred. If I had but as much title to her as to have breathed once on that   120
straight stomacher of hers, I would now assure myself to carry her yet, ere she went out of Smithfield. Or she should carry me, which were

102. *stone-puritan*] Male puritan, by analogy to 'stone-horse', stallion. Since 'stone' means 'testicle', the term implies an aggressive sex-drive.
103. *sorrel*] Chestnut (of horses).
108–10. Whit imitates the braggart's doggerel in the Whitsun folk-plays of St George.
111. *fear*] Frighten.
112. *the cause*] The puritan cause.
113. *pure*] Puritan.
115. *lay aboard*] Attack; nautical term for bringing one's ship alongside another for boarding.
117. *pig-box*] Pig-booth.
119. *the widow's hundred*] Equating the eligible widow with desirable property and jurisdiction, a 'hundred' being a subsection of the English shire having its own court.
120. *title*] Claim; evidence of the legal right to the possession of property.
121. *stomacher*] Stiff ornamental covering over the chest and the abdomen, worn to fill in the front opening of garments.   *carry*] Win, especially in face of opposition or argument.
122. *carry*] Bear Quarlous's weight during copulation.

the fitter sight, I confess. But you are a modest undertaker by circumstances and degrees. Come, 'tis disease in thee, not judgment. I should offer at all together. – Look, here's the poor fool again that was stung by the wasp ere while.   125

Act 3 scene 3*

[Enter] Justice [Overdo]

OVERDO   I will make no more orations shall draw on these tragical conclusions. And I begin now to think that, by a spice of collateral justice, Adam Overdo deserved this beating; for I, the said Adam, was one cause (a by-cause) why the purse was lost, and my wife's brother's purse too, which they know not of yet. But I shall make very good   5
mirth with it at supper – that will be the sport – and put my little friend Master Humphrey Wasp's choler quite out of countenance, when, sitting at the upper end o' my table, as I use, and drinking to my brother Cokes and Mistress Alice Overdo, as I will, my wife, for their good affection to old Bradley, I deliver to 'em it was I that was   10
cudgelled and show 'em the marks. To see what bad events may peep out o'the tail of good purposes! The care I had of that civil young man I took fancy to this morning – and have not left it yet – drew me to that exhortation, which drew the company, indeed, which drew the cutpurse, which drew the money, which drew my brother Cokes his   15
loss, which drew on Wasp's anger, which drew on my beating: a pretty gradation! And they shall ha' it i' their dish, i' faith, at night for fruit. I love to be merry at my table. I had thought once, at one special blow he ga' me, to have revealed myself! But then – I thank thee, fortitude – I remembered that a wise man (and who is ever so great a part o'the   20

123. *undertaker*] One who tackles a task or challenge.

124. *circumstances*] Roundabout methods.

125. *offer at*] Make a direct assault, gamble aggressively on winning.

*   In Overdo's private oration, Jonson wittily creates a bridge between the previous scene and the scenes that follow. While the puritan party is at table in Ursula's booth, Overdo imagines himself regaling his own table at home with the story of how his family beat him at the fair. Overdo ironically attributes his misfortune to his altruistic desire to protect 'that civil young man' Edgworth from corruption, and associates himself with all the martyrs of Smithfield in his willingness to endure even more suffering for his faith in justice and the commonwealth. Thanks to Edgworth, Overdo does suffer more in 3.5 and 4.1.

1.   *draw on*] Attract.

2.   *spice*] Kind.   *collateral*] Accompanying, ranking side by side with.

4.   *by-cause*] Secondary or concealed cause.

20–21. *and who ... himself*] And whoever plays a part in the running of the state.

commonwealth in himself) for no particular disaster ought to aban-
don a public good design. The husbandman ought not, for one
unthankful year, to forsake the plough. The shepherd ought not,
for one scabbed sheep, to throw by his tar-box. The pilot ought
not, for one leak i' the poop, to quit the helm, nor the alderman ought   25
not, for one custard more at a meal, to give up his cloak. The
constable ought not to break his staff and forswear the watch for one
roaring night, nor the piper o'the parish (*ut parvis componere magna
solebam*) to put up his pipes for one rainy Sunday. These are certain
knocking conclusions, out of which I am resolved, come what come   30
can – come beating, come imprisonment, come infamy, come banish-
ment, nay, come the rack, come the hurdle, welcome all – I will not
discover who I am till my due time, and yet still all shall be, as I said
ever, in justice' name and the king's, and for the commonwealth.

[*Exit*] *Overdo*

WINWIFE   What, does he talk to himself and act so seriously? Poor fool!   35
QUARLOUS   No matter what. Here's fresher argument; intend that.

Act 3 scene 4*

[*Enter*] *Cokes, Mistress Overdo, Grace,* [*followed by*] *Wasp* [*carrying
Fair purchases*]

21. *particular*] Personal.
24. *tar-box*] Container for tar-salve used to cure sores on sheep.
25. *poop*] Stern of a ship.
26. *one custard more*] An extra guest. Traditionally, open pies were served at civic dinners;
     cf. *Alch* 3.2.90.   *cloak*] Representing his official standing.
27. *roaring*] Tempestuous, or rowdy.
28. *piper o' the parish*] Piper hired by the parish to play at community functions.   *ut . . .
     solebam*] 'As I was accustomed to comparing great things to small ones', slightly
     revised from Virgil, *Eclogues* 1.23, where *sic* [= thus] appears instead of *ut* [= as].
29. *knocking*] Hard-hitting, decisive.
32. *hurdle*] A frame or sledge on which, until 1870, traitors were dragged through the
     streets to their execution.
35. *What*] Why.
36. *intend*] Pay attention to.
*   Cokes represents the inherent childishness Jonson ascribes to those who look with their
     senses instead of their understanding: 'What petty things they are, we wonder at! Like
     children, that esteem every trifle, and prefer a fairing before their fathers: what
     difference is between us and them, but that we are dearer fools, coxcombs, at a higher
     rate?' (*Disc*, Parfitt 1975: p. 417).

COKES   Come, Mistress Grace, come, sister, here's more fine sights yet, i'
 faith. God's lid, where's Numps?
LEATHERHEAD   What do you lack, gentlemen? What is 't you buy? Fine
 rattles! Drums? Babies? Little dogs? And birds for ladies? What do
 you lack?   5
COKES   Good honest Numps, keep afore. I am so afraid thou'lt lose
 somewhat. My heart was at my mouth when I missed thee.
WASP   You were best buy a whip i' your hand to drive me.
COKES   Nay, do not mistake, Numps, thou art so apt to mistake. I would
 but watch the goods. Look you now, the treble fiddle was e'en almost   10
 like to be lost.
WASP   Pray you take heed you lose not yourself. Your best way were e'en
 get up and ride for more surety. Buy a token's worth of great pins to
 fasten yourself to my shoulder.
LEATHERHEAD   What do you lack, gentlemen? Fine purses, pouches,   15
 pincases, pipes? What is't you lack? A pair o' smiths to wake you i'
 the morning? Or a fine whistling bird?
COKES   Numps, here be finer things than any we ha' bought, by odds! And
 more delicate horses, a great deal! Good Numps, stay, and come
 hither.   20
WASP   Will you scourse with him? You are in Smithfield, you may fit
 yourself with a fine easy-going street-nag for your saddle again'
 Michaelmas term, do. Has he ne'er a little odd cart for you to make
 a caroche on i' the country, with four pied hobbyhorses? Why the
 measles should you stand here with your train, cheaping of dogs,   25
 birds, and babies? You ha' no children to bestow 'em on? Ha' you?
COKES   No, but again' I ha' children, Numps, that's all one.
WASP   Do, do, do, do! How many shall you have, think you? An' I were
 as you, I'd buy for all my tenants too. They are a kind o' civil savages
 that will part with their children for rattles, pipes, and knives. You   30
 were best buy a hatchet or two, and truck with 'em.
COKES   Good Numps, hold that little tongue o' thine, and save it a labour.
 I am resolute Bat, thou know'st.
WASP   A resolute fool, you are, I know, and a very sufficient coxcomb.

10. *treble fiddle*] Violin, the string instrument playing the highest pitch
16. *a pair o' smiths*] Alarm clock with a striking device.
21. *scourse*] Bargain.
22. *again'*] In preparation for.
24. *caroche*] Luxurious town carriage. Wasp is ironic.
25. *cheaping of*] Haggling for.
27. *again'*] Anticipating when.
29. *a kind o' civil savages*] The sort of ignoramuses assumed to be standard in lower-class
 life; tractable brutes.
31. *truck*] Deal.

With all my heart – nay, you have it, sir, and you be angry – turd i'   35
your teeth, twice, if I said it not once afore, and much good do you!

WINWIFE   Was there ever such a self-affliction? And so impertinent?

QUARLOUS   Alas! His care will go near to crack him. Let's in and comfort
him.

WASP   Would I had been set i' the ground, all but the head on me, and had   40
my brains bowled at, or threshed out, when first I underwent this
plague of a charge!

QUARLOUS   How now, Numps! Almost tired i' your protectorship?
Overparted? Overparted?

WASP   Why, I cannot tell, sir, it may be I am. Does 't grieve you?   45

QUARLOUS   No, I swear does't not, Numps, to satisfy you.

WASP   'Numps'? 'Sblood, you are fine and familiar! How long ha' we been
acquainted, I pray you?

QUARLOUS   I think it may be remembered, Numps, that? 'Twas since
morning, sure.   50

WASP   Why, I hope I know 't well enough, sir. I did not ask to be told.

QUARLOUS   No? Why then?

WASP   It's no matter why. You see with your eyes now what I said to you
today? You'll believe me another time?

QUARLOUS   Are you removing the Fair, Numps?   55

WASP   A pretty question! And a very civil one! Yes, faith, I ha' my lading,
you see, or shall have anon. You may know whose beast I am by my
burden. If the pannier-man's jack were ever better known by his loins
of mutton, I'll be flayed and feed dogs for him when his time comes.

WINWIFE   How melancholy Mistress Grace is yonder! Pray thee let's go   60
enter ourselves in grace with her.

[*Cokes is shopping at Leatherhead's booth*]

COKES   Those six horses, friend, I'll have –

WASP   How!

COKES   – and the three Jew's trumps, and half a dozen o' birds, and that
drum – I have one drum already – and your smiths – I like that device   65

38. *crack*] Craze.

40–42. These lines may well express Jonson's own experience as a tutor, when he
accompanied Sir Walter Ralegh's son to France in 1612/13.

44. *Overparted*] Given too difficult a role to play.

45. *grieve*] Hurt.

55. *removing*] Packing up, referring to the number of packages Numps is carrying.

58. *pannier-man's jack*] Hawker's jackass, which would be skinned and sold for dogfood
when it died.

59. *for him*] In his place.

61. *grace*] Favour.

64. *trumps*] Harps.

o' your smiths very pretty well – and four halberts – and – le' me see
– that fine painted great lady, and her three women for state, I'll have.

WASP   No, the shop. Buy the whole shop, it will be best, the shop, the
shop!

LEATHERHEAD   If his worship please.   70

WASP   Yes, and keep it during the Fair, bobchin.

COKES   Peace, Numps. [*To Leatherhead*] Friend, do not meddle with
him, an' you be wise and would show your head above board. He will
sting thorough your wrought night-cap, believe me. A set of these
violins I would buy too, for a delicate young noise I have i' the country   75
that are every one a size less than another, just like your fiddles. I
would fain have a fine young masque at my marriage, now I think on
't, but I do want such a number of things. And Numps will not help
me now, and I dare not speak to him.

TRASH   Will your worship buy any gingerbread, very good bread, com-   80
fortable bread?

COKES   Gingerbread! Yes, let's see.

He runs to her shop

WASP   There's the t'other springe!

LEATHERHEAD   Is this well, Goody Joan? To interrupt my market? In the
midst? And call away my customers? Can you answer this at the Pie-   85
Powders?

TRASH   Why? If his mastership have a mind to buy, I hope my ware lies
as open as another's. I may show my ware as well as you yours.

COKES   Hold your peace. I'll content you both: I'll buy up his shop and thy
basket.   90

WASP   Will you, i' faith?

LEATHERHEAD   Why should you put him from it, friend?

WASP   Cry you mercy! You'd be sold too, would you? What's the price on
you? Jerkin and all, as you stand? Ha' you any qualities?

TRASH   Yes, Goodman Angry man, you shall find he has qualities if you   95
cheapen him.

WASP   God's so', you ha' the selling of him! What are they? Will they be
bought for love or money?

TRASH   No indeed, sir.

---

71. *bobchin*] Blabbermouth, one who talks idly out of turn.
73. *above board*] In company.
75. *noise*] Band of musicians.
77. *masque*] Group of masquers.
83. *springe*] Snare to catch birds.
95. *qualities*] Accomplishments.
96. *cheapen*] Are in the market for, ask the price of.
97. *God's so'*] Oath derived from *cazzo* = penis (Italian).

WASP   For what then? Victuals?   100

TRASH   He scorns victuals, sir. He has bread and butter at home, thanks
   be to God! And yet he will do more for a good meal, if the toy take
   him i' the belly. Marry, then they must not set him at lower end. If they
   do, he'll go away though he fast. But put him atop o' the table, where
   his place is, and he'll do you forty fine things. He has not been sent   105
   for and sought out for nothing at your great city-suppers, to put down
   Coryat and Cokely, and been laughed at for his labour. He'll play you
   all the puppets i' the town over, and the players, every company, and
   his own company too. He spares nobody!

COKES   I' faith?   110

TRASH   He was the first, sir, that ever baited the fellow i' the bear's skin,
   an 't like your worship. No dog ever came near him since. And for fine
   motions!

COKES   Is he good at those too? Can he set out a masque, trow?

TRASH   O Lord, master! Sought to far and near for his inventions, and he   115
   engrosses all: he makes all the puppets i' the Fair.

COKES   Dost thou, in troth, old velvet jerkin? Give me thy hand.

TRASH   Nay, sir, you shall see him in his velvet jerkin and a scarf too, at
   night, when you hear him interpret Master Littlewit's motion.

COKES   Speak no more, [*Turning to Leatherhead*] but shut up shop   120
   presently, friend. I'll buy both it and thee too, to carry down with me,
   and her hamper beside. Thy shop shall furnish out the masque, and
   hers the banquet. I cannot go less to set out anything with credit.

103. *lower end*] Of the table, where inferior guests sat.
104. *atop*] At the head, where the jester sat.
107. *Coryat*] Thomas Coryat, 1577–1617, Prince Henry's jester, and a great traveller.
   Coryat's Crudities (1611) is an anecdotal record of his 1608 journey through Europe;
   Jonson contributed mock-commendatory verses and a character-sketch of the author,
   but his references to him elsewhere are contemptuous (cf. *Epigrams* 139, *Underwoods*
   13).   *Cokely*] A jester who improvised at entertainments, mentioned also in *DisA* 1.1
   and *Epigrams* 129.
111. *baited the fellow i' the bear's skin*] An actor at the Fortune playing a two-legged bear
   was almost killed by 'Butchers (playing Dogs)', according to Samuel Rowlands' *The
   Knave of Hearts* (1612); the same year, a ballad on the incident was entered in the
   Stationers' Register.
113. *motions*] Puppet-shows.
114. *set out*] Produce.   *trow?*] Do you think?
115. *Sought to*] Sought out, applied to.
116. *engrosses*] Monopolises.
118–19. *at night*] Tonight.
123. *banquet*] Dessert.   *cannot go less*] Gambling term in primero, meaning 'match the
   highest bid'. See *Volp* 3.5.36–8 and *SW* 3.5.89.

What's the price, at a word, o' thy whole shop, case and all, as it
stands?   125

LEATHERHEAD   Sir, it stands me in six-and-twenty shillings, sevenpence
halfpenny, besides three shillings for my ground.

COKES   Well, thirty shilling will do all then! [*Pays Leatherhead, and turns
to Trash*] And what comes yours to?

TRASH   Four shillings and elevenpence, sir, ground and all, an 't like your   130
worship.

COKES   Yes, it does like my worship very well. [*Paying her*] Poor
woman, that's five shillings more. What a masque shall I furnish out
for forty shillings – twenty pounds Scotch! And a banquet of
gingerbread! There's a stately thing! Numps? Sister? And my wedding   135
gloves too – that I never thought on afore! All my wedding gloves –
gingerbread? O me! What a device will there be! To make 'em eat their
fingers' ends! And delicate broaches for the bride-men! And all! And
then I'll ha' this posy put to 'em: *For the best grace*, meaning Mistress
Grace, my wedding posy.   140

GRACE   I am beholden to you, sir, and to your Barthol'mew-wit.

WASP   You do not mean this, do you? Is this your first purchase?

COKES   Yes, faith, and I do not think, Numps, but thou'lt say it was the
wisest act that ever I did in my wardship.

WASP   Like enough! I shall say anything, I!   145

Act 3 scene 5*

[*Enter*] *Justice* [*Overdo, following*] *Edgworth, Nightingale*

126. *stands me in*] Costs, is worth to me.
134. *twenty pounds Scotch*] At the union of Scotland and England on King James'
accession to the English throne in 1603, the Scots pound was evaluated at one-twelfth of a
pound sterling (1s 8d).
136. *wedding gloves*] Traditional gift to guests at a wedding.
138. *bride-men*] The bridegroom's male attendants.
139. *posy*] Motto or engraved sentiment.

*   Renaissance popular literature abounds in urban folk-tales that celebrate the low-life
tricksters of London. This scene demonstrates the cony-catching expertise of Nightingale and Edgworth. Robert Greene tells a story that might be a direct source in *The
Third and Last Part of Cony-Catching* (1592), available in Judges (1930).

The lighthearted exposé of cony-catchers is shadowed by the more serious but
legally sanctioned crime committed by a profit-seeking guardian who gains control over
an heir or heiress through the Court of Wards. As Grace explains below, she must either
give up her freedom by marrying against her will, or give up most of her fortune as the

OVERDO   [*Aside*] I cannot beget a project with all my political brain yet;
my project is how to fetch off this proper young man from his
debauched company. I have followed him all the Fair over, and still I
find him with this songster. And I begin shrewdly to suspect their
familiarity, and the young man of a terrible taint, poetry! With which   5
idle disease, if he be infected, there's no hope of him in a state-course.
Actum est of him for a commonwealth's-man, if he go to 't in rime
once.

EDGWORTH   [*Pointing out Cokes to Nightingale*] Yonder he is buying o'
gingerbread. Set in quickly before he part with too much on his   10
money.

NIGHTINGALE   [*Sings*]
My masters and friends and good people, draw near, etc.

COKES   Ballads! Hark, hark! [*To Leatherhead*] Pray thee, fellow, stay a
little. Good Numps, look to the goods.

He runs to the ballad-man

What ballads hast thou? Let me see, let me see myself!   15

WASP   Why so! He's flown to another lime-bush. There he will flutter as
long more, till he ha' ne'er a feather left. Is there a vexation like this,
gentlemen? Will you believe me now, hereafter? Shall I have credit
with you?

QUARLOUS   Yes, faith, shalt thou, Numps, and thou art worthy on 't, for   20
thou swearst for 't.

[*Wasp follows Cokes*]

I never saw a young pimp errant and his squire better matched.

penalty for disobedience. Her relationship to Justice Overdo has far more devastating
implications than has Cokes's to his guardian Wasp. Cokes spends his fortune as he
pleases, simply shrugging off Wasp's interference. Wasp's 'authority', such as it is, is
moral rather than legal.

1. *political*] Shrewd, apt in pursuing a policy.
2. *fetch off*] Rescue.   *proper*] Good-looking, respectable.
6. *state-course*] Career in public service (?).
7. *Actum est of him for*] It's all over for him as.   *commonwealth's-man*] Agent of the
commonwealth, analogous to 'statesman', government agent (see *Volp* 2.1.78); a citizen
devoted to the interests of the state.   *go to 't*] Indulge.
16. *lime-bush*] A bush smeared with birdlime to snare birds.
22. *pimp*] Perhaps Quarlous uses the term loosely as an epithet of contempt. Hibbard
(1977) suggests it is a printer's misreading of Jonson's *puny*, 'novice, ninny', but Jonson
favoured the spelling *puisne*, which does not seem to allow for that particular
misreading. Another alternative is that the word means 'spoilt brat', adapted from
pimper, 'pamper, coddle'; such a term would accord with Winwife's earlier reference to

WINWIFE   Faith, the sister comes after 'em well too.

GRACE   Nay, if you saw the Justice her husband, my guardian, you were
fitted for the mess. He is such a wise one his way –   25

WINWIFE   I wonder we see him not here.

GRACE   O! He is too serious for this place, and yet better sport than the
other three, I assure you, gentlemen, where'er he is, though 't be o' the
bench.

COKES   [*To Nightingale*] How dost thou call it? 'A Caveat against   30
Cutpurses'! A good jest, i'faith. I would fain see that demon, your
cutpurse you talk of, that delicate-handed devil. They say he walks
hereabout. I would see him walk now. [*Turns to Mistress Overdo*]
Look you, sister, here, here, let him come, sister, and welcome.

He shows his purse boastingly

Ballad-man, does any cutpurses haunt hereabout? Pray thee raise me   35
one or two. Begin, and show me one.

NIGHTINGALE   Sir, this is a spell against 'em, spick and span new, and 'tis
made as 'twere in mine own person, and I sing it in mine own defence.
But 'twill cost a penny alone, if you buy it.

COKES   No matter for the price. Thou dost not know me, I see. I am an   40
odd Bartholomew.

MISTRESS OVERDO   Has 't a fine picture, brother?

COKES   O sister, do you remember the ballads over the nursery-chimney
at home o' my own pasting up? There be brave pictures. Other
manner of pictures than these, friend.   45

WASP   Yet these will serve to pick the pictures out o' your pockets, you
shall see.

COKES   So I heard 'em say. Pray thee mind him not, fellow. He'll have an
oar in everything.

NIGHTINGALE   It was intended, sir, as if a purse should chance to be cut   50
in my presence now, I may be blameless though, as by the sequel will
more plainly appear.

COKES   We shall find that i' the matter. Pray thee begin.

NIGHTINGALE   To the tune of 'Paggington's Pound', sir.

Cokes as 'the cosset', 1.5.42. Like Cokes, foolish self-absorption and self-indulgence
also characterise Wasp, Mistress Overdo, and Justice Overdo, making them all
comprise a well-matched 'pampered' foursome.

25.   *mess*] A party of four who dine together.

32.   *walks*] Lurks, but playing on the idea of a demonic spirit haunting the fair.

35.   *raise*] Conjure.

46.   *pictures*] The king's head, stamped on the coins in his purse.

51.   *though*] Nevertheless.   *sequel*] That is, the song about to be sung.

54.   *'Paggington's Pound'*] Or 'Packington's Pound', an old dance-tune in Chappel's *Old
English Popular Music* (1893: vol. 1, p. 259), and elsewhere.

COKES [*Sings*] *Fa, la la la, la la la, fa la la la.* Nay, I'll put thee in tune and   55
   all! Mine own country dance! Pray thee begin.

NIGHTINGALE It is a gentle admonition, you must know, sir, both to the
   purse-cutter and the purse-bearer.

COKES Not a word more out o' the tune, an' thou lov'st me. *Fa, la la la,
   la la la, fa la la la* – Come, when?   60

   [*While Nightingale sings, Cokes comments on the lyrics*]

NIGHTINGALE *My masters and friends and good people draw near,*
   And look to your purses, for that I do say –

COKES Ha, ha, this chimes! Good counsel at first dash.

NIGHTINGALE *– And though little money in them you do bear,*
   It cost more to get than to lose in a day.   65

COKES Good!

NIGHTINGALE   *You oft have been told,*
         Both the young and the old,
      And bidden beware of the cutpurse so bold.
   Then if you take heed not, free me from the curse   70
   Who both give you warning, for and the cutpurse.

COKES Well said! He were to blame that would not, i'faith.

NIGHTINGALE *Youth, youth, thou hadst better been starved by*
         thy Nurse,
      Than live to be hanged for cutting a purse.   75

COKES Good, i' faith! How say you, Numps? Is there any harm i' this?

NIGHTINGALE *It hath been upbraided to men of my trade*
      That oftentimes we are the cause of this crime.

COKES The more coxcombs they that did it, I wusse.

NIGHTINGALE *Alack and for pity, why should it be said?*   80
   As if they regarded or places or time!
         Examples have been
         Of some that were seen
   In Westminster Hall, yea the pleaders between.
   Then why should the judges be free from this curse   85
   More than my poor self for cutting the purse?

59. *out o'*] Outside of, not part of.
62. *for that*] Because of what.
63. *chimes*] Rings true.
71. *for and*] And also.
77–8. *It hath … crime*] Greene's pamphlet makes this accusation also.
82–4. *Examples … between*] In Thomas Dekker's *Jests to Make you Merry* (1607), a
   compassionate juror acquitted a cutpurse who, on his way out of the courtroom, picked
   the juror's pocket.
84. *Westminster Hall*] Where the Courts of Common Pleas, King's Bench, and Chancery
   sat, in the great hall of Westminster Palace. *pleaders*] Lawyers.

COKES   God a mercy for that! Why should they be more free indeed?

NIGHTINGALE   *Youth, youth, thou hadst better been starved by*
        thy Nurse
    Than live to be hanged for cutting a purse.   90

COKES   That again, good ballad-man, that again.

He sings the burden with him

O rare! I would fain rub mine elbow now, but I dare not pull out my hand. On, I pray thee! He that made this ballad shall be poet to my masque.

NIGHTINGALE   *At Worcester 'tis known well, and even i' the jail,*   95
    A knight of good worship did there show his face
    Against the foul sinners in zeal for to rail,
    And lost (ipso facto) his purse in the place.

COKES   Is it possible?

NIGHTINGALE   *Nay, once from the seat*   100
      Of judgment so great,
    A judge there did lose a fair pouch of velvet.

COKES   I'faith?

NIGHTINGALE   *O Lord for thy mercy, how wicked or worse*
    Are those that so venture their necks for a purse!   105
    Youth, youth, etc.

COKES   [*Singing with him*] *Youth, youth, etc!* Pray thee stay a little, friend. – Yet o' thy conscience, Numps, speak: is there any harm i' this?

WASP   To tell you true, 'tis too good for you, 'less you had grace to follow   110
it.

OVERDO   [*Aside, writing*] It doth discover enormity. I'll mark it more. I ha' not liked a paltry piece of poetry so well a good while.

COKES   *Youth, youth, etc!* Where's this youth now? a man must call upon him for his own good, and yet he will not appear? Look here, here's   115
for him: handy-dandy, which hand will he have?

92. *rub mine elbow*] As a sign of mirth.

100–102. *Nay ... velvet*] Alluding to a trick played by Sir Thomas More. Irritated by a judge who blamed the cutpurses' negligent victims for the rise in crime, More struck a bargain with a cutpurse who, during his trial, agreed to steal the judge's purse. The cutpurse approached the bench to consult privately with the judge, cut his purse while talking to him, and passed it to More. When More then requested alms for a poor man in court, the judge was shocked to find his purse missing. More restored it, advising him not to reproach the innocent in future. A version of this incident appears in the play partly written by Shakespeare, *Sir Thomas More*, 1.2.

107. *stay*] Wait, pause.

116. *handy-dandy*] Children's guessing game, choosing in which hand an item is hidden.

He shows his purse

> On, I pray thee, with the rest. I do hear of him, but I cannot see him,
> this Master Youth, the cutpurse.

NIGHTINGALE   *At plays and at sermons and at the sessions,*
> > *'Tis daily their practice such booty to make;*   120
> > *Yea, under the gallows, at executions,*
> > *They stick not the stare-abouts' purses to take.*
> > > *Nay, one without grace*
> > > *At a better place,*
> > *At court, and in Christmas, before the King's face –*   125

COKES   That was a fine fellow! I would have him now.

NIGHTINGALE   *Alack then for pity, must I bear the curse*
> > *That only belongs to the cunning cutpurse?*

COKES   But where's their cunning now when they should use it? They are
> all chained now, I warrant you. [*Again singing the refrain with*   130
> *Nightingale*] Youth, youth, thou hadst better, etc. The rat-catcher's
> charm! Are all fools and asses to this? A pox on 'em, that they will not
> come! That a man should have such a desire to a thing, and want it!

QUARLOUS   'Fore God, I'd give half the Fair, and 'twere mine, for a
> cutpurse for him, to save his longing.   135

COKES   Look you, sister, here, here –

He shows his purse again

> Where is 't now? Which pocket is 't in? For a wager?

WASP   I beseech you leave your wagers, and let him end his matter, an't
> may be.

COKES   O, are you edified, Numps?   140

OVERDO   [*Aside*] Indeed he does interrupt him too much. There Numps
> spoke to purpose.

COKES   Sister, I am an ass.

[He shows his purse] again

123–5. *Nay ... face*] John Selman cut a purse valued at one halfpenny during the
celebration of the sacrament in the King's Chapel at Whitehall, Christmas Day 1611;
he was tried before Sir Francis Bacon, and hanged 7 January 1612. Two pamphlets and
a ballad relating the story were registered within three days of the execution.

131–2. *The rat-catcher's charm!*] Irish peasants believed that their poets could destroy rats
with magically vituperative verses. Cokes attributes a similar power to Nightingale's
ballad as effectively making the cutpurses vanish.

132. *Are all fools and asses to this?*] Are all cutpurses made fools of by this ballad?
(Hibbard 1977).

133. *to*] For   *want*] Lack.

138. *matter*] Performance.

I cannot keep my purse. On, on, I pray thee, friend.

NIGHTINGALE   *But O you vile nation of cutpurses all,*   145
          Relent and repent and amend and be sound,
          And know that you ought not, by honest men's fall,
          Advance your own fortunes, to die above ground.

WINWIFE   Will you see sport? Look, there's a fellow gathers up to him,
mark.   150

*Edgworth gets up to him and tickles him in the ear with a straw twice to
draw his hand out of his pocket*

NIGHTINGALE   *And though you go gay*
          In silks as you may,
          It is not the high way to heaven, as they say.

QUARLOUS   Good, i' faith! O, he has lighted on the wrong pocket.

NIGHTINGALE   *Repent then, repent you, for better, for worse,*   155
          And kiss not the gallows for cutting a purse.
          Youth, youth, thou hadst better been starved by thy
             Nurse
          Than live to be hanged for cutting a purse.

[*Edgworth takes Cokes's purse*]

WINWIFE   He has it! 'Fore God, he is a brave fellow. Pity he should be   160
detected.

ALL   An excellent ballad! An excellent ballad!

EDGWORTH   Friend, let me ha' the first, let me ha' the first, I pray you.

[*He conveys the purse to Nightingale*]

COKES   Pardon me, sir. First come, first served. And I'll buy the whole
bundle too.   165

WINWIFE   That conveyance was better than all. Did you see't? He has
given the purse to the ballad-singer.

QUARLOUS   Has he?

EDGWORTH   Sir, I cry you mercy. I'll not hinder the poor man's profit.
Pray you mistake me not.   170

COKES   Sir, I take you for an honest gentleman. If that be mistaking, I met
you today afore – Ha! Humh! O God! My purse is gone, my purse,
my purse, etc.!

WASP   Come, do not make a stir and cry yourself an ass thorough the Fair
afore your time.   175

---

146. *Relent*] Yield, give up your criminal course.
148. *die above ground*] Be hanged.
174. *thorough*] Throughout.

COKES   Why, hast thou it, Numps? Good Numps, how came you by it? I
    mar'l!

WASP   I pray you seek some other gamester to play the fool with. You may
    lose it time enough, for all your Fair-wit.

COKES   By this good hand, glove and all, I ha' lost it already, if thou hast   180
    it not: feel else. And Mistress Grace's handkercher too, out o' the
    t'other pocket.

WASP   Why, 'tis well, very well, exceeding pretty and well.

EDGWORTH   Are you sure you ha' lost it, sir?

COKES   O God! Yes, as I am an honest man, I had it but e'en now, at   185
    Youth, youth.

NIGHTINGALE   I hope you suspect not me, sir.

EDGWORTH   Thee? That were a jest indeed! Dost thou think the
    gentleman is foolish? Where hadst thou hands, I pray thee? Away, ass,
    away.   190

    [*Exit Nightingale*]

OVERDO   [*Aside, slipping away*]   I shall be beaten again if I be spied.

EDGWORTH   Sir, I suspect an odd fellow, yonder, is stealing away.

MISTRESS OVERDO   Brother, it is the preaching fellow! You shall suspect
    him. He was at your t'other purse, you know! – Nay, stay, sir, and
    view the work you ha' done. An' you be beneficed at the gallows and   195
    preach there, thank your own handiwork.

COKES   Sir, you shall take no pride in your preferment. You shall be
    silenced quickly.

OVERDO   What do you mean, sweet buds of gentility?

COKES   To ha' my pennyworths out on you, bud. No less than two purses   200
    a day serve you? I thought you a simple fellow, when my man Numps
    beat you i' the morning, and pitied you –

MISTRESS OVERDO   So did I, I'll be sworn, brother, but now I see he is
    a lewd and pernicious enormity, as Master Overdo calls him.

OVERDO   [*Aside*]   Mine own words turned upon me like swords!   205

COKES   Cannot a man's purse be at quiet for you i' the master's pocket,
    but you must entice it forth and debauch it?

WASP   Sir, sir, keep your debauch and your fine Bartholomew-terms to
    yourself, and make as much on 'em as you please. But gi' me this from
    you i' the mean time: I beseech you, see if I can look to this.   210

177. *mar'l*] Marvel.

178. *gamester*] Playmate.

193. *shall*] Ought to.

195–6. *beneficed at the gallows and preach*] Condemned to be hanged and sermonise on
    repentance before your execution.

200. *pennyworths*] Money's worth in revenge.

[Wasp tries to take the licence-box from him]

COKES Why, Numps?

WASP Why? Because you are an ass, sir. There's a reason the shortest way, and you will needs ha' it. Now you ha' got the trick of losing, you'd lose your breech, an't 'twere loose. I know you, sir. Come, deliver.

Wasp takes the licence from him

You'll go and crack the vermin you breed now, will you? 'Tis very fine.   215
Will you ha' the truth on't? They are such retchless flies as you are, that blow cutpurses abroad in every corner. Your foolish having of money makes 'em. An' there were no wiser than I, sir, the trade should lie open for you, sir, it should, i'faith, sir. I would teach your wit to come to your head, sir, as well as your land to come into your hand,   220
I assure you, sir.

[Exeunt Cokes and Mistress Overdo, forcing Overdo along]

WINWIFE Alack, good Numps.

WASP Nay, gentlemen, never pity me. I am not worth it. Lord send me at home once to Harrow o'the Hill again, if I travel any more, call me Coryat, with all my heart.   225

[Exit Wasp, following the others]

QUARLOUS *[To Edgworth]* Stay, sir, I must have a word with you in private. Do you hear?

EDGWORTH With me, sir? What's your pleasure, good sir?

QUARLOUS Do not deny it. You are a cutpurse, sir. This gentleman here and I saw you, nor do we mean to detect you – though we can   230
sufficiently inform ourselves toward the danger of concealing you – but you must do us a piece of service.

EDGWORTH Good gentlemen, do not undo me. I am a civil young man and but a beginner, indeed.

QUARLOUS Sir, your beginning shall bring on your ending, for us. We are   235
no catchpoles nor constables. That you are to undertake is this: you saw the old fellow with the black box here?

212. *the shortest way*] Briefly.
215. *crack*] Boast about.
216. *retchless*] Heedless.
217. *blow*] Breed, deposit eggs like flies.
218–19. *An' there ... open for you*] If other people did not interfere with my authority, you would be apprenticed to some trade.
224–5. *call me Coryat*] Call me a fool.
233. *civil*] Respectable.
235. *for us*] For all we care.

EDGWORTH   The little old governor, sir?

QUARLOUS   That same. I see you have flown him to a mark already. I
would ha' you get away that box from him and bring it us.   240

EDGWORTH   Would you ha' the box and all, sir? Or only that that is in
't? I'll get you that, and leave him the box to play with still – which
will be the harder o' the two – because I would gain your worships'
good opinion of me.

WINWIFE   He says well. 'Tis the greater mastery, and 'twill make the more   245
sport when 'tis missed.

EDGWORTH   Ay, and 'twill be the longer a-missing, to draw on the sport.

QUARLOUS   But look you do it now, sirrah, and keep your word, or –

EDGWORTH   Sir, if ever I break my word with a gentleman, may I never
read word at my need. Where shall I find you?   250

QUARLOUS   Somewhere i' the Fair hereabouts. Dispatch it quickly.

[Exit Edgworth]

I would fain see the careful fool deluded! Of all beasts, I love the
serious ass. He that takes pains to be one and plays the fool with the
greatest diligence that can be.

GRACE   Then you would not choose, sir, but love my guardian, Justice   255
Overdo, who is answerable to that description in every hair of him.

QUARLOUS   So I have heard. But how came you, Mistress Welborn, to be
his ward? Or have relation to him, at first?

GRACE   Faith, through a common calamity: he bought me, sir, and now
he will marry me to his wife's brother, this wise gentleman that you   260
see, or else I must pay value o' my land.

239. *flown him to a mark*] Identified him (cf 2.4.40).

241–4. The empty-box trick is an amusing variation on Kyd's black-box scene in *The
Spanish Tragedy* 3.6; it employs the same cocky humour against life's injustice, and
echoes Pedringano's fate by metaphorically executing the joke's victim, when Wasp
'*misseth the licence*' and cries, 'I'll be hanged then' (5.6.79.1, 81). Jonson had acted in
Kyd's play in the mid-1590s and Henslowe paid Jonson to write additional scenes for
a revival in 1601/2.

245. *mastery*] Master-stroke.

250. *read word*] Plead benefit of clergy (cf. 1.4.6).

259. *he bought me*] Purchased her guardianship from the Crown in the Court of Wards.
This court administered the estates of all wards of the crown (minors and lunatics
inheriting from the king's tenants), and had the power to sell control over a ward,
including the right to force a marriage, to any buyer. The Court of Wards was
abolished in 1646 for abusing the system.

261. *pay value*] Make financial amends to her guardian if she refuses to marry the selected
spouse, or marries another without consent while she is still a minor.

QUARLOUS   'Slid, is there no device of disparagement? Or so? Talk with
    some crafty fellow, some picklock o' the law! Would I had studied a
    year longer i' the Inns of Court, and 't had been but i' your case.

WINWIFE   [*Aside*] Ay, Master Quarlous, are you proffering?   265

GRACE   You'd bring but little aid, sir.

WINWIFE   [*Aside*] I'll look to you, i' faith, gamester. – [*To Grace*] An
    unfortunate foolish tribe you are fallen into, lady. I wonder you can
    endure 'em.

GRACE   Sir, they that cannot work their fetters off must wear 'em.   270

WINWIFE   You see what care they have on you, to leave you thus.

GRACE   Faith, the same they have of themselves, sir. I cannot greatly
    complain, if this were all the plea I had against 'em.

WINWIFE   'Tis true! But will you please to withdraw with us a little and
    make them think they have lost you? I hope our manners ha' been   275
    such hitherto, and our language, as will give you no cause to doubt
    yourself in our company.

GRACE   Sir, I will give myself no cause. I am so secure of mine own
    manners as I suspect not yours.

QUARLOUS   Look where John Littlewit comes.   280

WINWIFE   Away, I'll not be seen by him.

QUARLOUS   No, you were not best. He'd tell his mother, the widow.

WINWIFE   Heart, what do you mean?

QUARLOUS   Cry you mercy, is the wind there? Must not the widow be
    named?   285

    [*Exeunt Grace, Winwife, Quarlous*]

Act 3 scene 6*

    [*Enter*] *John* [*Littlewit,*] *Win*

LITTLEWIT   Do you hear, Win, Win?

WIN   What say you, John?

LITTLEWIT   While they are paying the reckoning, Win, I'll tell you a
    thing, Win. We shall never see any sights i' the Fair, Win, except you
    long still, Win. Good Win, sweet Win, long to see some hobbyhorses,
    and some drums, and rattles, and dogs, and fine devices, Win. The   5

---

262. *disparagement*] The legal plea that her guardian intends to marry her to a socially
    inferior husband.

263. *picklock o' the law*] A lawyer adept at finding legal loop-holes.

265. *proffering*] Making advances.

276–7. *doubt yourself*] Fear for your safety.

279. *manners*] Behaviour.

*   Busy's assault on the idols of the fair offers a ludicrously reductive version of anti-
    Roman Catholic iconoclasm in the name of the 'afflicted saints' of the puritan 'cause'.

bull with the five legs, Win, and the great hog. Now you ha' begun
with pig, you may long for anything, Win, and so for my motion, Win.

WIN   But we sha'not eat o' the bull and the hog, John. How shall I long
then?   10

LITTLEWIT   O yes! Win, you may long to see, as well as to taste, Win.
How did the pothecary's wife, Win, that longed to see the anatomy,
Win? Or the lady, Win, that desired to spit i' the great lawyer's mouth
after an eloquent pleading? I assure you they longed, Win. Good Win,
go in, and long.   15

   [Exeunt Littlewit and Win]

TRASH   I think we are rid of our new customer, brother Leatherhead. We
shall hear no more of him.

LEATHERHEAD   All the better. Let's pack up all and be gone before he
find us.

   They plot to be gone

TRASH   Stay a little. Yonder comes a company. It may be we may take   20
some more money.

   [Enter] Knockem, Busy

KNOCKEM   Sir, I will take your counsel, and cut my hair and leave
vapours. I see that tobacco, and bottle-ale, and pig, and Whit, and
very Ursula herself, is all vanity.

BUSY   Only pig was not comprehended in my admonition; the rest were.   25
For long hair, it is an ensign of pride, a banner, and the world is full
of those banners, very full of banners. And bottle-ale is a drink of
Satan's, a diet-drink of Satan's, devised to puff us up and make us
swell in this latter age of vanity, as the smoke of tobacco to keep us

The attack follows his proselytising of Knockem, who agrees compliantly with Busy's
rants against long hair, ale, tobacco, and Ursula, the compendious representative of the
World, the Flesh, and the Devil. It ends with Busy's being sold into 'martyrdom' in the
Smithfield stocks for a shilling. This scene suggests that in Busy Jonson is caricaturing
the famous puritan preacher William Whately, known as the roaring boy of Banbury,
who frequently sermonised at fairs.

7. *bull ... hog*] 'Monsters' or curiosities of the fair; cf. 3.1.10.
12. *anatomy*] Skeleton.
13. *spit ... mouth*] Proverbial reward and encouragement.
22. *cut my hair*] In *EMO*, Induction 40–41, puritans are described as having 'their hair /
Cut shorter than their eye-brows'.
25. *Only*] Except.
26. *For*] As for.
28. *diet-drink*] Prescription.
29. *latter age*] The era culminating in the end of the world, a millenarian belief.

in mist and error. But the fleshly woman which you call Ursula is   30
above all to be avoided, having the marks upon her of the three
enemies of man: the World, as being in the Fair; the Devil, as being in
the fire; and the Flesh, as being herself.

[*Enter*] *Purecraft*

PURECRAFT   Brother Zeal-of-the-land! What shall we do? My daughter
Win-the-fight is fallen into her fit of longing again.   35
BUSY   For more pig? There is no more, is there?
PURECRAFT   To see some sights i' the Fair.
BUSY   Sister, let her fly the impurity of the place swiftly, lest she partake
of the pitch thereof. Thou art the seat of the Beast, O Smithfield, and
I will leave thee. Idolatry peepeth out on every side of thee.   40
KNOCKEM   [*Aside*] An excellent right hypocrite! Now his belly is full, he
falls a-railing and kicking, the jade. A very good vapour! I'll in and joy
Ursula with telling how her pig works. Two and a half he ate to his
share! And he has drunk a pailful. He eats with his eyes as well as his
teeth.   45

[*Exit Knockem*]

LEATHERHEAD   What do you lack, gentlemen? What is 't you buy?
Rattles, drums, babies –
BUSY   Peace with thy apocryphal wares, thou profane publican: thy bells,
thy dragons, and thy Toby's dogs. Thy hobbyhorse is an idol, a very
idol, a fierce and rank idol. And thou, the Nebuchadnezzar, the proud   50
Nebuchadnezzar of the Fair, that set'st it up for children to fall down
to and worship.
LEATHERHEAD   Cry you mercy, sir. Will you buy a fiddle to fill up your
noise?

[*Enter Littlewit and Win*]

LITTLEWIT   Look, Win. Do look, i' God's name, and save your longing.   55
Here be fine sights.
PURECRAFT   Ay, child, so you hate 'em, as our brother Zeal does, you may
look on 'em.

32–3. *Devil … fire*] Tribulation Wholesome (*Alch* 3.1.21–7) makes the same argument
that fire is the devil's element.
42. *jade*] Vicious horse.
48. *apocryphal*] Spurious, in keeping with the puritan rejection of the Apocrypha.   *publican*] Heathen (derived from Matthew 18:17).
48–9. *bells … dragons … dogs*] Alluding to *Bel and the Dragon* and the dog in Tobit 5:16
in the Apocrypha.
50. *Nebuchadnezzar*] The king of Babylon who forced his people to worship an idol
(Daniel 3).
53–4. *fill up your noise*] Add to a band of musicians; sneeringly, cover up or add a counter-
din to Busy's puritanical outburst.

LEATHERHEAD   Or what do you say to a drum, sir?

BUSY   It is the broken belly of the Beast, and thy bellows there are his   60
    lungs, and these pipes are his throat, those feathers are of his tail, and
    thy rattles the gnashing of his teeth.

TRASH   And what's my gingerbread, I pray you?

BUSY   The provender that pricks him up. Hence with thy basket of popery,
    thy nest of images, and whole legend of gingerwork.   65

LEATHERHEAD   Sir, if you be not quiet the quicklier, I'll ha' you clapped
    fairly by the heels for disturbing the Fair.

BUSY   The sin of the Fair provokes me. I cannot be silent.

PURECRAFT   Good brother Zeal!

    [She draws him aside]

LEATHERHEAD   Sir, I'll make you silent, believe it.   70

LITTLEWIT   I'd give a shilling you could, i'faith, friend.

LEATHERHEAD   Sir, give me your shilling. I'll give you my shop if I do
    not, and I'll leave it in pawn with you i'the mean time.

LITTLEWIT   A match, i'faith, but do it quickly then.

    [Exit Leatherhead]
    [Busy meanwhile] speaks to the widow

BUSY   Hinder me not, woman. I was moved in spirit to be here this day in   75
    this Fair, this wicked and foul Fair, and fitter may it be called a foul
    than a Fair. To protest against the abuses of it, the foul abuses of it,
    in regard of the afflicted saints that are troubled, very much troubled,
    exceedingly troubled, with the opening of the merchandise of Babylon
    again, and the peeping of popery upon the stalls here, here, in the high   80
    places. See you not Goldilocks, the purple strumpet there? In her
    yellow gown and green sleeves? The profane pipes, the tinkling
    timbrels? A shop of relics!

    [Begins to throw down the goods]

LITTLEWIT   Pray you, forbear! I am put in trust with 'em.

64. *pricks him up*] Spurs him on, stimulates him.

64–5. *popery ... images ... legend*] Because of the association of the Fair with St
    Bartholomew, Busy sees the gingerbread shapes as miniature effigies of saints and
    reminders of saints' lives, remnants of which had been purged from the reformed
    churches as vestiges of Roman Catholicism.

78. *the afflicted saints*] The puritan elect.

81–2. *Goldilocks ... purple ... yellow ... green*] Puritans considered bright colours
    profane; 'green sleeves' in particular were associated with 'strumpets' who rolled in the
    grass with lovers, thus staining their gowns.

82–3. *pipes ... timbrels*] Puritans also objected to elaborate music in the church, especially
    organs; hence the ludicrous opposition to penny-whistles and tambourines here.

BUSY   And this idolatrous grove of images, this flasket of idols! Which I   85
will pull down –

Overthrows the gingerbread

TRASH   O my ware, my ware, God bless it!
BUSY   – in my zeal and glory to be thus exercised.

Leatherhead enters with officers

LEATHERHEAD   Here he is. Pray you lay hold on his zeal. We cannot sell
a whistle, for him, in tune. Stop his noise first!   90
BUSY   Thou canst not: 'tis a sanctified noise. I will make a loud and most
strong noise till I have daunted the profane enemy. And for this
cause –
LEATHERHEAD   Sir, here's no man afraid of you or your cause. You shall
swear it i' the stocks, sir.   95
BUSY   I will thrust myself into the stocks, upon the pikes of the land.
LEATHERHEAD   Carry him away.

[*Officers seize him*]

PURECRAFT   What do you mean, wicked men?
BUSY   Let them alone. I fear them not.

[*Exeunt Busy and officers, followed by Purecraft*]

LITTLEWIT   Was not this shilling well ventured, Win, for our liberty?   100
Now we may go play, and see over the Fair, where we list, ourselves.
My mother is gone after him, and let her e'en go and loose us.
WIN   Yes, John, but I know not what to do.
LITTLEWIT   For what, Win?
WIN   For a thing I am ashamed to tell you, i' faith, and 'tis too far to go   105
home.
LITTLEWIT   I pray thee be not ashamed, Win. Come, i' faith, thou shalt
not be ashamed. Is it anything about the hobbyhorse-man? An't be,
speak freely.
WIN   Hang him, base bobchin, I scorn him. No, I have very great what-   110
sha'callum, John.

85. *flasket*]   Long shallow basket.
90. *for*]   Because of.
96. *I will thrust . . . land*]   That is, as a martyr.
102. *loose*]   Let us loose.
110. *bobchin*]   Blabbermouth.
110–11. *what-sha'callum*]   Bladder (euphemism).

LITTLEWIT   O! Is that all, Win? We'll go back to Captain Jordan, to the
pig-woman's, Win. He'll help us, or she, with a dripping-pan, or an
old kettle, or something. The poor greasy soul loves you, Win, and
after we'll visit the Fair all over, Win, and see my puppet-play, Win.   115
You know it's a fine matter, Win.

[Exeunt Littlewit and Win]

LEATHERHEAD   Let's away. I counselled you to pack up afore, Joan.
TRASH   A pox of his Bedlam purity. He has spoiled half my ware. But the
best is we lose nothing, if we miss our first merchant.
LEATHERHEAD   It shall be hard for him to find or know us, when we are   120
translated, Joan.

[They gather up their wares, and exeunt]

ACT 4

Act 4 scene 1*

[Enter] Trouble-all, Bristle, Haggis, Cokes, Overdo

TROUBLE-ALL   My masters, I do make no doubt but you are officers.
BRISTLE   What then, sir?
TROUBLE-ALL   And the King's loving and obedient subjects.
BRISTLE   Obedient, friend? Take heed what you speak, I advise you.
Oliver Bristle advises you. His loving subjects, we grant you, but not   5
his obedient, at this time; by your leave, we know ourselves a little
better than so. We are to command, sir, and such as you are to be

113. *dripping-pan*] Wittily apt substitute for a chamber-pot.
119. *miss*] Avoid.   *merchant*] Customer.
121. *translated*] Moved; altered their appearance.
*   Trouble-all emerges late in the play to act as a belated warning, a call to the conscience,
or to the conscientious, to do nothing without proper authorisation. His quest for
'warrant' echoes through the last two acts: it becomes a search for protection or shelter
against inexplicable victimisation, for which Overdo is responsible. His is the warrant
Trouble-all seeks, because Overdo had dismissed him from his job as an officer in the
Pie-Powders court apparently in a fit of pique (60–72), but when Overdo tries to make
restitution, he gives his blank warrant to the wrong man (5.2. 91–115), and Trouble-all
is stripped of the little he has left (5.6. 42.1–2 – 56). As a commentary on justice, it is
not far removed from the mordant irony of *Volp* or the letter-of-the-law abuses in *SW*
and *Alch*, where possession counts for more than rights.
5. *Oliver*] Called 'Davy' at 3.1.7, presumably a generic nickname for any Welshman,
after the patron saint of Wales, St David, just as 'Paddy' connects any Irishman with St
Patrick.

obedient. Here's one of his obedient subjects going to the stocks, and
we'll make you such another, if you talk.

TROUBLE-ALL   You are all wise enough i' your places, I know.   10

BRISTLE   If you know it, sir, why do you bring it in question?

TROUBLE-ALL   I question nothing, pardon me. I do only hope you have
warrant for what you do, and so quit you, and so multiply you.

He goes away again

HAGGIS   What's he? Bring him up to the stocks there. Why bring you him
not up?   15

[Trouble-all] comes again

TROUBLE-ALL   If you have Justice Overdo's warrant, 'tis well: you are
safe. That is the warrant of warrants. I'll not give this button for any
man's warrant else.

BRISTLE   Like enough, sir, but let me tell you, an' you play away your
buttons thus, you will want 'em ere night, for any store I see about   20
you. You might keep 'em, and save pins, I wusse.

[Trouble-all] goes away

OVERDO   [*Aside*] What should he be, that doth so esteem and advance
my warrant? He seems a sober and discreet person! It is a comfort to
a good conscience to be followed with a good fame in his sufferings.
The world will have a pretty taste by this how I can bear adversity, and   25
it will beget a kind of reverence toward me hereafter, even from mine
enemies, when they shall see I carry my calamity nobly, and that it
doth neither break me nor bend me.

HAGGIS   Come, sir, here's a place for you to preach in. Will you put in
your leg?   30

They put him in the stocks

OVERDO   That I will, cheerfully.

BRISTLE   O' my conscience, a seminary! He kisses the stocks.

COKES   Well, my masters, I'll leave him with you. Now I see him
bestowed, I'll go look for my goods and Numps.

HAGGIS   You may, sir, I warrant you.   35

[Exit Cokes]

---

13.   *so quit you, and so multiply you*] God forgive you and increase your family.

20.   *want*] Need, miss.   *store*] Abundant supply.

22.   *advance*] Praise, promote.

30.   *leg*] Apparently these stocks hold the prisoner by one leg only; see 4.6.68.1–2.

32.   *seminary*] Recusant priest; cf. 2.1.29.

Where's the t'other bawler? Fetch him too – you shall find 'em both
fast enough.

OVERDO   [*Aside*] In the midst of this tumult, I will yet be the author of
mine own rest and, not minding their fury, sit in the stocks in that calm
as shall be able to trouble a triumph.   40

[*Trouble-all*] *comes again*

TROUBLE-ALL   Do you assure me upon your words? May I undertake for
you, if I be asked the question, that you have this warrant?

HAGGIS   What's this fellow, for God's sake?

TROUBLE-ALL   Do but show me 'Adam Overdo', and I am satisfied.

Goes out

BRISTLE   He is a fellow that is distracted, they say, one Trouble-all: he was   45
an officer in the Court of the Pie-Powders here last year, and put out
on his place by Justice Overdo.

OVERDO   Ha!

BRISTLE   Upon which, he took an idle conceit, and 's run mad upon 't. So
that ever since, he will do nothing but by Justice Overdo's warrant. He   50
will not eat a crust, nor drink a little, nor make him in his apparel
ready. His wife, sir-reverence, cannot get him make his water or shift
his shirt without his warrant.

OVERDO   [*Aside*] If this be true, this is my greatest disaster! How am I
bound to satisfy this poor man that is, of so good a nature to me, out   55
of his wits, where there is no room left for dissembling!

[*Trouble-all*] *comes in*

TROUBLE-ALL   If you cannot show me 'Adam Overdo', I am in doubt of
you. I am afraid you cannot answer it.

Goes again

39. *rest*] Peace of mind, punning on 'arrest'.
47. *on*] Of.
49. *idle conceit*] Foolish delusion.
51–2. *make ... ready*] Get dressed.
52. *make his water*] Urinate.   *shift*] Change.
55. *of so good a nature to me*] As a result of his admiration for me.
56. *where*] So that, to the extent that.
58. *answer*] Justify, defend.

HAGGIS   Before me, Neighbour Bristle, and now I think on't better, Justice
    Overdo is a very parantory person.   60
BRISTLE   O! Are you advised of that? And a severe justicer, by your leave.
OVERDO   [*Aside*]   Do I hear ill o' that side too?
BRISTLE   He will sit as upright o' the bench, an' you mark him, as a candle
    i' the socket, and give light to the whole court in every business.
HAGGIS   But he will burn blue and swell like a boil, God bless us, an' he   65
    be angry.
BRISTLE   Ay, and he will be angry too, when him list, that's more, and
    when he is angry, be it right or wrong, he has the law on's side ever.
    I mark that too.
OVERDO   [*Aside*]   I will be more tender hereafter. I see compassion may   70
    become a justice, though it be a weakness, I confess, and nearer a vice
    than a virtue.
HAGGIS   Well, take him out o' the stocks again. We'll go a sure way to
    work. We'll ha' the ace of hearts of our side, if we can.

   They take the Justice out
   [*Enter*] *Pocher, officers with Busy, Purecraft*

POCHER   Come, bring him away to his fellow, there. Master Busy, we shall   75
    rule your legs, I hope, though we cannot rule your tongue.
BUSY   No, minister of darkness, no, thou canst not rule my tongue. My
    tongue it is mine own, and with it I will both knock and mock down
    your Bartholomew-abominations till you be made a hissing to the
    neighbour parishes round about.   80
HAGGIS   Let him alone. We have devised better upon 't.
PURECRAFT   And shall he not into the stocks then?
BRISTLE   No, mistress, we'll have 'em both to Justice Overdo and let him
    do over 'em as is fitting. Then I and my gossip, Haggis, and my beadle,
    Pocher, are discharged.   85
PURECRAFT   O, I thank you, blessed honest men!
BRISTLE   Nay, never thank us, but thank this madman that comes here. He
    put it in our heads.

   [*Trouble-all*] *comes again*

PURECRAFT   Is he mad? Now heaven increase his madness and bless it

---

60. *parantory*] Peremptory.
67. *when him list*] Whenever he pleases.
73–4. *go a sure way to work*] Play it safe.
74. *the ace of hearts*] The winning trick, in terms of showing a kindly disposition. *of*]
    On.
79. *hissing*] Object of contempt and derision.
85. *discharged*] Released from responsibility.

and thank it. – Sir, your poor handmaid thanks you.   90
TROUBLE-ALL   Have you a warrant? An' you have a warrant, show it.
PURECRAFT   Yes, I have a warrant out of the word to give thanks for
    removing any scorn intended to the brethren.
TROUBLE-ALL   It is Justice Overdo's warrant that I look for. If you have
    not that, keep your word, I'll keep mine. Quit ye, and multiply ye.   95

[*Exeunt all but Trouble-all*]

Act 4 scene 2*

[*Enter*] Edgworth, Nightingale

EDGWORTH   Come away, Nightingale, I pray thee.
TROUBLE-ALL   Whither go you? Where's your warrant?
EDGWORTH   Warrant for what, sir?
TROUBLE-ALL   For what you go about. You know how fit it is. An' you
    have no warrant, bless you, I'll pray for you. That's all I can do.   5

Goes out

EDGWORTH   What means he?
NIGHTINGALE   A madman that haunts the Fair. Do you not know him?
    It's marvel he has not more followers after his ragged heels.
EDGWORTH   Beshrew him, he startled me. I thought he had known of our
    plot. Guilt's a terrible thing! Ha' you prepared the costardmonger?   10
NIGHTINGALE   Yes, and agreed for his basket of pears. He is at the corner
    here ready. And your prize, he comes down sailing that way, all alone,
    without his protector: he is rid of him, it seems.
EDGWORTH   Ay, I know. I should ha' followed his protectorship for a feat
    I am to do upon him. But this offered itself so i' the way, I could not   15

92. *the word*] The bible.
95. *keep your word*] Hold your tongue.
*   The chief irony of Trouble-all's role as conscience or duty is his ineffectiveness; he
    cannot plant scruples or accountability in the barren ground of the fair, where law and
    order are foreign soil. He accidentally startles Edgworth into feeling guilt (9–10), but
    not enough to make him stop stealing; and he refuses to help Cokes without official
    permission. Like all the other standards of the fair, conscience too is debased.
9. *Beshrew*] Curse.
10. *prepared*] Instructed.
11. *agreed*] Settled on a price.
12. *prize*] Ship worth plundering.

let it scape. Here he comes. Whistle! Be this sport called 'Dorring the Dottrel'.

Nightingale whistles

NIGHTINGALE   *Wh, wh, wh, wh, etc.*
COKES   By this light, I cannot find my gingerbread-wife, nor my hobbyhorse-man in all the Fair now, to ha' my money again. And I do   20
not know the way out on 't to go home for more. Do you hear, friend, you that whistle? What tune is that you whistle?
NIGHTINGALE   A new tune I am practising, sir.
COKES   Dost thou know where I dwell, I pray thee? Nay, on with thy tune. I ha' no such haste for an answer. I'll practise with thee.   25

[*While they whistle together, enter Costardmonger*]

COSTARDMONGER   Buy any pears, very fine pears, pears fine!

Nightingale sets his foot afore him, and he falls with his basket

COKES   God's so! A muss, a muss, a muss, a muss!

[*He scurries after the fruit, tripping over his sword and cloak, his hat falling over his eyes*]

COSTARDMONGER   Good gentleman, my ware, my ware! I am a poor man. Good sir, my ware!
NIGHTINGALE   [*To Cokes*] Let me hold your sword, sir; it troubles you.   30
COKES   Do, and my cloak, an' thou wilt, and my hat too.

Cokes falls a-scrambling whilst they run away with his things

EDGWORTH   A delicate great boy! Methinks he out-scrambles 'em all. I cannot persuade myself but he goes to grammar-school yet, and plays the truant today.
NIGHTINGALE   Would he had another purse to cut, 'Zekiel!   35
EDGWORTH   Purse? A man might cut out his kidneys, I think, and he never feel 'em, he is so earnest at the sport.
NIGHTINGALE   His soul is halfway out on 's body at the game.
EDGWORTH   Away, Nightingale, that way.

[*Exit Nightingale with Cokes's sword, cloak, and hat*]

16–17. '*Dorring the Dottrel*'] Hoaxing the simpleton. To 'give someone the dor' was to hoodwink or make a fool of him; literally, the dor was a jeer made by resonating the tongue between the lips, imitating the buzz of a beetle or bee, a sound also known as a 'raspberry' or 'Bronx cheer'. A *dottrel* is a species of plover, proverbially known for its stupidity and the ease with which it is caught.
27. *muss*] Scramble.

COKES   I think I am furnished for Cather'ne pears for one under-meal. Gi'   40
me my cloak.

COSTARDMONGER   Good gentleman, give me my ware.

COKES   Where's the fellow I ga' my cloak to? My cloak? And my hat? Ha!
God's lid, is he gone? Thieves, thieves! Help me to cry, gentlemen!

He runs out

EDGWORTH   Away, costermonger, come to us to Ursula's.   45

[*Exit Costardmonger*]

Talk of him to have a soul? 'Heart, if he have any more than a thing given
him instead of salt, only to keep him from stinking, I'll be hanged afore
my time presently. Where should it be, trow? In his blood? He has not so
much to'ard it in his whole body, as will maintain a good flea. And if he
take this course, he will not ha' so much land left as to rear a calf   50
within this twelvemonth. Was there ever green plover so pulled! That his
little overseer had been here now and been but tall enough to see him
steal pears in exchange for his beaver hat and his cloak thus! I must go
find him out next for his black box and his patent, it seems, he has of his
place, which I think the gentleman would have a reversion of, that   55
spoke to me for it so earnestly.

[*Exit Edgworth*]
[*Cokes*] *comes again*

COKES   Would I might lose my doublet and hose too, as I am an honest
man, and never stir if I think there be anything but thieving and
cozening i' this whole Fair! 'Bartholomew Fair', quoth he! An' ever
any Bartholomew had that luck in't that I have had, I'll be martyred   60
for him, and in Smithfield too! I ha' paid for my pears. A rot on 'em,
I'll keep 'em no longer.

Throws away his pears

40. *under-meal*] Afternoon snack.

46–7. *Talk ... stinking*] Just as salt preserves meat, so the soul was thought to preserve man
from rotting.

51. *green*] Inexperienced, innocent. *pulled*] Plucked.

54–5. *patent ... place*] Edgworth thinks the document he is to steal is a document assuring
Wasp of his office as Cokes's governor.

55. *reversion*] Right to succeed an incumbent in an office.

60–61. *martyred ... in Smithfield*] Protestant martyrs were executed there during the reign
of Mary Tudor, but the last Smithfield martyr was Bartholomew Legate, burned in
1611 for his radical separatist beliefs. Cokes seems to be identifying with this
Bartholomew as being as luckless as himself.

You were choke-pears to me – I had been better ha' gone to
mumchance for you, I wusse. Methinks the Fair should not have used
me thus, and 'twere but for my name's sake. I would not ha' used   65
a dog o' the name so. O, Numps will triumph now!

Trouble-all comes again

Friend, do you know who I am? Or where I lie? I do not myself, I'll
be sworn. Do but carry me home, and I'll please thee. I ha' money
enough there. I ha' lost myself, and my cloak and my hat, and my fine
sword, and my sister, and Numps, and Mistress Grace, a gentle-   70
woman that I should ha' married, and a cut-work handkercher she ga'
me, and two purses today. And my bargain o' hobbyhorses and
gingerbread, which grieves me worst of all.

TROUBLE-ALL   By whose warrant, sir, have you done all this?

COKES   Warrant? Thou art a wise fellow indeed! As if a man need a   75
warrant to lose anything with!

TROUBLE-ALL   Yes, Justice Overdo's warrant a man may get and lose
with, I'll stand to 't.

COKES   Justice Overdo? Dost thou know him? I lie there, he is my brother-
in-law, he married my sister. Pray thee show me the way. Dost thou   80
know the house?

TROUBLE-ALL   Sir, show me your warrant. I know nothing without a
warrant, pardon me.

COKES   Why, I warrant thee, come along. Thou shalt see I have wrought
pillows there, and cambric sheets, and sweet bags too. Pray thee guide   85
me to the house.

TROUBLE-ALL   Sir, I'll tell you. Go you thither yourself first alone, tell
your worshipful brother your mind, and but bring me three lines of his
hand, or his clerk's, with 'Adam Overdo' underneath. Here I'll stay
you, I'll obey you, and I'll guide you presently.   90

COKES   [*Aside*] 'Slid, this is an ass, I ha' found him. Pox upon me, what
do I talking to such a dull fool? – Farewell, you are a very coxcomb,
do you hear?

---

63. *choke-pears*] Unpalatable variety of pear; hence, something difficult to swallow, like a
    severe reproof.
64. *mumchance*] A dicing game.   *for*] Instead of.
67. *lie*] Lodge (that is, at the Overdo house, where he is visiting).
68. *carry*] Escort.   *please*] Reward.
71. *cut-work*] With a pattern cut out and embroidered like lace.
84. *wrought*] Embroidered.
85. *sweet bags*] Filled with herbs to perfume the linen.
89. *stay*] Wait for.
91. *found him*] Found him out, discovered his true character.

TROUBLE-ALL   I think I am. If Justice Overdo sign to it, I am, and so we
   are all. He'll quit us all, multiply us all.   95

   [*Exeunt*]

Act 4 scene 3*

   [*Enter*] *Grace* [*with*] *Quarlous* [*and*] *Winwife*, [*who*] *enter with their
   swords drawn*

GRACE   Gentlemen, this is no way that you take. You do but breed one
   another trouble and offence, and give me no contentment at all. I am
   no she that affects to be quarrelled for, or have my name or fortune
   made the question of men's swords.
QUARLOUS   'Slood, we love you.   5
GRACE   If you both love me as you pretend, your own reason will tell you
   but one can enjoy me, and to that point there leads a directer line than
   by my infamy, which must follow if you fight. 'Tis true, I have
   professed it to you ingenuously, that rather than to be yoked with this
   bridegroom is appointed me, I would take up any husband, almost   10
   upon any trust. Though subtlety would say to me, I know, he is a fool,
   and has an estate, and I might govern him and enjoy a friend beside.
   But these are not my aims. I must have a husband I must love, or I
   cannot live with him. I shall ill make one of these politic wives!
WINWIFE   Why, if you can like either of us, lady, say which is he, and the   15
   other shall swear instantly to desist.
QUARLOUS   Content, I accord to that willingly.
GRACE   Sure you think me a woman of an extreme levity, gentlemen, or

---

*   The epithets chosen by Quarlous and Winwife have an odd bearing on the marriage
       plots. Winwife chooses the romantic hero in Shakespeare and Fletcher's *Two Noble
       Kinsmen* (1613), 'Palemon', who is devoted to love and guided by destiny to succeed
       over his less worthy rival, his friend Arcite. Broadly speaking, Winwife seems fated by
       both his names to win Grace. Quarlous selects 'Argalus', a knight in Sidney's *Arcadia*,
       who remains faithful to his love even when his vindictive rival destroys her beauty and
       she runs away; later her beauty is miraculously restored, and the lovers are reunited.
       This version of the 'loathly lady' story has no application to Grace, but does have some
       ironic pertinence to Quarlous's later decision to wed Dame Purecraft instead, despite
       his malevolent views on widows (1.3.52ff.): her 'six thousand pound' makes her
       attractive.
  3.   *affects*] Aspires, likes.
  6.   *pretend*] Claim.
 10.   *is*] Who is.
10–11. *almost upon any trust*] Virtually without credentials.
 12.   *friend*] Lover.
 14.   *politic*] Scheming.

a strange fancy that – meeting you by chance in such a place as this,
both at one instant and not yet of two hours' acquaintance, neither of   20
you deserving, afore the other, of me – I should so forsake my
modesty – though I might affect one more particularly – as to say,
'This is he', and name him.

QUARLOUS   Why, wherefore should you not? What should hinder you?

GRACE   If you would not give it to my modesty, allow it yet to my wit.   25
Give me so much of woman and cunning as not to betray myself
impertinently. How can I judge of you so far as to a choice without
knowing you more? You are both equal and alike to me yet, and so
indifferently affected by me as each of you might be the man, if the
other were away. For you are reasonable creatures, you have   30
understanding and discourse. And if fate send me an understanding
husband, I have no fear at all but mine own manners shall make him
a good one.

QUARLOUS   Would I were put forth to making for you then.

GRACE   It may be you are. You know not what's toward you. Will you   35
consent to a motion of mine, gentlemen?

WINWIFE   Whatever it be, we'll presume reasonableness, coming from
you.

QUARLOUS   And fitness, too.

GRACE   I saw one of you buy a pair of tables e'en now.   40

WINWIFE   Yes, here they be, and maiden ones too, unwritten in.

GRACE   The fitter for what they may be employed in. You shall write,
either of you, here, a word or a name, what you like best, but of two
or three syllables at most, and the next person that comes this way –
because Destiny has a high hand in business of this nature – I'll   45
demand which of the two words he or she doth approve and,
according to that sentence, fix my resolution and affection without
change.

QUARLOUS   Agreed. My word is conceived already.

WINWIFE   And mine shall not be long creating after.   50

GRACE   But you shall promise, gentlemen, not to be curious to know

25. *wit*] Intelligence.
26. *cunning*] Worldly knowledge, social skill.
27. *impertinently*] Unsuitably.
29. *indifferently affected*] Impartially esteemed.
31. *discourse*] Rationality.
32. *manners*] Moral character.
34. *put forth to making for*] Apprenticed to.
35. *toward*] Ahead of.
36. *motion*] Proposal.
40. *pair of tables*] Notebook, writing-tablet.
43. *either*] Each.

which of you it is, taken, but give me leave to conceal that till you have
brought me either home or where I may safely tender myself.

WINWIFE   Why, that's but equal.

QUARLOUS   We are pleased.   55

GRACE   Because I will bind both your endeavours to work together,
friendly and jointly, each to the other's fortune, and have myself fitted
with some means to make him that is forsaken a part of amends.

QUARLOUS   These conditions are very courteous. Well, my word is out of
the *Arcadia* then: 'Argalus'.   60

WINWIFE   And mine out of the play: 'Palemon'.

Trouble-all comes again

TROUBLE-ALL   Have you any warrant for this, gentlemen?

QUARLOUS, WINWIFE   Ha!

TROUBLE-ALL   There must be a warrant had, believe it.

WINWIFE   For what?   65

TROUBLE-ALL   For whatsoever it is, anything indeed, no matter what.

QUARLOUS   'Slight, here's a fine ragged prophet dropped down i' the
nick!

TROUBLE-ALL   Heaven quit you, gentlemen.

QUARLOUS   Nay, stay a little. – Good lady, put him to the question.   70

GRACE   You are content then?

WINWIFE, QUARLOUS   Yes, yes.

GRACE   [*To Trouble-all*] Sir, here are two names written –

TROUBLE-ALL   Is 'Justice Overdo' one?

GRACE   How, sir? I pray you read 'em to yourself – it is for a wager   75
between these gentlemen– and with a stroke or any difference, mark
which you approve best.

TROUBLE-ALL   They may be both worshipful names for aught I know,
mistress, but 'Adam Overdo' had been worth three of 'em, I assure
you, in this place. That's in plain English.   80

GRACE   This man amazes me! I pray you, like one of 'em, sir.

TROUBLE-ALL   I do like him there: that has the best warrant, mistress, to
save your longing and multiply him – it may be this. [*Marks a*

---

53. *tender*] Offer formally to discharge an obligation.
54. *equal*] Fair.
58. *forsaken*] Rejected.
60. *Argalus*] A heroic knight in Sir Philip Sidney's *Arcadia* (1.5 and 7) whose love for
Parthenia endures despite the revenge of a jealous rival.
61. *Palemon*] In Shakespeare and Fletcher's *Two Noble Kinsmen* (1613), the rival of Arcite
for the love of a lady.
67–8. *i' the nick*] At the right moment.
76. *any difference*] Distinguishing mark.

name] But I am still for 'Justice Overdo', that's my conscience. And
quit you.   85

[*Exit Trouble-all*]

WINWIFE Is't done, lady?
GRACE Ay, and strangely as ever I saw! What fellow is this, trow?
QUARLOUS No matter what, a fortune-teller we ha' made him. Which is
't, which is 't?
GRACE Nay, did you not promise not to inquire?   90
QUARLOUS 'Slid, I forgot that. Pray you pardon me.

[*Enter Edgworth*]

Look, here's our Mercury come. The licence arrives i' the finest time
too! 'Tis but scraping out Cokes his name, and 'tis done.
WINWIFE How now, lime-twig? Hast thou touched?
EDGWORTH Not yet, sir. Except you would go with me and see 't, it's not   95
worth speaking on. The act is nothing without a witness. Yonder he
is, your man with the box, fallen into the finest company, and so
transported with vapours that they ha' got in a northern clothier and
one Puppy, a western man that's come to wrestle before my Lord
Mayor anon, and Captain Whit, and one Val Cutting, that helps   100
Captain Jordan to roar, a circling-boy – with whom your Numps is so
taken that you may strip him of his clothes, if you will. I'll undertake
to geld him for you, if you had but a surgeon ready to sear him. And
Mistress Justice there is the goodest woman! She does so love 'em all
over, in terms of justice and the style of authority, with her hood 105
upright – that I beseech you come away, gentlemen, and see't.
QUARLOUS 'Slight, I would not lose it for the Fair. What'll you do, Ned?
WINWIFE Why, stay hereabout for you. Mistress Welborn must not be
seen.
QUARLOUS Do so, and find out a priest i' the mean time. I'll bring the 110
licence. – Lead. Which way is 't?

---

84. *conscience*] Conviction.

94. *lime-twig*] Sticky-fingered thief; cf. 3.5.16, 'lime-bush'.

99. *western*] From Cornwall.

99–100. *wrestle before my Lord Mayor*] A regular after-dinner feature of Bartholomew
Fair. The Lord Mayor opened the fair in the morning, dined at noon, and in the
afternoon watched wrestlers compete for prizes awarded by magistrates.

101. *circling-boy*] A bully who quarrels by daring victims to step into a circle which he
draws on the ground, as Cutting does Quarlous in 4.4.109–17.

104. *goodest*] Epithet of courtesy or respect (as in *Goodwife* or *my good lady*), expanded
deprecatingly. *love*] Evaluate or appraise. See 4.4.93–6. The word also suggests the
pleasure Mistress Overdo takes in her quasi-judicial function.

EDGWORTH   Here, sir, you are o' the backside o' the booth already. You may hear the noise.

[*Exeunt*]

Act 4 scene 4*

[*Enter*] *Knockem, Nordern, Puppy, Cutting, Whit, Mistress Overdo, Wasp*

KNOCKEM   Whit, bid Val Cutting continue the vapours for a lift, Whit, for a lift.

NORDERN   I'll ne mare, I'll ne mare. The eale's too meeghty.

KNOCKEM   How now, my Galloway nag! The staggers? Ha! Whit, gi' him a slit i' the forehead. Cheer up, man, a needle and thread to stitch his   5
ears. I'd cure him now, an' I had it, with a little butter and garlic, long pepper, and grains. Where's my horn? I'll gi' him a mash presently shall take away this dizziness.

PUPPY   Why, where are you, zurs? Do you vlinch and leave us i' the zuds, now?   10

NORDERN   I'll ne mare. I's e'en as vull as a paiper's bag, by my troth, I!

PUPPY   Do my northern cloth zhrink i' the wetting? Ha?

---

*   Like 3.1, this scene also achieves part of its effect through its variety of regional accents: here Jonson adds the dialects of the Border (Nordern) and of Cornwall (Puppy), and the hectoring of Val Cutting, the London street bully. The game of vapours is not a harmless pastime: aside from exciting profanity and violence, its object is theft (the licence and the cloaks) and kickbacks to the watch, fetched by Whit to break up the game and blame the remaining victim, once the stolen property has vanished.

1. *lift*] Theft.

3. *ne maire ... too meeghty*] Jonson's attempt at a Border accent: 'no more. The ale's too mighty.'

4. *Galloway nag*] Small sturdy riding-horse bred in SW Scotland.   *staggers*] Dizziness in horses, causing a staggering gait.

4–7. *gi' ... mash*] Remedies for the staggers. The cures listed in Markham, *Cavelarice* (1607), include cutting the horse's forehead, applying a warm salve made of garlic to the forehead, neck, and inner ears, stitching the tips of the ears together, and feeding the animal warm mashes of malt and water.

6–7. *long pepper*] Very strong pepper, presumably to generate more heat in the salve.

7. *grains*] Refuse of malt.   *horn*] Drenching-horn, used for dosing horses.

9. *zurs ... vlinch ... zuds*] Stage-Cornish. Edgar uses the same accent in *King Lear* 4.6.232–42.   *vlinch*] Flinch, draw back (from the drinking and quarrelling competition in progress).   *i' the zuds*] In the suds, in difficulty.

11. *paiper's*] Piper's.

12. *northern cloth ... wetting*] Common regional jeer that northern material shrank easily.

KNOCKEM   Why, well said, old flea-bitten, thou'lt never tire, I see.

They fall to their vapours again

CUTTING   No, sir, but he may tire, if it please him.
WHIT   Who told dee sho? That he vuld never teer, man?   15
CUTTING   No matter who told him so, so long as he knows.
KNOCKEM   Nay, I know nothing, sir, pardon me there.

[Enter] Edgworth, Quarlous

EDGWORTH   They are at it still, sir, this they call vapours.
WHIT   He shall not pardon dee, Captain. Dou shalt not be pardoned.
   Predee, shweetheart, do not pardon him.   20
CUTTING   'Slight, I'll pardon him, an' I list, whosoever says nay to 't.
QUARLOUS   [*To Edgworth*]   Where's Numps? I miss him.
WASP   Why, I say nay to 't.
QUARLOUS   O, there he is!

Here they continue their game of vapours, which is nonsense: every man
to oppose the last man that spoke, whether it concerned him or no

KNOCKEM   To what do you say nay, sir?   25
WASP   To anything whatsoever it is, so long as I do not like it.
WHIT   Pardon me, little man, dou musht like it a little.
CUTTING   No, he must not like it at all, sir. There you are i' the wrong.
WHIT   I tink I be. He musht not like it indeed.
CUTTING   Nay, then he both must and will like it, sir, for all you.   30
KNOCKEM   If he have reason, he may like it, sir.
WHIT   By no meansh, captain, upon reason. He may like nothing upon
   reason.
WASP   I have no reason, nor I will hear of no reason, nor I will look for no
   reason, and he is an ass that either knows any or looks for 't from me.   35
CUTTING   Yes, in some sense you may have reason, sir.
WASP   Ay, in some sense, I care not if I grant you.
WHIT   Pardon me, thou ougsht to grant him nothing, in no shensh, if dou
   do love dyshelf, angry man.
WASP   Why, then, I do grant him nothing, and I have no sense.   40
CUTTING   'Tis true, thou hast no sense indeed.
WASP   'Slid, but I have sense, now I think on 't better, and I will grant him
   anything, do you see?
KNOCKEM   He is i' the right, and does utter a sufficient vapour.
CUTTING   Nay, it is no sufficient vapour neither. I deny that.   45
KNOCKEM   Then it is a sweet vapour.
CUTTING   It may be a sweet vapour.

---

13. *flea-bitten … never tire*] Based on the proverb, 'A flea-bitten [dappled] horse never
   tires.'

WASP   Nay, it is no sweet vapour neither, sir. It stinks, and I'll stand to 't.

WHIT   Yes, I tink it dosh shtink, captain. All vapour dosh shtink.

WASP   Nay, then it does not stink, sir, and it shall not stink.   50

CUTTING   By your leave, it may, sir.

WASP   Ay, by my leave, it may stink. I know that.

WHIT   Pardon me, thou knowesht nothing. It cannot, by thy leave, angry
man.

WASP   How can it not?   55

KNOCKEM   Nay, never question him, for he is i' the right.

WHIT   Yesh, I am i' de right, I confesh it; so ish de little man too.

WASP   I'll have nothing confessed that concerns me. I am not i' the right,
nor never was i' the right, nor never will be i' the right, while I am in
my right mind.   60

CUTTING   Mind? Why, here's no man minds you, sir, nor anything else.

They drink again

PUPPY   Vriend, will you mind this that we do?

QUARLOUS   [*To Edgworth*] Call you this vapours? This is such belching
of quarrel as I never heard. Will you mind your business, sir?

EDGWORTH   You shall see, sir.   65

NORDERN   I'll ne maire. My waimb warks too mickle with this aureudy.

EDGWORTH   Will you take that, Master Wasp, that nobody should mind
you?

WASP   Why? What ha' you to do? Is 't any matter to you?

EDGWORTH   No, but methinks you should not be unminded, though.   70

WASP   Nor I wou'not be, now I think on 't. Do you hear, new acquaintance, does no man mind me, say you?

CUTTING   Yes, sir, every man here minds you, but how?

WASP   Nay, I care as little how as you do. That was not my question.

WHIT   No, noting was ty question. Tou art a learned man, and I am a   75
valiant man, i' faith la! Tou shalt speak for me, and I vill fight for tee.

KNOCKEM   Fight for him, Whit? A gross vapour – he can fight for
himself.

WASP   It may be I can, but it may be I wou' not. How then?

CUTTING   Why, then you may choose.   80

WASP   Why, and I'll choose whether I'll choose or no.

KNOCKEM   I think you may, and 'tis true, and I allow it for a resolute
vapour.

WASP   Nay, then, I do think you do not think, and it is no resolute vapour.

CUTTING   Yes, in some sort he may allow you.   85

64. *business*] That is, stealing the licence.

66. *waimb warks too mickle*] Stomach churns too much.

70. *unminded*] Ignored.

KNOCKEM   In no sort, sir, pardon me, I can allow him nothing. You
   mistake the vapour.
WASP   He mistakes nothing, sir, in no sort.
WHIT   Yes, I predee now, let him mistake.
WASP   A turd i'your teeth, never 'predee' me, for I will have nothing   90
   mistaken.
KNOCKEM   Turd, ha? Turd? A noisome vapour! Strike, Whit!

They fall by the ears; [Edgworth steals the licence from the box and exit]

MISTRESS OVERDO   Why gentlemen, why gentlemen, I charge you upon
   my authority, conserve the peace! In the King's name and my
   husband's, put up your weapons. I shall be driven to commit you   95
   myself else.
QUARLOUS   Ha, ha, ha!
WASP   Why do you laugh, sir?
QUARLOUS   Sir, you'll allow me my Christian liberty. I may laugh, I hope.
CUTTING   In some sort you may, and in some sort you may not, sir.   100
KNOCKEM   Nay, in some sort, sir, he may neither laugh nor hope in this
   company.
WASP   Yes, then he may both laugh and hope in any sort, an't please him.
QUARLOUS   Faith, and I will then, for it doth please me exceedingly.
WASP   No exceeding neither, sir.   105
KNOCKEM   No, that vapour is too lofty.
QUARLOUS   Gentlemen, I do not play well at your game of vapours, I am
   not very good at it, but –
CUTTING   Do you hear, sir? I would speak with you in circle!

He draws a circle on the ground

QUARLOUS   In circle, sir? What would you with me in circle?   110
CUTTING   Can you lend me a piece, a Jacobus? In circle?
QUARLOUS   'Slid, your circle will prove more costly than your vapours,
   then. Sir, no, I lend you none.

89. *predee*] Prithee = I pray thee.
92.1 *fall by the ears*] Fight
95. *commit*] Send to prison; but Quarlous laughs at the bawdy implication, 'commit
   adultery'.
105. *exceeding*] Going too far.
109. *in circle*] Both a literal reference to the circle he draws on the ground, daring his victim
   to enter and fight, and a metaphor for insulting circumlocution, or indirect incitement
   to a fight, as in Cutting's request for a large sum of money, knowing Quarlous will
   refuse, and his disparaging Quarlous's beard. The objects of 'circling' are pleasurable
   violence and theft.
111. *piece*] Coin. *Jacobus*] Gold sovereign issued by James I, worth 24 shillings in 1612.

CUTTING   Your beard's not well turned up, sir.

QUARLOUS   How, rascal? Are you playing with my beard? I'll break circle   115
with you.

They draw all, and fight

PUPPY, NORDERN   Gentlemen, gentlemen!

KNOCKEM   Gather up, Whit, gather up, Whit! Good vapours!

[Exit Whit with the discarded cloaks]

MISTRESS OVERDO   What mean you? Are you rebels? Gentlemen? Shall
I send out a sergeant-at-arms or a writ o' rebellion against you? I'll   120
commit you, upon my womanhood, for a riot, upon my justice-hood,
if you persist.

WASP   Upon your justice-hood? Marry, shit o' your hood, you'll commit?
Spoke like a true Justice of Peace's wife, indeed, and a fine female
lawyer! Turd i' your teeth for a fee now!   125

MISTRESS OVERDO   Why, Numps, in Master Overdo's name, I charge
you.

WASP   Good Mistress Underdo, hold your tongue.

MISTRESS OVERDO   Alas, poor Numps!

WASP   Alas! And why 'alas' from you, I beseech you? Or why 'poor   130
Numps', Goody Rich? Am I come to be pitied by your tuftaffeta now?
Why, mistress, I knew Adam the clerk, your husband, when he was
Adam Scrivener, and writ for twopence a sheet, as high as he bears his
head now, or you your hood, Dame.

*[Exeunt Knockem, Quarlous, and Cutting;] the watch comes in [with
Whit, who still holds the bundle of discarded cloaks]*

What are you, Sir?   135

BRISTLE   We be men and no infidels. What is the matter here, and the
noises? Can you tell?

WASP   Heart, what ha' you to do? Cannot a man quarrel in quietness? But
he must be put out on't by you? What are you?

114. *Your beard's not well turned up*] This may be an implicit stage direction for Cutting
to pull Quarlous's beard, thus forcing the fight.

119. *rebels*] Rioters.

120. *writ o' rebellion*] Warrant charging disobedience to a legal command.

131. *Goody*] Goodwife.   *Rich*] A sneer inverting her 'poor' and accusing her of pretending to have the same power as a member of the Rich family who owned the
fairground.   *tuftaffeta*] Taffeta woven with raised stripes or spots, which were cut to
leave a pile like velvet. The tufted parts were a different colour from the ground.

133. *Adam Scrivener*] Possibly alluding to Chaucer's poem, 'Chaucer's Words unto Adam,
his own Scriven', chastising Adam's careless copying.

139. *put out on't*] Interrupted in the course of it.

BRISTLE   Why, we be his Majesty's watch, sir.   140

WASP   Watch? 'Sblood, you are a sweet watch indeed. A body would think, and you watched well o'nights, you should be contented to sleep at this time o'day. Get you to your fleas and your flock-beds, you rogues, your kennels, and lie down close.

BRISTLE   Down? Yes, we will down, I warrant you! – [*To the other*   145
officers] Down with him in his Majesty's name, down, down with him, and carry him away to the pigeon-holes.

MISTRESS OVERDO   I thank you, honest friends, in the behalf o' the Crown and the peace, and in Master Overdo's name, for suppressing enormities.   150

WHIT   Stay, Bristle, here ish anoder brash o' drunkards, but very quiet, special drunkards, will pay dee five shillings very well. Take 'em to dee, in de graish o' God. One of 'em does change cloth for ale in the Fair here; te t'oder ish a strong man, a mighty man, my Lord Mayor's man, and a wrastler. He has wrashled so long with the bottle here that   155
the man with the beard hash almosht streek up hish heelsh.

BRISTLE   'Slid, the Clerk o' the Market has been to cry him all the Fair over, here, for my Lord's service.

WHIT   Tere he ish, predee taik him hensh, and make ty best on him.

[*Exeunt watch with* Wasp, Puppy, Nordern]

How now, woman o'shilk, vat ailsh ty shweet faish? Art tou   160
melancholy?

MISTRESS OVERDO   A little distempered with these enormities. Shall I entreat a courtesy of you, Captain?

WHIT   Entreat a hundred, velvet voman, I vill do it. Shpeak out.

MISTRESS OVERDO   I cannot with modesty speak it out, but –   165

[*She whispers to him*]

WHIT   I vill do it and more, and more, for dee. – What, Ursula, and't be bitch, and't be bawd, and't be!

[*Enter Ursula*]

URSULA   How now, rascal? What roar you for, old pimp?

142. *watched*] Stayed alert; served as watchmen.
147. *pigeon-holes*] Stocks.
151. *brash*] Brace.
156. *the man with the beard*] A Bellarmine drinking-jug, pot-bellied with a bearded face on its narrow neck caricaturing Cardinal Bellarmine, opponent of the reformers in Holland.   *streek up hish heelsh*] Knocked him off his feet.
157. *Clerk o' the Market*] City official who inspects the market and collects dues.
158. *Lord's*] Lord Mayor's.
162. *distempered with*] Unnerved or disturbed by.

WHIT   [*Handing her the cloaks*] Here, put up de cloaks, Ursh, de
  purchase. Predee now, shweet Ursh, help dis good brave voman to a   170
  jordan, and't be.
URSULA   'Slid, call your Captain Jordan to her, can you not?
WHIT   Nay, predee leave dy consheits and bring the velvet woman to de –
URSULA   I bring her, hang her! Heart, must I find a common pot for every
  punk i' your purlieus?   175
WHIT   O good voordsh, Ursh! It ish a guest o' velvet, i' fait la!
URSULA   Let her sell her hood and buy a sponge, with a pox to her. My
  vessel? Employed, sir. I have but one, and 'tis the bottom of an old
  bottle. An honest proctor and his wife are at it within. If she'll stay her
  time, so.   180
WHIT   As soon ash tou cansht, shweet Ursh. Of a valiant man I tink I am
  the patientsh man i' the world, or in all Smithfield.

  [*Enter Knockem*]

KNOCKEM   How now, Whit? Close vapours? Stealing your leaps? Covering in corners, ha?
WHIT   No, fait, Captain, dough tou beesht a vishe man, dy vit is a mile   185
  hence now. I vas procuring a shmall courtesy for a woman of fashion
  here.
MISTRESS OVERDO   Yes, Captain, though I am Justice of Peace's wife, I
  do love men of war and the sons of the sword when they come before
  my husband.   190
KNOCKEM   Say'st thou so, filly? Thou shalt have a leap presently. I'll
  horse thee myself, else.
URSULA   Come, will you bring her in now? And let her take her turn?
WHIT   Gramercy, good Ursh, I tank dee.
MISTRESS OVERDO   Master Overdo shall thank her.

  [*Exit Mistress Overdo*]

171. *jordan*] Chamber-pot.
175. *punk i' your purlieus*] Whore in your string of brothels.
183. *Stealing your leaps?*] Sneaking samples of your own merchandise? Having sexual
  relations with the whores you should be selling to others?
183–4. *Covering*] Copulating (used of stallions).

Act 4 scene 5*

[*Enter*] John [*Littlewit*], Win

LITTLEWIT   Good Gammer Urs, Win and I are exceedingly beholden to you, and to Captain Jordan and Captain Whit. Win, I'll be bold to leave you i' this good company, Win, for half an hour or so, Win, while I go and see how my matter goes forward, and if the puppets be perfect, and then I'll come and fetch you, Win.   5

WIN   Will you leave me alone with two men, John?

LITTLEWIT   Ay, they are honest gentlemen, Win, Captain Jordan and Captain Whit. They'll use you very civilly, Win. God b'w'you, Win.

[*Exit Littlewit*]

URSULA   What, 's her husband gone?

KNOCKEM   On his false gallop, Urs, away.   10

URSULA   An' you be right Bartholomew-birds, now show yourselves so. We are undone for want of fowl i' the Fair here. Here will be 'Zekiel Edgworth and three or four gallants with him at night, and I ha' neither plover nor quail for 'em. Persuade this, between you two, to become a bird o' the game while I work the velvet woman within, as   15
you call her.

KNOCKEM   I conceive thee, Urs! Go thy ways.

[*Exit Ursula*]

Dost thou hear, Whit? Is 't not pity, my delicate dark chestnut here with the fine lean head, large forehead, round eyes, even mouth, sharp ears, long neck, thin crest, close withers, plain back, deep sides, short   20
fillets, and full flanks, with a round belly, a plump buttock, large thighs, knit knees, straight legs, short pasterns, smooth hooves, and short heels, should lead a dull honest woman's life, that might live the life of a lady?

---

*   This scene plays punningly on 'green women': the 'green' or naive Win and Mistress Overdo will be transformed into 'Guests o' the game' in green gowns and scarlet petticoats, temporary versions of Ramping Alice, the punk who resents their intrusion on her trade.

1. *Gammer*] Courtesy title for an old woman, short for 'grandmother'.
4–5. *be perfect*] Know their parts.
7. *honest*] Respectable.
8. *use*] Treat, but with inadvertent bawdy innuendo.
10. *false gallop*] Canter; figuratively, mistaken assumption.
12. *fowl*] Prostitutes.
14. *plover, quail*] Wenches.
18–24. Knockem equivocally describes the perfect mount.
20. *plain*] Flat.

WHIT   Yes, by my fait and trot, it is, Captain. De honesht woman's life is   25
   a scurvy dull life, indeed la!

WIN   How, sir? Is an honest woman's life a scurvy life?

WHIT   Yes, fait, shweetheart, believe him, de leef of a bond-woman! But
   if dou vilt harken to me, I vill make tee a free-woman and a lady. Dou
   shalt live like a lady, as te Captain saish.   30

KNOCKEM   Ay, and be honest too sometimes: have her wires, and her
   tires, her green gowns, and velvet petticoats.

WHIT   Ay, and ride to Ware and Rumford i' dy coash, shee de players, be
   in love vit 'em, sup vit gallantsh, be drunk, and cost de noting.

KNOCKEM   Brave vapours!   35

WHIT   And lie by twenty on 'em, if dou pleash, shweetheart.

WIN   What, and be honest still? That were fine sport.

WHIT   'Tish common, shweetheart, tou may'st do it, by my hand. It shall
   be justified to ty husband's faish, now. Tou shalt be as honesht as the
   skin between his hornsh, la!   40

KNOCKEM   Yes, and wear a dressing, top and topgallant, to compare with
   e'er a husband on 'em all, for a foretop. It is the vapour of spirit in
   the wife to cuckold nowadays, as it is the vapour of fashion in the
   husband not to suspect. Your prying cat-eyed citizen is an abominable
   vapour.   45

WIN   Lord, what a fool have I been!

WHIT   Mend then, and do everyting like a lady hereafter: never know ty
   husband from another man.

27. *honest*] Chaste.

29. *lady*] Woman of rank; lady of pleasure.

31. *wires*] Frames to stiffen ruffs.

32. *tires*] Head-dresses. *green gowns*] Worn by prostitutes and loose women; see 3.6.82
   and this scene, 83–5.

33. *Ware*] 24 miles N of London, a town noted for its 'Great Bed' measuring almost 11 feet
   square and taken to be symbolic of Ware's notoriety as a lovers' rendezvous; cf.
   SW] 3.2.63 and 5.1.53. *Rumford*] An Essex village 13 miles NE of St Paul's, a
   favourite place for summer excursions by fashionable merrymakers.

39–40. *honesht as the skin between his hornsh*] proverbially, 'honest as the skin between
   his brows', meaning obvious honesty, but Whit's substitution of cuckold's horns
   suggests that Littlewit's carelessness with his wife's honour will have the obvious result.

41. *dressing*] Attire. *top and topgallant*] Topsail and topgallant sail, nautical phrase
   meaning 'in full array'.

42. *foretop*] A nautical term for the top of the foremast, but also referring either to the
   forelock of a horse or to a fashionable man who wore his hair elaborately curled and
   stiffened over his forehead. A 'foretop' in this latter sense was a fop. According to
   Knockem, modern couples dress for adultery, and the wife who wastes her sexual
   opportunities behaves foolishly.

47. *Mend*] Amend, set yourself right. *know*] Recognise socially or indulge sexually.

KNOCKEM   Nor any one man from another, but i' the dark.

WHIT   Ay, and then it ish no dishgrash to know any man.   50

  [*Enter Ursula*]

URSULA   Help, help here!

KNOCKEM   How now? What vapour's there?

URSULA   O, you are a sweet ranger and look well to your walks! Yonder
  is your punk of Turnbull, Ramping Alice, has fallen upon the poor
  gentlewoman within, and pulled her hood over her ears, and her hair   55
  through it.

  Alice enters, beating the Justice's wife

MISTRESS OVERDO   Help, help, i'the King's name!

ALICE   A mischief on you! They are such as you are, that undo us and take
  our trade from us, with your tuftaffeta haunches!

KNOCKEM   How now, Alice!   60

ALICE   The poor common whores can ha' no traffic for the privy rich ones.
  Your caps and hoods of velvet call away our customers and lick the
  fat from us.

URSULA   Peace, you foul ramping jade you –

ALICE   Od's foot, you bawd in grease, are you talking?   65

KNOCKEM   Why, Alice, I say!

ALICE   Thou sow of Smithfield, thou!

URSULA   Thou tripe of Turnbull!

KNOCKEM   Cat-a-mountain vapours! Ha!

URSULA   You know where you were tawed lately; both lashed and slashed   70
  you were in Bridewell.

ALICE   Ay, by the same token, you rid that week, and broke out the bottom
  o' the cart, night-tub.

58. *undo*] Ruin.

59. *tuftaffeta haunches*] Fashionable silk skirts, worn over a farthingale which exaggerated
  the spread of the hips. See 4.4.131.

61. *common*] Available to all customers.   *privy*] Private, exclusive.

62–3. *lick the fat from us*] Deprive us of our best customers (proverbial).

65. *in grease*] Fat enough to kill, used of swine ready for slaughter.

69. *Cat-a-mountain*] wildcat, colloquial for whore. The 'vapours' Knockem so describes
  involve the yowling, hissing, spitting, and scratching associated with a cat-fight.

70. *tawed*] Flogged; see *Alch* 4.3.100.   *slashed*] Cut with a scourge.

71. *Bridewell*] A prison for vagrants and whores, on the west side of the Fleet Ditch.

72. *rid*] Rode in a cart for whores, a public punishment.

73. *night-tub*] Container for excrement, so called because workers emptied household tubs
  during the night.

KNOCKEM   Why, lion-face! Ha! Do you know who I am? Shall I tear ruff,
slit waistcoat, make rags of petticoat? Ha! Go to, vanish, for fear of   75
vapours! Whit, a kick, Whit, in the parting vapour.

[Exit Alice, kicked out by Knockem and Whit]

[To Mistress Overdo] Come, brave woman, take a good heart. Thou
shalt be a lady too.

WHIT   Yes, fait, dey shall all both be ladies, and write Madam. I vill do't
myself for dem. 'Do' is the vord, and D is the middle letter of   80
'Madam'. DD: put 'em together and make deeds, without which all
words are alike, la!

KNOCKEM   'Tis true. Ursula, take 'em in, open thy wardrobe, and fit 'em
to their calling. Green gowns, crimson petticoats, green women! My
Lord Mayor's green women! Guests o'the game, true bred. I'll provide   85
you a coach to take the air in.

WIN   But do you think you can get one?

KNOCKEM   O, they are as common as wheelbarrows where there are great
dunghills. Every pettifogger's wife has 'em, for first he buys a coach
that he may marry, and then he marries that he may be made cuckold   90
in 't. For if their wives ride not to their cuckolding, they do 'em no
credit. 'Hide and be hidden, ride and be ridden', says the vapour of
experience.

[Exeunt Ursula, Win, Mistress Overdo]

Act 4 scene 6*

[Enter] Trouble-all

TROUBLE-ALL   By what warrant does it say so?
KNOCKEM   Ha! Mad   child   o'the   Pie-Powders,   art   thou   there?

74–5. *tear ... petticoat*] Threats to rip Alice's clothes off. Whores, also called 'waist-
coaters', wore a *waistcoat*, a more recent fashion than the stomacher, but without the
shift or outer gown that covered up modest women.
79. *write*] Style themselves.
80. *'Do'*] Copulate.
81. *deeds*] Sexual acts.
84. *Green ... women*] The outfits of whores.
89. *pettifogger*] Rascally small-time lawyer.
92. *ridden*] Mounted sexually.
*   The paradoxes of this scene help to prepare for the inversions of the final act. Knockem
cheats, pimps, and brawls, but, in an act of casual compassion, forges a warrant to buy
Trouble-all a drink. Quarlous rejects any notion of parity with Edgworth, but steals,
commits fraud by impersonation, forges a licence, and breaks faith with his friends, acts
that exceed Edgworth's and Knockem's crimes. So too this scene depicts Overdo as a

– [*Calling*] Fill us a fresh can, Urs, we may drink together.
TROUBLE-ALL I may not drink without a warrant, Captain.
KNOCKEM 'Slood, thou'll not stale without a warrant shortly. Whit, give 5
    me pen, ink, and paper. I'll draw him a warrant presently.

[*Whit exits and re-enters with pen, ink and paper*]

TROUBLE-ALL It must be Justice Overdo's!
KNOCKEM I know, man. Fetch the drink, Whit.
WHIT I predee now, be very brief, Captain, for de new ladies stay for dee.
KNOCKEM O, as brief as can be. 10

[*Exit Whit; Knockem writes*]

    Here 'tis already: 'Adam Overdo'.

[*Enter Whit with a can of ale for Trouble-all*]

TROUBLE-ALL Why, now I'll pledge you, Captain.
KNOCKEM Drink it off. I'll come to thee anon again.

[*Exeunt Knockem and Whit into booth; Trouble-all roams off*]
[*Enter Quarlous, talking*] to the cutpurse [*Edgworth*]

QUARLOUS Well, sir. You are now discharged. Beware of being spied
    hereafter. 15
EDGWORTH Sir, will it please you enter in here at Ursula's and take part
    of a silken gown, a velvet petticoat, or a wrought smock? I am
    promised such, and I can spare any gentleman a moiety.
QUARLOUS Keep it for your companions in beastliness. I am none of 'em,
    sir. If I had not already forgiven you a greater trespass, or thought you 20
    yet worth my beating, I would instruct your manners, to whom you
    made your offers. But go your ways, talk not to me. The hangman is
    only fit to discourse with you; the hand of beadle is too merciful a
    punishment for your trade of life.

[*Exit Edgworth*]

truant judge, Busy as a reprobate minister, and Wasp as a delinquent guardian: they
    deserve but escape punishment.
 5. *stale*] Urinate.
14. *spied*] Observed picking pockets.
16–17. *take part of*] Partake of.
18. *moiety*] Share.
21. *instruct your manners*] Improve your behaviour, teach you a lesson.
23. *hand of beadle*] Public whipping administered by the parish officer, who punished
    petty offenders.

I am sorry I employed this fellow, for he thinks me such: *Facinus*   25
quos inquinat aequat. But it was for sport. And would I make it
serious, the getting of this licence is nothing to me, without other
circumstances concur. I do think how impertinently I labour, if the
word be not mine that the ragged fellow marked. And what
advantage I have given Ned Winwife in this time now of working   30
her, though it be mine. He'll go near to form to her what a debauched
rascal I am, and fright her out of all good conceit of me. I should
do so by him, I am sure, if I had the opportunity. But my hope is
in her temper yet, and it must needs be next to despair that is
grounded on any part of a woman's discretion. I would give, by my   35
troth now, all I could spare – to my clothes and my sword – to
meet my tattered soothsayer again who was my judge i' the
question, to know certainly whose word he has damned or saved.
For, till then, I live but under a reprieve. I must seek him. Who
be these?   40

Enter Wasp with the officers

WASP   Sir, you are a Welsh cuckold, and a prating runt, and no constable.
BRISTLE   You say very well. – Come put in his leg in the middle roundel,
and let him hole there.

[*They put Wasp in the stocks*]

WASP   You stink of leeks, metheglin, and cheese. You rogue!
BRISTLE   Why, what is that to you, if you sit sweetly in the stocks in the   45
mean time? If you have a mind to stink too, your breeches sit close
enough to your bum. Sit you merry, sir.
QUARLOUS   How now, Numps?
WASP   It is no matter how. Pray you look off.
QUARLOUS   Nay, I'll not offend you, Numps. I thought you had sat there   50
to be seen.
WASP   And to be sold, did you not? Pray you mind your business, an' you
have any.
QUARLOUS   Cry you mercy, Numps. Does your leg lie high enough?

25. *such*] The same type of fellow as he is.
25–6. *Facinus quos inquinat aequat*] 'Crime puts those it corrupts on the same footing'
(Lucan, *Pharsalia* 5.290).
28. *impertinently*] Pointlessly.
30. *working*] Prejudicing.
31. *form*] Draw an image of.
32. *conceit*] Impression.
41. *runt*] Ox or cow of a small breed raised in Wales; a slur on persons of inferior size or
of uncouth manners.
44. *leeks*] Symbol of St David, patron saint of Wales. *metheglin*] Welsh mead.

[Enter] Haggis [with] Overdo, Busy

BRISTLE How now, neighbour Haggis, what says Justice Overdo's   55
    worship to the other offenders?
HAGGIS Why, he says just nothing. What should he say? Or where should
    he say? He is not to be found, man. He ha' not been seen i'the Fair here
    all this live-long day, never since seven o'clock i' the morning. His
    clerks know not what to think on 't. There is no Court of Pie-Powders   60
    yet. Here they be returned.
BRISTLE What shall be done with 'em then? In your discretion?
HAGGIS I think we were best put 'em in the stocks, in discretion – there
    they will be safe in discretion – for the valour of an hour or such a
    thing, till his worship come.   65
BRISTLE It is but a hole matter, if we do, neighbour Haggis. – Come, sir,
    here is company for you. – *[To the officers]* Heave up the stocks.
WASP *[Aside]* I shall put a trick upon your Welsh diligence, perhaps.

As they open the stocks, Wasp puts his shoe on his hand and slips it in
for his leg

BRISTLE *[To Busy]* Put in your leg, sir.
QUARLOUS What, Rabbi Busy! Is he come?   70

They bring Busy and put him in

BUSY I do obey thee. The lion may roar, but he cannot bite. I am glad to
    be thus separated from the heathen of the land, and put apart in the
    stocks for the holy cause.
WASP What are you, sir?
BUSY One that rejoiceth in his affliction, and sitteth here to prophesy the   75
    destruction of fairs and May-games, wakes, and Whitsun-ales, and
    doth sigh and groan for the reformation of these abuses.

[They put Overdo in the stocks]

WASP *[To Overdo]* And do you sigh and groan too, or rejoice in your
    affliction?
OVERDO I do not feel it, I do not think of it, it is a thing without me.   80

---

62. *discretion*] Opinion.
63. *discretion*] Prudence; separation.
64. *valour*] Value, length.
76. *May-games, wakes*] Considered heathen survivals by Puritans. *Whitsun-ales*] Parish
    festivities held at Whitsuntide, marked by feasting, sports, and merrymaking.
80. *without me*] Outside of myself, having nothing to do with me. Overdo speaks stoically
    as one whose integrity external mishap cannot damage.

Adam, thou art above these batteries, these contumelies. *In te manca ruit fortuna*, as thy friend Horace says. Thou art one *Quem neque pauperies, neque mors, neque vincula terrent*. And therefore, as another friend of thine says – I think it be thy friend Persius – *Non te quaesiveris extra*.   85

QUARLOUS   What's here! A stoic i' the stocks? The fool is turned philosopher.

BUSY   Friend, I will leave to communicate my spirit with you, if I hear any more of those superstitious relics, those lists of Latin, the very rags of Rome and patches of popery.   90

WASP   Nay, an' you begin to quarrel, gentlemen, I'll leave you. I ha' paid for quarrelling too lately. Look you, a device: but shifting in a hand for a foot.

He gets out

God b'w'you.

BUSY   Wilt thou then leave thy brethren in tribulation?   95

WASP   For this once, sir.

[Exit Wasp]

BUSY   Thou art a halting neutral – Stay him there, stop him! – that will not endure the heat of persecution!

BRISTLE   How now, what's the matter?

BUSY   He is fled, he is fled, and dares not sit it out.   100

BRISTLE   What, has he made an escape? Which way? Follow, neighbour Haggis!

[Exit Haggis; enter] Purecraft

PURECRAFT   O me! In the stocks! Have the wicked prevailed?

BUSY   Peace, religious sister. It is my calling, comfort yourself, an

81. *batteries*] A succession of heavy blows.

81–2. *In te manca ruit fortuna*] 'In assaulting you, Fortune maims herself' (Horace, *Satires* 2.7.88).

82–3. *Quem ... terrent*] 'Whom neither poverty, nor death, nor fetters can terrify' (Horace, 84).

84–5. *Non te quaesiveris extra*] 'Do not seek to know anything outside yourself' (Persius, *Satires* 1.7).

86–7. Quarlous's crack is an ironic reminder that 'mad Arthur' Overdo's insensitivity to his predicament is foolish, not wise.

88. *leave*] Stop.

89. *lists*] Shreds.

92. *shifting in*] Exchanging, replacing.

97. *halting*] Limping, presumably because Wasp is carrying one shoe.   *neutral*] One who supports neither side in a dispute.

extraordinary calling, and done for my better standing, my surer   105
standing hereafter.

The madman enters

TROUBLE-ALL   By whose warrant, by whose warrant, this?
QUARLOUS   O, here's my man dropped in, I looked for!
OVERDO   Ha!
PURECRAFT   O good sir, they have set the faithful here to be wondered at,   110
and provided holes for the holy of the land.
TROUBLE-ALL   Had they warrant for it? Showed they Justice Overdo's
hand? If they had no warrant, they shall answer it.

[Enter Haggis]

BRISTLE   Sure you did not lock the stocks sufficiently, neighbour Toby!
HAGGIS   No? See if you can lock 'em better!   115
BRISTLE   They are very sufficiently locked, and truly, yet something is in
the matter.
TROUBLE-ALL   True, your warrant is the matter that is in question. By
what warrant?
BRISTLE   Madman, hold your peace. I will put you in his room else, in the   120
very same hole, do you see?
QUARLOUS   How! Is he a madman?
TROUBLE-ALL   Show me Justice Overdo's warrant, I obey you.
HAGGIS   You are a mad fool. Hold your tongue.
TROUBLE-ALL   In Justice Overdo's name, I drink to you, and here's my   125
warrant.

Shows his can [to the watchmen, who walk aside]

OVERDO   [*Aside*]   Alas, poor wretch! How it earns my heart for him!
QUARLOUS   [*Aside*]   If he be mad, it is in vain to question him. I'll try
though. — [*To Trouble-all*]   Friend, there was a gentlewoman showed
you two names some hour since, 'Argalus' and 'Palemon', to mark in   130
a book. Which of 'em was it you marked?
TROUBLE-ALL   I mark no name but 'Adam Overdo'. That is the name of
names, he only is the sufficient magistrate, and that name I reverence.
Show it me.
QUARLOUS   [*Aside*]   This fellow's mad indeed. I am further off now than   135
afore.
OVERDO   [*Aside*]   I shall not breathe in peace till I have made him some
amends.
QUARLOUS   [*Aside*]   Well, I will make another use of him is come in my

108. *I looked for*] That is, 'man ... [whom] I looked for'.
127. *earns*] Grieves.

head. I have a nest of beards in my trunk, one something like his.   140

[Exit Quarlous;] the watchmen come back again

BRISTLE   This mad fool has made me that I know not whether I have
locked the stocks or no. I think I locked 'em.

TROUBLE-ALL   Take Adam Overdo in your mind, and fear nothing.

BRISTLE   'Slid, madness itself, hold thy peace, and take that!

TROUBLE-ALL   Strikest thou without a warrant? Take thou that!   145

The madman fights with 'em and they leave open the stocks

BUSY   [*To Overdo*] We are delivered by miracle. Fellow in fetters, let us
not refuse the means; this madness was of the spirit. The malice of the
enemy hath mocked itself.

[Exeunt Busy and Overdo]

PURECRAFT   Mad do they call him! The world is mad in error, but
he is mad in truth. I love him o' the sudden – the cunningman said all   150
true – and shall love him more and more. How well it becomes a man
to be mad in truth! O, that I might be his yoke-fellow and be mad with
him! What a many should we draw to madness in truth with us!

[Exit Purecraft;] the watch, missing them, are affrighted

BRISTLE   How now! All scaped? Where's the *woman*? It is witchcraft! Her
velvet hat is a witch, o' my conscience, or my key, t' one! The madman   155
was a devil, and I am an ass. So bless me, my place, and mine office!

[Exeunt]

140. *nest*] Collection, each one set within the next.   *trunk*] Trunk hose, wide breeches to
the knee, stuffed with hair to suggest thighs of enormous size.

154–6. The watchman's fears at the disappearance of his prisoners make him accuse Dame
Purecraft, an independent and outspoken woman, of witchcraft. See 2.2.20n.

155. *t' one*] The one or the other.

ACT 5

Act 5 scene 1*

[*Enter*] [*Leatherhead as*] *Lantern* [*the puppet-master,*] *Filcher, Shark-*
well [*at the puppet-theatre*]

LEATHERHEAD   Well, luck and Saint Bartholomew! Out with the sign of
our invention, in the name of wit, and do you beat the drum the
while.

[*Filcher and Sharkwell hang the banner advertising the puppet-show, and*
proceed to drum up business]

All the fowl i' the Fair, I mean, all the dirt in Smithfield – that's one
of Master Littlewit's carwhitchets now – will be thrown at our banner   5
today, if the matter does not please the people. O, the motions that I,
Lantern Leatherhead, have given light to i'my time, since my Master
Pod died! *Jerusalem* was a stately thing, and so was *Nineveh*, and *The*
City of Norwich, and *Sodom and Gomorrah*, with the rising o'
the prentices and pulling down the bawdy-houses there upon   10

---

*   Leatherhead's new persona, Lantern, requires a change of costume (see note at
3.6.121); Littlewit, as a theatre buff, has no problem recognising him, but Cokes and
the others seem not to identify him with the toy-stall. Lantern speaks for the puppets
as well as for himself in the performances that follow in 5.4 and 5.5, but he is not
backstage manipulating them. He is the interpreter standing in front of the stage to tell
the story and to backchat with the puppets. See Speaight 1955: pp. 66–9.
1.   *sign*] See 'banner', l.5, usually a painted cloth.
2.   *invention*] Original puppet-play.
5.   *carwitchets*] Puns.
6   *motions*] Puppet-shows.
8.   *Pod*] F notes in the margin, 'Pod was a Master of motions before him'. Jonson
mentions 'Captain Pod' in *EMO* (4.5.62), written in 1599, and in *Epigrams* 97.2 ('On
the New Motion') and 129.16 ('To Mime').
8–9.   *Jerusalem, Nineveh, The City of Norwich, Sodom and Gomorrah*] Jacobean puppet-
shows depicted (a) travesties of Bible stories like the destruction of Jerusalem or the
annihilation of Sodom and Gomorrah, but modernised them to include events like the
Shrove-Tuesday riots as relevant contemporary equivalents; (b) corruptions of stage-
plays, like the fall of Nineveh including a scene of Jonah and the whale, borrowed from
Lodge and Green's *A Looking Glass for London and England* (1598) (the death of
Julius Caesar, based on Shakespeare's 1599 play, was also popular); or (c) telescoped
national events such as the building of Norwich, raised in an hour, according to legend,
or the Gunpowder Plot (see below).
9–11.   *rising . . . Shrove-Tuesday*] Apprentices traditionally rioted on the last Tuesday before
Lent, wrecking brothels and play-houses; cf. *SW* 1.1.137.

Shrove-Tuesday, but *The Gunpowder Plot*, there was a get-penny! I
have presented that to an eighteen- or twenty-pence audience, nine
times in an afternoon. Your home-born projects prove ever the best:
they are so easy and familiar. They put too much learning i'their
things nowadays, and that, I fear, will be the spoil o'this. Littlewit? I
say,   15
Micklewit! If not too mickle! Look to your gathering there, Goodman
Filcher.

FILCHER   I warrant you, sir.

LEATHERHEAD   And there come any gentlefolks, take twopence a piece,
Sharkwell.

SHARKWELL   I warrant you, sir, threepence, an' we can.

[*Exit Leatherhead*]

Act 5 scene 2*

The Justice comes in like a porter

OVERDO   This later disguise I have borrowed of a porter shall carry me
out to all my great and good ends, which, however interrupted, were
never destroyed in me. Neither is the hour of my severity yet come to
reveal myself, wherein cloud-like I will break out in rain and hail,
lightning and thunder, upon the head of enormity. Two main works   5
I have to prosecute: first, one is to invent some satisfaction for the
poor kind wretch who is out of his wits for my sake, and yonder I see
him coming. I will walk aside and project for it.

[*Enter*] *Winwife, Grace*

---

11. *The Gunpowder Plot*] Another current-event play, which continued to be performed as
a Punch-and-Judy show well into the eighteenth century, based on Guy Fawkes's
conspiracy to blow up James I and his parliament on 5 November 1605. *get-
penny*] Money-maker.

13. *home-born projects*] Shows using current English material.

14. *easy*] Credible.   *familiar*] Well-known, readily understood.   *too much learning*] A
charge frequently levelled at Jonson.

15. *spoil*] Undoing.

16. *mickle*] Great.   *gathering*] Collecting of entrance money.

*   Once Quarlous becomes the madman, his luck changes: 'mad' at the loss of Grace, he
stumbles into a bride with money and a blank warrant to get more, opportunities he
would be crazy not to make use of.

1–2. *carry me out to*] Win or obtain for me.

3. *severity*] Harsh rebuke of others.

8. *project*] Form a plan.

WINWIFE   I wonder where Tom Quarlous is, that he returns not. It may
    be he is struck in here to seek us.   10
GRACE   See, here's our madman again.

   [Enter] Quarlous, Purecraft; Quarlous, in the habit of the madman, is
   mistaken by Mistress Purecraft

QUARLOUS   [*Aside*]   I have made myself as like him as his gown and cap
    will give me leave.
PURECRAFT   Sir, I love you, and would be glad to be mad with you in
    truth.   15
WINWIFE   [*Aside*]   How! My widow in love with a madman?
PURECRAFT   Verily, I can be as mad in spirit as you.
QUARLOUS   By whose warrant? Leave your canting. – [*To Grace*] Gen-
    tlewoman, have I found you? – Save ye, quit ye, and multiply ye! –
    Where's your book? 'Twas a sufficient name I marked. Let me see 't,   20
    be not afraid to show 't me.

   He desires to see the book of Mistress Grace

GRACE   What would you with it, sir?
QUARLOUS   Mark it again, and again, at your service.
GRACE   Here it is, sir. This was it you marked.
QUARLOUS   'Palemon'? Fare you well, fare you well.   25
WINWIFE   How, 'Palemon'!
GRACE   Yes, faith, he has discovered it to you now, and therefore 'twere
    vain to disguise it longer. I am yours, sir, by the benefit of your
    fortune.
WINWIFE   And you have him, mistress, believe it, that shall never give you   30
    cause to repent her benefit, but make you rather to think that in this
    choice she had both her eyes.
GRACE   I desire to put it to no danger of protestation.

   [Exeunt Grace, Winwife]

QUARLOUS   [*Aside*]   'Palemon' the word, and Winwife the man?
PURECRAFT   Good sir, vouchsafe a yoke-fellow in your madness. Shun   35
    not one of the sanctified sisters that would draw with you in truth.

---

10. *is struck*]   Has turned.
18. *canting*]   Puritan jargon.
28. *benefit*]   Agency, kindness.
32. *she had both her eyes*]   Fortune is proverbially blind, or depicted as blindfolded.
33. *protestation*]   In law, a protest at an allegation, the truth of which the pleader can
    neither affirm, deny, nor ignore without self-incrimination. Here, Grace would appear
    immodest if she agreed with Winwife directly, foolish if she disagreed, and smug if she
    made no reply. She takes the politic route of declining protest.

QUARLOUS   Away! You are a herd of hypocritical proud ignorants, rather
wild than mad. Fitter for woods and the society of beasts than houses
and the congregation of men. You are the second part of the society
of canters, outlaws to order and discipline, and the only privileged   40
church-robbers of Christendom. Let me alone. – 'Palemon' the word,
and Winwife the man?

PURECRAFT   [*Aside*] I must uncover myself unto him, or I shall never
enjoy him, for all the cunningmen's promises. – Good sir, hear me. I
am worth six thousand pound. My love to you is become my rack. I'll   45
tell you all, and the truth, since you hate the hypocrisy of the parti-
coloured brotherhood. These seven years, I have been a wilful holy
widow only to draw feasts and gifts from my entangled suitors. I am
also, by office, an assisting sister of the deacons, and a devourer
instead of a distributor of the alms. I am a special maker of marriages   50
for our decayed brethren with our rich widows for a third part of their
wealth, when they are married, for the relief of the poor elect; as also
our poor handsome young virgins, with our wealthy bachelors or
widowers, to make them steal from their husbands when I have
confirmed them in the faith and got all put into their custodies. And   55
if I ha' not my bargain, they may sooner turn a scolding drab into a
silent minister than make me leave pronouncing reprobation and
damnation unto them. Our elder, Zeal-of-the-land, would have had
me, but I know him to be the capital knave of the land, making himself
rich by being made feoffee in trust to deceased brethren and coz'ning   60
their heirs by swearing the absolute gift of their inheritance. And thus
having eased my conscience and uttered my heart with the tongue of
my love, enjoy all my deceits together. I beseech you. I should not have

39–40. *second part of the society of canters*] The first part being the rogues and vagabonds
who spoke thieves' cant. For details of their jargon, see Thomas Harman, *A Caveat or
Warning for common Cursitors* (1566), in Judges (1930).

46–7. *parti-coloured*] Specious in defending their cause; or puritanically dyed-in-the-wool.
A 'colour' means a trick or pretence, as well as a dye; 'parti-' derives from 'party' in the
sense of being one-sided in an argument.

47–58. *These seven ... unto them*] Compare this confession to *SW* 2.2.67–72 and *Alch*
3.2.69-73.

52. *elect*] Those predestined by God for salvation (puritan cant).

56. *scolding drab*] Foul-mouthed slut.

57. *silent minister*] Puritan clergyman who lost his licence to preach. See *SW* 2.2.68 and
Alch 3.1.38.   *reprobation*] Condemnation to eternal damnation (Puritan cant).

59. *capital*] Chief.

60. *feoffee in trust*] Trustee invested with a freehold estate in land.

61. *absolute*] Unconditionally deeded to another, as opposed to being held in trust for the
heirs.

revealed this to you, but that in time I think you are mad, and I hope
you'll think me so too, sir?   65

QUARLOUS Stand aside. I'll answer you presently.

He considers with himself of it

Why should not I marry this six thousand pound, now I think on't?
And a good trade, too, that she has beside, ha? The t'other wench
Winwife is sure of; there's no expectation for me there! Here I may
make myself some saver yet, if she continue mad – there's the   70
question. It is money that I want. Why should I not marry the money
when 'tis offered me? I have a licence and all. It is but razing out one
name and putting in another. There's no playing with a man's fortune!
I am resolved! I were truly mad an' I would not! –
[*To Purecraft*] Well, come your ways, follow me. An' you will be   75
mad, I'll show you a warrant!

He takes her along with him

PURECRAFT Most zealously, it is that I zealously desire.

The Justice calls him

OVERDO Sir, let me speak with you.

QUARLOUS By whose warrant?

OVERDO The warrant that you tender and respect so. Justice Overdo's! 80
I am the man, friend Trouble-all, though thus disguised – as the careful
magistrate ought – for the good of the republic in the Fair and the
weeding out of enormity. Do you want a house or meat, or drink, or
clothes? Speak whatsoever it is, it shall be supplied you. What want
you?   85

QUARLOUS Nothing but your warrant.

OVERDO My warrant? For what?

QUARLOUS To be gone, sir.

OVERDO Nay, I pray thee stay. I am serious, and have not many words,
nor much time to exchange with thee. Think what may do thee good.   90

QUARLOUS Your hand and seal will do me a great deal of good; nothing
else in the whole Fair that I know.

OVERDO If it were to any end, thou should'st have it willingly.

---

64. *in time*] Propitiously, as by God's design.

70. *make myself some saver*] Break even, recoup previous losses (gambling term); see *Volp*
    4.1.20 and *SW* 3.3.27.

80. *tender*] Have tender regard for, esteem.

81–2. *as the careful magistrate ought*] As befits the painstaking or scrupulous magistrate.
    Overdo is still attempting to follow Whetstone's advice in *A Mirror for Magistrates of
    Cities* (see Induction 120 and note).

82. *republic*] State.

QUARLOUS   Why, it will satisfy me; that's end enough to look on. An' you
will not gi' it me, let me go.   95

OVERDO   Alas! Thou shalt ha' it presently. I'll but step into the scrivener's
hereby and bring it. Do not go away.

The Justice goes out

QUARLOUS   Why, this madman's shape will prove a very fortunate one, I
think! Can a ragged robe produce these effects? If this be the wise
Justice, and he bring me his hand, I shall go near to make some use   100
on't. He is come already!

And [Overdo] returns

OVERDO   Look thee! Here is my hand and seal, 'Adam Overdo'. If there
be anything to be written above in the paper that thou want'st now
or at any time hereafter, think on't. It is my deed; I deliver it so. Can
your friend write?   105

QUARLOUS   Her hand for a witness, and all is well.

OVERDO   With all my heart.

He urgeth Mistress Purecraft [to sign]

QUARLOUS   [*Aside*] Why should not I ha' the conscience to make this a
bond of a thousand pound now, or what I would else?

OVERDO   Look you, there it is, and I deliver it as my deed again.   110

QUARLOUS   [*To Purecraft*] Let us now proceed in madness.

He takes her in with him

OVERDO   Well, my conscience is much eased; I ha' done my part. Though
it doth him no good, yet Adam hath offered satisfaction! The sting is
removed from hence. Poor man, he is much altered with his affliction:
it has brought him low! Now for my other work, reducing the young   115
man I have followed so long in love from the brink of his bane to the
centre of safety. Here, or in some such-like vain place, I shall be sure
to find him. I will wait the good time.

108. *conscience*] Good sense.
115. *reducing*] Leading back.

Act 5 scene 3*

[*Enter*] *Cokes* [*to*] *Sharkwell, Filcher*

COKES   How now? What's here to do? Friend, art thou the Master of the
Monuments?
SHARKWELL   'Tis a motion, an't please your worship.
OVERDO   [*Aside*] My fantastical brother-in-law, Master Bartholomew
Cokes!   5
COKES   A motion, what's that?

He reads the bill

'The ancient modern history of *Hero and Leander*, otherwise called
The Touchstone of True Love, with as true a trial of friendship bet-
ween Damon and Pythias, two faithful friends o'the Bankside'?
Pretty, i'faith! What's the meaning on't? Is't an interlude? Or what   10
is't?
FILCHER   Yes, sir. Please you come near. We'll take your money within.
COKES   Back with these children! They do so follow me up and down.

The boys o' the Fair follow him
[*Enter*] *John* [*Littlewit*]

LITTLEWIT   By your leave, friend.

---

*   The puppet-play, described in this scene and performed in the next, travesties two
English treatments of classical myth celebrating romantic love and male friendship.
Marlowe's unfinished poem *Hero and Leander*, completed by Jonson's close friend
George Chapman and printed in 1598, had also been burlesqued in Nashe's *Lenten
Stuff* (1599). Richard Edwardes's interlude *The Excellent Comedy of Two the most
Faithfullest Friends, Damon and Pythias* (1565 and 1571) was 'very tragical mirth', like
the mechanicals' interlude of 'Pyramus and Thisbe' in Shakespeare's *A Midsummer
Night's Dream*. Jonson reduces both sources to the level of cheap sex and gratuitous
violence characteristic of Punch-and Judy shows. His rationale appears at lines 91–107,
as Lantern and Littlewit explain that 'too learned and poetical' works have to be
lowered in tone 'to a more familiar strain' to make them accessible for the audience ('a
little easy and modern for the times'). Ironically, the puppet-show distorts, by pushing
it to a ludicrous extreme, the very method Jonson used to 'English' his borrowings from
Aristophanes and the Roman verse satirists. At the same time, the puppets also distort
the Grace–Winwife–Quarlous plot of two friends quarrelling over a woman, and the
contagious contrariness that infects the whole fair, already represented reductively in
the game of vapours.
  1. *What's here to do?*] 'What's going on here?'
1–2. *Master of the Monuments*] Cokes mistakes Sharkwell for an official tour-guide, like
the keeper of the tombs at Westminster Abbey.
  4. *fantastical*] Capricious, absurd.
 10. *interlude*] Farce, light comedy.

FILCHER   You must pay, sir, an' you go in.   15

LITTLEWIT   Who, I? I perceive thou knowst not me. Call the master o' the
motion.

SHARKWELL   What, do you not know the author, fellow Filcher? You
must take no money of him; he must come in *gratis*. Master Littlewit
is a voluntary: he is the author.   20

LITTLEWIT   Peace, speak not too loud. I would not have any notice taken
that I am the author till we see how it passes.

COKES   Master Littlewit, how dost thou?

LITTLEWIT   Master Cokes! You are exceeding well met. What, in your
doublet and hose, without a cloak or a hat?   25

COKES   I would I might never stir, as I am an honest man, and by that fire!
I have lost all i' the Fair, and all my acquaintance too. Didst thou meet
anybody that I know, Master Littlewit? My man Numps, or my sister
Overdo, or Mistress Grace? Pray thee, Master Littlewit, lend me some
money to see the interlude here. I'll pay thee again, as I am a   30
gentleman. If thou'lt but carry me home, I have money enough there.

LITTLEWIT   O, sir, you shall command it. What, will a crown serve you?

COKES   I think it well. – What do we pay for coming in, fellows?

FILCHER   Twopence, sir.

COKES   Twopence? There's twelvepence, friend. Nay, I am a gallant, as   35
simple as I look now, if you see me with my man about me and my
artillery again.

LITTLEWIT   Your man was i' the stocks e'en now, sir.

COKES   Who, Numps?

LITTLEWIT   Yes, faith.

COKES   For what, i' faith? I am glad o' that. Remember to tell me on't   40
anon – I have enough now! What manner of matter is this, Master
Littlewit? What kind of actors ha' you? Are they good actors?

LITTLEWIT   Pretty youths, sir, all children both old and young.

[*Enter Leatherhead*]

Here's the master of 'em –   45

20. *voluntary*] Amateur contributor.
22. *passes*] Goes over with or pleases the audience.
26. *by that fire*] Presumably Ursula's.
36. *simple*] Humbly outfitted.
37. *artillery*] That is, his sword.
44. *Pretty youths … all children*] Playing on the popularity of child-actors, who, after an
earlier period of success in the 1580s, reached their peak in the first fifteen years of the
seventeenth century and then, because of increasing scandal and litigation, especially
after 1608, ceased to operate on a scale that threatened adult companies. Periodic
attempts to revive children's companies during Charles I's reign were not so successful.
See the note to the title page of *SW* on the Children of her Majesty's Chapel.

Leatherhead whispers to Littlewit

LEATHERHEAD   Call me not Leatherhead, but Lantern.

LITTLEWIT   – Master Lantern, that gives light to the business.

COKES   In good time, sir. I would fain see 'em. I would be glad drink with the young company. Which is the tiring-house?

LEATHERHEAD   Troth, sir, our tiring-house is somewhat little. We are but   50
beginners yet, pray pardon us. You cannot go upright in 't.

COKES   No? Not now my hat is off? What would you have done with me, if you had had me, feather and all, as I was once today? Ha' you none of your pretty impudent boys now, to bring stools, fill tobacco, fetch ale, and beg money, as they have at other houses? Let me see some o'   55
your actors.

LITTLEWIT   Show him 'em, show him 'em. Master Lantern, this is a gentleman that is a favourer of the quality.

OVERDO   [*Aside*] Ay, the favouring of this licentious quality is the consumption of many a young gentleman: a pernicious enormity!   60

[*Leatherhead*] *brings them out in a basket*

COKES   What, do they live in baskets?

LEATHERHEAD   They do lie in a basket, sir. They are o' the small players.

COKES   These be players minors indeed. Do you call these players?

LEATHERHEAD   They are actors, sir, and as good as any, none dispraised, for dumb shows. Indeed, I am the mouth of 'em all!   65

COKES   Thy mouth will hold 'em all. I think one Taylor would go near to beat all this company with a hand bound behind him.

16. *not Leatherhead, but Lantern*] Leatherhead needs to preserve his disguise before Cokes, whom he has already bilked of 30 shillings.

48. *In good time*] A conventional greeting, like 'How do you do?' or 'Well met'. *glad drink*] Glad to drink.

54–5. *pretty impudent boys ... houses*] For satirical commentary on the behaviour of stage-sitters at the theatre, see Sir Francis Beaumont's *The Knight of the Burning Pestle*, a children's company play first performed in 1607, and Thomas Dekker's *The Gull's Hornbook* (1609), an exposé of fashionable manners.

58. *quality*] Acting profession.

60. *consumption*] Financial ruin.

65. *dumb shows*] Mimes; in early drama, action without speech offered as prologues or scenes in plays, summarising or emblematising a part of the plot. *mouth*] Interpreter, speaker, perhaps ventriloquist.

66. *Taylor*] Punning on the proverbial cowardice of tailors, and alluding either to the actor Joseph Taylor, a member of Lady Elizabeth's Men and a member of the original cast of this play; or to John Taylor the water-poet, who accepted a challenge from William Fennor to a contest of wit at the Hope Theatre on 7 October 1614, and won by default when Fennor failed to appear.

LITTLEWIT   Ay, and eat 'em all too, an' they were in cake-bread.
COKES   I thank you for that, Master Littlewit! A good jest! – Which is your
    Burbage now?   70
LEATHERHEAD   What mean you by that, sir?
COKES   Your best actor. Your Field?
LITTLEWIT   Good, i' faith! You are even with me, sir.
LEATHERHEAD   This is he, that acts young Leander, sir. He is extremely
    beloved of the womenkind, they do so affect his action, the green   75
    gamesters that come here, and this is lovely Hero; this with the beard,
    Damon; and this, pretty Pythias. This is the ghost of King Dionysius
    in the habit of a scrivener, as you shall see anon at large.
COKES   Well, they are a civil company. I like 'em for that: they offer not
    to fleer, nor jeer, nor break jests, as the great players do. And then,   80
    there goes not so much charge to the feasting of 'em, or making 'em
    drunk, as to the other, by reason of their littleness. Do they use to play
    perfect? Are they never flustered?
LEATHERHEAD   No, sir, I thank my industry and policy for it. They are
    as well governed a company, though I say it – And here is young   85
    Leander is as proper an actor of his inches, and shakes his head like
    an hostler.
COKES   But do you play it according to the printed book? I have read that.
LEATHERHEAD   By no means, sir.
COKES   No? How then?   90

68. *eat 'em all*] Tailors were proverbially voracious. *an' they were in cake-bread*] If they
    were gingerbread-men.
70. *Burbage*] Richard Burbage, 1567–1619, the leading actor in Shakespeare's company,
    and the most celebrated player of his day.
72. *Field*] Nathan Field, 1587–1620? or 1633?, a leading actor in Lady Elizabeth's Men,
    formerly a boy-actor and subsequently a playwright, strongly influenced by Jonson.
75. *affect his action*] 'Desire his love-making' as well as 'admire his acting'.
75–6. *green gamesters*] Either eager young women affected by greensickness (experiencing
    their first pangs of sexual desire, after puberty), or green-gowned whores, birds o' the
    game.
80. *great*] Adult, human-sized.
83. *perfect*] Word-perfect, knowing their parts.
86. *as proper an actor of his inches*] An excellent actor for his size.
87. *hostler*] Perhaps alluding to William Ostler (d. 1614), an actor with the King's Men,
    formerly a boy-actor. See the note on *Alch* Actors 8.
88. *printed book*] Chapman's continuation of Marlowe's *Hero and Leander* (1598), went
    through five printings between 1598 and 1613.

LEATHERHEAD   A better way, sir. That is too learned and poetical for our
audience. What do they know what Hellespont is? 'Guilty of true
love's blood'? Or what Abydos is? Or 'the other Sestos hight'?

COKES   Th'art i' the right. I do not know myself.

LEATHERHEAD   No, I have entreated Master Littlewit to take a little   95
pains to reduce it to a more familiar strain for our people.

COKES   How, I pray thee, good Master Littlewit?

LITTLEWIT   It pleases him to make a matter of it, sir. But there is no such
matter, I assure you. I have only made it a little easy and modern for
the times, sir, that's all. As, for the Hellespont, I imagine our Thames   100
here, and then Leander I make a dyer's son about Puddle Wharf, and
Hero a wench o'the Bankside, who, going over one morning to Old
Fish Street, Leander spies her land at Trig Stairs and falls in love with
her. Now do I introduce Cupid, having metamorphosed himself into
a drawer, and he strikes Hero in love with a pint of sherry, and other   105
pretty passages there are o' the friendship that will delight you, sir,
and please you of judgment.

COKES   I'll be sworn they shall. I am in love with the actors already, and
I'll be allied to them presently. – They respect gentlemen, these fellows
– Hero shall be my fairing. But which of my fairings? – Le' me see. –   110
I' faith, my fiddle! And Leander, my fiddlestick. Then Damon, my
drum, and Pythias, my pipe, and the ghost of Dionysius, my
hobbyhorse. All fitted!

92–3. *Hellespont ... 'Guilty of true love's blood' ... Abydos ... 'the other Sestos hight'*]
References to the first four lines of Chapman's continuation:

On Hellespont, guilty of true love's blood,
In view and opposite two cities stood,
Sea-borderers, disjoin'd by Neptune's might·
The one Abydos, the other Sestos hight

93. *hight*] Called.

101. *Puddle Wharf*] A landing on the north shore of the Thames between Blackfriars and
Paul's Stairs. According to Stow, the wharf was named either after the horses which
used the water-gate here for bathing and drinking and which fouled the water with their
urine; or perhaps merely after a man named Puddle who lived nearby.

102. *Bankside*] Area of theatres and brothels south of the Thames.

102–3. *Old Fish Street*] The site of London's first fish-market, running west from Bread
Street.

103. *Trig Stairs*] Stairs going down to the river about a quarter-mile east of Puddle Wharf,
near Paul's Stairs.

105. *drawer*] Tapster, waiter in a tavern.

109. *be allied to them*] 'Make them members of my family' by matching them with his
earlier purchases.

113. *fitted*] Suited agreeably, furnished with something apt.

Act 5 scene 4*

[Enter] to them, Winwife, Grace

WINWIFE   Look, yonder's your Cokes gotten in among his play-fellows. I
    thought we could not miss him at such a spectacle.
GRACE   Let him alone. He is so busy, he will never spy us.

Cokes is handling the puppets

LEATHERHEAD   Nay, good sir.
COKES   I warrant thee I will not hurt her, fellow. What, dost think me   5
    uncivil? I pray thee be not jealous. I am toward a wife.
LITTLEWIT   Well, good Master Lantern, make ready to begin, that I may
    fetch my wife, and look you be perfect. You undo me else i' my
    reputation.
LEATHERHEAD   I warrant you, sir. Do not you breed too great an   10
    expectation of it among your friends. That's the only hurter of these
    things.
LITTLEWIT   No, no, no.

[Exit Littlewit]

COKES   I'll stay here and see. Pray thee let me see.
WINWIFE   How diligent and troublesome he is!   15
GRACE   The place becomes him, methinks.
OVERDO   *[Aside]* My ward, Mistress Grace, in the company of a stran-
    ger? I doubt I shall be compelled to discover myself before my time!

*[Enter] Knockem, Whit, Edgworth, Win, Mistress Overdo [the women
    masked and dressed as punks;] the doorkeepers speak*

FILCHER   Twopence apiece, gentlemen, an excellent motion!
KNOCKEM   Shall we have fine fireworks and good vapours?   20

---

*   The puppets in Lantern's theatre are probably hand-puppets, since there is no reference
    to wires or strings here or in the previous scene when Cokes was handling them in their
    basket. Also, the violence and speed of the scenario suggest hand-puppets in a Punch-
    and-Judy routine; strings might tangle and ruin the credibility of the performance. Early
    usage of 'puppet' generally referred to a living actor in a dumbshow, a dwarf, or a hand-
    puppet. Lantern does all the voices, using his own voice as the narrator, and adopting
    a falsetto which Cokes finds at first almost incomprehensible, but gradually learns to
    interpret. See the notes on 5.5 for more information on puppet voices.
  5. *her*] Hero.
  6. *uncivil*] Impolite.   *toward a wife*] Engaged to be married.
15. *diligent*] Persistent, tenacious.   *troublesome*] Causing disturbances, meddling.
18. *doubt*] Suspect, or fear.   *discover*] Uncover, reveal.

SHARKWELL   Yes, Captain, and waterworks too.

WHIT   I preedee, take a care o' dy shmall lady there, Edgworth. I will look to dish tall lady myself.

LEATHERHEAD   Welcome, gentlemen, welcome, gentlemen.

WHIT   Predee, Mashter o' de Monshtersh, help a very sick lady here to a   25
chair to shit in.

LEATHERHEAD   Presently, sir.

They bring Mistress Overdo a chair

WHIT   Good fait, now, Ursula's ale and *aqua vitae* ish to blame for 't. Shit down, shweetheart, shit down and shleep a little.

[*Mistress Overdo collapses on to the chair*]

EDGWORTH   [*To Win*] Madam, you are very welcome hither.   30

KNOCKEM   Yes, and you shall see very good vapours.

[*Overdo is*] *by Edgworth*

OVERDO   [*Aside*] Here is my care come! I like to see him in so good company, and yet I wonder that persons of such fashion should resort hither!

The cutpurse courts Mistress Littlewit

EDGWORTH   This is a very private house, madam.   35

LEATHERHEAD   Will it please your ladyship sit, madam?

WIN   Yes, goodman. – They do so all-to-be-madam me, I think they think me a very lady!

EDGWORTH   What else, madam?

WIN   Must I put off my mask to him?   40

EDGWORTH   O, by no means!

WIN   How should my husband know me, then?

KNOCKEM   Husband? An idle vapour! He must not know you, nor you him. There's the true vapour.

OVERDO   [*Aside*] Yea, I will observe more of this. – [*To Whit*] Is this a   45

21. *waterworks*] Pageant on the Thames, where the action of the puppet-play is set. Splashing puppets and spectators with water may have been part of the farce activity in the sculler scene, 110–50 below.

22. *dy shmall lady*] Win Littlewit.

23. *dish tall lady*] Mistress Overdo.

31.1. *by*] Close to; also, referring to.

35. *private house*] Small indoor playhouse like Blackfriars, as opposed to the large public theatres like the Globe or the Hope. Edgworth is joking about the abbreviated size of the puppet-stage and of the spectators' area.

37. *all-to-be-madam me*] Literally, 'madam' me all to pieces; keep flattering me with their courteous addresses.

lady, friend?

WHIT   Ay, and dat is anoder lady, shweeheart. If dou hasht a mind to 'em, give me twelvepence from tee, and dou shalt have eder-oder on 'em.

OVERDO   I? – [*Aside*] This will prove my chiefest enormity. I will follow this.   50

EDGWORTH   Is not this a finer life, lady, than to be clogged with a husband?

WIN   Yes, a great deal. When will they begin, trow, in the name o'the motion?

EDGWORTH   By and by, madam. They stay but for company.   55

KNOCKEM   Do you hear, puppet-master? These are tedious vapours. When begin you?

LEATHERHEAD   We stay but for Master Littlewit, the author, who is gone for his wife, and we begin presently.

WIN   That's I, that's I.   60

EDGWORTH   That was you, lady, but now you are no such poor thing.

KNOCKEM   Hang the author's wife, a running vapour! Here be ladies will stay for ne'er a Delia o' em all.

WHIT   But hear me now, here ish one o' de ladish ashleep. Stay till she but vake, man.   65

   [*Enter*] *to them Wasp*

WASP   How now, friends! what's here to do?

   The doorkeepers [*speak*] *again*

FILCHER   Twopence apiece, sir, the best motion in the Fair.

WASP   I believe you lie. If you do, I'll have my money again, and beat you.

WINWIFE   Numps is come!

WASP   Did you see a master of mine come in here, a tall young squire of   70
   Harrow o' the Hill, Master Bartholomew Cokes?

FILCHER   I think there be such a one within.

WASP   Look he be, you were best, but it is very likely. I wonder I found him not at all the rest. I ha' been at the eagle, and the black wolf, and the

48. *eder-oder on 'em*] Either the one or the other of them.
53. *trow*] I wonder.
63. *Delia*] The lady addressed in Samuel Daniel's sonnet sequence, *Delia* (1592), probably an anagram of 'ideal'. Knockem points out that other ladies do not want to be kept waiting just because someone's sweetheart is late.
74–6. *eagle ... wolf ... bull ... dogs ... hare*] Attractions at the fair, including the 'monsters' at 3.1.10. The bull with the extra leg, first mentioned at 3.6.6–7, is now endowed with an extra pizzle (penis) as well; the leg and the pizzle may both refer to the same extra appendage. A hare trained to play the tabor was apparently not an uncommon spectacle, mentioned in Thomas Heywood's *The Wise-woman of Hogsden*, 2.2, and in John Taylor's *The Bawd* (*Works*, 1630).

bull with the five legs and two pizzles – he was a calf at Uxbridge Fair   75
two years agone – and at the dogs that dance the morris, and the hare
o' the tabor, and missed him at all these! Sure this must needs be some
fine sight that holds him so, if it have him.

COKES   Come, come, are you ready now?

LEATHERHEAD   Presently, sir.   80

WASP   Hoyday, he's at work in his doublet and hose. – Do you hear, sir?
Are you employed, that you are bare-headed and so busy?

COKES   Hold your peace, Numps! You ha' been i' the stocks, I hear.

WASP   Does he know that? Nay, then the date of my authority is out. I must
think no longer to reign; my government is at an end. He that will   85
correct another must want fault in himself.

WINWIFE   Sententious Numps! I never heard so much from him before.

LEATHERHEAD   Sure, Master Littlewit will not come. Please you take
your place, sir. We'll begin.

COKES   I pray thee do. Mine ears long to be at it, and my eyes too. O   90
Numps, i' the stocks, Numps? Where's your sword, Numps?

WASP   I pray you intend your game, sir. Let me alone.

COKES   Well, then we are quit for all. Come, sit down, Numps; I'll
interpret to thee. Did you see Mistress Grace? It's no matter neither,
now I think on't. Tell me anon.   95

WINWIFE   A great deal of love and care he expresses!

GRACE   Alas! Would you have him to express more than he has? That
were tyranny.

COKES   Peace, ho! Now, now.

LEATHERHEAD   *Gentles, that no longer your expectations may wander,*   100
Behold our chief actor, amorous Leander,
With a great deal of cloth lapped about him like a scarf,
For he yet serves his father, a dyer at Puddle Wharf,
Which place we'll make bold with, to call it our Abydus,
As the Bankside is our Sestos, and let it not be denied us   105
Now, as he is beating to make the dye take the fuller,
Who chances to come by but fair Hero in a sculler;
And, seeing Leander's naked leg and goodly calf,

---

84. *the date of my authority is out*] My period of control [over Cokes] has expired.
86. *want*] Lack.
92. *intend your game*] Watch your show.
93. *quit*] Even.
94. *interpret*] Explain, but his intention is not clear, whether to define how they are even
with each other, or to comment on the puppet-show.
101. *amorous Leander*] Marlowe's description, *Hero and Leander* 1.51.
106. *fuller*] More completely.
108. *leg … calf*] Marlowe, *Hero and Leander* 1.61.

Cast at him from the boat a sheep's eye and a half.
Now she is landed and the sculler come back; 110
By and by you shall see what Leander doth lack.

PUPPET LEANDER   *Cole, Cole, old Cole!*

LEATHERHEAD   *That is the sculler's name, without control.*

PUPPET LEANDER   *Cole, Cole, I say, Cole!*

LEATHERHEAD   *We do hear you.*

PUPPET LEANDER   *Old Cole!*

LEATHERHEAD   *Old Cole? Is the dyer turned collier? How do you*
sell?

PUPPET LEANDER   *A pox o' your manners! Kiss my hole here and*
smell. 115

LEATHERHEAD   *Kiss your hole and smell? There's manners indeed!*

PUPPET LEANDER   *Why, Cole! I say, Cole!*

LEATHERHEAD   *It's the sculler you need!*

PUPPET LEANDER   *Ay, and be hanged.*

LEATHERHEAD   *Be hanged! Look you yonder.*
Old Cole, you must go hang with Master Leander.

PUPPET COLE   *Where is he?*

PUPPET LEANDER   *Here, Cole, what fairest of fairs* 120
Was that fare that thou landedst but now a' Trig Stairs?

COKES   What was that, fellow? Pray thee tell me. I scarce understand 'em.

LEATHERHEAD   *Leander does ask, sir, what fairest of fairs*
Was the fare that he landed but now at Trig Stairs. 125

PUPPET COLE   *It is lovely Hero.*

PUPPET LEANDER   *Nero?*

PUPPET COLE   *No, Hero.*

LEATHERHEAD   *It is Hero*
Of the Bankside, he saith, to tell you truth without erring,
Is come over into Fish Street to eat some fresh herring.
Leander says no more, but as fast as he can
Gets on all his best clothes, and will after to the Swan. 130

109. *sheep's eye*] Lecherous glance (proverbial).

112. *old Cole*] A pander or bawd. In John Marston's *The Malcontent*, 2.2.2, Malevole calls
Maquerelle 'old coal', and goes on to explain that, as an ageing whore-turned-bawd,
she has become the charred remains of her former fiery lust, reduced to lighting
'virgins' tapers' by coaxing young women into prostitution.   *without control*] U-
sually means 'freely', but here the expression seems to mean 'believe it or not', or 'no
kidding', thus acknowledging the crudeness of the name.

114. *collier*] A coal-seller; hence a term of abuse because colliers were dirty of necessity and
cheats by reputation.   *How*] At what price.

130. *Swan*] A common tavern name; the full name of the Old Fish Street tavern was the
Swan on the Hoop, near Bread Street Hill.

COKES   Most admirable good, is't not?

LEATHERHEAD   *Stay, sculler.*

PUPPET COLE   *What say you?*

LEATHERHEAD   *You must stay for Leander*
And carry him to the wench.

PUPPET COLE   *You rogue, I am no pander!*

COKES   He says he is no pander. 'Tis a fine language. I understand it
    now.   135

LEATHERHEAD   *Are you no pander, Goodman Cole? Here's no man*
    says you are.
    You'll grow a hot Cole, it seems. Pray you, stay for your fare.

PUPPET COLE   *Will he come away?*

LEATHERHEAD   *What do you say?*

PUPPET COLE   *I'd ha' him come away.*

LEATHERHEAD   *Would you ha' Leander come away? Why, 'pray, sir,*
    stay.
    You are angry, Goodman Cole. I believe the fair maid   140
    Came over w'you a' trust. Tell us, sculler, are you paid?

PUPPET COLE   *Yes, Goodman Hogrubber o' Pict Hatch!*

LEATHERHEAD   *How, Hogrubber o' Pict Hatch?*

PUPPET COLE   *Ay, Hogrubber o' Pict Hatch! Take you that!*

The puppet strikes him over the pate

LEATHERHEAD   *O, my head!*

PUPPET COLE   *Harm watch, harm catch.*

COKES   'Harm watch, harm catch', he says. Very good, i'faith.   145
    The sculler had like to ha' knocked you, sirrah.

LEATHERHEAD   Yes, but that his fare called him away.

PUPPET LEANDER   *Row apace, row apace, row, row, row, row, row!*

LEATHERHEAD   *You are knavishly loaden, sculler, take heed where*
    you go.

PUPPET COLE   *Knave i' your face, Goodman Rogue!*   150

PUPPET LEANDER   *Row, row, row, row, row, row!*

COKES   He said 'knave i' your face', friend.

LEATHERHEAD   Ay, sir, I heard him. But there's no talking to these
    watermen. They will ha' the last word.

COKES   God's my life! I am not allied to the sculler yet. He shall be   155

141. *a' trust*] On trust, on credit.

142. *Hogrubber*] Swineherd; an insult to Leatherhead's taste in social or sexual com-
    panions.   *Pict Hatch*] A rendezvous of thieves and prostitutes, not far from Turnbull
    Street.

144. *Harm watch, harm catch*] If you look for trouble, you'll get it.

146. *had like to ha' knocked you*] Almost beat you up.

Dauphin my boy. But my fiddlestick does fiddle in and out too much.
I pray thee speak to him on't. Tell him I would have him tarry in my
sight more.

LEATHERHEAD   I pray you be content. You'll have enough on him, sir.

> *Now gentles, I take it, here is none of you so stupid,*   160
> *But that you have heard of a little god of love called Cupid,*
> *Who out of kindness to Leander, hearing he but saw her,*
> *This present day and hour doth turn himself to a drawer.*

[Enter Puppet Jonas as the drawer]

> *And because he would have their first meeting to be merry,*
> *He strikes Hero in love to him with a pint of sherry,*   165
> *Which he tells her from amorous Leander is sent her,*
> *Who after him into the room of Hero doth venter.*

Puppet Leander goes into Mistress Hero's room

PUPPET JONAS   *A pint of sack, score a pint of sack i' the Coney.*
COKES   Sack? You said but e'en now it should be sherry.
PUPPET JONAS   *Why so it is: sherry, sherry, sherry!*   170
COKES   'Sherry, sherry, sherry!' By my troth, he makes me merry. I must
have a name for Cupid too. Let me see ... Thou mightst help me now,
an' thou wouldest, Numps, at a dead lift, but thou art dreaming o' the
stocks still! Do not think on't, I have forgot it. 'Tis but a nine days'
wonder, man. Let it not trouble thee.   175
WASP   I would the stocks were about your neck, sir, condition I hung by
the heels in them till the wonder were off from you, with all my heart!
COKES   Well said, resolute Numps. – But hark you, friend, where is the
friendship all this while between my drum, Damon, and my pipe,
Pythias?   180
LEATHERHEAD   You shall see by and by, sir.

---

156. *Dauphin my boy*] Snatch from a lost ballad, also quoted by Edgar in *King Lear*,
3.4.98: 'Dolphin my boy, boy; sessa! let him trot by'. Perhaps Cokes is matching the
sculler with one of the ballads he has bought, or perhaps he is referring to another of
his hobbyhorses. *my fiddlestick*] Leander (cf. 5.3.111).

167. *venter*] Venture.

168. *Coney*] Name of the room in the inn; also suggests the indecent purposes for which
the room is used. *OED* cites Massinger's *The Virgin Martyr* (1602) 2.1: 'A pox on
your Christian cockatrices! They cry, like poulterers' wives, "No money, no coney"'.
See also 'sack', 239 and note below.

169. *Sack? ... sherry*] Cokes does not realise that sack was the generic name for all white
wine, including sherry.

173. *at a dead lift*] As a last resort (proverbial).

174–5. *a nine days' wonder*] A short-lived sensation (proverbial).

176. *condition*] On condition that.

COKES You think my hobbyhorse is forgotten too. No, I'll see 'em all
    enact before I go. I shall not know which to love best, else.
KNOCKEM This gallant has interrupting vapours, troublesome vapours.
    Whit, puff with him.   185
WHIT No, I predee, Captain, let him alone. He is a child, i' faith la.
LEATHERHEAD *Now, gentles, to the friends who in number are two,*
    And lodged in that alehouse in which fair Hero does do.
    Damon, for some kindness done him the last week,
    Is come fair Hero in Fish Street this morning to seek.   190
    Pythias does smell the knavery of the meeting,
    And now you shall see their true friendly greeting.
PUPPET PYTHIAS *You whoremasterly slave, you!*
COKES 'Whoremasterly slave you'? Very friendly and familiar, that.
PUPPET DAMON   *Whoremaster i' thy face!*   195
    Thou hast lain with her thyself. I'll prove't i' this place.

COKES Damon says Pythias has lain with her himself. He'll prove't in
    this place.
LEATHERHEAD *They are whoremasters both, sir, that's a plain case.*
PUPPET PYTHIAS *You lie like a rogue.*
LEATHERHEAD   *Do I lie like a rogue?*   200
PUPPET PYTHIAS *A pimp and a scab.*
LEATHERHEAD   *A pimp and a scab?*
    I say, between you, you have both but one drab.
PUPPET DAMON *You lie again.*
LEATHERHEAD   *Do I lie again?*
PUPPET DAMON *Like a rogue again.*
LEATHERHEAD   *Like a rogue again?*
PUPPET PYTHIAS *And you are a pimp again.*   205
COKES 'And you are a pimp again', he says.
PUPPET DAMON   *And a scab again.*
COKES 'And a scab again', he says.
LEATHERHEAD *And I say again, you are both whoremasters again,*
    And you have both but one drab again.   210

   They fight

PUPPETS DAMON, PYTHIAS *Dost thou, dost thou, dost thou?*

---

182. *my hobbyhorse is forgotten*] Frequently quoted refrain from a lost ballad. Cokes
    refers to the puppet Dionysius, who has not yet appeared in the puppet-play.
185. *puff*] Threaten to brawl or bicker.
188. *do*] Work as a prostitute.
201. *scab*] Syphilitic knave.
202. *drab*] Whore.

LEATHERHEAD   *What, both at once?*
PUPPET PYTHIAS   *Down with him, Damon!*
PUPPET DAMON   *Pink his guts, Pythias!*
LEATHERHEAD   *What, so malicious?*
    Will ye murder me, masters both, i' mine own house?
COKES   Ho! well acted, my drum! Well acted, my pipe! Well acted still!   215
WASP   Well acted, with all my heart!
LEATHERHEAD   *Hold, hold your hands!*
COKES   Ay, both your hands, for my sake! For you ha' both done well.
PUPPET DAMON   *Gramercy, pure Pythias.*
PUPPET PYTHIAS   *Gramercy, dear Damon.*
COKES   Gramercy to you both, my pipe and my drum.   220
PUPPETS DAMON, PYTHIAS   *Come now, we'll together to breakfast to*
    Hero.
LEATHERHEAD   *'Tis well you can now go to breakfast to Hero.*
    You have given me my breakfast, with a 'hone and 'honero!
COKES   How is't, friend. Ha' they hurt thee?
LEATHERHEAD   *O no!*
    Between you and I, sir, we do but make show.   225
    Thus, gentles, you perceive, without any denial,
    'Twixt Damon and Pythias here, friendship's true trial.
    Though hourly they quarrel thus and roar each with other,
    They fight you no more than does brother with brother.
    But friendly together, at the next man they meet,   230
    They let fly their anger, as here you might see't.
COKES   Well, we have seen't, and thou hast felt it, whatsoever thou sayest.
    What's next, what's next?
LEATHERHEAD   *This while, young Leander with fair Hero is drinking,*
    And Hero grown drunk to any man's thinking!   235
    Yet was it not three pints of sherry could flaw her
    Till Cupid, distinguished like Jonas the drawer,
    From under his apron, where his lechery lurks,

212. *Pink*] Pierce, stab.
213. *malicious*] The word should be drawn out into four syllables (ma-li-ci-ous) to rhyme with 'Pythias' and to fit the very ragged quadrimeter of the verse (four measures to a line).
219. *pure*] Sweet.
221. *to*] With.
223. *'hone and 'honero*] Alas! (Gaelic, *ochone, ochonarie*).
236. *flaw her*] Make her drunk.
237. *distinguished*] Disguised.

Put love in her sack. Now mark how it works.

PUPPET HERO   *O Leander, Leander, my dear, my dear Leander,*   240
I'll forever be thy goose, so thou'lt be my gander.

COKES   Excellently well said, fiddle. She'll ever be his goose, so he'll be
her gander. Was't not so?

LEATHERHEAD   Yes, sir, but mark his answer now.

PUPPET LEANDER   *And, sweetest of geese, before I go to bed,*   245
I'll swim o'er the Thames, my goose, thee to tread.

COKES   Brave! He will swim o'er the Thames and tread his goose tonight,
he says.

LEATHERHEAD   Ay, peace, sir. They'll be angry if they hear you eavesdropping, now they are setting their match.   250

PUPPET LEANDER   *But lest the Thames should be dark, my goose, my*
dear friend,
Let thy window be provided of a candle's end.

PUPPET HERO   *Fear not, my gander. I protest, I should handle*
My matters very ill, if I had not a whole candle.

PUPPET LEANDER   *Well then, look to't, and kiss me to boot.*   255

[*They kiss*]

LEATHERHEAD   *Now here come the friends again, Pythias and Damon,*
And under their cloaks they have of bacon a gammon.

Damon and Pythias enter

PUPPET PYTHIAS   *Drawer, fill some wine here.*

LEATHERHEAD   *How, some wine there?*
There's company already, sir, pray forbear!

PUPPET DAMON   *'Tis Hero.*

LEATHERHEAD   *Yes, but she will not be taken,*   260
After sack and fresh herring, with your Dunmow bacon.

239. *sack*] Wine, quibbling on vagina. Henke (1979) quotes the seventeenth-century 'A
Ballad of all the Trades', in A. J. Bradley and John W. Duarte (eds), *Sixty Ribald Songs
from Pills to Purge Melancholy* (London, 1968), p. 25:

> O the miller, the dusty, musty miller,
> The miller that beareth on his back:
> He never goes to measure meal
> But his maid, but his maid,
> But his maid holds ope the sack.

246. *tread*] Copulate with (used especially of birds).

250. *setting their match*] Fixing a date for their love-making.

261. *Dunmow bacon*] In Little Dunmow, Essex, a jury of six bachelors and six spinsters
awarded a flitch of bacon to the couple who could prove that they had neither
quarrelled nor regretted their wedding after one year of marriage. Leatherhead implies
that Hero is already sated with food (and food for amorous thought) supplied by

PUPPET PYTHIAS   *You lie, it's Westfabian!*

LEATHERHEAD   *Westphalian, you should say.*

PUPPET DAMON   *If you hold not your peace, you are a coxcomb, I would*
    say.

    Leander and Hero are kissing

PUPPET PYTHIAS   *What's here? What's here? Kiss, kiss, upon kiss!*

LEATHERHEAD   *Ay, wherefore should they not? What harm is in this?*   265
    'Tis Mistress Hero.

PUPPET DAMON   *Mistress Hero's a whore.*

LEATHERHEAD   *Is she a whore? Keep you quiet, or, sir knave, out of*
    door!

PUPPET DAMON   *Knave, out of door?*

PUPPET HERO   *Yes, knave, out of door!*

PUPPET DAMON   *Whore, out of door!*

PUPPET HERO   *I say, knave, out of door!*

PUPPET DAMON   *I say, whore, out of door!*

PUPPET PYTHIAS   *Yea, so say I too!*   270

PUPPET HERO   *Kiss the whore o' the arse!*

    Here the puppets quarrel and fall together by the ears

LEATHERHEAD   *Now you ha' something to do:*
    You must kiss her o' the arse, she says.

PUPPETS DAMON, PYTHIAS   *So we will, so we will!*

    [They kick her]

PUPPET HERO   *O my haunches, O my haunches! Hold, hold!*

LEATHERHEAD   *Stand'st thou still?*
    Leander, where art thou? Stand'st thou still like a sot,
    And not offer'st to break both their heads with a pot?   275
    See who's at thine elbow there! Puppet Jonas and Cupid.

PUPPET JONAS   *Upon 'em, Leander! Be not so stupid!*

    They fight

PUPPET LEANDER   *You goat-bearded slave!*

PUPPET DAMON   *You whoremaster knave!*

PUPPET LEANDER   *Thou art a whoremaster!*

PUPPET JONAS   *Whoremasters all!*

LEATHERHEAD   *See, Cupid with a word has ta'en up the brawl.*   280

Leander; she will not be interested in what Damon and Pythias have to offer. Also,
since the flitch is awarded for marital fidelity, Leatherhead suggests that Damon and
Pythias's friendship is a homosexual union.

262. *Westphalian*] From Westphalia, Germany, famous for cured ham.

278. *goat-bearded*] The goat was a symbol of lechery, one of the seven deadly sins.

KNOCKEM   These be fine vapours!

COKES   By this good day, they fight bravely! Do they not, Numps?

WASP   Yes, they lacked but you to be their second all this while.

LEATHERHEAD   *This tragical encounter, falling out thus to busy us,*

    It raises up the ghost of their friend Dionysius,   285

    Not like a monarch, but the master of a school,

    In a scrivener's furred gown which shows he is no fool,

    For therein he hath wit enough to keep himself warm.

    'O Damon,' he cries, 'and Pythias, what harm

    Hath poor Dionysius done you in his grave,   290

    That after his death you should fall out thus and rave,

    And call amorous Leander whoremaster knave?'

PUPPET DIONYSIUS   *I cannot, I will not, I promise you, endure it!*

Act 5 scene 5*

[Enter] to them Busy

283. *second*] Supporter in a duel.

285. *Dionysius*] God of wine and wild revelry; also patron of festivals at which ancient dramatic performances were judged.

286. *master of a school*] Dionysius the Younger, tyrant of Syracuse, 367–43 BC, became a schoolmaster after his abdication.

*   Busy's heated debate with the puppet Dionysius absurdly reduces the puritan anti-theatrical stance, argued in many tracts and sermons since the 1580s, to childish contradiction: 'It is profane', 'It is not profane', 'It is profane', 'It is not profane'. Busy's charges of profanity depend on two common accusations. One is that players, by definition, do not work and therefore, because they do not develop their God-given talents and follow a vocation or 'calling', deserve punishment as rogues and vagabonds. By law, actors were liable to be arrested unless they could show either that they were servants of a powerful patron, or that they were members of a guild (Jonson himself was a bricklayer). The other puritan argument is that, through their transvestism on the stage, actors contravene Deuteronomy 22:5, 'A woman shall not wear that which pertaineth unto a man, neither shall a man put on a woman's garment; for whosoever doeth these things is an abomination unto the Lord thy God'. The puppet disproves this charge of gender-perversion by demonstrating its sexlessness, and Busy is 'confuted', forced to recognise the folly of his dogmatic and intolerant creed.

    Part of the comedy of this scene depends on the sound of the voices: Busy makes 'a base [= bass] noise', and Dionysius [= Lantern] squeaks, 'neigheth and hinnyeth' in a 'treble creaking' like a wheel that needs oil. Puppeteers on the continent spoke through a tube concealed in the mouth (*pivetta* in Italian; *sifflet-pratique* in French), which helped to create different voices for each puppet, although all the voices had a piercingly high pitch. But English puppetmasters apparently altered their vocal tone by clipping their noses and speaking in a twanging falsetto. Thus, Dionysius's encounter

BUSY   Down with Dagon, down with Dagon! 'Tis I will no longer endure
    your profanations.

LEATHERHEAD   What mean you, sir?

BUSY   I will remove Dagon there, I say, that idol, that heathenish idol, that
    remains, as I may say, a beam, a very beam, not a beam of the sun, nor   5
    a beam of the moon, nor a beam of a balance, neither a house-beam,
    nor a weaver's beam, but a beam in the eye, in the eye of the brethren:
    a very great beam, an exceeding great beam, such as are your stage-
    players, rhymers, and morris-dancers, who have walked hand in hand
    in contempt of the brethren and the cause, and been borne out by   10
    instruments of no mean countenance.

LEATHERHEAD   Sir, I present nothing but what is licensed by authority.

BUSY   Thou art all licence, even licentiousness itself, Shimei!

LEATHERHEAD   I have the Master of the Revels' hand for't, sir.

BUSY   The Master of Rebels' hand, thou hast: Satan's! Hold thy peace, thy   15
    scurrility shut up thy mouth! Thy profession is damnable and, in
    pleading for it, thou dost plead for Baal. I have long opened my mouth
    wide and gaped, I have gaped as the oyster for the tide after thy
    destruction, but cannot compass it by suit or dispute, so that I look for
    a bickering ere long, and then a battle.   20

KNOCKEM   Good Banbury-vapours.

COKES   Friend, you'd have an ill-match on't, if you bicker with him here.
    Though he be no man o'the fist, he has friends that will go to cuffs for
    him. Numps, will not you take our side?

with Busy would have a further mocking edge for the contemporary audience, since
puritan preachers too were famed for speaking through the nose in a whine to project
their orations.

1. *Dagon*] The god of the Philistines, an idol whose destruction is described in 1
    Samuel 5.

6. *beam of a balance*] The bar from which the scales of a balance are suspended.

7. *weaver's beam*] Cylinder in a loom. *beam in the eye*] Figuratively, a very great
    offence, alluding to the mote (speck) and the beam (large timber) in Matthew 7:3–5.

10. *borne out*] Supported.

11. *instruments*] Agents (of the devil). *countenance*] Social or political position (alluding
    to court patronage of theatres).

13. *Shimei*] King David permitted Shimei to curse and stone him with impunity, declaring
    that Shimei was licensed to do so by God's authority (2 Samuel 16:5–13). Busy's name-
    calling is not apt; he himself is the Shimei.

14. *Master of the Revels*] Court official who censored and licensed plays.

15–16. *thy scurrility shut up thy mouth!*] May your scurrility choke you into silence!

17. *Baal*] God of the Midianites, whose altar was destroyed by Gideon at God's command
    (Judges 6:25–32).

20. *bickering*] Skirmish.

EDGWORTH   Sir, it shall not need. In my mind, he offers him a fairer   25
    course, to end it by disputation! Hast thou nothing to say for thyself
    in defence of thy quality?

LEATHERHEAD   Faith, sir, I am not well studied in these controversies
    between the hypocrites and us. But here's one of my motion, Puppet
    Dionysius, shall undertake him, and I'll venture the cause on't.   30

COKES   Who? My hobbyhorse? Will he dispute with him?

LEATHERHEAD   Yes, sir, and make a hobby-ass of him, I hope.

COKES   That's excellent! Indeed he looks like the best scholar of 'em all.
    Come, sir, you must be as good as your word now.

BUSY   I will not fear to make my spirit and gifts known! Assist me, zeal,   35
    fill me, fill me; that is, make me full.

WINWIFE   What a desperate profane wretch is this! Is there any ignorance
    or impudence like his? To call his zeal to fill him against a puppet?

GRACE   I know no fitter match than a puppet to commit with an
    hypocrite!   40

BUSY   First, I say unto thee, idol, thou hast no calling.

PUPPET DIONYSIUS   *You lie. I am called Dionysius.*

LEATHERHEAD   The motion says you lie, he is called Dionysius i'the
    matter, and to that calling he answers.

BUSY   I mean no vocation, idol, no present lawful calling.   45

PUPPET DIONYSIUS   *Is yours a lawful calling?*

LEATHERHEAD   The motion asketh if yours be a lawful calling?

BUSY   Yes, mine is of the spirit.

PUPPET DIONYSIUS   *Then idol is a lawful calling.*

LEATHERHEAD   He says then idol is a lawful calling! For you called him   50
    idol and your calling is of the spirit.

COKES   Well disputed, hobbyhorse!

BUSY   Take not part with the wicked, young gallant. He neigheth and
    hinnyeth, all is but hinnying sophistry. I call him idol again. Yet I say

28–9. *controversies between the hypocrites and us*] That is, the diatribes in the puritan anti-
    theatrical tracts by Stephen Gosson and Philip Stubbes, among others, and the anti-
    puritan replies written by actors and playwrights including Lodge, Nashe, Field, and
    Heywood.

30. *Dionysius*] The appropriate speaker in this debate, because he is named for the god of
    theatre, in whose honour the Dionysiac festivals (including drama competitions) of
    ancient Athens were held. Dionysius represents the spiritual release invited by holiday
    conditions of parades, drinking and feasting, play-watching, and invocations of the
    god.   *undertake him*] Take him on.

39. *commit*] Perpetrate a folly; oppose in a contest or involve in hostility; offend against
    morality (as in 'commit adultery').

41. *no calling*] No vocation or recognised profession that serves society and develops the
    individual's God-given talents.

44. *matter*] Puppet-play text.

his calling, his profession, is profane, it is profane, idol.   55
PUPPET DIONYSIUS   *It is not profane!*
LEATHERHEAD   It is not profane, he says.
BUSY   It is profane.
PUPPET DIONYSIUS   *It is not profane.*
BUSY   It is profane.   60
PUPPET DIONYSIUS   *It is not profane.*
LEATHERHEAD   Well said! Confute him with 'not' still. You cannot bear
   him down with your base noise, sir.
BUSY   Nor he me, with his treble creaking, though he creak like the
   chariot-wheels of Satan. I am zealous for the cause –   65
LEATHERHEAD   As a dog for a bone.
BUSY   And I say it is profane, as being the page of Pride and the waiting-
   woman of Vanity.
PUPPET DIONYSIUS   *Yea? What say you to your tire-women then?*
LEATHERHEAD   Good!   70
PUPPET DIONYSIUS   *Or feather-makers i' the Friars that are o' your
   faction of faith? Are not they with their perrukes and their puffs, their
   fans and their huffs, as much pages of Pride and waiters upon Vanity?
   What say you? What say you? What say you?*
BUSY   I will not answer for them.   75
PUPPET DIONYSIUS   *Because you cannot, because you cannot. Is a bugle-
   maker a lawful calling? Or the confect-maker's? Such you have there.
   Or your French fashioner? You'd have all the sin within youselves,
   would you not? Would you not?*
BUSY   No, Dagon.   80
PUPPET DIONYSIUS   *What then, Dagonet? Is a puppet worse than these?*
BUSY   Yes, and my main argument against you is that you are an

63. *base*] Vile; also 'bass', low-pitched.
64. *treble creaking*] High-pitched falsetto; the shrill grating of axles. The contrast is to
   Busy's 'base noise', l.63.
69. *tire-women*] Dressmakers, particularly milliners.
71. *feather-makers i' the Friars*] Puritans in Blackfriars controlled the trade in feathers for
   hats and fans. Their ministering to and profiting from vanity despite their austere
   religious beliefs was perceived as an instance of their hypocrisy.
72. *puffs*] Little vanities or trinkets, such as rosettes of ribbons or little bunches of feathers
   to ornament the hair or dress.
73. *huffs*] Shoulder-pads.
76–7. *bugle-maker*] Maker of ornamental glass beads, usually black.
77. *confect-maker*] Maker of sweets.
78. *fashioner*] Tailor or dressmaker.
81. *Dagonet*] The name of King Arthur's fool.

abomination, for the male among you putteth on the apparel of the female, and the female of the male.

PUPPET DIONYSIUS *You lie, you lie, you lie abominably!* 85

COKES Good, by my troth, he has given him the lie thrice.

PUPPET DIONYSIUS *It is your old stale argument against the players, but it will not hold against the puppets, for we have neither male nor female amongst us. And that thou may'st see, if thou wilt, like a malicious purblind zeal as thou art!* 90

The puppet takes up his garment

EDGWORTH By my faith, there he has answered you, friend, by plain demonstration.

PUPPET DIONYSIUS *Nay, I'll prove against e'er a rabbin of 'em all that my standing is as lawful as his, that I speak by inspiration as well as he, that I have as little to do with learning as he, and do scorn her* 95 *helps as much as he.*

BUSY I am confuted. The cause hath failed me.

PUPPET DIONYSIUS *Then be converted, be converted.*

LEATHERHEAD Be converted, I pray you, and let the play go on!

BUSY Let it go on. For I am changed, and will become a beholder with 100 you!

COKES That's brave, i' faith. Thou hast carried it away, hobbyhorse. On with the play!

The Justice discovers himself

OVERDO Stay! Now do I forbid, I, Adam Overdo! Sit still, I charge you.

COKES What, my brother-i'-law! 105

GRACE My wise guardian!

84. *the female of the male*] Since there were no women on the Renaissance stage in England, this reference must be to such cross-dressing roles as Rosalind in *As You Like It*, or Viola in *Twelfth Night*, in which the boy-actor plays a female who disguises herself as a male. Jonson subverts this popular convention in *SW*.

86. *the lie*] the ultimate insult; cf. *Alch* 3.4.39 and note.

88–9. *neither male nor female*] The puppet defeats Busy with his own weapon, the Bible, quoting from St Paul (Galatians 3:28): 'There is neither Jew nor Greek, there is neither bond nor free, there is neither male nor female: for ye are all one in Christ Jesus' (M. Butler 1989).

90. *purblind*] Dimsighted, nearly blind.

90.1. *takes up*] Pulls up.

93. *rabbin*] Rabbi.

94. *standing*] Profession.

95. *as little to do with learning*] Puritans believed that inner conviction ('inspiration') and independent interpretation of the Bible, not scholarly study, led one to God's truth.

102. *carried it away*] Won a decisive victory, triumphed.

EDGWORTH   Justice Overdo!
OVERDO   It is time to take enormity by the forehead and brand it, for I
     have discovered enough.

Act 5 scene 6*

   [Enter] to them Quarlous (like the madman), Purecraft

QUARLOUS   Nay, come, Mistress Bride. You must do as I do now. You
     must be mad with me, in truth. I have here Justice Overdo for it.
OVERDO   Peace, good Trouble-all, come hither, and you shall trouble
     none. I will take the charge of you, and your friend too.

   To the cutpurse and Mistress Littlewit

     You also, young man, shall be my care. Stand there.   5
EDGWORTH   Now mercy upon me.

   The rest are stealing away

KNOCKEM   Would we were away, Whit. These are dangerous vapours.
     Best fall off with our birds for fear o' the cage.
OVERDO   Stay! Is not my name your terror?
WHIT   Yesh, faith, man, and it ish sot tat we would be gone, man.   10

   [Enter] John [Littlewit]

LITTLEWIT   O gentlemen! Did you not see a wife of mine? I ha' lost my
     little wife, as I shall be trusted, my little pretty Win. I left her at the
     great woman's house in trust yonder, the pig-woman's, with Captain
     Jordan and Captain Whit, very good men, and I cannot hear of her.
     Poor fool, I fear she's stepped aside. Mother, did you not see Win?   15
OVERDO   If this grave matron be your mother, sir, stand by her, *et digito
     compesce labellum*. I may perhaps spring a wife for you anon. –
     Brother Bartholomew, I am sadly sorry to see you so lightly given and
     such a disciple of enormity, with your grave governor Humphrey, but

---

*   This final scene has a full stage, Jonson's favourite finale: at least eighteen people,
     twenty counting Filcher and Sharkwell, plus extras and puppets. By the end, all the
     spoilsports have been silenced (Busy, Wasp, Overdo), and all disguises stripped off.
     Though Cokes may recover his goods from Edgworth (if not from Trash and
     Leatherhead), other characters simply have to accept their losses, as at the end of *Alch.*
   8. *fall off*] Slip away.   *cage*] That is, prison.
  15. *fool*] Sweet.   *stepped aside*] Wandered away.
  16–17. *et digito compesce labellum*] From Juvenal, *Satires* 1.160, 'and restrain your lips
     with your finger'.
  17. *spring*] Cause to rise from hiding (used of partridge).

stand you both there in the middle place: I will reprehend you in your   20
    course. – Mistress Grace, let me rescue you out of the hands of the
    stranger.
WINWIFE   Pardon me, sir, I am a kinsman of hers.
OVERDO   Are you so? Of what name, sir?
WINWIFE   Winwife, sir.   25
OVERDO   Master Winwife? I hope you have won no wife of her, sir. If you
    have, I will examine the possibility of it at fit leisure. – Now to my
    enormities. Look upon me, O London, and see me, O Smithfield, the
    example of justice and mirror of magistrates, the true top of formality
    and scourge of enormity! Harken unto my labours and but observe   30
    my discoveries, and compare Hercules with me, if thou dar'st, of old,
    or Columbus, Magellan, or our countryman Drake of later times.
    Stand forth, you weeds of enormity and spread. (*To Busy*) First, Rabbi
    Busy, thou superlunatical hypocrite. (*To Lantern Leatherhead*) Next,
    thou other extremity, thou profane professor of puppetry, little better   35
    than poetry. (*To the horse-courser and cutpurse*) Then, thou strong
    debaucher and seducer of youth: witness this easy and honest young
    man. (*Then Captain Whit*) Now thou esquire of dames, madams, and
    twelvepenny ladies. (*And Mistress Littlewit*) Now my green madam
    herself of the price. Let me unmask your ladyship.   40
LITTLEWIT   O my wife, my wife, my wife!
OVERDO   Is she your wife? *Redde te harpocratem!*

21. *course*] Turn.
23. *kinsman*] Used of any relationship by marriage.
28–9. *Look upon me, O London ... mirror of magistrates*] alluding to Richard Johnson's
    pamphlet, *Look on me London: I am an Honest Englishman, ripping up the Bowels of
    Mischief, lurking in thy Sub-urbs and Precincts. Take Heed. 'The Hangman's Halter,
    and the Beadle's Whip, / Will make the Fool dance, and the Knave to skip'*, dedicated
    to Lord Mayor Middleton, on whom Jonson loosely models Overdo. Johnson's
    pamphlet was plagiarised from Whetstone's *A Mirror for Magistrates of Cities* (1584;
    rpt 1586), in which Whetstone admonished Lord Mayors and magistrates to follow
    ancient Roman example in putting on disguises to see vice at first hand. For further
    discussion of how Jonson expands his satire, refer to the notes to 2.1, and to McPherson
    1976. pp 225–8.
29. *formality*] Accordance with legal form.
32. *Magellan*] Ferdinand Magellan, 1489–1521, Portuguese explorer who died in the
    Philippines while circumnavigating the globe; one of his fleet made it back to Spain on
    6 September 1522.   *Drake*] Sir Francis Drake, 1540–96, circumnavigated the globe in
    1577–80 on the *Golden Hind* and helped defeat the Spanish Armada in 1587–88.
33. *enormity and spread*] Widespread enormity (Hibbard 1977).
37. *easy*] Compliant.
42. *Redde te harpocratem!*] Another warning to be silent, 'Imitate Harpocrates', the god of
    silence, depicted with his finger on his lips.

Enter Trouble-all [nearly naked and covering himself with a dripping pan, pursued by] Ursula, Nightingale

TROUBLE-ALL   By your leave, stand by, my masters, be uncovered.
URSULA   O stay him, stay him! Help to cry, Nightingale! My pan, my
    pan!   45
OVERDO   What's the matter?
NIGHTINGALE   He has stol'n Gammer Ursula's pan.
TROUBLE-ALL   Yes, and I fear no man but Justice Overdo.
OVERDO   Ursula? Where is she? O the sow of enormity, this! (*To Ursula
    and Nightingale*) Welcome. Stand you there; you, songster, there.   50
URSULA   An' please your worship, I am in no fault. A gentleman stripped
    him in my booth and borrowed his gown and his hat, and he ran away
    with my goods here for it.
OVERDO   (*To Quarlous*) Then this is the true madman, and you are the
    enormity!   55
QUARLOUS   You are i' the right. I am mad but from the gown outward.
OVERDO   Stand you there.
QUARLOUS   Where you please, sir.
MISTRESS OVERDO   [*Waking up*] O lend me a basin – I am sick, I am
    sick! Where's Master Overdo? Bridget, call hither my Adam.   60

Mistress Overdo is sick, and her husband is silenced

OVERDO   How – ?
WHIT   Dy very own wife, i' fait, worshipful Adam.
MISTRESS OVERDO   Will not my Adam come at me? Shall I see him no
    more then?
QUARLOUS   Sir, why do you not go on with the enormity? Are you   65
    oppressed with it? I'll help you. Hark you, sir, i' your ear: your
    'innocent young man' you have ta'en such care of all this day is a
    cutpurse that hath got all your brother Cokes his things, and helped
    you to your beating and the stocks. If you have a mind to hang him
    now and show him your magistrate's wit, you may, but I should think   70
    it were better recovering the goods and to save your estimation in him.

43. *be uncovered*] Remove your hats.
51. *in no fault*] Not to blame.
60. *Bridget*] Apparently Mistress Overdo's maid, whom she calls as she awakens from her
    drunken stupor, imagining herself at home.
63. *at*] To.
66. *oppressed with*] Distressed or crushed by.
71. *save*] Spare. *estimation*] Reputation. *in him*] Engaged on his behalf, liable to loss
    because of him.

I thank you, sir, for the gift of your ward, Mistress Grace: look you, here is your hand and seal, by the way. Master Winwife, give you joy. You are Palemon, you are possessed o' the gentlewoman, but she must pay me value: here's warrant for it. And, honest madman, there's thy 75 gown and cap again; I thank thee for my wife. (*To the widow*) Nay, I can be mad, sweetheart, when I please still, never fear me. And careful Numps, where's he? I thank him for my licence.

WASP How!

Wasp misseth the licence

QUARLOUS   'Tis true, Numps. 80
WASP   I'll be hanged then.
QUARLOUS   Look i' your box, Numps. – [*To Overdo*] Nay, sir, stand not you fixed here like a stake in Finsbury to be shot at, or the whipping-post i' the Fair, but get your wife out o' the air – it will make her worse, else – and remember you are but Adam, flesh and blood! 85 You have your frailty; forget your other name of Overdo, and invite us all to supper. There you and I will compare our discoveries, and drown the memory of all enormity in your bigg'st bowl at home.
COKES   How now, Numps, ha' you lost it? I warrant 'twas when thou wert i' the stocks. Why dost not speak? 90
WASP   I will never speak while I live again, for aught I know.
OVERDO   Nay, Humphrey, if I be patient, you must be so too. This pleasant conceited gentleman hath wrought upon my judgment and prevailed. I pray you take care of your sick friend, Mistress Alice – [*To them all*] and, my good friends all – 95
QUARLOUS   And no enormities.
OVERDO   – I invite you home with me to my house to supper. I will have none fear to go along, for my intents are *ad correctionem, non ad*

---

72.   *the gift of your ward*] Quarlous has apparently used the blank warrant obtained in 5.2 to transfer Grace's guardianship from Overdo to himself.
75.   *pay me value*] Quarlous uses the warrant to demand the guardian's share of Grace's fortune for marrying without permission (see 3.5.261 and note), an unnecessary and ungentlemanly ploy on his part since Grace had already promised to compensate the man she did not marry (see 4.3.56–8). Quarlous had then made a gentleman's agreement to her 'conditions' as 'very courteous' (l.59).
77.   *fear*] Doubt, distrust.
83.   *stake in Finsbury*] Archery butt in Finsbury Fields, a sporting ground used by citizens for archery and other recreations.
84.   *whipping-post*] At which offenders were tied for public whipping.
93.   *pleasant*] Merry, jocular.   *conceited*] Ingenious, full of ideas.
98–9. *ad ... diruendum*] 'To correct, not to destroy; to build up, not to tear down'.

destructionem; ad aedificandum, non ad diruendum. So lead on.

COKES   Yes, and bring the actors along. We'll ha' the rest o' the play at   100
home.

THE END

THE EPILOGUE*

[*Delivered at the court performance*]

Your Majesty hath seen the play, and you
Can best allow it from your ear and view.
You know the scope of writers and what store
Of leave is given them, if they take not more,
And turn it into licence. You can tell   5
If we have used that leave you gave us well,
Or whether we to rage or licence break,
Or be profane, or make profane men speak!
This is your power to judge, great sir, and not
The envy of a few. Which if we have got,   10
We value less what their dislike can bring,
If it so happy be t' have pleased the King.

---

*   Addressed to the king, these lines excuse the limitations of playwright and actors, and
      rely on the king's superior judgment to give the final verdict. Like the play itself, the
      epilogue depends on the idea of 'licence' or 'warrant'.

2. *allow*] Sanction.

4. *leave*] Permission, warranted by law or protocol.

5. *licence*] Unwarranted liberty, improper freedom unrestrained by prudence or decorum.

7. *to rage or licence break*] Break into madness or impropriety.

10. *envy*] Ill-will, malice.   *Which*] Referring to the king's 'leave' indicating approval.

11. *their dislike*] The discord created by the 'few' envious.

12. *it*] The play.

SELECT BIBLIOGRAPHY

Adams, Robert M. (ed.) (1979), *Ben Jonson's Plays and Masques*, Norton Critical Edition, New York.

Aubrey, J. (1982), *Brief Lives*, ed. Richard Barber, Woodbridge, Suffolk.

Baines, B. J. and Williams, M. C. (1977), 'The Contemporary and Classical Antifeminist Tradition in Jonson's *Epicoene*', *Renaissance Papers*, pp. 43–58.

Barish, J. A. (1959), '*Bartholomew Fair* and its Puppets', *Modern Language Quarterly* 20, pp. 3–17.

Barish, J. A. (1960), *Ben Jonson and the Language of Prose Comedy*, New York.

Barton, A. (1984), *Ben Jonson, Dramatist*, Cambridge.

Beaumont, F. and Fletcher, J. (1912), *The Works of Beaumont and Fletcher*, ed. A. R. Waller, Cambridge.

Beaurline, L. A. (ed.) (1966), *Ben Jonson: Epicoene or The Silent Woman*, Regents Renaissance Drama, Lincoln and London.

Beaurline, L. A. (1978), *Jonson and Elizabethan Comedy*, San Marino.

Benson, P. J. (1992), *The Invention of the Renaissance Woman: The Challenge of Female Independence in the Literature and Thought of Italy and England*, University Park, PA.

Bergeron, D. M. (1986), '"Lend Me Your Dwarf": Romance in *Volpone*', *Medieval and Renaissance Drama in England* 3, pp. 99–113.

Blissett, W. (1974), 'Your Majesty is Welcome to a Fair', *Elizabethan Theatre* 4, pp. 80–105.

Bradley, J. and Adams, J. Q. (eds) (1922), *The Jonson Allusion-Book*, New Haven.

Brady, J. (1991), '"Noe Fault, but Life": Jonson's Folio as Monument and Barrier', in J. Brady and W. H. Herendeen (eds), *Ben Jonson's 1616 Folio*, Newark, London, and Toronto, pp. 192–216.

Brockbank, P. (ed.) (1968), *Ben Jonson: Volpone*, New Mermaids, London.

Brown, D. (ed.) (1966), *The Alchemist*, New Mermaids, London.

Brown, S. (1990), 'The Boyhood of Shakespeare's Heroines: Notes on Gender Ambiguity in the Sixteenth Century', *Studies in English Literature* 30, pp. 243–63.

Bruster, D. (1992), *Drama and the Market in the Age of Shakeseare*, Cambridge.

Burt, R. A. (1987), '"Licensed by authority": Ben Jonson and the Politics of Early Stuart Theatre', *English Literary History* 54.3, pp. 529–60.

Butler, J. (1990), *Gender Trouble: Feminism and the Subversion of Identity*, New York and London.

Butler, M. (ed.) (1989), *The Selected Plays of Ben Jonson*, vol. 2, Cambridge.

Carlton, C. (1978), 'The Widow's Tale: Male Myths and Female Reality in 16th and 17th Century England', *Albion* 10, pp. 118–29.

Carr, C. A. (1982), 'Play's the Thing: A Study of Games in *The Alchemist*', *Colby Library Quarterly* 18.2, pp. 113–25.

Cartelli, T. (1983), '*Bartholomew Fair* as Urban Arcadia: Jonson Responds to Shakespeare', *Renaissance Drama* 14, pp. 151–72.

Chalfant, F. S. (1978), *Ben Jonson's London: A Jacobean Placename Dictionary*, Athens, GA.

Cohen, R. (1978), 'The Setting of *Volpone*', *Renaissance Papers*, pp. 65–75.

Contarini, Gasparo (1599), *The Commonwealth and Government of Venice*, trans. Lewis Lewkenor, London.

Cook, E. (ed.) (1991), *The Alchemist*, New Mermaids, London and New York.

Cope, J. I. (1965), '*Bartholomew Fair* as Blasphemy', *Renaissance Drama* 8, pp. 127–56.

Coryat, T. (1611; rpt 1905), *Coryat's Crudities*, 2 vols, Glasgow.

Cox, G. H. (1983), 'Apocalyptic Projection and the Comic Plot of *The Alchemist*', *English Literary Renaissance* 13, pp. 70–87.

Creaser, J. (1975), 'Volpone: The Mortifying of the Fox'. *Essays in Criticism* 25, pp. 329–56.

Creaser, J. (1976), 'A Vindication of Sir Politic Would-be', *English Studies* 57, pp. 502–14.

Creaser, J. (ed.) (1978), *Ben Jonson: Volpone, or The Fox*, London Medieval and Renaissance Series, London.

Davidson, C. (1989), 'Judgment, Iconoclasm, and Anti-Theatricalism in Jonson's *Bartholomew Fair*', *Papers on Language and Literature* 25.4, pp. 349–63.

Davidson, C., Giankaris, C. J., and Stroupe, J. H. (1986), *Drama in the Renaissance: Comparative and Critical Essays*, New York.

Davis, N. Z. (1978), 'Women on Top: Symbolic Sexual Inversion and Political Disorder in Early Modern Europe', in B. A. Babcock (ed.), *The Reversible Art: Symbolic Inversion in Art and Society*, Ithaca and London, pp. 147–90.

De Luna, B. N. (1967), *Jonson's Romish Plot: A Study of 'Cataline' and its Historical Context*, Oxford, chs 4 and 5.

de Sousa, G. U. (1986), 'Boundaries of Genre in Ben Jonson's *Volpone* and *The Alchemist*', *Essays in Theatre* 4.2, pp. 134–46.

Donaldson, I. (1970), *The World Upside-Down: Comedy from Jonson to Fielding*, London.

Donaldson, I. (1971), 'Volpone: Quick and Dead', *Essays in Criticism* 21, pp. 121–34.

Donaldson, I. (1986), 'Jonson's Magic Houses', *Essays & Studies*, pp. 39–61.

Donne, J. (1912), *The Poems of John Donne*, ed. Herbert J. C. Grierson, Oxford.

Duncan, D. (1979), *Ben Jonson and the Lucianic Tradition*, Cambridge.

Dusinberre, J. (1975), *Shakespeare and the Nature of Women*, London.

Elliott, R. C. (1960), *The Power of Satire*, Princeton.

Evans, R. C. (1989), 'Thomas Sutton: Ben Jonson's Volpone?', *Philological Quarterly* 68.3, pp. 295–314.

Ezell, M. J. M. (1987), *The Patriarch's Wife: Literary Evidence and the History of the Family*, Chapel Hill and London.

Ferns, J. (1970), 'Ovid, Juvenal, and "The Silent Woman"', *Modern Language Review* 65, pp. 248–53.

Fisher, F. J. (1962), 'The Development of London as a Centre of Conspicuous Consumption in the Sixteenth and Seventeenth Centuries', in E. M. Carus-Wilson (ed.), *Essays in Economic History*, London, vol. 2, pp. 197–207.

Flachmann, M. (1977), 'Ben Jonson and the Alchemy of Satire', *Studies in English Literature* 17, pp. 259–80.

Florio, J. (1598), *A World of Words*, London.

Foley, H. (1982), 'The "Female Intruder" Reconsidered: Women in Aristophanes' *Lysistrata* and *Ecclesiazusae*', *Critical Philology* 77, pp. 1–20.

Freud, S. (n.d.), *Wit and its Relation to the Unconscious*, trans. A. A. Brill, London.

Furnivall, F. J. (ed.) (1882), *The Anatomy of Abuses*, by Phillip Stubbes, London.

Gifford, W. (ed.) (1816), *The Works of Ben Jonson*, 9 vols, London.

Goldberg, J. (1983), *James I and the Politics of Literature: Jonson, Shakespeare, Donne, and their Contemporaries*, Baltimore and London.

Green, A. E. (ed.) (1971), *Witches and Witch-hunters*, Wakefield, Yorkshire.

Gurr, A. (1987), *Playgoing in Shakespeare's London*, Cambridge.

Haining, P. (ed.) (1974), *The Witchcraft Papers: Contemporary Records of the Witchcraft Hysteria in Essex, 1560–1700*, London.

Halio, J. L. (ed.) (1968), *Volpone*, Fountainwell Drama Texts, Edinburgh.

Hall, J. (1969), *The Discovery of a New World*, trans. J. Healey (1609), Amsterdam and New York.

Hall, J. (1981), *Another World and Yet the Same: Bishop Joseph Hall's 'Mundus Alter et Idem'*, trans. and ed. J. M. Wands, New Haven and London.

Hallahan, H. D. (1977), 'Silence, Eloquence, and Chatter in Jonson's *Epicoene*', *Huntington Library Quarterly* 40, pp. 117–27.

Hamel, G. (1973), 'Order and Judgment in *Bartholomew Fair*', *University of Toronto Quarterly* 43, pp. 48–67.

Haynes, J. (1989), 'Representing the Underworld: *The Alchemist*', *Studies in Philology* 86, pp. 18–41.

Haynes, J. (1992), *The Social Relations of Jonson's Theater*, Cambridge.

Heffner, R. L. (1961), 'Unifying Symbols in the Comedy of Ben Jonson', in M. Bluestone and N. Rabkin (eds), *Shakespeare's Contemporaries*, Englewood Cliffs, NJ, pp. 196–202.

Henderson, K. U. and McManus, B. F. (1985), *Half Humankind: Contexts and Texts of the Controversy about Women in England, 1540–1640*, Urbana and Chicago.

Henke, James T. (1979), *Courtesans and Cuckolds: A Glossary of Renaissance Dramatic Bawdy (Exclusive of Shakespeare)*, New York and London.

Henry, A. (ed.) (1906), *Epicoene, or The Silent Woman*, Yale Studies in English 31, New York.

Herford, C. H. and Simpson, P. and E. (eds) (1925–52), *Ben Jonson*, 11 vols, Oxford.

Hibbard, G. R. (ed.) (1977), *Bartholmew Fair*, New Mermaids, London.

Hoenselaars, A. J. (1992), *Images of Englishmen and Foreigners in the Drama of Shakespeare and his Contemporaries: A Study of Stage Characters and National Identity in English Renaissance Drama, 1558–1642*, London and Toronto.

Holdsworth, R. V. (ed.) (1979), *Ben Jonson: Epicoene*, New Mermaids, London and New York.

Horsman, E. A. (ed.) (1960), *Bartholomew Fair*, Revels Plays, London.

Hotine, M. (1991), 'Ben Jonson, Volpone, and Charterhouse', *Notes and Queries* 38, pp. 79–81.

James, K. (1980), 'Ben Jonson's Way with Widows: Dame Pliant and Dame Purecraft', *Tennessee Studies in Literature* 25, pp. 24–34.

Jankowski, T. A. (1992), *Women in Power in the Early Modern Drama*, Urbana and Chicago.

Jardine, L. (1983), *Still Harping on Daughters: Women and Drama in the Age of Shakespeare*, Brighton, Sussex.

Jensen, E. J. (1985), *Ben Jonson's Comedies on the Modern Stage*, Ann Arbor.

Jones, D. (1976), ' "Th'Adulteries of Art": A Discussion of *The Silent Woman*' in A. Brissenden (ed.), *Shakespeare and Some Others: Essays on Shakespeare and Some of his Contemporaries*, Adelaide.

Jones, E. (1982), 'The First West End Comedy', *Proceedings of the British Academy* 48, pp. 215–58.

Jones, M. (1969), 'Sir Epicure Mammon: A Study in Spiritual Fornication', *Renaissance Quarterly* 22, pp. 233–42.

Jonson, Ben (1607), *Volpone*, London.

Jonson, Ben (1612; rpt 1971), *The Alchemist*, Amsterdam and New York.

Jonson, Ben (1616), *Works*, London.

Jonson, Ben (1640), *Works*, London.

Judges, A. V. (ed.) (1930), *The Elizabethan Underworld*, London.

Juneja, R. (1978), 'Eve's Flesh and Blood in Jonson's *Bartholomew Fair*', *Comparative Drama* 12, pp. 340–55.

Juneja, R. (1984), 'Rethinking about Alchemy in Jonson's *The Alchemist*', *Ball State University Forum* 25, pp. 3–14.

Kahn, C. (1991), 'Whores and Wives in Jacobean Drama', in D. Kehler and S. Baker (eds), *In Another Country: Feminist Perspectives on Renaissance Drama*, Metuchen, NJ and London, pp. 246–60.

Kaplan, J. H. (1970), 'Dramatic and Moral Energy in Ben Jonson's *Bartholomew Fair*', *Renaissance Drama* 3, pp. 137–56.

Kastan, D. S. and Stallybrass, P. (eds) (1991), *Staging the Renaissance: Reinterpretations of Elizabethan and Jacobean Drama*, New York and London.

Kay, W. D. (1976), '*Bartholomew Fair*: Ben Jonson in Praise of Folly', *English Literary Renaissance* 6, pp. 299–316.

Kay, W. D. (1995), *Ben Jonson: A Literary LIfe*, Macmillan Literary Lives, London.

Kernan, A. (ed.) (1962), *Ben Jonson's Volpone*, The Yale Ben Jonson, New Haven and London.

Kernan, A. (ed.) (1974), *The Alchemist*, The Yale Ben Jonson, New Haven.

Kieckhefer, Richard (1989), *Magic in the Middle Ages*, Cambridge.

King, M. L. (1991), *Women of the Renaissance*, Chicago and London.

Knapp, P. (1991), 'Ben Jonson and the Publicke Riot', in Kastan and Stallybrass (1991), pp. 164–80.

Leggatt, A. M. (1976), 'Morose and his Tormenters', *University of Toronto Quarterly* 45, pp. 221–35.

Leggatt, A. M. (1981), *Ben Jonson: His Vision and His Art*, London.

Leinwand, T. B. (1986), *The City Staged: Jacobean Comedy, 1603–1613*, London and Madison.

Levin, C. and Robertson, K. (eds) (1991), *Sexuality and Politics in Renaissance Drama*, Lewiston.

Levin, R. (1965), 'The Structure of *Bartholomew Fair*', *PMLA* 80, pp. 172–9.

Lorenz, K. (1967), *On Aggression*, trans. M. Latzke, London.

Maclean, I. (1980), *The Renaissance Notion of Woman: A Study in the Fortunes of Scholasticism and Medical Science in European Intellectual Life*, Cambridge.

Marchitello, H. (1991), 'Desire and Domination in *Volpone*', *Studies in English Literature* 31, pp. 287–308.

Marcus, L. S. (1991), 'Pastimes and the Purging of Theater: *Bartholomew Fair* (1614)', in Kastan and Stallybrass (1991), pp. 196–209.

Mares, F. H. (ed.) (1967), *The Alchemist*, Revels Plays, London.

Marston, J. (1856), *The Works of John Marston*, ed. J. O. Halliwell, London.

McLeish, K. (trans.) (1979), *The Clouds* by Aristophanes, Cambridge.

McLuskie, K. (1989), *Renaissance Dramatists*, New York, London, and Toronto.

McPherson, D. (1976), 'The Origins of Overdo: A Study in Jonsonian Invention', *Modern Language Quarterly* 37, pp. 221–33.

McPherson, D. (1990), *Shakespeare, Jonson, and the Myth of Venice*, Newark.

Mebane, John (1989), *Renaissance Magic and the Return of the Golden Age*, Lincoln and London.

Middleton, T. (1885), *The Works of Middleton*, ed. A. H. Bullen, London.

[Middleton, T.] (1974), *The Puritan, or The Widow of Watling Street*, in W. Kozlenko (ed.), *Disputed Plays of William Shakespeare*, New York.

Miles, R. (1986), *Ben Jonson: His Life and Work*, London.

Millard, B. C. (1984), '"An Acceptable Violence": Sexual Contest in Jonson's *Epicoene*', *Medieval and Renaissance Drama in England* 1, pp. 143–58.

Mirabelli, P. (1989), 'Silence, Wit, and Wisdom in *The Silent Woman*', *Studies in English Literature* 29, pp. 309–36.

Monsarrat, G. D. (1983), 'Editing the Actor: Truth and Deception in *The Alchemist* V.3–5', *Cahiers élisabethains* 23, pp. 61–71.

Morley, H. (1880; rpt 1968), *Memoirs of Bartholomew Fair*, Detroit.

Newman, K. (1991), *Fashioning Femininity and English Renaissance Drama*, Chicago.

Ostovich, H. (1986), '"Jeered by Confederacy": Group Aggression in Jonson's Comedies', *Medieval and Renaissance Drama in England* 3, pp. 115–28.

Ostovich, H. (1993), 'Ben Jonson and the Dynamics of Misogyny: A Creative

Collaboration', *Elizabethan Theatre* 15.

Parfitt, G. (ed.) (1975), *Ben Jonson: The Complete Poems*, including *Timber; or Discoveries*, Appendix 1, and *Conversations with William Drummond*, Appendix 2, London.

Park, B. A. (1981), '*Volpone* and Old Comedy', *English Language Notes* 19.2, pp. 105–9.

Parker, D. (trans.) (1961), *The Wasps* by Aristophanes, Ann Arbor.

Parker, R. B. (1970), 'The Themes and Staging of *Bartholomew Fair*', *University of Toronto Quarterly* 39.4, pp. 293–309.

Parker, R. B. (1976a), '*Volpone* and *Reynard the Fox*', *Renaissance Drama* 7, pp. 3–42.

Parker, R. B. (1976b), 'Wolfit's Fox: An Interpretation of *Volpone*', *University of Toronto Quarterly* 45, pp. 200–20.

Parker, R. B. (1978), '*Volpone* in Performance: 1921–1972', *Renaissance Drama* 9, pp. 147–73.

Parker, R. B. (ed.) (1983), *Volpone, or The Fox: Ben Jonson*, Revels Plays, Manchester.

Partridge, E. B. (1958), *The Broken Compass: A Study of the Major Comedies of Ben Jonson*, London.

Partridge, E. B. (ed.) (1964), *Bartholomew Fair*, Lincoln.

Partridge, E. B. (ed.) (1971), *Epicoene*, The Yale Ben Jonson, New Haven.

Partridge, Eric (1947; rev and enl 1968), *Shakespeare's Bawdy: A Literary and Psychological Essay and a Comprehensive Glossary*, London.

Paster, G. K. (1985), *The Idea of the City in the Age of Shakespeare*, Athens, GA.

Paster, G. K. (1987), 'Leaky Vessels: The Incontinent Women of City Comedy', *Renaissance Drama* 18, pp. 43–65.

Paster, G. K. (1993), *The Body Embarrassed: Drama and the Disciplines of Shame in Early Modern England*, Ithaca, NY.

Prior, M. (1985), *Women in English Society 1500–1800*, London and New York.

Procter, J. (ed.) (1989), *The Selected Plays of Ben Jonson*, vol. 2, Cambridge.

Rackin, P. (1987), 'Androgyny, Mimesis, and the Marriage of the Boy Heroine on the English Renaissance Stage', *PMLA* 102, pp. 29–41.

Rea, J. D. (ed.) (1919), *Volpone, or The Fox*, Yale Studies in English 59, New Haven.

Rebhorn, W. A. (1980), 'Jonson's "Jovy Boy": Lovewit and the Dupes in *The Alchemist*', *Journal of English and Germanic Philology* 79, pp. 355–75.

Rhodes, N. (1980), *Elizabethan Grotesque*, London and Boston.

Riddell, J. A. (1981), '*Volpone*'s Fare', *Studies in English Literature* 21, pp. 307–18.

Riggs, D. (1989), *Ben Jonson: A Life*, Cambridge and London.

Robinson, J. E. (1961), '*Bartholomew Fair*: Comedy of Vapours', *Studies in English Literature* 1.2, pp. 65–80.

Rose, M. B. (ed.) (1986), *Women in the Middle Ages and the Renaissance: Literary and Historical Perspectives*, Syracuse, NY.

Ross, C. L. (1988), 'The Plague of *The Alchemist*', *Renaissance Quarterly* 41, pp. 438–58.

Rubinstein, Frankie (1989), *A Dictionary of Shakespeare's Sexual Puns and their Significance*, London.

Salingar, L. (1986), *Dramatic Form in Shakespeare and the Jacobeans*, Cambridge.

Schuler, R. M. (1985), 'Jonson's Alchemists, Epicures, and Puritans', *Medieval and Renaissance Drama in England* 2, pp. 171–208.

Scot, R. (1584; 1964), *The Discoverie of Witchcraft*, intro. J. R. Williamson, Arundel.

Shepherd, S. (1981), *Amazons and Warrior Women: Varieties of Feminism in Seventeenth-Century Drama*, Brighton, Sussex.

Shipley, N. R. (1992), 'A Possible Source for *Volpone*', *Notes and Queries* 39, pp. 363–9.

Shuger, D. K. (1984), 'Hypocrites and Puppets in *Bartholomew Fair*', *Modern Philology* 82, pp. 70–73.

Skulsky, H. (1989), 'Cannibals vs. Demons in *Volpone*', *Studies in English Literature* 29, pp. 291–307.

Slights, W. W. E. (1985), 'The Play of Conspiracies in *Volpone*', *Texas Studies in Literature and Language* 27, pp. 369–89.

Smallwood, R. L. (1981), 'Here in the Friars': Immediacy and Theatricality in *The Alchemist*', *Review of English Studies* 32 pp. 143–60.

Smith, C. C. (1972), '*Bartholomew Fair*: Cold Decorum', *South Atlantic Quarterly* 71, pp. 548–56.

Speaight, George (1955), *The History of the English Puppet Theatre*, London.

Stallybrass, P. (1991), 'The World Turned Upside Down: Inversion, Gender, and the State', in V. Wayne (ed.), *The Matter of Difference: Materialist Feminist Criticism of Shakespeare*, Ithaca, NY, pp. 201–20.

Steane, J. B. (ed.) (1967), *The Alchemist*, London.

Stow, J. (1908; rpt 1971), *A Survey of London: Reprinted from the Text of 1603*, 2 vols, intro. C. L. Kingsford, Oxford.

Sweeney, J. (1982), '*Volpone* and the Theater of Self-Interest', *English Literary Renaissance* 12, pp. 220–41.

Sweeney, J. G. (1985), *Jonson and the Psychology of Public Theater: To Coin the Spirit, Spend the Soul*, Princeton.

Teague, F. (1978), 'Ben Jonson's Stagecraft in *Epicoene*', *Renaissance Drama* 9, pp. 175–92.

Teague, F. (1985), *The Curious History of 'Bartholomew Fair'*, Lewisburg.

Thomas, K. (1971), *Religion and the Decline of Magic: Studies in Popular Beliefs in Sixteenth and Seventeenth Century England*, London.

Tietze-Conrat, Erica (1957), *Dwarfs and Jesters in Art*, London.

Trussler, S. (ed.) (1986), *Ben Jonson: Bartholomew Fair*, London and New York.

van Lennep, Jacques (1984), *Alchimie: contribution a l'histoire de l'art alchimique*, Brussels.

Veltz, J. W. (1984), 'Scatology and Moral Meaning in Two English Renaissance Plays', *South Central Review* 1.1–2, pp. 4–21.

Waith, E.M. (ed.) (1963), *Ben Jonson: Bartholomew Fair*, The Yale Ben Jonson, New Haven and London.

Watson, R. N. (1987), *Ben Jonson's Parodic Strategy: Literary Imperialism in the Comedies*, Cambridge.

Welsford, Enid (1935), *The Fool: His Social and Literary History*, London.

Wheeler, Charles F. (1938), *Classical Mythology in the Plays, Masques, and Poems of Ben Jonson*, Princeton.

Wiltenburg, J. (1992), *Disorderly Women and Female Power in the Street Literature of Early Modern England and Germany*, Charlottesville and London.

Woodbridge, L. (1984), *Women and the English Renaissance: Literature and the Nature of Womankind 1540–1620*, Urbana and Chicago.

Woodbridge, L. (1994), *The Scythe of Saturn: Shakespeare and Magical Thinking*, Urbana and Chicago.

Woodman, D. (1973), *White Magic and Renaissance Drama*. Rutherford, Madison, and Teaneck.

Zeitlin, F. I. (1980, 1981, 1982), 'Travesties of Gender and Genre in Aristophanes' *Thesmophoriazousae*', in Elizabeth Abel (ed.), *Writing and Sexual Difference*, Chicago, pp. 131–58.